HARPER'S NEW TESTAMENT COMMENTARIES

GENERAL EDITOR: HENRY CHADWICK, D.D.

THE GOSPEL ACCORDING TO ST. JOHN

A COMMENTARY ON
THE GOSPEL ACCORDING TO
ST. JOHN

J. N. SANDERS

LATE FELLOW AND DEAN OF PETERHOUSE, CAMBRIDGE

Edited and completed by
B. A. MASTIN

LECTURER, UNIVERSITY COLLEGE OF NORTH WALES, BANGOR

1817

HARPER & ROW PUBLISHERS
NEW YORK AND EVANSTON

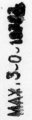

CONTENTS

PREFACE

When, in 1938, P. Gardner-Smith published *Saint John and the Synoptic Gospels*, the sole acknowledgement contained in the book was 'to Mr J. N. Sanders of Peterhouse for his kindness in reading proofs and for his helpful criticisms and suggestions'. Shortly afterwards F. N. Davey, in the Preface to E. C. Hoskyns' posthumous work *The Fourth Gospel* (1940), wrote of the assistance he had received from several of Hoskyns' former pupils, including 'the Rev. J. N. Sanders, Bye-Fellow of Peterhouse', whose contribution in the field of textual criticism was specially noted. The first book which Sanders himself wrote was *The Fourth Gospel in the Early Church: Its Origin and Influence on Christian Theology up to Irenaeus* (1943). This embodied research for which he had been awarded the Kaye Prize at Cambridge in 1939, and was followed by *The Foundations of the Christian Faith* (1950), a more general treatment of the New Testament in which some development in his thought on the Fourth Gospel can be traced.

In September 1954 the first issue of *New Testament Studies* contained a paper by Sanders entitled '"Those Whom Jesus Loved" (John xi. 5)', and in 1957 he contributed an article on a similar theme, 'Who was the Disciple whom Jesus Loved?', to the symposium *Studies in the Fourth Gospel* edited by F. L. Cross. He wrote a review article on 'Commentaries on the Gospel according to St John' for *Theology* (Vol. LXI, 1958), but his only other contributions to the study of the Fourth Gospel appeared posthumously: articles on 'Gospel of John' and 'Lazarus of Bethany' in *The Interpreter's Dictionary of the Bible* (1962), and 'St John on Patmos', in the January 1963 issue of *New Testament Studies*.

At the time of Sanders' death the Introduction and the Commentary on chapters i–xv had already been completed, though it was clear from the state of the manuscript that a few matters had been left for attention later. Some notes on chapters xviii and xix were available, and these have been fully utilised, though unfortunately only a few additional scraps of information about what would have gone into the final section of the Commentary were to hand. I am therefore responsible for what is written on chapters xvi-xxi and for the Appendix on vii. 53–viii. 11. I have also added a few notes bearing my initials in square brackets earlier in the Commentary where recent discussions of various topics seem to demand notice.

It is hardly possible for one born in the year in which Mr Gardner-Smith's book appeared to bring to the study of the Fourth Gospel the wide range of erudition with which the whole of this Commentary should have been endowed. Equally, it is extremely difficult to complete a book begun by someone else, especially when that other person had distinctive views of his own to express. I could not myself by any means accept all the positions maintained by my former teacher, but have seen it as the major part of my task to permit him to speak for himself; it is not my function to comment on his views or to rewrite his conclusions. I have, however, endeavoured to suggest in my own section of the Commentary the lines along which my own thought would develop.

I should have valued longer for the completion of this work, and in many ways feel that all I have done now is equip myself for its satisfactory performance. None the less this book is offered to the scholarly world in the conviction that, even though several years have passed since its original author's death, what he has to say about the Fourth Gospel is still worthy of attention.

I am grateful to Mr D. R. Ap-Thomas, Mr A. J. M. Bray, Mr C. E. Chaffin, Mr R. T. Davies, Mr P. J. S. Edwards, Mr M. J. Johnson, Dr A. Marshall, Mr A. C. Pick, the Reverend D. G. Selwyn, the Reverend P. W. Speck, and Mr A. M. Suggate for assistance and advice of various kinds. The Reverend Canon D. G. Hill and the Reverend R. L. Sturch generously made available notes taken at the Holy Week Lectures delivered by the Reverend J. N. Sanders at Ely Theological College in 1961. The Reverend Professor H. Chadwick, the Reverend Dr D. Inman, and the Reverend Professor C. F. D. Moule kindly lent me books which I would otherwise have found it difficult to obtain, and Professor Chadwick has advised me in the course of my work.

I am deeply indebted to my colleagues at Bangor, the Reverend S. I. Buse, the Reverend I. Thomas, and Dr M. E. Thrall, who have allowed me to consult them on a wide variety of matters. I am also grateful to the authorities of the University College of North Wales who have awarded me grants which enabled me to study away from Bangor during two Long Vacations.

Finally, Mrs D. G. Sanders has given me access to all her husband's papers, and has encouraged me in every possible way during the preparation of this book.

B. A. MASTIN

University College of North Wales,
Bangor.
St Patrick's Day, 1968.

ABBREVIATIONS

Barrett	C. K. Barrett, *The Gospel According to St John* (1955).
Bauer	W. Bauer, *Das Johannesevangelium* (1925).
Bauer⁵	W. Bauer, *Griechisch-Deutsches Wörterbuch zu den Schriften des Neuen Testaments und der übrigen urchristlichen Literatur* (⁵1958). W. F. Arndt and F. W. Gingrich, *A Greek-English Lexicon of the New Testament and Other Early Christian Literature* (1957) is a translation of the fourth edition of Bauer, with some adaptations and additions.
B.-D.	*A Greek Grammar of the New Testament and Other Early Christian Literature* by F. Blass and A. Debrunner: a translation and revision of the ninth-tenth German edition (incorporating supplementary notes of A. Debrunner) by R. W. Funk (1961).
BFBS²	The British and Foreign Bible Society's text of the Greek New Testament (²1958).
Black	M. Black, *An Aramaic Approach to the Gospels and Acts* (²1954).
Bultmann	R. Bultmann, *Das Evangelium des Johannes* (1941).
Dodd, *Interpretation*	C. H. Dodd, *The Interpretation of the Fourth Gospel* (1953).
J.T.S.	*The Journal of Theological Studies* (o.s. = old series, n.s. = new series).
Lagrange	M. J. Lagrange, *Évangile selon Saint Jean* (⁵1936).
LS⁹	H. G. Liddell and R. Scott, *A Greek-English Lexicon*, 9th edition revised by H. S. Jones (1925-40).
Moule	C. F. D. Moule, *An Idiom Book of New Testament Greek* (²1959).
Moulton, *Prolegomena*	J. H. Moulton, *A Grammar of New Testament Greek*, Vol. I. Prolegomena (³1908).
Moulton–Howard	J. H. Moulton and W. F. Howard, *A Grammar of New Testament Greek*, Vol. II. Accidence and Word-Formation (1929).

ix

Moulton and Milligan	J. H. Moulton and G. Milligan, *The Vocabulary of the Greek Testament* (1914–29).
N.T.S.	*New Testament Studies.*
Strack–Billerbeck	H. L. Strack and P. Billerbeck, *Kommentar zum Neuen Testament aus Talmud und Midrasch* (1922–28).
Turner	J. H. Moulton's *A Grammar of New Testament Greek*, Vol. III. Syntax, by N. Turner (1963).
T.W.z.N.T.	*Theologisches Wörterbuch zum Neuen Testament*, ed. G. Kittel and G. Friedrich (1933–19), now appearing in translation as *Theological Dictionary of the New Testament* (1964–).
Z.N.W.	*Zeitschrift für die Neutestamentliche Wissenschaft.*

INTRODUCTION

1. THE CONTENTS AND STRUCTURE OF THE FOURTH GOSPEL

The FG may be divided into the following parts:

(a) Prologue (i. 1-18), the nature and incarnation of the divine Word, or Logos, the agent of God in creation, revelation, and redemption;

(b) Testimony (i. 19 – xi. 54) of John the Baptist and other witnesses, and of Jesus' own acts and words, that he is the Christ, i.e. the incarnate Logos;

(c) Passion and Resurrection of Jesus (xi. 55 – xx. 31); and

(d) Epilogue (xxi), the final meeting of Jesus with his disciples.

In greater detail, (b) and (c) may be subdivided as follows:

(b) i. 19-51. Testimony of John the Baptist, Andrew, Nathanael, and Jesus (in Judaea).

ii. 1-12. FIRST SIGN. Jesus changes water into wine (at Cana in Galilee).

13-25. Cleansing of the Temple (Jerusalem).

iii. 1-21. Dialogue with Nicodemus, at 16 turning into a meditation by the evangelist, interrupted by,

22-24, a note on Jesus baptising, and,

25-30, the final testimony of John the Baptist to Jesus, but resumed iii. 31-36.

iv. 1-42. Dialogue with a Samaritan woman (on the way from Judaea to Galilee).

43-54. SECOND SIGN. Jesus heals the son of a 'royal official' (at Cana).

v. 1-9. THIRD SIGN. Jesus heals a man who has been ill for thirty-eight years (in Jerusalem).

10-47. Controversy with the Jews.

vi. 1-15. FOURTH SIGN. Jesus feeds five thousand men with five loaves and two fish (in Galilee). An attempt to make him king.

I

[1] It is not clear whether the evangelist intended this as a miracle, and so a 'sign', or not. For reasons for not regarding it as a sign, see the Commentary, p. 183.

[2] The passage vii. 53 - viii. 11 is most probably not an original part of the text of the FG (see below, pp. 459 f.).

This outline shows that whereas (c) contains a more or less continuous narrative, (b) contains what are at first sight a series of disconnected episodes, loosely strung together, and occasionally with very abrupt transitions. The impression of incoherence which this gives has led many critics to propose more or less drastic rearrangements of the text in order to improve the flow of the narrative, on the assumption that the text has suffered accidental or deliberate dislocation. A further motive for rearrangement of the text of the FG is that it makes it easier to harmonise the Gospels.

The following are some of the rearrangements that have been suggested:

(a) iii. 22-30 should follow either ii. 12 or iii. 36, so as not to interrupt iii. 16-21 and 31-36, which reads better as a whole.

(b) v should follow vi, so that the Feeding of the Multitude in Galilee follows immediately after the events in Galilee described in iv.

(c) vii and viii should be rearranged as follows: vii. 15-24 (which follows naturally after v. 47); viii. 12-20; vii. 1-14, 25-52; viii. 21-59.

(d) x. 1-18 should follow x. 29, so as to avoid the abrupt opening of x.

(e) xii. 36 ('When Jesus had said this')—43 should follow xii. 50, so that the evangelist's comments do not interrupt Jesus' discourse.

(f) xiii. 31 ('Now is the Son of man glorified')—xiv. 31 should follow xvi. 33, so that 'Get up, let us go from here', meaningless at xiv. 31, since it is not apparently acted upon until much later, does not interrupt Jesus' discourse.

These will be discussed as they arise in the course of the Commentary, but it may be said now that they undeniably improve the flow of the narrative, if it is assumed that the evangelist was interested in producing the kind of narrative which they give. It is this assumption which is questionable. It may well be that the suggested rearrangements do in some cases restore connexions that existed in the source used by the evangelist, but it may also be argued that the present arrangement is deliberate, and reflects the peculiar interests of the evangelist, as the following considerations may show.

The clue to the understanding of the structure of the FG is provided by the Prologue. If these verses are compared with Luke i. 1-4, the only other Gospel prologue, it will be seen at once that their purpose is different. They do not explain the evangelist's motives and qualifications for writing, as Luke's opening verses do. The FG does not explain its purpose until xx. 30 f. Instead, the Prologue of the FG summarises the subject-matter of the Gospel, and sets it in the context of the eternal purpose of God. Its function is more like that of the prologue to a Greek tragedy, or even that of the overture to an opera.

The analogy to an overture is particularly appropriate, since the Prologue states the main themes which are developed in the course of the Gospel, and which give it a unity which is neither chronological nor geographical, but theological and dramatic.

Some of these unifying and recurrent themes are as follows:

(a) Jesus is the incarnate Logos. Though Logos is not used in the main part of the Gospel as a title, many references to the word or words[1] of Jesus or of God have a deeper significance because Logos is used as it is in the Prologue: cf. ii. 22; iv. 41, 50; v. 24, 38; vi. 63, 68; viii. 31, 37, 47; xii. 48; xv. 3; xvii. 17.

[1] λόγος, ῥῆμα.

(b) Jesus is the source of life. The signs, particularly the raising of Lazarus, display him as such: cf. i. 4; iii. 15 f.; v. 24, 26, 29, 39, 40; vi. 35, 63, 68; viii. 12; x. 10, 28; xi. 25; xiv. 6; xvii. 2, 3; xx. 31.

(c) Jesus is the source of light. The sign of the healing of the man born blind particularly illustrates this; cf. also i. 4, 5; iii. 19-21; viii. 12; ix. 5; xii. 35, 36, 46.

(d) Jesus is the source of truth, cf. i. 14, 17; iv. 23, 24; v. 33; viii. 32, 40, 44-46; xiv. 6, 17; xv. 26; xvi. 13; xvii. 17, 19; xviii. 37, 38.

Others that can be traced through the Gospel from the Prologue onwards are indicated by the words 'witness', 'believing', 'world', 'flesh'; others are introduced as the Gospel develops.

The structure of the Gospel then is theological and dramatic. Incidentally this implies that the Prologue, whatever its source may be, is an integral part of the Gospel. That the motive for the selection of the six signs in ii-xi is theological is indicated by xx. 30 f. They all illustrate the creative and redemptive power of the incarnate Logos, and by their number (one less than the perfect number 7) lead up to the final sign, the resurrection of Jesus himself. The signs are the backbone of the narrative.

The incidents which are related in the FG are relatively few, in comparison with those in the other Gospels, but also much more fully developed. They may be compared to the successive scenes of a tragedy. No one complains if the successive scenes of a tragedy of Shakespeare's take one rapidly from one place to another. The alternation between Judaea and Galilee in the FG has the same dramatic purpose. Each scene is so placed as to carry forward the exposition of the themes which it is the theological purpose of the FG to expound.

A further aspect of the theological and dramatic character of the FG is its use of symbolism. It is difficult to avoid the conclusion that just as the themes of life, light, etc., run through the FG, so also do certain symbols. 'Night' for instance is both theologically and dramatically appropriate for Nicodemus' entry at iii. 2, and Judas' exit at xiii. 30. Or again, water appears to have a symbolical significance; in the miracle at Cana and the healing of the man by the pool in Jerusalem, it represents the old dispensation (cf. also Jacob's well, iv. 6); but it is also the medium of the sacrament of baptism—hence the washing of the disciples' feet (xiii. 5 ff.). Other examples will be noted in the Commentary.

The FG, then, if this exposition is correct, is very far from being loose and incoherent in structure. It is a closely-knit theological and dramatic unity, and to rearrange its parts would be to lose the effect which the evangelist intended.

Finally it must be noted that while we do right to recognise the theological and dramatic motives in the FG, we should not infer from them that the author was indifferent to the historicity of the events which he narrates. His fundamental theological principle, that 'the Logos became flesh', guarantees his concern for historicity.[1]

2. THE FOURTH GOSPEL AND THE SYNOPTIC GOSPELS

The summary of the contents of the FG given above illustrates some of the ways in which the FG differs from the other three. Thus it mentions incidents and persons not found in the other Gospels, though they are of considerable importance in the FG: e.g. the miracle at Cana (ii. 1-12); the fact that Jesus and his disciples baptised (iii. 22-24); his frequent visits to Jerusalem and his preaching and miracles there (v. 1-47; vii. 1-x. 42); the raising of Lazarus and its consequences (xi); Nicodemus (iii. 1-15), the woman of Samaria (iv. 1-42), and the Greeks at the feast (xii. 20-36). Then when what are apparently the same events as some in the Synoptic Gospels are described, they are placed at different points in the narrative: e.g. the Cleansing of the Temple (John ii. 13-25) which occurs in the Synoptic Gospels after the Entry into Jerusalem; the Anointing at Bethany (John xii. 1-11, 'six days before the Passover', cf. Mark xiv. 3-8—Mark xiv. 1 is 'two days before the Passover'); and perhaps the Draught of Fishes (John xxi. 4-8, cf. Luke v. 1-11). There are also alternative versions of the same events, e.g. the first encounter of John the Baptist with Jesus (John i. 29, cf. Mark i. 9), and of Jesus with some of his disciples (John i.

[1] For a further discussion of this aspect of the FG, see pp. 56-65 below.

37 ff., cf. Mark i. 16 ff.—in the FG this occurs in Judaea, in the Synoptic Gospels in Galilee); and of the trial of Jesus and his resurrection appearances. Events of considerable importance in the Synoptic Gospels are also ignored by the FG; e.g. Jesus' birth and baptism, his temptations and exorcisms, his Transfiguration, and the institution of the Lord's Supper.

These by no means exhaust the differences. The standpoint of the FG is Judaea, of the Synoptic Gospels, Galilee. Thus John iv. 43-45 appears to imply that Judaea is Jesus' own country, while Mark vi. 4, Matt. xiii. 57, and Luke iv. 24 have versions of the saying about a prophet's own country which imply that it is Galilee.[1] There is also a striking difference (which a summary of contents cannot illustrate) between the teaching attributed to Jesus in the FG and in the Synoptic Gospels.

In the latter the teaching of Jesus, both in content and form, resembles most closely that of the Hebrew prophets. In the FG, the dialogues and discourses have a close formal resemblance to those in the Hermetic literature, while its characteristic vocabulary resembles that of Hellenistic theosophy rather than Hebrew prophecy or the teaching of Jesus in the Synoptic Gospels.[2] Genuine parables of the type found in the Synoptic Gospels, if they occur in the FG at all, are far more drastically transformed by allegorical interpretation than the Synoptic parables ever are (see the Commentary on x. 1 ff. and xv. 1 ff.). A great deal of teaching in the FG is about Jesus' own person— sayings beginning 'I am . . .' are characteristic—as it is not in the Synoptic Gospels.

These differences must raise three important questions:

(i) Did the author of the FG use the Synoptic Gospels as sources for his own book?

(ii) What is the relationship between the teaching of Jesus in the FG and in the Synoptic Gospels?

(iii) What is the relative historical value of the FG and the Synoptic Gospels?

These questions will be dealt with in detail as opportunity

[1] But see further the note *ad loc.*
[2] The fact that the vocabulary of the FG has parallels to that of the Dead Sea Scrolls also does not make it any easier to understand its relationship to the Synoptic Gospels, though it has an important bearing on the question of the historicity of the FG.

offers in the course of the Commentary. The following observations may however be in place here.[1]

(i) *Possible Use of the Synoptic Gospels as Sources of the Fourth Gospel*

The answers which are given to the question whether any material in the FG is actually derived from the Synoptic Gospels must depend to some extent on the critics' general estimate of the probabilities of the case. If one is inclined to the view that the Gospels are on the whole historically reliable, then correspondences between them are only what one might expect, and not necessarily evidence for literary borrowing. If on the other hand one takes the view that there is very little in the Gospels that can be called historical, and that that little has been worked over and amplified in the course of transmission, then correspondences, even when rather far-fetched, are the more easily interpreted as evidence for literary dependence. And since the FG is commonly regarded as the latest of the four, it follows that, if there is any literary dependence, it is on the side of the FG. These considerations must be borne in mind in examining particular passages.

Correspondences between the FG and Matthew are so slight that there is general agreement that the FG cannot be dependent on it. The case, however, is different with Mark and Luke.

(*a*) *The Fourth Gospel and Mark.* (a) John i. 19-34. At first sight, the resemblance of this passage to Mark i. 2-11 is very slight indeed. It does, however, incorporate a number of verses more or less parallel to some in Mark, cf. John i. 23 = Mark i. 3; John i. 26 = Mark i. 8; John i. 27 = Mark i. 7; John i. 34 = Mark i. 11. If it is assumed that the FG has no authentic tradition of its own on John the Baptist, the suggestion that these verses were adapted from Mark may well seem plausible, but on no other hypothesis.

(b) John ii. 13-22. This narrative of the Cleansing of the Temple resembles that in Mark xi. 15-17, but the difference in

---

[1] For a discussion of the significance of the differences between the FG and Synoptic Gospels for our understanding of the purpose of the FG, see pp. 52 f.

date and in the details of the two accounts tells against a direct borrowing from Mark.

(c) John iii. 24 may be taken as a cross reference to Mark's comment (i. 14) that Jesus' Galilean ministry only began after the arrest of John the Baptist, designed to date everything before John iii. 24 before Mark i. 14. If so, it may be taken as a harmonising editorial comment.

(d) John vi. 1-21. Here there is at first sight the strongest case for the dependence of John on Mark, since both here and in Mark vi. 35-52 the Feeding of the Five Thousand is followed by Jesus dismissing the disciples to cross the lake alone, and then appearing to them walking 'on' the lake. Note especially the two hundred pennyworth of bread, five loaves and two fish, the men sitting on the grass, Jesus giving thanks, the twelve baskets full of pieces, and the five thousand men in both John and Mark. John has, however, details which can hardly have come to him independently of the main story—e.g. the parts played by Philip and Andrew, and the boy who provided the loaves and fish—and, unless he made these up himself, he must have had a version of the Feeding independent of Mark vi. If Mark vi and Mark viii. 1-10 give variant versions of the same incident, as is widely maintained, then, if John borrows from anywhere, it may be from the source of both Mark vi and viii. Moreover, the mention in John vi. 15 of the attempt to make Jesus king, which explains the otherwise unexplained action of Jesus in Mark in sending off the disciples by themselves, has an air of authenticity about it, and tells in favour of the independence of John.

In the miracle of Jesus walking 'on' the water (if it is such), the miraculous element is less emphasised in John than in Mark. This is contrary to what we are led to suppose was the tendency in the development of Gospel tradition, and this (for what it is worth) again favours the independence of the FG.

(e) John vi. 66-71. Here Peter confesses that Jesus has 'words of eternal life', and Jesus warns the disciples that one of them is a 'devil'. In Mark viii. 29-33 (after Mark's second Feeding) Peter confesses that Jesus is Christ, and Jesus later calls Peter 'Satan'. Since a confession that Jesus is Christ would be nothing new in the FG—it is already found in John i. 41—it may be argued that this passage is a Johannine paraphrase of Mark, with a correction of Mark thrown in—it was Judas who played the part of Satan, not Peter.

(f) John xii. 1-8. The anointing of Jesus here recalls that in Mark xiv. 3-9. In particular the description of the ointment and its value are the same in both Gospels. But again John has details not found in Mark, the origin of which is a mystery if John is here borrowing from Mark.

(g) John xviii. 10, 11. The account of the arrest and trials of Jesus in the FG is so different from Mark's that it is difficult to resist the conclusion that John here follows an independent source. This would not of course necessarily prevent him using the other Gospels occasionally, if he knew them. This passage is a case in point. In Mark xiv. 47 an anonymous disciple cuts off an anonymous servant's ear. In Luke xxii. 50 f., the two characters are still anonymous, but it is his right ear which the servant loses, and Jesus heals him. In the FG Peter strikes Malchus. Are the extra details in Luke and John legendary accretions to the tradition found in Mark, or do they come from independent sources? Luke may well have had an independent source for his Passion narrative. And likewise John: if the disciple 'known to the High Priest' (John xviii. 15 f.) was a real person (surely not a wild hypothesis), and the source of the FG's information for the Passion, then he might well have known the High Priest's servant Malchus.

These are intended only as a sample—it is hoped a fair one— of those passages which call for consideration in this connexion. Neither individually nor cumulatively do they compel us to suppose that Mark is a source for the FG. At most John may have had it in mind as he wrote his own Gospel (cf. (c) and (e) in particular).

John of Ephesus indeed must have known St Mark's Gospel, if Papias was correct in quoting the comment of *the Elder* on Mark (Eusebius, *H.E.*, III. 39), and if John of Ephesus was the editor of the FG. But knowing Mark, and using it as a source, are two different things.

(*b*) *The Fourth Gospel and Luke.* Such points of contact as there are between the FG and Luke which may suggest that one is dependent on the other are all between the FG and the material peculiar to Luke, i.e., that which he did not derive either from Mark or from the hypothetical source which he shared with Matthew. If John in fact borrowed from Luke, this is very odd, for John had no synopsis of the first three Gospels to help him in his selection of material, and there is nothing in the material itself to suggest why John should have chosen just that, with all Luke before him.

The main correspondences are:

(a) the use of 'the Lord' instead of 'Jesus' in the course of the narrative (Luke vii. 13; x. 1; xi. 39; xii. 42; xiii. 15; xviii. 6; xix. 8; xxii. 61; John iv. 1; vi. 23; xi. 2; xx. 20);

(b) the absence of exorcisms;

(c) the disciple 'Judas of James', Luke vi. 16, who is presumably the 'Judas (not Iscariot)' of John xiv. 22;

(d) Martha and her sister Mary, Luke x. 38-42; John xi. 1 ff.; xii. 1 ff.;

(e) the name Lazarus in the parable, Luke xvi. 19-31, and the story, John xi. 1 ff., both connected with the idea of resurrection;

(f) the appearances of the risen Christ in Jerusalem, Luke xxiv. 36-43; John xx. 19-29; and

(g) the miraculous draught of fish, Luke v. 1-11; John xxi. 1-14.

Of these, (a), (b), and (f) are evidence for nothing more than a similarity of outlook between the FG and Luke's special source—suggesting (say) a Sadducee from Jerusalem familiar with the Gentile mission; the rest may suggest a common source. Of them, (e) and (g) raise important issues.

It is often maintained that John's information about the family at Bethany represents a conflation of material from Mark xiv. 3-9; Luke vii. 36-50 (where an anonymous woman washed Jesus' feet with tears, and anointed them with ointment); Luke x. 38-42; and Luke xvi. 19-31; and that the story of the raising of Lazarus arose as an illustration of the lesson of the parable that those who would not listen to Moses and the prophets would not listen even if one rose from the dead. But there is nothing in Luke to suggest the association of Martha and Mary with Lazarus, or the identification of Mary with the anonymous sinner of the earlier story. On the other hand, it is conceivable that the use of the name Lazarus in the parable is an example of Jesus' irony. The lesson of the parable is in fact what happened as a result of the raising of Lazarus—according to the FG, it produced the decision to put Jesus to death. It is not without significance that Luke xvi. 19-31 is the only parable in which a proper name is used.

The two stories involving miraculous draughts of fish (g) have often been regarded as variants of the same legend. But, if so, which is the more primitive is a nice question. In any case, the theory that the FG here actually borrowed from Luke seems far-fetched, and much less probable than that each evangelist found the story in more or less the form in which he gives it in the source which he used.

These questions will be considered further in the Commentary. Here it is sufficient to say that the case for John's direct use of Luke is hardly established, and that the most natural explanation of the phenomena is that John and Luke used sources which to some extent overlapped. It will be argued in the Commentary that, in the case of Martha, Mary, and Lazarus, the FG had a source superior to Luke's.[1]

(ii) *The Teaching of Jesus in the Fourth Gospel and the Synoptic Gospels*

On the basis of the investigations carried out in the previous section of this Introduction, it may be accepted, at least as a working hypothesis, that the FG is substantially independent of the other three. This conclusion has important consequences for the discussion of the relationship of the teaching attributed to Jesus in the FG to that found in the Synoptic Gospels. The differences between them are obvious, and call for some explanation. If it were likely that the FG had used the Synoptic Gospels extensively, then the natural conclusion would be that the evangelist had drastically refashioned the teaching of Jesus found in the Synoptic tradition, and had added to it from the common stock of Hellenistic religious teaching. This is what many critics in fact think happened. But if the FG is independent, then in its teaching material it may well represent an independent tradition.

[1] See pp. 276 f. below.

Now the fact that the bulk of the Synoptic teaching is ascribed to Jesus' Galilean ministry, and of the Johannine to that in Jerusalem may offer a partial solution to the problem. But only partial, for though the emphasis on the different aspects of Jesus' teaching may have been different in Galilee and in Jerusalem, he can hardly have altered his style as radically as the differences between the FG and the Synoptic Gospels suggest. It must therefore be recognised that the form of the Johannine teaching at any rate is due to the evangelist. Has he also influenced it in substance as well as in form?

Though differences must be recognised, they must not be exaggerated. The significance of Jesus' acts of healing, etc., as signs of the power of God active in the world which is so important in the FG is found also in Matt. xii. 28, and Luke xi. 20. That of his death found in John xv. 13 is also in Mark x. 45. His words at the Feeding of the Multitude in John vi. 53 recall those at the Last Supper in Mark xiv. 22 ff.; his claim to be the only mediator in John xiv. 6 is found also in Matt. xi. 27 and Luke x. 22. His description of the Holy Spirit as Paraclete (Παράκλητος, 'advocate, champion') and the functions which he attributes to him in John xiv. 16 ff.[1] find at least a partial parallel in Mark xiii. 11, where the Holy Spirit is to be a kind of counsel for the defence of the disciples, i.e. a παράκλητος, though of course the actual term is not used. The FG agrees with the Synoptic Gospels in recording Jesus' use of the title 'Son of man' for himself, though it differs from them in attributing to him also the use of the title 'Son of God'. In the Synoptic Gospels Jesus does not indeed disclaim the title, but he does not actually use it of himself since 'Son of man' is by itself quite adequate to describe his eschatological function. In the FG however there has been a shift of emphasis from his eschatological function to his ontological status, and the two titles 'Son of man' and 'Son of God' are used as complementary descriptions of his status, of which the one would be misleading without the other.[2]

This is one significant aspect of an important feature of the thought of the FG, which may be called its transvaluation of eschatology. Whereas in the Synoptic Gospels there is a basic

---

[1] See also the notes *ad loc.*   [2] See also pp. 103-106 below.

contrast of present and future, which holds good even if the future is visualised as imminent, in the FG the contrast is between the temporal and the eternal, i.e. it is ontological rather than eschatological. This comes out in many other ways, e.g. in the shift in the meaning of ζωὴ αἰώνιος from 'the life of the (coming) age' to 'eternal life',[1] in the demythologising of the idea of judgement in John iii. 19, 'This is the judgement, that the light has come into the world, etc.', and in the affirmation that Christ has already overcome the world (John xvi. 33).

In the FG, however, nothing is quite as simple as it seems at first sight, and this must be qualified by two further observations, namely that though the FG has shifted the emphasis from eschatology to ontology, a future resurrection and judgement still feature in its teaching (cf. John v. 29; vi. 39 ff.), and that its transvaluation of eschatology preserves something in the actual teaching of Jesus which the Church had tended to distort or misunderstand, his conviction that the power of God was already at work, that the decisive moment had come.[2]

Thus there is at once similarity in substance and difference in emphasis and terminology between the teaching of Jesus in the FG and in the Synoptic Gospels.

Much that is only implicit in the Synoptic Gospels becomes quite explicit in the FG. The crucial case is that of Jesus' claim to be Messiah. In Mark the title is only accepted by Jesus when Peter makes his confession at Caesarea Philippi (Mark viii. 29), and then Jesus immediately warns the disciples to keep silent about it. He does not publicly accept the title until his trial before Caiaphas (Mark xiv. 62). In the FG he claims to be Messiah to the Samaritan woman (John iv. 26), and argues with the crowds in Jerusalem who ask him to tell them if he is the Christ (John x. 24). But in Mark Jesus is continually acting in a way which constitutes an implicit claim to be Messiah—and the words of Bartimaeus, who hails him as 'Son of David'—surely a Messianic title (Mark x. 48)—suggest that the 'Messianic Secret' was not so complete as Mark might lead us to suppose.

Now it is possible that the FG may help us to understand the

---

[1] See on iii. 14 f. below.
[2] See the note on iv. 23, and Dodd, *Interpretation*, p. 447.

reserve which Mark attributes to Jesus in making his claim to be Messiah by implication rather than openly. If the belief that Jesus was a descendant of David, which the Nativity stories attest, was already current in his own lifetime, as Bartimaeus' words imply, then it might also have been expected that he would come forward, as heir of David, to claim his throne.[1] The attempt to make Jesus king, which John vi. 15, records, shows that had he done so, he would have had a ready welcome. In Jerusalem the enthusiasm for a militant Messiah might well have been kindled more quickly than in Galilee, and Jesus' own refusal to be the kind of Messiah that Jerusalem would have welcomed may be the explanation of his abandonment of Jerusalem in order to make a fresh start in Galilee. There he carefully avoided making any overt claims to Messiahship, in order to let his actions show what kind of Messiah he intended to be. But his disciples, some of whom had already been with him in Judaea, continued to nurse the nationalist hope (which they had not abandoned even after the Resurrection, as Acts i. 6, suggests). If Andrew did tell his brother that he had found the Messiah, as John i. 41, relates, he meant by Messiah the militant leader of popular expectation.[2] The Galilean ministry, and Jesus' delay in opening his Messianic campaign (as it must have seemed to his disciples), must have tried their faith in him. Simon Peter's confession at Caesarea Philippi may be not so much a new discovery, a sudden revelation of the truth (though Matthew so represents it, reflecting a later point of view—Matt. xvi. 17), as the triumph of faith over disappointment—'You *are* the Christ (in spite of your apparent unwillingness to behave as such)'.[3]

In this, then, the FG may well faithfully preserve an aspect of Jesus' ministry that we would not have known had we only had the other Gospels. In other respects also John may help us to form a truer picture of Jesus' ministry and his teaching. This does not mean, however, that we can accept everything in the FG at its face value. For what a modern critic means by 'words of Jesus' we have to go to the Synoptic Gospels rather than the FG. The teaching in the FG may be closer to that of Jesus in

[1] But see the note on vii. 42.   [2] See also pp. 99 f. below.
[3] See also p. 100 below.

substance than has commonly been recognised, but its *form* has very largely been imposed upon it by the evangelist, or by the principal source from which he drew his material. Such characteristic Johannine utterances as the 'I am . . .' sayings can hardly be taken as 'words of the Lord' in any literal sense.

The clue to the understanding of the form of the Johannine teaching attributed to Jesus may be that the material in the FG consisted originally of sermons, preached by a man who was a Christian prophet, whose own words were as truly 'words of the Lord' as those spoken by Jesus beside the sea of Galilee or in the Upper Room. In his sermons the prophet not only quoted what we mean by 'the words of the Lord', but also paraphrased and adapted them. In John xvi. 14, which refers to the Spirit taking what is Christ's and telling it to the disciples, we have the explanation and justification of the way in which the prophet handled the teaching of Jesus. He would no doubt have regarded the scruples of the modern critic as miserable pedantry.[1]

(iii) *The Relative Historical Value of the Fourth Gospel and the Synoptic Gospels*

Any answer to the question of the relative historical value of the FG and the Synoptic Gospels can be, at this stage, only provisional. The more fundamental question of the historical

---

[1] This suggestion that the sermons of a Christian prophet underlie the FG may also make other features of it more intelligible. Chapter vi, which begins with the account of the Feeding of the Multitude, and attaches to it the discourse on Jesus as the Bread of Life, reads like a Passover sermon. The story is the text for the discourse. If it was a Passover sermon, the Eucharistic references are appropriate. Then when John came to relate the Last Supper, he used for it another Passover sermon on the other 'Sacrament of the gospel', based on the washing of the disciples' feet.

The frequent mention of feasts in the FG may be an indication of the occasions on which the sermons utilised in the Gospel were delivered. The Church inherited the Jewish festivals; we still keep Passover and Pentecost, and a Jewish Christian prophet could find a new significance in other feasts as well. The recurrent emphasis on 'light' and 'water' in John vii–ix may recall the ritual of the feast of Tabernacles with which these chapters are associated.

Form-criticism has directed attention to the rôle of preaching in the preservation of the gospel tradition. The narrative *pericopai* in the Gospels are perhaps 'sermon-texts' rather than 'sermon-illustrations'.

value of the Gospels as such still awaits a satisfactory answer.[1] It may be said here, however, that if the independence of the FG with regard to the others is established, the way is clear for taking its claim to be a source of historically reliable material much more seriously than has often been done in the past. The FG does not just preserve a few scraps of authentic information, by accident, as it were, but a source, independent of the Synoptic Gospels, which reveals aspects of the ministry of Jesus on which the others hardly touch, though they contain indications that their own information is incomplete. Thus, for instance, Matt. xxiii. 37-39 = Luke xiii. 33-35, suggests that Jesus had been active in Jerusalem at times of which the Synoptic tradition gives no information.

The nineteenth-century opinion that the Synoptic Gospels, and Mark in particular, are historical, as opposed to the FG, which is theological, must be given up.[2] The Marcan outline of Jesus' ministry is as much governed by dogmatic and theological considerations as is John's. To reconcile them, and extract from them a coherent account that does justice both to the Synoptic and Johannine evidence must be a difficult and delicate task. Possibly it is one that cannot be expected to succeed. But it is quite certain that any attempt which ignores the contribution which the FG can make is doomed to failure.

It may be that one should distinguish between the narrative parts of the FG and the discourses here. Though the *structure* of the narrative is controlled by the interests which are made apparent in the discourses, it does not follow that the *contents* of each narrative section are not historically reliable, and that one cannot unpick the FG and rearrange the episodes in the order which their internal evidence suggests. This would have a greater prospect of success if it were clear that the authority for the narrative (i.e. the 'eye-witness') was not also the prophet who was responsible for the discourses.[3] But even if the whole Gospel, narrative and discourses alike, are the work of the same hand and brain, we may still hope, paradoxical as it may sound

[1] For some observations on this, see pp. 61 ff. below.
[2] On this, see further p. 61 below.
[3] On this, see further p. 48 below.

to say so, for some degree of success since John's evident theo·
logical motives, as has already been noted,[1] are fully compatible
with a genuine concern for historicity on his part. If Mark has
theological motives too, we may nevertheless still have the same
hope about his Gospel. So, delicate as the task may be of reconstructing the ministry of Jesus from the evidence of the
Gospels, it is not inherently hopeless. To attempt it in the
course of the present Commentary would take it beyond its
proper limits and purpose, but it is hoped that it may do something to indicate the contribution which the FG can make to
such a reconstruction.

The relative value of Mark and the FG for this task presents
a remarkable analogy to that of Xenophon and Plato for the
understanding of Socrates. Like Jesus, Socrates wrote nothing,
and we are dependent on the records left by his disciples for our
knowledge of his thought. Xenophon was a practical and un-
imaginative man, and though he knew Socrates well, he failed
to understand him fully. Mark was not of course himself an eye-
witness, but his information appears to have come in the main
from one who was as well placed with regard to Jesus as
Xenophon had been with Socrates, and who, moreover, resembled Xenophon in character. Plato, on the other hand, only
knew Socrates for a comparatively short time, and learnt a lot
from his own relations who had known him better. But he was
as original and profound a thinker as Socrates himself, fully
capable of understanding his master, but unable to limit himself to a literal reproduction of his views. Being the man he was,
he inevitably developed, and to some extent modified Socrates'
teaching. Similarly John (or the writer whose work he uses) was
a thinker at once more profound and original than any of the
Synoptic evangelists or their sources. His Gospel reflects this,
but it is probably also true that his insight into the meaning of
Jesus' teaching and ministry is greater than theirs. But we shall
probably never finally settle how much of the teaching in the
FG is due to Jesus, and how much to John, just as we shall
probably never finally settle how much in Plato's *Dialogues* is
due to Socrates, and how much to Plato. But this has not, and
indeed should not, put an end to discussion.

[1] See p. 6 above.

INTRODUCTION

3. THE THEOLOGY OF THE FOURTH GOSPEL AND ITS SOURCES

The teaching of the FG, while based ultimately upon that actually given by Jesus, differs from it in ways which suggest that it contains elements derived from other sources. It has in fact a theology of its own, seen most clearly, in the Prologue and the meditations which interrupt the narrative, but also informing and pervading the whole Gospel, and the question must be asked what were the sources from which this distinctive theology was derived.

The FG teaches that God is unknown and unknowable unless and until he is made known by his Logos, his agent not only in revelation, but also in the creation of the world and the salvation of mankind. The chief end of man is to know God, which is attained by belief in the Logos, whereby men become sons of God, and so receive the gift of eternal life. To accomplish the Father's loving purpose, the Logos became man, so uniting flesh and spirit, and making possible the gift of holy spirit to men. Holy spirit is released, as it were, by the death of the incarnate Logos, and mediated to men by Baptism and the Lord's Supper. The theology of the FG is an ethical dualism: it deals in contrasts—light and darkness, life and death, spirit and flesh, the world and God, the temporal and the eternal. Sometimes it seems to approach a metaphysical dualism, but it is saved from this by its recognition that the purpose of God is to save the world, and by its central, characteristic, and unique affirmation that the Logos became flesh.

The question of the sources of this distinctive theology has received a great variety of answers.

The most obvious source is the Wisdom Literature of the Old Testament and Apocrypha, as will be noted as occasion offers in the Commentary. Others have, however, also been suggested. One is the teaching of the Jewish philosopher Philo, an approximate contemporary of St Paul who taught in Alexandria, and expounded in his voluminous allegorical commentaries on the Pentateuch a Platonised Stoicism in which the Logos played an important part. The Alexandrian Fathers who shared his philosophical opinions recognised the affinity of his teaching to that of the FG, and in consequence regarded him as a kind of honorary Christian.

Nineteenth-century critics, adopting the then novel doctrine of evolution, and inheriting from their Lutheran tradition a tendency to interpret the FG in Pauline terms, saw the FG as a thorough-going Hellenisation of the gospel, carrying the process a stage farther than St Paul had done. Later in the century, the comparative study of the religions of the Near East contemporary with the rise of Christianity drew attention to the affinities of the theology of the FG with those of contemporary religious movements. One such was that which produced the *Hermetica*, a collection of tracts (in style very like the discourses in the FG) advocating an Egyptian syncretistic theosophy—a blend of Platonic mysticism and cosmogony fused with elements of unorthodox Judaism—the earliest of which may have been written as early as the middle of the first century A.D. Another was the pre-Christian Gnostic movement, the existence of which it was thought necessary to postulate in order to account for the later rise of Gnosticism within the Church. It was also suggested that the ideas which appeared to underlie the practices of the mystery cults of the period, syncretistic religions founded on the worship of a dying and rising Saviour God, such as Attis or Osiris, could throw light on those of the FG. Then when later the writings of the Mandaeans, a bizarre sect still surviving in the Near East, which may have originated in the first century A.D. in Transjordan, were made accessible to European scholarship, they too were claimed to have influenced the theology of the FG.[1] More recently still, the same claim has been made for the Dead Sea Scrolls, the writings of a sect which was active in Palestine in the first century A.D.

The period which saw the rise of Christianity and the writing of its first literature was one of great religious activity. The conquests of Alexander the Great had produced a great mingling of races and cultures, fostered by the deliberate policy of Hellenisation which Alexander himself began. The new Greek cities which he founded, of which the Egyptian Alexandria was the most famous among the many scattered throughout his empire, were centres of a new civilisation, the language of which was

[1] For details, see Dodd, *Interpretation*, pp. 10-130.

Greek, while its ideas were an exotic combination of Greek and barbarian elements. Native gods were identified with members of the Greek pantheon, and their worship and mythology were adopted by the conquerors. A great variety of syncretistic cults and theologies arose in consequence. Judaism itself was at first deeply influenced by Hellenism, and the Wisdom Literature of the Old Testament and Apocrypha bears many traces of Greek philosophical notions. The Maccabean revolt was a conscious reaction against Hellenism, but even in Palestine it could not entirely obliterate the effects of early Greek influence. The Hellenic leaven continued to work in the Jewish lump. Outside Palestine, Hellenic influence was less hampered, and the philosophy of Philo is a monument to its effect. How soon after its origin within Judaism Christianity felt the influence of contemporary syncretism is disputed, but it is undeniable that Christian heresies arose at an early date which exhibited many of its characteristic features. The heresy which arose at Colossae in the time of St Paul is perhaps the earliest known example. In the second century the Gnostic movement threatened to undermine the very foundations of the faith, and it may be regarded as significant that some of the earliest evidence for the use of the FG comes from Gnostic sources.[1] But lest it should be too readily assumed that the FG itself is a monument of early Gnosticism (as the so-called Alogi[2] supposed), it should be remembered that Irenaeus[3] successfully built his refutation of Gnosticism very largely on the FG. He may have understood it better than the Gnostics did.

All these religions and theosophies had certain characteristic features in common. All were pessimistic about the present state of the world, and looked for salvation *from* it rather than *for* it. In consequence, they tended towards a dualism sometimes ethical, but often metaphysical (e.g. the Mandaeans and some Christian Gnostics). God was thought of as remote and transcendent, knowable only through a divine or angelic intermediary (e.g. the Logos in Philo, Hermes in the Hermetic literature, Jesus in the Gnostic systems). They all tend to use the same terminology. 'Life', 'light', and 'truth' are used in

---

[1] See below, pp. 37 f.   [2] See below, p. 25.   [3] See below, pp. 39-42.

them in much the same sense as in the FG. It does not, however, follow from all this that the FG is very deeply influenced by them. Their importance for the study of the FG is not so much that they indicate the sources of its theology as that they illustrate the beliefs of those to whom it was designed to appeal. For its most characteristic affirmation, that the Logos became flesh, there is no analogy in Philo, for whom the Logos is a personified abstraction, or anywhere else. That Christ has come in the flesh was the great stumbling-block to the Gnostics. John boldly used the language of his contemporaries in order to help them to understand a faith radically different from their own, however similar it may sound superficially.

Here the Dead Sea Scrolls are of great importance. They use the characteristic language of contemporary syncretism as the FG does, yet they emanate from a sect which was as firmly Jewish as the Maccabees had been. They in fact provide the closest comparison, both chronologically and geographically, to the FG, and illustrate its fundamentally Jewish and scriptural character. The distinctive theology of the FG is to be explained from within Judaism, particularly from the Wisdom Literature,[1] and from the new insights which the experience of Christ had given men. If John expressed these in language which his pagan contemporaries could understand, it only shows how successful he was in solving the problem of communication which is so difficult for the Church today. There is no need to relegate the FG to the second century A.D. and to a Hellenistic environment to account for its characteristic vocabulary. The Dead Sea Scrolls show that it could perfectly well have been written by a man who had been born in Palestine early in the first century A.D.[2]

---

[1] Through which such Greek influence as he received came to him. There is no real evidence that John was directly influenced by Greek philosophy.

[2] For the significance of the Dead Sea Scrolls for the study of the FG, see (amongst others) A. Dupont-Sommer, *The Jewish Sect of Qumran and the Essenes* (1954), pp. 151, 155 f.; Millar Burrows, *The Dead Sea Scrolls* (1956), pp. 338-340, *More Light on the Dead Sea Scrolls* (1958), pp. 123-130; J. M. Allegro, *The Dead Sea Scrolls* (1956), pp. 128 f.; W. F. Albright, 'Recent Discoveries in Palestine and the Gospel of St John', in *The Background of the New Testament and its Eschatology*, ed. W. D. Davies and D. Daube (1956), pp. 153-171; R. E. Brown, 'The Qumran Scrolls and the Johannine Gospel and Epistles', in *The Scrolls and the New Testament*, ed. K. Stendahl (1958), pp. 183-207.

It remains to consider the relationship of the FG to the Epistles of St Paul and to the Hebrews. John, Paul, and the writer to the Hebrews were all confronted with the same problem, that of making their message intelligible to men for whom the simple title 'Christ' was inadequate or unintelligible, because the background of hope and belief which gave it its meaning was not theirs. This problem had arisen as soon as the first Christian missionaries addressed themselves to the Gentiles. The use of the title 'Lord' (Κύριος) was an attempt to explain the significance of 'Christ'. St Paul's words, '. . . there are many "gods" and many "lords"—yet for us there is one God . . . and one Lord, Jesus Christ' (1 Cor. viii. 5, 6), show that Κύριος was familiar as a divine title, intelligible to Gentiles. They also were all compelled to realise that if Jesus was in fact the Christ, the Son of God, these titles were not even for them self-explanatory. However averse they may have been to speculation for its own sake, they were bound to consider the relationship of the Son to the Father, and to produce a Christology. The materials for constructing a Christology which lay to their hand were roughly the same for them all—their experience of Christ, the Scriptures of the Old Testament, and the terms and concepts of contemporary religious speculation. It is not surprising that their teaching on the person of Christ is similar. But it requires a very close resemblance between them to prove that John is actually dependent on St Paul or the writer to the Hebrews.

The fact that all assert Christ's pre-existence is hardly sufficient to prove it. The terms which they use are sufficiently dissimilar to suggest that the Pauline and Johannine Christologies are independent but analogous responses to the same basic problem.

The thought of Paul and John is closest in Col. i. 15-19 and the Prologue to the FG. St Paul describes Christ as the 'image of the invisible God': the thought is similar to that of John i. 18, but the terminology is different. St Paul's word *'image'* (εἰκών) occurs in the Johannine literature only in Revelation, where it means an idol. Paul and John agree that all things were created through Christ (Col. i. 16, 17; John i. 3), and they both use the technical term 'fulness' (πλήρωμα) used in Gnostic theology for the sum-total of divine attributes, cf. 'In him all the fulness of God was pleased to dwell' (Col. i. 19); 'Of his fulness did we all accept' (John i. 16). But St Paul expresses the uniqueness of Christ consistently by the term 'first-begotten' (πρωτότοκος), the FG by 'only-begotten' (μονογενής), and neither uses the other's word at all.

There are similar resemblances between the FG and Hebrews. 'God has spoken to us by a Son, whom he appointed heir of all things, through whom also he made the worlds' (Heb. i. 2) and indeed the whole Epistle for Christmas Day harmonises beautifully with the Gospel, John i. 1–14, but it is not close enough in language to prove the literary dependence of the Gospel on the Epistle. Hebrews comes very close to calling Christ the Word, but it is only the FG that takes the decisive step. And the Fourth Evangelist could have got to the point reached by Hebrews independently. Thus, if these conclusions are sound, they vindicate the essential originality and independence of the Fourth Evangelist. The distinctive teaching in his Gospel is essentially his own—the product of his reflexions on the Old Testament, the teaching of Jesus, and the needs of his contemporaries.

4. THE ORIGIN, PURPOSE, AND VALUE OF THE FOURTH GOSPEL[1]

From the third century A.D. until the beginning of the modern period in New Testament criticism the Gospel, three Epistles, and Revelation of John have been ascribed to the apostle John, the son of Zebedee. The earliest evidence of the ascription of any of these works to the apostle is in the writings of Justin Martyr, who died about A.D. 165. He attributes the Revelation to 'a man named John, one of the apostles of Christ' (*Dialogus*, lxxxi. 15), but though he apparently knew of the FG he never mentions it explicitly. The FG existed in his time, for

[1] [Cf. D. M. Smith, Jr., 'The Sources of the Gospel of John: An Assessment of the Present State of the Problem', *N.T.S.*, Vol. X, 1963–64, pp. 336-351, and *The Composition and Order of the Fourth Gospel* (1965), for an exposition and critique of Bultmann's theory of the sources used by the Evangelist and the various stages which have led to the production of the FG in its present form. The book contains an extremely full and valuable account of recent contributions to the debate.—B. A. M.]

there is a tiny fragment of papyrus,[1] bearing some parts of six verses of the FG, which is assigned on palaeographical grounds to the early second century. It is in fact the earliest surviving portion of a manuscript of any part of the New Testament. But for the ascription of the FG to John we have to wait until later.

In the course of the second century certain otherwise orthodox Christians ascribed both the Gospel and the Revelation to the Gnostic Cerinthus. Epiphanius in consequence gave them the nickname 'Alogi' (which can mean both 'without reason' and 'without the Logos'). This was probably due to the popularity of both works in heretical circles at that time.[2] In the case of the FG, scruples had been silenced by the end of the century, but in the third century Dionysius, bishop of Alexandria, who died about A.D. 264, questioned the ascription of the Revelation to the author of the FG, on the grounds of the great difference between the two works, particularly in style—grounds which most modern critics accept as conclusive. His observations on the Revelation are preserved by Eusebius (*H.E.*, VII. 25), who was himself reluctant, on dogmatic grounds, to ascribe the book to an Apostle. As Dionysius regarded the FG as the work of the Apostle John, he had to look elsewhere for an author of the Revelation. After hinting that the book may be a pseudepigraph, he mentions, only to reject, John Mark as a possible author, and appears finally to recommend the suggestion that there may have been two Johns in Asia, 'since indeed they say that there are two tombs in Ephesus, and that each is called John's'. But Dionysius' critical scruples were not enough to overcome the tradition, and Eusebius finally, though with obvious reluctance, included the Revelation among the 'acknowledged' books of the New Testament (*H.E.*, III. 25). Dionysius' second Asian John has survived to haunt and confuse the critics. There was only one John in Asia, but one may well question whether he was the son of Zebedee.

If one follows Dionysius in ascribing the FG and the Revelation to different authors, one must also admit that it is the Revelation which has the prior claim to be considered the work of the son of Zebedee, on the strength of Justin Martyr. To

---

[1] The Rylands Papyrus 457, John xviii. 31-34 on one side, 37 and 38 on the other.　　　　　[2] For this, see pp. 37 f. below.

accept the traditional authorship of the FG and reject that of the Revelation is to prefer a subjective opinion of what an apostolic work ought to be to the objective evidence of external testimony. And it is on the external testimony that the case for the authorship of the FG by the son of Zebedee mainly relies. All this goes to show that the problem of the authorship of these works cannot be solved piecemeal. If the tradition is to be rejected for one, it is only logical and consistent to reject it for all. A satisfactory theory of the origin of the FG must also take account of the Epistles and the Revelation, which have more in common than the authorship which the tradition ascribes to them all.

The ascription of the FG to John the son of Zebedee is consistent with the internal evidence. John xxi. 24, ascribes the Gospel to the disciple whom Jesus loved, and it is in this chapter only in the FG (xxi. 2) that the sons of Zebedee are mentioned, along with Simon Peter, Thomas, Nathanael, and two other unnamed disciples. The Revelation claims to be the work of a man named John (Rev. i. 1, 4, 9; xxii. 8), though, as Dionysius noticed, he never claims to be an apostle. 1 John is anonymous, but 2 and 3 John are the work of a man who calls himself 'the elder' (πρεσβύτερος), whom the tradition identified with John the son of Zebedee. It may be noted that 1 Pet. v. 1, makes Peter address the elders as their 'fellow-elder' (συμπρεσβύτερος), so that this description of John (if it is he) is not necessarily incompatible with his being an apostle. The tradition does, however, involve certain difficulties, and in order to estimate its value it will be necessary to discuss first the relationship of the FG to the Epistles and the Revelation, then the internal evidence of the FG, and then the external evidence for its use and authorship in writers of the second century A.D. Only then will it be possible to draw together the results of the enquiry and propose a theory to account for them.

(i) *The Literary Relationship of the Fourth Gospel,*
   Epistles, and Revelation

Evidence for the common authorship of these works is furnished by the close resemblance between the language and theology of the FG and the Epistles, by certain similarities (along with marked differences) in language and theology between the FG and the Revelation, and by the formal similarity between the Epistles and the letters to the seven churches in the Revelation. In English the resemblances appear closer, and the differences less, than they are in the Greek.

The FG and the Revelation are the only books in the New Testament which use Logos as a title of Christ, though the conquering Logos of Rev. xix. 13 is closer to Wisd. xviii. 15 ff., than to John i. 1-14. Both describe Christ as the Lamb (John i. 29; Rev. v. 6 and many other instances). But the word in the FG (as in Acts viii. 32, and 1 Pet. i. 19) is ἀμνός, in Revelation ἀρνίον, which occurs only once in the rest of the New Testament, in the plural and in its literal sense, in John xxi. 15. Both show an interest in symbolism, particularly numerical symbolism. The 'living water' of John iv. 10 and vii. 38, recalls the 'water of life' of Rev. xxi. 6; xxii. 17. Both use the verb σκηνόω of the divine *tabernacling* among men (John i. 14; Rev. xxi. 3). Both attach the same significance to such concepts as 'life', 'death', 'thirst', 'victory'. There is a difference in their treatment of the Holy Spirit, unitary and personal in the FG, and more of an impersonal power in the Revelation, symbolised by the seven lamps 'which are the seven spirits of God' (Rev. iv. 5; cf. i. 4; iii. 1). This may, however, be due in part to the exigencies of symbolism in the Revelation. The eschatology of the FG is based on a distinction between the temporal and eternal, that of the Revelation on one between present and future. The eschatology of the Revelation is not however wholly futurist, nor is that of the FG completely indifferent to the future, and here the difference may be more apparent than real, due to the fact that the Revelation is 'myth' (μῦθος), while the FG is rational discourse (λόγος). In its eschatology 1 John is closer to the Revelation than to the FG, and forms a kind of bridge between them.

The language of the Revelation presents a difficult problem. In common with the FG it has a Semitic simplicity of construction, but otherwise it is very different from it, and indeed quite unlike any other book written in Greek. It is almost a private language, with a grammar and a syntax which are quite unique, but it is used with perfect consistency and great effectiveness. It seems to have been deliberately fashioned for the purpose of writing the Revelation. So anyone presumably could have written the Revelation—if he was eccentric enough to have invented its language—even the author of the FG! In a special case such as this, it is difficult to apply the ordinary criteria of vocabulary, style, etc., for determining common authorship. There are, however, some features of the vocabulary of the Revelation and of the FG where the two show marked preferences for alternatives both of which are quite normal Greek.[1]

This would seem to make it difficult to admit common authorship, unless indeed there were some considerable lapse of time between the writing of the two books, or the author wrote the Revelation himself and dictated the Gospel and Epistles to a secretary to whom he allowed some freedom of expression.

The resemblances in thought and language between the FG and the Epistles are so close that it has generally been thought unnecessary to argue in detail for identity of authorship. There are nevertheless some differences,[2] and it is a nice question how much significance should be attached to them. C. H. Dodd has

[1] Thus for 'call' or 'name' Revelation uses καλέω 5 times, λέγω once, FG καλέω once, λέγω 13 times: for 'dwell' Revelation uses κατοικέω 13 times, FG μένω 15 times—while in other senses 1 and 2 John have several examples of μένω (some of which can be translated 'dwell' in a metaphorical sense), and Revelation only one; for 'a little while' both Revelation and FG have 2 examples each of μικρὸν χρόνον, while Revelation uses ὀλίγον once, and FG μικρόν 9 times (7 of them in xvi. 16-19); for 'no longer' Revelation has 13 examples of οὐκ .... ἔτι and 3 of οὐκέτι, FG 12 of οὐκέτι; for 'as' (conjunction) Revelation has ὡς 6 times, FG καθώς over 30 times (ὡς occurs only in John vii. 46 in a passage which may be spurious); for 'until' Revelation has 6 examples of ἄχρι and 2 of ἕως, FG 9 and 1 John one of ἕως and none of ἄχρι.

[2] Thus (to give only some examples) contrast 'It is the last hour' (ἐσχάτη ὥρα, 1 John ii. 18) with the teaching of the FG that the decisive 'hour' is that of Christ's death (e.g. John xvi. 23). Of other eschatological terms,'the last day' occurs 6 times in the FG, but not in the Epistles; the 'coming' (παρουσία) of Christ once, and 'Antichrist' 5 times in the Epistles, but not in the FG. Christ is represented as a 'propitiation' in 1 John iv. 10, but the idea does not occur explicitly in the FG. παράκλητος is used of the Holy Spirit in the FG, of Christ in 1 John ii. 1; in 1 John it means 'Advocate', in the FG it has a wider sense. The phrase 'the real light' (τὸ φῶς τὸ ἀληθινόν) occurs both in John i. 9, and in 1 John ii. 8, but 'light' has a different connotation in John i. 4, 'The life was the light of men', and 1 John i. 5, 'God is light'. Such important words in the FG as 'Lord' (Κύριος), 'glory' (δόξα), 'scripture' (γραφή), 'save' (σώζω), are not in the Epistles. 'Faith' (πίστις) is in 1 John v. 4, but not in the FG.

argued against common authorship,[1] and W. F. Howard[2] with equal ingenuity and learning for it. In any case, there is some close connexion between the FG and the Epistles, and the question of authorship may perhaps best be answered by the suggestion[3] that the author of the Epistles was responsible for the final form of the FG, but preserved in it the characteristics of its sources, which account for the differences between the FG and Epistles.

(ii) *The Internal Evidence for the Authorship of the Fourth Gospel*

The FG identifies its author, 'the disciple who bore witness about these things and wrote these things' (xxi. 24), with 'the disciple whom Jesus loved . . . who also leant back against his chest at the supper' (xxi. 20; cf. xiii. 23-25). This disciple was standing by the Cross, and Jesus gave his mother into his care (xix. 25-27). He was thus the witness who saw the blood and water come out of Jesus' side (xix. 35). This is emphasised by the occurrence of the words, 'his witness is true', both in xix. 35, and xxi. 24.[4] It is clear from xxi. 23, 'This saying went out to the brethren, that that disciple was not going to die', that the disciple had in fact died when these words were written. It follows from this that he cannot have written xxi. 24, or indeed the whole of xxi.

From the association of this disciple with Peter both here and at the Last Supper it is a natural inference that he is the 'other disciple', also associated with Peter, in xviii. 15 f., and in xx. 2 ff. It may, however, be that this natural inference is incorrect, since in xiii. 23; xix. 26; xxi. 7, 20, the verb used for 'loved' is ἠγάπα, whereas in xx. 2, it is ἐφίλει. Unless the FG uses these verbs simply as synonyms,[5] there is a case for distinguishing the

[1] 'The First Epistle of John and the Fourth Gospel', *Bulletin of the John Rylands Library*, XXI (1937), pp. 129-156.

[2] 'The Common Authorship of the Johannine Gospel and Epistles', *J.T.S.*, o.s., Vol. XLVIII (1947), pp. 12-25.   [3] For this, see pp. 47 f.

[4] Though, curiously enough, 'true' in xix. 35, is ἀληθινή, and in xxi. 24, ἀληθής. See p. 75, n. 3.

[5] This is unlikely. In xxi. 15-17 it is possible that John uses both verbs in a way which suggests that he distinguishes between them. See the note on iii. 16, p. 130, n. 2.

THE GOSPEL ACCORDING TO ST JOHN

'other disciple' of xviii. 15, and xx. 2, from the disciple whom Jesus loved.

The Beloved Disciple, whether or not he is the same as the Other Disciple, could be any one of the seven mentioned in xxi. 1, 2, but the choice may in fact be narrowed down to the two sons of Zebedee and the two other disciples who are un-named. The tradition fixed on John the son of Zebedee, and there is nothing in the rest of the FG which absolutely prevents this identification. It does, however, involve certain difficulties.

Thus there is the question whether a Galilean fisherman, even a wealthy one, perhaps with trading interests in Jerusalem, would be known to the High Priest. This can easily be overcome if the distinction between the Beloved Disciple and the Other Disciple is accepted, or alternatively if one supposes (as is not inconceivable) that John the son of Zebedee was in fact a priest who earned his living as a fisherman in Galilee when he was not on duty in the Temple.[1]

But there are others also. The Beloved Disciple was by the Cross, yet Mark xiv. 50, echoed by Matt. xxvi. 56, says that the disciples who were in the Garden (i.e. the Twelve) forsook Jesus and fled; Luke xxii. 54, 'Peter followed a long way behind', implies the same. Admittedly there are other differences be-tween the accounts of the Crucifixion in the Synoptic Gospels and the FG, but this is a particularly obvious one. Then again the FG mentions none of the incidents in the Synoptic Gospels in which John the son of Zebedee figured. This is not difficult to understand if the FG was written as a kind of supplement to the Synoptic Gospels, but it is if the FG is substantially inde-pendent of them. Then again in the FG Jesus entrusts his mother to the care of the Beloved Disciple. Would he have done this if the Beloved Disciple had been one whom he had called to leave all the joys and duties of family life to be an apostle? Finally there is the fact that the standpoint of the FG is Judaean rather than Galilean. It is Judaea which is Jesus' 'own country' (John iv. 44),[2] and in Jerusalem and its environs that most of the incidents in the Gospel are located. The Twelve also are by no means as prominent in the FG as they are in the Synoptic

---

[1] This suggestion I owe to Prof. H. Riesenfeld.
[2] But see also the note *ad loc.*

Gospels. In the FG they are mentioned, as a group, only in vi. 67-71, and in xx. 24, though individuals are mentioned elsewhere.

None of these difficulties is insuperable, and even taken together they would not rule out the identification of the Beloved Disciple with John the son of Zebedee, if two important conditions were fulfilled. One of these is that the external evidence were clear and unanimous from the start; this will be considered in the next section of the Introduction. The other is that there were nothing in the FG pointing to a different identification of the Beloved Disciple.

Now I would maintain that a clear indication of his identity is given in John xi. 5, 'Jesus loved (ἠγάπα) Martha and her sister and Lazarus'. He is therefore Lazarus, and the fact that, according to the FG, Lazarus had already died once provides a natural explanation for the belief that the Beloved Disciple was not going to die, based on the misunderstanding of Jesus' words recorded in John xxi. 22. This involves supposing that the Twelve were not the only disciples present at the Last Supper, but there is nothing in the FG to compel us to think that they were; this difficulty is no greater than those which are involved in the traditional view of authorship.

The great stumbling-block is of course the raising of Lazarus. But if one can believe that Lazarus was raised from the dead (as I suppose most defenders of the traditional authorship do), it is straining at the gnat and swallowing the camel to think that he could not have written any of the material incorporated in the FG, if there is any indication that he did so. And even if one cannot accept the raising of Lazarus as historical fact, to believe that the evangelist (who certainly so regarded it) intended him to be identified as the Beloved Disciple is only to add one more to the already long list of fictions which (according to the sceptics) the evangelist was responsible for propagating.

I do, however, happen to believe that Lazarus was raised from the dead, and to accept him as the Beloved Disciple does account for certain features of the FG which cannot be explained so well on the traditional theory of authorship, such as the Judaean standpoint of the Gospel and the centrality of the raising of Lazarus in the scheme of the Gospel. Moreover, since

Lazarus had not been called to be an apostle, he could take Jesus' mother into his own home more easily than the son of Zebedee could have done—and incidentally we may infer from the absence of any mention of her in the household at Bethany, that Lazarus' own mother was dead (which John's was not [1]).

Finally, since there is nothing to prevent us supposing that Lazarus was known to the High Priest, it is not necessary on the hypothesis that he was the Beloved Disciple to draw a distinction between the Beloved Disciple and the Other Disciple. There are, however, indications in the external evidence [2] which may point to this distinction being a real one, and to the possibility that the John who published the Gospel in Ephesus was the Other Disciple.

(iii) *The External Evidence for the Authorship of the Fourth Gospel*

The earliest indisputable evidence for the existence of the FG is the Rylands Papyrus 457 [3] (No. 52 in the list of New Testament papyri). The date of this is about A.D. 125. Of approximately the same date is a fragment of an unknown gospel (Egerton Papyrus 2) which appears to have been based on the FG. Before this date there are only what appear to be echoes of the phraseology of the FG which may indicate that the writers in whose books they appear had read the FG. In the nature of the case it is hard to estimate the significance of such possible allusions.

In 1 Clement, written probably about A.D. 96 in Rome, there are four passages with some resemblances in phraseology to the FG:

xliii, 'That the name of the true and only Lord may be glorified', recalls two passages of the FG, John xii. 28, 'Father, glorify thy name', and xvii. 3, where 'only' and 'true' are applied together to God; here δοξάζω, ὄνομα, μόνος, and ἀληθινός are common to 1 Clement and the FG.

xlix, 'Let him that hath love in Christ keep the commandments of Christ', recalls John xiv. 15, 'If you love me, keep my

---

[1] According to Matt. xxvii. 56, she was among the women who had followed Jesus from Galilee, and were watching the crucifixion from a distance.   [2] See pp. 33-44.   [3] See p. 25 and n. 1.

commandments', where the noun ἀγάπη in 1 Clement corresponds to the verb ἀγαπάω in the FG, but both have different words for 'keep' and 'commandments'.

ibid. '(Jesus gave) his flesh for our flesh' cf. John vi. 51, 'The bread which I shall give is my flesh, for the life of the world'.

lx, 'Cleanse us with the cleansing of thy truth' cf. John xvii. 17, 'Sanctify them in the truth'.

Since 1 Clement is virtually contemporary with the FG,[1] these resemblances between them cannot be more than co-incidental. But they are included because they provide some standard by which to judge the probability of passages in later writings, no closer to the FG than these, being in fact dependent on it.

The Epistle of Barnabas, written probably in Alexandria not much later than 1 Clement, interprets the Brazen Serpent of Num. xxi. 9, as a type of Christ, as does John iii. 14. As this is the only passage in the New Testament to use this rather recondite typology, Barnabas xii. 7 may be dependent on it.

In the Epistles of Ignatius, written shortly before his martyrdom, which took place not later than A.D. 110, there are many resemblances in thought and language to the FG, though nothing that can be called a quotation. A good example of these resemblances between them is Magnesians viii. 2, 'There is one God who revealed himself through Jesus Christ his Son, who is his Word that proceeded from silence, who in all things pleased him who sent him', which recalls John i. 18, and viii. 29. There are so many of these passages in Ignatius that it seems reasonable to suppose that he knew the FG. If so, the FG was in Antioch by A.D. 110. It may be significant that when he wrote to Ephesus Ignatius mentioned St Paul, but said nothing of John. John is said to have survived into the reign of Trajan (A.D. 98–117), and cannot have been long dead when Ignatius wrote. One might have expected some mention of the last survivor of the Twelve, if John had been such. But perhaps Ignatius was so preoccupied with his own impending martyrdom that only the martyr Paul seemed worth his mention.

The earliest evidence to link the FG with John as author and with Asia Minor is that provided by information about Polycarp

[1] For the date of the FG see below, pp. 44-47, 51.

and Papias. Polycarp was already bishop of Smyrna at the time of Ignatius' martyrdom, and Papias, bishop of Hierapolis, was his contemporary. Of Polycarp Irenaeus, who became bishop of Lyons about A.D. 178, says that 'not only was he instructed by apostles, and associated with many who had seen the Christ, but also was appointed by apostles in Asia bishop in the church in Smyrna', and that he himself had seen him when he was young and Polycarp very old.[1] Polycarp died a martyr about A.D. 156. Irenaeus gives some further details of Polycarp in a letter[2] to Florinus, a former companion of his who had fallen into heresy. In this he mentions by name John as one of those who had seen the Lord and with whom Polycarp had been associated, and whose words he related. Of Papias Irenaeus says that he was a hearer of John and a companion of Polycarp,[3] though Eusebius, when quoting this statement of Irenaeus (*H.E.*, III. 39), adds that Papias' own words show that he had not himself heard or seen the apostles, but had received the faith from those who had been acquainted with them. He then quotes a passage from Papias which includes the following sentence, from which apparently he concluded that Papias had not actually met any apostles:

'If by chance anyone came who had been a follower of the elders, I asked him the words of the elders; what Andrew or what Peter said, or what Philip, or what Thomas, or James; or what John, or Matthew, or any other of the Lord's disciples; and what Aristion and the elder John, the disciples of the Lord, say.'[4]

Eusebius himself concluded from this passage that the inclusion of the name of John twice, once in the list of apostles,

---

[1] Καὶ Πολύκαρπος δὲ οὐ μόνον ὑπὸ ἀποστόλων μαθητευθείς, καὶ συναναστραφεὶς πολλοῖς τοῖς τὸν Χριστὸν ἑωρακόσιν, ἀλλὰ καὶ ὑπὸ ἀποστόλων, καταστασθεὶς εἰς τὴν Ἀσίαν ἐν τῇ ἐν Σμύρνῃ ἐκκλησίᾳ ἐπίσκοπος, ὃν καὶ ἡμεῖς ἑωράκαμεν ἐν τῇ πρώτῃ ἡμῶν ἡλικίᾳ. ἐπιπολὺ γὰρ παρέμεινε, καὶ πάνυ γηραλέος . . . (*adv. Haer.*, III. iii. 4, ed. Harvey, Vol. II, p. 12).

[2] Preserved by Eusebius (*H.E.*, V. 20). Irenaeus speaks of Polycarp telling of his association with John, τὴν μετὰ Ἰωάννου συναναστροφὴν ὡς ἀπήγγελλε.

[3] Ἰωάννου μὲν ἀκουστής, Πολυκάρπου δὲ ἑταῖρος γεγονώς.

[4] Εἰ δέ που καὶ παρηκολουθηκώς τις τοῖς πρεσβυτέροις ἔλθοι, τοὺς τῶν πρεσβυτέρων ἀνέκρινον λόγους· τί Ἀνδρέας, ἢ τί Πέτρος εἶπεν, ἢ τί Φίλιππος, ἢ τί Θωμᾶς, ἢ Ἰάκωβος· ἢ τί Ἰωάννης, ἢ Ματθαῖος, ἤ τις ἕτερος τῶν τοῦ κυρίου μαθητῶν· ἅ τε Ἀριστίων καὶ ὁ πρεσβύτερος Ἰωάννης οἱ τοῦ κυρίου μαθηταὶ λέγουσιν.

and again with the epithet 'elder' and in association with Aristion, supported the view of Dionysius of Alexandria[1] that there had been two men named John in Asia. Eusebius' motive in this is obvious: he wants to find an author for the Revelation who is not an apostle. But this does not necessarily mean that Eusebius has misunderstood Papias, though he has read more into his words than they say. Papias does not suggest that both Johns were in Asia. One might even infer from his having to rely on hearsay that neither of them was—why did he not take the short journey from Hierapolis to Ephesus to find out for himself what John was saying? We cannot tell. He may indeed have met John, and still have been anxious to collect records of what he had said to others.

It is sometimes argued that Eusebius was mistaken in supposing that Papias meant to distinguish the two men named John, and was exploiting his looseness of expression in the interests of his own ideas. But the facts that the first John is in a list of men who were all apparently members of the Twelve, and that the second is called 'the elder', are more naturally explained on the assumption that they were different persons, and that John 'the elder' was indeed a disciple, but not one of the Twelve. If so, then it was this John whom Papias knew (and presumably Polycarp also), since Papias writes of those in his first list in the past tense—'what Andrew or what Peter said'—and of Aristion and the elder John in the present. This suggests that only the latter were alive at the time when Papias made his enquiries.

Eusebius also says of Papias that 'he used testimonies from the first epistle of John'.[2] Polycarp also seems to have known it, for his own Epistle to the Philippians contains many echoes of 1 John.[3] It is often argued that this must mean that they also knew the FG. Though this argument is not conclusive, it is quite probable.[4]

[1] See above, p. 25.
[2] H.E., III. 39, ad fin.
[3] E.g. 'Whoever does not confess that Jesus Christ came in the flesh is Antichrist' (Polycarp, Phil. vii. 1), cf. 1 John iv. 2 f.
[4] Is it only a coincidence that the order of the first three Apostles in Papias' Preface (quoted above, p. 34)—Andrew, Peter, Philip—is that also in John i. 40-43?

Papias indeed is said to have been John's amanuensis. The authority for this surprising assertion is the so-called Anti-Marcionite Prologue to the FG. This is found in a number of Latin manuscripts, and is thought to be a translation of a Greek original of the period A.D. 150–200 but it should be used with caution. It states:

'The Gospel of John was revealed to the churches by John while he was still in the body, as Papias of Hierapolis, John's dear disciple, recorded in his five exegetical books. He wrote down the Gospel correctly at John's dictation. But the heretic Marcion, after he had been reproved by him for his contrary opinions, was rejected by John. He had brought him writings or letters from the brethren who were in Pontus.'[1]

This has an obvious apologetic motive, to clear the FG of imputations of heresy, such as the 'Alogi' were making at the period. Its claim that John had met and rebuked Marcion is incredible—their dates do not allow it.[2] How much else must be rejected is uncertain. If Papias did in fact mention John's authorship of the FG it is surprising that Irenaeus does not quote him.[3] If he was John's secretary, Eusebius can hardly have had the effrontery to deny that he knew John. The most one can accept from this Prologue is the publication of the FG during the lifetime of John, and the possibility that Papias had been associated at some time with him. But it is also possible that the Prologue is based on nothing more than the statement of Irenaeus[4] that John published the Gospel at Ephesus and the

[1] *Evangelium Iohannis manifestatum est ecclesiis a Iohanne adhuc in corpore constituto sicut Papias nomine Hierapolitanus, discipulus Iohannis carus, in †exotericis, id est in extremis†, quinque libris rettulit. Descripsit vero evangelium dictante Iohanne recte. Verum Marcion haereticus, cum ab eo fuisset improbatus, eo quod contraria sentiebat, abiectus est ab Iohanne. Is vero scripta vel epistulas ad eum pertulerat a fratribus qui in Ponto fuerunt.* I have ventured to replace *in exotericis, id est in extremis* by 'exegetical' in the translation on the assumption that *exotericis* is a mistake for *exegeticis*, and *id est in extremis* a gloss attempting to explain the corrupt and unintelligible *exotericis*. Papias' book was Λογίων Κυριακῶν Ἐξηγήσεις.

[2] But, as Irenaeus' story of Polycarp's rebuke of Marcion shows (*Adv. Haer.*, III. iii. 4; E.T. in *A New Eusebius*, ed. J. Stevenson (1957), p. 119), Marcion had dealings with John's disciples.

[3] But Irenaeus does not quote Papias or any other authority for his statements on Matthew and Mark either, though he may well have taken them from him. See below, p. 40.

[4] See below, p. 39.

belief that Papias had been associated at some period with
him.[1]

Papias is also referred to by two late writers as their source for
the statement that John the Apostle was killed by the Jews. One
is the fifth-century historian Philip of Side, the other the ninth-
century chronicler George the Sinner. Though neither says that
he was killed along with his brother James, it is sometimes
claimed that this is what happened, and that the present text
of Acts xii. 2, 'He killed James the brother of John with the
sword', which admittedly is an odd way of referring to James
the son of Zebedee, read originally, 'He killed James and John
his brother with the sword', and has been altered to comply
with the dominant tradition. Yet both Irenaeus and Eusebius
had read Papias (which probably neither Philip of Side nor
George had done), and it is difficult to believe that they would
have suppressed this information, even in the interests of their
view of the origin of the FG.[2] It is safer to leave the death of
John the son of Zebedee unexplained than to rely on such
dubious information.

The evidence of Papias and Polycarp then, while by no means
indisputable, suggests the presence in Asia of a disciple of the
Lord named John as late as the early second century A.D. But
for the final assessment of the meaning and value of their
evidence we must wait to consider Irenaeus, the interpretation of whose statements is of crucial importance in this
enquiry.

To the same period as Papias and Polycarp belongs the Alexandrian Gnostic Valentinus. He radically transformed Christianity into an elaborate Hellenistic theosophical system, which
proved very popular. The FG was known in Egypt in his time,
and it is very probable that Valentinus himself knew and used
it. The Jung Codex, a Coptic MS. discovered with several
others at Nag Hammadi in Egypt, contains (with other matter)
a 'Gospel of Truth' which appears to be the work of Valentinus,

---

[1] The fact that it does not claim John as *Jesus*' 'dear disciple' may,
however, tell in favour of its independence of, and priority to, Irenaeus.

[2] Though if Irenaeus did not in fact attribute the FG to the son of
Zebedee (see below, pp. 41 f.), his early martyrdom would have been no
difficulty to him. But even so, this would still leave Eusebius guilty of a
serious suppression of the truth.

and shows that he (if he was indeed its author) was familiar with the FG.[1]

His pupil Heracleon wrote the first known commentary on the FG about A.D. 160; Irenaeus[2] preserves an exposition of part of the Prologue by another pupil of his, Ptolemaeus, and Clement of Alexandria[3] yet another, by Theodotus, another of Valentinus' pupils.[4] Ptolemaeus certainly ascribed the FG to 'John', and we may perhaps infer that Heracleon also did from the fact that Origen, who usually quotes Heracleon only when he disagrees with him, says nothing of his opinion on the authorship of the FG. Valentinus and later Heracleon visited Rome, and if it was known there that they used the FG, it is not surprising that Catholic Christians later in the century ascribed the FG to Cerinthus, or that the Anti-Marcionite Prologue is so anxious to dissociate the FG from heresy. It seems clear, however, that the first known ascription of the FG to 'John' was made by Ptolemaeus. And, knowing how fond the Gnostics were of claiming that their speculations were really the secret doctrine handed down by the Apostles to their favourite disciples, we may infer that by 'John' Ptolemaeus meant the son of Zebedee. This is why the Anti-Marcionite Prologue refers to Papias as 'John's *dear* disciple'. It was through him, not through any heretic, that the authentic tradition came.

Justin Martyr, who, as we have seen, ascribed the Revelation to 'John, one of the apostles of Christ', can be shown, from the many resemblances to its phraseology in his writings, to have known the FG, but he never mentions it, or its author, by name.

---

[1] See *The Jung Codex*, three studies ed. F. L. Cross (1955), and particularly the article in it by W. C. van Unnik, 'The "Gospel of Truth" and the New Testament'. On pp. 115-121 van Unnik lists allusions to the NT found in this document, including several from the FG. See also *Evangelium Veritatis*, ed. M. Malinine, H.-C. Puech, and G. Quispel (1956). [Cf. also R. E. Brown, 'The Gospel of Thomas and St John's Gospel', *N.T.S.*, Vol. IX, 1962–63, pp. 155-177, who argues that the Gospel of Thomas—which may or may not be properly described as a Gnostic work—'does show some contact with ideas and vocabulary such as those found in John', though he does not think the compiler of this document himself knew the FG.—B. A. M.]

[2] *adversus Haereses*, I. viii. 5 (ed. Harvey, Vol. I, pp. 75-80).

[3] Ed. Stählin, Vol. III, pp. 107-109.

[4] Irenaeus is therefore quite justified in speaking of the Valentinians using the FG very fully. *Hi autem qui a Valentino sunt, eo quod est secundum Iohannem plenissime utentes* (*adv. Haer.*, III. xi. 10, ed. Harvey, Vol. II, p. 46).

Yet he had been in Ephesus, and was in Rome at the same time as Valentinus. This may provide the clue to his silence. If he believed the FG to be the work of John the Apostle, and had an authority for this belief other than Valentinus, it is curious that he does not mention it.

Some time, perhaps not a long time, after A.D. 150 the Acts of John by Leucius Charinus identifies the Beloved Disciple with John the Apostle, but denies that he wrote a Gospel.[1] Though worthless as history, this book is nevertheless evidence for the belief that the Apostle had been active in Ephesus and the surrounding country. Its denial that he wrote a Gospel is simply a heretical attempt to discredit the FG, from which some of its material is clearly borrowed, but which contradicted the favourite thesis of the Acts of John that the Christ had only a spiritual body.

After this, evidence becomes much more detailed. Tatian, the disciple of Justin Martyr, who was in Rome until about A.D. 170, furnishes the first exact quotations of the FG—of John i. 5, in his *Oratio ad Graecos* xiii. 1, and of John i. 3, *ibid*. xix. 4. He also used the FG along with the other three Canonical Gospels in his *Diatessaron*, a Gospel harmony which, in a Syriac version, was long popular in the East. He says nothing, however, of the authorship of the FG.

The first quotation by an orthodox writer of the FG as Scripture and the work of John is by Theophilus of Antioch, about A.D. 180.[2] But by this time Irenaeus was already at work on (if he had not already published) his great treatise against heresy, in which he describes the origin of the FG as follows:

'Then (i.e. after the other three canonical Gospels) John the disciple of the Lord, who also had leaned against his breast, himself also published the Gospel when he was living at Ephesus in Asia.'[3]

He also states that it was written to exclude the heresy of

[1] See *The Apocryphal New Testament*, ed. M. R. James (1924), p. 251.

[2] *Ad Autolycum*, II. xxii. ὅθεν διδάσκουσιν ἡμᾶς αἱ ἅγιαι γραφαί, καὶ πάντες οἱ πνευματοφόροι, ἐξ ὧν Ἰωάννης λέγει· Ἐν ἀρχῇ ἦν ὁ λόγος· καὶ ὁ λόγος ἦν πρὸς τὸν θεόν.

[3] Ἔπειτα Ἰωάννης ὁ μαθητὴς τοῦ κυρίου, ὁ καὶ ἐπὶ τὸ στῆθος αὐτοῦ ἀναπεσών, καὶ αὐτὸς ἐξέδωκε τὸ εὐαγγέλιον, ἐν Ἐφέσῳ τῆς Ἀσίας διατρίβων (*adv. Haer.*, III. i. 2, ed. Harvey, Vol. II, p. 6).

Cerinthus and the Nicolaitans, and to establish a rule of truth in the Church.[1] This is clearly aimed at the 'Alogi'. Elsewhere he says that John survived until the time of Trajan.[2]

His authority for these statements must be supposed to come from the elders who had associated with John, to whom he refers from time to time for support, as for example, for the opinion that the ministry of Jesus lasted more than ten years.[3] Elsewhere he refers to a single unnamed elder as his authority for various opinions. But when he gives his account of the origin of the Gospels he does not appeal to any authority.

These elders included Polycarp and probably also Papias. Irenaeus' accounts of the Gospels of Matthew and Mark[4] are close enough to those of Papias as recorded by Eusebius[5] to suggest that Irenaeus was here dependent on Papias.[6] If so, he may also have taken his account of the FG from him. Against this the silence of Eusebius has to be set, but Eusebius may not have quoted Papias on the FG because he did not think he gave an adequate account of it. This may help to vindicate the Anti-Marcionite Prologue's account of Papias' witness to John. If Irenaeus derived his information, at least in part, from Papias, it is of less account than it would otherwise be that he never

---

[1] *Hanc fidem annuntians Iohannes Domini discipulus, volens per Evangelii annuntiationem auferre eum qui a Cerintho inseminatus erat hominibus errorem, et multo prius ab his qui dicuntur Nicolaitae* . . . . . . *et regulam veritatis constituere in Ecclesia* (adv. Haer., III. xi. 7, ed. Harvey, Vol. II, pp. 40 f.).

[2] Παρέμεινε . . . μέχρι τῶν Τραϊανοῦ χρόνων (adv. Haer., II. xxxiii. 3, ed. Harvey, Vol. I, p. 331); cf. adv. Haer., III. iii. 4 (ed. Harvey, Vol. II, p. 15).

[3] 'As the Gospel and all the elders who had associated with John in Asia testify that John had handed down', *sicut Evangelium et omnes seniores testantur, qui in Asia apud Iohannem discipulum Domini convenerunt, id ipsum tradidisse eis Iohannem* (adv. Haer., II. xxxiii. 3). These words immediately precede the passage quoted in the previous note. These 'elders' are also his authority for the prophecy about the marvellous vines in the Millennium (adv. Haer., V. xxxiii. 3, ed. Harvey, Vol. II, p. 417 f.)—just before his mention of Papias.

[4] adv. Haer., III. i. 2 (ed. Harvey, Vol. II, pp. 3-6); Eusebius, H.E., V. 8.

[5] H.E., III. 39.

[6] Cf. (on Matthew) Irenaeus Ὁ μὲν δὴ Ματθαῖος ἐν τοῖς Ἑβραίοις τῇ ἰδίᾳ διαλέκτῳ αὐτῶν καὶ γραφὴν ἐξήνεγκεν εὐαγγελίου with Papias Ματθαῖος μὲν οὖν Ἑβραΐδι διαλέκτῳ τὰ λόγια συνεγράψατο; and (on Mark) Irenaeus Μάρκος ὁ μαθητὴς καὶ ἑρμηνευτὴς Πέτρου, καὶ αὐτὸς τὰ ὑπὸ Πέτρου κηρυσσόμενα ἐγγράφως ἡμῖν παραδέδωκε with Papias' report of 'the elder's' (John's?) words Μάρκος μὲν ἑρμηνευτὴς Πέτρου γενόμενος, ὅσα ἐμνημόνευσεν, ἀκριβῶς ἔγραψεν.

claims that he got his information from Polycarp, the only one of the two whom apparently he had actually heard.

There is, however, no hint in all that Irenaeus says that either Polycarp or Papias was the source of his own identification of the author of the FG with the Beloved Disciple. This would seem to be his own inference from the testimony of the elders that John had seen the Lord, taken in conjunction with that of the FG itself. An alternative possibility is that he got it from a tradition which had grown up in Asia after the period of the elders, the first indication of which is found in the Leucian Acts of John.[1] Irenaeus, however, nowhere asserts that the Beloved Disciple *was* the son of Zebedee, and when in one passage[2] he is clearly referring to John the son of Zebedee, he does not say that he was the Beloved Disciple. This is when, alluding to Gal. ii. 9, he names Peter, James, and John as 'the apostles whom the Lord made witnesses of his whole ministry and his whole teaching, for they are everywhere found associating with him'.[3] He had the names in this order in his text of Galatians,[4] and his words show that by James and John he understood the sons of Zebedee. Since he is arguing against Marcion's attempt to set Paul against the other apostles, it would have strengthened his case to call John the Beloved Disciple, if he had thought that he was.

It is thus not even certain that Irenaeus himself regarded John as the son of Zebedee. There is no evidence that Papias or Polycarp did. When Irenaeus says that Polycarp had been appointed Bishop by the apostles, he does not say that Polycarp himself said this. All that can be derived from the testimony of Polycarp and Papias is that there was a former disciple of the Lord in Asia in the early second century named John. This 'elder' John is not a 'shadowy figure', or a *Doppelgänger*, as is sometimes said. It is John the son of Zebedee about whom we know nothing apart from what is in the New Testament.

---

[1] See above, p. 39. Later evidence for this is given by Polycrates, for whom see below, pp. 42 f.

[2] *adv. Haer.*, III. xii. 9 (ed. Harvey, Vol. II, p. 72).

[3] *Apostoli, quos universi actus et universae doctrinae Dominus testes fecit, ubique enim simul cum eo assistentes inveniuntur Petrus et Iacobus et Iohannes.*

[4] As have also P[46] D G, the Old Latin, Marcion, Tertullian, and some later Latin Fathers.

When Irenaeus was writing, it is probable that the Valentinians were claiming the apostolic authority of the FG for their doctrines. Irenaeus could either tacitly admit the correctness of their exegesis and repudiate the FG, which is what the 'Alogi' did, or else he could accept the Gospel as the work of a disciple, as the Anti-Marcionite Prologue did, and refute the Valentinians' exegesis. His loyalty to his vivid (but not necessarily accurate) boyhood memories of Polycarp as well as the soundness of his instinct as an exegete inclined him inevitably to the latter course. In the circumstances it is surprising that, if he thought John was the son of Zebedee, he did not say so. The suspicion must remain that he did not think that he was.

Another account of the origin of the FG is given in the so-called *Muratorian Canon*,[1] a fragmentary document in barbarous Latin and with a corrupt text, but important because it appears to be the translation of a Greek original contemporary with, but independent of, Irenaeus. Of the FG it says:

'The fourth of the Gospels ⟨is by⟩ John, one of the disciples. When his fellow disciples and bishops exhorted him ⟨to write it⟩, he said, "Fast with me today for three days, and whatever is revealed to any one of us, let us tell it to one another." In the same night it was revealed to Andrew, one of the apostles, that, with the approval of them all, John should write down everything in his own name.'[2]

John, it may be noted, is only called a disciple, while Andrew is called an apostle. This account can hardly be accepted as historical. It looks rather like an attempt to provide apostolic authority for a work that was known not to be of strictly apostolic authorship, interpreting John xxi. 24, 'We know that his witness is true,' as a kind of apostolic *imprimatur*.

Some curious information about the Asian John is preserved by Polycrates, bishop of Ephesus towards the end of the second

---

[1] An emended text is given in A. Souter, *The Text and Canon of the New Testament* (2nd ed., 1954) pp. 191-193, and a translation in H. Bettenson, *Documents of the Christian Church* (1943), pp. 40 f.

[2] *Quartum evangeliorum Iohannis ex decipolis (i.e. discipulis). Cohortantibus condescipulis et ep⟨iscopi⟩s suis, dixit, Conieiunate mihi ⟨h⟩odie triduo et quid cuique fuerit revelatum alterutrum nobis ennarremus. Eadem nocte revelatum Andreae ex apostolis ut recogniscentibus cun⟨c⟩tis Iohannis suo nomine cuncta discriberet.*

century A.D. In a letter to Pope Victor defending the Asian method of keeping Easter, he appeals to the saints of Asia as his authorities. He mentions 'Philip, one of the twelve apostles, who sleeps in Hierapolis, and his two daughters, aged virgins, and his other daughter who lived in the Holy Spirit and rests in Ephesus. And moreover John, who leaned against the Lord's breast, who had been a priest wearing the *petalon*,[1] both a martyr (or simply 'witness') and teacher; he sleeps in Ephesus.'[2]

This has no more claim to be considered historical than the *Muratorian Canon* has, but is nevertheless highly significant. Polycrates is anxious to find witnesses sufficiently impressive to counterbalance the Roman witnesses, Peter and Paul. So he first cites 'Philip, one of the twelve apostles'. Doubtless Philip did live and die in Hierapolis, but a reference to Acts xxi. 8 f., will show that he was Philip, one of the seven deacons, who had four virgin daughters who were prophetesses—unless by some extraordinary coincidence Philip the Apostle and Philip the deacon *both* had virgin daughters who were prophetesses. Doubtless the local patriotism of Hierapolis is responsible for the promotion.

Only after Philip does he mention John, as if tacitly admitting that John was not one of the Twelve, since in every list of the Twelve the sons of Zebedee take precedence over Philip.[3] His claims to consideration are the facts that he was the Beloved Disciple of the FG, and that he had been (apparently, if Polycrates means what he says) High Priest. He can therefore hardly have thought that he was the son of Zebedee, whatever the origin or value may be of his statement. It may only be an inference, considerably embroidered, from John xviii. 15 f., or

---

[1] I.e. the gold plate worn on the High Priest's turban (Exodus xxviii. 36-38).

[2] Φίλιππον τῶν δώδεκα ἀποστόλων, ὃς κεκοίμηται ἐν Ἱεραπόλει, καὶ δύο θυγατέρες αὐτοῦ γεγηρακυῖαι παρθένοι, καὶ ἡ ἑτέρα αὐτοῦ θυγάτηρ ἐν Ἁγίῳ Πνεύματι πολιτευσαμένη ἐν Ἐφέσῳ ἀναπαύεται. Ἔτι δὲ καὶ Ἰωάννης, ὁ ἐπὶ τὸ στῆθος τοῦ κυρίου ἀναπεσών, ὃς ἐγενήθη ἱερεὺς τὸ πέταλον πεφορεκώς, καὶ μάρτυς καὶ διδάσκαλος· οὗτος ἐν Ἐφέσῳ κεκοίμηται (Eusebius, *H.E.*, III. 31, repeated V. 24).

[3] Though in the incomplete list which Papias gives Philip comes before James and John, after Andrew and Peter. This may reflect the honour in which Asia held Philip, and perhaps also Andrew, if the legend in the *Muratorian Canon* rests on an Asian foundation. See also p. 34.

possibly an indication that the Asian John was indeed of high priestly family. This may suggest that he was the Other Disciple of John xviii. 15 f., and xx. 2, if this Other Disciple is indeed to be distinguished from the Beloved Disciple. If nevertheless Polycrates *did* think that the Asian John was the son of Zebedee (as Irenaeus also may have done, though neither actually says so), it was in the face of the evidence which he himself cites. John, as well as Philip, was promoted apostle by the imagination and zeal of the Church of Asia.

The conclusion to which this investigation has led is that there was no such continuous, clear, and unanimous tradition that the Beloved Disciple was John the son of Zebedee as was stated above[1] to be necessary before this identification could be accepted. Instead, it appears probable that it began as a heretical opinion, designed to add weight to the theories which the Valentinians sought to support by its authority. At the same period the church in Asia Minor accepted it as flattering to their local pride and a useful support to their peculiar, but possibly primitive, method of keeping Easter. There was, however, in Asia Minor a former disciple named John, who was known to Papias and Polycarp, and who, according to the Anti-Marcionite Prologue, the *Muratorian Canon*, and Irenaeus, published the FG. If this John had been the Beloved Disciple, one might have expected this fact to emerge in an earlier and less tendentious authority than the Leucian Acts of John. I conclude therefore that it is not unreasonable to distinguish the Other Disciple, John, from the Beloved Disciple, Lazarus, and to attempt an account of the origin of the Johannine literature on that assumption. I have already said[2] that a satisfactory theory of the origin of the FG must also take account of the Epistles and Revelation. The following hypothesis is designed to do this.

(iv) *The Origin of the Gospel, Epistles, and Revelation of St John*[3]

The author of the Revelation is named John, and the close

---

[1] See p. 31.　　　[2] See p. 26.
[3] [Cf. the paper by J. N. Sanders, published posthumously, 'St John on Patmos', *N.T.S.*, Vol. IX, 1962–63, pp. 75–85.—B. A. M.]

connexion of the book with the Roman province of Asia suggests that this John is to be identified with the John who was buried at Ephesus; this is a reasonable conclusion even if the Revelation is in fact a pseudepigraph.

Of him we are told that he was 'on the island called Patmos on account of the word of God and the testimony of Jesus' (Rev. i. 9). He had therefore been sentenced to banishment, *relegatio*, for his activity as a Christian. This comparatively mild punishment was generally given to eminent persons who had been indiscreet rather than positively criminal, and was designed to put them out of harm's way, far from their old associations. The Roman poet Ovid had been banished to Tomi on the Black Sea; Augustus' daughter Julia to the island of Pandateria; Herod Antipas to Lyons, to quote only a few examples. It may therefore be inferred from the nature of his punishment that John was a person of some eminence—a Jewish aristocrat 'known to the High Priest' was more likely to suffer *relegatio* than a Galilean fisherman; that he had not lived so near to Patmos as Ephesus before his banishment; and that he was exiled before Christianity had become a capital offence. It looks therefore as though John was banished to Patmos for his activities in Judaea in, say, the early sixties, rather than as late as the reign of Domitian.

While he was in Patmos, he learned of the condition of the churches in Asia, and wrote the Seven Letters incorporated in the Revelation, none of which contains anything which requires us to suppose that he knew the seven churches personally or had ever lived in any one of them. According to Eusebius (*H.E.*, III. 23, *ad init.*) he was released after the death of Domitian,[1] and according to Irenaeus,[2] survived in Ephesus until the reign of Trajan.

Domitian died in A.D. 96, and a milder regime began during the brief reign of Nerva, and continued under Trajan (A.D. 98–117). Thus, if Eusebius is correct, John's first *personal* acquaintance with Ephesus was in A.D. 96 or 97. By that time he must have been very old. If he was a lad of fifteen at the time of the crucifixion, he would be about eighty in A.D. 96. The tradition

---

[1] ἀπὸ τῆς κατὰ τὴν νῆσον μετὰ τὴν Δομετιανοῦ τελευτὴν ἐπανελθὼν φυγῆς.

[2] See p. 40 above.

agrees that he lived to a great age, and it would not have been impossible for him to have lived for some years into the reign of Trajan. Polycarp himself was at least eighty-six when he was executed about A.D. 156, and could well have met John after his release from Patmos, when he himself would have been about twenty-six.

When John arrived in Ephesus the church there had been in existence for more than a generation. It had been founded by Paul, and according to Eusebius (*H.E.*, III. 4) its first bishop had been Timothy. Onesimus was bishop when Ignatius wrote his Epistle to the Ephesians. The arrival of so venerable a survivor of the church of Jerusalem in a church founded by St Paul, whose relations with Jerusalem had been difficult, must have been something of an embarrassment to Timothy or Onesimus, particularly as John appeared anxious to exercise some control over the churches of Asia. So much is clear from 2 and 3 John, which also show that his intervention was resented by some.[1] It is unlikely that in his lifetime he had much influence, beyond the circle of his immediate disciples. To the churches of Asia he must have been a remote, if formidable, figure, and it was only after he was safely dead that they realised what an asset they had in him. Ignatius ignores his presence in Ephesus, but after his time the tradition arose of John the Apostle as the authority for the Asian method of keeping Easter, and the source of traditions about the Lord. This had happened within a generation of his death.[2]

The Revelation was the first of the works attributed to him to have any popularity in orthodox circles, as Justin Martyr shows. Can it be regarded as the work of John? 'Revelations' generally are pseudonymous, and if John's Revelation were such it might be easier to attribute the FG and Epistles to its reputed author. But it is not beyond the bounds of possibility that the Revelation is the work of John, written in Patmos, probably during the stress of the latter years of Domitian. Its difference from the FG is more in style than in substance, and this can be accounted for on the assumption that in the Revelation we have the actual words of John, perhaps written by him-

[1] See 3 John 9 ff.
[2] See p. 43.

self, and in the FG and Epistles the paraphrases of the secretaries to whom he dictated them. It probably contains material from different periods of John's long life,[1] and shows signs of a certain amount of interpolation and rearrangement, particularly at the end.

2 and 3 John belong to the latest period of John's life, when he was free to travel (cf. 3 John 10), and striving to establish his authority in Asia. 1 John is not an epistle in the same sense as 2 and 3 John, but rather an introduction to the FG, emphasising those aspects of its message which John thought particularly relevant to the churches of Asia, namely the importance of the truth that Christ came in the flesh, and of love as the mainspring both of Christ's ministry and of the Christian life. The letters to the Seven Churches, revealing the lukewarmness and heretical notions of the Christians in Asia, show how necessary these lessons were for them. Their moral and intellectual failings are what one might expect from the successors of those to whom St Paul's Epistle to the Colossians was addressed. It is noteworthy also how the Revelation as a whole never loses sight of the humanity of Jesus, while the final verse of 1 John, 'keep yourselves from idols', repeats a warning implicit also throughout the Revelation.

It is the unanimous, and probably independent, affirmation of the Anti-Marcionite Prologue, the *Muratorian Canon*, and Irenaeus, that John published the FG in Ephesus, i.e. after his release from Patmos, and so after he had published the Revelation. The final verses of the FG, xxi. 24 and 25, are his editorial comments on the book which he is publishing.

'(24) This is the disciple who bore witness about these things, and wrote these things, and we know that his witness is true.

'(25) And there are many other things which Jesus did: if these were written down one by one, I do not think that the world itself would hold the books which would be written.'

The last verse, repeating what has already been said at xx. 30, that the FG contains only a selection of Jesus' deeds, is the

---

[1] Thus, for example, the situation of the Churches is by no means as desperate in the letters to the Seven Churches as in the rest of the book. Persecution does not yet look like becoming universal.

47

comment of John himself (and the only time that he uses the First Person Singular in the FG), and not, as is often supposed, of some amanuensis or redactor.

Verse 24 identifies the Beloved Disciple as the witness upon whom John relies. 'We know that his witness is true', is not the comment of a kind of editorial committee (as the *Muratorian Canon* appears to understand it), but an instance of an author taking his readers into his confidence, and assuming that they share his opinion. That the Beloved Disciple also 'wrote these things' (καὶ ὁ γράψας ταῦτα) may be a gloss introduced to reconcile the authorship of the FG by John of Ephesus with the later (erroneous) identification of John with the Beloved Disciple. It can however be taken as an acknowledgement by John that he possessed a written source which he believed to be the work of the Beloved Disciple. That he had 'written these things' does not necessarily mean that he had written the whole FG as it stands, down to xxi. 23, or even to the end of chapter xx. 'These things' which the Beloved Disciple wrote can be taken as the same 'things' about which he bore witness ('who bore witness about *these things*, and wrote *these things*'). There is no indication of the Beloved Disciple's presence in the FG before chapter xi (or xiii if he is not in fact Lazarus), except for the possibility that he is the unnamed disciple of John the Baptist who makes a brief and isolated appearance along with Andrew in i. 35-40.[1] From this it may be inferred that the written testimony of the Beloved Disciple only covered that part of Jesus' ministry of which he was an actual eye-witness, i.e. principally his last days in Jerusalem, his Crucifixion, and Resurrection. Even in the latter part of the FG the Beloved Disciple may not be John's only source, for if John himself is to be identified with the Other Disciple of xviii. 15 and xx. 2, he had memories of his own upon which he could draw.

It follows from this that the form and structure of the FG as we have it is the work of John. He must have had other sources for the earlier part of his Gospel, but it is probably impossible to identify them. Everything in the FG has been thoroughly assimilated by its author, even the testimony of the Beloved Disciple himself.

[1] See the Commentary, p. 99.

One further question remains. Can John of Ephesus be identified with anyone mentioned in the New Testament? The suggestion that he is John Mark, whose mother's house was the headquarters of the Jerusalem Church, and who was a relation of Barnabas, and companion of both Paul and Peter[1] at various times, is worth serious consideration. It would account satisfactorily for his Judaean point of view, his acquaintance with the thought of St Paul and with the theology of the first 'Hellenists' in the Church, of whom Barnabas was no doubt one, and also for his knowledge of the Galilean ministry of Jesus, which he could have got direct from Peter, rather than from the Synoptic Gospels. It involves the assumption that, if the Second Gospel is the work of a man called Mark who was also an associate of Peter's, there were two men called Mark who were associated with him at different periods. But this is not a serious difficulty. Mark is a very common name, and the Second Gospel itself does not read like the work of a man who actually knew Palestine himself, though he had good sources of information. Such resemblances as there are between the Second and Fourth Gospels may be due, in whole or in part, to the fact that Peter is a common source for them both.

If the distinction between the Other Disciple and the Beloved Disciple, and the identification of Lazarus with the Beloved Disciple, cannot be maintained, then John Mark is both the eyewitness and the author of the FG. He was at the Last Supper, which may well have been held in his mother's house, so that he, as the man of the house, though only by modern reckoning an adolescent, could well have had his place at the Supper next to Jesus himself, the principal guest.

At this point the reader may well feel prompted to ask why, if the author of the FG was in fact John Mark, and if either he or Lazarus was the Beloved Disciple, these facts have left so little trace in the tradition, and have not been recognised much earlier than this.

To the first part of the question the answer is, I believe, that John was only resident in Ephesus at the very end of his life, and did not make much impression on the churches of Asia.

[1] See Acts xii. 12, 25; xv. 37, 39; Col. iv. 10; 2 Tim. iv. 11; Philem. 24; 1 Pet. v. 13.

His Gospel was popular first with the Valentinians, who were only interested in it as a support for their doctrines. They therefore ascribed it to John the Apostle. The Church of Ephesus, when it came to realise that it too could find the FG useful, accepted that attribution. So Lazarus was completely ignored, and only a few traces were left of the real identity of John. To the second part the answer is that in the modern period conservative scholars have been content to accept the authorship of John the son of Zebedee as the best guarantee of the authenticity of the FG, and to minimise the difficulties which it entails, without seriously considering alternative possibilities. Those on the other hand who have denied or doubted the traditional view have usually done so because they doubted the authenticity and primitive character of the FG. They generally date it too late for it to have been written by anyone who had ever seen Jesus, and those who doubt the historicity of the raising of Lazarus can hardly believe that he was the Beloved Disciple.

Today, however, the situation is changed. The Dead Sea Scrolls show that the language and ideas of the FG do not make it inconceivable that it is the work of a man born in Judaea early in the first century A.D. They thus powerfully reinforce the other indications, too slight in themselves to be decisive, of the primitive and authentic character of the tradition embodied in the FG. So the way had been opened for a fresh approach to the problem of the FG. The difficulties in the traditional authorship largely remain. John the son of Zebedee could have written the FG, but neither the internal evidence of the FG nor the early tradition make it likely that he did. Studying this evidence, however, in the conviction that the FG does contain primitive and authentic material, and reliable clues to the authorship, I have been gradually led to formulate my conclusions. I am well aware that to both the upholders and the opponents of the tradition they may seem perverse and far-fetched, but I would maintain that they do account for the facts which we know, and I hope that the statement of them may stimulate others to reconsider the problem for themselves.

It may be convenient here to recapitulate. The FG is the work of John, known in the New Testament as John Mark or

Mark, and to Papias as the Elder. Born about A.D. 15, a member of the priestly aristocracy at Jerusalem, he became acquainted with Jesus and his disciples through his mother Mary, whose house in Jerusalem was probably the scene of the Last Supper, and is mentioned in Acts xii. 12, as a meeting place of the Jerusalem Church. He let Peter into the High Priest's house on the night of Jesus' arrest, and went with him to the sepulchre. Peter may well have been staying in his mother's house. He may have been the John who accompanied Peter to Samaria (Acts viii. 14). Later he went with his uncle Barnabas and Paul to Cyprus. When Barnabas and Paul separated, he again accompanied his uncle to Cyprus. Later still, he was with Paul in Rome (Col. iv. 10): it was presumably in Rome, after Paul's death (A.D. 62?) that he again met Peter. It is interesting to note that Peter refers to Rome as 'Babylon' in the same verse in which he mentions the author of the Revelation (1 Peter v. 13). John returned to Jerusalem, and was sent into exile to Patmos. There he 'saw' the Revelation, and meditated on the life and teaching of Jesus, preaching to a small circle of disciples. Somehow he possessed a copy of what he believed to be the memoirs of Lazarus, which eventually he incorporated into his Gospel. Released at last from Patmos in A.D. 96, he went to Ephesus, the nearest place to Patmos where there was a Christian Church. Timothy, the first bishop of Ephesus, must have known him, but it is doubtful if he was then still alive. In Ephesus his friends prevailed on him to put his Gospel into writing (if we may rely thus far on the *Muratorian Canon*), and he dictated it to an amanuensis, Papias, if the Anti-Marcionite Prologue is to be trusted. The first Epistle is an introduction to the FG, 2 and 3 John letters which he wrote from Ephesus. There, in the reign of Trajan, he died and was buried.[1] His memory was treasured by his immediate disciples, Papias and Polycarp among them, but at first his Gospel would seem to have made little impression, even upon them. The Gnostics were the first to make extensive use of it. By the time that the Church had

[1] The 'two tombs' of John at Ephesus which misled Dionysius of Alexandria into inferring that two Johns had lived in Ephesus may be due to the fact that the remains of John were translated to a new tomb, perhaps after the Church of Ephesus had come to realise the value of John as one of the great lights of Asia.

realised its true value, the precise circumstances of its origin had been forgotten, and an understandable anxiety to confer on it the apostolic origin which its merits seemed to require prevented any critical enquiries. John was himself identified with the Beloved Disciple, and Lazarus fell into the oblivion which he may well have desired. Then John was further identified with the Apostle, the son of Zebedee, for whose presence in Asia there is no shred of early or authentic evidence. Though the evidence for his death at the hands of the Jews (which must mean before A.D. 70) is late and dubious,[1] yet the existence of such an opinion so late, when the Johannine writings were all unhesitatingly ascribed to him, must leave a lurking suspicion that there may be something in it.

(v) *The Purpose of the Fourth Gospel*

In xx. 30 f., 'Now there were many other signs which Jesus also performed in front of his disciples, but they are not written in this book; but these are written in order that you may believe that Jesus is the Christ, the Son of God, and that, so believing, you may have life in his name', John states his purpose in writing. He has made a selection of those Acts of Jesus which showed most clearly that he was the Christ. The verse which comes immediately before these contains the words of the risen Christ, 'Blessed are they who have not seen, and yet have believed'. John offers evidence that will help those who have not seen to believe.

Primarily, though not exclusively, he intended his Gospel for Christian readers. The deficiencies in the faith and practice of the Christians of Asia which the letters to the Seven Churches and the Epistles of John reveal or imply would all find correction in the FG. It is reasonable to infer that it was intended to provide it. The Christians of Asia found a Christ who had come in the flesh hard to accept. They would doubtless have welcomed a Saviour-God after the pattern of those worshipped in the Hellenistic mystery-cults. John tells them of the Logos become flesh, in a way that will reveal to them the man as well as the Logos. This is the purpose of the 'signs'. The Gospels

[1] See p. 37.

already in circulation (of which John must have known of Mark at least, though he did not need to use it as a source) would not be equally effective. Hellenistic Christians did not have the familiarity with their Jewish background which alone would enable them to understand their theological implications. To them they would seem simply collections of marvels, or absurdities. The other evangelists, no less than John, intended their stories to be 'signs', but they could no longer be seen to be such.

John also stresses the importance of the new commandment to love one another. Paul also had found it necessary to emphasise this, when addressing the same kind of readers.

Now what would correct the misunderstandings of Gentile Christians would also serve to commend the gospel to pagans, and John must also have visualised them as readers of his Gospel.

But there were also Jewish communities in the cities of Asia —cf. the references to 'those who say that they are Jews and are not, but are a synagogue of Satan' in Smyrna and Philadelphia (Rev. ii. 9 and iii. 9). Their hostility was a danger both to the faith and peace of the Christian Churches, but there was also the prospect that they too might be converted—cf. Rev. iii. 9, 'I will make them come and bow down before your feet, and learn that I have loved you'. The careful exposition of Jesus' Messianic claims in the FG suggests that one of its purposes is to further the conversion of the Jews.

John also seems to have in mind the threat to the peace and faith of the Church from the pretensions of the Imperial power and the Imperial cult, and in some respects anticipates the apologetic literature of the second century. The Revelation was given its final form at a time when it seemed likely that persecution would annihilate the Church on earth. Though with the death of Domitian the worst danger was past, the threat of it still remained, and John is still sensitive to it in his Gospel, though it no longer dominates his thinking as it did in the Revelation. Against the Emperor's claim to man's worship he emphasises the kingship of Christ. Thomas' confession of faith, 'My Lord and my God' (John xx. 28) vindicates as belonging to Christ the title which Domitian had blasphemously assumed,

Dominus et Deus. But, as John makes clear in his record of Jesus' conversation with Pilate, the kingship of Christ does not impair the legitimate authority of the Empire—'My kingdom is not of this world' (John xviii. 36). Here also he has the Jews in mind; their hostility to the Christians may endanger their own allegiance to the God of Israel. He records the blasphemy of Jesus' enemies, 'We have no king but Caesar' (John xix. 15), to remind them of this danger.

These concerns determine the contents and structure of the FG, in which John shows that Jesus is the divine Logos become man, vindicates and defines his status and function as Messiah, and elucidates his relationship both to Judaism and the Roman Empire.

First[1] (i. 1-18) he lays down that the Logos is God's sole agent in creation, revelation, and redemption, and became man. Then, after the testimony of John the Baptist, Andrew, Nathanael, and Jesus himself (i. 19-51), from which it is made clear that Jesus is the Messiah, the first sign, the changing of water into wine (ii. 1-12), and its corollary, the cleansing of the Temple (ii. 13-25), expound the relationship of Jesus to Judaism: he replaces the water of the old dispensation with the wine of the new, and supersedes the Temple; at the same time the new dispensation is the old purified. Then follow two conversations, with Nicodemus (iii), and the Samaritan woman (iv. 1-42), in which Jesus confronts representatives of those within and without the old dispensation, and then the second and third signs, two acts of healing (iv. 43-54, and v), which show Christ as the Saviour and giver of life. After the controversy provoked by the third sign there follows the fourth (vi. 1-15), the feeding of the multitude, which, like the first, has a corollary (vi. 16-21), Jesus walking 'on' the lake. The discourse in vi. 22-59, shows Jesus as the Moses of the new dispensation, who gives the real manna to feed God's people, his own flesh and blood. The corollary shows Jesus ever ready to succour his disciples, lost in the dark without him. This marks a turning-point in the ministry; vi. 60-71, shows how many of Jesus' disciples were offended at his claims, and henceforth hostility gradually intensifies. Chapters

[1] See 1. *The Contents and Structure of the FG.*, and, for details, the Commentary *passim*.

vii and viii deal with the claims of Jesus made at the feast of
Tabernacles, and are followed appropriately by the fifth sign
(ix. 1-12), the healing of a man born blind, which shows Jesus
as the giver of light, and the controversy which it provokes
(ix. 13-41), in which Jesus condemns the blindness of the unbelieving Jews. Chapter x, which begins with Jesus' discourse
(1-18) on the theme of the shepherds, true and false, and the
sheep, is in place here, in spite of its abrupt opening, since it
contrasts Jesus, the good shepherd, with the blind leaders of the
Jewish people. After a final denunciation (x. 22-42) Jesus withdraws from Jerusalem, but returns for the sixth sign (xi. 1-44),
the raising of Lazarus, which both shows Jesus as the giver of
life, and, by its character and its place in the series of signs,
prepares for the final, seventh, and so perfect sign, the Resurrection of Christ himself. The four scenes which follow (xi. 45-57,
the plot to kill Jesus; xii. 1-11, the anointing; 12-19, the triumphal entry into Jerusalem; and 20-26, the approach of the
Gentiles which Jesus recognises as the sign that his time has
come) are a good example of the dramatic structure of the FG.
They contain a series of contrasts—enemies and friends, Jews
and Gentiles take the stage in turn—and lead on to a comment
by the evangelist (xii. 37-43), followed by a discourse (xii. 44-50)
on the theme of belief and unbelief suggested by the preceding
scenes. Chapters xiii-xvii show Jesus among his disciples, at
supper, when he washes their feet (xiii. 1-20), and (xiii. 21-30)
points out the traitor to the disciple whom he loved, and afterwards, where he gives his final charge to them (xiii. 31–xvi. 33)
and prays (xvii) for them and those whom they will bring to
him. These chapters form the heart of the FG. Though it is
impossible to regard them as a literal record of what Jesus said,
they are dramatically appropriate, gathering up the themes in
the earlier part of the Gospel, and preparing for the final manifestation of the glory of Christ in his Crucifixion and Resurrection. The rest of the Gospel is in the main a straightforward
narrative of events, in which the special concerns of the evangelist become only occasionally explicit, as when, for instance,
in the conversation between Christ and Pilate (xviii. 28–xix. 16)
he confronts the representative of the earthly Emperor with the
divine King, and expounds the nature of his kingdom, or when

he draws attention to the parallel between the Christ and the Passover lamb (xix. 33-37). The Gospel culminates in Thomas' confession (xx. 28) and Jesus' response to it, while chapter xxi, which forms an epilogue (though it is the work of the evangelist, and not an appendix added by a later hand), both looks to the future of the Church and provides the quiet ending so often found in ancient tragedy.[1]

(vi) *The Value of the Fourth Gospel*

If this is a fair account of the evangelist's purpose, and of the methods which he used to accomplish it, it must raise the question of the value of the Gospel, both theological and historical. The two can be distinguished, but not ultimately separated. The FG could have theological value of a kind, even if it were devoid of historical value, but it would be different in kind from the theological value it would have if it also possessed historical value as well.

The question of its historical value relative to the Synoptic Gospels has already been touched on;[2] the more important and difficult question of its absolute value must now be considered. Is it simply a missionary, apologetic, and polemical treatise presented in the form of a Gospel, or is it indeed all this, and at the same time historically reliable?

Until the early nineteenth century the FG was generally accepted as not only historically reliable, but also as theologically the most valuable of the four. It is nevertheless probable that its historical value was inferred from its theological value rather than independently established. Both were guaranteed by its apostolic authorship, but that, as has been shown, does not depend on any authentic tradition, but is again an inference from its theological value. It was Irenaeus who, by using the FG for the refutation of Gnosticism, established its authority in the Church, and, once accepted as orthodox and apostolic, it exerted an influence on the development of early Christian doctrine greater than that of any other book of the New Testa-

---

[1] I do not mean by this that John was deliberately imitating the style of Aeschylean tragedy. The analogy, though genuine, is quite unconscious.

[2] See 2, (iii) above, p. 16.

ment. Even the Arian preference for the term Logos to describe the status of Christ did not diminish the esteem in which the orthodox held the Gospel which first used it, though it did ensure the exclusion of Logos from orthodox confessions of the faith.

While the FG was dominant in the East, it also contributed an important element to the complex synthesis of St Augustine's theology. It was not, however, that element which was to prove most influential in later Western theology. The steady divergence between the theological traditions of the Eastern and Western Churches in the Middle Ages, is, at least in part, due to the difference between Johannine and non-Johannine conceptions of Christianity.

At the Reformation it was the theology of St Paul, as interpreted by St Augustine, which exercised the decisive influence upon the continental Reformers, and though they continued to regard the FG as the most valuable of the four, it was because they found it the one which could most easily be interpreted in terms of their own distinctive theology. This was later to have important consequences. In England, however, the fortunes of the FG were rather different. There the Augustinianism characteristic of the continental Reformers, though influential, was not so dominant; Anglican interest in a theology that was Catholic but not Romanist led to the study of the Greek Fathers and opened the way for a tradition of Johannine theology that had not been subjected to interpretation in Pauline terms. The effect of this tradition in English theology, though its introduction was due to a specifically Anglican interest, has not been confined to Anglicans. It is found for instance in the Cambridge Platonists. Its distinctive result has been the emphasis which English theology has always tended to place upon the Incarnation as the central doctrine of the faith. Westcott's Commentary on St John is a typical product of this tradition, and owes to this fact its place as the classical exposition of the Gospel in English.

For long the pre-eminence of the FG was unchallenged. The two leading philosophers in Germany, and indeed in Europe, in the early nineteenth century, Schleiermacher and Hegel, both regarded it as the most valuable of the four Gospels, though for different reasons, and on grounds which were hardly those of orthodox Christians. But because they approved of what they believed to be its teaching they were no more disposed than their more orthodox predecessors and contemporaries to question the traditional view of its origin and value. Schleiermacher valued the FG because he found his favourite concept of Christ's 'filial consciousness' expressed in it more clearly than in the others, and Hegel because the text 'God is Spirit' (John iv. 24) seemed to him an anticipation of his own philosophy.

But their pupils and successors thought differently. The critics of the Tübingen School, F. C. Baur and D. F. Strauss, and the later Liberal theologians in Germany all abandoned the traditional view of the FG, primarily, it is important to realise, on dogmatic grounds. Critical grounds were discovered in order to vindicate conclusions reached on other grounds. This has produced a controversy which still continues, and in which dogmatic motives continually confuse the critical issue. The traditional ascription of the FG to John the son of Zebedee is very vulnerable, and opponents of the tradition have often been content to demonstrate this, and think that then they have destroyed the grounds for accepting the FG as historically reliable, while orthodox defenders of the FG have clung to an untenable position in the equally mistaken, but understandable, conviction, that the value of the FG as a bulwark of traditional orthodoxy is involved in the tradition of its authorship, and that to deny the latter is to imperil the former. Dogmatic presuppositions on both sides have largely determined the course of the controversy, and have made it difficult for those who are not partisans on one side or the other to secure a hearing.

Baur and Strauss were both Hegelians, who adapted Hegel's dialectical pattern of thesis, antithesis, and synthesis to their own special purposes (as Karl Marx also did). Baur used it to interpret the history of the early Church and of the literature of the New Testament in which it was reflected. The faith of the Jerusalem Church was the thesis, Paulinism the antithesis, and Johannine theology the synthesis, in which dogma is purveyed as history. This estimate of Johannine theology was facilitated by the traditional tendency in German theology to read John through Pauline spectacles. But the consequence of Baur's dogmatic scheme was that the FG could no longer be regarded as apostolic.

Strauss reached the same conclusion by a different route. He applied the Hegelian formula to the elucidation of the development of Gospel criticism. Here the traditional acceptance of the Gospels as they stand as historically true is the thesis. The antithesis to this is the rationalist criticism of the eighteenth century, which denied the possibility of miracles, and by ingenious rationalisations of the Gospel miracles save the historical credibility of the rest of their contents. To these Strauss opposed his own view of their nature, the synthesis which transcends the two opposing views. The Gospels are mythological, the products of the faith of the early Church: they cannot be accepted either as historical or as the work of apostles or their disciples.

The Liberal theologians who succeeded the Tübingen School abandoned its Hegelianism, which had provided the grounds for denying the traditional view of the authorship and character of the Gospels, but kept its scepticism about the tradition. In abandoning Hegelianism, they felt that they were approaching their critical task of recovering the Jesus of History in a truly objective spirit. But the critic who supposes that he is free of presuppositions is in fact the victim of the deadliest of them all. And the Liberals had others also—in particular their assumption that religion is a phenomenon that can be explained on naturalistic and evolutionary lines.

They were impressed by the obvious differences, in both form and contents, between the FG and the Synoptic Gospels, and attributed them to the influence of theological interests in the FG which were absent from the Synoptic Gospels. So they used the Synoptic Gospels almost exclusively as the source from which they drew their materials for reconstructing the Jesus of History. Mark provided the outlines of the ministry, and Q the teaching, of the martyred prophet of the fatherhood of God and the brotherhood of man, whom the Church had converted into the object of its faith. The FG was, for them, a document which illustrated this change in the character of the faith, and was only incidentally of any value for their particular purpose.

But the Jesus of History proved an elusive quarry. The variety of mutually incompatible reconstructions produced by the ingenuity of Liberal scholarship led to a certain scepticism about the feasibility of the project. Then, at the end of the century came A. Schweitzer's devastating criticism of the whole Liberal attempt at the reconstruction of the Jesus of History in *The Quest of the Historical Jesus*.[1] This, however, did nothing to rehabilitate the FG. For Schweitzer's own doctrine of the 'Messianic Secret', and his emphasis on the futurist eschatology of Jesus only made the FG seem more remote than ever from historical fact. Schweitzer himself, consistently enough, regarded the FG as a document of a thoroughly Hellenised Christianity.[2]

Meanwhile, however, both in Germany and England the traditional view of the FG had been vigorously maintained, and it seemed as though a state of deadlock had been reached, the one party remaining unshaken in its conviction that the FG was apostolic and so must be historical, the other that it was unhistorical and so could not be apostolic.

For British theology a way out of this impasse was provided by E. F. Scott's book, *The Fourth Gospel, its Purpose and Theology* (1906), which has exercised a lasting—and perhaps excessive—influence on the approach to the problem of the FG. Scott recognised that the problem of the FG involves more than deciding its authorship and historical value; a prior question is that of its purpose, its meaning, and the sources of its theology. It has been to this prior question that British scholarship has in the main addressed itself, and the fruitfulness of Scott's approach, and the validity of his assessment of priority, may be illustrated by such major and distinguished works as C. H. Dodd's *The Interpretation of the Fourth Gospel* (1953) and C. K. Barrett's *Commentary* (1955). But the interest found, and success achieved, in answering Scott's prior question seem to

---

[1] E.T. by W. Montgomery (1910) of *Von Reimarus zu Wrede. Geschichte der Leben-Jesu-Forschung* (1906).

[2] See *The Mysticism of Paul the Apostle* (E.T. of *Die Mystik des Apostels Paulus* by W. Montgomery, 1931), chapter xiii, 'The Hellenization of Paul's Mysticism by Ignatius and the Johannine Theology'.

have diverted attention from the questions of historicity and authorship.[1]

One reason for the comparative neglect of the question of historicity may be found in the influence of Form Criticism. By drawing attention to the motives which led to the preservation and moulding of the gospel tradition it has emphasised more clearly than was done in the past the difficulty of establishing the historical substratum in the narratives and of discovering the original form and occasion of the sayings of Jesus. By stressing the influence of the community it has tended to minimise the importance of the original eye-witnesses, without whom the tradition could not have begun, but who must also have been continuing members of the first Christian community. By revealing that theological motives have moulded the Synoptic Gospels no less than the FG it has fostered the sceptical conclusion that Mark is no more historical than the nineteenth-century Liberals supposed the FG to be. To concentrate on the ideas of the Fourth Evangelist at the expense of other aspects of the FG is a tendency consonant with that of Form Criticism. But the other questions still remain.

The sceptical attitude to the historicity of the Gospels which is characteristic of Form Criticism (though by no means confined

[1] [Cf. now C. H. Dodd, *Historical Tradition in the Fourth Gospel* (1963), who argues that 'behind the Fourth Gospel lies an ancient tradition independent of the other gospels, and meriting serious consideration as a contribution to our knowledge of the historical facts concerning Jesus Christ' (p. 423). It should be noted that Dodd assumes throughout that 'the tradition we are trying to track down was oral' (p. 424); he is in fact dealing with a severely limited question, and, as he often hints, one has to ask next what the Evangelist did with the material on which he drew before any valid exegesis of the FG in its present form is possible. One has also to enquire about the likelihood of written sources intervening, and consider what difference, if any, this would make. Dodd's book does not represent thoroughgoing conservatism; it is an unfashionable attempt to ask the sort of question which historians have a right to ask about any ancient document. Dodd is well aware that there is a 'theological interest which all through this gospel prevails over the purely historical' (p. 217), and it is perverse to attack him because this is a different sort of book from *The Interpretation of the Fourth Gospel*. While one may not accept in their entirety Dodd's apparent presuppositions about the relationship of history to faith, he does observe pertinently that 'the historian might be pardoned for thinking that we throw up the sponge too readily, and for overhearing, when we sing the praises of the new approach to the gospels, a half-smothered sigh of relief at escaping from a peculiarly difficult and embarrassing problem' (p. 2.)—B. A. M.]

to it) is only justifiable if it can be shown to be impossible for the evangelists' aims to be at once historical and theological. The two evangelists, however, who have mentioned their purpose in writing, Luke and John, seem quite unaware of any incompatibility between their historical and theological interests. Luke claims both that he has made diligent enquiry from eyewitnesses of Jesus' ministry, and that he writes in order that Theophilus may have a secure basis for his faith (Luke i. 1-4). John emphasises that the events which he describes really happened, and that he writes in order that his readers may believe that Jesus is the Christ, the Son of God (John xx. 30 f.).

In order to answer the question whether these aims are compatible, whether, in other words, an evangelist is precluded by the nature of his mission from also being a historian, it is necessary first to consider briefly the nature of historical narrative. The task of the historian both resembles and differs from that of the newspaper reporter. Neither (one hopes) would write anything which he knew to be untrue. Neither can find space to report everything that happens, or more than a tiny fraction of what happens. Beyond definite, though differing, limits, each would defeat his own object by trying to include too much. Both must employ certain criteria for the inclusion of material. It is in the nature of their criteria that the historian and the journalist part company. Not only must the historian restrict his selection of facts much more severely than the journalist, but he must also adopt a different perspective, and realise the significance of events which at the time when they happened seemed unworthy of notice. An extreme example would be the Crucifixion. No Roman at the time could have dreamed that the death of Jesus would have more momentous consequences for the world than the death of Tiberius was to have a few years later. And this is true whatever one thinks to have been the significance of his death.

The historian then must not only discover what happened but also select from the facts which he has discovered those which he believes to be significant. And his criteria of significance will depend on something which he cannot acquire simply from an investigation of the raw material of history, however diligent in that he may be. His criteria are judgements of value, which may be modified by his study of the facts, but are never simply derived from them. A historian without such criteria is not a historian, but an antiquarian. History cannot be written without presuppositions. The 'good' historian is not one without presuppositions, but the one with sufficient humility to recognise that his presuppositions are not infallible simply because they are his own, and sufficient honesty not to distort or suppress evidence that does not fit in with them, but to modify his presuppositions to account for the facts. If one disagrees with a historian whom one has to recognise as honest, it is because one cannot accept his presuppositions.

Now the evangelists, and John in particular, are, I would maintain, 'good' historians in the sense of the preceding paragraph. Persuaded by their own experience, or by that of witnesses whom they believed to be trustworthy, of the truth that Jesus is the Christ, the Son of God, they adopted as their criterion of significance in selecting and arranging the material in their Gospels, that it should illustrate this truth, which alone made satisfactory sense of the facts which they knew. From this it would seem to follow that only those who can share the evangelists' presuppositions are capable of admitting that their Gospels are historically reliable. The converse of this can be amply illustrated from the attempts made to write a life of Jesus in the nineteenth century.

The truly heroic attempt then made by scholars who did not in fact share the evangelists' presuppositions to disentangle the Jesus of History from the Christ of Faith ended in a scepticism which was inherited not only by the exponents of Form Criticism, but more recently also by the advocates of a kind of neo-Orthodoxy, for whom the fact that Jesus was crucified under Pontius Pilate seems to supply all that the Christian faith requires as historical basis.

But such scepticism is not inevitable. That it is the result of attempting to distinguish the Jesus of History from the Christ of Faith may rather suggest that the attempt to distinguish them is misconceived. The ministry of Jesus can be understood, and the Gospels which record it accepted as historical, only if one accepts the presuppositions of the evangelists. This is what Origen meant when he said that no one could perceive the meaning of the FG who had not leaned on Jesus' breast and taken from Jesus Mary as his own mother.[1] This does not mean the end of criticism, as the example of Origen himself shows. He was quite capable of recognising, for example, that it is impossible to harmonise all the Gospel narratives. The critic must still ask himself whether the evidence which the evangelists adduce will bear the significance which they find in it, and whether they have committed mistakes of fact or interpretation. In particular, the Gospel which presents Christ as the truth ought to be able to stand up to the most rigorous investigation, and the critic would be failing in his duty, not only as a critic, but also as a Christian, if he hesitated to apply it.

John's fundamental doctrine, that 'the Logos became flesh', implies for him that the events which he describes as 'signs' really happened. His narrative cannot be theologically significant unless it is also historically true. Equally, unless its theological significance is recognised, it is in itself quite trivial.[2]

The critic cannot, however, accept the historical truth of the FG simply on the grounds that John's theology seems to entail it. John may have had untrustworthy sources, or may have made mistakes, perhaps under the influence of illegitimate theological motives. But, while the critic must take these considerations into account, he can at least acquit John of indifference to historical truth. Detailed consideration of his success in conveying both the 'Logos' and the 'flesh', the facts and their meaning, without distorting the facts, must be left for the Commentary. But some further general observations may be in place here.

Attention has already[3] been drawn to two probable consequences of the fact (if it be such) that the FG was fashioned out of sermons preached by the evangelist—namely that the structure of the Gospel is determined by theological considerations,

---

[1] οὗ (i.e. of the FG) τὸν νοῦν οὐδεὶς δύναται λαβεῖν μὴ ἀναπεσὼν ἐπὶ τὸ στῆθος Ἰησοῦ, μηδὲ λαβὼν ἀπὸ Ἰησοῦ τὴν Μαρίαν γινομένην καὶ αὐτοῦ μητέρα. *in Iohannem* I. 6 (ed. Brooke, Vol. I, p. 7).

[2] It is instructive to compare what the FG says about 'flesh' and 'Spirit' in vi. 53, 'Unless you eat the flesh of the Son of man and drink his blood, you do not have life in yourselves', and 63, 'It is the Spirit which gives life; the flesh is no use', i.e. merely as flesh, unless it is recognised as the vehicle of the Spirit.

[3] See pp. 15 ff. above.

and that the discourses contain primarily the words of the evangelist, speaking indeed in the name of the Lord, but not by any means always reproducing actual words spoken during his ministry.

That the structure of the FG is determined by theological considerations does not of course rule out the possibility that the order of events is chronological, but it does tend to make it questionable. Even so, however, the actual incidents may be historical.

It is sometimes said that the extraordinary vividness of some at least of the passages in the FG is an argument for their historical truth. But this is an argument that must be used with caution. The story of Jesus' encounter with the woman of Samaria is most vivid and lifelike. But it is difficult to suppose that either Jesus or the woman herself would have told the story in its present form, and no other witness was present. The vividness of some incidents may therefore be due not to the accuracy of an eye-witness' memory, but to the vividness of the evangelist's imagination.[1] And if the author of the FG was also the seer and hearer of the Revelation, we may well credit him with such an imagination. But it does not follow from this that all the incidents which he describes are products of his imagination, or that any one of them can safely be dismissed as wholly imaginary. In the Revelation also John saw and heard things which he had to use his imagination to describe—but this does not mean that even they are simply imaginary. The Revelation is not just a literary exercise by an imaginative person learned in apocalyptic literature, but the product of visions and auditions which the prophet was convinced he had received. Similarly the FG is not historical fiction. But the prophet's imagination has played a necessary part in both.

[1] But see the note on iv. 29.

COMMENTARY

A. PROLOGUE, i. 1-18

The Prologue is written in rhythmical prose, though it does not seem possible to arrange it in any generally acceptable metrical scheme. Its style, appropriate to its solemn theme, has the simplicity and grandeur characteristic of the classical Christian liturgies. It has indeed been suggested that a hymn to the divine Logos, or to Sophia, the divine Wisdom, was incorporated by the evangelist into the Prologue. The difference in vocabulary between the Prologue and the rest of the FG lends colour to this suggestion. But if the evangelist is using an already existing hymn, he has made of it an integral and organic part of his own work, which develops from it like an opera of Wagner's from its overture.

i. (1) **In the beginning there was the Logos, and the Logos was with God, and was God: (2) this Logos was in the beginning with God. (3) All things came into being through him; and without him not a single thing came into being. (4) As for that which is in being, in it he was the life; and the life was the light of men. (5) And the light shines in the darkness; and the darkness did not master it.**

1. **In the beginning there was the Logos.** Since λόγος does not correspond exactly to 'word', which is its primary meaning in this context, but has a range of other meanings, of which 'reason' is here most significant, it is better to transliterate it than to give a translation which conveys only a part of its meaning.

John introduces the term **Logos** quite without explanation, showing that he expects his readers to understand it. For those who were familiar with the Old Testament, his opening phrase, **In the beginning,** would recall Gen. i. 1, and indicate that he is offering an interpretation of the story of creation in Genesis. God called the world into being by his word of command. This is suggested by Gen. i. 3, 'God said, "Let there be light"; and

67

there was light', and is familiar also to the Psalmists, cf. Ps. xxxiii. 6, 'By the word of the Lord the heavens were made', and cxlviii. 5, 'He commanded and they were created'.

For the Christian reader his words could have another meaning. The gospel of Jesus Christ was also *logos*, and to the proclamation of this *logos* the Church, the new creation, owed its existence. John suggests—perhaps with a glance at Mark i. 1, 'The beginning of the gospel of Jesus Christ'—that this can only be properly expressed by recognising that Jesus Christ is not only the subject-matter of the Christian *logos*, but (as will be obvious later) himself the Logos of God, his agent in the creation of the world as well as in the new creation, and that the Logos was active long before the preaching of John the Baptist which for Mark was the beginning of the gospel. Christianity is in a sense as old as creation, a thought which John expresses in the pictorial language of his Revelation under the figure of the Lamb slain before the foundation of the world (Rev. xiii. 8).

Readers unfamiliar both with Genesis and the Christian Gospel would not have found John's opening words unintelligible, however much his subsequent statements might surprise them. To them they would affirm the absolute priority of the divine Reason which is the principle of law in the cosmos. For Logos was familiar in this sense in the Platonised Stoicism of the period, and in the theologies and philosophies which had come under its influence. Logos was first used as a technical term in the philosophy of Heraclitus of Ephesus in the sixth century B.C. But it is most improbable that his use of it in any way anticipated John's. There was no Ephesian tradition of Logos-theology, as some have supposed. The impression that there was such a tradition was the result of the Stoics' reading back their own conception of the Logos into Heraclitus' notoriously enigmatic utterances. John may, however, have been indirectly influenced by Stoicism, by way of the Wisdom Literature of the Old Testament and Apocrypha, and perhaps also of Philo. In the pre-Maccabean period such ideas found a ready welcome in Israel, and have left their permanent mark upon its literature. Of all Greek influences, that of Stoicism was the deepest— perhaps because its founder, Zeno, from Citium in Cyprus, was of Semitic stock, and his origin showed itself in his deep moral earnestness. Originally hostile to popular religion, the Stoics came to terms with it, and made it a vehicle for propagating their own ideas by allegorising its myths and deities. Thus, for example, Hermes, the messenger of the gods, and his Egyptian counterpart, Thoth, were identified with the Stoic Logos. This reduction of mythical persons to abstractions went along with an opposite tendency in religion to personify abstractions, a tendency carried to absurd lengths in some later Gnostic systems.

Under Stoic influence the Hebrew Wisdom Literature interpreted the 'word of the Lord' in terms of the Stoic Logos, and personified both Logos and Sophia (Wisdom) as intermediaries between God and the world. The Logos appears fully personified in Wisdom xviii. 15 f., 'Thy all-powerful word leaped from heaven, from the royal throne, into the midst of the land that was doomed, a stern warrior carrying the sharp sword of thy authentic command, and stood and filled all things with death.' Wisdom is closely associated with Logos, indeed almost interchangeable with it, cf. the prayer in Wisdom ix. 1 ff. 'O God of my fathers and Lord of mercy, who hast made all things by thy word, and by thy wisdom hast formed man . . . give me the wisdom that sits by thy throne.' Wisdom is here personified as a kind of assessor in the divine court. As such, she was present when God made the world (*ibid.*, 9), cf. the words of Wisdom in Prov. viii. 22 ff., 'The Lord created me at the beginning of his work, the first of his acts of old. Ages ago I was set up, at the first, before the beginning of the earth . . . (27) when he established the heavens, I was there.'

Thus Wisdom and Logos have here a part very like that of the Logos in John's Prologue, and it is likely that he was influenced by the Wisdom Literature. In the philosophy of Philo also the Logos is God's agent in creation and revelation, but is never more than a personified abstraction. When John goes on to his further affirmations about the Logos, he goes beyond anything in the Old Testament or in Philo, as when he says

and the Logos was with God, and was God: 2. this Logos was in the beginning with God. This passage is usually punctuated so as to give the sense 'and the Logos was God:

this . . .' (καὶ θεὸς ἦν ὁ λόγος. οὗτος). The punctuation adopted here (καὶ θεὸς ἦν. ὁ λόγος οὗτος) seems to give a better balance to verses 1 and 2 by lengthening the final, recapitulatory clause. The manuscripts give little guidance in matters of punctuation. The phrase 'this word' (ὁ λόγος οὗτος) occurs also in John vi. 60, and vii. 36,[1] and is thus in accordance with John's usage.

As John will show more clearly later, when he uses 'Father' and 'Son' instead of 'God' and 'Logos', the Logos is more than a personified abstraction, an entity, indeed a person, distinct from God, though not different in nature from him. It is sometimes argued that John draws a subtle distinction between **was with God** and **was God** in a way which English cannot reproduce, by using the definite article in the first clause (ἦν πρὸς τὸν θεόν), thus making **God** here fully substantival, and leaving it out of the second (καὶ θεὸς ἦν), thus making it rather adjectival, and refraining from asserting the complete deity of the Logos. But the absence of the article in the second clause can be as well explained by the fact that θεός is the predicate.[2] John means here what later orthodoxy was to express by the unity of the substance and distinction between the persons of the Father and the Son. As John xx. 28, shows, he could use ὁ θεός of Christ—'My Lord and my God' (ὁ κύριός μου καὶ ὁ θεός μου).

3. **All things came into being through him; and without him not a single thing came into being.** Virtually all pre-Nicene quotations of this passage, whether made by orthodox or heretical writers (including the Valentinians Ptolemaeus and Theodotus, Tatian, Irenaeus, Clement of Alexandria, Origen, and Tertullian) end with **not a single thing came into being** (ἐγένετο οὐδὲ ἕν), and usually make this quite explicit by not quoting any further. This means that the following relative clause, **which is in being,** must be construed as part of the following sentence. It was appended to the previous clause so as to add a qualification to **not a single thing**— 'without him was not anything made that was made'—in order to prevent verse 3 being interpreted in such a way as to include

---

[1] According to Westcott and Hort, who read οὗτος ὁ λόγος in John xxi. 23. Souter, oddly enough, has οὗτος ὁ λόγος in vi. 60, and vii. 36, but ὁ λόγος οὗτος in xxi. 23.

[2] Cf. ζωή in the first clause of verse 4, 'in it he was the life'.

the Holy Spirit among the things which came into being through the Logos.

John asserts as emphatically as possible the sole agency of the Logos in creation. This recalls not only what is said in the Old Testament and Apocrypha about Logos and Sophia, but, more directly, what is said elsewhere in the New Testament about the part of Christ in creation, cf. 1 Cor. viii. 6, 'For us there is one God, the Father, from whom are all things and for whom we exist, and one Lord, Jesus Christ, through whom are all things and through whom we exist', Col. i. 16, 'In him all things were created', and Heb. i. 2, 'Through whom also he created the world'. The Hebrews passage comes very near to calling Christ the Logos, for it begins 'God . . . has in these last days spoken to us by a Son, whom he appointed the heir of all things, through whom also he created the world.'

4. **As for that which is in being, in it he was the life.** In the clause **which is in being** the verb is in the perfect tense,[1] which is used for a present state which is a consequence of a past action or event. To translate it as if it were a past tense, 'that was made', is a misrepresentation which must, however, be accepted if the clause is read as part of the previous verse. On the other hand, an argument for this punctuation may be drawn from the fact that the translation of the main clause as 'in *him* was life' (which would follow if this punctuation were adopted) may seem to be supported by John v. 26, 'As the Father has life in himself, so also he gave to the Son to have life in himself.' But John elsewhere states that Christ *is* the life, cf. xi. 25, 'I am the resurrection and the life', and xiv. 6, 'I am the way, the truth, and the life'.

Harsh as the expression ὃ γέγονεν, ἐν αὐτῷ ζωὴ ἦν may seem, it must be accepted as what John wrote, provided that a satisfactory interpretation can be found. Of the various possibilities the one most probable (that adopted here) is that which is suggested by a comparison with verse 12, which is similar in construction and quite unambiguous in meaning. In it, as in this verse, the relative clause which begins the sentence depends on a pronoun which is part of the predicate of the main clause— 'As for those who received him (ὅσοι δὲ ἔλαβον αὐτόν), to them

[1] γέγονεν; contrast ἐγένετο (aorist) in the previous clause: cf. γέγονεν in i. 15.

he gave (ἔδωκεν αὐτοῖς).'[1] Hence **As for that which is in being** (ὃ γέγονεν), **in it** (ἐν αὐτῷ) **he was the life** (ζωὴ ἦν). Notice also how in verse 4 in the relative clause **is in being** (γέγονεν) echoes the previous main verb in 3, **came into being** (ἐγένετο), just as in 12 'received' (ἔλαβον) echoes 'accepted' (παρέλαβον) in 11, and how in both an affirmative relative clause follows a negative main clause.[2]

Thus the Logos was not only God's agent in creation, but he is in the world (as John states explicitly in verse 10) sustaining it in being, as the principle of life within it. He 'gives life to the world' (John vi. 33). This is also true of the new creation, which lives because Christ lives in it, cf. John xiv. 19 f. Here John agrees with Paul; cf. Gal. ii. 20, 'It is no longer I who live, but Christ who lives in me', Col. iii. 4, 'Christ who is our life' etc.

And the life was the light of men. Since he is immanent in the world as its life, he is also its light, cf. John viii. 12, 'I am the light of the world. He who follows me shall have the light of life.' That is, he is the source of revelation.

That the Logos is the life and that he is the light are two of the major themes in the FG.[3] Used in the same metaphorical sense as in the FG, they are also found in other religious writings, pagan as well as Jewish, of the period—the *Hermetica*, the Mandaean and Gnostic literature, and the Dead Sea Scrolls. Since they are very natural metaphors, it may well seem superfluous to suppose that John required literary sources from which to borrow them. They occur in the Old Testament—cf. Ps. xxxvi. 9, 'With thee is the fountain of life;[4] in thy light do we see light'—as well as in the teaching attributed to Jesus in the Synoptic Gospels—e.g. Matt. vii. 14, 'the way which leads to life', and Luke xvi. 8, 'the sons of light'. If, however, a source for the use of 'light' and 'life' in the FG (and the Synoptic Gospels) is to be sought other than that in the Old Testament, the Dead Sea Scrolls are more likely to provide it than any other literature.

---

[1] The same construction also occurs in vi. 39, ἵνα πᾶν ὃ δέδωκέν μοι, μὴ ἀπολέσω ἐξ αὐτοῦ; xviii. 9 (where Barrett notes that the construction is 'very characteristic of John's style', p. 435).

[2] See also p. 77 n. 1 on i. 10.

[3] See Introduction, p. 5.

[4] Cf. John iv. 14.

5. And the light shines in the darkness; and the darkness did not master it. Under the metaphor of **the darkness** John confronts us with that which is unresponsive to, and rebellious against, the divine light. The tenses here are significant—the light continues to shine (φαίνει, present), because the darkness failed to master it (οὐ κατέλαβεν, aorist). While this can be understood in a general sense, John may also intend a more specific allusion. The gospel can be represented as 'light' (cf. 2 Cor. iv. 4), and he may be thinking of the failure of persecution to suppress it. In his Revelation he had described in apocalyptic and pictorial terms the attempt of the powers of evil to destroy the Church, and had foretold their failure. This verse sums up the lesson of the Revelation, though in different terms.[1]

John is fond of using words with two meanings, both of which are applicable. Of this characteristic of his style **master** (κατέλαβεν) is an example. The verb καταλαμβάνω means both 'overcome, overtake' (as in xii. 35, where 'darkness' is the subject of καταλάβῃ[2]), and 'understand, comprehend'. Here 'overcome' is the primary meaning, with 'understand' as an overtone—the darkness failed to overcome the light, and would not have attempted to do so if it had understood it. The failure of understanding on the part of Jesus' enemies, and their utter defeat at the moment of apparent triumph are emphasised in the FG, which also stresses that the Cross, the moment of Christ's apparent failure in the eyes of the world, is in fact his glorification.

John's contemporaries were much concerned with the problem of evil. Many adopted a dualist solution of it. But not John. For him, nothing exists apart from God, but God's creatures are capable of turning away from him. The rebellious creature,

[1] Though the word 'darkness' never occurs in the Revelation, and 'light' only four times (xviii. 23; xxi. 24; xxii. 5 (twice)), yet the contrast of light and darkness is there, though in pictorial terms—cf. the description of the throne of God (Rev. iv. 2 ff.) and of the heavenly city (xxi. 10 ff.), where there is no need of the sun or moon (xxi. 23), since the glory of God lights it, and its lamp is the Lamb (cf. xxii. 5), and also where there is no night (xxi. 25; xxii. 5)—which has the same symbolical significance in the FG (cf. John iii. 2, etc.).

[2] Cf. vi. 17, where κατέλαβεν δὲ αὐτοὺς ἡ σκοτία is read by ℵ D d instead of καὶ σκοτία ἤδη ἐγεγόνει.

turned away from God, sees as it were its own shadow—the projection of itself—and endows it with a spurious reality, so that, in a sense, nothing *does* exist—apart from God.[1]

'Light' and 'darkness' were used in fully dualist systems (deriving ultimately from Zoroastrianism) to describe the two opposing, and equally real, principles of good and evil. But John's use of these terms does not imply anything more than an ethical dualism, fully compatible with monotheism, such as is found also in the Dead Sea Scrolls, with their war of the children of light and the children of darkness.

(6) There came into being a man sent from God, by name John. (7) He came for witness, in order to bear witness about the light, in order that all should believe through him. (8) He was not ⟨himself⟩ the light, but came in order to bear witness about the light. (9) The real light was that which lights every man as it comes into the world.

The abrupt introduction of John the Baptist, and the change to a more prosaic style in this passage, lend colour to the view that there is here an interpolation into an already existing hymn. But John the Baptist comes in here because his ministry provides the historical context for the beginning of the gospel, and heralds the appearance of the incarnate Logos in the world, which is the theme of the following verses (cf. Mark i. 1, again, and Acts x. 36 ff.).

It is equally unnecessary to suppose that the mention of the Baptist has any polemical intention, against a supposed 'Baptist' sect in Asia Minor, who placed John above Jesus in importance. The evidence for the existence of such a sect is scanty. The twelve men at Ephesus who had received John's baptism (Acts xix. 2 ff.) are not really evidence for Asia Minor a generation or more later, when the FG was written, even if it is certain that they were members of a 'Baptist' sect. There is no trace of 'Baptists' in the other Johannine writings. The importance which the Mandaeans attributed to John the Baptist, even if it is an original feature of their belief, is equally inconclusive for

[1] The same idea can be read into the Collect for the Fourth Sunday after Trinity in the Book of Common Prayer, 'O God ... without whom nothing is strong'.

Asia Minor at this period. The fact that the evangelist is concerned only with John the Baptist's status and function in relationship to Jesus is not evidence of any polemical intention. He is writing a Gospel, not a history of religion.

John was **sent**[1] **from God,** i.e. his accredited representative, just as Jesus was 'sent', and in turn 'sent' his disciples (John xvii. 18). But this does not put the Baptist on an equality with Jesus, since their commissions were different. Whereas Jesus was the light, the Baptist was but a 'lamp' (John v. 35), useful only until the dawn. 7. His function was to bear **witness,** and to elicit belief. 'Witness' (μαρτυρία), and the belief which it elicits are two important themes in the FG.[2] The principal purpose of the Gospel is to cite the evidence on which the belief may be based that Jesus is the Christ (xx. 30 f.). Of all this evidence that of John is primary, and so the next main section of the FG begins with his witness, first to himself (i. 19 ff.), and then to Jesus (i. 29 ff.).

9. **The real**[3] **light was that which lights every man as it comes into the world.** It would be possible to understand 'the Logos' as the subject of the main clause, and **the real light** as the predicate, but to make **the light** the subject seems

---

[1] ἀπεσταλμένος. 'Apostle' (ἀπόστολος) is derived from this verb, and in the LXX translates the participle which is the Hebrew equivalent of ἀπεσταλμένος (3 Kingdoms, i.e. 1 Kings, xiv. 6, 'I am sent to you with heavy tidings'). For the 'sending' of the Son see note on iii. 17.

[2] John does not use the noun πίστις in the FG, but the verb πιστεύω is very common. Πίστις occurs in 1 John v. 4, and four times in the Revelation (ii. 13, 19; xiii. 10; xiv. 12). Πιστεύω, common in 1 John, is not found in the Revelation. Μαρτυρία and cognate words are, however, almost as frequent in the Revelation as in the FG.

[3] The adjective ἀληθινός, used here, occurs 9 times in the FG (4 in the Epistles, and 10 in the Revelation); its cognate ἀληθής 14 times in the FG (3 in the Epistles, none in the Revelation). Outside the Johannine literature both are comparatively rare in the New Testament, but the distinction in meaning between them is clear and consistent—ἀληθής means 'true' (as in Mark xii. 14) and ἀληθινός 'real' (as in Luke xvi. 11, and Heb. ix. 24).

In the FG the distinction is not at first sight consistently preserved. If ἀληθής is read in vi. 55, it must mean 'real'; but the true reading may be ἀληθῶς (see note *ad loc.*). In xix. 35 ἀληθινή is used with μαρτυρία, in viii. 14, ἀληθής; in vii. 28 ἔστιν ἀληθινὸς ὁ πέμψας με, in viii. 26 ὁ πέμψας με ἀληθής ἐστιν. But if ἀληθινός is translated either 'reliable' or 'real' and ἀληθής 'true, truthful', there is a consistent usage. A person can be both, and so can a statement. The noun ἀλήθεια has the double meaning 'truth' and 'reliability, reality'. See on i. 14.

to fit the context better. It would also be possible to translate
ἐρχόμενον εἰς τὸν κόσμον not (as here) as a description of **the
light, as it comes into the world,** but as 'coming into the
world',[1] and so applying to **every man.** But John iii. 19, and
xii. 46, support the former alternative.

The world (ὁ κόσμος) is the created order, which is the object
of God's love (cf. iii. 16), but rebellious against him, and so
fallen under the power of the 'ruler of this world' (cf. xii. 31,
and 1 John v. 19) who is hostile to God, but whose power is
broken by the death of Christ. The world hates Christ (vii. 7),
and his disciples (xv. 18 f., cf. 1 John iii. 13), and so incurs
judgement, though this is the consequence rather than the
purpose of Christ's coming into the world (cf. iii. 17 ff.; xii. 47).
His purpose was to conquer, and, in conquering, to save the
world.[2]

In this verse, which repeats in other words the first clause of
verse 5, John is thinking of the general revelation available at
all times, if only men could see it (cf. Rom. i. 19 f.), as he is also
in verse 5. So he uses the present tenses 'shines' (5) and 'lights'
(9). Then in the following verses 10-13 he becomes progress-
ively more specific, leading up to the particular and decisive
revelation made through the Logos become flesh, which is the
climax of the Prologue.

**(10) He was in the world, and the world came into
being through him, and the world did not know him.
(11) He came into his own ⟨property⟩, and his own
⟨people⟩ did not accept him. (12) But as for all those who
did receive him, he gave to them authority to become
children of God, that is, to those who believe in his name.
(13) These were not begotten from ⟨the mixture of⟩
bloods, nor from the will of flesh, nor from the will of a
husband,[3] but from God.**

10. Just as verse 9 paraphrases and expands the first clause
of verse 5, so the clauses of verse 10 recall other previous state-

[1] Cf. the Vulgate *venientem*.
[2] See also (on viii. 23) p. 223.
[3] The phrase οὐδὲ ἐκ θελήματος ἀνδρός is omitted by the first hand of B and a
few other authorities. But this is almost certainly an accidental omission, as it
begins with the same three words as the previous phrase, rather than a gloss
on it which has become established in the vast majority of MSS.

ments—**he was in the world** verse 4,[1] **the world was made by him** verse 3, and **the world did not know him** the second clause of verse 5, drawing out the secondary meaning of **master,** and virtually identifying the **world** with 'the darkness' of 5.

Knowledge is an important concept in the FG, though John avoids the noun $\gamma\nu\hat{\omega}\sigma\iota s$, perhaps because of its misleading associations in Hellenistic religion. But he uses the verb frequently. He avoids 'faith' and uses 'believe' in the same way, and perhaps for the same reason, that it had come to have misleading associations.[2] For John, knowledge is not merely intellectual. It is closely connected with faith. The man who believes in God has eternal life (John vi. 47), and eternal life can be described as knowing God, and Christ (John xvii. 3). Faith leads to knowledge, and imparts to it something of its own quality.

11. **He came into his own ⟨property⟩** presents another aspect of the matter. The phrase **into his own ⟨property⟩** ($\epsilon\grave{\iota}s\ \tau\grave{\alpha}\ \emph{ἴδια}$) occurs also in John xix. 27, 'The disciple took her *into his own home.*' **His own ⟨people⟩** ($o\acute{\iota}\ \emph{ἴδιοι}$) refers primarily to the Jews 'of whom is Christ as far as the flesh is concerned' (Rom. ix. 5). The blindness and apostasy of Christ's own people is as much a matter of anxious concern to the evangelist as it had been to Paul more than a generation earlier (cf. John xii. 37-43).

A reader familiar with Stoicism might have understood these words differently. The whole of mankind can be described as the people of the Logos, since man is a 'rational animal' ($\zeta\hat{\omega}ον\ \lambda o\gamma\iota\kappa\acute{o}ν$). It would not be unlike John to intend this as a secondary meaning, for he certainly did not think that those who did receive the Logos were Jews only.

12. Though the Jews, as a nation, and the Gentiles, as represented by the Roman Empire, rejected the Logos (in the sense both of 'the Christ' and 'the gospel'), there were some **who did receive him,** to whom **he gave authority** ($\emph{ἐξουσία}$—not 'power') **to become children of God.** These are described as

---

[1] Thus incidentally vindicating the translation of verse 4 given above, in which the Logos is understood as the subject of the clause.

[2] As the slogan of a degenerate Paulinism? (See Introduction, pp. 52 f.)

those who believe in his name, i.e. trust and obey him, and accept him as what he claims to be.

In holding that faith is what enables men to become children of God John agrees with Paul (cf. 'Sons of God through faith', Gal. iii. 26) and differs from the Gnostics. Neither Paul nor John teaches that Christians are children of God in the same way that Christ is the Son of God. The Valentinians, however, held that the 'spiritual' are 'of the same substance' (ὁμοούσιοι) with God, using the very term which Athanasius was later (against understandable opposition, in view of its heretical antecedents) to insist upon using of the Son. 1 John has something which sounds like Gnostic doctrine in its idea of the divine 'seed' which the faithful possess (iii. 9, etc.), but this is no more than a picturesque way of saying, as John does in verse 13, that the faithful are **begotten from God.**

That Christians are sons of God, owing their new life as completely to the creative act of God as they owed their natural life to the procreative act of their parents, seemed the only adequate expression for their sense of regeneration and utter dependence upon the Father's power. And, according to Matt. v. 9 and 45, they had Jesus' own authority for their description of themselves as sons of God.

13. John explains as emphatically as possible that the faithful do not become children of God by physical descent, i.e. by membership of a particular race,[1] but by the direct intervention of God, in a manner which he will explain more fully later (John iii. 3 and 5).[2] Physical parentage cannot bestow spiritual status (cf. John iii. 6). The use of the plural **bloods** is most probably due to the ancient belief that animal seed is derived from the blood, and that conception follows on the mingling of the seed of the father and the mother; **the will of the flesh** means simply 'human desire'; if John had thought **flesh** inherently or necessarily *sinful* he would not have said that the Logos became flesh.

[1] In viii. 33 ff., John dismisses as irrelevant the Jews' claim that Abraham is their father, and asserts that their attitude to him belies their further claim that God is their Father. It is true that *spiritual* ancestry alone is relevant—and their actions show that theirs is from the Devil. Cf. also Matt. iii. 9 = Luke iii. 8, Rom. ix. 7 f.

[2] See the notes on these passages, pp. 123-125.

John would hardly have expressed himself so elaborately if all that he wanted to say here was that one does not become a child of God by the process of natural reproduction. To intend a secondary meaning is a characteristic feature of his style, and the precise correspondence between what he says here and the doctrine of the virginal conception of Jesus, whose birth was not due to normal conception, to human desire, or to the will of a husband, but to the direct creative act of God, strongly suggests that John means us to take this allusion, and recognise in the manner of Jesus' birth the pattern of the Christians' spiritual rebirth.[1] This is more probable than that John intended by this allusion to deny the doctrine of the virginal conception of Jesus by the emphatic assertion that it is *Christians* who are spiritually born, not Christ. There is nothing in John's theology incompatible with the doctrine.

(14) And the Logos became flesh, and dwelt among us, and we watched his glory, glory as of one only-begotten of a father, full of grace and truth.

By saying that **the Logos became flesh** (cf. 'Christ came in the flesh', 1 John iv. 2; 2 John 7), John means that Christ was both divine, being **the Logos,** and, in the full sense of the word, human, being **flesh.** He uses **flesh** in its Hebrew sense. It is not for him, as it was for Greek philosophy, the material envelope in which the real man is temporarily confined, the real man being the soul or mind, but it is man in his entirety—body and soul—as a created and temporal being. The antithesis to 'flesh' is 'spirit'; to the Greek 'spirit' would mean the highest element in man, the spark of the divine which distinguishes him from animals and links him to the gods; to John 'spirit' is supernatural—'God is spirit' (John iv. 24). He follows in this Old Testament usage, cf. 'The Egyptians are men, and not God; and their horses are flesh, and not spirit' (Isa. xxxi. 3). Man is

---

[1] One ancient and valuable Old Latin MS. (*b*), Irenaeus, Tertullian, Augustine, and a few other authorities, read, '. . . who believe in the name of him who was begotten . . .' (ὃs . . . ἐγεννήθη, with 'of him' (αὐτοῦ) as antecedent, instead of oἳ . . . . ἐγεννήθησαν, with 'who believe' (τοῖς πιστεύουσιν) as antecedent). This makes quite good sense, but cannot be accepted as the true reading because it is difficult to see why the plural should have been substituted for it, whereas the change from the plural to the singular is easy to understand.

indeed capable of receiving the spirit,[1] but as a divine endowment, not a natural faculty, and as given to those who believe in Christ (cf. John vii. 39; xiv. 17; etc.). To receive the spirit is to become a child of God.

This teaching about the Logos is something quite new. It is not the same as, or derived from, the pagan belief in 'heroes' who were half gods and half men, the offspring of the union of divine and human parents (goddesses could be mothers of half-human children, as gods could be fathers). The doctrine of the incarnation is the result of reflection upon the significance of Jesus Christ, and of the recognition that in him God had made himself known to men in quite a new way. In Christ God spoke to men; in his actions were displayed at once divine compassion and divine creative power. Moreover it was impossible to distinguish the message from the man. Christ was more than a prophet, for it was not just what he said and did, but what he *was*, that constituted the revelation of God in Christ. And so, since it was already a commonplace of Hellenistic-Jewish theology that God spoke and acted through his Logos, John takes the decisive and revolutionary step of identifying the Logos with the man Jesus.

Up to this point both Jew and Greek could have followed John quite happily. But this assertion that **the Logos became flesh** would be a shock to both. The Cross, said St Paul, was a scandal to the Jews, and foolishness to the Gentiles (1 Cor. i. 23); the incarnation was just as much. Hence there arose two early heresies, the Jewish, Ebionism, which denied the divinity of Christ, and the Greek, Docetism, which denied the reality of Christ's humanity. Both already existed, at least in principle, in John's time, and his writings are careful to exclude them both. In the Epistles, for instance, he maintains that 'Christ came in the flesh' (1 John iv. 2; 2 John 7), and that those that deny this are on the side of Antichrist, and even in the Revelation he

[1] The possibility of the gift of the spirit, making men children of God, as of the incarnation of the Logos, depends upon the fact that man is made in the image of God. Christ is the perfect 'image' of the Father—in him we see God—and so perfect man, man as God intended him to be, 'Son of man' as well as 'Son of God'. An analogy to the union of man and God in the incarnate Logos may be seen in the no less mysterious union of animal and man in man.

never loses sight of the humanity of Christ, and appears to use for preference his human name.[1] The Gospel is not so explicitly antidocetic as the Epistles, but seems rather, by its careful record of Jesus' disputes with the Jews, to be concerned with excluding the opposite heresy of Ebionism. Its material reflects an earlier stage in the development of Christianity than the Epistles, though it was written at much the same period as the Epistles.

The following clause, **and dwelt among us,** emphasises that the Logos really shared our human lot, and also, as the verb **dwelt** ($\dot{\epsilon}\sigma\kappa\dot{\eta}\nu\omega\sigma\epsilon\nu$) indicates, that in him God was present among men. The verb $\sigma\kappa\eta\nu\acute{o}\omega$ is found in the New Testament only here and in the Revelation, and is used by John because it has the same consonants, S, K, N, as the Hebrew root שָׁכַן (also meaning 'dwell') from which the noun מִשְׁכָּן, 'tabernacle' is derived.[2] The tabernacle was the place where God was believed to make his presence felt. Ezekiel had prophesied to the exiles deprived of the tabernacle and the comfort of God's presence in it, 'My tabernacle shall be with them, and I will be their God, and they shall be my people' (xxxvii. 27), and John suggests that this prophecy is fulfilled, not in the restored Temple, but in the incarnate Logos, who is the true Temple (cf. John ii. 21). John quotes the text from Ezekiel in Rev. xxi. 3, and asserts explicitly that there was no temple in the new Jerusalem, 'for its temple is the Lord God the Almighty and the Lamb' (Rev. xxi. 22).

This allusion is made more explicit by **and we watched his glory,** for the tabernacle was the place where the glory of the Lord was manifested, cf. Exod. xl. 34, 'The glory of the Lord filled the tabernacle.'

We watched[3] appeals to the collective witness of the first generation of Christians, of whom John of course was one, cf. 1 John i. 1.

---

[1] 'Jesus' alone occurs 9 times, 'Jesus' with 'Christ' or 'Lord' 5 times, 'Christ' alone 4 times (for Romans the figures are 2, 36, 34 respectively).

[2] And also the word *Shekinah*, used in Rabbinic Hebrew as a reverential periphrasis for God.

[3] $\dot{\epsilon}\theta\epsilon\alpha\sigma\acute{a}\mu\epsilon\theta\alpha$: $\theta\epsilon\acute{a}o\mu\alpha\iota$ describes what one does in a *theatre* ($\theta\acute{\epsilon}\alpha\tau\rho o\nu$); see also i. 32, 38; iv. 35; vi. 5; xi. 45. In 1 John i. 1, John uses both $\dot{o}\rho\acute{a}\omega$ 'see' and $\theta\epsilon\acute{a}o\mu\alpha\iota$.

For the meaning of the rather similar verb $\theta\epsilon\omega\rho\acute{\epsilon}\omega$ see p. 191.

The **glory** of Christ is an important theme in the FG. The distinctive feature of John's thought about it is that it is manifested throughout his earthly ministry, particularly in his miracles (cf. ii. 11) but supremely in the Cross (cf. vii. 39; xii. 23; xiii. 31; xvii. 1, a series of passages in which John uses the verb 'glorify' (δοξάζω), and of which the meaning is gradually revealed). In the rest of the New Testament the glory of Christ is something which follows his sufferings, cf. Luke xxiv. 26, 'Was it not necessary that the Christ should suffer these things and enter into his glory?', Heb. ii. 9, 'Jesus crowned with glory and honour because of the suffering of death', and 1 Pet. i. 11, 'the sufferings of Christ and the subsequent glory'. So John does not mention the Transfiguration (if he knew of it), since the glory of Christ manifested in it was merely transitory. For him the glory of Christ was manifest throughout his ministry.

The translation **glory as of one only-begotten of a father** is an attempt to reproduce the Greek, which does not have definite articles with **only-begotten** and **father** here (though it does in verse 18), more accurately than does '*the* only-begotten of *the* Father'. It is John's habit to disclose his meaning gradually. The analogy of a father's only son brings out the closeness of the relationship of the Logos to God. This is further stressed in 18, where 'only-begotten' and 'Father' are no longer the terms of an analogy, but actual titles.

Finally, the incarnate Logos, the true tabernacle, and place of God's revelation of himself, is described as **full**[1] **of grace and truth.** John probably intends these qualities to be taken as equivalents of the 'mercy and truth' (חסד ואמת) which are ascribed to God in Exod. xxxiv. 6, Ps. lvii. 3, etc. If so, John is translating direct from Hebrew, and not following the LXX, which translates חסד by ἔλεος (pity), not χάρις (grace).

Χάρις occurs in the Johannine writings only here and in John i. 16 and 17, and in formulas of greeting in 2 John 3 and Rev. i. 4, and xxii. 21. Thus it might seem that, like πίστις (faith) and γνῶσις (knowledge) it is a characteristically Pauline term which

---

[1] The adjective πλήρης (full) is often indeclinable in the Greek of John's period. It may therefore be taken as qualifying αὐτοῦ 'of him who was full...' The Valentinians took it as qualifying δόξαν (glory), but Irenaeus is probably correct in taking it as qualifying Λόγος.

John generally avoids. Its appearance in the Prologue may lend colour to the suggestion that the Prologue was not originally the work of John. It may, however, be noted that χάρις only occurs in the other Gospels in eight passages in Luke, four of which do not record sayings of Jesus (i. 30; ii. 40, 52; iv. 22), while, in the other four which do, it does not mean 'grace' (vi. 32, 33, 34; xvii. 9). Its absence from the vocabulary of Jesus may be a sufficient explanation of its absence from the body of the FG.

᾽Αλήθεια (truth) on the other hand is an important word in the FG.[1] John uses it not only in the sense which it has in classical Greek, which corresponds to that in normal English usage ('truth'), but also in the sense of the Hebrew אמת, 'reliability, faithfulness'. This is derived from the same root (found also in *Amen*) as 'faith', אמונה, and accordingly ἀλήθεια in the FG often has a meaning very close to that of πίστις (faith), as a body of revealed doctrine. Thus John the Baptist and Jesus 'bear witness to the truth' (v. 33; xviii. 37); this truth has a liberating and sanctifying power (viii. 32; xvii. 17); it is closely connected with the Spirit (cf. 'spirit of truth' xiv. 17; xv. 26; xvi. 13; I John iv. 6); men will worship in spirit and truth, iv. 23 f. Jesus himself (as the Logos) *is* the truth (xiv. 6). 'Truth' is used in the same sense, almost as a technical term, in other contemporary religious literature, including the Dead Sea Scrolls.

(15) John bore witness about him, and cried out[2] saying, 'This is the man of whom I said, He who comes after me is before me; because he was first in comparison with me'.[3]

This verse comes in awkwardly, breaking the connexion between 14 and 16, but this does not necessarily mean that it is an interpolation. If John the Baptist has any place in the Prologue, and the evangelist knew of a saying attributed to him which could be interpreted as a testimony to Jesus as the

---

[1] It does not, however, occur in the Revelation, though it is frequent in the Epistles.

[2] κέκραγεν, perfect; for its force here see Moulton, *Prolegomena*, p. 147. [Cf. B.-D. §§321, 341.—B. A. M.]

[3] πρῶτός μου. This may be only an example of a superlative with a comparative force, cf. xv. 18, and see Moulton, *Prolegomena*, pp. 79, 245. [Cf. B.-D. §62, Turner, p. 32.—B. A. M.]

pre-existent Logos dwelling among men, this is the most suitable place for it.

In **this is the man** the verb is in the imperfect tense ($\tilde{\eta}\nu$), as required by Greek idiom when one recognises something which has been there for some time. John had been saying that he would have a successor who would be his superior, and then realised that Jesus was the man to whom his words applied.

M. Black[1] has pointed out that the two clauses **is before me** and **was first in comparison with me** could both be translations of the same Aramaic original. If so, the evangelist, who delights in double meanings, may be supposed to have put in both in order to bring out both the superiority in status of Jesus to the Baptist, and his absolute priority as the eternal Logos to him, a mere man. What may be presumed to have been the original saying of the Baptist would then be an example of the parallelism characteristic of Semitic poetry such as Black also discerns in the speech attributed to the Baptist in John iii. 27-36.[2]

(16) Because of his fulness did we all accept, and grace instead of grace. (17) Because the law was given through Moses, grace and truth came into being through Jesus Christ.

The word **fulness** takes up **full** in verse 14. The Logos was **full of grace and truth,** and, by watching his glory, we Christians participated in his grace and truth. The word translated **fulness** ($\pi\lambda\acute{\eta}\rho\omega\mu\alpha$) was used by the Valentinians for the sum-total of the divine attributes personified as the *Aeons* (of which Logos was one). Its use here, in connexion with **grace and truth**—divine attributes—may suggest that already in John's time the word had some such quasi-technical sense as that which the Valentinians attached to it. The word is found in a similar sense in Col. i. 19; ii. 9, where Paul, writing against a heresy current in Asia Minor, asserts that the 'fulness' is in Christ. John also uses it to emphasise the completeness of Christ's revelation of God.

Verse 17 is best understood as an explanation of **grace**

---

[1] Black, pp. 107 f.

[2] If, however, the Baptist thought he was preparing for Elijah, his superior, and one who had preceded him in time, both clauses could have had a natural meaning in this saying (see on i. 21).

instead of grace. Its contrast between **Moses** and **Jesus Christ** and between **the law** and **grace and truth** should not be interpreted so precisely as to obscure the fact that all God's dealings with his people are gracious. The gift of the law was an act of divine grace, though less so than the grace given through Jesus Christ. It was also a revelation of divine truth, at least in its witness to Christ (cf. John v. 39). To make law and grace mutually exclusive may be Pauline, but it does not follow that it is also Johannine.

The name **Jesus** is appropriately used here for the first time; as the human name borne by the incarnate Logos it emphasises that it was through the *man* that the divine revelation was given.

(18) No one has ever yet seen God; the only-begotten,[1] who is in the bosom of the Father, is the one that[2] revealed him.

Though there are occasions in the Old Testament when men are said to have seen God (e.g. Jacob, Gen. xxxii. 30; Moses, Aaron, Nadab, Abihu, and seventy elders, Exod. xxiv. 9; Isaiah, Isa. vi. 1, 5), it was thought to be dangerous, even when possible (cf. Isa. vi. 5), and in later Judaism it was held not just that no man could see God and live (cf. Exod. xxxiii. 20), but that it was not in fact *God* whom the recipients of the Old Testament visions had seen.[3] Outside Judaism one tendency was (as

---

[1] P66 ℵ BC* LW*Θ, a few Versions (*pesh hl* mg *boh*), the Valentinians and most of the early Fathers, read 'God only-begotten', ὁ μονογενὴς θεός; the majority of Greek MSS. (headed by A), of the Versions, and of the Fathers (of whom Tertullian appears to be the earliest) 'the only-begotten Son', ὁ μονογενὴς υἱός. The reading 'the only-begotten', ὁ μονογενής, is supported only by two MSS. of the Latin Vulgate, and by Ephrem, Aphraat, Cyril of Jerusalem and Nestorius, but is nevertheless to be preferred. It is consistent with the context, following naturally on John i. 14, and best accounts for the other two variants, of which ὁ μονογενὴς υἱός, being an easier reading, with inferior support, is clearly an emendation of ὁ μονογενὴς θεός. This is unlikely to have been a Valentinian alteration, or the early Fathers would hardly have accepted it. It was probably due to an accidental repetition of two letters at a very early stage in the tradition—ΜΟΝΟΓΕΝΗΣΟΩΝ became ΜΟΝΟΓΕΝΗΣΟΣΟΩΝ which was 'corrected' to ΜΟΝΟΓΕΝΗΣ Θ̄Σ̄ (contraction for ΘΕΟΣ) ΟΩΝ. The same confusion of ΟΣ and ΘΕΟΣ occurs in 1 Tim. iii. 16.

[2] This is an attempt to represent the redundant, but emphatic, ἐκεῖνος which is quite frequent in the FG: cf. i. 33; v. 11, 37; ix. 37; x. 1; xii. 48; xiv. 12, 21, 26; xv. 26.

[3] See on xii. 41, p. 300.

in some forms of Gnosticism) to deny the possibility of seeing or even understanding the supreme God, who was completely beyond all human knowledge. But in the mystery religions the vision of the god or gods into whose mysteries one was initiated was the culmination of the initiation, and conferred divinity upon the initiate.

In saying that **no one has ever yet seen God** John may still be thinking of the contrast between Moses (in spite of Exod. xxiv. 9) and Jesus. But he may also have the mysteries in mind; the word **revealed** (ἐξηγήσατο) may suggest this, since it was a technical term in the mysteries, used of the priest who conducted the initiation.

John's theology is sacramental rather than mystical—i.e. he teaches consistently that the divine is perceived and received through the material, the flesh, and, conversely, that what is perceived and received through the flesh *is* the divine. Man would like to see God (cf. John xiv. 8, 'Show us the Father'), and so transcend the limits of his humanity and become 'as God' (cf. Gen. iii. 5, 22), as he was thought to do in the mysteries, but the fullest vision of God attainable to man as he now is comes only through the incarnate Logos—**the only-begotten, who is in the bosom of the Father, is the one that revealed him** (cf. John xiv. 9, 'He who has seen me has seen the Father'). But by adding **yet** John leaves open the possibility of direct vision in some future state, when the union of the faithful with God in Christ (cf. John xvii. 21 ff.) has been accomplished (cf. 1 Cor. xiii. 12). By describing the only-begotten as **in the bosom of the Father** John indicates their intimate relationship, as of friends reclining together at a banquet (cf. Jesus and the disciple whom he loved, John xiii. 23, where the same word κόλπος (bosom) is used).

Father, as a title of God, is characteristic of the FG, in which there are more than a hundred instances of God addressed or referred to as Father (Matthew has 45). In this it no doubt reflects the usage of Jesus himself. Passages particularly important are ii. 16; iii. 35; iv. 23; v. 17-23, 26, 36; vi. 57; viii. 38-44; x. 30, 38; xiv. 2, 6, 9 ff.; xv. 1; xvii. 1, 5, 21; xviii. 11; xx. 17, 21.

B. TESTIMONY, i. 19-xi. 54

1. FIRST TESTIMONY OF THE BAPTIST, i. 19-34

(19) And this is the witness of John, when the Jews sent to him from Jerusalem[1] priests and Levites, to ask him 'Who are you?' (20) And he confessed, and did not deny, and confessed, 'I am not the Christ'. (21) And they asked him, 'What then? Are you Elias?' and he said 'I am not.' 'Are you the prophet?' and he answered, 'No'. (22) So they said to him, 'Who are you?—so that we may give an answer to those who sent us. What do you say about yourself?' (23) He said, 'I am a voice of one crying, "In the wilderness make straight the way of the LORD", as Esaias the prophet said'. (24) And they had been sent from the Pharisees. (25) And they asked him, and said to him, 'Why then do you baptise, if you are not the Christ, or Elias, or the prophet?' (26) John answered them saying, 'I baptise in water; amongst you there stands one whom you do not know, (27) he who comes after me,[2] the strap of whose sandal I am not worthy to undo'. (28) This happened in Bethany[3] beyond the Jordan, where John was baptising.

19. After the Prologue, the FG proceeds almost without a break (note **And**), taking up first the theme, stated in the Prologue (i. 6-8, 15) of **the witness of John.** The occasion when this was given was the arrival of a deputation of **priests and Levites** from **the Jews,** or, as John adds in an afterthought, **the Pharisees** (24).

It is often said that John shows little knowledge of the state

---

[1] In the FG John uses consistently the Hellenised form of the name Ιεροσόλυμα and in the Revelation the transliterated and indeclinable form Ἰερουσαλήμ (iii. 12; xxi. 2, 10), thus making a nice distinction between the actual and the ideal cities.

[2] ὁ ὀπίσω μου ἐρχόμενος. ℵ* B omit ὁ, which Barrett approves; but the fact that it is found also in verse 15, and read here by P⁶⁶ CWΘ and the vast majority of MSS., probably means that it is correct. The omission of one of two similar adjacent letters could easily happen.

[3] The variant *Bethabara* appears to be due to Origen's mistaken archaeological zeal.

of parties within Judaism, and lumps together all Jesus' opponents as **the Jews**. It is true that when John wrote down the
FG, the Jews as a nation had repudiated Jesus and his Church,
and that the distinction of parties within the nation (which in
any case had had little effect on their attitude to Jesus) can have
had little interest to the readers whom John had in mind. This
does not, however, necessarily imply that John himself was
ignorant of the state of affairs during Jesus' ministry. He mentions the Pharisees several times in the FG, and in three passages (vii. 32 and 45; xi. 47 and 57; xviii. 3) uses the phrase 'the
highpriests and Pharisees' to describe the parties in the Sanhedrin whose temporary alliance had made possible the arrest
and execution of Jesus. He avoids the name 'Sadducees', and
this may be due to the fact that he himself would once have
been counted as a Sadducee, and, disliking the party-label, preferred to describe his old associates as 'the leading members of
the priesthood'. His mention of the Pharisees here is as likely
to be due to a correct memory of a rather unusual incident as
to an ignorant attempt to add verisimilitude to his narrative by
using a name familiar in the Synoptic Gospels. The mention of
priests and Levites[1] may also be accepted as due to an accurate
memory.

This deputation is unlikely to have been an official one, since
the Pharisees did not control the Sanhedrin. But if they were
interested in the Baptist (as well they might be), they might
have thought it tactful to choose members of their party who
were also priests as their representatives, since the Baptist himself was of priestly family.

20. **'I am not the Christ'** implies that some believed him
to be one of the Messianic figures of popular expectation. Luke
iii. 15, explicitly states that all wondered whether he could be
the Christ, but does not report any denial of this on the part of
the Baptist, except indirectly, by quoting in verse 16, 'I baptise
in water, etc.' (cf. John i. 26). To argue that the report of an
explicit denial in the FG is meant as polemic against a 'Baptist'
sect contemporary with the evangelist is only plausible if this
whole incident is regarded as unhistorical.

[1] This phrase which occurs nowhere else in the New Testament occurs
often in the *Manual of Discipline*.

The Christ (both here and in Luke iii. 15) sounds like a specifically Christian usage. It was natural for Christians to speak of **the Christ,** since for them he was identifiable with a single known person. But when there were a number of different Messianic figures expected by different sects and parties, it would have been more natural for John to say rather, 'I am not any one of the Messiahs who are expected', or words to that effect. Since he was of priestly family, he might have been thought to be the priestly 'Messiah of Aaron'—whom the Dead Sea Sect expected, along with 'The Prophet' (Elijah?) and the 'Messiah of Israel' (the heir of David).[1] The expectation of two Messiahs, a priest and a king, rests on Zech. iv. 14.

21. The expectation of the return of Elias (Elijah) as a forerunner of a Messiah, or as himself a Messiah, is based on Mal. iii. 1 ff.; iv. 5 (=iii. 23 in the Hebrew text). 'Malachi' himself does not mention any Messiah, and expects apparently that Elijah will be the forerunner of the LORD himself. Jesus was sometimes identified with Elijah (cf. Mark vi. 15; viii. 28 = Matt. xvi. 14), or expected to behave like him (cf. Luke ix. 54), but he apparently cast John the Baptist for the rôle of Elijah[2] (cf. Mark ix. 11 ff. = Matt. xvii. 10 ff.; and—much more explicit —Matt. xi. 14). This suggests that the Baptist's denial that he is Elijah, recorded in the FG, rests on something more substantial than a guess of the evangelist's.

Since the Baptist spoke of a successor who was his superior (i. 15 and 26 f.), he may have believed that he was preparing for the return of Elijah from the desert into which he had gone before he was taken up into heaven. Baptising in fire[3] would seem a congenial occupation for a resuscitated Elijah.

The prophet was expected in fulfilment of Deut. xviii. 18-19, a text included in a collection made by the Dead Sea Sect,[4]

---

[1] See *Manual of Discipline,* ix. 11. [Cf. the very full discussion by M. Black, 'The Qumran Messiah and Related Beliefs', in *The Scrolls and Christian Origins* (1961), pp. 145-163.—B. A. M.]

[2] His hairy garment and leather girdle (Mark i. 6) recall Elijah's (2 Kings i. 8). Is this why they are not mentioned in the FG?

[3] This (or 'in wind and fire') was probably the original form of the Baptist's prediction.

[4] See T. H. Gaster, *The Scriptures of the Dead Sea Sect* (1957), p. 353.

presumably to support their theory of the pattern of future events. For them, the prophet was distinct from the two Messiahs.[1] John vii. 40 f. distinguishes him from 'the Christ', and Mark vi. 15, from Elijah. The Baptist's questioners here distinguished him both from 'the Christ' and Elijah, whereas John vi. 14, may equate the prophet either with Elijah or the Messiah—or indeed with Elijah interpreted as a Messianic figure.[2] It is difficult to keep the various figures distinct in the kaleidoscope of Jewish apocalyptic expectation.

Having repudiated all his questioners' suggestions, the Baptist nevertheless claims that he has a function foretold in the Old Testament. He is **a voice of one crying, "In the wilderness make straight the way of the LORD"** (a quotation of Isa. xl. 3, which compresses into one the two clauses of the original). This text is quoted in a fuller form by the Synoptic evangelists (Mark i. 3, Matt. iii. 3, Luke iii. 4), who punctuate the text, 'The voice of one crying in the wilderness, . . .' They do not attribute it to the Baptist himself, but it is at least as likely that they used it because he had done so, as that the FG attributes it to the Baptist because the Synoptic evangelists had quoted it. There seems no reason to depart from Isaiah's punctuation in the FG. This text was used by the Dead Sea Sect[3] to justify their withdrawal into the wilderness, and they therefore kept to Isaiah's punctuation. Their understanding of what was involved in preparing the way of the LORD was admittedly different from the Baptist's, but the use of this text is nevertheless a link between them. The Sect's aim was to form a spiritual élite, the Baptist's to initiate a mass movement of repentance.

25. The question **'Why then do you baptise?'** shows that John's baptism was recognised as a preparation for the coming of the LORD. In this it resembled that practised by the Dead Sea Sect, from which it may have been derived, though the Sect would not have approved the Baptist's indiscriminate administration of the rite. His baptism was a symbolic action, like those of the prophets (cf. Jer. xix. 10 f., and many other

---

[1] *Manual of Discipline*, ix. 11.
[2] See note on vi. 14.
[3] *Manual of Discipline*, viii. 14.

examples), and, like them, was meant to effect what it symbolised, in this case, a purification which would preserve its recipient from the imminent baptism in fire.[1] It may thus be called an eschatological sacrament. But the Baptist had denied that he was any of the recognised eschatological persons who were to prepare for the coming of the LORD. Hence the question, which does not imply that any of these persons were expected to baptise.

26. For the complete answer to the question, verse 33 must be read with 26 and 27. Baptism in water[2] is a preparation for a baptism in holy spirit to be administered by one already present, but unrecognised, the Baptist's successor, for whom he himself is unworthy to perform the most menial of services. That the Baptist had promised, or threatened, baptism in fire, destroying the wicked, seems clear from the Synoptic tradition (cf. Matt. iii. 12 = Luke iii. 17). Matt. iii. 11 (= Luke iii. 16) adds to the words 'I baptise in water' the antithetical parallel clause 'He shall baptise you in holy spirit and fire', which probably meant for the Baptist the wind which blew the chaff from the grain and the fire that burnt it. But Mark i. 8, and John i. 33 (neither of which has any equivalent of Matt. iii. 12 = Luke iii. 17), do not mention fire, and so make of the Baptist's words a prophecy of that gift of the Holy Spirit which the Church was conscious of possessing through Christ.[3]

'**There stands among you one whom you do not know**' has no equivalent in the Synoptic Gospels, though verse 27 has—in Mark i. 7 = Matt. iii. 11 = Luke iii. 16, with some variations. It is a nice question whether John's account of the Baptist is a drastic remodelling of Mark's, or whether he is following an independent, but in part parallel source. He certainly had a considerable amount of material dealing with the Baptist, much of which is independent of the Synoptic tradition (cf. John iii. 27 ff.), and this may support the view that he

---

[1] See below.

[2] 'Water' is important in the symbolism of the FG, (i) as representing the old covenant, ii. 7; iv. 7, 13; v. 4; (ii) as the medium of the future Christian Sacrament, iii. 5; iv. 10 ff.; vii. 38; xiii. 5 ff.; xix. 34. The point of contact between the two is the water of John's baptism.

[3] And which the Dead Sea Sect also had expected, cf. *Manual of Discipline*, iv. 20-22.

has taken all his material from sources other than the Synoptic Gospels. He may also of course have used Mark, to an extent which cannot precisely be determined, or at least have written with an eye on his Gospel. It seems clear that Mark, the common source of Matthew and Luke other than Mark, and John all had independent access to traditions about the Baptist, and that all have something to contribute to an adequate understanding of his work.

28. **Bethany beyond the Jordan** (so called to distinguish it from Bethany near Jerusalem, John xi. 1, 18) is not otherwise known or identifiable. But it seems difficult to see why John mentioned it if it did not stand in his source. It can have no allegorical or symbolic significance. John seems to have had a fairly detailed knowledge of the topography of Southern Palestine.

(29) On the next day he saw Jesus coming towards him, and said, 'See, the Lamb of God, who takes away [1] the sin of the world! (30) This is he of whom I said, "After me there comes a man who is before me, because he was first in comparison with me." (31) And I did not know him; but ⟨now I realise that⟩ it was in order that he should be made manifest to Israel that I came baptising in water.' (32) And John bore witness, saying, 'I watched [2] the Spirit coming down like a dove out of heaven, and it remained upon him. (33) And I did not know him ⟨then⟩; but it was the one who sent me to baptise in water that [3] said to me, "Upon whomsoever you see the Spirit descending and remaining, he it is who baptises in Holy Spirit." (34) And I have seen and borne witness that this is the Elect [4] of God.'

John gives only the barest outline of his story. The date is given, and the place is presumably Bethany, but there is no

---

[1] 'Who takes away' (ὁ αἴρων) can also mean 'who bears'. John probably intends both senses. The Lamb takes away the sin of the world by bearing it.

[2] θεάομαι. See on i. 14, p. 81, n. 3.   [3] See p. 85, n. 2.

[4] The vast majority of authorities read 'Son'. But **Elect** is to be preferred; it is supported by P[5] ℵ* 77 218 ff[2] sin cur, and the conflated reading 'Elect Son' in 57 a b ff[2] corr sah; and the change from the unusual **Elect** to the familiar 'Son' (cf. Mark i. 11, Matt. iii. 17, Luke iii. 22) is more probable than that in the other direction.

mention of any audience. Jesus makes his first appearance,[1] but says nothing. John sees him, and utters his testimony. He recognises Jesus as **the Lamb of God who takes away the sin of the world,** who has **the Spirit remaining upon him, baptises in Holy Spirit,** and is **the Elect of God.**

It is commonly argued that this whole incident is quite un-historical, and is an adaptation of the account of the baptism of Jesus in Mark i. 9-11. In Mark, the Baptist does not appear to have recognised Jesus as anyone out of the ordinary; Jesus alone saw the descent of the Spirit,[2] and alone heard the divine declaration 'Thou art my beloved Son; with thee I am well pleased'. The evangelist was embarrassed by the fact that the Baptist baptised Jesus,[3] and so suppressed it (anti-'Baptist' polemic again!), turning the descent of the dove into a sign to the Baptist that the Christ had come, and reducing the Baptist to the rôle of a mere witness to the fact, who declared publicly what the divine voice had revealed to Jesus alone, according to Mark.[4] Matthew similarly objectifies the divine voice by making it declare 'This is my beloved Son, with whom I am well pleased' (Matt. iii. 17).

It is further argued that any recognition of Jesus as Christ by the Baptist at this stage is incompatible with the enquiry which he made from prison, 'Are you he who is to come (i.e. the Messiah), or shall we look for another?' (Matt. xi. 3, Luke vii. 19).

If this line of argument is adopted, it follows that the description of Jesus as **the Lamb of God who takes away the sin of the world** is due, not to the Baptist, but to the evangelist, and is to be interpreted in terms of his teaching. If Revelation

---

[1] The data are insufficient to fix this incident in Jesus' ministry. It was after his Baptism (cf. 32 ff.), but whether before or after the Temptations (which John does not mention) it is impossible to say.

[2] The phrase 'like a dove' is probably adverbial, qualifying 'descending', and describing the manner of its descent, like a bird alighting. If so, it is futile to look for analogies of the Spirit to a dove. Luke, however, seems to have taken this as a description of the appearance of the Spirit, adding 'in bodily form' to Mark's account (Luke iii. 22).

[3] As, it is also argued, was Matthew (hence Matt. iii. 14 f.).

[4] 'The Elect of God' (John i. 34) is the equivalent of 'beloved Son' in Mark i. 11. 'With thee I am well pleased' is an echo of Isa. xlii. 1, 'In whom my soul delights', which refers to God's Elect.

offers any clue, it is that the Lamb is at once a sacrifice (cf. Rev. v. 6, etc.) and the leader of God's people, the Messiah (cf. Rev. vii. 17, etc.). The Lamb as sacrifice suggests the Passover (cf. the Passover allusion in John xix. 33, 36—and 1 Cor. v. 7), and the scapegoat (which did 'bear' and so 'take away' sin, as the Passover lamb did not, cf. Lev. xvi. 21 f.), and perhaps also the ram caught in the thicket and sacrificed in place of Isaac (Gen. xxii. 8). The lamb led to the slaughter in Isa. liii. 7 (where LXX has the word ἀμνός used in John i. 29 and 36), which refers to the Servant of the LORD, forms a link connecting the sacrificial Lamb with the Messianic Lamb. The representation of the Messiah as the Lamb which leads the flock derives from Jewish apocalyptic.[1] The ingenious suggestion that 'Lamb' is a mistranslation of an Aramaic word טליא meaning 'servant' (i.e. the Servant-Messiah), due to its similarity to the Hebrew טלה, 'lamb', lacks sufficient evidence.[2]

The evangelist may well have intended his readers to pick up some—or all—of these allusions, but the question remains whether **the Lamb of God** can have meant anything in the context of the Baptist's expectations, and so can have been used by him. If it can, then the way becomes clear for the recognition of the substantial historicity of this testimony of the Baptist to Christ.

It appears from John i. 35 ff., that Andrew at any rate is represented as understanding that **the Lamb of God** meant the Messiah (cf. verse 41). If the Baptist intended this, he most probably used the term in the sense it bore in the apocalyptic tradition. He saw in Jesus, who was of Davidic descent, the destined leader of God's people. **'I did not know him'** does not mean, 'He was a stranger to me', but 'I did not recognise him as Messiah when I baptised him.' He had been looking for the return of Elijah to baptise in wind and fire, and it was then revealed to him that the descent of the Spirit and its remaining on the man whom he had baptised was the sign that his expectation had been fulfilled. His successor had appeared, but he was the Messiah. He would take away the sin of the world by slaying the sinners. Isa. xi. 1-4, may be relevant here. It is a prophecy

---

[1] See Dodd, *Interpretation*, pp. 231 ff.
[2] See Dodd, *Interpretation*, pp. 235 f.

about the 'shoot from the stump of Jesse', and speaks of the
Spirit of the LORD resting upon him (verse 2, cf. John i. 32 f.),
and of him slaying the wicked with the breath of his mouth
(verse 4). For 'breath' Isaiah has רוח, which also means
'spirit', and the baptism in Holy Spirit[1] may be the evangelist's
substitution for a 'baptism' which was in fact the overwhelming
of the wicked by wind and fire.[2] The Baptist may also have
meant by **the Elect of God** to allude to Isa. xlii. 1 (where the
Spirit is also spoken of as being upon the Elect).

That the Baptist could have said all this is borne out by the
fact that these statements correspond to some extent with the
expectations of the Dead Sea Sect. The Sect applied Isa. xi. 1-4,
to their 'Messiah of Israel', as is shown by a fragment of a
Commentary on Isaiah found in one of the Dead Sea caves.[3] The
members of the Sect were 'elect', and believed that their task
was to make atonement for the world by punishing the wicked.[4]
What applied to the individual members of the Sect (or to
the community as a whole) could apply *a fortiori* to
their war-leader. The Baptist was not a member of the Sect,
but he may well have learnt some of his teaching from
them.

His enquiry addressed to Jesus from prison may then have
been due to his surprise that Jesus was not behaving as he
expected. Jesus knew himself to be the Messiah, but he repudiated the Baptist's conception of his rôle. The Baptist's prophecy
may be compared with that of Caiaphas (John xi. 50), inasmuch
as both spoke better than they knew. Jesus rejected the conquest of the world as a temptation of the Devil (cf. Matt. iv. 8 f.,
Luke iv. 6 f.); he *did* conquer the world (cf. John xvi. 33), but
not by military force; his kingdom was not of this world (cf.
John xviii. 36).

The evangelist preserved the description of Jesus as **the
Lamb of God** most probably because it was susceptible of a
sacrificial as well as a Messianic interpretation, but gave the
prophecy of Jesus' baptising in a form more susceptible than

---

[1] See *Manual of Discipline*, iv. 20-22.
[2] For the metaphorical use of 'baptise' and 'baptism' cf. Mark x. 38 f.,
and Luke xii. 50.
[3] See Gaster, *op. cit.*, p. 346.
[4] See *Manual of Discipline*, viii. 6.

the original to his own interpretation.[1] He thus gives this saying in the Marcan form, but probably independently, rather than in that found in Matthew and Luke.[2] He omitted the actual baptism of Jesus, as he also omitted other events important in the Synoptic Gospels,[3] and for the same reason, that it had no theological significance for him. But he has to keep the descent of the Spirit because it was the sign which made possible the Baptist's testimony, which is important for him. The evangelist has therefore modified his account of Jesus' encounter with the Baptist in this passage, but, even so, it is very far from being the product of his imagination. Mark too may have modified his account, and omitted the Baptist's recognition of Jesus as incompatible with his own view that the fact that Jesus was Messiah was kept a secret until Peter revealed it at Caesarea Philippi—and was bidden to keep silent about it[4] (Mark viii. 29 f.). It is not by any means only in the FG that theological considerations influence the narrative.

32. This is the first mention of the Spirit in the FG. The doctrine of the Spirit is an important and distinctive feature of John's theology,[5] and it is surprising that John did not introduce it into his Prologue. This may have been because the Logos and the Spirit were virtually indistinguishable before the Incarnation (cf. John vii. 39). The purpose of the Incarnation of the Logos may be described as the uniting of flesh and spirit, so that men might receive life and light through the spirit, which was to be made available for them by the death of Christ, and be conveyed to them by the sacraments. John distinguishes the spirit as a gift to men from the Spirit who gives it, speaking of the latter as *him* (though the word πνεῦμα is neuter), thus indicating that the Spirit is as personal as the Logos, and not just an impersonal force (cf. John xvi. 13, 'When he (ἐκεῖνος, masculine) comes, the Spirit of truth . . .'). He also distinguishes the Spirit from the Logos, whose work

[1] As preparatory to the action of Jesus breathing on the disciples and saying, 'Receive Holy Spirit' (John xx. 22).

[2] See above, p. 91.

[3] As, for example, the Transfiguration. See above, p. 82.

[4] For an explanation of Peter's confession at Caesarea Philippi see below, p. 100.

[5] See on iii. 5-8; iv. 23 f.; vi. 63; vii. 39; xiv. 17, 26; xv. 26; xvi. 13 ff.; xx. 22.

he continues among the faithful. But this distinction only became possible through the revelation of God made through the incarnate Logos.

2. THE FIRST DISCIPLES, i. 35-51

(35) The next day John was again standing, and two of his disciples; (36) and looking at Jesus walking he said, 'See, the Lamb of God!' (37) And the two disciples heard him speaking, and followed Jesus. (38) But Jesus, turning and noticing[1] them following, said to them, 'What do you seek?' And they said to him, 'Rabbi (which means "Teacher"), where are you staying?' (39) He said to them, 'Come, and you will see'. So they went and saw where he was staying, and stayed with him that day (it was about four o'clock in the afternoon). (40) Andrew, the brother of Simon Peter, was one of the two who heard John and followed him. (41) In the morning[2] he found his brother Simon, and said to him, 'We have found the Messiah (which means "Anointed"[3])'. (42) He took him to Jesus. Jesus looked at him and said, 'You are Simon, the son of John; you shall be called Cephas (which means "Rock"[4]).'

35. Again the evangelist gives only the bare essentials of his story, as in the previous episode, subordinating everything

---

[1] θεάομαι. See on i. 14, p. 81, n. 3.

[2] Reading πρωΐ, implied by b e r¹ sin. πρῶτον ('first', adverb) is read by P66 A B Θ fam 1 fam 13 etc.; πρῶτος ('first', adjective) by ℵ* W etc. All are found elsewhere in the FG (πρωΐ, xviii. 28; xx. 1: πρῶτον, ii. 10; vii. 51; xv. 18; xviii. 13: πρῶτος, xx. 4, 8, and in two passages which are probably interpolations, v. 4; viii. 7), and all make good sense, so that decision between them is difficult. As between πρῶτον and πρῶτος the greater weight of evidence would support πρῶτον. As between πρωΐ and πρῶτον the fact that πρῶτον is more easily explicable as a corruption of πρωΐ than πρωΐ of πρῶτον favours πρωΐ. The next word in the Greek text is τόν, which suggests that πρῶτον τόν arose from πρωΐ τόν by an accidental doubling of τόν (cf. note on μονογενής, p. 85, n. 1).

[3] 'Christ' (Χριστός).

[4] 'Peter' (Πέτρος, a masculine formed from the proper word for 'rock', πέτρα).

else to his main purpose of showing the effect of the Baptist's
testimony. 36. The Baptist sees **Jesus walking**—why or where
the evangelist does not say—and repeats his declaration, **'See,
the Lamb of God'.** 37. The two disciples then leave the
Baptist, and follow Jesus, thus beginning the process which will
end in Jesus drawing all men to himself (cf. John xii. 32). The
Baptist has begun to decrease, Jesus to increase (cf. John iii. 30).

38. Jesus' first recorded words in the FG, the question,
'What do you seek?' is answered by another, **'Rabbi, where
are you staying?'**—natural enough, if they feel that their
business is too important to be mentioned in public. **Rabbi**
subtly emphasises the paradox of the incarnation. It is intended
to show reverence (the more so since Jesus was not a regular
Rabbi, cf. John vii. 15), yet fails utterly to express the true
dignity of him to whom it is addressed.[1] 39. Jesus' answer,
'Come, and you will see' is also quite natural—and so is the
consequence of the invitation—**they went, and saw . . . and
stayed with him.** But this simple episode may have a deeper
meaning, as conforming to, and illustrating, the pattern of
man's quest for Christ and its outcome. Moved by prophecy (in
this case the testimony of the Baptist) the disciple begins his
quest (cf. 'Seek and you will find', Matt. vii. 7 = Luke xi. 9, and
the warning in John vii. 34, 36, not to put off the quest until it
is too late). Meeting Christ, he is invited to see for himself
where Christ is staying, and stays with him. John xv. 4 ff. will
at last make clear that the place where Christ 'stays' (the verb
μένω is used in both passages) is in the Christian community,
and that where the Christian 'stays' is in Christ.[2]

39. **They stayed with him that day** probably means that
they stayed not only for the brief period of daylight that
remained—it was already **four o'clock in the afternoon** (literally, 'the tenth hour', calculated from dawn)—but also over-
night. If the reading **in the morning** in verse 41 is correct,[3]
they must have done so. The evangelist says nothing of their
further conversation. His account of the instruction which Jesus
gave his disciples must wait until later in his narrative.

[1] Cf. its use by Nicodemus, iii. 2.
[2] See also vi. 56; viii. 31, and xiv. 2, 23, which have the cognate noun μονή.
[3] See p. 97, n. 2.

Andrew is mentioned again in the FG at vi. 8 and xii. 22, as well as in the next episode. In the Synoptic Gospels, apart from the story of his call, he is mentioned only at Mark xiii. 3 and in the lists of the Twelve. His relative importance in the FG may account for his mention in the *Muratorian Canon*.[1]

The mention of **Andrew** naturally raises the question who the other disciple was. The answer is often given that he was John the son of Zebedee, and in support of this it is argued that in verse 41 πρῶτος ('first', adjective) should be read,[2] and the verse translated, 'He was the first to find his own brother[3] Simon...', implying that John next found *his* own brother. Thus the four disciples whose call is recorded in Mark i. 16-20, figure also in John i. 35-42. But this is rather subtle, even for the FG.

Another suggestion is that of M. C. Perry,[4] that the other disciple, unnamed here, is Philip, the sequel to whose first encounter with Jesus is described in verses 43 ff. If any comparison is to be made between Mark and the FG here, it is just as plausible to see the call of *five* disciples in John i. 35-51 (Andrew, the unnamed disciple, Simon, Philip, and Nathanael), designed as an equivalent or alternative to the five called in Mark (Simon and Andrew, James and John in i. 16-20, plus Levi the publican in ii. 14). The unnamed disciple may still be the Beloved Disciple, but it is impossible to prove from this passage that he was John the son of Zebedee.

On the other hand it may be argued that our evangelist is not thinking of Mark at all in this passage. Strictly speaking, it is incorrect to say that Andrew and his unnamed companion were called: they offered to follow Jesus, and, unlike other volunteers (Matt. viii. 19-22, Luke ix. 57-62), were accepted. This incident may help to explain the prompt response of Simon and Andrew in Mark i. 16-18.[5]

41. Andrew's announcement to his brother, **'We have**

---

[1] See Introduction, p. 42.   [2] See p. 97, n. 2.

[3] Giving to ἴδιον in τὸν ἀδελφὸν τὸν ἴδιον the emphatic sense 'his *own* brother'. But in *Koiné* Greek the unemphatic sense, 'his', is more frequent.

[4] *Theology*, Vol. LXIV, 490 (April 1961), pp. 153 f. [The same identification is argued for by M.-É. Boismard, 'Les Traditions johanniques concernant le Baptiste: note additionnelle', *Revue Biblique*, Vol. 70, 1963, pp. 39-42.—B. A. M.]

[5] For a discussion of the relationship of this episode to the call of the disciples in Luke v. 1-11, see pp. 443 f., 449 ff. below.

found the Messiah' is not incompatible with Peter's later confession at Caesarea Philippi (Mark viii. 29), though it may be with Mark's presentation of it. Andrew meant no more than John the Baptist did by 'the Lamb of God', i.e. the 'Messiah of Israel' as the Dead Sea Sect called him. Peter's subsequent confession was not a new discovery, but the triumph of faith over appearances. Jesus refused the rôle for which the Baptist designed him, and which Peter, like his brother, had expected him to play. When Jesus asks him 'Who do you say that I am?' Peter replies, 'You *are* the Christ' (even if nothing that Jesus had done so far appeared to support the belief).

42. This is not the giving of the name Cephas to Simon, but a prophecy that he will receive the name. None of the Gospels states explicitly the occasion when Simon actually received it. Mark iii. 16, simply says 'Simon he surnamed Peter' (cf. Luke vi. 14). Matt. xvi. 18, 'You are Peter', may be intended as the formal bestowal of his new name. Jesus' recognition of Simon, and prophecy about him, mark him as possessing the clairvoyant power of the ancient prophets—cf. how Samuel knows Saul and his business at their first meeting (1 Sam. ix. 15 ff.)[1]

John transliterates and translates Semitic names and titles[2] more frequently than any other New Testament author. It is not because he likes the glamour of barbaric names (cf. the Gnostics' *Hachamoth, Ialdabaoth*, etc.), or thinks of them as potential ingredients in spells (cf. the magical papyri),[3] or is conscientiously (or unscrupulously!) adding local colour to his narrative. They reflect quite unconsciously the Semitic character of the tradition upon which he draws.

(43) The next day he wished to go away to Galilee, and found Philip; and Jesus said to him, 'Follow me'. (44) Now Philip was from Bethsaida, the city of Andrew and Peter. (45) Philip found Nathanael, and said to him, 'We

[1] For further examples of, or references to, Jesus' clairvoyant power, cf. i. 47; ii. 24 f.; iv. 17-19, 50; v. 42; vi. 61, 64; xi. 4, 11-14.

[2] Rabbi (i. 38), Messias (i. 41), Cephas (i. 42), Siloam (ix. 7), Thomas (xi. 16; xx. 24), Gabbatha (xix. 13), Golgotha (xix. 17), Rabboni (xx. 16).

[3] *Talitha cumi* (Mark v. 41) and *Ephphatha* (Mark vii. 34) may, however, have conceivably been preserved as words of power which Christian exorcists might use.

have found him of whom Moses[1] and the prophets wrote,
Jesus the son of Joseph from Nazareth'. (46) And Nathanael said to him, 'Can anything good come out of
Nazareth?' Philip said to him, 'Come and see'. (47) Jesus
saw Nathanael coming to him, and said of him, 'See, one
who is truly an Israelite, in whom there is no guile'.
(48) Nathanael said to him, 'How do you recognise me?'
Jesus answered and said to him, 'Before Philip called
you, as you were under the fig-tree, I saw you'. (49) Nathanael answered him, 'Rabbi, you are the Son of God, you
are the King of Israel'. (50) Jesus answered and said to
him, 'Is it because I said to you, "I saw you under the
fig-tree", that you believe? You shall see greater things
than these'. (51) And he said to him, 'Amen, amen, I say
to you, you shall see heaven opened, and the angels of
God ascending and descending upon the Son of man'.

43. The mention of Jesus' projected visit to Galilee is introduced to account for the otherwise abrupt change of scene
between chapters i and ii, but is at once forgotten. Jesus' words
to Philip,[2] '**Follow me**', sound like an invitation to accompany
him on his journey—an impression which verse 44 might seem
to confirm—but are in fact a summons to become a disciple
(cf. viii. 12; x. 4 f., 27; xii. 26; xxi. 19, 22). Jesus cannot have
been asking Philip to go with him, for Philip at once goes away,
and

45. **found Nathanael,[3] and said to him, 'We have found
. . .'**—why **We** when no one else has been mentioned? It looks
as though the source which John is using in i. 19-51, and which
did not contain the story of the marriage at Cana (ii. 1-11),

---

[1] The vast majority of the authorities add 'in the law'; but it is omitted by
e r[1] *sin* and once by Origen. It is probably a very early gloss.

[2] Philip is mentioned again in vi. 5, 7; xii. 21 f.; xiv. 8 f.; in the Synoptic
Gospels he only figures in the lists of the Twelve Apostles. The greater
interest shown in him by the FG may have helped to foster the belief that
Philip of Hierapolis was one of the Twelve (for which see Introduction,
p. 43.)

[3] Nathanael is not mentioned in the Synoptic Gospels. He is usually
identified with Bartholomew, whose name follows Philip's in the lists of
Apostles in Mark iii. 18, Matt. x. 3, and Luke vi. 14. Bartholomew means
'Son of Ptolemy' and so could be Nathanael's patronymic, as Barjonas was
Simon Peter's (Matt. xvi. 17).

originally continued after 42 with an account of one of the two disciples mentioned in 35-42—probably Andrew[1]—finding Philip and bringing him to Jesus. Then it would be natural for Philip to say, **'We have found . . .'**, meaning, 'Andrew (or whoever it was) and I . . .' If so, Philip's enlistment follows the same pattern as those of Peter and Nathanael, as part of the chain-reaction started by the Baptist's testimony. This suggestion would also account for another feature of 43—the mention of Jesus as subject of **said to him.** As the verse now stands, this is unnecessary, for Jesus is the subject of all the main verbs since 42. But if in the source Jesus was not the subject of **found Philip,** it would be necessary to mention him in the next clause. Thus it seems that the mention of the projected visit to Galilee, necessary to weld together two distinct sources, has caused a certain amount of confusion in the narrative at this point.

Philip's testimony to Jesus, as **him of whom Moses and the prophets wrote,** is probably meant to allude principally to Deut. xviii. 18-19, and Isa. xi. 1-4; xlii. 1. For the witness of the Scriptures to Jesus in the FG cf. v. 39.

His description of Jesus as **son of Joseph** (cf. John vi. 42) does not mean that John denied, or was ignorant of, the virginal conception of Jesus.[2] Whatever else may be true of his birth, Jesus was legally Joseph's son, as he is also described by Luke.[3]

Though Nazareth[4] is not mentioned in the Old Testament, Mishnah, or Talmud, or by Josephus, the independent witness of Mark (i. 9), the birth narratives of Matthew (ii. 23) and Luke (i. 26 etc.), and John, is sufficient to refute the suggestion that it is a place-name invented to account for the titles *Nazarēnos*

[1] Andrew is mentioned both in John vi and xii where Philip is named, and Philip follows Andrew in the list of the Twelve in Mark (iii. 18).

[2] See on i. 13.

[3] Luke iv. 22, 'Is not this Joseph's son?' Cf. Mark vi. 3, 'Is not this the carpenter, the son of Mary?' and Matt. xiii. 55, 'Is not this the carpenter's son? Is not his mother called Mary?' 'Son of Mary', as used in Mark, might imply that Jesus' paternity was unknown or disputed, and so Matthew and Luke avoid it. That Jesus was the illegitimate son of Mary is the only plausible alternative to the traditional view of his birth. The slander was propagated by anti-Christian writers in antiquity, and may underlie the remark attributed to Jesus' opponents in John viii. 41, '*We* were not born of fornication'.

[4] Or Nazara (Matt. iv. 13, Luke iv. 16).

and *Nazōraios* given to Jesus, the true meaning of which had been forgotten or suppressed.[1]

46. Nathanael came from Cana of Galilee (John xxi. 2), and cannot believe that an obscure village near his own town can be the home of the Messiah.[2] Philip does not argue with him, but invites him to put his prejudice to the test of experience. Nathanael's willingness to do this, shown by his going to Jesus (47) merits Jesus' description of him as **one in whom there is no guile.** Jesus recognises Nathanael, as he had Simon,[3] and greets him as **one who is truly an Israelite,**[4] i.e. a member of the true Israel, as opposed to the unbelievers—the Jews.

48. By explaining that he had seen where he was, **under the fig-tree,**[5] before Philip called him, Jesus indirectly answers Nathanael's question **'How do you recognise me?'** Both are due to his supra-normal faculty of perception.[3] 49. Convinced by this demonstration that Jesus has powers which ordinary men have not, Nathanael sees the truth of Philip's testimony, and confesses that Jesus is **the Son of God, King of Israel.** The true Israelite acknowledges the true King of Israel. For Nathanael, at this time, these two titles must have been virtually synonymous. The King of Israel became, in virtue of his anointing, 'Son of God', cf. Ps. ii. 7. But Nathanael, like the Baptist and these other early witnesses, spoke better than he knew. **Son of God** and **King of Israel** are both titles which John claims for Jesus, but in a sense rather different from that which Nathanael gave to them.

This is the first time in the FG that Jesus is actually described as **Son of God,** but John has, in his characteristic manner, carefully prepared for it (cf. i. 14 and 18), so that his readers may understand the title now that it is given to him. It is found in the Synoptic Gospels, but only rarely. In Mark it occurs in the title (i. 1) and in the centurion's confession (xv.

[1] *Nazarēnos* is a natural formation from *Nazara*. For a discussion of *Nazōraios* see note on xviii. 5.

[2] Cf. John vii. 41.

[3] See p. 100, n. 1 above.

[4] **Israelite** is used only here in the Gospels. It occurs five times in Acts (each time in the vocative plural), and three times in Paul's Epistles (Rom. ix. 4; xi. 1, 2 Cor. xi. 22).

[5] It is unnecessary to speculate about what Nathanael was doing there. Merely to know where he was is a sufficient indication of Jesus' clairvoyance.

39), and is used otherwise only by supernatural speakers, divine or diabolical. Nowhere in the Synoptic Gospels does Jesus use it himself, though in Matt. xi. 27, Luke x. 22, he speaks of himself as 'the son' and of God as 'the Father'. In the FG, however, 'Son of God', 'his Son', 'the Son', occur not only in the evangelist's meditations (as in iii. 16 ff.), but also in sayings of Jesus addressed both to believers (cf. xi. 4) and to opponents (cf. v. 19 ff.; viii. 35 f.; x. 36). This raises the question whether John has imported the title wholesale into the FG, or whether the Synoptic Gospels have deliberately avoided it, as they do the title 'Christ', with which it is, for both the FG and the Synoptic Gospels, synonymous (cf. John xi. 27, Matt. xvi. 16, Mark xiv. 61). The question does not admit of a simple answer. The bulk of the Synoptic material is independent of the Johannine tradition, which deals mainly with Jesus' teaching in Jerusalem, and it is in John's Jerusalem material that the title mainly occurs. Its historical credibility is part of the larger question of that of this Jerusalem material as a whole, which will be considered in due course. The use of 'Son of God' by Nathanael here, in the sense which he must have given to it, is quite as credible as the rest of this early testimony.

That Jesus is **King of Israel** is also claimed by John. In his account of Jesus' entry into Jerusalem he uses the title (xii. 13), where Mark has 'the coming kingdom of our father David' (xi. 10) and Luke 'the king who comes in the name of the LORD' (xix. 38), while Matthew has 'Hosanna to the son of David; blessed is he who comes in the name of the LORD' (xxi. 9). Here the other evangelists may well have paraphrases of the words preserved most accurately by John. John of course knew quite well that Jesus would not be the kind of king which the crowds expected. He had already once avoided an attempt to make him king (vi. 15). Nevertheless, as his conversation with Pilate is designed to show, he is a king, though his kingdom is not of this world (xviii. 36). The description which Pilate wrote, 'King of the *Jews*' (xix. 19), shows his misunderstanding of Jesus' claim, as can be seen by one who bears in mind the distinction which the FG draws between 'the Jews' and 'Israel'.[1]

50. Jesus asks Nathanael, with gentle irony, whether so trivial

[1] See on iii. 10, below.

a thing has convinced him, and promises that he shall **see greater things than these** (which will, incidentally, show him to be greater than Nathanael has so far realised). This saying forms an appropriate introduction to the 'signs' which occupy the greater part of chapters ii-xi. But the evangelist then adds a further statement.

51. **'Amen, amen, I say to you, you shall see heaven opened, and the angels of God ascending and descending upon**[1] **the Son of man.'** The double **Amen, amen** is characteristic of, and peculiar to, the FG, and is used to introduce solemn, almost oracular, declarations (cf. iii. 3, 5, 11; v. 19, 24, 25; vi. 26, 32, 47, 53; viii. 34, 51, 58; x. 1, 7; xii. 24; xiii. 16, 20, 21, 38; xiv. 12; xvi. 20, 23; xxi. 18), usually in passages of which the form and phraseology often suggest the prophetic activity of the evangelist himself or of his authority.[2] Its introduction here, the change from **you** in the singular in verse 50 to the plural, and the character of the saying to which it is a preface, all suggest that this verse is an addition made by John to the source which he has hitherto been following. The mention of **angels** is something unusual in the FG—apart from v. 4 (which in any case is unlikely to be part of the true text), and the comment of the crowd in xii. 29, 'An angel spoke to him', the only other mention of an angel is in the account of the Resurrection, xx. 12. Angels, however, feature in apocalypses, and it is possible that this saying was originally part of a prophecy of the Second Coming similar to that in Matt. xxv. 31.[3] By introducing it at this point John gives a new interpretation to it. Its clear allusion to the story of Jacob's ladder in Gen. xxviii. 11-17, enables him to show that Jesus is more than **King of Israel**. He is the second Jacob, i.e. the true Israel in his own person.[4] Moreover the title **Son of man** comes in as the climax

---

[1] Black (p. 85) suggests that underlying ἐπί (here translated **upon**) is the Aramaic ‘*al*, used in the sense of the Hebrew ’*ĕl*, ‘towards’, suggesting the picture of the angels converging upon the Son of man. But the sense **upon** (which has Rabbinic precedent in the exegesis of Gen. xxviii. 12) suggests an idea congenial to the FG, of the Son of man as the place of communication between heaven and earth.

[2] Cf. the use of 'Amen, I say to you/thee' in the Synoptic Gospels, and particularly in Luke. See J. C. O'Neill, 'The Six Amen Sayings in Luke', *J.T.S.*, n.s., Vol. X, 1959, pp. 1-9.

[3] Cf. also Acts vii. 56.   [4] Cf. xv. 1.

to the series of confessions in verses 29-49, and, in a sense, as a corrective, since it was the title by which Jesus himself had preferred to be known. The saying implies that it is in the ministry of Jesus that the real manifestation of the glory of the Son of man is to be seen, and not in some future apocalyptic event (cf. i. 14; ii. 11, etc.). It thus adds force and precision to the general statement, **'You shall see greater things than these'**.

Son of man occurs elsewhere in the FG twelve times, each time in a saying attributed to Jesus, except for two questions addressed to him (both in xii. 34). The Son of man came down from heaven (iii. 13), and will return there (vi. 62), after he has been lifted up (iii. 14; viii. 28; cf. xii. 34a), i.e. crucified, and thereby glorified (xii. 23; xiii. 31); he is the object of faith (ix. 35; cf. iii. 15), and has power to execute judgement (v. 27); he will feed men with a lasting food (vi. 27), namely his flesh (vi. 53). As used in the FG the title preserves clear traces of its origin in Jewish apocalyptic imagery. It is ultimately connected in some way with Dan. vii. 13, where 'one like a son of man'[1] represents the kingdom of the saints of the Most High, i.e. the righteous remnant, or true Israel; hence its appropriateness in John i. 51. Jesus himself seems to have preferred it because its somewhat enigmatic character (cf. John xii. 34b, which shows that it puzzled his hearers) enabled him to give it the content and meaning which he himself intended, whereas Messianic titles in current use had connotations which he himself repudiated. John seems to use the title 'Son of man' very much in the sense which Jesus intended it to have, for in the FG, as in the Synoptic Gospels, it expresses the paradoxical status of him who was both the humiliated and the exalted Christ.

[1] I.e. *kᵉbar 'ᵉnāsh*, translated with barbaric literalness in Rev. i. 13 and xiv. 14, ὅμοιον υἱὸν ἀνθρώπου. Apart from Acts vii. 56, these are the only passages in the New Testament outside the Gospels where the periphrasis 'Son of man' is found.

3. THE FIRST SIGN, AT CANA, AND ITS COROLLARY, THE CLEANSING OF THE TEMPLE, ii. 1-25

ii. (1) **And on the third day there was a wedding at Cana of Galilee; and Jesus' mother was there; (2) and Jesus and his disciples were also invited to the wedding. (3) And they did not have any wine, because the wine provided for the wedding had come to an end; then[1] Jesus' mother said to him, 'They have not any wine'. (4) And Jesus said to her, 'Do not interfere with me, mother; my time[2] has not yet come'. (5) His mother said to the servants, 'Do whatever he tells you'. (6) And there were six stone waterpots standing there for the Jews' purification, holding twenty gallons or more each. (7) Jesus said to them, 'Fill the pots with water'. And they filled them to the brim. (8) And he said to them, 'Draw some out now, and take it to the head waiter'. And they took it. (9) The head waiter tasted the water which had become wine, and did not know where it came from— but the servants who had drawn the water knew. So the head waiter called the bridegroom, (10) and said to him, 'Every man serves the good wine first, and the inferior when they are drunk; but you have kept the good wine until the present moment[3]'. (11) Jesus made this beginning of his signs at Cana of Galilee, and showed forth his glory; and his disciples believed in him.**

1. John's remark that the wedding took place **on the third day** serves to emphasise that though it marks a fresh start in

---

[1] Reading οἶνον οὐκ εἶχον, ὅτι συνετελέσθη ὁ οἶνος τοῦ γάμου· εἶτα with ℵ* *a b ff*² *r hl* ᵐᵍ. The reading of the majority of the MSS., 'when the wine had failed', ὑστερήσαντος οἴνου, is an early 'improvement' of the rather rambling, but characteristic, style of the original. The sense which ὑστερέω must have here is not exactly paralleled elsewhere in the New Testament, though the verb occurs in fifteen other passages. 'Then', εἶτα, is also found in John xiii. 5; xix. 27; xx. 27, and in the other Gospels twice in Mark and once in Luke.

[2] ὥρα means both '⟨a period of⟩ time' and '⟨the right⟩ time'. 'Season' in English has a similar double meaning.

[3] ἕως ἄρτι. ἄρτι is more emphatic than the usual word νῦν. Cf. v. 17; ix. 19, 25; xiii. 7, 19, 33, 37; xiv. 7; xvi. 12, 24, 31.

his narrative, as the first of the signs, it is nevertheless connected with, and the culmination of, the series of events described in i. 19-51. The disciples have been gathered, and their faith is at once confirmed: the promise of i. 50, that they should see greater things, is beginning to be fulfilled. John carefully dovetails together the sections of his narrative. He probably means us to understand that there was an interval of a day between i. 43-51, and ii. 1-11. Had he meant otherwise,[1] he would have repeated 'on the next day', as he had done previously at i. 35 and 43. There is thus a blank day between i. 43-51, and ii. 1-11, which is probably to be taken as a Sabbath, so that the first sign is given on the Lord's Day. Though the Lord's Day is strictly the first day of the week, it is also, as Christians can never forget, in a special sense **the third day,** and John may mean us to take this allusion to the day of resurrection. Now if we count from i. 19, and assume that a fresh day starts at i. 41,[2] we find that i. 19–ii. 11 covers a week, from a Monday to a Sunday. Towards the end of the FG we find a similar week, also including a blank Sabbath, and culminating in the Lord's Day on which occurred the final and greatest sign, that of Christ's resurrection (cf. xii. 1; xx. 1). Thus the beginning and ending of Christ's ministry conform to the same pattern.

This strongly suggests that the arrangement of the material in chapters i and ii is artificial, and that the events described in i. 19–ii. 11 did not in fact fall within an actual week. This is corroborated by the difficulty of fitting in the journey from wherever Jesus was at i. 43 to Cana in the time which John's scheme allows. We must suppose that Jesus would not have travelled on the Sabbath, and so must have been at Cana, or very close to it, by the Friday evening. Weddings took place after sunset (cf. Matt. xxv. 6)—this one, if the calculation given above is correct, immediately after the Sabbath, on what we call Saturday night. So if Jesus was outside Galilee at i. 43 (as he appears to be), he would have had to travel on the Friday. Cana was the home of Nathanael (cf. John xxi. 2), and John may mean

[1] 'On the third day', following 'the next day' (i. 43), could mean 'on the day after that', as the ancients counted inclusively.
[2] See p. 98.

us to suppose that he was at home when Jesus 'saw' him under the fig-tree (i. 48). According to John iii. 23, the Baptist was at Aenon near Salim. This is either just south of Scythopolis, in the north-east corner of Samaria, or (more probably) south-east of Shechem.[1] From Shechem Jesus would have had some difficulty in reaching Cana between Thursday morning and Friday evening. From Scythopolis the journey is just feasible. He must have been just outside Galilee at i. 43, and must have fallen in with Philip on his way to Cana. But the difficulty of visualising the time-table of i. 19–ii. 11 suggests that John is not here concerned with details of chronology and topography.

2. We are probably meant to infer that it was due to their newly-formed friendship with Nathanael that Jesus and the other disciples were invited to the wedding.

A wedding-feast was an appropriate occasion for the first manifestation of the glory of the Christ, since a wedding-feast is a parable of the Messianic kingdom (cf. Matt. xxii. 2 ff.; xxv. 1 ff.; Mark ii. 19; Rev. xix. 9). This may have determined John's choice of it as the beginning of the signs, and so confirms the suspicion that the arrangement of the material here is artificial.[2] But it does not follow that either John himself or his source concocted the story simply for its parabolic significance.

On the contrary, if one can allow the possibility of the miracle, the story itself, if not its context, has an air of verisimilitude. The feast takes place in a modest household, which did not normally drink wine, but had provided it specially for the feast (cf. verse 3). Its hospitable instincts overcame its prudence, and the sudden addition of unexpected guests to the party must have contributed to, if it did not entirely cause, the sudden failure of the wine.

Here **the mother of Jesus** (not given her own name, either here or at xix. 25, but the more honourable appellation of mother of her son) intervenes, anxious lest her son has failed to

---

[1] See W. F. Albright, *art. cit.*, p. 159.

[2] In his comparison of the Johannine and Synoptic accounts of the opening of Jesus' public ministry Origen admits the artificiality of John's arrangement of his material (*In Iohannem*, X, on John ii. 12 ff., ed. Brooke, Vol. I, pp. 181 ff.). He justifies what he calls John's 'physical lie' by the 'spiritual truth' which it illustrates (p. 187).

notice the crisis, and confident that he can do something to meet it.

4. Jesus' reply, translated literally, 'What have I to do with you, woman?', gives quite a wrong impression. Though intended to check his mother's enthusiasm, and to claim his right to make his own decision, it is not as harsh as it sounds in English. 'What to me and thee?' (τί ἐμοὶ καὶ σοί;) is the literal translation of a Semitic idiom, as uncouth in Greek as it is in English. It occurs, for example, at 2 Sam. xvi. 10, when David rejects Abishai's offer to kill Shimei, and at Mark v. 7 = Luke viii. 28, on the lips of the Gerasene demoniac, when the devils try to stop Jesus casting them out. Its precise force depends entirely on the tone of voice with which it is uttered. 'Woman' (γύναι) is also used by Jesus in addressing his mother at xix. 26, and is clearly compatible both with affection and respect.[1] In both passages **mother** is the best English equivalent.

My time has not yet come gives expression to a hesitation on Jesus' part. He will do nothing without his Father's will (cf. John v. 19). Later in the FG these words will take on a deeper meaning; the time will be seen to be that of Jesus' death, which is also that of his glorification.[2] He will not now by any independent or premature action appear to be seeking his own glory (cf. v. 30; vii. 18; viii. 50, 54). And this is why the miracle, when he has decided that he may perform it, shows forth his glory.

Another factor in his hesitation may reasonably be supposed to have been a scruple about using the power which he was conscious of possessing for so apparently trivial an object; cf. also the temptation to satisfy his own hunger by turning stones into bread (Matt. iv. 3 f. = Luke iv. 2-4). In the present case, however, the miracle is not done for Jesus' own convenience, but to save his host from an embarrassment which, in view of the high value then attached to the virtue of hospitality, would have been felt more keenly perhaps than we can fully appreciate. The motive would not have seemed so trivial then as it may

[1] It is also used to the Samaritan woman (iv. 21) and to Mary Magdalene (xx. 13, 15).
[2] For the further development of this theme see the notes on iv. 21; v. 25, 28; vii. 30; viii. 20; xii. 23, 27; xiii. 1; xvi. 2, 32; xvii. 1.

appear to us. Moreover the miracle does not violate the order of nature in the way that changing stones into bread would do.[1] So, after a moment's hesitation, Jesus in fact complies with his mother's implied suggestion. There is a parallel to this in vii. 1-10. There Jesus' brethren challenge him to show himself in Jerusalem, so that his disciples may see his works. Jesus at first refuses, but after a time goes up to Jerusalem. We may suppose that on both occasions his hesitation was due to the same reluctance to act merely in response to a challenge, even to one given so discreetly as here.

5. Jesus' mother apparently assumes, in spite of this rebuff, that he will do something to meet the situation, and warns the servants to do whatever he tells them. Such familiarity between guests and servants, unusual perhaps in polite society, is natural enough here, as it would be at a village wedding-party today.

The word for **servants** (διάκονοι) has been thought to have been used because it also means 'deacons', and so contains an allusion to their duties at the Eucharist.[2] But this is by no means conclusive, since the word simply describes the *function* of servants, while 'slave' (δοῦλος), the commoner word in the New Testament, describes their *status*. The word is used in sayings of Jesus in Matt. xx. 26; xxii. 13; xxiii. 11; Mark ix. 35; x. 43; John xii. 26. In Matt. xxii. 13, it describes servants at a wedding-feast (as here), but their function there is not eucharistic—unless the exclusion of an unworthy recipient can be so described. There is another possible (and equally inconclusive) eucharistic allusion in vi. 9 (which see), p. 178.

6. The **six stone waterpots** were to hold the water for the ritual washing obligatory before meals (cf. Mark vii. 1-4). In view of the symbolical significance of water elsewhere in the FG,[3] it is possible that, for John, the water in the pots represented the old dispensation, superseded by the wine of the gospel. But detailed allegorical interpretation of the whole story does not seem plausible. It is a standing temptation to read an allegorical interpretation into all numbers in the FG;[4] many no

[1] Cf. C. S. Lewis, *Miracles* (1947), pp. 163 f.
[2] Διάκονος was also a title of pagan cult-ministers.
[3] Cf. p. 91, n. 2.   [4] See on iv. 18, below, p. 144.

doubt have a symbolic significance, but **six** here does not seem to be one of them. There just *were* six.[1]

The pots held (literally) 'two or three *metrētai* each'. A *metrētēs* was a little more than nine gallons, so that the six pots held altogether something between 108 and 162 gallons. We are not to suppose that this huge amount all became wine, but only the water actually drawn from the waterpots.

7. The pots would presumably be nearly empty, as the water would have been used for washing before the feast. John mentions that **they filled them to the brim** both to show the prompt obedience of the servants to a command which must have puzzled them, and to indicate how the fact of the miracle might be established. It would be easy to see the water remaining in the pots after the wine had been drawn off.

8. The verb translated **draw out** (ἀντλέω) is not, *pace* Westcott, 'applied most naturally to drawing water from the well'. Though John uses it in this sense in iv. 7 and 15, its original meaning appears to have been to 'bale out' a ship,[2] which is appropriate for ladling wine out of the pots. Westcott's idea that the water which was to become wine was taken direct from the well lacks foundation.

The **head waiter** (ἀρχιτρίκλινος) is taken by Barrett to have been, not a servant, but one of the guests appointed by the party as chairman to supervise the drinking. But this was a Gentile custom, and it is unlikely that it would be followed at a village wedding, even in Galilee, or that Jesus would have provided the means for the mere drinking-party that it would imply. But any large party needs someone to organise the waiting, and this was the function of the ἀρχιτρίκλινος.[3] Neither the head waiter's ignorance of the source of the wine nor his familiarity with the bridegroom is a decisive argument against his being a servant. He was probably an old family slave, accorded the freedom of speech found in many an old retainer at the present day. His ignorance is not surprising in the hubbub of the party, but it is mentioned partly in order to draw attention to the miracle, partly to contrast with the knowledge of those who had

---

[1] Six, as 7 (the perfect number) – 1, may perhaps represent the imperfection of the old covenant. But there is no 7 in the story to symbolise the new.

[2] LS⁹ s.v. ἀντλέω.   [3] LS⁹ s.v. ἀρχιτρίκλινος 2; Bauer⁵ s.v.

heard and obeyed Jesus (cf. John vii. 17, for knowledge as the result of obedience).

9. John lays stress on the fact that a miracle happened, but says nothing of the way in which Jesus worked it. This indifference to the mechanics of the miracle and the unobtrusiveness of the man responsible for it distinguish this from pagan miracle-stories.

10. The head waiter's comment is a bit of peasant humour: there is no evidence that the practice which he describes was in fact followed then any more than it is today. His words do not imply that the guests were already drunk. They are quoted simply to prepare for the testimony—all the more effective for the ignorance of the witness—to the goodness of the wine.

11. The miracle thus attested, but recognised as such only by Jesus' immediate circle, and by the servants whose obedience includes them with the disciples, was **the beginning of his signs,** and, like all his signs, **showed forth,** to those who had eyes to see it, **his glory,**[1] and confirmed his disciples' faith (cf. xx. 30 f.). It would be wrong to say that it *created* faith, for the disciples had, by following Jesus, shown their readiness to trust him. It was not an ostentatious display of power to overawe the unbelieving. According to the Synoptic Gospels, when Jesus was challenged to show such a 'sign', he refused (cf. Mark viii. 11 f., and the passages parallel to it, Matt. xii. 38 f.; xvi. 1 ff.; Luke xi. 16, 29 f.).[2] The Synoptic Gospels do not use the term 'sign' ($\sigma\eta\mu\epsilon\hat{\iota}o\nu$) for the miracles of Jesus, though the evangelists clearly regard them as being such in effect (cf. Matt. xii. 28 = Luke xi. 20). They use it, however, in two classes of passage (additional to those quoted above)—(1) of the signs which will be wrought by false Christs and false prophets before 'the end' (Mark xiii. 22 = Matt. xxiv. 24), and (2) of the genuine signs which will indicate that 'the end' is imminent (Luke xxi. 11, 25; cf. 'the sign of the Son of man', Matt. xxiv. 30, and the questions of the disciples about the 'sign of the end', Matt. xxiv. 3 = Mark xiii. 4, Luke xxi. 7). It is, however, consistent with

[1] Cf. John i. 14, and comment.
[2] Cf. also Herod's expectation of a 'sign' from Jesus (Luke xxiii. 8). Traces of the belief that unbelievers are likely to expect signs occur also in John ii. 18; iv. 48; vi. 30.

John's transvaluation of eschatology[1] that he should use of the actions of Jesus during his ministry the term which, in its legitimate Christian sense, the Synoptic Gospels reserve for the signs of the end: they are the true signs of the end, of the coming of the Son of man, and of God's intervention through his Son.

The sign of the changing of water into wine displays, before the public ministry of Jesus is due to begin, the meaning of that ministry, which is the supersession of the old covenant by the new. One important question remains. Can it be regarded as historical?

It is argued that it is an example of allegory presented as history. The story itself (it is said) is full of improbabilities; it has no parallel or echo in the Synoptic Gospels, and is different in kind from the Synoptic miracles; it is an amalgam of themes from the Synoptic Gospels[2] and from Hellenistic religion. Philo interprets Melchizedek as the Logos who offers wine instead of water[3] (but does not *change* water into wine). The changing of water into wine appears in the legends of the wine-god Dionysus,[4] and is alleged to have happened in some of his temples. Thus Bauer cites from Pliny a story that a spring in his temple on the island of Andros flowed with wine every year on the nones of January[5]—i.e. at about the time of the Christian feast of the Epiphany; the miracle at Cana is of course an 'epiphany' of the glory of Christ, and, as such, features in the Epiphany liturgy.

In the detailed discussion already undertaken the attempt has been made to meet the criticism that the story is full of improbabilities. Granted the possibility of miracle, it is a reasonable and coherent narrative. It is Jewish in character and setting. It has no parallel in the Synoptic Gospels because it falls outside the public ministry of Jesus, which, for John, began in

[1] See Introduction, pp. 13 f.

[2] Cf. the parables of the wedding-feast, etc. (quoted above) and the words of Jesus at the Last Supper (Mark xiv. 24 and parallels), identifying the wine with his blood. This explains, according to Bauer, the otherwise enigmatic allusion to Jesus' 'hour' in verse 4—it is the hour of Jesus' death, from which the Eucharist derives its potency.

[3] Philo, *Leg. Alleg.*, III. 82 (quoted by Bauer, p. 44, and Barrett, p. 157).

[4] Cf. Euripides, *Bacchae* 704 ff. (Bauer, Barrett *ibid.*).

[5] Pliny, *Nat. Hist.*, II. 231: *Andro in insula templo Liberi patris fontem nonis Ianuariis semper vini saporem fundere.*

Jerusalem, ii. 13 ff. But it resembles the miracle of the Feeding of the Multitude (found also in the Synoptic Gospels) more closely than it does those connected with the legend and cult of Dionysus. It was performed in response to human need, and unostentatiously, not as a mere display of power and prodigality to confound the sceptical. Moreover, if it had originated in an allegory, one would expect the details of the story to be more susceptible of allegorical interpretation than in fact they are. The attempt, for example, to see the mother of Jesus as an allegory of the old Israel, repudiated by Jesus, lacks all probability. The story is not an allegory, but the account of an actual event, in which John saw an acted parable.

(12) After this[1] he went down to Capernaum[2]—he and his mother and brothers and his disciples—and stayed there not many days.

This verse marks a brief interlude between the testimony to Jesus which preceded the public ministry (i. 19–ii. 11), and the opening of the ministry itself. The fact that Jesus' mother and brothers were with him as well as his disciples may suggest that the few days at Capernaum were spent in making up a party for the journey to Jerusalem. Jesus' brothers appear again at vii. 3, as here, just before a festival. There is nothing in the FG to indicate what their exact relationship was to Jesus.

(13) And the Jews' Passover was near, and Jesus went up to Jerusalem. (14) And he found in the Temple those who were selling oxen and sheep and pigeons, and the money-changers sitting; (15) and he made a whip of cords and drove[3] them all out of the Temple—sheep and oxen as well—and spilt the money-changers' cash and upset their tables, (16) and said to those who were selling the pigeons, 'Take these away; stop making[4] my Father's house a house of trade'. (17) His disciples remembered that it is written, 'Zeal for thy house shall consume me'.

13. In the Synoptic Gospels also there is an account of Jesus

---

[1] See on p. 131, n. 4.

[2] Cana is a hill-village, and Capernaum considerably below sea-level.

[3] Literally, 'threw . . . out', cf. vi. 37, p. 189, n. 2.

[4] μὴ ποιεῖτε, cf. v. 14, 28; vi. 20, 27, 43; vii. 24; xii. 15; xiv. 1 = 27; xx. 17, 27, and (for a different nuance) v. 45; x. 37; xix. 21. See Moulton, *Prolegomena*, pp. 122-125. [Cf. Turner, pp. 76, 77.—B. A. M.]

cleansing the Temple (Mark xi. 15-17, Matt. xxi. 12 f., Luke xix. 45 f.), but just before the Passover at which he was crucified, whereas John uses his account of it to open Jesus' public ministry. The critical problems which this poses will be considered later.

By speaking of **the Jews' Passover** John may wish to remind his readers of the *Christian* Passover (1 Cor. v. 7) which has superseded the old one. This dissociation of himself from Judaism is characteristic of John (cf. v. 1; vi. 4; vii. 2; xi. 55; and the note on i. 19, above).

14. The **oxen and sheep and pigeons** were sold for sacrifice, and their suitability for that purpose was guaranteed by the Temple authorities. The **money-changers** provided (for a discount) the coinage which alone could be used for Temple dues and offerings, since it was free of idolatrous images. Thus both traders and money-changers provided services which, if not indispensable, were a great convenience to worshippers.

15. We can hardly suppose that Jesus cleared the Temple court single-handed. His use of a whip[1] and his upsetting of the tables suggest that his action was resisted, and that resistance was overcome by force, presumably with the help of his disciples and sympathisers.

16. Jesus' objection is, in the other Gospels, to the dishonesty of the traders, but in John it is to trade as such within the Temple precincts. It could easily be represented as an attack on the sacrificial worship of the Temple, and John may intend us to understand it as such. For he clearly indicates later (verses 19 ff.) that Jesus is to supersede the Temple. It may be recalled that members of the Dead Sea Sect also objected to the Temple worship. But by calling the Temple **my Father's house** Jesus showed clearly that he regarded the Temple as still worthy of respect. In the Synoptic accounts of the cleansing he calls it 'a house of prayer', and this should perhaps be understood as excluding sacrifice.

By his words Jesus claims, in passing, as it were, and appar-

[1] Staves and other weapons were forbidden in the Temple. Jesus' action seems to have been spontaneous and unpremeditated. When it met with resistance, he picked up a handful of cords to serve as an improvised whip—for men apparently, as well as beasts. The whip is not mentioned in the other Gospels.

ently without provoking any adverse comment, that God is his Father. Later (v. 18) this is made a ground of complaint against him. Though characteristic of John, and absent from the Synoptic accounts of this incident, this claim is by no means confined to the FG. It is particularly frequent in Matthew (cf. vii. 21, etc.), and is also found in Luke (x. 22, etc.), while Mark preserves the Aramaic *Abba* (xiv. 36).[1]

17. The disciples recall Ps. lxix. 9, '**Zeal for thy house shall consume me**'. The AV rendering, 'hath eaten me up', corresponds more closely to the Hebrew, and is the reading of some MSS. of the LXX and of John (κατέφαγε). But the Future (καταφάγεται) is undoubtedly original in John, and has probably influenced the text of those MSS. of the LXX which exhibit it. The psalm is an urgent appeal to God to vindicate the righteous man who has been oppressed for his zeal and faithfulness to God, but here the verse is to be understood as a prophecy that the zeal which Jesus then showed would later lead to his destruction. In the Synoptic Gospels (though not in John) the cleansing of the Temple is the immediate occasion for the decision to kill Jesus. This verse may therefore indicate that in the source[2] which John used the cleansing of the Temple was much closer to the arrest of Jesus than it is now in the FG.

(**18**) **So the Jews answered and said to him, 'What sign do you show us ⟨as authority⟩ for doing this?' (19) Jesus answered and said to them, '⟨If you⟩ destroy this temple, I will raise it up in three days'. (20) So the Jews said, 'This temple took forty-six years to build, and will you raise it up in three days?' (21) But he was speaking of the temple of his body. (22) So when he was raised from the dead, his disciples remembered that he said this, and believed the scripture and the word which Jesus spoke.**

18. The demand for a **sign** to justify Jesus' challenge to the established order is not in itself surprising. If Isaiah, for example, could offer Ahaz a sign (Isa. vii. 11 ff.), Jesus might well be expected to offer a similar authentication. In the Synoptic Gospels it is not only opponents who ask for a sign (cf. Mark viii. 11; Matt. xii. 38; xvi. 1; Luke xi. 16), but also the

---

[1] See also the notes on i. 18, and i. 49.
[2] See also p. 208 below.

disciples (cf. Mark xiii. 4 = Matt. xxiv. 3 = Luke xxi. 7). Jesus
is also asked to state the authority for his actions (cf. Mark xi.
28 = Matt. xxi. 23 = Luke xx. 2). Though this demand in
Mark comes shortly after his account of the cleansing of the
Temple, it is not necessary to suppose, as Barrett does, that
John is here combining the demand for a sign from Mark viii.
11, and the question about Jesus' authority of Mark xi. 28. It
could well have stood in John's source, and be independent of
Mark.

19. Jesus' answer must have seemed to his hearers both
enigmatic and evasive. In the Synoptic Gospels Jesus refuses to
give signs (Mark viii. 12, Matt. xii. 39 = xvi. 4 = Luke xi. 29) or
to state the authority for his actions (Mark xi. 33 = Matt. xxi. 27
= Luke xx. 8). Those who cannot see for themselves cannot be
helped by signs.[1] The most he does is to make an enigmatic
reference to 'the sign of Jonah' (Matt. xii. 39 = xvi. 4 = Luke
xi. 29), which Matthew interpreted as an allusion to Jesus'
resurrection (xii. 40). Here too Jesus' answer contains an allusion to his resurrection, but it is unlikely that John is here
dependent upon Matthew.

In John, Jesus does of course perform signs, but they are
designed to confirm faith, not to convince sceptics. So he in
effect refuses a sign, and gives a warning instead. The unbelief
which inspired the Jews' demand for a sign will in fact lead to
the destruction of the Temple. But Jesus will, by his resurrection, have brought into being a new spiritual temple to replace
the old, namely, as John explains (verse 21), **the temple of his
body.** In John iv. 21, Jesus predicts in effect the supersession
of the Jerusalem Temple, and Rev. xxi. 22, states that there
will be no temple in the new Jerusalem.

Mark xiv. 58, records the testimony of false witnesses that
Jesus had said, 'I will destroy this temple that is made with
hands, and in three days I will build another, not made with
hands', and Mark xv. 29 f., the taunt, 'Aha! You who would
destroy the temple and build it in three days, save yourself,
and come down from the cross!' (cf. Matt. xxvi. 61 and xxvii.
40). It seems clear that Jesus did say something about the

[1] Though Jesus does answer his disciples' request—in the discourse of
Mark xiii and its parallels.

destruction of the Temple, but it is hard to say what precisely it was or what he meant. The most probable explanation of the form of words in the FG is that Jesus challenged the Jews to show their faith in him by destroying the Temple, and offered them in return the sign of raising it again in three days. John may therefore preserve the saying which the false witnesses distorted, but his interpretation of it is not that which Jesus intended. Verse 22 implies that the disciples only saw this meaning in Jesus' words after the resurrection.

20. The Jews misunderstand Jesus' words—a theme which recurs frequently in the FG (cf. iii. 4; iv. 11, etc.), and is of a piece with the tragic irony which pervades the whole story of Jesus' ministry, cf. i. 10 f.

Herod began his rebuilding of the Temple in the eighteenth year of his reign (Josephus, *Antiquities*, XV. 380), i.e. about 20 B.C. Forty-six years thus give a date about A.D. 26.[1] But Josephus also says (*Ant.*, XV. 421) that the *naos* (the word which John uses here) was finished in a year and five months, and (*Ant.*, XX. 219) that the whole complex of buildings was not finally completed until the procuratorship of Albinus was nearly at an end, about A.D. 63. These data, if reliable, can only be reconciled with the plain sense of John's words if Josephus used *naos* of the sanctuary proper, and John of a larger group of buildings, and if operations had been suspended in A.D. 26 when this larger group of buildings was nearly complete. This is not difficult to accept if one regards John's historical information as generally sound.[2]

21. The primary reference in **the temple of his body** is to the body of Jesus which was raised from the tomb. But it is conceivable that there is a secondary allusion to the Church,

---

[1] This is not necessarily the date of the cleansing of the Temple, but only that before which it cannot have taken place.

[2] Otherwise the forty-six years may be taken as the age of Jesus at this time. A three years' ministry then gives his age at the Crucifixion as 49 (the square of the 'perfect' number 7), and the Resurrection can be regarded as inaugurating the Jubilee. This fits in neatly with John viii. 57, 'You are not yet fifty years old'—more appropriate if he was over forty rather than just over thirty—and with the tradition preserved by Irenaeus (*adv. Haer.*, II. xxxiii, ed. Harvey, Vol. I, p. 331), on the authority of the elders of Asia who had known John, that Jesus lived until he was nearly fifty. But there is nothing in John ii. 20, to support this interpretation.

the new Israel, which may be said to have come into being with
the resurrection of Jesus. But the thought is Pauline rather than
Johannine—cf. 1 Cor. iii. 16; vi. 19; 2 Cor. vi. 16, Eph. ii. 22,
taken in conjunction with the passages which describe the
Church as the body of Christ, Rom. xii. 5; 1 Cor. xii. 12, 27.
For John, however, it is clear that the body of Jesus is the focus
of God's presence among men, and so the reality which the old
Temple foreshadowed (cf. the significance of 'dwelt'—ἐσκήνωσεν
—in i. 14).

22. The comment that the disciples **believed**[1] is a characteristic conclusion to a Johannine narrative. For other examples of
belief as the response to Jesus' words and actions cf. ii. 11; iv.
39, 41, 50, 53; vi. 69; vii. 31; viii. 30; ix. 38; x. 42; xi. 27, 45;
xii. 11, 42; xvi. 30; xx. 8. John uses here the Singular **scripture**
(γραφή), which elsewhere refers to a particular passage (cf. vii.
38, 42; x. 35; xiii. 18; xvii. 12; xix. 24, 28, 36, 37). For the
Scriptures as a whole he uses the Plural γραφαί (v. 39). Thus
presumably he means here that after the Resurrection the
disciples understood that the prophecy of Ps. lxix. 9, indeed
applied to Jesus, and saw the meaning of his enigmatic words
reported in verse 19.

John thus begins his narrative of Jesus' public ministry with
the Cleansing of the Temple in Jerusalem. But the close articu-
lation of his Gospel is shown by the fact that though this incident marks in a sense a fresh start, the narrative is subordinate
and complementary to that of the First Sign. The Cleansing of
the Temple is not a miracle, and so, strictly speaking, not a
sign. But John puts it here as a corollary to the First Sign, the
lesson of which it underlines. As the Gospel replaces the Law,
so Jesus replaces the Temple as the place where God dwells
among men. But the fact that the wine of the Gospel is made
from the water of the Law, and that Jesus cleanses the actual
Temple and calls it his Father's house, shows that there is also

[1] John, however, here uses the verb πιστεύω with a dative. 'Believe' so used
means 'to accept as true, or as speaking the truth', cf. iv. 21, 50; v. 24, 38,
46 f.; vi. 30; viii. 31, 45 f.; x. 37 f.; xii. 38; xiv. 11, and is to be distinguished
from 'believe *in*' (πιστεύω εἰς), i. 12; ii. 11, 23; iii. 16, 18, 36; iv. 39; vi. 29, 35,
40; vii. 5, 31, 38 f., 48; viii. 30; ix. 35 f.; x. 42; xi. 25 f., 45, 48; xii. 11, 36 f., 42,
44, 46; xiv. 1, 12; xvi. 9, which implies trust and faith. When used absolutely
the verb may mean either according to the context. See also on i. 12.

some continuity between old and new. The new is, in a sense, the old purified.

John's motive for placing it here is therefore theological, and, unless we are to accept the unlikely view that Jesus twice cleansed the Temple, it is probable that the Synoptic Gospels are correct in placing the incident towards the end of Jesus' ministry. It is true that it was only there that Mark could place it, as he apparently knew only of one journey of Jesus to Jerusalem—his last. But on the other hand John's own narrative suggests the close proximity of the Passion—cf. in particular Jesus' saying about the destruction of the Temple. If this was used as the basis of an accusation made against him at his trial, it is likely that it had been uttered only recently.[1]

Since John's narrative contains several features absent from Mark's (notably the whip, the quotation from Ps. lxix. 9, and the saying about the destruction of the Temple), it is unlikely that he derived it from Mark. They have, however, sufficient similarity to suggest that both derive ultimately from a common source. If so, it is conceivable that originally the story had no fixed place in the tradition, and that both Mark and John put it in where it was most convenient.[2]

(23) And while he was in Jerusalem at the Passover keeping the feast,[3] many believed in his name,[4] when they observed[5] his signs which he did; (24) but Jesus himself did not trust himself to them because he recognised them all, (25) and had no need of anyone to bear witness about any man; for he himself recognised what was in the man.

This brief section serves, like ii. 12, as a transition from one scene in the drama to the next, and prepares for Jesus' conversation with Nicodemus by describing how Jesus' signs had

---

[1] See also the note on verse 17 above.

[2] This suggests the further possibility that Jesus in fact cleansed the Temple, not at the Passover, but at the feast which was the most effective occasion for such a demonstration, namely that of the Dedication, which commemorated the cleansing of the Temple by the Maccabees, or at Tabernacles. On this, see further pp. 254 f. below.

[3] ἐν τῇ ἑορτῇ is so taken by Bauer[5], s.v. ἑορτή. Barrett takes it as 'in the festival crowd', which is the sense it most probably bears at vii. 11. It is possible, however, that ἐν τῷ πάσχα is simply an early gloss on ἐν τῇ ἑορτῇ.

[4] Cf. i. 12.   [5] θεωροῦντες. For θεωρέω see p. 191.

kindled an imperfect faith in the men of Jerusalem. Nicodemus himself was impressed by these signs (iii. 2), and his own faith was imperfect.

23. Faith produced by signs alone is inadequate because the proper function of signs is to confirm a faith which already exists. 24. Jesus knew intuitively that the faith of the men of Jerusalem was imperfect, and so he could not **trust himself to them.** With the slightest encouragement they might have been led to try to make him King, as did the men whom he was later to feed miraculously in Galilee (vi. 15).

25. Jesus' clairvoyant power has already been noted (see p. 100 above). To know what is in man is the prerogative of God (cf. Ps. cxxxix. 1-4, Jer. xvii. 10, Acts i. 24, etc.). The power to do this was claimed by Apollonius of Tyana, and ascribed to the Redeemer in the Mandaean liturgy.[1] In Jesus also it is a mark of divinity.

4. CONVERSATION WITH NICODEMUS, iii. 1-21

iii. (1) And there was a man of the Pharisees, Nicodemus by name, a ruler of the Jews; (2) he came to him by night and said to him, 'Rabbi, we know that you are come a teacher from God; for no one can do these signs which you do, unless God were with him'.

1. The name **Nicodemus,** though Gentile in origin, is attested for Jews independently of the FG.[2] This Nicodemus was **a ruler of the Jews,** i.e. a member of the Sanhedrin (cf. vii. 50), a Pharisee, and a Rabbi (iii. 10). He thus represents the old dispensation, the passing away of which has been foretold in chapter ii. But it does not follow that he was not a historical person. John may even have been acquainted with him.

2. His coming **by night** may have been due to caution, or simply to a desire for privacy. But John probably singles this fact out for mention (when so many other details are omitted— notably the purpose of Nicodemus' visit) because the night is an

---

[1] See Bauer, p. 50.
[2] For details, see Strack–Billerbeck, II, pp. 412 ff.

apt symbol of his spiritual state.[1] He is the spokesman of those Jews mentioned in ii. 23, and so says **'We know . . .'**, but by calling Jesus **Rabbi** and **a teacher from God,** Nicodemus only shows that they had failed to grasp the full significance of Jesus.[2] They had been impressed by his signs, as evidence of God's approval—unlike the Jews in ix. 16. But their faith was still inadequate. Nicodemus' meeting with Jesus provides John with an opportunity of enlarging on the theme of renewal stated in chapter ii. But Nicodemus soon disappears from view, and the conversation turns into a meditation by the evangelist.

(3) Jesus answered and said to him, 'Amen, amen I say to you, unless a man is born[3] from above,[4] he cannot see the kingdom of God'.

The supersession of the old by the new is accomplished for the individual by a new birth, **from above.** The description of conversion as a second birth or a divine begetting[5] is foreign to Judaism, but familiar in the Hellenistic mystery religions. The evidence for this is assembled and discussed by Barrett,[6] and in greater detail by Bauer.[7] The conclusion is usually drawn from this that this verse reproduces the teaching of John rather than of Jesus. But without challenging the evidence assembled by Bauer (as Lagrange[8] does—and with some success), it may still be possible to question the conclusion drawn from it.

The mention of **the kingdom of God,** a characteristic theme of Jesus' teaching in the other Gospels, but found in John only in iii. 3 and 5, does not seem probable in a free composition of the evangelist's. From Matt. xviii. 3, 'Unless you turn and become like children, you will never enter the kingdom of

---

[1] See note on i. 5, 'darkness', and cf. John xiii. 30.

[2] See note on i. 38, 'Rabbi'.

[3] The verb γεννάω is used both of the father, 'to beget', and of the mother, 'to bear'. Verse 4 suggests that 'born' is preferable here.

[4] ἄνωθεν. This means both 'from above', which appears to be its primary significance here (cf. verse 5), and 'again'. Of the other twelve instances of the use of ἄνωθεν in the New Testament, in only one (Gal. iv. 9) does it clearly mean 'again'. It occurs in John iii. 7, 31; xix. 11, 23. John, however, is fond of using words with a double meaning (e.g. κατέλαβεν, 'overcome' and 'comprehend', i. 5, and πνεῦμα, 'wind' and 'spirit', iii. 8, etc.) and intends both meanings here.

[5] See also the notes on i. 12 f.

[6] Pp. 171 ff.   [7] Pp. 51 ff.   [8] Pp. 83-86.

heaven', to the thought of this verse is not a long step. The faithful are described in Matt. v. 9 and 45, as 'sons of God'. The fact that Jesus is not reported to have spoken of the new birth in his public preaching, either in John or in the other Gospels, does not exclude the possibility of his having done so in private. The idea of a new birth derives its cogency from the actual experience of conversion. Jesus was not of course himself 'converted', but he had enough insight into what conversion involved to have been capable of describing it as a new birth.

What he probably said was, 'Unless a man is born *again*, he cannot see the kingdom of God'. Then John, finding this saying in Greek, took it as 'born from above', quite conceivably under the influence of Hellenistic ideas, and made it the basis of this dialogue with Nicodemus, most of which admittedly represents his own meditations.

(4) Nicodemus said to him, 'How can a man be born when he is old? He cannot enter his mother's womb a second time and be born, can he?' (5) Jesus answered, 'Amen, amen, I say to you, unless a man is born of water and spirit,¹ he cannot enter the kingdom of God'.

In reply to Nicodemus' somewhat sarcastic questions, which show that he has taken ἄνωθεν to mean 'again', Jesus is made to explain that birth ἄνωθεν means birth **of water and spirit.** This I take to be John's own gloss on Jesus' words, identifying baptism, which he believed to convey the gift of the spirit, as the occasion of the new birth, and seeing in it the fulfilment of the Baptist's prophecy in i. 33, of the baptism in holy spirit. The change from **see** to **enter the kingdom of God** is a stylistic variation with no change of meaning.

It has been argued that **water and** is an editorial addition. It is true that **born of spirit** would adequately paraphrase **born from above,** and that **water** is not mentioned again. But if this whole passage is in a sense 'editorial'—and John is the editor—the hypothesis is superfluous.

(6) 'What is born of flesh is flesh, and what is born of

---

¹ Not 'the Spirit', the giver, but the gift which he gives. See the note on i. 32, above.

spirit is spirit. (7) Do not be astonished[1] that I said to you, "You must be born from above." '

6. Here **flesh** and **spirit** are the human and divine, or natural and supernatural, orders of existence.[2] Birth is a feature of them both. But, though here as elsewhere the natural is a parable of the supernatural, the two orders must not be confused. One's birth within the natural order cannot confer any spiritual status;[3] to be born a Jew does not exempt a man from the need for spiritual birth.

7. The Plural in **You must be born from above** corresponds to that in 'We know' in verse 2. Jesus addresses through Nicodemus the men whom he represents.

(8) 'The wind blows where it wishes, and you hear its sound, but do not know where it comes from and where it goes; so is everyone who is born of spirit.'

The point of this verse is unavoidably lost in translation, for $\pi\nu\epsilon\hat{\upsilon}\mu\alpha$, like the Hebrew רוּחַ, means both **wind** and 'spirit'. The wind is a parable of spirit, as natural birth of supernatural. One can of course find out which way the wind is blowing, but not its source or its destination. Similarly spirit is discernible in its effects, but mysterious in its character. It does not belong to the natural order.

In English **so is everyone who is born of spirit** has the appearance of a *non sequitur*, but this is only because the double meaning of the previous clause cannot be reproduced. Spirit can enter the natural order, and impart its own qualities to men.

(9) Nicodemus answered and said to him, 'How can these things happen?' (10) Jesus answered and said to him, 'Are you the ⟨famous⟩ teacher[4] of Israel and do not recognise these things? (11) Amen, amen I say to you that what we know we speak and to what we have seen we bear witness, and you do not accept our witness. (12) If I told you earthly things, and you do not believe, how, if I tell you heavenly things, will you believe?'

[1] Aorist subjunctive. Contrast v. 28, and see Moulton, *Prolegomena*, pp. 122-126. [Cf. B.-D. § 337 (3), Turner, p. 77.—B. A. M.]

[2] See note on i. 14, above.   [3] See note on i. 13, above.

[4] In Greek when a noun in the predicate has the Article (as ὁ διδάσκαλος here) it has a force rather like that of the emphatic *the* in colloquial English. Cf. '*the* prophet' (i. 21).

10. There is a certain irony in Jesus' answer to Nicodemus' repeated, 'How can . . .?' (cf. verse 4). Surely a famous teacher of God's people *must* understand these things. **Israel** (contrasted with 'ruler of the *Jews*' in verse 1) underlines the irony. It is used by John for God's faithful people (cf. 'Israelite' in i. 47), while 'the Jews' implies those who are unfaithful (see on i. 19).

11. Though formally it is still Jesus who is speaking to Nicodemus (as **Amen, amen I say to you** indicates), the Plurals **we know**, etc., show that in these words we are also meant to hear the echoes of later controversy between Church and Synagogue. The language of this verse has many parallels in 1 John i. 1-3.

12. The **earthly things** can best be interpreted as the parables of birth (verse 6) and the wind (verse 8). Nicodemus did not have the insight necessary to understand them, and so would not be able to understand the heavenly things—the realities of which they are parables, even if Jesus were to speak of them without using parables, or 'plainly', as it is called in xvi. 29.

(13) And no one has gone up into heaven, except the one who came down from heaven, the Son of man who is in heaven.

Just as verse 11 echoes later controversy, so this verse also reflects the standpoint of the Church after the Ascension. John is gradually moving from the report of a conversation to the reflections inspired by it. The transition is not, however, complete until verse 16, and these words are still capable of being understood as a saying of Jesus that could have been uttered during his earthly ministry. The double meaning which they are thus capable of bearing was no doubt intended by John.

If these words are to be taken as continuing the conversation with Nicodemus it is necessary to assume that a step in the argument has been omitted. It can be supplied as follows: since **no one has gone up into heaven,** there is no one on earth who can speak from his own experience of 'heavenly things', **except the one who came down from heaven,**[1] **the Son**

[1] See, for the further development of this theme, vi. 33, 38, 41, 42, 50, 51, 58.

of man who is in heaven. The title **Son of man** is particularly appropriate here (see on i. 51).

The clause **who is in heaven** is at first sight difficult to interpret, except on the assumption that this whole passage simply reflects the standpoint of an age later than that of the ministry of Jesus. It is omitted by an important group of witnesses—though one exclusively Egyptian in character or origin (P⁶⁶ ℵ BLW 33 *sah* Origen), but occurs in the majority of Greek MSS. (including AΘ *fam* 1 *fam* 13 579) and in several Versions (*lat pesh boh arm*). The early Syriac readings 'who *was* in heaven' (*cur*) and 'who is *from* heaven' (*sin*) presuppose the longer text. The difficulty of this suggests that it is original, and that the omission of the words is an Alexandrian emendation.[1]

As part of a saying attributable to Jesus the words may be taken either as implying that heaven is to be understood as a state rather than a place—cf. Bishop Ken's 'Heaven is, dear Lord, where'er thou art'—or as a symbolic expression of the unity of the Father and the Son unbroken by the Incarnation. But here again John no doubt intends a double meaning.

(14) And just as Moses lifted up the serpent in the wilderness, so must the Son of man be lifted up; (15) in order that everyone who believes may have eternal life in him.[2]

This at last answers Nicodemus' question, 'How can these things happen?' (verse 9), though Nicodemus is by now forgotten. Jesus is again made to claim that he fulfils an Old Testament type (cf. i. 51)—this time, that of the serpent of brass which Moses was commanded to set up upon a standard, so that whoever was bitten by one of the fiery serpents might look at it, and live (Num. xxi. 8 f.). The point of the comparison is in the 'lifting up' of the Son of man, and in the result of this act— that **everyone who believes may have eternal life in him,** just as those who looked at the serpent of brass lived. It may

---

[1] Clauses beginning with 'who is . . .' (ὁ ὤν) are a feature of John's style— cf. i. 18; iii. 31; vi. 46; viii. 47; xii. 17; xviii. 37; and ὁ ὤν καὶ ὁ ἦν of Rev. i. 4, 8; iv. 8; xi. 17; xvi. 5.

[2] 'In him' (ἐν αὐτῷ) should be taken with 'have eternal life' rather than 'believes', for 'believe in' in John is elsewhere εἰς αὐτόν (cf. Lagrange, p. 82).

be noted that in Palestinian Aramaic and in Syriac the verb which is equivalent to 'to be lifted up' (ὑψωθῆναι) has the special meaning 'to be crucified'.[1] John intends this double meaning, here and in the other passages where the word occurs (viii. 28; xii. 32, 34). The fact that it is only perceptible in Aramaic suggests that even if this is not an actual word of Jesus, it comes from an Aramaic source.

Belief in the crucified Son of man is thus the means to **eternal life**. **To have eternal life** is virtually equivalent to 'seeing' or 'entering the kingdom of God'. This is the first example of the use of **eternal life** (ζωὴ αἰώνιος) in the FG,[2] though 'life' has already occurred in i. 4. In the Synoptic Gospels ζωὴ αἰώνιος means 'the life of the ⟨coming⟩ age' (e.g. Mark x. 30 = Luke xviii. 30, '... in the coming age the life of the ⟨coming⟩ age'),[3] but in John **eternal life** gives the correct meaning. No doubt the two concepts ultimately coincide, but the difference in outlook which they imply is significant.[4]

(16) For God so loved the world, that he gave his only-begotten Son, in order that everyone who believes in him may not be lost,[5] but have eternal life. (17) For God did not send his Son into the world, in order that he might judge the world, but in order that the world might be saved through him. (18) The man who believes in him is not judged; the man who does not believe is already judged, because he has not believed[6] in the name of the only-begotten Son of God. (19) And this is the judgement, that light is come into the world, and men loved darkness rather than light; for their deeds were wicked. (20) For everyone who does evil hates the light, and does not come to the light, in order that his deeds may not be examined; (21) but the man who behaves honestly comes to the light, in order that his deeds may be shown to have been done in God.

[1] See Black, p. 103.
[2] See also iii. 16, 36; iv. 14, 36; v. 24, 39; vi. 27, 40, 47, 54, 68; x. 28; xii. 25, 50; xvii. 2 f.
[3] ἐν τῷ αἰῶνι τῷ ἐρχομένῳ ζωὴν αἰώνιον.
[4] See above pp. 13 f.   [5] See on vi. 39.
[6] Perfect. Cf. vi. 69, and see note *ad loc.*

In this passage, which has a function in the Gospel similar
to that of a chorus in a Greek tragedy, John, now speaking in
his own person (as in i. 1-18), draws together themes which have
already been stated, and introduces new ones, in a meditation
inspired by the conversation between Jesus and Nicodemus,
and developing out of it.

16. That **God loved the world** introduces the first new
theme, that of love (ἀγάπη, ἀγαπάω), which is also of cardinal
importance in the rest of the New Testament. In John i. 9 f.,
the world has already been described as the creation of God
through the agency of his Logos, which nevertheless had failed
to recognise the light. Here, but here only in the FG, **God** is
said to have **loved the world,** and shown his love by sending[1]
his Son[2] to save it (verse 17, cf. Rom. v. 8; viii. 32). Elsewhere
in the FG God is only said to love his Son (iii. 35; x. 17; xv. 9;
xvii. 23 f., 26) or those who love the Son (xiv. 21, 23; xvii. 23);
similarly Jesus loves the Father (xiv. 31), and never men in
general, but only 'his own' (xiii. 1), or his disciples (xiii. 34;
xv. 9, 12)—among them Martha, Mary, and Lazarus (xi. 5), and
the disciple 'whom he loved' (xiii. 23; xix. 26; xxi. 7, 20)—or
'the man who loves him' (xiv. 21). The disciples are spoken of
as loving Jesus (xiv. 15, 21, 23, 28), but never God (contrast
1 John iv. 20 f.; v. 2; Matt. xxii. 37, Rom. viii. 28, etc.), and,
while they are commanded to love *one another* (xiii. 34; xv. 12,
17; cf. Rom. xiii. 8; 1 Thess. iv. 9), they are never told to love
anyone else (contrast Matt. v. 44 and 46). John thus appears to
restrict the scope of a Christian's love to Christ and the Church,
in noticeable contrast to the teaching of Jesus in the other
Gospels; he nevertheless is firmly convinced that love is the

---

[1] The sending of the Son is a frequent theme of the FG. The verb used
here is ἀποστέλλω (as in i. 6; iii. 28; of John the Baptist), cf. iii. 34; v. 36, 38;
vi. 29, 57; vii. 29; viii. 42; x. 36; xi. 42; xvii. 3, 8, 18, 21, 23, 25; xx. 21. The
verb πέμπω is also used (of John the Baptist, i. 33) of the Son, iv. 34; v. 23 f.,
30, 37; vi. 38 f., 44; vii. 16, 18, 28, 33; viii. 16, 18, 26, 29; ix. 4; xii. 44 f.,
49; xiii. 20; xiv. 24; xv. 21; xvi. 5. These words seem to be completely
synonymous, as xx. 21, indicates, where both are used. But see C. C.
Tarelli, 'Johannine Synonyms', *J.T.S.*, o.s., Vol. XLVII, 1946, pp.
175-177.

[2] Note that 'only-begotten' (μονογενής) occurs in the FG only in i. 14, 18;
iii. 16, 18, and in 1 John iv. 9. See also on i. 14. The word is characteristic of
John's own style, rather than of his source's.

most adequate description of God's attitude to man.[1] Those, however, who reject God's love, as made known in his gift of his Son, find judgement and wrath (iii. 36). Hence John's emphasis on the need of faith and love for the Son, through whom indeed men love God.[2]

17 f. Judgement is not, however, the purpose of the Son's coming, but only its inevitable result for those who reject him.[3] His purpose was that the world **might be saved** (cf. xii. 47).[4] Thus the believer **is not judged,** the unbeliever **judged already**—by a judgement he has passed upon himself.

This introduces a new theme—that of 'judgement', already familiar in the Synoptic Gospels. But John refashions the concept drastically: he may well be said to demythologise it.[5] The Father does not judge (v. 22), but has committed judgement to the Son (v. 22, 27): even the Son can be said not to judge (viii. 15; xii. 47), though if he does, his judgement is just (v. 30; viii. 16). Men judge themselves, by their response to the light (iii. 19) i.e. Christ, or are judged by his word (xii. 48). Thus the moment of judgement can be described as that of the lifting up of the Son of man (xii. 31). John does not, however, discard

[1] See also on xiii. 34.

[2] John also uses $\phi\iota\lambda\acute{\epsilon}\omega$ for 'love' in the following passages: v. 20, 'the Father loves the Son'; xi. 3, 'he whom you love is sick'; xi. 36, 'See how he loved him'; xii. 25, 'he who loves his own life'; xv. 19, 'the world would love its own'; xvi. 27, 'the Father loves you, because you love me'; xx. 2, 'the other disciple whom Jesus loved'; and in the conversation between Jesus and Peter in xxi. 15-17. Whereas $\phi\iota\lambda\acute{\epsilon}\omega$ is used for the spontaneous feeling of friendship, $\dot{\alpha}\gamma\alpha\pi\acute{\alpha}\omega$ describes an activity of the will. It would be pointless to command anyone to have a feeling of friendship, and so $\phi\iota\lambda\acute{\epsilon}\omega$ is never used in a command; but $\dot{\alpha}\gamma\alpha\pi\acute{\alpha}\omega$ is (cf. John xiii. 34; xv. 12, 17).

See further pp. 29 f. above, the notes on these passages, and E. Evans, 'The Verb 'ΑΓΑΠΑιΝ in the FG', in *Studies in the FG*, ed. F.L. Cross (1957), pp. 64-71.

[3] In ix. 39, Jesus says that he came into the world for judgement. This sounds like purpose, but should probably be understood rather as foreseen result.

[4] The word 'save' ($\sigma\acute{\omega}\zeta\omega$) and its cognates 'saviour' ($\sigma\omega\tau\acute{\eta}\rho$) and 'salvation' ($\sigma\omega\tau\eta\rho\acute{\iota}\alpha$) are comparatively rare in the Johannine literature. The verb occurs in the same sense as here only in John v. 34; x. 9; xii. 47, and never in the Epistles or Revelation. 'Saviour' occurs once in John iv. 42, and in 1 John iv. 14, 'salvation' in John iv. 22, and three times in liturgical formulae in Rev. vii. 10; xii. 10; xix. 1. There seems to be a deliberate tendency on the part of John to avoid the words as much as possible.

[5] See Introduction, pp. 13 f.

entirely the idea of a future judgement (cf. v. 29; xii. 48), though he shifts the emphasis away from it. In this he is perhaps more faithful to the teaching of Jesus than the other evangelists.[1]

19 f. The theme of **light** is taken up from i. 4 ff., and linked with that of judgement (cf. Eph. v. 13). The idea, though not the language, resembles Paul's teaching that the purpose of the Law was to reveal the sinfulness of men (cf. Rom. iii. 20; etc.). Just as all cats are black in the dark, so men do not show up in their true colours until the light of Christ shines upon them.

This is not necessarily predestinarian doctrine, though it is consistent with it. It is true that John divides men into two classes, and says nothing of the conversion of men from one class to the other; but he does not say that it is by an inscrutable decree of Providence that some shun, and others welcome, the light. A man's character is his destiny.[2]

21. **The man who behaves honestly** is a paraphrase of the Greek ὁ ποιῶν τὴν ἀλήθειαν, literally, 'doing the truth', which is as uncouth in Greek as in English. It is a translation of the Hebrew עשה אמת (Ezek. xviii. 9, etc., 'deal truly' RV), which is also used in the Dead Sea Scrolls (*Manual of Discipline*, i. 5; v. 3). For the meaning of 'truth' in the FG see the comment on i. 14.[3]

The thought of this verse resembles that of Matt. v. 16, 'Let your light so shine before men, that they may see your good works and give glory to your Father who is in heaven'.

5. JESUS AND THE BAPTIST, iii. 22-36

(22) After this[4] Jesus and his disciples went into the land of Judaea; and he spent some time[5] with them there, and baptised. (23) And John also was baptising in Aenon near Salim, because there were many springs there; and

---

[1] See Introduction, pp. 13 f.

[2] For the opposite view, see Barrett, p. 182.   [3] P. 83, above.

[4] μετὰ ταῦτα. The plural implies an interval of unspecified length, as in v. 1, 14; vi. 1; vii. 1; xiii. 7; xix. 38; xxi. 1. Contrast the singular μετὰ τοῦτο, ii. 12; xi. 7, 11; xix. 28, which implies immediate succession.

[5] διέτριβεν, cf. xi. 54.

**people kept coming and being baptised. (24) For John
had not yet been thrown into prison.**

22 ff. The whole passage iii. 22-30 gives the impression of
an interruption, breaking the continuity between 16-21 and 31-
36, which can be regarded as two parts of a single meditation.
There is almost certainly a change of source at verse 22;
possibly that used in i. 19-51, is again being followed. In the
source **the land of Judaea** was presumably meant as a contrast to 'Galilee' in i. 43, but as it now stands it must be taken
as a contrast to Jerusalem, the last place to be mentioned (ii. 23).
The passage is often regarded as an intrusion, accidental or
deliberate, disturbing the original order of the FG. It is, however, more probable that the appearance of disturbance is only
due to the abrupt change of source, and that it was the evangelist himself who put this passage here.[1] The mention of Jesus
baptising comes in appropriately after his words to Nicodemus
about being born of water and spirit (iii. 5). Moreover, the
Baptist's final testimony to Jesus (iii. 28-30) is dramatically
appropriate after the scene with Nicodemus.[2] His faith contrasts with Nicodemus' lack of it. This juxtaposition of contrasting scenes is a characteristic device of the evangelist's,[2]
used in a somewhat similar fashion to *montage* in Russian films
like Eisenstein's *The Battleship Potemkin*.

That **Jesus** (or, as iv. 2, explains, his disciples) **baptised** for
a time in Judaea while **John was also baptising** elsewhere[3] is
not improbable, in spite of the silence of the Synoptic Gospels
on the subject. Jesus may have believed at first that the mass
movement of repentance begun by the Baptist would be sufficient to bring in the kingdom of God, and so was content to
follow his example. After the Baptist's arrest, however, he saw
that something different was required, and made an entirely
fresh start in Galilee. Though the evangelist preserves here a
piece of genuine historical information, it is not for this that he
mentions it, but because the baptism administered by Jesus is
important for him as a kind of acted parable of the baptism of
the Spirit which will eventually be given.[4]

---

[1] See Introduction, pp. 3 f.   [2] See also the note on iii. 31.
[3] For Aenon (which means 'springs') see note on ii. 1, above, p. 109.
[4] It thus resembles the washing of the disciples' feet, xiii. 2 ff.

24. The comment that **John had not yet been thrown into prison** may have been added by the evangelist as a cross-reference to Mark i. 14, to show that the ministry of baptism was earlier than anything recorded in Mark of Jesus' ministry.[1]

(25) Now there arose a dispute among the disciples of John with Jesus about purification. (26) And they came to John and said to him, 'Rabbi, the man who was with you on the other side of the Jordan, to whom you bore witness —see, this man is baptising, and they are all going to him'.

25. **Jesus.** The MSS. vary between 'a Jew' ('Ιουδαίου, ABW, etc.) and 'the Jews' ('Ιουδαίων, P66 ℵ* Θ, etc.). Of these readings the former seems preferable, since it is the only example of the Singular 'Jew' in the FG, in which the Plural is common, and so is less likely to be a correction than the Plural. But neither reading makes very good sense. The complaint of the Baptist's disciples is against *Jesus*, which presupposes that their dispute is with him. A number of emendations have therefore been suggested, of which Baldensperger's **Jesus** gives the best sense, and is adopted above.[2]

The dispute about purification may have been, as Barrett says,[3] about 'Jewish purification in general'—of which Jesus was very critical[4]—but can hardly have excluded all reference to baptism, since the point of the disciples' grievance (whether or not their dispute had been with Jesus) is the apparent rivalry of Jesus with the Baptist. The evangelist says nothing of the nature of the dispute, since his sole concern is to record the testimony of the Baptist to Jesus.

26. John's disciples are annoyed at the apparent eclipse of their master by his former associate, and exaggerate his success in their annoyance.

(27) John answered and said, 'No man can accept

[1] John could well have known Mark without necessarily using it as a source. See Introduction, pp. 8 ff.

[2] The reading 'Ιουδαίου could have been due to an accident, rather than to deliberate alteration. The last four letters of the phrase 'with Jesus' (ΜΕΤΑ‾Ι‾Ο‾Υ‾, ΙΟΥ being the contraction for ΙΗΣΟΥ) could have been repeated (ΜΕΤΑΙΟΥΑΙΟΥ) and ΙΟΥΑΙΟΥ 'corrected' to ΙΟΥΔΑΙΟΥ.

[3] P. 184.

[4] Cf. Mark vii. 1 ff. =Matt. xv. 1 ff., and Luke xi. 37-41, part of which is also found in Matt. xxiii. 25 f.

anything unless it is given him from heaven. (28) You yourselves bear me witness that I said, "I am not the Christ", but, "I am sent before him". (29) It is the man who has the bride who is the bridegroom; but the friend of the bridegroom, who stands and listens to him, rejoices greatly at the bridegroom's voice; this then is my joy which is fulfilled. (30) He must increase, but I must diminish.'

27 f. John refuses to share his disciples' annoyance. Jesus' success, and his own eclipse, are in accordance with the will of God. John has already explained that he was **not the Christ** (i. 20), but was **sent before him** (cf. i. 23-34).

29. Indeed, John rejoices at their news. He likens himself to the friend of the bridegroom, one of those whose duty it was to escort the bridegroom to the bride's house and announce his coming (cf. Matt. xxv. 6, 'Behold, the bridegroom!'). His joy is in the evidence of the bridegroom's joy. Jesus then is the bridegroom. In Mark ii. 19, Jesus claims this status for himself. The specific mention of **the bride** here may be intended to recall the idea of the Church as the bride of Christ, found not only in 2 Cor. xi. 2; Eph. v. 22-32, but also in Rev. xxi. 2, 9; xxii. 17.

(31) He who comes from above is above all; he who is of the earth is of the earth, and speaks of the earth; he who comes from heaven[1] (32) bears witness of that which he saw and heard; and no one accepts his witness. (33) He who does accept his witness has confirmed that God is true.[2] (34) For he whom God sent speaks the words of God; for he does not give by measure. (35) The Father loves the Son, and has given all things by his means. (36) He who believes in the Son has eternal life; but he who is disobedient to the Son shall not see life, but the wrath of God remains upon him.

31. The change from the First Person in verse 30, 'I must diminish', to the Third in 31, **he who is of the earth,** when

[1] This is the reading of ℵ* D *fam* 1 565, etc.; P⁶⁶ A B W Θ *fam* 13 28, etc. add 'is above all'. While the longer reading is in the style of the FG, it may, nevertheless, be due to the accidental repetition after the second ἐρχόμενος of the words which follow the first (but see Barrett, p. 188).

[2] ἀληθής. See on i. 9.

both refer to the Baptist, marks the transition from the Baptist's speech to the evangelist's meditation. Verses 31-36 both take up the thread of 16-21, interrupted by 22-30, and develop out of the Baptist's speech, as 16-21 does out of Jesus' previous words. To move 22-30 to another position in the Gospel, while removing the abruptness of its opening, would also break its connexion with 31-36. Moreover, if Black's view is correct, that a Greek translation of an Aramaic poem, already utilised in the Prologue,[1] underlies both 27-30 and 31-36,[2] it would confirm the impression that 31-36 is continuous with 22-30, and show that the evangelist is not just composing freely either the Baptist's speech or the meditation which develops out of it.

Christ **comes from above** (cf. iii. 13), and so John, who is a man, **of the earth,** cannot enter into competition with him. The sentence **he who is of the earth is of the earth** is such a bald tautology, even for a work so full of repetition as the FG, that there is much force in Black's suggestion[3] that the latter clause is due to a corruption of the Aramaic original, which he restores as 'he that is of the earth is inferior to him'.

John **speaks of the earth,** for even he did not fully realise the true status of him whose forerunner he was.[4] Jesus, by contrast (32) **bears witness of that which he saw and heard** (cf. iii. 11).

That **no one accepts his witness** again echoes iii. 11, and looks still further back to i. 11. The evangelist is haunted by the unbelief of the Jews, and returns to the theme in v. 43, and xii. 37.

33. But just as the generalisation of i. 11, 'His own did not accept him', is modified immediately by i. 12, 'But as for all those who did receive him', so here also John allows that there are exceptions. **He who does accept his witness has confirmed** (literally, 'sealed', ἐσφράγισεν) **that God is true.** The words **that God is true** are not quite what would be expected here, and once again Black produces an apt emendation of the assumed Aramaic original, 'that God sent him'.[5] This makes good sense, but 1 John v. 10, 'He who does not believe God has made him a liar, because he has not believed in the witness

---

[1] See note on i. 15.   [2] Black, pp. 108-111.   [3] Black, pp. 109 f.
[4] See above, pp. 94 f.   [5] Black, p. 110.

which God bore about his Son', may vindicate the accepted text. To accept the witness of Jesus is to acknowledge its truth, and so to recognise that it comes from God.

34. For he whom God sent[1] (the incarnate Logos) **speaks the words** ($\dot{\rho}\dot{\eta}\mu\alpha\tau\alpha$) **of God; for he** (i.e. God) **does not give by measure.** The text of the second clause is uncertain. Some excellent authorities (including A D Θ *fam* 13 28 *a vg pesh hl eg*) add 'God' as Subject; *cur* adds 'the Father', *sin* 'God the Father'. While 'God' gives the sense intended by the evangelist, it is almost certainly a gloss and is omitted by P⁶⁶ ℵ BW *fam* 1 565 *vt*. The vast majority of MSS. and Versions also add 'the spirit' as Object: the shorter reading is attested only by B* *sin*; but the addition is so natural, and the omission so unlikely, that the shorter reading is to be preferred. It has the advantage of leaving open the possibility of a double meaning such as John loves. The Son **speaks the words of God** because God has given his gifts so bountifully to *him*; but he also gives bountifully to *us*, who have received from Christ's fulness (i. 16), as the next two verses show.

35. The love of the Father for the Son[2] explains why **he has given all things by his means.** The Father loves not only the Son, but also those who love and believe in the Son (cf. xiv. 23; xvii. 23), and so he has made his Son the sole intermediary between himself and the faithful (cf. i. 18). The words translated **by his means** ($\dot{\epsilon}\nu$ $\tau\hat{\eta}$ $\chi\epsilon\iota\rho\dot{\iota}$ $\alpha\dot{\upsilon}\tau o\hat{\upsilon}$) are usually understood as equivalent to 'into his hands' (xiii. 3, with which cf. Matt. xi. 27 = Luke x. 22; Matt. xxviii. 18). But in xiii. 3, 'into his hands' is $\epsilon\dot{\iota}s$ $\tau\dot{\alpha}s$ $\chi\epsilon\hat{\iota}\rho\alpha s$. It is true that in Hellenistic Greek the Prepositions $\epsilon\dot{\iota}s$ and $\dot{\epsilon}\nu$ are not clearly distinguished, and true also that God gives to the Son before he gives to the faithful through him. But John's changes of phrase are sometimes intentional, and $\dot{\epsilon}\nu$ $\tau\hat{\eta}$ $\chi\epsilon\iota\rho\dot{\iota}$ $\alpha\dot{\upsilon}\tau o\hat{\upsilon}$ here recalls Gal. iii. 19, 'Ordained through angels by means of ($\dot{\epsilon}\nu$ $\chi\epsilon\iota\rho\dot{\iota}$) a mediator'. And if John is thinking primarily of the Son's function as mediator, his words here provide the best connexion between the text of verse 34, which has been adopted on other grounds, and verse 36.

---

[1] See p. 129, n. 1.
[2] For 'love' in the FG see note on iii. 16.

36. He who believes in the Son has the supreme gift of God, which is **eternal life** (cf. iii. 16), and, as 1 John v. 11 f., shows, 'God gave us eternal life, and this life is in his Son. He who has the Son has life; he who does not have the Son of God does not have life.' On the other hand, **he who is disobedient**[1] **to the Son shall not see life** (cf. iii. 18). Upon him **the wrath of God remains.** This is the only occasion in the FG where the word **wrath** ($\dot{o}\rho\gamma\acute{\eta}$) occurs, though it is found six times in the Revelation.[2] It is the consequence of man's rejection of the light and of the love of God.

Thus John's meditation upon the encounter of Jesus with the two representatives of the old Israel, Nicodemus and the Baptist, reaches its climax in this solemn warning of the consequence of disobedience—a warning particularly appropriate to the Jews (cf. xii. 37 ff., where John returns to this theme).

6. JESUS IN SAMARIA, iv. 1-42

iv. (1) So when the Lord[3] **knew that the Pharisees had heard that Jesus was making and baptising more disciples than John (2) (though Jesus himself was not baptising, but his disciples), (3) he left Judaea, and went away again into Galilee. (4) And he had to go through Samaria.**

The scene now changes from Judaea to Samaria. In Judaea, Jesus had found popularity, but hardly real faith: in apostate Samaria, however, he is to find faith. The Samaritan woman provides an effective foil to the Rabbi Nicodemus. Contrast and irony are familiar dramatic devices in the FG. Equally familiar, too, is the careful way in which the new episode is linked to those that have gone before, in particular by the further development of the themes of 'water' and 'spirit'.

These opening verses explain why Jesus left Judaea. He

---

[1] $\dot{o}$ $\dot{a}\pi\epsilon\iota\theta\hat{\omega}\nu$. John uses this verb only here; it is rather more emphatic than its equivalent, 'he who does not believe' ($\dot{o}$ $\mu\dot{\eta}$ $\pi\iota\sigma\tau\epsilon\acute{\nu}\omega\nu$) in iii. 18.

[2] It belongs therefore to the vocabulary of John rather than to that of his source.

[3] The reading **Lord** of P^{66} A B W *fam* 13 28 700 *f q sin sah* is to be preferred to 'Jesus' read by א D Θ *fam* 1 *lat cur boh*, as being less common in the FG.

knew (not necessarily by supernatural means) that the Pharisees
were aware that his success was greater than the Baptist's. He
is to be presumed to have feared their hostility, and to have
withdrawn in order to avoid a premature conflict. We are not
told, but it is not unlikely,[1] that the Baptist was by now in
prison. One dangerously popular prophet had been eliminated;
it would be prudent for one who was apparently even more
popular to withdraw. Jesus knew the value of popularity (ii. 24).

1. This verse looks back to iii. 30, 'He must increase, but I
must diminish', and serves to bind together the two sections of
the narrative.

2. The qualification that **Jesus himself was not baptising,
but his disciples,** is often regarded as an interpolation. But if
it is so, why was it not put in at iii. 22, where it would fit
equally well? It is better to regard it as a comment put into his
source by the evangelist himself. Here **disciples** must be understood in a more restricted sense than in verse 1, as referring to
the five whom he had collected in i. 37-51, and who had followed
him to Judaea (iii. 22), and were still with him (iv. 8). There is
no reason to doubt that it was the disciples who actually baptised during Jesus' ministry in Judaea. If they had done so then,
it would account for their resumption of the practice after the
day of Pentecost (Acts ii. 41), even if they had had no specific
command to do so. But Matt. xxviii. 19 (the fact of the command to baptise, if not the precise wording) may also be historical, and is then to be understood, not as commanding something quite new, but as telling the disciples to resume, with a
new significance, the practice which Jesus had abandoned, as
ineffectual as yet, when he made his fresh start in Galilee. Both
in John iv. 1, and Matt. xxviii. 19, 'making disciples' and
'baptising' occur together.

4. Jesus **had to go through Samaria,** if he wanted to take
the shortest route to Galilee—and perhaps also to avoid pursuit.
The Pharisees might be less likely to follow him into Samaria.

It is not impossible that this withdrawal through Samaria
should be dated later than this—perhaps after the visit which
Jesus made to Jerusalem for the feast of the Dedication (x. 22-

[1] Mark i. 14, dates the opening of Jesus' Galilean ministry after John's
arrest.

42)—and that John has again abandoned a chronological order of events for one dramatically and theologically more appropriate, as in the case of the Cleansing of the Temple, which may have come at the beginning of that visit.[1]

(5) So he came to a city of Samaria, called Sychar, near the piece of land which Jacob gave to his son Joseph; (6) and Jacob's Spring was there. So Jesus, exhausted by the journey, just sat down by the spring. It was about noon.

5. Sychar is usually identified with 'Askar, an Arab village about a mile north of Jacob's Spring. But this has been questioned by W. F. Albright,[2] who maintains that the **city** in question was the ancient Shechem (in Greek *Sychem*), the site of which has been established by excavation as at Balaṭah, close to the spring. As the ancient Shechem was destroyed and the site abandoned about A.D. 67, when a new city was founded some two miles to the northwest (Flavia Neapolis, now Nablus), it would seem that, if Albright is correct, the tradition found in the FG was formulated before A.D. 67. He also proposes, following the Old Syriac, to read *Sychem* for **Sychar,**[3] but this may be an unnecessary complication. **Sychar** may be a distortion of *Shechem*, originally intended as an insult to the Samaritans.[4]

The identification of **the piece of land which Jacob gave to his son Joseph** near the site of Shechem appears to depend upon an inference from two texts in Genesis, xxxiii. 19, which relates the purchase of land by Jacob from the sons of Hamor, the father of Shechem, and xlviii. 22, where Jacob says to Joseph, 'I have given to thee one portion (in Hebrew *shechem*, literally 'shoulder') above thy brethren' (RV).

---

[1] See above, p. 121, and the notes on iv. 10 and x. 22 below.

[2] *art. cit.*, p. 160.

[3] Jerome also claimed that *Sychem* was the correct reading here (though Albright does not mention this). Bauer[5] (s.v. Συχάρ) is inclined to follow Jerome. Both Jerome and the Old Syriac may be accepted as witness to a tradition about the site, without it being necessary to suppose that the text of the FG is in fact corrupt here.

[4] It may represent the Hebrew *Shikkor*, 'drunkard' (or its Aramaic equivalent), suggested perhaps by Isa. xxviii. 1, 'Woe to . . . the drunkards (*shikkore*) of Ephraim'. Strack–Billerbeck (II, p. 431) regards this as improbable, and prefers 'Askar, as does Lagrange (pp. 103 f.). But they wrote before the identification of Balaṭah with the site of Shechem.

6. The traditional **Jacob's Spring**[1] seems well authenticated. It is not mentioned in the Old Testament, but a water-supply of his own would have been a necessity to anyone occupying land in an alien country.

It was by, or on, the wall surrounding this spring that **Jesus, exhausted by the journey, just**[2] **sat down.** He appears to have been more fatigued than the disciples, who went on into the city to buy food; he was perhaps not of robust physique,[3] and the walk in the noontide heat made rest necessary. The evangelist depicts a truly human Jesus.

(7) There came a woman of Samaria to draw water. Jesus said to her, 'Give me a drink'. (8) For his disciples had gone away into the city to buy food. (9) Then the Samaritan woman said to him, 'How can you, a Jew, ask a drink of me, a Samaritan woman?'[4]

7. This unexpected meeting by Jacob's Spring—noon was an unusual time to draw water—recalls the idyllic scene from the patriarchal age, when Jacob himself met Rachel by the well (Gen. xxix. 2-12). But there are of course differences. Jesus,

[1] I.e. πηγή, a natural spring (cf. verse 14) at the bottom of a well (φρέαρ, cf. verses 11 and 12) nearly 100 feet deep (Lagrange, p. 106).

[2] This is an attempt to represent οὕτως (literally 'thus'). It may perhaps be translated 'like this', and be a survival from oral tradition, when the speaker suited his action to his words (cf. xiii. 25).

[3] He died on the cross much more rapidly than was usual.

[4] The majority of MSS. and Versions add here οὐ γὰρ συγχρῶνται ᾿Ιουδαῖοι Σαμαρείταις (P66 ABWΘ *fam* 1 *fam* 13 *lat syr eg*, etc.), which ℵ* D *a b e* omit. If it is part of the text, it is a comment of the evangelist's, not of the Samaritan woman's. The usual translation, 'Jews have no dealings with Samaritans', is far too sweeping a generalisation. Jesus' disciples expected to buy food in the Samaritan city. Accordingly, C. K. Barrett (p. 194) accepts D. Daube's view that it means, 'Jews do not use together with Samaritans' (the Object 'drinking-vessels' being understood from the context), in accordance with a rabbinic regulation of about A.D. 65 that Samaritan women were always to be regarded as ritually unclean, and would defile any vessel from which they drank. Barrett concludes that 'John has added to his material an editorial note applicable to his own day'.

But would John's readers have known enough about Jewish ritual regulations to appreciate a statement no more explicit than this? In the sense in which the passage has usually been taken, however, it is readily intelligible as a second-century gloss. By the time it was added to the text, relations between Jews and Samaritans had deteriorated.

Barrett asserts that 'there is no evidence whatever' for συγγράομαι meaning 'to have dealings with'; but LS9 quotes Diogenes of Oenoanda (second century A.D.) *Fragment* 64.

who has already likened himself to Jacob (i. 51), and is indeed
greater than Jacob (iv. 12, 25 f.), instead of drawing water for
the woman, as Jacob did for Rachel, asks her for a drink. There
is an equally ironical contrast between the maiden Rachel and
the much-married Samaritan.

Jesus' request for a drink also recalls that of Abraham's
servant to Rebekah (Gen. xxiv. 17), but instead of complying
promptly, as Rebekah did, 9. the Samaritan woman hesitates.
She recognises Jesus as a Jew—presumably from his dress—
and asks him how he can make such a request of a Samaritan
woman. Her surprise is perhaps due not only to their difference
of religion, but also of sex—Jewish Rabbis did not enter into
conversation in public with strange women (cf. verse 27).[1] She
wants to justify her implicit refusal of his request by picking a
quarrel.

**(10) Jesus answered and said to her, 'If you knew the
gift of God, and who it was who said to you, "Give me a
drink," you would have asked him, and he would have
given you living water'.**

10. Jesus avoids a quarrel by ignoring the woman's refusal
of his request and by changing the subject. He hints, in the
enigmatic fashion characteristic of the FG, that he is not as
helpless as he looks; if she knew **the gift of God,** i.e., as Origen
well says,[2] that God only gives to those who ask (cf. Matt. vii.
7), and realised that he himself was in fact God's agent (cf. iii.
35) in the giving of his gifts, it would not be Jesus, but the
woman, who would be asking the favour.

The gift which Jesus offers is **living water.**[3] This means
ostensibly water from a river or spring, not stagnant water from
a cistern (cf. Jer. ii. 13). But it also has a deeper meaning. In the
FG water symbolises the old covenant, as the medium of John's
baptism (i. 26), in the water-pots at Cana (ii. 7), and in Jacob's
Spring (iv. 7, 13); but it is also the means whereby the spirit is
given in Christian baptism (cf. iii. 5), and so, when given by
Jesus, is itself a symbol of the spirit (as becomes apparent in
vii. 38 f.). The contrast between the two covenants, and the

---

[1] Cf. p. 149.
[2] *In Iohannem*, XIII. 1 (ed. Brooke, Vol. I, p. 247).
[3] Cf. 'water of life', Rev. vii. 17; xxi. 6; xxii. 1, 17.

two kinds of water which symbolise them, helps to explain why John has introduced this episode at this point in his Gospel. Its position is determined by the themes which it expounds.

(11) The woman said to him, 'Sir, you have nothing to draw water with, and the well is deep; whence then have you this living water? (12) You are not greater, are you, than our father Jacob, who gave us the well, and drank from it himself, and his sons, and his beasts?'

11. Like the Jews in the Temple (ii. 20) and Nicodemus (iii. 4), the woman takes Jesus' words at their face value. It is characteristic of the FG to draw attention to such misunderstanding. There is **living water** at the bottom of the **well,**[1] but Jesus cannot reach it.

12. How then can he provide **living water?** Is he counting on a miracle, like that which Moses performed (Exod. xvii. 5)? The well was good enough for Jacob and his sons, and sufficient for his cattle. This stranger could not be more important than Jacob,[2] who had had to dig the well to secure his water-supply. The Samaritans were proud of their descent from the Patriarchs, to whom their attitude was rather like that of High Anglicans to the Fathers of the Church.

(13) Jesus answered and said to her, 'Everyone who drinks of this water will thirst again; (14) but whoever shall drink of the water which I shall give him will not thirst ⟨again⟩ for ever;[3] but the water which I shall give him will become in him a spring of water issuing in eternal life'.[4]

13. Jesus begins to explain himself. By 'living water' he did not mean actual spring-water, which quenches thirst only tem-

---

[1] φρέαρ. See the footnote to verse 6 above. John distinguishes this from the spring (πηγή) by which it was fed. According to Lagrange (p. 104), 'Ces puits bâtis pour capter une source profonde ne sont point rares en Palestine.' It is odd that Barrett should think that 'it is probable that John intended no difference between the words' (p. 196).

[2] The form of the question in Greek implies that the answer expected is 'No', as in iii. 4; iv. 29, 33; viii. 53.

[3] οὐ μὴ ... εἰς τὸν αἰῶνα is the most emphatic way of saying 'never': cf. viii. 51, 52; x. 28; xi. 26; xiii. 8. εἰς τὸν αἰῶνα also occurs in vi. 51, 58; viii. 35; xii. 34; xiv. 16. For αἰών see Bauer[5], s.v., and on ix. 32.

[4] Literally, 'springing to (or 'into') eternal life'. The phrase εἰς ζωὴν αἰώνιον, 'to eternal life' recurs in iv. 36; vi. 27; xii. 25. See pp. 185 f.

porarily. 14. He offers a new kind of water, one draught[1] of
which will quench thirst for ever. Though the woman does not
realise it, this is the thirst for God to which many passages in
the Old Testament refer—e.g. Ps. xlii. 1, 2; lxiii. 1; cxliii. 6;
Isa. lv. 1 ff.; Amos viii. 11. Jesus is offering to quench this thirst
by providing **a spring of water issuing in eternal life.** The
mention of **eternal life** recalls iii. 36. Later (vi. 27, 35, 58)
Jesus will make a similar claim for the bread which he offers.

His words here, and in vii. 37 ff.[2] recall Isa. xliv. 3; xlix. 10;
lviii. 11, and especially Ps. xxxvi. 9. This water is the life-giving
spirit, as vii. 39, will make clear.

The use in the Old Testament of water and thirst in this
metaphorical sense makes it unnecessary to look further afield
for the origin of the thought of this passage. The many parallels
which Bauer and Bultmann adduce in their Commentaries here
from Philo and Gnostic and Mandaean literature are rather
parallel developments of the same metaphors than direct sources
of the FG at this point. The Old Testament ideas may well
rest ultimately on a primitive mythological belief in a 'water of
life', but by the time of the FG (or of Jesus himself!) these
ideas are metaphorical and no longer mythological.

**(15) The woman said to him, 'Sir, give me this water,
so that I neither thirst, nor come here to draw'.**
She does not yet understand Jesus, but has at least reached
the point where it is she who makes the request.

**(16) Jesus said to her, 'Go; call your husband, and
come here'. (17) The woman answered and said to him,
'I have not any husband'. Jesus said to her, 'Rightly did
you say, "I have not any husband"; (18) for you had five
husbands, and now the one whom you have is not your
husband; this is true[3] that you said.'**

16. Jesus appears to ignore both her misunderstanding and
her request. But his motive in telling her to call her husband
is to provide the opportunity of bringing her to realise her true
position, so that she may understand that Jesus can satisfy
needs of which she is not yet conscious.

---

[1] This is implied by the tense of the verb πίη (Aorist).
[2] Cf. also Rev. vii. 17; xxi. 6; xxii. 17.
[3] ἀληθής. See on i. 9.

17 f. The woman's answer is intended to be misleading, but with characteristic irony Jesus tells her that she has spoken the truth. He knows, by the same power by which he was enabled to see Nathanael under his fig-tree (i. 48), that she had been married five times, and was now living with a sixth 'husband'. It is natural to suppose that she had been divorced so many times that no respectable man would marry her, and that her sixth union was irregular. But there is no hint of this in the story; it might be that her husbands had died, and that, like Raguel's daughter Sara (Tobit vii. 11), she was thought to have been the involuntary cause of their deaths. Some man had then taken her into his house, but did not treat her as his wife.[1]

The **five husbands** are commonly taken to be an allegory of the gods worshipped by the five nations settled in Samaria by the Assyrians,[2] and the sixth man either of the God of Israel, whom the Samaritans did not worship properly, or of some deity whose cult had recently been introduced into Samaria, as, for instance, by Simon Magus (Acts viii. 9 f.).[3] But lawful wedlock is not an apt allegory for idolatrous worship, which figures in the Old Testament as adultery (cf. Ezek. vi. 9, etc.). And in any case allegory is not John's method, but symbolism.[4] The Samaritan woman is a symbol of mankind outside the covenant which God had made with his people (as Nicodemus is of those within it), and the parallel between Jesus' encounter with her and that of Jacob with Rachel may suggest the symbolism which (if any) was in the mind of the evangelist, namely that of the Saviour seeking the Church, his Bride (cf. Rev. xxi. 9), among those outside the old covenant—and in the event the woman proves to be more responsive to Jesus than Nicodemus had been. The **five husbands** then are no more allegorical than the six stone water-pots of ii. 6. The point of mentioning the exact number **five** is to emphasise Jesus' supernatural knowledge of the woman's affairs.

(19) The woman said to him, 'Sir, I perceive[5] that you

[1] See also on verse 29 below.
[2] 2 Kings xvii. 24.
[3] See Barrett, p. 197.
[4] As Bultmann points out in rejecting this allegory (p. 138, n. 4).
[5] θεωρῶ. See p. 191.

are a prophet. (20) Our fathers worshipped on this mountain; and you say that in Jerusalem is the place where men ought to worship.'

If the woman is supposed to have been a sinner, **I perceive that you are a prophet** may be taken as a sarcastic attempt to change the subject. Any priest who has had occasion to talk to backsliding parishioners will recognise the technique of raising some religious grievance in order to divert his attention. But this has nothing in the text to support it. The woman really wants to know the answer, and thinks that a man who was evidently both free from Jewish prejudices (as shown by his request for a drink) and endowed with supernatural insight will be able to give her an answer. Jesus has thus achieved what he intended. He has overcome the woman's indifference, and by putting her problem to him she has enabled him to tell her the saving truth about himself in a way which she will understand.

There had been a Samaritan temple on Mount Gerizim, the lower slopes of which are visible from Jacob's well, and though it had been destroyed by John Hyrcanus about 128 B.C.[1] the site was used for worship for centuries afterwards. The Samaritans claimed that by 'the place which the Lord your God will choose . . . to put his name . . . there' (Deut. xii. 5) was meant *Gerizim*, which they read instead of *Ebal* in Deut. xxvii. 4, for the place where the Israelites were to offer their first sacrifices in the Promised Land.[2] Gerizim was the mount of blessing (Deut. xi. 29; xxvii. 12), and so an appropriate place of worship. Moreover, both Abraham (Gen. xii. 7) and Isaac (Gen. xxxiii. 18-20) had built altars near Shechem. So the Samaritan woman could appeal to the practice of the common ancestors of Jews and Samaritans **(our fathers)** against later Jewish opinion **(you say).**

(21) Jesus said to her, 'Believe me, woman,[3] that the

[1] Josephus, *Antiquities*, XIII. 255 f.
[2] Another Samaritan variant reading was *Moreh* (Gen. xxii. 2) for *Moriah*, for the place where Abraham was to sacrifice Isaac. Moreh was identified with Gerizim, for according to Gen. xii. 6, it was near to Shechem. 2 Chron. iii. 1 (which the Samaritans did not acknowledge as Scripture) claims that Moriah was the site of Solomon's Temple.
[3] γύναι. See on ii. 4 (p. 110).

time¹ is coming, when ⟨it will be⟩ neither on this mountain nor in Jerusalem ⟨that⟩ you will worship the Father.²
(22) You worship what you do not know; we worship
what we know; because salvation is from the Jews.
(23) But the time is coming, and is now, when real³
worshippers shall worship the Father in spirit⁴ and
truth;⁵ for indeed the Father seeks such as his worshippers. (24) God is spirit, and his worshippers must worship
in spirit and truth.'

21. The woman has just described Jesus as a prophet, and
his words **Believe me, woman,** introduce what is in effect a
prophecy. He refuses to judge the dispute between the Jews
and Samaritans, as on another occasion (Luke xii. 13-15) he
refused to divide an inheritance between two brothers; as then
he warned the brothers to beware of covetousness, so now he
bids the Samaritan woman to forget her grievance, for **the time
is coming** when all particularist worship will disappear. In
both cases he calls attention to a matter of fundamental importance underlying the obvious issue.

22. Jesus does, however, give a hint of judgement by saying
that the Samaritans worship in ignorance (cf. Acts xvii. 23),
while the Jews do not. By rejecting all but the Pentateuch, for
instance, the Samaritans had wilfully denied themselves access
to the revelation of God given through the prophets, and they
had shown themselves prone to error, particularly to idolatry.
The Jews were by no means perfect: they rejected Jesus, and
Nicodemus could not understand his teaching. But they were still
Jesus' 'own people' (i. 11), and when he says **We worship what
we know,** he is the spokesman of Israel—and aptly so, since he
fulfils the type of Jacob (i.e. Israel, cf. i. 51). The old covenant
may have been incomplete, but it was (unlike the Samaritan
schism) on the right lines—and so **salvation⁶ is from the Jews.**

---

¹ ὥρα. See on ii. 4 (p. 110, n. 2).   ² See on i. 18 (p. 86 above).
³ ἀληθινοί. See on i. 9 (p. 75, n. 3).   ⁴ See on i. 32 (p. 96).
⁵ See on i. 14 (p. 83).
⁶ σωτηρία. This is the only occurrence of the word in the FG. It is perhaps
significant that it occurs only once in the Synoptic Gospels in a saying of
Jesus (Luke xix. 9), and elsewhere in them only in the *Benedictus* (Luke i. 69,
71, 77). John appears to avoid it, as having formed no part of Jesus' normal
vocabulary. See also the notes on the verb 'save' (σώζω, iii. 17, p. 130, n. 4
above) and 'grace' (i. 14) above.

23. Jesus has already said that **the time is coming** for a new kind of worship (verse 21); he now expands this by the paradoxical qualification **and is now,** and describes the new worship in positive terms, as he had done before in negative. A real, spiritual worship replaces local, particularist worship.

Verses 21 and 23 take up a number of themes already announced. That of **the time** occurs first in ii. 4,[1] where it simply refers to the proper time for Jesus' intervention. Here, and later, it refers to the time for God's intervention, which, as eventually becomes clear, is effected through the death of Jesus.[2] This repeated emphasis on **the time** brings out sharply the providential character of Jesus' ministry. From the standpoint of Jesus' ministry, **the time** for God's decisive intervention is future. But here (and in v. 25) **the time is now** come— before the death of Jesus is imminent (contrast xii. 23; xvi. 32). For to be confronted with Jesus is the ultimate challenge. Thus the FG preserves the double emphasis on future consummation and present reality found in the teaching of Jesus on the kingdom of God in the Synoptic Gospels.[3]

The new worship, now possible because Jesus is come, is real, as opposed to that of the Temple no less than of Mount Gerizim,[4] because it is **in spirit and truth** (i.e. 'reality'). Thus two further themes are taken up again.[5] That of **spirit** takes us back to iii. 5—the **real worshippers** are those reborn of water and spirit—and back again to i. 33, John's prophecy of the baptism in Holy Spirit. That of **truth** takes us back to iii. 21, and, beyond that, to i. 14, 17; the real worshippers are those who 'do the truth,' and discern the truth revealed in the incarnate *Logos*.

24. That **God is spirit** is not meant as a definition of God's being—though this is how the Stoics would have understood it. It is a metaphor of his mode of operation, as life-giving power, and it is no more to be taken literally than i John i. 5, 'God is light', or Deut. iv. 24, 'Your God is a devouring fire'.[6]

---

[1] See p. 107, n. 2, and p. 110, n. 2.
[2] See v. 25, 28; xii. 23, 27; xiii. 1; xvii. 1. In vii. 30, and viii. 20, John notes that attacks on Jesus failed because his time had not yet come.
[3] See Introduction, p. 14.   [4] Cf. Heb. ix. 24, etc.
[5] To reappear together in xiv. 17; xv. 26; xvi. 13, 'the spirit of truth'.
[6] See the discussion in Origen, *In Ioh.* xiii. 21 (ed. Brooke, Vol. I, pp. 267 f.).

It is only those who have received this power through Christ who can offer God a real worship. 'Spiritual' worship is not necessarily that which does without rites and ceremonies. The Christian sacraments draw their validity from the union of flesh and spirit in the incarnate *Logos*.[1]

(25) The woman said to him, 'I know that Messiah (which means Christ) is coming; when he comes, he will announce[2] all things to us.' (26) Jesus said to her, 'I am ⟨he, I⟩ who speak to you'.

25. The woman is puzzled, and resigns herself to understanding this eventually—when Messiah comes. Little is known of the Samaritan expectation of him whom they called *Ta'eb*, the Restorer.[3] Since they did not accept the prophets, this expectation was probably based on Deut. xviii. 15, Moses' prediction of a prophet like himself. Such a prophet might well be expected to settle the questions in dispute between Jew and Samaritan.

26. The woman's assumption that her problem cannot be solved for the present is at once challenged by Jesus' claim that *he* is the Christ.

His apparently simple words **I am** may be meant by the evangelist to recall the divine self-revelation in the Old Testament (cf. Exod. iii. 14), and so to point to Christ's divinity. This might sound over-subtle, even for the FG, were it not that this is the first of a series of self-revelatory sayings, characteristic of the FG, and all echoing the Old Testament formula. This is particularly striking in those sayings (vi. 20; viii. 24, 28, 58; xiii. 19; xviii. 5-8) in which Jesus uses the words 'I am' (Ἐγώ εἰμι) without any predicate. These have a parallel in the Synoptic Gospels only in two passages, when Jesus reveals himself to his disciples as he walks on the water (Mark vi. 50 = Matt. xiv. 27; cf. John vi. 20), and in his discourse on the Mount of Olives, in which he speaks of those who will come saying 'I am' (Mark xiii. 6 = Luke xxi. 8; cf. 'I am the Christ', Matt. xxiv. 5).[4]

---

[1] Cf. vi. 53 ff.   [2] ἀναγγελεῖ, used also of the Holy Spirit, xvi. 13 ff.

[3] Lagrange (p. 115) suggests that the anonymous Samaritan who promised to reveal the sacred vessels hidden by Moses on Mount Gerizim (Josephus, *Ant.*, XVIII. 85) was a claimant to Messiahship.

[4] In other passages a predicate is expressed (vi. 35 = 48, 41, 51; viii. 12; x. 7 = 9, 11 = 14; xi. 25; xiv. 6; xv. 1 = 5). To these there is no Synoptic parallel. For a discussion of their significance see the note on vi. 35.

The apparent echo of the Old Testament formula in these passages does not of itself make it impossible to accept them as historical, though it is highly improbable that Jesus himself intended the allusion. The form of words is quite natural in the passages in which it occurs. A greater difficulty about the present verse is that Jesus' claim to be Christ is in striking contrast to his injunction to the disciples in the Synoptic Gospels (Mark viii. 30 = Matt. xvi. 20 = Luke ix. 21) not to tell anyone who he is. But Jesus may have felt that he could say openly in Samaria what would have caused serious misunderstanding in a Jewish environment. For Jesus was not prepared to accept the rôle of King of Israel for which his birth qualified him, and which John the Baptist apparently expected him to assume.[1] 'Christ' had for him a special connotation, and he never says openly that he is the Christ to a Jewish audience even in the FG.[2]

(27) And at this his disciples came, and were surprised that he was talking with a woman; yet no one said, 'What do you seek?' or 'Why do you talk with her?' (28) So the woman left her waterpot and went away into the city, and said to the men, (29) 'Come, see a man who told me all I have done. This man is not the Christ, is he?' (30) They went out of the city and came to him.

27. The conversation has reached its dramatic climax with Jesus' claim to be the Christ, and is broken off by the arrival of the disciples. The disciples' silence indicates their embarrassment at finding Jesus talking with a woman.[3] He was noticeably free from Jewish prejudice in this, cf. Mark vii. 25 ff. = Matt. xv. 22 ff.; John vii. 53–viii. 11; xi. 20-27.

28. There is no deeper significance in the fact that **the woman left her waterpot;**[4] it simply indicates her haste to tell her news.

29. The woman's candour, and the absence of any suggestion of penitence on her part, may tend to support the interpretation of verse 18 suggested above. Her story evidently made a great impression, and this may help to account for the vivid record

---

[1] See note on i. 29.   [2] See note on x. 24 f.   [3] See note on iv. 9.
[4] Loisy, however, suggests that this indicates that she has not received the water of the spirit (*Le Quatrième Évangile* (1903), p. 361).

of this conversation, to which at the time there was no witness. It was remembered and repeated, so that we do not need to ascribe it simply to John's talent for dramatic dialogue.[1]

The form of the question, **'This man is not the Christ, is he?'** (expecting the answer 'No', cf. iv. 12) does not necessarily indicate any lack of faith on the woman's part, but rather deference to the opinion of those whom she asks to see for themselves who this man is.[2]

(31) In the meantime his disciples asked him, saying, 'Rabbi, eat'. (32) But he said to them, 'I have food[3] to eat which you do not know'. (33) So the disciples said to one another, 'No one has brought him anything to eat, has he?' (34) Jesus said to them, 'My food[4] is to do[5] the will of him who sent me and to complete his work. (35) You say, do you not, "There are still four months before the harvest comes"? See, I say to you, raise your eyes and watch[6] the fields—they are bright for harvest. (36) The reaper is already receiving wages and gathering fruit for eternal life,[7] so that the sower may rejoice as well as the reaper. (37) For in this the saying is reliable[8] that one is the sower and another the reaper. (38) I sent you to reap where you have not toiled: others have toiled, and you have entered into their toil.'

31-33. The disciples naturally enough misunderstand[9] Jesus' refusal of the food which they have brought. But 34. Jesus proceeds at once to explain that the food which sustains his life is his obedience to his Father and devotion to the completion of his task.[10] His words bring together a number of themes which

---

[1] John could have heard the story himself if it was indeed he who accompanied Peter to Samaria (see p. 51).

[2] [Cf. Turner, p. 283.—B. A. M.]

[3] βρῶσις.

[4] βρῶμα. There seems to be no significance in the variation.

[5] ἵνα ποιῶ. In the FG ἵνα, which originally means only 'in order that' has become extended in meaning and lost its sense of purpose: cf. viii. 56; xv. 8, 13. See Moule, p. 146.

[6] θεάομαι. See on i. 14, p. 81 n. 3.

[7] εἰς ζωὴν αἰώνιον. See p. 142, n. 4.

[8] ἀληθινός. See p. 75, n. 3 above (on i. 9).

[9] See the note on iv. 11.

[10] The thought is similar to that underlying Jesus' quotation of Deut. viii. 3, in his reply to Satan (Matt. iv. 4 = Luke iv. 4).

run through the FG—his obedience to his Father's will,[1] his mission[2] and the completion[3] of his Father's work.[4]

35. **"There are still four months before the harvest comes"** is not meant to date this incident. In ancient times (and until the drilling of seed enabled cultivation to continue while the crops were growing[5]) the period from seed time to harvest was one of relative idleness.[6] As four months was the shortest possible time for a crop to reach maturity, this could be a proverbial saying indicating that there is still plenty of time in hand. But Jesus insists that this comfortable doctrine is inapplicable. The harvest is already ripe; **the fields . . . are bright.**[7]

36. The only point in mentioning the reaper's **wages** appears to be that it shows that the harvest is really being gathered.[8] The harvest is that of those who believe as a result of the apostles' preaching,[9] and so gain **eternal life.** The fact that there is no interval in this harvest between sowing and reaping such as there is in one of grain means that **the sower** sees an immediate return for his efforts and so **may rejoice as well as the reaper.** Normally, however, it is sorrow which is the sower's lot, and joy the reaper's, as in Ps. cxxvi. 5 f.

37. The proverb **that one is the sower and another the reaper** reflects the bitter truth that men are often deprived of the reward of their labours. Barrett's argument[10] that this proverb is Greek rather than Jewish (so that this cannot be an authentic saying of Jesus) overlooks the fact that the contrast of sowing and reaping is also found in Matt. xxv. 24 = Luke

---

[1] Cf. v. 30; vi. 38-40.   [2] See p. 129, n. 1 (on iii. 17).

[3] τελειόω, v. 36; xvii. 4. Cf. also the cognate τελέω, xix. 28, 30.

[4] For '(God's) work' cf. vi. 29; xvii. 4 (with τελειόω). Jesus' 'works' (his miracles) are also God's, cf. v. 36 (again with τελειόω), ix. 3 f.; x. 32, 37; xiv. 10.

[5] So that the tares had to remain among the wheat until the harvest, Matt. xiii. 29.

[6] While the crop is growing all the husbandman can do is to get up and go to bed, Mark iv. 27.

[7] λευκός. Greek colour-adjectives express degree of brightness rather than tint. The former is more apparent under the strong Mediterranean sun; the latter in our own climate. So λευκός means 'bright' rather than 'white'.

[8] Contrast the wages in the parable of the Labourers in the Vineyard, Matt. xx. 8.

[9] As in Matt. ix. 37 = Luke x. 2.   [10] Barrett, p. 203.

xix. 21, 'Reaping where you did not sow'. The proverb, says Jesus, is true, but not in this case in its obvious sense.[1]

38. The work for which the disciples have been sent out (cf. John xvii. 18; xx. 21) has already been started by others. Thus the distinction of sower and reaper remains valid, though both rejoice in the harvest.

Who then are the **others,** the fruit of whose toil the disciples reap? Do these sayings reflect a situation later than the ministry of Jesus, when the **others** are Jesus and the first apostles, whose toil has produced the harvest which the second generation reaps? The past tense **I sent** is curious in a saying of Jesus, since the disciples have not yet done any preaching, and this may seem to support this suggestion. If so, this passage must be regarded as the utterance of a Christian prophet elaborating and adapting harvest themes from the Synoptic Gospels.

But these conclusions are not inevitable. The readiness with which the Samaritan woman has gone to tell her friends of Christ has made him see that the harvest is already beginning. When the disciples go out on their mission they will find that the work of preparation has been done, and so realise that Jesus **sent** them **to reap where** they **have not toiled**—hence the tense of **I sent.** The parallels to Synoptic themes then vindicate, rather than challenge, the authenticity of this passage. It is rather the deferment of the harvest to the end of the world (as in Matt. xiii. 39) which reflects later ideas. The **others** are all those who have prepared for the harvest—the prophets, for example, and John the Baptist—of whom the Samaritan woman is an example.

(39) And from that city many of the Samaritans believed on him through the word of the woman who bore witness, 'He told me all I have done'. (40) So when the Samaritans came to him they asked him to stay with them: and he stayed there two days. (41) And many more believed through his word, (42) and said to the woman, 'We no longer believe through your talk; for we have heard ourselves, and know that this is truly the Saviour of the world.'

[1] Cf. the way in which Jesus recognises the truth of the Samaritan woman's saying that she has no husband, in a sense which she did not intend (iv. 18).

39. Note how the themes of 'belief' and 'witness' are once again brought out, and (41 f.) the contrast between belief as the result of witness and of personal knowledge.[1]

40. For the possible significance of the fact that Jesus **stayed** with the Samaritan believers see the note on i. 38.[2] That he stayed only **two days** may be mentioned in order to suggest that their conversion was not permanent, as indeed it cannot have been if the evidence of the rest of the New Testament is taken into account. For there is no evidence outside the FG for the conversion of Samaritans before the preaching of Philip (Acts viii. 5 ff.). In Matt. x. 5, Jesus forbids his disciples to preach in any Samaritan city, and in Luke ix. 52 f., some Samaritans refuse to entertain Jesus and his disciples because he was on his way to Jerusalem. Is this Samaritan episode then an invention of our evangelist's? If it is, he has shown an indifference to the prevailing tradition which it is quite as difficult to credit as it is that he preserves an isolated episode which the rest of the New Testament has overlooked. Jesus' command to avoid Samaritan cities is no more incompatible with this than is his command to avoid the Gentiles (in the same verse of Matthew) with his encounter with the Gentile woman (Mark vii. 26 = Matt. xv. 22). His meeting with the Samaritan woman was equally fortuitous with this, and no more of a precedent. Moreover, a welcome in one place is not incompatible with a hostile reception in a different place and in different circumstances.

42. The confession that Jesus is **the Saviour of the world** is the climax of the whole passage, and the counterpart of the self-revelation of Christ in verse 26. It takes up the theme of iii. 17. The same confession occurs in 1 John iv. 14, but this is the only other example of the word **Saviour** in the Johannine literature.[3] In the rest of the New Testament it is used of God (Luke i. 47; 1 Tim. i. 1; ii. 3; iv. 10; Titus i. 3; ii. 10; iii. 4; Jude 25) and of Christ (Luke ii. 11; Acts v. 31; xiii. 23; Eph. v. 23; Phil. iii. 20; 2 Tim. i. 10; Titus i. 4; ii. 13; iii. 6; 2 Pet. i. 1, 11; ii. 20; iii. 2, 18). Its use is thus much more frequent in the later than the earlier literature. The reluctance to use it

---

[1] Cf. xx. 29.   [2] P. 98 above.
[3] See the note on iii. 17 (p. 130, n. 4).

in the earlier period may have been because of its use as a pagan cult title, particularly in emperor-worship.[1] This does not mean, however, that its use in the FG here is a sign of lateness; the Samaritans cannot be supposed to have shared the scruples of the early Christians. The title may have come into use later as a conscious counterblast to pagan pretensions, rather than as a sign of syncretism.

7. JESUS IN GALILEE. THE SECOND SIGN, AT CANA, iv. 43-54

iv. (43) And after the two days he went out from there into Galilee. (44) For Jesus himself bore witness that a prophet does not have any honour in his own country. (45) So when he came to Galilee, the Galileans welcomed him, for they had seen all the things that he had done in Jerusalem during the feast; for they also had gone to the feast.

This is an editorial paragraph designed, like ii. 12 and ii. 23-25, to link two episodes—possibly from different sources—and to supply a motive for the change of scene, the necessity for which is dramatic and theological rather than historical. Its artificiality is revealed by the obscurity of its logic.

44. The motive for Jesus' going to Galilee is **that a prophet does not have any honour in his own country.**[2] In iv. 1-3, it was to avoid antagonising the Pharisees—by a success which this paragraph appears to ignore. Jesus' **own country** is apparently Judaea, though John seems aware of the tradition which put Jesus' home in Galilee—his mother is there (ii. 1), and his brethren (vii. 3). Moreover, Jesus' success in Galilee is not markedly different from that in Judaea. 45. The faith of the Galileans is based on **the things that he had done in Jerusalem**—cf. ii. 23, 'While he was in Jerusalem . . . many be-

---

[1] **Saviour of the world** was used as a title of Hadrian: see Barrett (p. 204) and Bauer[5] s.v. σωτήρ.

[2] Cf. i. 11, 'He came into his own property, and his own people did not accept him'.

lieved in his name when they saw the signs which he did'. John may wish to indicate that though Galilee was Jesus' home and Judaea the proper scene for his ministry, no place on earth can be his **own country**: his **country** (πατρίς, literally 'father-land') is with his Father, who alone honours the Son (cf. viii. 54).[1]

The saying which John utilises here is also found in the Synoptic Gospels (Mark vi. 4; Matt. xiii. 57; Luke iv. 24); but since the parallels with these passages are in substance rather than form, it is more probable that this was a saying which had no fixed context in the tradition or stereotyped form than that John has adapted it from Mark, and deliberately changed its reference from Galilee to Judaea.

(46) So he came back to Cana of Galilee, where he had made the water wine. And there was a certain royal official[2] whose son was ill in Capernaum. (47) This man heard that Jesus had come from Judaea to Galilee, went to him, and asked him to go down[3] and heal his son; for he was going to die. (48) So Jesus said to him, 'Unless you see signs and wonders, you will not believe'. (49) The official said to him, 'Sir, come down before my child dies'. (50) Jesus said to him, 'Go, your son lives'. The man believed the word which Jesus spoke to him, and went. (51) And when he was already on the way down his slaves met him saying that his child lived. (52) So he enquired from them the hour[4] in which he got better; so they said to him, 'Yesterday at one o'clock[5] the fever left him'. (53) So the father knew that it was in that hour in which Jesus had said to him, 'Your son lives'; and he

[1] See the illuminating discussion in R. H. Lightfoot, *St. John's Gospel: A Commentary* (ed. C. F. Evans, 1956), pp. 34-36.

[2] βασιλικός. The variant reading βασιλίσκος (diminutive of βασιλεύς, 'king') found here in D *a d* and some MSS. of *boh*, and in verse 49 (D *l* 184 and some MSS. of *boh*) is worth serious consideration. It is implied by Heracleon's comment (preserved in Origen, *In Ioh.*, XIII. 60, ed. Brooke, Vol. I, p. 321), 'As it were a little king appointed by a universal king over a little kingdom'. It cannot just be dismissed as due to the influence of the Latin *regulus*. The reading βασιλικός may have prevailed because it makes John's story easier to harmonise with Matt. viii. 5-13, and Luke vii. 1-10.

[3] See p. 115, n. 2 (on ii. 12).

[4] ὥρα. See p. 110, n. 2 (on ii. 4) for other senses of the word in the FG.

[5] Literally, 'the seventh hour'.

**himself believed, and his whole household. (54) This
second sign**[1] **Jesus did when he had come from Judaea
to Galilee.**

46. The mention of **Cana** here, while in verse 54 it is emphasised that this was the second sign at Cana, invites us to compare the two signs. Both elicit faith and relieve need, though in
the second the need is far more urgent than in the first; Jesus,
now recognised as the Saviour of the world (iv. 42), saves a
child from imminent death. The themes illustrated in the story
are thus 'belief' and 'life'. Now the six signs wrought by Jesus
fall into two groups, each headed by a nature-miracle (with a
corollary attached to it) and comprising two healing-miracles
as well. This healing, the second miracle in the first group,
illustrates i. 4, 'As for that which is in being, in it he was the
life', and the second in the second group the following clause,
'and the life was the light of men' (the healing of the man born
blind, ix. 1-12). Moreover, within the first group the second
sign is not only linked to the first (as has been shown), but also
to the third (v. 1-9), by a series of contrasts—one is done at a
distance, the other in the presence of the patient; one is of a
child suffering from an acute attack of fever, the other of an
adult with a chronic complaint. Thus John dovetails each story,
by parallelism and contrast, into the structure of the Gospel.

The resemblance of the healing of the royal official's son to
Matt. viii. 5-13, and Luke vii. 1-10, is obvious, though there are
noticeable differences between them (as indeed there are also
between Matthew and Luke[2]). If all three versions refer to the
same incident, the tradition followed by John had diverged at
an early stage from that in the other Gospels, and it is a nice
question[3] which of the three is closest to the facts.

In Matthew and Luke the man who asks Jesus' help is a
centurion and a Gentile (cf. Matt. viii. 10 = Luke vii. 9, and
Luke vii. 5); in John he is a **royal official** (not necessarily
military) and there is nothing to indicate that he is a Gentile.
He is only assumed to be one because he is in the other Gospels.

---

[1] πάλιν δεύτερον. The πάλιν is redundant.

[2] Principally that in Matthew the centurion approaches Jesus himself,
while in Luke he sends a deputation of Jews.

[3] And probably unanswerable.

But if he was in the service of Herod Antipas (called a king, Mark vi. 14, though one only by courtesy), he was quite as likely to be a Jew. And Gentiles only appear in John xii. 20 ff., and then in so roundabout a way that John could hardly have introduced one as early as this without making the fact quite explicit.

In John the patient is the official's **son**; in Matthew the centurion's 'boy' ($\pi\alpha\hat{\iota}s$, which can mean either 'child' or 'slave'); in Luke his 'slave' ($\delta o\hat{\upsilon}\lambda os$). **Capernaum** is the scene of the miracle in all three, but only John mentions **Cana**.

48. Jesus' answer implies that he regards the request to heal the man's son as an example of the mere seeking of a sign[1] (note the Plural **you**—his words do not apply only to the official), and so of a faith no more adequate than that noted at ii. 23, and iv. 45. 49. Undeterred, the official repeats his request more urgently (note the diminutive **child** instead of 'son' in 47), and so 50. Jesus puts his faith to the test by declining to go with him[2] and simply telling him his son is cured. The man rose to the occasion and **believed the word**[3] . . . and went.

52. It is not much more than 20 miles from Cana to Capernaum, no long journey, particularly if, as one would expect, the official rode. The meeting with Jesus had been at 1 p.m. (verse 53), and the man had presumably left home early that morning. Why did he not return the same day? John may intend to emphasise his complete confidence in Jesus by this indication of his delay.[4]

53. That **he believed** indicates a completeness of faith, more than the acceptance of what Jesus says as correct (as in verse 50); cf. i. 7 and 50, for this absolute use of 'believe'. The mention of **his whole household** sharing his faith underlines the impressiveness of the miracle. The only close parallel to this elsewhere in the New Testament is in Acts xviii. 8, but this is no reason for doubting the fact on this occasion.

[1] The phrase **signs and wonders** occurs in Mark xiii. 22 = Matt. xxiv. 24, of the devices used by 'false Christs and false prophets'.

[2] In Matt. viii. 7, Jesus says, 'I will come and heal him', and Luke says that he went with the deputation (vii. 6).

[3] This may be an allusion to Jesus as the *Logos*. See Introduction, p. 4.

[4] This is more probable than that he mentions the time of the cure (literally 'the seventh hour') because 7 is appropriate, as the perfect number.

54. After this John ceases to enumerate the signs. This is probably because, in his rearrangement of his material, he has disturbed their original order.

8. THE THIRD SIGN, IN JERUSALEM, AND CONTROVERSY WITH THE JEWS, v

v. (1) After this[1] there was the feast of the Jews,[2] and Jesus went up to Jerusalem. (2) Now there is in Jerusalem by the Sheep ⟨Gate⟩ a pool, called in Aramaic[3] Beth-zatha, which has five porticoes. (3) In these there lay a crowd of invalids, blind, lame, withered. (5) And there was a man there who had been ill for thirty-eight years. (6) When Jesus saw him lying ⟨there⟩, and knew that he had already been[4] ⟨there⟩ a long time, he said to him, 'Do you wish to become well?' (7) The invalid answered him, 'Sir, I have not got a man to put me in the pool when the water is stirred; but while I am on my way, someone else goes down before me'. (8) Jesus said to him, 'Get up, take up your pallet, and walk'. (9) And immediately the man became well, took up his pallet, and walked.

1. This verse serves to introduce the story, and accounts for the change of scene by the journey of Jesus to the feast in Jerusalem, as in ii. 13 and vii. 10. John does not say which feast it was, and conjecture on this point is futile. It is likely that in John's source chapter v followed vi, and if so, the feast would then be the Passover, mentioned as near in vi. 4. John did not alter this when he transposed vi and v in order to pair off this miracle with that of iv. 46–54.[5]

---

[1] Μετὰ ταῦτα, implying an interval of unspecified length; see p. 131, n. 4.

[2] See note on ii. 13.

[3] Literally 'in Hebrew' ('Εβραϊστί). The word occurs in the New Testament only here, John xix. 13, 17, 20; xx. 16, and Rev. ix. 11; xvi. 16.

[4] To describe a state continuing up to the present, Greek uses the present tense (ἔχει) where English uses the perfect; cf. viii. 58; xiv. 9.

[5] Hence the reading ἡ ἑορτή ('the feast', א C L fam 1 33 eg) is to be preferred to the correction ἑορτή ('a feast', P66 ABDWΘ fam 13 cur) in spite of its inferior attestation.

2. The text here is uncertain at two points.

The reading **by the Sheep ⟨Gate⟩ a pool**[1] is probably to be preferred to the less strongly attested 'a sheep pool',[2] though Origen[3] and other early writers do in fact refer to this as 'the sheep pool'. Barrett's suggestion that we should translate, 'There is in Jerusalem, by the Sheep Pool, that which in Aramaic is called . . .', is worth consideration, in spite of its awkwardness.[4]

The second problem is the Aramaic place-name. The majority of MSS.[5] read *Bethesda*; the alternatives are *Beth-saida*,[6] *Be(th)zatha*,[7] and *Belzetha*.[8] Now whenever John transliterates a Semitic name elsewhere in the FG he gives its Greek equivalent,[9] and it is surprising that he does not do so here. But the exception to the rule is more understandable if we read **Bethzatha,** which may represent בֵּית שִׁיתָא 'the House of the Sheep', i.e. the building surrounding the Sheep Pool,[10] so called, according to Origen,[11] because sheep for sacrifice were collected there, and their entrails were washed in it after the sacrifice. It was to the north of the old city, not far from the Sheep Gate.[12] *Bethsaida* is then to be regarded as a very early corruption, due to the substitution of a familiar word (found in John i. 44; xii. 21) for an unfamiliar one: *Bethesda* as a 'correction' of this, perhaps favoured because it could represent בֵּית חִסְדָּא 'the House of Mercy': and *Belzetha* as another corruption, perhaps with an intermediate stage *Bezetha*, the name, according to Josephus,[13] of the new quarter north of the old city.

The Sheep Pool, again according to Origen,[14] was double,

---

[1] ἐπὶ τῇ προβατικῇ κολυμβήθρα P⁶⁶ BW *fam* 1 *fam* 13, etc. (ADΘ have ἐν in place of ἐπί).

[2] προβατικὴ κολυμβήθρα ℵ *e*.

[3] *In Ioh.*, Fragment 61 (ed. Brooke, Vol. II, p. 273).

[4] P. 210. This implies ἐπὶ τῇ προβατικῇ κολυμβήθρᾳ. See n. 10 below.

[5] AΘ *fam* 1 *fam* 13 *f q cur pesh*, etc.   [6] P⁶⁶ B W *c ff* ² *vg hl eg*.

[7] ℵ 33 *e l*.   [8] D, and (with some variations) some Latin MSS.

[9] As in i. 38, 41, 42; ix. 7; xi. 16; xx. 16, where the Semitic word precedes the Greek translation, and in xix. 13 and 17, where they are the other way round.

[10] It is just possible that the original text was ἐπὶ τῇ προβατικῇ κολυμβήθρᾳ τὸ λεγόμενον (read by ℵ instead of ἡ ἐπιλεγομένη) Ἑβραϊστὶ Βηθζαθά, i.e. 'at the Sheep Pool the ⟨building⟩ called in Aramaic Bethzatha'.

[11] *Loc. cit.*   [12] Neh. iii. 1, 32; xii. 39.

[13] *B.J.*, V. 149.   [14] *Loc. cit.*

with porticoes on the four sides and the fifth between the two parts of the pool. What could be the remains of such a building have been discovered near the church of St Anne, not far from the Antonia.[1] This seems to be another example of the accuracy of John's topography. It is unlikely that John meant the **five porticoes** to symbolise the five books of the Law, which cannot take away sin.[2]

3. The **crowd of invalids**[3] was attracted by the reputed curative property of the pool, available, according to verse 7, only when the water was disturbed. The pool was presumably fed by a spring which flowed intermittently.[4]

6. Jesus takes the initiative, and singles out a man whom he knew (not necessarily by supernatural means) to be in a hopeless plight. He had been ill for thirty-eight years,[5] and had nobody to give him a helping hand. 8. Without waiting for any sign of faith, Jesus bids him get up, pick up his pallet and walk. His words here are identical with those addressed to the paralytic in Mark ii. 9, and it is not surprising that some critics have regarded John's narrative here as a free adaptation of Mark's. But the details of the two incidents are so different[6] that direct

[1] See Lagrange, p. 133, and J. Jeremias, *Die Wiederentdeckung von Bethesda* (1949). Photograph in M. Join-Lambert, *Jerusalem* (1958), p. 113.

[2] So Bultmann, p. 180, n. 8, and Barrett, p. 211. Loisy, *op. cit.*, p. 386, takes the opposite view, following St Augustine, *Aqua illa iudaïcus populus erat, quinque porticus lex* (*In Ioh.* XVII).

[3] D and some Old Latin MSS. add 'paralysed' to the list.

[4] Many MSS. (including DWΘ *fam* 1 *fam* 13 *lat pesh*) add at the end of verse 3 'waiting for the moving of the waters' (P[66] א A*B*C* *q cur sah* omit). Many also add, with minor variations, verse 4, 'For an angel of the Lord came down from time to time into the pool and stirred the water; the first therefore to enter after the stirring of the water became well, whatever was the disease by which he was held' (A L Θ *fam* 1 *fam* 13 *pesh*, etc., but not P[66] א BC* DW 33 *f l q cur*). While there is nothing in these passages incompatible with Johannine usage, the strength of the evidence for their omission suggests that they are glosses.

[5] John does not say what his illness was. The thirty-eight years are no more likely to be allegorical than the five porticoes.

[6] In Mark the incident is in Capernaum, in John in Jerusalem; in Mark the man has four friends, in John nobody; in Mark they take the initiative, in John Jesus does; in Mark Jesus sees their faith, in John faith is not mentioned; in Mark Jesus forgives the man before telling him to get up, in John (v. 14) he tells him not to go on sinning, after healing him; in Mark Jesus gives offence by telling the man he is forgiven, in John (v. 18) by cancelling the Sabbath (not mentioned in Mark) and making himself equal to God (though this latter charge occurs also in Mark ii. 7, by implication at least).

borrowing is unlikely. If the two incidents are ultimately the same, the traditions followed by Mark and John must have diverged at an early stage.

This third sign is placed here as a foil to the second.[1] Its main theme is the same—that of life given by the word of Jesus— but it says nothing of faith (though the man's obedience to Jesus' command implies that he possessed it). Instead, it shows for the first time how Jesus provoked open hostility, thus preparing for the signs which follow. It also carries forward the subsidiary theme of 'water' (verse 7); that in the pool, like that in the waterpots at Cana and in Jacob's well, symbolises the old covenant, which Jesus supersedes.

(9) Now it was Sabbath on that day. (10) So the Jews said to the man who had been healed, 'It is Sabbath, and it is not lawful for you to take up your pallet'. (11) But he answered them, 'It was the man who made me well that[2] said to me, "Take up your pallet, and walk"'. (12) They asked him, 'Who is the man who said to you "Take it up, and walk"?' (13) But the man who was cured did not know who it was; for Jesus had withdrawn, there being a crowd in the place. (14) After this[3] Jesus found him in the Temple, and said to him, 'See, you have become well; do not go on sinning any longer, lest something worse happen to you'. (15) The man went away, and reported to the Jews that it was Jesus who had made him well. (16) And for this the Jews persecuted Jesus, because he did these things on Sabbath. (17) But Jesus answered them, 'My Father has been working until the present moment,[4] and I work'. (18) So for this the Jews sought to kill him more than ever, because he was not only cancelling the Sabbath, but also saying that God was his own Father, making himself equal to God.

9. The **Sabbath** is a point of similarity between this sign and the fifth (cf. ix. 14, where it is again mentioned after the healing); the pattern is continued by the interrogation of the man who had been healed (undertaken here by the Jews, in ix by the Pharisees[5]), by the further meeting of Jesus with the

---

[1] See above, p. 156.　　[2] See p. 85, n. 2.　　[3] See p. 158, n. 1.
[4] ἕως ἄρτι. See p. 107, n. 3.　　[5] See on i. 19, pp. 87 f. above.

man (v. 14 and ix. 35 ff.), and by the concluding discourse which develops out of the controversy (v. 19 ff. and x).

10. The carrying of burdens on the Sabbath was not specifically forbidden by the Pentateuch, but the Mishnah classified it as work, with some precedent in Num. xv. 32-36; Jer. xvii. 21; and Neh. xiii. 15-19. Thus the complaint against the man carrying his pallet was by no means merely captious.

11. The man appeals to the authority of his healer, and so shifts the blame. He is quite ready to co-operate with Jesus' enemies, and when he discovers who his healer was, he tells them (15). They thereupon transfer their attack to Jesus (16 ff.). This man is a poor creature, unlike the formerly blind man of the fifth sign, who defends Jesus, and suffers for it.

13. We are perhaps meant to infer that Jesus **had withdrawn** to avoid a demonstration by the **crowd** (cf. vi. 15). His motive could not yet be to avoid hostility, as it was later (e.g. viii. 59; x. 39).

14. Jesus' words contain the first reference to **sin** since i. 29, and imply that he is concerned not only with the conquest of physical evil (as the acts of healing themselves might lead us to suppose) but also of moral evil. By telling the man that he is not to **go on sinning any longer,**[1] Jesus implies that his sins up to date are forgiven (cf. his words to the paralytic, Mark ii. 5), and also that there is a causal connexion between sin and disease, though it is not so simple as was popularly supposed. Men are ill because all men are sinners , but we do not suffer disease or other natural calamities in precise proportion to our sins (cf. ix. 1-3, and Luke xiii. 1-5). The warning **lest something worse happen** need mean no more than that to continue to sin after so signal a mercy would invite reprisal (cf. what happened to the man in the parable, Luke xi. 24-26).

16. The verbs **persecuted** and **did** (and **sought, was cancelling,** and (was) **saying** in 18) are Imperfects, and can be taken to imply that this is a typical example of something that had already happened on other occasions, though John only mentions it now for the first time.[2] This iterative sense of the

---

[1] The precise words (μηκέτι ἁμάρτανε) are also found in viii. 11. For the force of the present imperative in negative commands cf. ii. 16, and p. 115, n. 4.

[2] The signs which he actually records are only a selection, cf. xx. 30.

Imperfect may be borne out by the fact that strictly Jesus himself had not yet *done* anything on this occasion. The Synoptic Gospels, however, show that, in the eyes of his opponents, he habitually infringed the Sabbath law.[1] But **persecuted** at least may have a conative[2] rather than an iterative force, and imply that they now tried to persecute Jesus (but did not succeed for some time). If so, John means that a new phase of the ministry has now begun—and in fact controversy now begins to play a large part in the FG.

17. Jesus' answer to the implicit charge that he works on the Sabbath is an explicit admission of its truth—**I work**; but in this (he says) he is only imitating his Father,[3] who **has been working**[4] **until the present moment** (i.e. whose activity is unceasing). Jesus in effect repudiates any crudely anthropomorphic understanding of God's rest after his six days labour of creation, the aetiological myth which explained the command to rest from labour on the seventh day.[5] That God is by his very nature continually active is a Greek philosophical commonplace, found at least as early as Aristotle,[6] and adopted by the Hermetic writers[7] and Philo,[8] who was well aware of its

---

[1] Cf. Mark ii. 23-28; iii. 1-6, etc.

[2] A good example of the conative Imperfect is in Acts xxvi. 11, where ἠνάγκαζον βλασφημεῖν means that Paul tried to make the Christians blaspheme, but did not succeed (cited by Moulton, *Prolegomena*, pp. 128 ff., which see).

[3] See on i. 18, p. 86 above for God as 'Father' in the FG.

[4] This represents the present ἐργάζεται used to describe an action continuing up to the present time, where English uses the Perfect: cf. xv. 27, ἀπ᾽ ἀρχῆς μετ᾽ ἐμοῦ ἐστε, 'You have been with me from the beginning' (cited by Moulton, *Prolegomena*, p. 119, which see).

[5] Cf. Gen. ii. 1-3; Exod. xx. 11; xxxi. 17.

[6] In whose philosophy the doctrine that God is pure activity (ἐνέργεια) is of cardinal importance: cf. 'There is something which moves without being moved, that is eternal and is both substance and activity' (ἔστι τι ὃ οὐ κινούμενον κινεῖ, ἀίδιον καὶ οὐσία καὶ ἐνέργεια οὖσα, *Metaphysics* Λ 1072a 25, 26). This 'unmoved mover' is God, whom he defines as the 'eternal best living being' (φαμὲν δὴ τὸν θεὸν εἶναι ζῷον ἀίδιον ἄριστον, *ibid.*, 1072b 29, 30).

[7] Cf. *C.H.*, ix. 9 'the sense and thought of God is this, that he is always moving all things' (καὶ τοῦτό ἐστιν ἡ αἴσθησις καὶ νόησις τοῦ θεοῦ, τὸ τὰ πάντα ἀεὶ κινεῖν).

[8] In addition to the passage quoted by Barrett (p. 213) cf. *De Cherubim* 87, where Philo points out that God's 'rest' does not mean that he ceases to do good, 'since that which is the cause of all things is by nature active and never has any respite from doing the best' (ἐπειδὴ φύσει δραστήριον τὸ τῶν ὅλων αἴτιον παῦλαν οὐδέποτε ἴσχον τοῦ ποιεῖν τὰ κάλλιστα).

incompatibility with earlier ideas, as were also the Rabbis.[1]
This does not necessarily mean that Jesus could not have used
the words attributed to him. The claim which they imply to a
sovereign freedom with regard to the Sabbath does not go
beyond his assertion that 'the Son of man is Lord even of the
sabbath' (Mark ii. 28).

18. Jesus' answer is regarded by the Jews as aggravating his
offence. Not content with commanding an infringement of the
Law, he has now denied the scriptural basis of the Sabbath rest,
thus **cancelling the Sabbath,**[2] by an assertion that **God
was his own Father** which is in effect a claim to equality
with God[3] (cf. x. 33). To John this claim was of course fully
justified ('the Logos . . . was God', i. 1), and it is merely
another example of the irony latent in the whole Gospel
that the Jews should regard it as blasphemy, and so seek
to exact the appropriate penalty, which was death by
stoning.

Under the circumstances, however, it was as natural for the
Jews to regard the claim as blasphemy as it would be for
Christians if anyone but Jesus made it,[4] though Jewish exegetes
did recognise that God had on occasion bestowed the title
Elohim on men as a mark of favour.[5] Pagans of course had no
such scruples, and men like Empedocles and Apollonius of

---

[1] Cf. Barrett (*ibid.*) and also the observation in *Bereshith Rabba* xi that the
statement that God rested on the seventh day from all his work refers only
to the creation of the world, and not to God's dealings with the sinners and
the righteous (i.e. his government of the world) (cited by Bauer, p. 82).

[2] ἔλυεν. See Bauer[5], s.v. λύω, 4. It means literally 'loosen', and, with
words like 'law' as object means either 'infringe, break' (cf. John vii. 23);
'give a lax interpretation to' (?Matt. v. 19; xvi. 19; xviii. 18); 'cancel, abrogate'
(cf. John x. 35)—senses which easily shade into one another.

[3] This is so whether or not ἴδιος, 'own', has the reduced sense here which
is common in Hellenistic Greek. See note on i. 41.

[4] For Jewish ideas cf. Philo, *Legum Allegoriae*, I. 49. For him it is the hall-
mark of selfishness and atheism to think oneself equal with God (φίλαυτος δὲ
καὶ ἄθεος ὁ νοῦς οἰόμενος ἴσος εἶναι θεῷ). For Christian, cf. 2 Thess. ii. 4. The
hope of becoming 'like God' was the temptation to which Eve succumbed
(cf. Gen. iii. 5, 22). This is probably alluded to in Phil. ii. 6, '(Christ)
did not think equality with God something at which to grasp'. Herein
lies the difference between Christ and Antichrist.

[5] Examples of such an interpretation of Exod. iv. 16; vii. 1; xxii. 27; Ps.
lxxxii. 6 (quoted by Jesus, John x. 34) are given in Strack–Billerbeck, II,
pp. 462 ff. To *claim* the title is of course always blasphemy.

Tyana could claim to be gods without incurring anything worse than amused scepticism.

This is the first time that John refers to any intention to kill Jesus, whose death has hitherto only been hinted at (ii. 19); but from now on he records repeated threats of, and attempts at, violence (vii. 30; viii. 59; x. 31, 39)—all abortive, because Jesus' time had not yet come—and then the final decision (xi. 53) which led to the crucifixion.

The discourse which follows develops from the controversy in v. 10-18, particularly from Jesus' words in 17, just as iii. 16-21, 31-36 does from the conversation with Nicodemus (iii. 1-15). The hostility of the Jews here serves the same purpose as the misunderstanding of Nicodemus, and provides the opportunity for expounding the significance of the two signs which have just been related and defining the relationship of Jesus to his Father. It sums up the first phase of the ministry, and looks forward to the next. As it stands it can hardly be taken as an actual sermon addressed by Jesus to men who were seeking to kill him, but rather as the pronouncement of a Christian prophet, John himself, or his source, cf. iii. 16 ff.

(19) So Jesus answered and said to them,

'Amen, amen, I say to you,[1] **the Son cannot do anything by himself, but only whatever he sees the Father doing; for whatever he does the Son also does likewise. (20) For the Father loves the Son, and shows him all that he himself does; and he will show him greater works than these, in order that you may be astonished. (21) For as the Father raises the dead and makes them live, so also the Son makes live those whom he wills.'**

19. Jesus' claim that God's continuous activity is a precedent for his own (17) is not blasphemous presumption, for he does not act on his own initiative (cf. v. 30), which guarantees that his imitation of his Father is not presumptuous, as was that of Phaethon driving the chariot of the Sun.

20. For, out of his affection[2] for his Son, God **shows him all that he himself does,** which he would not do unless he

---

[1] See on i. 51, p. 105.
[2] The verb used here is φιλέω; in iii. 35, it is ἀγαπάω. For the distinction between them see p. 130, n. 2.

intended his Son to imitate him. And he has **greater works** (cf. i. 50) to show him than those already done, and these, if they cannot make the Jews believe (which is not the purpose of signs), will at least astonish them (cf. vii. 21).

21. For the Father allows the Son to share his prerogative of raising the dead and making them live (cf. Deut. xxxii. 39; 1 Sam. ii. 6; 2 Kings v. 7; Wisdom xvi. 13). In Rev. i. 18, Christ has the keys of death and Hades. The Father sent the Son to give life (iii. 16); this has already been exemplified by the two signs, iv. 46 ff., and v. 1 ff., and is to be even more strikingly in the raising of Lazarus, of which this is the first hint.

Though **the Son makes live those whom he wills** yet it is not by an exercise of his own will in opposition to his Father's —for he does not seek his own will (v. 30b, cf. iv. 34; vi. 38). His will is his Father's, and in this paradox is the secret of true freedom.

(22) 'For the Father does not judge anyone either, but has given all judgement to the Son, (23) in order that all may honour the Son as they honour the Father. He who does not honour the Son does not honour the Father who sent him. (24) Amen, amen, I say to you,[1] that the man who listens to my word and believes him who sent me has eternal life, and does not come to judgement, but has passed from death into life.'

22 f. To God also belongs the prerogative of judgement,[2] but he has given this also to his Son. Here, as in iii. 16 f., the theme of 'judgement' occurs in the same context as that of 'life'. There is, however, a *prima facie* inconsistency in what the FG says of judgement. For just as **the Father does not judge anyone,** so too Christ does not judge (viii. 15; xii. 47); but it is also said that Christ *does* judge (v. 30; viii. 16; ix. 39). This apparent inconsistency is due to the fact that judgement was not the primary purpose of the Son's coming, but is its inevitable result. In so far as this result is foreseen, it can on occasion be described as if it were intentional.[3]

---

[1] See on i. 51, p. 105.

[2] That God is the Judge is a recurrent theme of the Old Testament, Ps. l. 6; lxxv. 7; xcvi. 13; xcviii. 9, etc.

[3] See on iii. 17, p. 130 above.

The intention behind this surrender of the Father's prerogative of judgement is that the Son may receive the same honour as the Father.[1] Men can indeed only honour the Father if they honour his Son, who is in all things, and in both directions, the intermediary between God and man.[2] So conversely to hate the Son is to hate the Father (xv. 23).

That the Father **sent** the Son is a frequent theme of the FG,[3] emphasising both the Son's utter dependence on the Father and, paradoxically enough, at the same time his sovereign freedom[4] as his accredited representative.[5]

24. This saying draws together several important themes. That of **eternal life**[6] comes in naturally after the mention of resurrection in verse 21. Here it is explained that **eternal life** is not simply a hope for the future (as verse 21 might be taken to imply), but is the present possession of **the man who listens to**[7] the Son's **word and believes him who sent** him. Here the themes of the 'word'[8] and 'belief'[9] are again woven into the pattern. Believing the Father is the natural consequence of listening to the Son, and is impossible without it, cf. xii. 44. Conversely, to believe in the Father involves believing in Christ (xiv. 1), so close in their collaboration.

Since the believer already possesses eternal life, he **does not come into judgement** (cf. iii. 18), **but has passed from death into life** (cf. iii. 16; viii. 51).[10] That this is indeed the

---

[1] Cf. 1 John ii. 23; Phil. ii. 10 f.

[2] Cf. xiii. 20, and the similar Synoptic saying, Mark ix. 37 = Matt. x. 40 = Luke ix. 48, and John xiv. 6 b.

[3] See p. 129, n. 1, above.

[4] Cf. v. 21.

[5] See on i. 6, p. 75 .

[6] See on iii. 15, p. 128.

[7] This is the first time in the FG that ἀκούω ('hear') has this characteristic Old Testament meaning, virtually equivalent to 'obey' (cf. Gen. xlii. 21; Jer. vii. 13, etc.; with 'the word of the Lord' as object cf. Amos vii. 16, etc.); for further examples, cf. vi. 60 'Who can listen to it (i.e. 'this word')?'; viii. 43 (again with 'my word' as object), 47; ix. 27; x. 3, 8, 16, 20, 27; xii. 47; xviii. 37. A closely related use occurs in ix. 31; xi. 41 f., with 'God' as subject. In iv. 42 'hearing' is contrasted with believing on someone else's authority. For the connexion between hearing and believing cf. Rom. x. 14 ff.

[8] See Introduction, p. 4. For the words of Jesus giving life cf. vi. 63, 68.

[9] Cf. i. 7, 12, and, for the connexion between belief and life, iii. 15 f., 36; vi. 40, 47; xi. 25 f.; xx. 31. For 'word' as object of 'believe' cf. ii. 22 (see note ad loc., p. 120); iv. 41, 50; v. 47.

[10] The same verb (μεταβαίνω) is used of Jesus' passing from this world (xiii. 1).

actual experience of Christians John testifies in his own person,
1 John iii. 14, though it is love, not faith, which is the ground
of this experience in the Epistle.

(25) 'Amen, amen, I say to you[1] that the time is coming
and is now, when the dead shall hear the voice of the
Son of God, and those who have heard shall live. (26) For
as the Father has life in himself, so also he gave to the
Son to have life in himself; (27) and gave him authority to
pass judgement, because he is Son of man. (28) Stop being
astonished at this, because the time is coming in which
all who are in the tombs shall hear his voice, (29) and
will come out, those who have done good to the resurrection of life, and those who have done evil to the resurrection of judgement.'

25. John elaborates on the previous verse, bringing in a
fresh theme, that **the time**[2] for attaining life is indeed imminent: **the spiritually dead shall hear the voice of the Son
of God, and . . . live.** There is in these words, characteristically,
also an allusion to the physically dead, made explicit in verse
28, and designed to carry on from verse 21 the preparation for
the sixth sign, the calling of the physically dead Lazarus from
his tomb, the acted parable of the life-giving power of Christ
both in the rousing of the spiritually dead and in the general
resurrection. This is the first mention of the **voice** of Jesus (i.e.
his spoken word), except for a passing reference in iii. 29. Like his
word (verse 24, cf. vi. 63), it is charged with power—thus Jesus
calls 'with a loud voice' to raise Lazarus (xi. 43). For the significance of hearing Jesus' voice cf. also x. 3, 16, 27; xviii. 37.

26. This verse restates and amplifies 21, as 27 does 22, and
28 f. 24 f. Since **the Father** is the living God (cf. Deut. v. 26;
Ps. xlii. 2; Jer. x. 10; etc.) with whom is the fountain of life
(Ps. xxxvi. 9), he **has life in himself,** and **gave to the Son
to have life in himself,** whereby he is the principle of life in
all that exists (i. 4).

27. He also has **authority**[3] **to pass judgement, because he
is Son of man.**[4] So also in the Synoptic Gospels **the Son of
man** is judge—both in the present, for it is as judge that he

---

[1] See on i. 51, p. 105.   [2] ὥρα. See on iv. 23.
[3] ἐξουσία cf. i. 12.   [4] See on i. 51.

has authority to forgive sins (Mark ii. 10), and in the Last
Judgement (Matt. xxv. 31 ff.).

28. The form of the prohibition[1] suggests that there were
some signs of astonishment among Jesus' hearers. It was his
assertion that he would come 'with the clouds of heaven', like
the 'one like a son of man' in Dan. vii. 13, which the High
Priest condemned as blasphemy (Mark xiv. 62). This involves
taking **this** as referring to the previous verse, and rejecting the
translation, 'Do not be astonished at this, that[2] the time is
coming . . .', which is grammatically possible, but inferior.

This time, thinking exclusively of the general resurrection,
Jesus says only **the time is coming** (cf. iv. 21, and contrast v. 25).
The mention of **the tombs** makes this reference quite explicit,
and also completes the preparation for the raising of Lazarus.

29. The alternatives of **life** and **judgement** recall the
separation of the sheep and the goats in Matt. xxv. 31 ff., and
especially 46, as well as John iii. 16 f.

Bultmann[3] regards 28 f., as a redactional addition, belonging
neither to the source nor to the evangelist himself, but designed
to bring the passage more into line with popular eschatology.
But this passage is not inconsistent with the previous verses.
The **resurrection of life** is the public recognition of what has
already been granted to the believers; at the general resurrection
those who have done evil will no longer be able to shun the
light (cf. iii. 20), but will be condemned. If the passage is an
addition, it was made by John himself.

**(30) 'I cannot do anything of my own accord;[4] as I hear,
I judge; and my judgement is just, because I do not seek
my own will but the will of him who sent me.'**

This verse recapitulates the previous paragraph, and leads up
to the one which follows.

Just as Jesus did not perform his acts of healing on his own

---

[1] μὴ θαυμάζετε, as in ii. 16, 'Stop making . . .' (see p. 115, n. 4) and v. 14.
Contrast μὴ θαυμάσῃς, iii. 7.

[2] ὅτι can mean 'because' and 'that' (introducing indirect speech).

[3] Pp. 196 f. He points out that 'do good', 'resurrection of life' and 'resurrection of judgement' do not occur elsewhere in the FG. But 'do evil' does
(iii. 20). His contention that κρίσις ('judgement') here means 'condemnation'
only in the FG is not correct: cf. verse 24.

[4] ἀπ' ἐμαυτοῦ, literally, 'from myself'. Cf. vii. 17, 28; viii. 28, 42; x. 18;
xiv. 10.

initiative (verse 19), so neither does he exercise the authority to judge which his Father has given him (verse 22) without reference to his Father's will, but he listens to him (cf. viii. 26, 40) and judges accordingly. So his **judgement is just** because it has nothing of self-interest in it; Jesus' sole aim is to do his Father's will (cf. iv. 34; vi. 38-40; and his words in Gethsemane in the Synoptic Gospels, and particularly Luke xxii. 42).

(31) **'If I bear witness about myself, my witness is not true.**[1] **(32) There is someone else who bears witness about me, and I know that the witness which he bears about me is true.**[1] **(33) You have sent to John, and he has borne witness to the truth. (34) But I do not** ⟨**mention him because I**⟩ **accept the witness from a man, but I say these things in order that you may be saved. (35) He was the lamp which is lit**[2] **and shines, and you were willing to rejoice for a time in his light. (36) But the witness which I have is greater than John's; for the works which the Father has given me to complete, the very works which I am doing, bear witness about me that the Father has sent me. (37) And it is the Father who sent me that**[3] **has borne witness about me. You have never yet heard his voice or seen his form. (38) And you do not have his word staying in you, because you do not believe him whom he sent. (39) You search the Scriptures, because you think that it is in them that you have eternal life; yet it is they which bear witness about me; (40) and you are not willing to come to me in order to have life.'**

31. The important theme of **witness**[4] is now brought into the discourse. Jesus has made, in the previous paragraph, a

---

[1] ἀληθής. See on i. 9.

[2] ὁ λύχνος ὁ καιόμενος. Not 'that burneth' (RV), but cf. Matt. v. 15, 'Nor do they light a lamp (καίουσιν λύχνον). . . .' [F. Neugebauer, 'Miszelle zu Joh 5.₃₅', *Z.N.W.*, Vol. LII, 1961, p. 130, finds here an allusion to Ps. cxxxii (LXX, cxxxi). 17b, 'I have prepared a lamp (λύχνον) for my anointed'; the previous verse in the LXX contains the verb 'to rejoice', which appears later in this verse in John. This is perhaps more probable than T. F. Glasson's suggestion (*Moses in the Fourth Gospel* (1963), p. 28, n. 2) that this description of the Baptist reflects Ecclus. xlviii. 1, 'Then the prophet Elijah arose like a fire, and his word burned like a torch (λαμπὰς ἐκαίετο).'—B. A. M.]

[3] See p. 85, n. 2.   [4] See on i. 7, etc.

number of claims about himself, hitherto uncorroborated by
other witnesses. He admits that his own claims are not acceptable as evidence, as the Pharisees also assert (viii. 13), though
he apparently contradicts himself by saying at viii. 14, that even
if he is bearing witness about himself his witness is true. But
the contradiction is more apparent than real. Jesus is so inti-
mately associated with his Father in all that he says and does
that he never is in fact a solitary, uncorroborated witness (cf.
viii. 16).

32. So here too, **there is someone else who bears witness,** whose **witness . . . is true. 33.** One might suppose that
this was **John** the Baptist, who had **borne witness to the
truth** (in what he had said about Jesus, i. 19 ff.; iii. 27 ff.) when
the Jews had sent their deputation to him. 34. But Jesus does
not need human witness; he only mentions John in the hope
that the Jews may still believe his witness and **be saved. 35.** For
though John's light was merely derivative (cf. i. 8), like that
of a **lamp,** yet he was sent from God (i. 6), and his ministry had
kindled an enthusiasm which, if it had not just lasted **for a time,**
could have led the Jews to salvation, for it pointed to Jesus.

36. Jesus appeals to a **witness . . . greater than John's,** i.e.
greater than that which John bore.[1] It is that of **the works
which the Father has given** him **to complete** (cf. iv. 34),
which are of course signs (cf. xx. 30 f.). Nicodemus had admitted their value as evidence (iii. 2), and Jesus will appeal to
them again (x. 25, 38; xiv. 11; xv. 24), as he did in his reply to
John the Baptist's messengers (Matt. xi. 4 f., Luke vii. 22). 37.
Thus the 'someone else' (verse 32) is **the Father who sent**[2]
him (cf. viii. 18).

But the Jews do not accept this witness because they do not
really know the Father at all (cf. vii. 28; viii. 19, 55; xv. 21).
They **have never yet heard his voice or seen his form.**
For this they can hardly be blamed, for no one has ever yet seen
God (i. 18). But they can be blamed for neglecting their oppor-
tunity of knowing him through his Son, to see whom is to see

---

[1] μείζω τοῦ Ἰωάννου, literally, 'greater than John'. This is best interpreted
as an example of a Semitic idiom found also, e.g., in Isaiah x. 10, literally,
'whose idols were greater than Jerusalem and Samaria' (so Black, p. 87).

[2] See p. 129, n. 1 (on iii. 17).

the Father (xiv. 9). When later a voice is heard from heaven, they misinterpret it (xii. 28 ff.). 38. Their refusal to accept the witness of Jesus' works shows that they **do not have his word staying in them.** There is here a possible allusion to Jesus as the Logos [1] who stays [2] in the believers.

39 f. Moreover, they misunderstand **the Scriptures,** which they study so diligently (cf. 2 Cor. iii. 13-16). As St Paul observes (Rom. x. 2), 'they have a zeal for God, but it is not enlightened'. The word translated **you search** could also be an Imperative 'search', and is so understood by the majority of ancient commentators. But the Indicative gives a better sense in the context. The Jews are quite right to **think that it is in them that** they have **eternal life,** but do not realise that this is only so because **they bear witness about** the Son, and so they do not go to him, the source of life (i. 4); cf. iii. 20 f.; vi. , 65; xiv. 6.

There is a close parallel to verse 39 in the Egerton Papyrus 2, a second-century fragment of an unknown Gospel, the precise relationship of which to the FG is obscure. It reads, 'You search the Scriptures *in which* you think that you have life': the variant 'in which' for 'because' in the FG is cited by Black [3] as an example of an alternative translation of the ambiguous Aramaic particle d^e, thus pointing to an Aramaic source for this passage.

(41) 'I do not accept glory from men. (42) But I know that you do not have love for God in yourselves. (43) I have come in my Father's name, and you do not accept me; if someone else comes in his own name, you will accept him. (44) How can you believe, when you accept glory from one another, and do not seek the glory ⟨that is⟩ from the One? [4] **(45) Do not think** [5] **that I will accuse you**

[1] See Introduction, p. 4.   [2] Cf. i. 38 and iv. 40.
[3] Pp. 54 f. Barrett, however, questions this, p. 223.
[4] Literally, 'the Only' (τοῦ μόνου), the reading of P⁶⁶ BW *a b eg arm.* Other authorities add 'God' (θεοῦ). The expression 'the Only' is unparalleled in the FG, and therefore more liable to emendation. The change of ΤΟΥΜΟ‾ΝΟΥΟΥ to ΤΟΥΜΟΝΟΥΘΥΟΥ by an accidental dittography is rather more likely than the omission of Θ‾Υ (cf. i. 18, p. 85, n. 1). For the opposite view, see Barrett, p. 224.
[5] μὴ δοκεῖτε. The force of the imperative here is, 'Do not, as you are liable to, think'. See on ii. 16, p. 115, n. 4, and Moulton, *Prolegomena*, p. 125. [Cf. B.-D. §336 (3), Turner, p. 76.—B. A. M.]

to the Father; there is someone who accuses you
—Moses, in whom you have placed your hope. (46)
For if you believed Moses, you would believe me; for
⟨it was⟩ about me ⟨that⟩ he wrote. (47) But if you do
not believe his writings, how will you believe my
words?'

41. Jesus does **not accept glory from men**—unlike the
Jews (verse 44)—but his glory is from the Father (cf. i. 14;
vii. 18; viii. 54; xvii. 1 ff.); he says this to explain that his criticism of them is not due to personal disappointment at not
receiving the glory he might have expected. 42. Then, with that
assured knowledge of character and motive which the evangelist has already noted (ii. 24 f.), he explains why the Jews are
unwilling to approach him (verse 40)—it is because they **do not
have love for God**; they prefer the darkness (iii. 19 f.). The
words **love for God** (τὴν ἀγάπην τοῦ θεοῦ) could also be translated 'God's love (for them)'; John may be intentionally ambiguous, but even if he is, the objective sense in the genitive is
probably predominant.

43. Jesus comes in his **Father's name**, i.e. as his representative, sent by him (iii. 17, etc.), and, as such, is rejected.
Here the 'coming' of the Christ, the complement of his
'sending', first becomes an explicit theme in the FG, though
there are many hints of it earlier.[1]

The illogicality of the Jews is shown by the fact that **if someone else comes** (i.e. as Messiah) **in his own name** (i.e. without the divine witness which Jesus has) they **will accept him**,
taking his claims at their face value. This in fact happened in
the case of Simon bar Kochba (or Kozeba), leader of the last
Jewish revolt (A.D. 132–135), and these words have been taken
as an allusion to him. This would, however, imply an impossibly
late date for the FG. The Fathers took this saying as a prophecy
of Antichrist (cf. Mark xiii. 22; Matt. xxiv. 5), but there is
probably no precise reference to any individual. There is a
close parallel in thought here to St Paul's prophecy of the

[1] Cf. i. 9, 11 (where the refusal of 'his own' to accept him, emphasised in
the present verse, is also stated); iii. 19; John's prophecies, i. 15, 27, 30; iii. 31;
Nicodemus, iii. 2; it recurs in vi. 14; vii. 27 f., 31; viii. 42; ix. 39; x. 10; xi. 27;
xii. 13, 46, 47.

'lawless one' (2 Thess. ii. 8-12), which is equally imprecise.
The main point is that the Jews are so impervious to
divine influence that they naturally accept one of their own
kind.

44. It is this which makes them unable to **believe.** The
word **believe** is probably used here, as in iv. 53, etc., to indicate real faith, something more than just accepting as true what
Jesus says (as in verse 38). The reason for their unbelief (and
the credulity mentioned in verse 43) is that they **accept glory
from one another** (cf. Matt. xxiii. 5 ff.) and forget the only
source of true glory (cf. Rom. x. 3). They have made of their
religion an idol which obscures God while it flatters their own
vanity, cf. xii. 43; Rom. ii. 29.

45. But Jesus will not complain to the Father of their treatment of his representative, any more than he judges men (iii.
17; viii. 15). Both are indeed unnecessary: men judge themselves (iii. 18 f.); the Jews already have an accuser, ironically enough, Moses, whose disciples they claim to be (ix.
28), the advocate of Israel (Jer. xv. 1), who stood before
the Lord to turn away his wrath (Ps. cvi. 23; Exod. xxxii. 11
ff.).

46. The Jews' unbelief is due to their misunderstanding of
Moses (cf. 39 f.). It was about Jesus that **he wrote** (cf. i. 45),
as did the prophets (cf. i. 45; xii. 38 ff.). 47. For the connexion
between believing the Scripture(s) and believing the word(s) of
Jesus cf. ii. 22. John, like St Paul, claims the Old Testament for
the Christian Church, and in this both follow the example of
Jesus, whose understanding of his mission was based upon it.
How far John is dependent here upon actual sayings of Jesus is,
however, impossible to decide.

This discourse deals with one of the main topics of the
FG—the problem of Israel's unbelief. It develops themes
from iii. 16 ff., and has many points of contact with the
passages of controversy which follow, particularly with vii.
15 ff. (which may well have followed v. 47 without a break in
John's source), as well as with xii. 37 ff. The connexion
between v. 47 and vii. 15 is broken by the insertion of vi, in
order to preserve the evangelist's pattern (see on iv. 46 and
v. 1).

**vi. (1) After this Jesus went away across the lake of
Galilee, ⟨that is⟩ of Tiberias. (2) And there was a great
crowd following him, because they observed** [1] **the signs
which he did on those who were ill. (3) And Jesus went
up into the hill-country, and was sitting there with his
disciples. (4) And the Passover, the feast of the Jews, was
near.**

1 f. The words **after this** [2] and the Imperfects **was . . .
following, observed** and **did** imply that there had been an
interval during which Jesus had performed many **signs** not
recorded in the FG, after which he **went away across the
lake.** For the enthusiasm engendered by Jesus' signs cf. ii.
23; iv. 45; his retirement suggests that he distrusted it (cf. ii.
24).

In John's source this section of the Gospel probably followed
immediately after iv. 46-54 (an example of Jesus' activity during
this period) and so did not have the *non sequitur* there is now
between v. 47 and vi. 1,[3] similar to that between iv. 54 and v. 1.

As in Mark, the Feeding of the Multitude which follows is
the climax of the Galilean ministry.[4]

3. Jesus' withdrawal **into the hill-country,** accompanied by
his **disciples,** and pursued by the crowd, recalls Mark iii.
13 = Matt. v. 1; Luke vi. 12; and Matt. xv. 29. The fact that
Jesus **sat down** (i.e. to teach) is one of the few points of
similarity between the FG and Matthew. The resemblance
to Matt. xv. 29 is particularly striking, for it is the introduction
to his second Feeding story, the Marcan version of which
(viii. 1) mentions neither the hill-country nor Jesus' sitting
down.

4. This is the second **Passover** mentioned in the FG (cf.

---

[1] ἐθεώρουν. See p. 191. [2] See p. 131, n. 4.

[3] Jerusalem is the last place mentioned as the FG now stands: vi. 1 would
be much more natural if it followed iv. 46-54, which describes an incident at
Cana in Galilee. See the notes on v. 1 and 47.

[4] For the question of the possible dependence of John on Mark see the
Introduction, p. 9. Points of detail will be noticed here as they arise.

ii. 13), and John's words **the feast of the Jews** recall the similar expression there.[1] In John's source it was presumably the feast also mentioned as near in v. 1. John preserves it for its symbolic value rather than from any concern for chronology. None of the other evangelists mentions it in any account of the Feeding, but this does not necessarily mean that John is responsible for importing it into his narrative. The mention of 'green grass' in Mark vi. 39 shows that it took place in the spring.

(5) Jesus then raised his eyes and noticing[2] that a great crowd was coming towards him said to Philip, 'Where are we to buy loaves for these to eat?' (6) But he said this to test him; for he knew himself what he was going to do. (7) Philip answered him, 'Two hundred shillings[3] worth of loaves is not enough for each of them to have a small piece.' (8) One of his disciples, Andrew, Simon Peter's brother, said to him, (9) 'There is a boy[4] here who has five barley loaves and two fish; but what ⟨use⟩ are these for so many?'

5. Mark vi. 34 and Matt. xiv. 14 both mention Jesus' seeing the approaching crowd, Luke ix. 11 his welcoming them. These three stories also confirm the impression given by John (see verse 3 above) that Jesus was on this occasion trying to escape the crowds (cf. Mark vi. 31-33, Matt. xiv. 13, Luke ix. 10, 11) but do not mention the hill-country—Matt. xv. 29 is unique in locating a Feeding there. In all the five Synoptic accounts of a Feeding the crowd has already spent a considerable time with Jesus (a whole day, Mark vi. 34, Matt. xiv. 14, Luke ix. 11; three days, Mark viii. 2, Matt. xv. 32). In John, however, they are apparently fed as soon as they come to Jesus, and there is no explanation either of their need or of Jesus' motive in feeding them. John does not mention Jesus' compassion, either in teaching (as in Mark vi. 34) or in feeding the crowd (as in Mark viii. 2). His narrative thus lacks verisimilitude in comparison

---

[1] See the note on ii. 13.

[2] θεασάμενος. See note on i. 14, p. 81, n. 3.

[3] δηνάρια. The *denarion* was a hired labourer's daily wage (cf. Matt. xx. 2): its silver content was rather less than a shilling, but its purchasing power must have been at least equal to a pound sterling today. Bread was probably much dearer, relatively to other goods, in the ancient world than it is today.

[4] παιδάριον. This word is ambiguous. It can mean either a youth or a slave.

with the Synoptic evangelists. His main interest is in the sign, and when he mentions details, it must be supposed to be for their symbolic significance rather than their historical value. The mention of the **crowd . . . coming towards him** may be for this reason, as vi. 35 will make clear.

The mention of **Philip** (as of Andrew later) has no parallel in the other Gospels. He has a relatively important rôle in the FG, cf. i. 43 ff.; xii. 21 f. (where Andrew also is mentioned); xiv. 8 f. This may indicate an interest in Philip as an apostle associated with Asia Minor—if the Asian Philip was indeed the apostle.[1]

Jesus' question, **'Where are we to buy loaves?'** contrasts with his command to the disciples in Mark vi. 37, and their question to him in Mark viii. 4. 6. As in his first sign at Cana, to which this corresponds in the pattern of the Gospel, Jesus (as indeed always) is in complete control of the situation, even when he accepts assistance and suggestions from others (as he does in both these signs).

7. **Philip** shows a similar, though not perhaps quite so understandable, lack of comprehension in xiv. 8. His remark closely resembles the disciples' question in Mark vi. 37, particularly in its estimate of **two hundred shillings worth of loaves.** This coincidence is striking, as is that of the numbers of loaves and fish used, men fed, and baskets of fragments. To some, these coincidences are sufficient to establish John's dependence on Mark. The argument that oral tradition would not preserve the numbers accurately would be more convincing if it was certain that Jesus only fed a crowd once during his ministry.

8 f. **Andrew** is more enterprising. Whereas in Mark vi. 38 and viii. 5 Jesus asks how much bread the disciples have, here **Andrew** produces **a boy** (whom the other Gospels do not mention) **who has five barley loaves** (the poorest kind) **and two fish** (Mark vi. 38 has the same numbers, but does not mention **barley,** and has a different word for **fish**[2]). Thus the initiative passes for a moment from Jesus. John is unlikely to

---

[1] See Introduction, p. 43.

[2] John uses ὀψάρια, as also in xxi. 9, 10, 13; Mark ἰχθύες, which John uses for the fish just caught by the disciples, xxi. 6, 8, 11. ὀψάρια can mean dried fish.

have allowed this unless it was in his source—which was not
Mark at this point. There may be here some symbolic significance, in that the **boy** anticipates the eucharistic offertory. The
parallel is not very close, but John must not be supposed to be
inventing for the sake of symbolism. There is a possibility of
eucharistic symbolism also in the first miracle at Cana, the
counterpart of this in the pattern of the FG.[1]

At this point some parallels may be noted to the story of
Elisha, who fed a hundred men with twenty **barley loaves**
(2 Kings iv. 42-44), provided by someone else, and assisted by
his servant. In John, however, the **boy** does not play the same
part as Elisha's servant, who rather resembles Philip in his
scepticism. So we need not suppose that the **boy** is in fact a
slave.[2] Nor does John appear to press the parallel.

**(10) Jesus said, 'Make the people sit down'. And there
was much grass in the place. So the men sat down, in
number about five thousand. (11) Then Jesus took the
loaves, gave thanks, and distributed them to them as
they were sitting down; and in the same way as much
of the fish as they wanted. (12) And when they had had
enough, he said to his disciples, 'Collect the pieces
which are left over, so that nothing is wasted'. (13) So
they collected them, and filled twelve baskets with the
pieces of the five barley loaves, which were left over
after they had eaten. (14) So when the people saw the
sign which he had done, they said, 'This is truly the
prophet who was to come into the world'.**

10. All five Synoptic accounts have the command to **sit
down,** in various forms, but only Mark vi. 39 and Matt. xiv. 19
mention the **grass,** and (with Luke ix. 14) give the number fed
as **five thousand.**

11. As host, Jesus **gave thanks, and distributed** the food,
as he would have done at any meal. The word translated **gave
thanks** ($\epsilon \dot{v} \chi \alpha \rho \iota \sigma \tau \acute{\eta} \sigma \alpha s$) is of course related to that from which
eucharist is derived, and it is found in all accounts of the Last
Supper (Mark xiv. 23, Matt. xxvi. 27, Luke xxii. 17, 19, 1 Cor.
xi. 24) and also in Mark viii. 6 and Matt. xv. 36. The other
Synoptic accounts of the Feeding use the synonym $\epsilon \dot{v} \lambda o \gamma \acute{\epsilon} \omega$,

[1] See on ii. 5, p. 111.   [2] See also Barrett, p. 229.

found also in Mark xiv. 22 and Matt. xxvi. 26, but there is little significance in the variant. John does not, however, mention two actions which have a possible eucharistic significance; the breaking of the bread, found in all accounts of the Last Supper (Mark xiv. 22, Matt. xxvi. 26, Luke xxii. 19, 1 Cor. xi. 24) as well as in Mark viii. 6, Matt. xiv. 19; xv. 36 (cf. for its eucharistic significance 1 Cor. x. 16); and the distribution of the food by the disciples, found in all Synoptic accounts of the Feeding (Mark vi. 41; viii. 6, Matt. xiv. 19; xv. 36, Luke ix. 16). Thus, if John is at all interested in eucharistic symbolism, he can hardly have been utilising Mark as a source. His narrative is probably less influenced by it than any of the other evangelists.

12 f. All the other evangelists' accounts agree that there was more than enough food for all, though instead of John's **had enough** (literally, 'were filled', ἐνεπλήσθησαν) they use the rather vulgar ἐχορτάσθησαν, used properly of feeding animals (cf. Rev. xix. 21),[1] which also occurs in John vi. 26 (Mark vi. 42; viii. 8, Matt. xiv. 20; xv. 37, Luke ix. 17); it was a real meal which Jesus gave the people. They also all relate the collection of the fragments, Mark vi. 43, Matt. xiv. 20, and Luke ix. 17 also agreeing that **they filled twelve baskets,** and using John's word κόφινος[2] for 'basket'. The careful avoidance of any waste of the bread was natural for a Jew (only a Gentile would let dogs eat bread from the table, Mark vii. 28 = Matt. xv. 27), but was also characteristic of the Eucharist.[3]

14. After the first sign at Cana, Jesus' disciples believed in him (ii. 11), as did the men at the passover in Jerusalem, when they saw the signs which he did (ii. 23). So now, **when the people saw the sign which he had done,** they confessed him **the prophet who was to come into the world,** but the sequel shows that their faith was no more secure than that of the men at Jerusalem (ii. 24).[4]

[1] It is connected with the word χόρτος, 'grass'.
[2] Apart from the Feeding stories, the word only occurs in a variant reading in Codex Bezae, Luke xiii. 8, 'a basket of manure'.
[3] Cf. *Apostolic Constitutions*, viii. 13, which mentions the deacons taking up the bread left over (τὰ περισσεύσαντα, the word used by John), as the disciples do in John. See Lagrange, p. 165. See also on vi. 38 f.
[4] See on vi. 30.

The following verse suggests that by **the prophet** they meant the Messiah—

(15) Then when Jesus realised that they were about to come and seize him, in order to make him King, he fled[1] back into the hill-country alone ⟨by⟩ himself.[2]

The miraculous powers which he had just displayed must have seemed to them to make him an excellent candidate for the throne of David. Both in i. 21 and vii. 40, however, as in the *Manual of Discipline*, ix. 11, 'the prophet' is distinguished from 'the Messiah' (or Messiahs). The feeding of the people in the wilderness would suggest that Jesus was the prophet like Moses promised in Deut. xviii. 15 ff., and in the discourse which follows the Mosaic precedent is brought out (vi. 31 f.). Again, Elijah, whose return had been prophesied by Mal. iv. 5, may have been in their minds. But we cannot expect theological precision from an excited crowd.[3]

15. Jesus was indeed king, but, as he explains to Pilate (xviii. 36) his kingship was not of this world, as it would have been if he had let the crowd have its way. It may indeed have been while Jesus was in the hills after this that he was tempted to aim at an earthly kingship (Matt. iv. 8 ff., Luke iv. 5 ff.). The location of all three Temptations in the wilderness after Jesus' Baptism, where only the first is naturally in place, may reasonably be ascribed to the tendency of the source common to Matthew and Luke to group its material by subject-matter.[4]

Thus the fourth sign ends like the third (v. 13) with Jesus quietly leaving the scene, conscious (as the discourses which follow both signs are intended to indicate) that he has failed to produce the effect he intended.

John here makes plain what Mark leaves unexplained, why Jesus abandoned his public ministry in Galilee when he was apparently at the height of his popularity. It was because he had conjured up a militant nationalistic Messianic hope. Is John's explanation then due to intelligent reading between the lines of

[1] Reading φεύγει (ℵ* a ff² vg cur) in preference to the colourless ἀνεχώρησεν, 'withdrew', of the other authorities, a word not used elsewhere by John.

[2] αὐτὸς μόνος. Cf. xii. 24.   [3] See also on i. 20 f.

[4] The other Temptation, located in the Temple, may belong to the period of the Triumphal Entry.

See also J. Ernest Davey, *The Jesus of St John* (1958), chapter 3.

Mark's story or to the fact that he had a superior source of information? Before this question can be answered, two more must be asked. What did Jesus do on this occasion? What did he mean by his action?

John obviously intends us to understand that Jesus performed a miracle, similar in principle to the first miracle at Cana. It is special pleading to argue, as R. A. Edwards[1] does, that because John does not actually say that Jesus multiplied the loaves, his narrative allows a non-miraculous interpretation. The parallel with the changing of water into wine rules this out. Nevertheless, John (and the Synoptic tradition) may be mistaken. If so, where did they get the story from? From some simple incident, such as Jesus and his disciples sharing their food with a hungry crowd, and by their example inducing others to do the same, so that all were fed? But could such an incident be the turning-point in Jesus' ministry? He must surely have done *something* to rouse the specifically Messianic hopes of the crowd. A more plausible explanation is that Jesus gave the food to the crowd as a token and pledge of their entry into the kingdom of God. It was an eschatological sacrament, and, in spite of the simplicity and coarseness of the food, a foretaste of the Messianic banquet.[2] It is as such that, in his own way, John interprets it in vi. 26 ff.; and it is not unreasonable to conclude that he does so because he is relying on a source with a better understanding of the situation than Mark had. It may be added that the Old Testament stories of the manna and of Elisha's miracle do not seem to have had much influence on the story in John or in the other Gospels, and that there are no obvious parallels to it in pagan sources.

The misunderstanding of Jesus' action marked the end of his attempt to lead a mass movement into the Kingdom of God. The alternative course which he now began to follow, and

---

[1] *The Gospel according to St John* (1954), p. 57.

[2] Cf. Matt. viii. 11 = Luke xiii. 29; Luke xiv. 15, and the parables in which the Kingdom is represented by a feast, Matt. xxii. 2 ff. = Luke xiv. 16 ff.; Matt. xxv. 1 ff. (cf. Rev. xix. 7). The same idea may underlie the petition in the Lord's Prayer, Matt. vi. 11 (= Luke xi. 3), 'Give us today our bread of the coming ⟨kingdom⟩' (ἄρτον . . . ἐπιούσιον). This is the explanation of A. Schweitzer (*The Quest of the Historical Jesus*, pp. 374 f., 377 f.) except that he regarded the meal as only a token one.

which led to the Cross, will be seen foreshadowed in the discourse, vi. 26 ff.

(16) But when it was evening, his disciples went down to the lake, (17) got into ⟨their⟩ boat, and crossed the lake towards Capernaum. And it was already dark, and Jesus had not yet come to them. (18) And the lake grew rough, for there was a gale blowing. (19) Then when they had sailed about three or four miles [1] they observed [2] Jesus walking by the lake [3] and getting near the boat; and they were afraid. (20) But he said to them, 'It is I; do not be afraid'. (21) Then they wanted to take him into the boat; and at once the boat got by the land to which they were going.

16. Jesus had gone up into the hills, leaving not only the crowd, but his disciples (contrast verse 3). At a loss what to do, the disciples waited until evening, and then (17) started back to Capernaum, whence apparently they had set out (though John does not say so). Mark vi. 45 f. and vii. 10 tell a different story. Both say that Jesus sent the crowd away, and vi. 45 that Jesus made his disciples get into the boat, while he himself went up into the hills to pray, and viii. 10 that he got into the boat with his disciples. John's version has the greater verisimilitude.

The mention of the darkness has a deeper significance; cf. i. 5; iii. 2; viii. 12; xi. 10; xii. 35 f.; xiii. 30. It symbolises the lost and bewildered state of the disciples when **Jesus had not yet come to them.**

18. Mark vi. 48 mentions that the wind was against the disciples, though Mark iv. 37 affords a closer parallel to this verse.

19. In Mark vi. 47 the disciples were in the middle of the lake, which has a maximum width of seven miles. But before it is assumed that there is here an undesigned coincidence be-

---

[1] Literally, 'twenty-five or thirty stades' The στάδιον was about two hundred yards, the length of the race-course at Olympia.

[2] θεωροῦσιν. See p. 191.

[3] ἐπὶ τῆς θαλάσσης, usually translated, 'on the lake', but the same preposition and construction is used in verse 21, where ἐπὶ τῆς γῆς must mean 'by the land'. For the question whether John meant a miracle here, see below, p. 183.

tween Mark and John, it should be remembered that the
disciples were making for Capernaum, which was nearly at the
head of the lake; three or four miles had nearly brought them
to their destination (cf. verse 21).

Meanwhile Jesus had apparently already started back to
Capernaum, taking the shortest route along the shore, **by the
lake.** If it were not for Mark's story, in which περιπατῶν ἐπὶ τῆς
θαλάσσης (the same phrase, admittedly, which John uses)
means 'walking *on* the lake', and for the assumption that John
is dependent on Mark, no one reading John would suppose that
he was describing a miracle.[1] It may seem like straining out a
gnat and swallowing a camel to accept John vi. 1-14 as describing a miracle, and then to boggle at vi. 16-21, but the same consideration in fact applies in both cases—the former corresponds,
in the pattern of the FG, to the first sign at Cana, which was a
miracle, the second to the Cleansing of the Temple, which was
not.

The fear of the disciples is sufficiently explained, not by
bringing in the ghost from Mark vi. 49, but by the fact that they
suddenly realised that they were off a lee shore, and at the
mercy of a gale.

20. Jesus' words need not have any deeper meaning; the
disciples had not recognised him (after all, it was at night), but
they would know his voice. So he shouts, 'It's me!' (cf. ix. 9).
But it is never safe to assume that John does not intend a deeper
meaning, and we should perhaps see here another instance of
the self-revelation of the Logos.[2] Mark vi. 50 has the identical
words, 'It is I; do not be afraid' ('Εγώ εἰμι· μὴ φοβεῖσθε[3]).

21. In John the disciples **wanted to take** Jesus **into the
boat,** but presumably did not, for they found they were at their
destination.[4] In Mark vi. 51, however, Jesus got into the boat,
and the wind fell. John does not mention the wind.

This little story was found by John in his source, and he kept
it because it could serve as a corollary to the Feeding miracle.
That shows Jesus as 'the life' (as the discourse will explain)

---

[1] But see Barrett, pp. 233 f.　　　　[2] See note on iv. 26.

[3] For the construction, cf. ii. 16; v. 28 and the notes *ad locc.*

[4] To see in these words an allusion to Ps. cvii. 30, 'So he bringeth them
unto the haven where they would be' (see Barrett, p. 234) is possible only
if one regards the episode as miraculous.

this appends an illustration of the fact that 'the life was the light of men', and so adds a modest *tessera* to the mosaic of the FG. In Mark, however, we see the story on the way to becoming the full-blown miracle of Matt. xiv. 22-33.

(22) The next day the crowd which was standing on the other side of the lake realised[1] that there had not been[2] any other boat there but one, and that Jesus had not got into it with his disciples, but that his disciples had gone away alone. (23) (Other[3] boats came from Tiberias near to the place where they had eaten the bread after the Lord had given thanks[4].) (24) So when the crowd saw that Jesus was not there, and that his disciples were not ⟨there⟩ either, they got into the boats themselves, and went to Capernaum seeking Jesus. (25) And when they had found him on the other side of the lake they said to him, 'Rabbi, how long[5] have you been here?'

This passage, which is very clumsily expressed, serves to connect the narrative of the Feeding with the dialogue and discourse in which its meaning is expounded. Its clumsiness is probably due to John's having introduced into his source an explanation of the way in which the crowd had reached Capernaum. If so, **on the other side of the lake** (22) referred originally to the *western* shore (as in 25); all that the source said was that the crowd at Capernaum knew that Jesus had not crossed the lake with his disciples, and that, when they found him there, they asked him, naturally enough, how long he had been there.[6] John (verse 23) introduced the **other boats** which came **from Tiberias** (about half way down the western side

[1] Literally, 'saw' ($\epsilon\tilde{\iota}\delta o\nu$).

[2] $\tilde{\eta}\nu$, imperfect, but with a pluperfect sense.

[3] The MSS. have ΑΛΛΑ, which can be accented either as $\dot{a}\lambda\lambda\dot{a}$ ('but') or $\ddot{a}\lambda\lambda a$ ('others'). In the 64 cases where John has $\dot{a}\lambda\lambda\dot{a}$ before a vowel, he elides the final a 50 times, so that the odds are in favour of the reading $\ddot{a}\lambda\lambda a$, in spite of the abruptness with which the sentence then begins.

[4] D *a d e sin cur* and a few other authorities omit 'after the Lord had given thanks'. Though this may be right, the words are in the style of John—cf. his use of 'the Lord' in similar editorial passages, iv. 1; xi. 2.

[5] $\pi\acute{o}\tau\epsilon$, literally 'When?' acquires the meaning, 'how long?' from the perfect tense of the verb $\gamma\acute{e}\gamma o\nu a s$. See Moulton, *Prolegomena*, p. 146.

[6] We are not meant to infer that they supposed that he had crossed the lake miraculously.

of the lake) to explain how the crowd got to Capernaum (24). But his explanation is not very likely. A whole fleet would have been needed. Then he repeats in 25 that the crowd was **on the other side of the lake,** thus giving to the phrase in 22 the meaning of the *eastern* side.[1]

(26) Jesus answered them and said, 'Amen, amen I say to you,[2] you are seeking me, not because you saw signs, but because you ate of the loaves and were filled.[3] (27) Work, not for the food which perishes, but for the food which lasts until eternal life, which the Son of man[4] shall give you; for him did the Father,[5] ⟨that is,⟩ God, seal.'

26. Instead of answering their question, Jesus accuses the crowd of misunderstanding his actions. Their eagerness for free food resembles the Samaritan woman's for the water which will save her the trouble of going to the well (iv. 15[6]). The plural **signs** is used here (contrast vi. 14) because of vi. 2. Their present misunderstanding is but one example of a general failure to see the real meaning of Jesus' actions, which makes them **signs.**[7] This was the reason for the Jews' failure to believe in Jesus (xii. 37).

The mention of **signs** here recalls Nicodemus' reference to them (iii. 2), and affords a clue to the place of the discourse which follows in the scheme of the FG. It corresponds to iii. 1-21, and its teaching on the Eucharist corresponds to that in iii. 1-21 on Baptism. It follows the corollary to the first sign in the second group of three as iii follows that to the first in the first group.

27. This explains more precisely the meaning of the previous verse. They are not concerned with temporal **food,** but eternal, cf. iv. 14. For this metaphorical use of **food** cf. iv. 34, which suggests that the only **food** which has eternal value is to do God's will—an interpretation which is borne out by verse 29. For **which lasts** ($\mu\acute{\epsilon}\nu\epsilon\iota$, literally 'remains') **until** ($\epsilon\acute{\iota}s$, literally 'into') **eternal life**[8] cf. viii. 35, 'the son remains for ever

---

[1] See Bultmann, pp. 160 f.
[2] See on i. 51, p. 105.
[3] $\dot{\epsilon}\chi o\rho\tau\acute{a}\sigma\theta\eta\tau\epsilon$. See on vi. 12.
[4] See on i. 51, p. 106.
[5] See on i. 18, p. 86.
[6] See Barrett, p. 237.
[7] See note on ii. 11.
[8] See p. 142, n. 4.

(εἰς τὸν αἰῶνα)', and xii. 34, 'the Christ remains for ever'.[1]
Further light is shed on this verse by 1 John ii. 17, 'The world
passes away, and its desire; but he who does God's will remains
for ever'(μένει εἰς τὸν αἰῶνα).

The sharp contrast **not . . . but** is characteristic of Hebrew;
cf. Hos. vi. 6, 'I desire mercy and not sacrifice'. Hosea no more
intends to deny all value to sacrifice than Jesus does to deny all
importance to actual food. A similar thought, expressed differently, is found in Matt. vi. 31-33.[2]

It is not clear whether **food** or **life** is the antecedent of the
relative clause **which the Son of man shall give you;** either
makes sense, but the analogy of 'the water which I shall give'
(iv. 14) suggests that it is in fact **food.**

Everyone who believes on the **Son of man** is to have **eternal
life** (iii. 15).[3] The discourse which follows takes up this theme,
and shows that **eternal life** is given to the believer who eats the
flesh of the Son of man and drinks his blood (vi. 53 f.). There is
no inconsistency between working for the heavenly food and
having it given (cf. verse 29).

That **him did the Father . . . seal** refers to the witness which
God bore to Jesus in his works (v. 36 f.), a witness which the
believer in his turn 'seals' (iii. 33).[4] For Jesus, **the Father** is
sufficient description; **God** is added for his hearers' benefit.[5]

**(28) So they said to him, 'What are we to do, in order
to do the works of God?' (29) Jesus answered and said to
them, 'This is the work of God, to believe in[6] him whom
he sent[7]'.**

[1] These are the only other examples of μένω followed by εἰς in the FG.
Apart from 1 John ii. 17, μένω . . . εἰς τὸν αἰῶνα occurs in 2 Cor. ix. 9 (=Ps.
cxii. 9), Heb. vii. 24, and 1 Pet. i. 25 (= Isa. xl. 8), which (apart from Heb.
vii. 3 μένει . . . εἰς τὸ διηνεκές, identical to it in meaning) are the only examples
of μένω . . . εἰς in the New Testament.

[2] See R. H. Lightfoot, *op. cit.*, p. 166.   [3] See note *ad loc.*

[4] Barrett (p. 238) suggests that there is also an allusion here to the descent
of the Spirit, 'sealing' Jesus as Christians are 'sealed' in baptism (cf. 2 Cor.
i. 22, Eph. i. 13; iv. 30). But the 'seal' metaphor is not one of those used of
baptism in John's Epistles, and the 'sealing' of God's servants in Rev. vii.
3-8 does not refer to their baptism. Bauer (p. 95—see also Bauer[5], s.v., 2 b)
rejects the parallel with iii. 33, and interprets the 'sealing' as Jesus' endowment with power to bestow the heavenly food.

[5] See Lagrange, p. 173.   [6] For the theme of 'belief' see on i. 7, 12; iii. 15 f.

[7] For the 'sending' of the Son see on iii. 17. This theme, found side-by-
side with that of 'belief' in iii. 15 ff. is now united with it.

28. The question takes up the verb 'work' from 27, but gives it a slightly different sense, not 'work for', but **do** (literally, 'work') **the works of God.** The questioners can hardly be expected to have understood the allusion to iv. 34 in verse 27, but they think of the eternal food as a reward of work, and so ask what **works** are expected of them. 29. Jesus answers that only one thing is necessary—**to believe in** God's representative (and so to go to him to receive, not a reward, but his gift). The Pauline antithesis of faith and works does not arise here. Believing in Jesus is more than just believing him (cf. v. 38), i.e. accepting what he says as true; it involves trust and obedience.

(30) So they said to him, 'What sign then are you doing, in order that we may see and believe you? What are you working? (31) Our fathers ate manna in the wilderness, as it is written, "He gave them bread from heaven to eat"'.

30. The Jews demand a **sign**—characteristically (cf. 1 Cor. i. 22)—if they are even to accept what Jesus says as true (**believe,** not 'believe in', as Jesus says in verse 29). The present tenses **are you doing ... are you working** have a future sense.[1] A **sign** had been demanded already (ii. 18)—and refused—as often in the Synoptic Gospels,[2] particularly Mark viii. 11, which follows Mark's second Feeding story. Barrett regards this as further evidence that John was following Mark.[3]

R. A. Edwards' contention that this demand indicates that the Feeding was not thought to be miraculous,[4] not only ignores vi. 14, but misrepresents the argument. The people had already seen one sign, and on the strength of it had confessed Jesus to be 'the prophet', and had tried to make him king (vi. 14 f.). That had apparently not satisfied his ambition. If then he claims to be more than they are so far prepared to admit, he must do something more impressive to prove it. 31. Moses gave their ancestors **manna—bread from heaven**[5]—not barley loaves—can Jesus do that? That would indeed prove him God's

[1] See Moulton, *Prolegomena*, p. 120.　　　[2] See notes on ii. 11 and 18 f.
[3] P. 239.　　　[4] *Op. cit.*, p. 57.
[5] The phrase **bread from heaven** occurs in Exodus xvi. 4, but there is no exact parallel to the quotation in the Old Testament. The closest is Ps. lxxviii. 24.

Messiah—for it was believed that in the days of the Messiah Israel would again be given manna.[1]

(32) So Jesus said to them, 'Amen, amen I say to you,[2] ⟨it was⟩ not Moses ⟨who⟩ gave you the bread from heaven, but ⟨it is⟩ my Father ⟨who⟩ gives you the real[3] bread from heaven. (33) For God's bread is that which comes down from heaven and gives life to the world.'

32. Jesus again does not answer a question put to him, but corrects the questioners' misunderstanding instead. His saying is very compressed, almost to obscurity. He first reminds them that it was **not Moses** who gave the manna, but God, and then (with the implication that, though it came from the *skies*, the manna was not really **bread from heaven)** adds that there is, however, a **real bread from heaven** which is given by God (and of which manna is the type.)

33. This verse is ambiguous—perhaps intentionally; **bread** (ἄρτος) is masculine, and so **that which comes down** (ὁ καταβαίνων) is also masculine, and could equally be translated, '*he who* comes down', which is what Jesus means, though his hearers take it the other way. There is a threefold contrast between the manna and **the real bread from heaven:** the former fed for a time the Hebrews only, and they afterwards died (cf. vi. 49); the latter feeds for ever (cf. vi. 27) the world (not just one people), and gives it life.[4] Now Jesus both came down from heaven (iii. 13), and is the means whereby the world attains to life (iii. 16). Hence verses 35 and 51, which explain how this is done.

(34) So they said to him, 'Sir,[5] give us this bread all the time'.[6] (35) Jesus said to them, 'I am the bread of life;[7]

---

[1] See Barrett, pp. 239 f.   [2] See on i. 51.

[3] ἀληθινός. See on i. 9, p. 75, n. 3.

[4] For 'life' in the FG see Introduction, p. 5 and note on i. 4.

[5] Κύριε, hardly 'Lord' in this context, but as in iv. 11, etc.

[6] πάντοτε, more emphatic than ἀεί (always); cf. vii. 6; viii. 29; xi. 42; xii. 8; xviii. 20.

[7] This is the first of seven sayings all in the same form, 'I am' (on which see note on iv. 26) followed by nouns, cf. viii. 12, 'the light of the world,' x. 7, 'the door of the sheep,' x. 11, 'the good shepherd,' xi. 25, 'the resurrection and the life,' xiv. 6, 'the way, the truth and the life,' xv. 1, 'the real vine'. The absence of parallels in the other Gospels (in which sayings of Jesus beginning with 'I' do occur, but have verbs like 'say', etc.), their occurrence in Hellenistic religious literature (as well as in Rev. i. 8 (=xxi. 6 and xxii. 13);

he who comes to me shall not be hungry, and he who
believes in me shall never be thirsty at any time. (36) But
I said to you that though you have seen[1] you do not
believe. (37) Everything which the Father gives me
shall come to me, and him who comes to me I shall not
reject;[2] (38) because I am come down from heaven, not
to do my own will, but the will of him who sent me. (39)
And this is the will of him who sent me, that of everything that the Father has given me I shall not lose anything, but shall raise it up on the last day. (40) For this is
the will of my Father, that everyone who observes the
Son and believes in him shall have eternal life; and I
shall raise him up on the last day.'

34. There is a note of irony in this request; the Jews do not
really believe, and yet they echo unconsciously not only iv. 15,
but also the Lord's Prayer. They suppose Jesus to be offering
them some kind of magic bread.[3] 35. But it is Jesus himself who
is **the bread of life**—and also the water of life, as the mention
of the **thirsty** as well as the **hungry** shows (cf. iv. 14; vii. 37
ff.).[4] He is available to satisfy once and for all the hunger and
thirst[5] of those who come to him[6] and believe in him.[7]

xxii. 16), and the fact that these sayings embody some of the most characteristic themes of the FG, all suggest the conclusion that these are not strictly
'sayings of Jesus' but of a Christian prophet speaking in his name. See also
Barrett, pp. 241 ff. and Bultmann, p. 167, n. 2, and L. Cerfaux ('Le Thème
littéraire parabolique dans l'évangile de saint Jean', *Coniectanea Neotestamentica, XI* (1947), pp. 15-25) whose thesis is that 'the formula *ego eimi*
introduces an explanation of a parable' (p. 25).

[1] All MSS. but א A *a b e q sin cur* add 'me'.

[2] Literally 'throw out', as in ii. 15 (cf. ix. 34 f.; xii. 31; xv. 6).

[3] Magic bread and water, and a 'tree of life' bearing magic fruit are
frequent themes in folklore, traces of which already appear in the Old
Testament (cf. the 'tree of life' the fruit of which confers immortality,
Gen. ii. 9; iii. 22).

[4] As there is nothing in the story of the Feeding to suggest that Jesus is
the water of life, it may be that in John's source this discourse was not as
closely connected with it as it is in the FG.

[5] Cf. Matt. v. 6, Rev. vii. 16; xxi. 6; xxii. 17.

[6] The words **he who comes to me** suggest that a deeper meaning may
be intended in previous references to men approaching Jesus, e.g. i. 47 f.; iv.
30, 40, 47; v. 40 (cf. 'come to the light', iii. 20 f.): they lead on to vi. 37,
44 f.; vii. 37; xii. 32 (men come because they are drawn to Jesus, cf. vi.
44).

[7] For 'belief' as a theme of the FG see notes on i. 7, 12; iii. 15 f.

The Eucharist is not yet clearly in view: the thought here is rather of the moment of conversion than of the continuing life nourished by the sacrament of the Lord's Supper.

36. This verse appears to interrupt the flow of the argument, and is thought by some critics[1] to be out of place. It has, however, some relevance here, before 37-40. After his revelation of himself as the answer to men's needs, Jesus recognises that, though they have seen (not 'him'[2] but) his signs (cf. verse 26), they **do not believe** him, and so cannot believe *in* him, and see him as the answer to their needs.

37. Yet men do not come to Jesus simply on their own initiative. God **gives** to Jesus, and draws to him (verse 44),[3] those who come to him. Yet this does not excuse them from blame if they refuse to be drawn. There is here an indication of the paradox of divine initiative and human response (in Pauline language, of grace and faith) that is inherent in the scheme of salvation, though at times both Paul and John so stress the divine initiative as to appear to destroy the paradox.

In verses 37-40 there is a curious alternation of neuter and masculine (37. **Everything . . . him** . . . 39. **everything . . . anything . . . it** . . . 40. **everyone . . . him** . . .); the neuter appears to have a collective sense, designed to emphasise the corporate unity of believers.[4]

38 f. It is God's will that men should be saved (iii. 16), and Jesus came down from heaven (iii. 13) **to do the will of him who sent**[5] him (cf. v. 30). So he will not **reject him who comes to** him (verse 37), but will **raise him up on the last day** (cf. v. 21, 25 f.). The belief that human history will end **on the last day**[6] is not (as has been supposed) out of place in the eschatology of the FG.[7] Jesus will **not lose anything that** his Father **has given him,** for it was God's purpose

[1] See Lagrange, pp. 176 f., Bultmann, pp. 163, 173.
[2] See p. 189, n. 1 (on the reading).
[3] In xii. 32 it is Jesus who draws men to himself.
[4] See the note on ii. 21.
[5] Cf. iv. 34, and p. 129, n. 1 (on iii. 17).
[6] A phrase found only in the FG, cf. vi. 44, 54; xi. 24; xii. 48.
[7] See Introduction, pp. 13 f. and notes on v. 21, 25 f., 28 f.

that no believer should be lost.[1] At the end of his ministry (xvii. 12; xviii. 9) Jesus will claim that this has been accomplished.

40. Finally, **everyone who observes the Son and believes in him** will **have eternal life.** For **observes** John uses here $\theta\epsilon\omega\rho\dot\epsilon\omega$,[2] which implies a greater degree of attention than the usual word for 'see', $\dot o\rho\dot a\omega$, but is also used less often for actual seeing. He uses the latter in verse 36, and the change appears to be deliberate. Mere sight is not sufficient if one is to believe in Jesus (cf. xv. 24), and ultimately is not even necessary (cf. xx. 29).

(41) So the Jews grumbled about him, because he said, 'I am the bread which came down from heaven'. (42) And they said, 'This man is Jesus, Joseph's son, is he not, whose father and mother we know? What does he mean now by saying,[3] "I am come down from heaven"?'

41. Grumbling at God's bounty was a frequent failing of the chosen people, cf. Ps. cvi. 25, and their complaint about the manna, Num. xxi. 5. John now speaks of Jesus' audience as **the Jews,**[4] though earlier he has used the more precise term 'Galileans' (iv. 45). He may intend to suggest that the Galileans are no better than the men of Jerusalem, whose lack of faith forms the theme of the last chapter. It is fantastic to suppose that John is thinking of a group of Judaeans who happened to be in Galilee.

42. The ground of their complaint is their familiarity with **Jesus, Joseph's son,** and his parents: cf. Mark vi. 3, Matt. xiii. 55, Luke iv. 22. This description of Jesus does not mean that John denied, or did not know of, the belief in his virginal conception,[5] any more than does the change from Mark's 'son

---

[1] It may be because of this that John records the collecting of the fragments at the Feeding (vi. 12). This would imply that John accepted Paul's equation, bread = body of Christ = believers (cf. 1 Cor. x. 17). On this, cf. vi. 51 (though John uses 'flesh', not 'body') and the note on ii. 21.

[2] $\theta\epsilon\omega\rho\dot\epsilon\omega$, 'observe, perceive', is used (with Jesus or his works, etc., as object) in ii. 23; iv. 19; vi. 2, 19, 62; vii. 3; xii. 45; xiv. 19; xvi. 10, 16, 17, 19; xvii. 24; xx. 14.

For the meaning of the rather similar verb $\theta\epsilon\dot a o\mu a\iota$ see p. 81, n. 3.

[3] Literally, 'How does he now say?'—cf. viii. 33; xii. 34; xiv. 9.

[4] See on i. 19. [5] See on i. 13.

of Mary'[1] to Matthew's 'the carpenter's son' or Luke's 'Joseph's son'. If John indeed held the doctrine of the virginal conception, the Jews' confidence is a good example of irony. They did not know Jesus' Father at all (cf. viii. 19, 55; xv. 21; xvi. 3; xvii. 25).

(43) Jesus answered and said to them, 'Stop grumbling[2] among yourselves. (44) No one can come to me unless the Father who sent me draws him; and I will raise him up on the last day. (45) It is written in the prophets, "And they shall all be taught by God." Everyone who has heard and learnt from the Father comes to me. (46) Not that anyone has seen the Father—it is only the one who is from God who has seen the Father. (47) Amen, amen, I say to you,[3] he who believes has eternal life. (48) I am the bread of life. (49) Your fathers ate the manna in the wilderness, and died. (50) This is the bread which comes down from heaven, so that anyone may eat of it and not die. (51) I am the living bread which came down from heaven; if anyone eats of this bread, he will live for ever[4]; and indeed the bread which I shall give for the life of the world is my flesh'.[5]

This paragraph amplifies the teaching already given, and at the end makes a further advance by an explicit allusion to the Eucharist.

43. Apart from the peremptory **'Stop grumbling'** Jesus ignores the interruption, and 44. again stresses the divine initiative (cf. verse 37) and the promise of resurrection (cf. verses 39, 40). 45. He then quotes **the prophets** (actually Isa. liv. 13) to support his contention—men have to be **taught by God.** That

[1] To call a man the son of his mother could be an insult, implying that his father was unknown. This could have been sufficient reason for Matthew and Luke to avoid the phrase, as well as John. Legally, of course, Joseph was Jesus' father.

[2] For the form of the prohibition, μὴ γογγύζετε, cf. ii. 16.

[3] See on i. 51.   [4] εἰς τὸν αἰῶνα. See on iv. 14.

[5] This order of words, which gives the sense intended, is in fact only found in אֵ *m* and Tertullian. The best attested reading is that of P66 B D W *lat sin cur*, 'the bread which I shall give is my flesh for the life of the world'. The majority of MSS. have a clearly secondary reading, adding a second 'which I shall give' after 'flesh'. It is because of the clumsiness of the best attested reading that Bultmann (p. 175, n. 1) suspects that 'for the life of the world' is a gloss. But the order is less harsh in Greek than in English.

is how he draws them, for the lessons which they learn from him—as, for example, in the Scriptures (cf. v. 39)—point them to Jesus, who can also be said to draw men (cf. xii. 32). 46. If men could see God, the intervention of Jesus would be unnecessary. But in fact only one man has seen God (cf. i. 18)—Jesus himself—and so really knows him. 47. So men must believe where they cannot see (cf. 2 Cor. v. 7), as Jesus most solemnly assures them, if they are to attain eternal life (cf. verse 40). As he will explain later (xiv. 9) to see Jesus *is* to see God.

48. Jesus then is indispensable. He is **the bread of life** (cf. verse 35), 49 f., the superiority of which to **the manna** (cf. verse 32) is shown by the fact that those who **ate the manna** afterwards **died,** while **the bread which comes down from heaven** preserves those who eat it from eternal death.

51. Jesus repeats the claim of verses 35 and 48, with a slight difference—he is **the living bread,** and, because **living,** life-giving (cf. verse 33). He has 'life in himself' (v. 26), and so imparts it.

In the repeated references to Jesus' descent from heaven three tenses of the verb 'come down' (καταβαίνω) are used—present (verses 33 and 50), perfect (38 and 42), and aorist (41, 51, and 58, as also in iii. 13). These emphasise respectively three aspects of Christ's coming—his repeated coming to the faithful (as in the Lord's Supper), his eternal status as the Incarnate,[1] and his coming as an event in history (i. 14).

Up to this point the references to **the bread which came down from heaven** can be understood simply as metaphor. But now the argument goes a stage further: **the bread** of which Jesus has been speaking is **his flesh,** given **for the life of the world.** The sacrificial and eucharistic reference in these words is unmistakable, and so we at last see how God is to accomplish his purpose of saving the world (iii. 16 ff.).

There is an obvious parallel here to the words spoken by Jesus over the bread at the Last Supper, as recorded in 1 Cor.

---

[1] Cf. the perfect participle ἐσφαγμένου, 'slain from the foundation of the world', in Rev. xiii. 8.

xi. 24 and the longer (and most probably authentic)[1] text of
Luke xxii. 19; though allowance must be made for the characteristically Johannine substitution of **flesh** for 'body'[2] and
expansion of 'for you' to **for the life of the world.**[3] The
preposition **for** (ὑπέρ) has a sacrificial connotation elsewhere
in John,[4] and occurs in the words spoken over the cup in Mark
xiv. 24.[5] It is only Paul and Luke who have it in the words
spoken over the bread. This is a noteworthy parallel between
Luke and the FG, but does not necessarily imply dependence
on Luke.[6] It is not surprising if John of Ephesus had indeed
been a companion of Paul.[7]

**(52) So the Jews argued[8] with one another, saying,
'How can this man give us flesh[9] to eat?' (53) So Jesus
said to them, 'Amen, amen I say to you,[10] unless you eat
the flesh of the Son of man and drink his blood, you do
not have life in yourselves. (54) He who eats[11] my flesh
and drinks my blood has eternal life, and I will raise him
up on the last day. (55) For my flesh really[12] is food, and
my blood really[12] is drink. (56) He who eats my flesh and**

---

[1] In Luke xxii. 19 D, several Old Latin MSS., and *sin cur* (which have the
verse after 16) read, 'This is my body', and omit the rest of the verse and the
whole of verse 20. But this is but one of the devices found in the MS. tradition
to suppress one of the two cups in Luke's account of the Last Supper.

[2] In the FG, except in ii. 21, the body (σῶμα) of Jesus is the crucified body
(xix. 38, 40; xx. 12—cf. 'the bodies', xix. 31). W. Bauer (p. 99) points out
that 'flesh' is found instead of 'body' in Ignatius, Rom. vii. 3, Philadelphians
iv. 1; xi. 2, Smyrneans vii. 1, and Justin, *Apology*, I. lxvi.

[3] This phrase is not found elsewhere in the New Testament. But cf. 'the
light of the world' (John viii. 12).   [4] x. 11, 15; xi. 50 ff.; xv. 13.

[5] The parallel passage in Matt. xxvi. 28 has περί for ὑπέρ.

[6] See Introduction, pp. 10 ff.   [7] See Introduction, p. 49.

[8] Literally, 'fought'.

[9] τὴν σάρκα. 'His flesh' (τὴν σάρκα αὐτοῦ) is read by B *lat sin cur*.

[10] See on i. 51.

[11] ὁ τρώγων (as in vi. 56, 57, 58; xiii. 18). In later Greek (cf. Matt. xxiv.
38) τρώγω replaces the classical ἐσθίω as the present tense of the aorist ἔφαγον.
ἐσθίω does not occur in the Johannine literature (see LS⁹). This would seem
to dispose of E. C. Hoskyns' attempt (*The Fourth Gospel* (ed. F. N. Davey,
1940), I, pp. 336 f.) to find some special meaning in τρώγω in the FG. But see
Bauer⁵, s.v.; Bauer, p. 98.

[12] ἀληθῶς ℵ* D Θ 28 *lat syr*: ἀληθής P⁶⁶ B W *fam* 1 *fam* 13 565 *q eg*. It is a
nice question which of these is the correct reading. The adverb ἀληθῶς is
consistent with John's usage—but may therefore be a correction. The adjective ἀληθής should strictly be ἀληθινός (see on i. 9)—and therefore may have
been replaced by ἀληθῶς. There is, however, no real difference in meaning.

drinks my blood stays in me, and I in him. (57) As the
living Father sent me, both I live through the Father, and
he who eats me—he also shall live through me. (58) This
is the bread which came down[1] from heaven; unlike[2]
the fathers ⟨who⟩ ate and died, he who eats this bread
shall live for ever.'[3]

(59) He said these things in synagogue[4] as he was
teaching in Capernaum.

52. This paragraph, like the previous one, amplifies, and
makes more explicit, teaching already given, and, again like the
previous paragraph, begins with an unintelligent interruption
which provides the opportunity for further teaching (cf. verse
42). The Jews, like their ancestors in the wilderness,[5] ask how
Jesus can give them meat. They have not grasped the meaning
of verse 51, which Jesus' reply now makes quite explicit.

53 f. Repeating, as in verse 47, his solemn formula of assurance, Jesus tells them that they must **eat the flesh of the Son
of man and drink his blood,** for it is this alone which guarantees **eternal life** as a present possession, and resurrection as
a future gift (cf. verses 39, 40, 44). 55. For the **flesh** and **blood**
of Christ (received—though John does not say this—under the
forms of bread and wine in the Lord's Supper) are real **food**
and **drink,** 56. effecting a real union with Christ, a mutual indwelling. Here we see how and where Christ really stays among
men.[6] 57. Then, taking up the theme of v. 26, Jesus explains
that **he who eats** him **lives through** him because **the Father
sent** him 58. as the real bread from heaven (cf. verses 32 f.),
incomparably more effective than the manna (cf. verse 49).

By recording this discourse here John clearly intends us to
understand the Feeding of the Multitude as taking the place of
the Last Supper as the occasion in the ministry of Jesus with
which the Church's celebration of the Eucharist was to be
connected. Consistently with this there is no eucharistic significance in John's account of the Last Supper.[7] In John's source

[1] For the significance of the aorist see on vi. 51.
[2] Literally 'not as'.   [3] εἰς τὸν αἰῶνα. See on iv. 14.
[4] ἐν συναγωγῇ, omitting the article, as we say 'in church'.
[5] Cf. Ps. lxxviii. 20.   [6] See on i. 38 and cf. xv. 4.
[7] See below, pp. 319 f. This discourse here may incorporate material found
in the account of the Last Supper in John's source.

the Feeding was no doubt presented as what in fact it was—an eschatological sacrament, a token and pledge to those who were fed that they would have a place in the kingdom—but it is unlikely that it had any specifically eucharistic significance. This suggestion is borne out by the fact that in the narrative of the Feeding itself the eucharistic features are not stressed as much even as in Mark.[1] So if vi. 26-59 formed part of the same source as vi. 1-25 it is probable that it was not originally in this position. Moreover, the emphasis on the blood, to which nothing in the Feeding corresponds, adds further support to the theory that the discourse is not in its original place. It may even not come from the same source at all, since the only mention of 'blood' in the FG (apart from the four instances in vi. 53-56) is in xix. 34,[2] and there it is not certain that any sacrificial or eucharistic reference is intended. In 1 John i. 7 and v. 6-8, however, as well as in Rev. i. 5; v. 9; vii. 14; xii. 11 the blood of Christ has an obviously sacrificial significance, and this suggests that the discourse here is in fact the composition of the evangelist, utilising (to an extent which cannot be precisely determined) actual words of Jesus spoken originally in a different context.

59. This verse marks the end of an episode. The public discourse **in synagogue** (i.e. during a synagogue service) is followed by a private discussion between Jesus and his disciples. Jesus takes more pains to enlighten them than the crowd in the synagogue.

(60) So when they heard ⟨this⟩ many of his disciples said 'This saying is a hard one! Who can listen to[3] it?' (61) But Jesus, knowing in himself that his disciples were grumbling about this, said to them, 'Does this offend you? (62) ⟨What⟩ then ⟨will you think⟩ if you perceive[4] the Son of man going up where he was before? (63) The spirit is that which gives life—the flesh is of no use; the words which I have spoken to you are spirit and are life. (64) But there are some of you who do not believe.' (For Jesus knew from the beginning who they were who did

---

[1] See above, p. 179.
[2] The use of αἷμα in i. 13 is irrelevant here.
[3] For this sense of ἀκούω see on v. 24, p. 167, n. 7.
[4] θεωρῆτε. See p. 191.

**not believe and who it was who would betray him.) (65)
And he said, 'This is why I said to you that no one can
come to me unless it is given him by the Father'.**

60. Disbelief now shows itself for the first time among the
disciples. 61. Jesus is aware of this—his understanding of men's
minds has already been remarked (ii. 24 f.[1])—and 62. puts a
question to them, designed, one must suppose, either to miti-
gate the offence caused by a literal understanding of eating his
flesh and drinking his blood, or (more subtly) to distinguish the
believers from the unbelievers among the disciples. This latter
is in fact the result, whether or not it was intended (cf. 66 ff.).

The Son of man came down from heaven to give life to the
world, by giving men his flesh as bread (vi. 51): but his work
will not be complete, and its benefits available to men, until he
has gone back up to the place where he was before. Ascent and
descent imply one another (cf. iii. 13). His going up will involve
both his lifting up (iii. 14), which will be seen to mean his
crucifixion (xii. 32 f.), as well as his return to the Father (xx.
17). Only after this will the Spirit be given (cf. vii. 39—Jesus'
glorification *is* his crucifixion—and xx. 22). The eating of which
Jesus has spoken is not to take place until Christ has gone back,
and so it cannot be understood in a crude and literal manner.
63. For the life which their eating of Jesus' flesh will give to men
will be the result of the gift of the Spirit, already seen as the
life-giving power in the new birth (iii. 5, etc.). The whole purpose of the Incarnation according to the FG was to effect the
union of flesh and Spirit in the person of Jesus, so that through
the flesh of Jesus the Spirit should be effectively available for
men. But **the flesh**—even that of the incarnate Christ—**is of
no use** apart from the Spirit, while equally the Spirit is only
given through the flesh (cf. vi. 53 ff., which is in no way contradicted by vi. 63). This is true both of **the flesh** understood as
the actual life of Jesus and as the food given in the Eucharist.
And the flesh (again in both senses) possesses this power of
imparting the Spirit by virtue of **the words** of Jesus, which
are spirit and are life (cf. i. 4 for the Logos—i.e. word—as
principle of life). If the original context of this saying was the
Last Supper, **the words** would be those spoken by Jesus in the

---

[1] See also on i. 42.

institution of the Eucharist. By placing them here, John gives them a more general sense. They are the discourses of Jesus by which the meaning of his life is expounded and faith is evoked.

64. Jesus now shows his awareness of the unbelief of some of his disciples—those for whom the flesh is of no use—and 65. explains that **this is why** he has already **said** (vi. 44 ff.) **that no one can come to** him **unless . . . the Father** gives him the power to do so (cf. iii. 27 and vi. 37). It sounds as if not only the initiative but also the outcome depended wholly on God, but this is not necessarily what the FG means. In it, as for St Paul, faith is of decisive importance; it is the condition of salvation (cf. i. 12; iii. 16). But John never actually says that faith is given (or withheld) by God. It is elicited by God, but man is free to respond or not to the divine initiative, and is so far responsible for his own salvation.[1] So Jesus is not here pronouncing the divine sentence upon the unbelievers, who can do nothing to reverse it, but is warning them that now is their opportunity. If they delay the decision it may be too late.

(66) In consequence[2] many of his disciples went away back, and did not accompany[3] him any longer. (67) So Jesus said to the Twelve, 'You do not want to go, do you[4]?' (68) Simon Peter answered him, 'Lord, to whom shall we go? You have words of eternal life; (69) and we are convinced[5] and know that you are the Holy One of God'. (70) Jesus answered them, 'I chose you, the Twelve, did I not? Even of you one is a devil.' (71) But he meant Judas, son of Simon Iscariot;[6] for he was going to betray him, though he was one of the Twelve.

66. Here a turning-point is reached in Jesus' ministry: he

---

[1] See also on iii. 19.

[2] ἐκ τούτου. This could mean 'from this time'. The phrase occurs elsewhere in the FG only in xix. 12, where also both meanings are possible. But John can say 'from this time' unambiguously, if he wants to (cf. xix. 27), and in 1 John iv. 6 ἐκ τούτου can only mean 'in consequence of this'.

[3] Literally, 'did not walk with him'.

[4] For the form of the question see on iv. 12, p. 142, n. 2.

[5] πεπιστεύκαμεν, Perfect of πιστεύω, 'believe', used also in iii. 18; viii. 31; xi. 27; xvi. 27; xx. 29.

[6] The other Gospels do not mention **Simon,** and give the surname **Iscariot** to Judas. **Iscariot** may mean 'man of Kerioth' (cf. the reading ἀπὸ Καρυώτου of ℵ*Θ *fam* 13 *hl*ᵐᵍ), or may be a corruption of *sicarius*, implying that he was a Zealot. See also xii. 4 and xiii. 2, 26.

has brought his disciples to the moment of decision, and in consequence **many of his disciples** abandoned him. The exact phrase **went away back** (ἀπῆλθον εἰς τὰ ὀπίσω) occurs again in xviii. 6, where it is used of the soldiers who recoiled from Jesus when he presented himself to them in Gethsemane. The parallel is no doubt intentional: in both passages the self-revelation of the Christ repels the unbelievers.

It is possible that in John's source it was Jesus' refusal to let himself be made king that offended the mass of his disciples.

In Mark also a turning-point is reached after the Feeding(s) of the Multitude, marked by Peter's confession and Jesus' first prediction of his death (Mark viii. 27 ff.), and, though John did not necessarily derive his material from Mark, it is hard to resist the conclusion that he writes with Mark in mind, and intends to give an alternative version of this episode in Jesus' ministry.

In the pattern of the FG this episode of Peter's confession corresponds to the final testimony of John the Baptist, following as it does vi. 22-65, which corresponds to the encounter with Nicodemus.[1]

67. The defection of the other disciples leaves Jesus with the Twelve. John does not actually record any call of the Twelve (though he refers to Jesus' choice of them in verse 70), or give any list of their names, or refer to them again as a group, except for a passing mention in xx. 24 ('Thomas, one of the Twelve'). They are not as important for John as they are for the other evangelists.

68. **Simon Peter,** as in the equivalent passage of Mark (viii. 27 ff.) is the spokesman for the others in answering Jesus' question (which is different in Mark). As Jesus, by the form of his question, expects, Peter scouts the idea of their deserting him, and confesses, first, that Jesus possesses **words of eternal life,** thus endorsing what Jesus himself has already said (verse 63), and, secondly, 69. that he is **the Holy One of God.** This is a Messianic title,[2] and thus in John, as in Mark, Peter confesses

---

[1] See above, p. 185.

[2] Used in Mark i. 24 = Luke iv. 34 by a man with an unclean spirit, and also in Acts iii. 14; iv. 27, 30. The word 'holy' (ἅγιος) is not used elsewhere in the FG of Jesus, though it occurs in 1 John ii. 20, and Rev. iii. 7. In John x. 36 and xvii. 19, the cognate verb ἁγιάζω, 'make holy, sanctify', is used— Jesus is he 'whom the Father sanctified', and he sanctifies himself for the sake of his disciples.

that Jesus is the Christ.[1] In Mark, and still more in Matt. xvi. 16 ff., this is represented as a new discovery by, or revelation to, Peter. But in John i. 41, Andrew has already told Peter that Jesus is the Messiah—after his first encounter with him. John has no doubt paraphrased Peter's confession, but it may well be that he represents its significance more accurately than Mark does. Coming, as it does, after the defection of all but the Twelve, Peter's confession is a re-affirmation of the conviction that Jesus *is* the Christ—even though he is not prepared to be the Christ of popular expectation.

70 f. Though Jesus had chosen the Twelve, his choice did not guarantee their faithfulness. One of them, Judas, was **a devil** (διάβολος), an appropriate description of one who betrayed his master to his enemies. In John xiii. 27, Satan is said to have entered Judas: here he is identified with him. Jesus chose Judas, knowing from the beginning of their association that he would betray him (cf. verse 64). Does this mean that Jesus chose Judas *in order that* he might betray him? Was Judas in fact a helpless instrument of the divine plan? Here again we are confronted by the mystery of divine fore-knowledge and human freedom. Judas' remorse—which John does not mention—shows that he at any rate felt responsible for his actions.[2]

In Mark viii. 33, Jesus calls Peter Satan when he tries to persuade him that he will not have to die. John seems to be correcting Mark by explaining that the real Satan among the Twelve is Judas.[3]

10. JESUS AT THE FEAST OF TABERNACLES, vii. 1-52; viii. 12-59

vii. (1) And after this[4] Jesus showed himself[5] in Gali-

---

[1] To have **words of eternal life** is natural for the Logos.

[2] On this topic see further pp. 310 f. (on xiii. 18).

[3] See Introduction, pp. 9 f.   [4] μετὰ ταῦτα. See on iii. 22, p. 131, n. 4.

[5] περιεπάτει, literally 'walk'. The sense in this verse (and in xi. 54) is half-way between the literal (common in the FG, cf. i. 36, etc.) and the metaphorical 'live', 'behave' (common in Paul, and found also in John xxi. 18 and the Epistles, e.g. 1 John ii. 6, 2 John 4, 6, 3 John 3, 4).

lee; for he was unable[1] to show himself[2] in Judaea,
because the Jews were seeking to kill him.

One would expect this verse to follow the account of an
incident in Judaea, instead of in Galilee (as does iv. 1 f., to
which it is parallel). In John's source vii. 1-14 may have
followed vii. 15-24 and viii. 12-20,[3] but when he rearranged this
material in the interests of the dramatic and theological development of his story he left this verse unchanged, in spite of its
illogicality, because it is a necessary part of the setting for the
next scene in his narrative. The Galilean ministry is now at an
end (as in the Synoptic Gospels), and there remains a series of
increasingly hazardous encounters in Jerusalem.

In the pattern of the FG vi. 22-71 corresponds to the encounter with Nicodemus and the final testimony of John the
Baptist (chapter iii),[4] and vii and viii to the encounter with the
Samaritans (iv. 1-42). The same arrangement of sign, corollary,
and discourses occurs in ii–iv. 42 and vii–viii, and in both cases
two further signs follow (iv. 46–v. 9 and ix–xi. 44). But the
scale expands as the Gospel proceeds.

**(2) Now the Jews' feast of Tabernacles was near. (3) So
his brothers said to him, 'Leave here and go to Judaea,
so that your disciples also may observe[5] the works that
you do. (4) For no one does anything in secret if he wants
it to be public.[6] If these ⟨are the things that⟩ you do,
show yourself to the world.' (5) For even his brothers did
not believe in him.**

2. As in ii. 13 and v. 1,[7] John speaks of **the Jews' feast.
Tabernacles** lasted for a week, and celebrated the vintage and
also commemorated the period when Israel dwelt in tents in

---

[1] Reading οὐ γὰρ εἶχεν ἐξουσίαν with W lat cur. The other authorities have
'for he was unwilling' (οὐ γὰρ ἤθελεν) which Barrett (p. 255) rightly regards
as less probable.   [2] περιπατεῖν; for this verb see above, p. 200, n. 5.
[3] See pp. 221 f. on viii. 20.   [4] See above, pp. 122 ff. and 131 ff.
[5] θεωρήσουσιν. See p. 191.
[6] In the clause 'if he wants it to be public' (καὶ ζητεῖ αὐτὸ ἐν παρρησίᾳ
εἶναι, literally 'and seeks it to be public') αὐτό, 'it', is read by P⁶⁶ BDW
and is to be preferred to αὐτός, 'himself' (ℵ Θ, etc.). αὐτό may, however, be
only a correct gloss, and the true reading καὶ ζητεῖ ἐν παρρησίᾳ εἶναι, as
attested by the two Old Latin MSS. b and e. But see Barrett ad loc. (p. 257).
(ἐν) παρρησίᾳ means (1) in public, openly, vii. 13, 26; x. 24; xi. 54; xviii.
20; (2) plainly (not in riddles) xi. 14; xvi. 25, 29.
[7] See the notes to these verses.

the wilderness. It attracted large crowds of pilgrims, and would give anyone seeking publicity excellent opportunities for exploiting the nationalist sentiments which were aroused by the feast.

3. Jesus' **brothers** have already appeared in ii. 12, just before the Passover. Then Jesus presumably went with them to the feast, and on this occasion they invite him to accompany them again. Their suggestion is in the nature of a challenge. They do not believe in him, but are not actively hostile. Their reference to **disciples** implies that they suppose Jesus to have followers in Jerusalem. They know that Jesus has failed to raise a mass movement in Galilee (as it must have appeared to them) —in spite of his miracles there. Then let him try again in Jerusalem. 4. Galilee is after all only an obscure province. Jesus' works only make sense to his unbelieving brothers if they are intended to gain publicity. It is only common sense then to display them to the widest possible audience. He must **show** himself **to the world** (by which they mean 'to everybody'). This, however, Jesus cannot yet do, since the world does not know him.[1] It will only be able to recognise him when he is lifted up on the Cross (xii. 32).

5. In the Synoptic Gospels Jesus' **brothers** show their lack of faith in him by their actions, cf. Mark iii. 31-35 and parallels, and perhaps also Mark iii. 21. But there is nothing in this verse to suggest dependence on Mark.

(6) So Jesus said to them, 'It is not yet the ⟨right⟩ time for me, but it is the ⟨right⟩ time for you all the time.[2] (7) The world cannot hate you, but me it does hate, because I bear witness about it, that its works are evil. (8) You go up to this feast: I am not going up to this feast, because

---

[1] Cf. i. 9, and the note to that verse on the meaning of 'the world' in the FG.

[2] Literally, 'My time (καιρός) is not yet present, but your time is ready all the time (πάντοτε, see p. 188, n. 6).' Καιρός, which means here the right time for doing anything, occurs in the FG only in vii. 6 and 8 (apart from the gloss at v. 4; see p. 160, n. 4). Elsewhere John uses ὥρα in this sense (e.g. ii. 4—on which see the note, p. 107, n. 2). Both words occur in the same sense in Revelation (καιρός i. 3 =xxii. 10; xi. 18; ὥρα iii. 10; xiv. 7, 15, etc.) and so must be regarded as synonymous, and equally Johannine. It is therefore unlikely that any inference can be drawn from the isolated occurrence of καιρός in vii. 6 and 8 that it comes from a special source.

the ⟨right⟩ time for me ⟨to go⟩ has not yet been reached.'¹ (9) And when he had said this he stayed by himself ² in Galilee.

6. Jesus' words recall ii. 4.³ As at Cana, Jesus will not do anything at merely human prompting, even from his nearest relatives. Yet in both cases he afterwards does what has been suggested, but in his own time.⁴ Jesus' **time** is, as xiii. 1 shows, that of his Crucifixion, before which he cannot be effectively shown to the world (cf. verse 4 above.) His brothers on the other hand belong to the world, as their lack of faith in Jesus shows. Like the world, they go their own way, and so they can go to the feast as and when they like. But not so Jesus.

7. Since they belong to the world, **the world cannot hate** them, as it does Jesus—and his disciples (cf. xv. 18 f.). Its hatred is due to its resentment at his testimony against its wickedness (cf. iii. 19 f.).

8. Since Jesus does in fact go up to the feast a few days later (cf. verses 10 and 14), several important authorities read, 'I am not yet going up . . .'⁵ in order to clear Jesus of any appearance of duplicity. But the words are not really misleading as they stand, and 'yet' must be dismissed as a gloss.⁶

To **go up** is almost a technical term for attending a feast (cf. ii. 13), and its use here is quite natural. It may, however, also have a deeper meaning, an allusion to the raising up of Jesus on the Cross. When his time has fully come, Jesus will be lifted up, and revealed to the world (cf. verses 4 and 6 above).

(10) But when his brothers had gone up to the feast, then he also went up, not openly, but as it were in secret. (11) Now the Jews were looking for him at the feast⁷ and

---

¹ Literally, 'fulfilled' (πεπλήρωται, used also in iii. 29).

² αὐτός is read by P⁶⁶ ℵ D*, etc., and is to be preferred to αὐτοῖς, 'to them', which the other MSS. read.

³ See the note *ad loc.*

⁴ Cf. also his behaviour at the news of Lazarus' illness (xi. 1-6).

⁵ ἐγὼ οὔπω ἀναβαίνω, P⁶⁶ B W Θ *fam* 1 *fam* 13 *f g²q pal hl sah*, etc: οὐκ ℵ D *lat sin cur boh arm.*

⁶ Black, however (¹ 1946, p. 126), argues that the word-play in Aramaic on *la . . . 'adh* ('not yet'), *'edha* ('feast'), and *'iddana* ('time') supports the reading 'not yet'. The force of this argument is diminished, however, by the fact that 'not yet' does occur once in any case.

⁷ ἐν τῇ ἑορτῇ may mean 'in the crowd attending the feast' (cf. Mark xiv. 2).

were saying, 'Where is he?' (12) And there was a lot of argument about him among the crowds: some were saying, 'He is a good man', but others, 'No, but he misleads the crowd'. (13) No one, however, talked about him in public[1] for fear of the Jews.

10. Barrett's suggestion[2] that Jesus' eventual departure from Galilee to Jerusalem, made **in secret,** is derived from Mark ix. 30 has little to commend it, since in Mark Jesus' arrival in Jerusalem is by no means secret—it was then that he made his Triumphal Entry (Mark xi. 1 ff.), which took place before the Passover, not Tabernacles, according to both Mark and John. In John, however, the arrival of Jesus in Jerusalem on this occasion was as unobtrusive as his departure from Galilee, and the Triumphal Entry is placed at xii. 12 ff., after a later journey to Jerusalem.[3]

11. John has already recorded the interest shown in Jesus in Jerusalem, favourable in ii. 23-25, and hostile in v. 16 ff. 12. Now there is a difference of opinion about him. He appears to have had some supporters **among the crowds,** but 13. these could not express their opinion **in public for fear of the Jews.** John here draws a distinction between **the crowds** and **the Jews.**[4] The latter are the experts in the law (cf. verse 15), the former the ignorant and despised commons, who did not know the law (cf. vii. 49), but who heard Jesus gladly (cf. Mark xii. 37, in which the same word ὄχλος occurs). The motive of secrecy **for fear of the Jews** recurs in xix. 38 and xx. 19.

The stage is now set for the entry of the protagonist and the beginning of the great controversy. It is often argued that the controversy about Jesus' status and mission in the FG reflects that between Jews and Christians at a later period. It may well be that John writes with an eye on later disputes, but this does not mean that his record is devoid of historical foundation.

(14) But when the feast was already half over Jesus went up into the Temple and taught. (15) So the Jews

---

[1] παρρησία. See p. 201, n. 6.   [2] Pp. 258 f.

[3] The Triumphal Entry may, however, have taken place in fact not before Passover, but before either Tabernacles or the Dedication. See further on x. 22 and xii. 12 ff.

[4] For John's use of the term 'Jews' see on i. 19 and ii. 13.

were surprised, saying, 'How ⟨is it that⟩ this¹ ⟨fellow⟩ knows ⟨his⟩ letters when he has not been ⟨anyone's⟩ disciple²?'

14. This is the first time that John refers to Jesus teaching in Jerusalem. This move from the synagogue of vi. 59 to the Temple marks the sharpening of the crisis. The Temple was the place of sacrifice, and the Father's house (ii. 16). It was Jesus' proper place, yet he was not welcome there (cf. i. 11). In vii and viii Jesus teaches *in* the Temple: in iv. 1-42 he teaches *about* it—which underlines the correspondence of the passages in the plan of the FG.³

15. Jesus' teaching surprised the Jews (cf. Mark i. 27); they admired its quality, but recognised (from its style, presumably) that the teacher was not a product of the rabbinical schools.⁴ The crowds in Galilee likewise recognised his difference from the scribes (Mark i. 22).

This verse forms a natural continuation to v. 47,⁵ and John may have found it following v. 47 in his source. By putting it here, he has made an abrupt transition from verse 14, and also has probably altered the sense of the Jews' question. Following immediately after v. 47, it would be an echo of Jesus' words, 'If you do not believe his writings (γράμμασιν), how will you believe my words?', and would mean 'How does he know the writings (γράμματα, i.e. the Scriptures)?' But in its present context γράμματα should probably be given its normal meaning of the subjects of elementary education.⁶

(16) So Jesus answered them and said, 'My teaching is not mine, but that of him who sent me. (17) If anyone is willing to do his will, he will know whether my teaching is from God or whether I am talking on my own authority.⁷ (18) The man who speaks on his own authority⁷ seeks his own glory: but it is the man who seeks the glory of him who sent him that is true, and there is no unrighteousness in him. (19) Moses gave you the law, did he not?

---

¹ οὗτος used (as here) by itself has a contemptuous sense. Hence ⟨fellow⟩.
² μὴ μεμαθηκώς, literally, 'not having learnt'.   ³ See above, p. 201.
⁴ Cf. the Sanhedrin's opinion of the Apostles (Acts iv. 13).
⁵ Cf. Bultmann, pp. 177 f.   ⁶ See Bauer⁵, s.v. 3.
⁷ ἀπ' ἐμαυτοῦ, ἀφ' ἑαυτοῦ, literally, 'from myself', 'from himself'; cf. v. 30; vii. 28; viii. 28, 42; x. 18; xiv. 10.

And yet not one of you is doing the law! Why are you seeking to kill me?'

16. Jesus begins by refuting the suggestion that his teaching is something which he has thought of by himself. It is true that it does not come from a Rabbi: he got it **from him who sent him,**[1] i.e. his Father. 17. From this it follows that the only man who can judge his credentials is one who is willing to do God's will, as Jesus does (cf. iv. 34; v. 30; vi. 38). And doing God's will means for men in general to believe in him whom God sent (cf. vi. 29, 1 John iii. 23). The man who is willing to listen to God comes to Jesus (cf. vi. 45).

18. A further test can be applied. **The man who speaks on his own authority seeks his own glory.** But Jesus does not seek his own glory: if he does not accept glory from men (cf. v. 41), he cannot be accused of seeking it for himself (cf. viii. 50). The fact that he **seeks the glory of him who sent him** proves his sincerity[2] and refutes the charge of **unrighteousness** implied by the complaint that he misleads the crowd (cf. viii. 46).

19. The Jews on the other hand claim to be righteous. They take their stand on the law which Moses gave them (cf. v. 45; ix. 28), which set forth the will of God for them. Yet they do not do what the law commands, as their refusal to believe in Jesus shows (cf. v. 39, 46 f.). Instead, they seek to kill him. This statement, which would be natural if vii. 15-19 followed v. 47 (cf. v. 18), is rather surprising as it stands, in spite of vii. 1, since there is nothing in the immediate context to suggest it.

(20) The crowd answered, 'You have a demon![3] Who is seeking to kill you?'

Jesus' charge that they are seeking to kill him is taken as a sign of madness (cf. viii. 48, 52; x. 20). That their words mean no more than this is suggested by x. 20, 'He has a demon and is mad'. They do not make the more sinister accusation of collusion with Beelzebub found in Mark iii. 22, etc. There is no

[1] See on iii. 17, p. 129, n. 1.
[2] The only other instances in the FG where a person is called ἀληθής are iii. 33; viii. 26 (referring to God). For the meaning of ἀληθής in the FG see p. 75, n. 3. Here it implies 'sincerity', 'truthfulness'.
[3] δαιμόνιον. This word occurs in the FG only in this connexion. In vi. 70 and viii. 44 the word is διάβολος.

place for this in the FG, which does not record any of Jesus' exorcisms. The crowd may have been genuinely ignorant of their rulers' plans, or simply seeking to beguile their victim.

(21) Jesus answered and said to them, 'I did one work and you are all surprised[1] at this.[2] (22) Moses gave you circumcision—not that it is from Moses but from the fathers—and you circumcise a man on the Sabbath. (23) If a man receives circumcision on the Sabbath in order that the law of Moses may not be broken,[3] are you angry with me because I made all of a man well on the Sabbath? (24) Stop judging[4] according to appearance, and give a just judgement.'

21. Jesus brings into the open the cause of their hostility—his healing of a man on the Sabbath (v. 2 ff.), which he proceeds to justify.

22 f. He employs a typical Rabbinic argument *from light to heavy*. This, like subsequent arguments between Jesus and the Jews in the FG, has been held to be a product of later controversy between Church and Synagogue, but it is hard to see why Jesus should not have used it. An argument of similar form is also found in Luke xiii. 15 f., again in a dispute about the Sabbath.

The argument (not all fully explicit) runs thus—**Moses** (the Jews' authority!—verse 19) **gave** them **circumcision** (which had in fact been first enjoined upon Abraham, cf. Gen. xvii. 10), with the command to administer it on the eighth day after birth, even if this were a Sabbath. This Jesus claims as justification for his healing on the Sabbath. There is a stage omitted from the argument, which should probably be understood as follows: circumcision cleanses one of a man's members; Jesus has

---

[1] θαυμάζω. This can have the connotation of a painful surprise, a shock.

[2] This is the punctuation of RV^mg and RSV. AV and RV punctuate 'at this' (διὰ τοῦτο) with the following sentence, in accordance with the otherwise invariable rule in the FG that διὰ τοῦτο comes first in the clause to which it belongs. But in at least 8 of its occurrences out of 14 (i. 31; vi. 65; ix. 23; xii. 27; xiii. 11; xv. 19; xvi. 15; xix. 11; contrast v. 16, 18; x. 17; xii. 39–viii. 47 and xii. 18 are doubtful) it refers to something previously mentioned. The AV punctuation is to be rejected because the reason why Moses gave circumcision is not stated, and it is not easy to infer what it was from the context.

[3] See p. 164, n 2.   [4] See p. 115, n. 4.

healed **all of a man**,[1] and, as v. 14 implies, cleansed him also
from sin. He is therefore entitled *a fortiori* to 'break' the
Sabbath. The unexpressed step in the argument resembles one
attributed to Rabbi Eli'ezer[2] (*c.* A.D. 90), that if one can ignore
the Sabbath for the sake of one member, one can for the sake
of all a man's members, i.e. when he is in danger of death. The
Jews' complaint was that Jesus cured *chronic* illnesses on the
Sabbath, but he contended that a cure was victory over Satan
and so should be won even on the Sabbath (cf. Luke xiii. 16).

**(25) Then some of the Jerusalemites said, 'This is the
man, is it not, whom they are seeking to kill? (26) And
see, he is talking openly,[3] and they are not saying anything to him. The rulers did not really discover,[4] did they,
that this is the Christ? (27) But we know where this man
comes from; but when the Christ is coming, nobody discovers where he is from.'**

If verses 15-24 are not in the place which they occupied in
John's source,[5] then originally verses 25-52 followed directly
after 14.[6] Now verse 25 does read a little strangely after the
denial of any knowledge of an attempt to kill Jesus (whether
feigned or not) in verse 20, but is entirely natural after 14,
giving the opinion of the local inhabitants after that of the
pilgrims attending the feast. This does not, however, mean that
the present order is not intentional. For it leads on from the
work to the person of Christ, and on again to his self-revelation
in vii. 37 ff. and viii. 12 ff., which correspond, in the pattern of
the FG, to his self-revelation to the Samaritan woman.[7]

25 f. The men of Jerusalem, better informed than the crowd
of pilgrims (which is how we must understand the contrast of
verses 20 and 25 in the present order of the passages), express
surprise at the inaction of the authorities, and wonder if somehow they have discovered that his claims are true.

27. But they dismiss the idea. Jesus does not fit the rôle of

---

[1] Literally, 'a whole man' (ὅλον ἄνθρωπον); 'whole' is, however, ambiguous
in English; hence the paraphrase.
[2] See Strack–Billerbeck, II, p. 488, and Barrett, p. 264.
[3] παρρησίᾳ. See p. 201, n. 6.
[4] ἔγνωσαν, 'got to know', Aorist of γινώσκω, used in 27, 'gets to know'
i.e. 'discovers'.
[5] See above, p. 205.   [6] Cf. Bultmann, p. 216.   [7] See above, p. 201.

the expected Christ. For **when the Christ is coming, no-body discovers where he is from.** This must not be taken to mean that they did not believe that the Christ would be a descendant of David, born in Bethlehem (cf. vii. 42), but that until he appears as Christ, his whereabouts will remain un-known.[1] There is irony in their admission that Christ's origin is mysterious. It is far more mysterious than they can imagine. But the men of Jerusalem **know where this man comes from**—Galilee! (cf. vii. 41, and i. 45 f.; vi. 42).

There is also irony in this claim to know Jesus' origin, par-ticularly if John shared the belief of Matthew and Luke that Jesus was in fact born in Bethlehem of David's line—and even if he did not, as the next verse makes clear.

(28) So Jesus cried out as he was teaching in the Temple, saying, 'You both know me and know where I am from! And I am not come on my own authority,[2] but I was sent by one who[3] is reliable,[4] though you do not know him. (29) I do know him, because I am from him,[5] and he sent me.'

28. Jesus' first remark could be punctuated as a question, but that would perhaps over-emphasise the irony. Jesus accepts the Jews' claim to knowledge about him, just as he accepts the Samaritan woman's statement that she has no husband (iv. 17 f.). Up to a point the Jews are right. It was well known that Jesus came from Galilee. But quite apart from the question whether they were accurately informed about his birthplace and parentage, they lacked the vital knowledge that he had not come on his own authority (cf. v. 43; viii. 42), but on another's, as **sent**[6] by one whom they should trust, but **do not know.**

---

[1] A similar opinion is expressed by Trypho the Jew in Justin Martyr's *Dialogus* (VIII. 4 cf. CX. 1), that even when Christ has been born he is unknown, even to himself, and has no power until Elias comes, anoints him, and makes him manifest to all. For Rabbinic parallels see Strack–Billerbeck, II, pp. 488 f.

[2] ἀπ' ἐμαυτοῦ, literally, 'from myself'; cf. v. 30; vii. 17; viii. 28, 42; x. 18; xiv. 10.

[3] Literally, 'but he who sent me . . .'.

[4] ἀληθινός. See on i. 9, p. 75, n. 3.

[5] With the implication, 'under his authority' or 'on his side', cf. viii. 44.

[6] For the sending of Christ, a recurrent theme in the FG, see on iii. 17, p. 129, n. 1.

Their ignorance is as great as the Samaritans', cf. iv. 22.[1] This
theme of Jewish ignorance is developed further in viii. 14, 19,
55; xv. 21.

29. Jesus on the other hand does **know him,** with a knowledge based on his affinity with him and on the commission
which he has from him, cf. vi. 46; viii. 13, 42; Matt. xi. 27. It is
through him that God makes himself known (i. 14).

**(30) So they sought to arrest him, and ⟨yet⟩ nobody laid
a hand on him, because his time[2] had not yet come. (31)
But many out of the crowd believed in him, and were
saying, 'When the Christ comes, he will not do more
signs, will he, than this man has done?' (32) The Pharisees heard the crowd muttering these things about him,
and the highpriests and the Pharisees sent officers[3] to
arrest him.**

30. At last the authorities decide to act. This verse is most
probably to be understood in the light of verse 32, which explains that the two parties in the Sanhedrin were for once in
agreement, provoked by the Pharisees' report of the favourable
impression which Jesus had made on the crowd. Their action
was, however, premature, since Jesus' **time had not yet come**
(cf. vii. 6, 8). Just as Jesus would do nothing on his own initiative (cf. ii. 4), so too nothing done by men on their own initiative
can affect him until the time is come (cf. xiii. 1). The repeated
mention of abortive attempts upon Jesus builds up the dramatic
tension as the Gospel proceeds, and emphasises the providential control under which he exercises his ministry.

31. Again, as in Samaria (iv. 41) **many . . . believed.** Jesus,
they argue, may not exactly fit the expected rôle of the Christ,
but even **the Christ . . . will not do more signs . . . than
this man has done.** For the effect of signs cf. ii. 23; iv. 48.

**(33) So Jesus said, 'For a little time longer I am ⟨to be⟩[4]
with you, and ⟨then⟩ I am going[4] to him who sent me.**

---

[1] Another point of resemblance between vii and viii and iv. 1-42, the
corresponding passage in the plan of the FG. See p. 201.

[2] ὥρα, as in ii. 4. See p. 107, n. 2.

[3] ὑπηρέται, servants, partly vergers, partly police, mentioned along with
slaves (δοῦλοι) in xviii. 18.

[4] These verbs are all in the present tense, but have a future sense; cf.
xiii. 6, 27, 33; xiv. 3, 17; xv. 27; xxi. 23. See Moule, p. 7.

(34) You will seek me, and not find ⟨me⟩, and where I am ⟨to be⟩[1] you cannot come.'

33. Though his enemies' attacks are at present abortive, they will not have long to wait before their apparent victory. Nor will his friends long enjoy his bodily presence (cf. xii. 35; xiii. 33; xiv. 19; xvi. 16 ff.). Jesus' prediction of his departure is intentionally vague: he is really referring to his death, and will do so increasingly in what follows (cf. viii. 21; xiii. 33; xiv. 2 ff.; xvi. 5, 10, 17). This again heightens the dramatic tension.

34. Though his enemies will look for him, they will not find him (vii. 36; viii. 21) until he surrenders himself to them (xviii. 1-9). Contrast the promise to the disciples, 'Everyone who seeks finds', Matt. vii. 8. His friends will also look for him (xiii. 33) but will not be able to follow him until he returns for them (xiii. 36; xiv. 2-4, 28). He is going to his Father (xvii. 11), with whom they also will eventually be (xvii. 24).

(35) So the Jews said to one another, 'Where is this[2] ⟨fellow⟩ about to go, that we shall not find him? He is not about to go, is he, into the Dispersion of the Greeks[3] and teach the Greeks?[3] (36) What does this saying of his mean,[4] "You will seek me, and not find ⟨me⟩, and where I am ⟨to be⟩ you cannot come"?'

35. His enemies wonder how he will escape them. Will he leave Palestine and transfer his attentions to the Jews scattered among the Gentiles, perhaps even to the Gentiles themselves? Like Caiaphas (xi. 49 ff.) they stumble unwittingly on the truth. For Christ will go to the Gentiles, in the apostolic mission. Their misunderstanding is typical; as on many previous occasions (cf. iii. 4; iv. 11; vi. 42, 52), Jesus' words are taken at their face value. 36. Though the Jews carefully repeat Jesus' words, they omit those which would have given them the

---

[1] *Ibid.*

[2] οὗτος. This is used contemptuously, as in verse 15 (p. 205, n. 1).

[3] In both cases the word used is Ἕλληνες. This is only used elsewhere in the FG in xii. 20. It can mean both Greeks by race, i.e. Gentiles, or Greek-speaking Jews. In **the Dispersion of the Greeks** it certainly means Gentiles, and so most probably has the same meaning in the other two instances (see also on xii. 20).

[4] Literally, 'What is this word which he said?'

clue to his meaning—those in which he speaks of going to him who sent him.

(37) On the last, the great, day of the feast Jesus stood and cried out, saying, 'If anyone thirsts, let him come,[1] and let him drink (38) who believes in me; as the scripture said, "Rivers of living water[2] shall flow from his innermost being.[3]"' (39) Now by saying this he referred to[4] the spirit which those who had believed[5] in him were about to receive; for the spirit was not yet[6] ⟨available⟩, because Jesus had not yet been glorified.

37. There appears to be some obscurity in the narrative here. The mention of a new **day** comes in awkwardly between the sending of the officers in verse 32 and their return in verse 45. It is possible that the rearrangement of this section of the FG, to which attention has already been drawn,[7] is responsible for this confusion.[8]

The feast of Tabernacles lasted for eight days, and one would naturally suppose that **the last** was therefore the eighth. But the eighth day could be considered a feast in its own right, and **the last, the great, day** may in fact be the seventh. It was marked by special ceremonies in the Temple, which would justify its description **great**.[9] The point of mentioning it is to stress the solemnity of the occasion on which Jesus made this pronouncement, and so of the pronouncement itself.

His invitation to the thirsty to **come,**[10] **and . . . drink** is particularly appropriate, since the pouring of libations of water

---

[1] This is the reading of P⁶⁶ ℵ* D *b e*. The other authorities add 'to me', which is of course implied. There is no apparent reason why these words should have been omitted, and it is best to regard them as a gloss.

[2] With this cf. Rev. xxii. 1, 'a river of water of life'.

[3] Literally, 'from his belly' (κοιλία), used, as e.g., in Job xv. 35, for 'the most secret part of a man as the seat of his innermost life' (Bauer, p. 114; Bauer⁵, s.v.): cf. the Rabbinic use of *guph* (belly) for 'person, self' (Strack–Billerbeck, II, p. 492), and the RSV translation, 'heart'.

[4] Literally, 'And this he said about . . .'.

[5] πιστεύσαντες, P⁶⁶ BW. Other authorities (ℵ D Θ *fam* 1 *fam* 13, etc.) have the easier 'those who believe'.

[6] οὔπω γὰρ ἦν πνεῦμα, P⁶⁶ ℵ Θ *eg arm*. This is expanded in various ways by the other authorities, to guard against the mistaken idea that John meant that the Spirit did not yet exist. [7] See pp. 201 and 205.

[8] The difficulty could be met by transposing 25-36 and 37-44. But see Introduction, p. 4. [9] See Strack–Billerbeck, II, pp. 490 f.

[10] For the significance of coming to Jesus, see p. 189, n. 6.

was a feature of the ritual of Tabernacles. Jesus is himself the true Temple (cf. ii. 21), and offers water far more effectual than that used in the ritual of Tabernacles (cf. iv. 14; vi. 35).[1]

37 f. The punctuation of these verses presents a difficult problem, the solution of which depends on their interpretation. The alternatives to the punctuation adopted above are:

(i) ... **let him drink.** ⟨As for the man⟩[2] **who believes in me, as the scripture said, 'Rivers ...'**

(ii) ... **let him drink who believes in me, as the scripture said. Rivers ...**

If (i) is adopted, it follows that it is from the believer that the **rivers of living water shall flow.** In support of this, iv. 14 may be cited, but it must be noted that there the believer only possesses the 'spring of water issuing in eternal life' because he has already drunk the water which Christ gives. Now in the FG **the scripture** (ἡ γραφή) is used of a particular passage,[3] and there is no passage of the Old Testament which obviously suggests that rivers of living water shall flow from the believer. Isa. lviii. 11, 'You shall be ... like a spring of water, whose waters fail not', is perhaps the best,[4] but could equally well be interpreted of the Christ. So, since (i) compels us to apply the passage to the believer, it should be rejected in favour of **let him drink who believes in me**—in spite of the formidable array of authorities which supports it.[5]

If (ii) is adopted, **the scripture** must be taken to refer to the

---

[1] See also the comments on these passages, pp. 143 and 189 f.

[2] Literally, 'The man who believes in me ... rivers shall flow from his belly'. This construction, a nominative which is not in fact the subject of the sentence, occurs elsewhere in the FG, e.g. vi. 39, which is, literally translated, 'so that everything which he gave me I might not lose of it ...'.

[3] See on ii. 22, p. 120.

[4] Barrett (p. 271) favours Zech. xiv. 8, 'Living waters shall flow out from Jerusalem', but this is rather far-fetched, and could be as well applied to Christ. See p. 214.

[5] Origen and the Greek Fathers (who may have disliked the idea of the Spirit proceeding from Christ—see Lagrange, p. 215), followed in the West by Augustine and Jerome, AV, RV, RSV, and many modern commentators, most recently Barrett (pp. 270 f.) and Lightfoot (p. 183). Bauer (p. 112) adopts this punctuation, but avoids the difficulty by taking the passage to mean, 'He who believes in me ⟨will realise that this is because⟩, as the Scripture said, "Rivers of living water will flow from his (i.e. Christ's) belly"'. The other punctuation was followed by Irenaeus and Cyprian, and more recently by Lagrange (pp. 214 ff.) and Bultmann (p. 228, n. 6).

invitation just given to the thirsty to come and drink, and will then allude to such Old Testament passages as Isa. xliv. 3 and lv. 1. Then **Rivers of living water,** etc., is a separate sentence, containing no Old Testament allusion, and can be applied to the believer, in accordance with iv. 14. It cannot apply to Jesus himself, for he would have used the First Person instead of the Third in a statement about himself—'Rivers of living water shall flow from *my* innermost being'. But the explanation given in verse 39, that Jesus **referred to the spirit** when he said this, seems to suggest that it is from Christ himself, and not from the believer, that the rivers flow, and so to be equally fatal to (i) and (ii).

This leaves the punctuation adopted above, . . . **let him drink who believes in me; as the scripture said, 'Rivers . . .'** to which it may be objected that it is almost as difficult to find an Old Testament passage that can be interpreted of Christ as the source of living water as it was to find one applicable to the believer. There are, however, two possibilities. There may be behind this a typological interpretation of the rock from which Moses produced water in the wilderness (Exod. xvii. 6), on the lines of 1 Cor. x. 4, 'They drank of a spiritual rock that followed them: and the rock was Christ'. However bizarre such interpretation may seem today, it was not alien to the FG, which can interpret the brazen serpent as a type of Christ (iii. 14). Moreover, the explicit contrast between Moses and Christ as givers of food (vi. 32 ff., 48 ff., 58) makes it less implausible to adopt an interpretation of the present passage which implies a contrast between them as givers of drink. Isa. xlviii. 21, in the LXX (where the verbs are future) promises the fugitives from Babylon a renewal of the miracle of water from the rock. Alternatively, since Christ is the real Temple (cf. ii. 21),[1] passages which refer to waters flowing from the Temple may be relevant here, cf. Ps. xlvi. 4; Ezek. xlvii. 1 ff.; Joel iii. 18; Zech. xiv. 8.[2]

Thus Jesus promises living water in abundance to those who believe in him. As coming **from his innermost being,** his very self, it will have the same effect as the flesh and blood which he has already designated as food and drink for the faithful (cf. vi. 53 f.), though the parallel is not quite exact, since

[1] See also p. 213.   [2] See also p. 213, n. 4.

the water which conveys the gift of the spirit in baptism is not drunk (cf., however, 1 Cor. xii. 13).

This passage may also point forward to xix. 34, to the water and blood which flowed from Christ's pierced side. It is true that there the primary reference is not to the gift of the spirit as such, but (if there is any symbolism to be detected there) rather to the sacraments, but nevertheless we already know that the sacraments are vehicles of the spirit (iii. 5; vi. 63).

39. The evangelist does not intend to leave his readers in any doubt about the meaning of Jesus' words: **by saying this he referred to the spirit.** (Note that Isa. xliv. 3 connects the pouring out of water with that of spirit.) Our attention is directed back to earlier references to **the spirit,** particularly to i. 32 f.; iii. 5-8; iv. 23 f.; vi. 63; and we are prepared for the further statements in xiv. 16 f., 26; xv. 26; xvi. 13 ff.; xx. 22.[1] We are told here that **the spirit** will not be available until **Jesus** has **been glorified.** Eventually it will be made clear that it is by his death that **Jesus** will be **glorified.**[2]

By saying that **the spirit was not yet** the evangelist does not mean that the spirit did not *exist* before the ministry of Jesus. It (or, as we shall later learn to say, he[3]) was 'from the beginning' just as much as the Logos. But it is not until Jesus, the Logos made flesh, has **been glorified** that the spirit will be an abiding possession, or rather a constant companion, of the faithful (xiv. 16).

(40) Then when they heard these words some of the crowd began to say, 'This is truly the prophet'. (41) Others were saying, 'This is the Christ'. But some said, 'Surely the Christ does not come from Galilee, does he? (42) The scripture said, did it not, that ⟨it is⟩ from the seed of David, and from Bethlehem, the village where David was, ⟨that⟩ the Christ comes?' (43) So a division

---

[1] See the notes on these passages, and particularly pp. 96 f.

[2] The present passage gives the first instance of the verb 'glorify' (δοξάζω) in the FG; its full significance is gradually revealed, xii. 23; xiii. 31; xvii. 1. The noun 'glory' (δόξα) on the other hand marks an important theme which first appears in i. 14 (see pp. 81 f.).

[3] xiv. 26 (ἐκεῖνος the masculine pronoun used in apposition to the neuter noun πνεῦμα).

arose in the crowd because of him. (44) And some wanted to arrest him, but nobody laid hands on him.

40 f. The conclusion reached by some of Jesus' hearers that he is **the prophet,** and by others that he is **the Christ** (cf. verse 26), recalls the questions put to John the Baptist in i. 21, which distinguish the prophet from the Christ,[1] rather than the confession of the Galileans in vi. 14, who appear to equate them.[2] Others, however, resemble the Galileans in vi. 42, and convinced that they know Jesus' origin (cf. verse 27), regard it as impossible for him to be the Christ.[3]

42. The passage of **scripture**[4] to which they refer is Mic. v. 2. These men of Jerusalem do not appear (or affect not) to know that Jesus was of Davidic descent, though Bartimaeus of Jericho did, according to Mark x. 47. It is a nice question whether the evangelist himself believed it. He never states it in so many words,[5] but it is probable that this is because the Davidic descent of Jesus was not theologically significant for him,[6] and had in fact caused misunderstanding during Jesus' ministry.[7] It would certainly add to the irony of this passage if he did in fact believe it to be true.

43. There are further mentions of **division** among Jesus' hearers (ix. 16; x. 19). They show that the light is beginning to have the effect predicted in iii. 20 f.[8]

44. The mention of this abortive desire to **arrest** Jesus— virtually a repetition of verse 30—comes in rather awkwardly between the sending of the officers in verse 32 and their return in verse 45. Perhaps the order here was originally different.[9] Nevertheless these repetitions are dramatically effective.[10]

(45) Then the officers came to the highpriests and Pharisees; and these said to them, 'Why did you not bring him?' (46) The officers answered, 'No human

---

[1] See pp. 89 f.   [2] See p. 180.   [3] See p. 209.

[4] For ἡ γραφή meaning a single passage of Scripture, see on ii. 22, p. 120.

[5] It is, however, clear that the author of Revelation accepted it, cf. Rev. v. 5; xxii. 16.

[6] Nor was it for St. Paul, who only refers to it once, quite incidentally, in Rom. i. 3.   [7] See Introduction, pp. 14 f.

[8] See p. 131 and cf. Luke xii. 51, though here a different word is used.

[9] See above, p. 212.   [10] See above, p. 210.

being[1] **ever spoke in the way in which this man**[1]**speaks'.**[2]
**(47) Then the Pharisees answered them, 'You also are
not misled, are you? (48) None of the rulers have believed
in him, have they, or of the Pharisees? (49) But this crowd
which does not study the law, they are accursed.'**[3]

45 f. The officers excuse their failure by appealing to the
superhuman impression made by Jesus' speech.[4] 47 ff. But the
Pharisees are not impressed. They hold the opinion already
expressed in verse 12, that Jesus misleads the crowd. It is only
those ignorant of **the law** who are taken in by him—i.e. those
whom the Rabbis called 'the people of the land' (*'ammē hā-'ārets*).[5]
Because they neglected the study of the law, they were considered *ipso facto* sinners, and liable to the curse pronounced in
Deut. xxvii. 26. Their evidence was not acceptable in a court of
law, and they could not have any right to an opinion on a religious
question. It is clear from the Synoptic Gospels, as well as the
FG, that these were the people who listened most readily to
Jesus, cf. Mark xii. 37, Luke vii. 34.

(50) Nicodemus, who had gone to him previously,[6]
⟨**and**⟩ **was one of them, said to them, (51) 'Our law does
not judge the man, does it, unless it first hears from him,
and knows what he is doing?' (52) They answered and
said to him, 'You are not also from Galilee, are you?
Search, and see that no prophet arises from Galilee.'**

50. The division in the crowd extends to the Sanhedrin.
Nicodemus, who was both a Pharisee and a 'ruler', i.e. a
member of the Sanhedrin (iii. 1), puts in a cautious word for
Jesus, 51. appealing to the principle that the law condemns
nobody unheard—cf. Deut. i. 16 f.; xiii. 14; xvii. 4; xix. 18, and
—for Roman practice—Acts xxv. 16. 52. But the Sanhedrin
cannot understand him—he is not even a fellow-countryman of

---

[1] The same word (ἄνθρωπος) is used in the Greek, but the emphatic
position which it occupies in the main clause appears to call for this paraphrase.

[2] A few authorities, including P[66] B W *boh*, omit the clause 'in which this
man speaks'. The words may be a gloss, but, since both clauses end with the
same word (ἄνθρωπος) the omission may be a very early mistake.

[3] In the Greek a singular noun has a plural verb, which this rendering
attempts to reproduce.   [4] Cf. xviii. 6.

[5] See Strack–Billerbeck, II, pp. 494-521 for a full account of the *'ammē
hā-'ārets*.   [6] This clause is omitted by ℵ* and may be a gloss.

the criminal! The claims made on his behalf are not supported by Scripture.

Jesus had bidden the Jews to search the scriptures (v. 39), and now the members of the Sanhedrin tell Nicodemus to do the same. Now 2 Kings xiv. 25 shows that a prophet did arise from Galilee—Jonah the son of Amittai. The Pharisees therefore presumably mean, not that no prophet *has ever arisen* from Galilee, but that there are no grounds in Scripture for expecting a prophet in the future from there. Just as in 41 ff. the origin of the Christ from Galilee is denied, so here, it may be, it is the origin particularly of 'the prophet' of verse 40 from Galilee that is denied.[1]

[For vii. 53–viii. 11 see the Appendix, pp. 458-466.]

viii. (12) Then Jesus spoke to them again, saying, 'I am the light of the world: he who follows me shall not walk[2] in darkness, but shall have the light of life'.

A new episode now opens, rather abruptly, but still within the context of the feast of Tabernacles. This abruptness may again be due to disturbance of the original order of the FG.[3] Nevertheless this declaration comes in effectively here, between the description of the division which arose among Jesus' hearers[4] and the healing of the man born blind. It is also appropriate in the feast of Tabernacles, since one of the features of the ritual of the feast was the illumination of the Temple. Jesus the true Temple is the true **light of the world.**[5] So also are his disciples (Matt. v. 14, Phil. ii. 15).[6]

For the form of Jesus' saying, which begins, **'I am . . .'** cf. vi. 35;[7] for Jesus as **the light** cf. i. 4 f.,[8] **of the world,** cf. i. 9 f.,[9] iii. 16 ff.[10] That his followers **shall not walk in darkness** has already been prepared for by vi. 16-21, particularly by 17, and

---

[1] On this interpretation, there is no reason for saying (as Barrett does, p. 275) that this raises the question whether John had any first-hand knowledge of Palestine in the first century, in view of the Rabbinic doctrine that each tribe had produced at least one prophet.

[2] See p. 200, n. 5. [3] See pp. 221 f.

[4] See on vii. 43, p. 216. [5] See on vii. 37, pp. 212 f.

[6] For the significance of 'following' Jesus see on i. 43 and xiii. 36.

[7] See p. 188, n. 7.

[8] See pp. 72-74 for the significance of 'light' in the FG.

[9] See p. 76 for the significance of 'the world' in the FG.

[10] See pp. 129 ff.

looks forward to xii. 35 f.; that they **shall have the light of life** follows naturally upon the collocation of **light** and **life** [1] in i. 4 f. and from iii. 16 and 19 ff. The actual phrase **the light of life** occurs in the Dead Sea Scrolls.[2] Thus several themes characteristic of the FG are drawn together here; others will make their appearance as the debate proceeds.

(13) Then the Pharisees said to him, 'You bear witness about yourself: your witness is not true '.[3]

The theme of witness[4] reappears, in a complaint of the Pharisees which recalls the saying of Jesus himself in v. 31. There he concedes the point that a man's testimony about himself is not true, but claims in verse 32 that he has corroboration. This latter the Pharisees deny.

(14) Jesus answered and said to them, 'Even if I am bearing witness about myself, my witness is true, because I know where I came from and where I am going; but you do not know where I came from, or where I am going.'

Jesus protests the truth of his testimony about himself, but does not repeat the claim of v. 32 until verse 18. Instead, using words which recall what is said of the spirit in iii. 8 he justifies his claim on the grounds that he knows, and the Pharisees do not, his own origin and destination (cf. vii. 27 f.). The relevance of this last remark of his is not immediately obvious. He is, however, preparing for the assertion in verse 18 that his Father who sent him corroborates his testimony (cf. v. 43), by claiming this knowledge of his origin which the Pharisees do not possess.

(15) 'You judge according to the flesh; I do not judge anyone. (16) But even if I do judge, my judgement is true;[5] **because I am not alone, but I have with me him who sent me.**[6] **(17) And even in your law it is written, that the**

---

[1] See Introduction, p. 5 and p. 72.

[2] *Manual of Discipline*, iii. 7. For the importance of the Scrolls for the study of the FG see Introduction, p. 22.

[3] The adjective here, and in verses 14, 16 (P⁶⁶ ℵ Θ), 17, is ἀληθής, on which see p. 75, n. 3.

[4] For the significance of 'witness' as a theme in the FG, see p. 75.

[5] A few MSS. here read ἀληθινή, 'reliable': see p. 75, n. 3.

[6] Literally, 'but I and he who sent me'.

witness of two men is true. (18) I am ⟨one⟩ who bear witness about myself, and ⟨the other who⟩ bears witness about me ⟨is⟩ the Father who sent me.'

15. Jesus explains that the Pharisees' ignorance is due to their judging **according to the flesh**,[1] i.e., from outward appearance; cf. vii. 24, and Jesus' ironical agreement in vii. 28 with the Jews' claim that they know where he is from. Then, from the mistaken judgement of the Pharisees, Jesus appears to go off at a tangent when he says **'I do not judge anyone'**; note that the themes of 'witness' and 'judgement' occur together in v. 30 ff. These words of Jesus appear to contradict v. 30, but the contradiction is more apparent than real. 16. For Jesus goes on at once to grant the possibility that he *does* judge—though judgement is not the purpose of his coming, but its inevitable result.[2] If then his coming does result in judgement, his **judgement is true,** since it is not a sentence imposed from outside, but the inevitable result of a man's own action and choice (cf. iii. 19 ff.).

This is not, however, the reason given here. Instead, Jesus says that it is **because I am not alone . . .,** which is at first sight a *non sequitur,* until it is realised that Jesus harks back to v. 30, and, by claiming that the Father corroborates his judgement, prepares for the claim that he also corroborates his testimony. In everything the Son acts in complete unanimity with the Father **who sent**[3] him (cf. v. 19 ff.).

17. Several texts in the Mosaic Law, particularly Deut. xix. 15, insist on more than one witness. By describing it as **your law** (cf. x. 34; xv. 25) Jesus seems to suggest a degree of detachment from Judaism which, it may be argued, should be attributed to the subsequent experience of the Church which appealed to the Old Testament in its polemic against Judaism.[4] Even in the Synoptic Gospels, however, Jesus appeals to Scripture against the Jews (cf. Mark ii. 26)[5] while Matt. v. 21 ff. suggests that Jesus' attitude to the law was critical.

[1] For the meaning of 'flesh' ($\sigma\acute{\alpha}\rho\xi$) in the FG see p. 79.
[2] For 'judgement' as a theme in the FG see on iii. 17 ff. (pp. 130 f.) and on v. 22 f. (p. 166).   [3] For the 'sending' of the Son see p. 129, n. 1.
[4] Cf. the attitude to the festivals in ii. 13; v. 1; vii. 2. See p. 116 and Barrett, p. 280. See also on x. 34 (pp. 259 f.) and xv. 25 (p. 345).
[5] See also on v. 47, p. 174.

18. Thus Jesus *has* a second witness—his Father (cf. v. 37; 1 John v. 9).

(19) So they said to him, 'Where is your father?' Jesus answered, 'You do not know either me or my Father; if you knew me, you would know my Father also'. (20) These words he spoke near[1] the treasury, while he was teaching in the Temple; and nobody arrested him, because his time[2] had not yet come.

19. The Pharisees misunderstand Jesus[3], and challenge him to produce his witness. It may be that they knew that Joseph was dead, or there may be in their words an implication that Jesus is illegitimate (cf. viii. 41). The latter suggestion is not inconsistent with the reference to Joseph as Jesus' father in vi. 42, since there the Jews are simply concerned to discount the claim that he is 'the bread which came down from heaven'.

In xiv. 8, Philip asks to be shown Jesus' Father, but, since he is prepared to believe that God is his Father, Jesus tells him, 'He who has seen me has seen the Father'. He cannot, however, say this to the Pharisees. They do not know his Father (v. 37; vii. 28), and so cannot know him.

20. The precise location of **the treasury,** which is also mentioned in Mark xii. 41; Luke xxi. 1, is not known exactly. It appears to refer to the part of the Court of the Women where the chests were placed to receive the freewill offerings of the worshippers.[4] Jesus' assertion that the Jews do not know God or his Son is all the more impressive—and provocative—for being made in God's house. Yet his hearers make no move against him, cf. vii. 30.[5]

This verse reads like the conclusion of an episode,[6] but as

---

[1] Literally 'in' (ἐν). Mark xii. 41 'opposite the treasury' is a more precise indication.   [2] ὥρα. See on ii. 4, p. 107, n. 2.

[3] For similar misunderstandings, which serve to advance the argument, cf. iii. 4; iv. 11; vi. 42, 52; vii. 35.

[4] So Strack–Billerbeck, II, p. 42. Barrett (p. 281) suggests that John 'had no precise conception of the plan of the Temple in his mind'. But this does not necessarily follow from the fact that we do not know exactly where it was. It may have been so familiar to him that it did not occur to him to explain it. Barrett does not mention the discussion of this question in Strack–Billerbeck, II, pp. 37-45, or the use of the word in the singular (as in the New Testament) in Josephus, *Antiquities*, XIX. 294.

[5] See p. 210.   [6] See Bultmann, p. 213.

such fits awkwardly into its present position. Since viii. 12 also
fits awkwardly on to vii. 52,[1] it is possible that viii. 12-20 is not
in its original position. It would come in better as the climax to
the account of a period in Jerusalem which comprised chapter v
and vii. 15-24.[2] The comment that **nobody arrested him,
because his time had not yet come** may be felt to be more
appropriate before than after the references to attempts to
arrest Jesus in vii. 30, 32, 44—for the order of the passages would
then be viii. 12-20; vii. 1-14;[3] vii. 25-52.[4] But the present order
of the passages is clearly intentional: **I am the light of the
world** is particularly appropriate to the feast of Tabernacles.[5]

(**21**) **Then he said to them again, 'I am going, and you
will seek me, and will die in your sin; where I am going,
you cannot come'.**

If the original order of the FG was as suggested in the previous
paragraph, viii. 21 once followed vii. 25-52, with which in fact
viii. 21 ff. has much in common. As it now stands, **again** makes
viii. 21 ff. read like an afterthought; but it would be more to the
point if it followed vii. 52.

Jesus' words are an obscure allusion to his death, as in the
parallel passage, vii. 33.[6] Here, however, his warning to his
enemies is more insistent than in vii. 34; instead of saying that
they will not find him, he tells them **you . . . will die in your sin**
— the sin of wilful refusal to accept the Christ. Here also **you
will seek me** may have an undertone that is not yet discernible
in vii. 34—they will one day look to him for salvation, but then
it will be too late. The mention of his enemies' death makes
clearer the allusion to his own death in **I am going.**

(**22**) **Then the Jews said, 'He will not kill himself, will
he, because he says, "Where I am going, you cannot
come"?'**

This is another characteristically ironical misunderstanding,[7]
parallel to, but more malicious than, that in vii. 35.[8] Confident
of their own salvation, the Jews ignore Jesus' warning, rudely
interrupt him, and suggest that it is he who will forfeit his own

---

[1] See p. 218.   [2] See p. 205.
[3] See p. 201.   [4] See p. 208.
[5] See p. 218.   [6] See p. 211.
[7] Cf. viii. 19, p. 221.   [8] See p. 211.

hope of salvation by committing suicide, which was to the Jews, though not to the Greeks and Romans, a particularly grievous sin.[1] But—like Caiaphas (xi. 50)—they have stumbled unawares on a profound truth. Jesus is to die a voluntary death (cf. x. 17 f.), but it will no more be suicide than those of the martyrs.[2]

(23) And he said to them, 'You are from the ⟨regions⟩ below, I am from the ⟨regions⟩ above;[3] you are from this world, I am not from this world. (24) So I said to you that you will die in your sins; for if you do not believe that I am, you will die in your sins.'

23. Jesus ignores the interruption, and proceeds to explain why he warned his hearers that they would die. It is because they **are from** (i.e. belong to) **the ⟨regions⟩ below, from this world,**[4] and are wrapped up in it, and unable to detach them-selves from it. For the contrast of **below** and **above** as earth and heaven cf. iii. 31.[5] In Hebrew thought **this world** is most naturally contrasted with *the world to come:* and since the Hebrew *ʿôlām* can mean both 'world' (κόσμος) and 'age' (αἰών) **this world** (κόσμος) in John corresponds to 'this age' (αἰών) in the Synoptic Gospels (cf. Matt. xii. 32) and Paul (cf. Rom. xii. 2).[6] For John the contrast is not temporal, but spatial, or perhaps between two simultaneously existing orders of being. This is in line with the transvaluation of eschatology in the FG.[7] It does not necessarily imply a crudely spatial or local conception of heaven[8] (though it no doubt originated in that way), any more than to say that the sun rises implies that one thinks that the earth does not move.

---

[1] See Josephus, *B.J.*, III. viii. 5, who describes it as 'impiety against God the Creator'.

[2] Marcus Aurelius, who as a Stoic approved of suicide, says men should not let themselves be killed 'like the Christians, from sheer obstinacy': cf. the final speech of the Fourth Knight in 'Murder in the Cathedral' (4th ed., p. 83).

[3] ἐκ τῶν ἄνω: cf. τὰ ἄνω Col. iii. 1, 'Seek the things that are above'. See also pp. 126 f.

[4] For the meaning of κόσμος ('world') in the FG, see p. 76.

[5] See p. 135.

[6] John has 9 instances of 'this κόσμος' in the FG and one in his Epistles, but none of 'this αἰών'. The corresponding figures for the Synoptic Gospels are 0 and 3, for Paul 1 (+ 1 in Ephesians) and 7 (+ 1 in Ephesians).

[7] See Introduction, pp. 13 f., and p. 128 (on iii. 15).

[8] See Barrett, p. 282.

24. Jesus repeats his warning, but in more general terms (**sins** instead of the singular), adding the explanation—oracular in its obscurity—that they will die unless they **believe** [1] **that I am.** The closest parallels to this absolute use of **I am** (ἐγώ εἰμι) in the FG are viii. 28, 58; xiii. 19, and, outside the FG, the LXX version of Isa. xliii. 10, 'that you may know and believe and understand that ἐγώ εἰμι,' [2] and Mark xiii. 6, the claim of those who will come and deceive many, saying ἐγώ εἰμι. [3] Matt. xxiv. 5 paraphrases this, 'I am *the Christ*'. This gives the clue to the meaning of the saying here, but it is noteworthy that both in Mark and John Jesus is not made to say 'I am the Christ'. He says it to the Samaritan woman, however (John iv. 26), since it would not have any misleading political associations for her. What Jesus means here is **I am** *the one who can save you* (cf. iii. 16). There is also in the words **I am** a possible allusion to the Divine Name (Exod. iii. 14). [4]

(25) So they said to him, 'Who are you?'
Having failed to understand Jesus, they ask him to complete his sentence. But Jesus cannot say anything that will help them, since they do not believe in him. Understanding comes after faith, not faith after understanding, cf. vii. 17; viii. 31 f. There is a similar situation in x. 24 ff. But in the case of the disciples things are different; Jesus can speak to them openly, cf. xvi. 29.

Jesus said to them, 'Why am I even speaking to you at all?' He gives expression to the hopelessness of even trying to explain to those whose refusal to believe makes them incapable of understanding. [5]

---

[1] For the significance of 'believing' in the FG see p. 75, n. 2, p. 78.
[2] See Bauer, p. 123, and Barrett, pp. 282 f.   [3] See Lagrange, p. 236.
[4] On the whole question of the meaning of ἐγώ εἰμι in the FG, see on iv. 26, pp. 148 f.
[5] Jesus' words τὴν ἀρχὴν ὅτι καὶ λαλῶ ὑμῖν can be taken as either (i) a question, or (ii) a statement answering the Jews' question.
Of these, (i) is followed by the Greek exegetes, and by Westcott, who regards it as 'a sad exclamation which is half interrogative' (p. 142); by RV ᵐᵍ, RSV ᵐᵍ, Lagrange (pp. 236 ff.), and Bauer (pp. 122 f.). This gives τὴν ἀρχήν a well-attested adverbial sense, 'at all' (see LS⁹ s.v. I. 1c), though it does not occur elsewhere in the New Testament; its position in the sentence is, however, the same as that of ἀκμήν, another adverbial accusative, in Matt. xv. 16. The interrogative sense of ὅτι has a parallel in Mark ix. 28.
Barrett (p. 283) objects to (i) on the grounds that it 'goes so badly with the next verse, and seems so pointless', and so follows RV and RSV in adopting

(26) 'I have many things to speak and to judge about you; but he who sent me is true, and the things which I heard from him, these I speak to the world.' (27) They did not know that he was telling them of the Father.

26. This feeling of hopelessness is only momentary. Jesus has indeed much to say about the Jews, not, however, for their salvation, but only in judgement upon their obduracy (cf. iii. 18 ff.; viii. 16; ix. 39). He must speak because he has a message which he **heard**[1] from him who **sent**[2] him; this message is true, because he who sent him is **true**[3], and he is to deliver it **to the world**[4] which he was sent to save (iii. 16 ff.), over the heads, as it were, of his immediate audience, 27. whose lack of understanding John is careful once again to mention.

(28) Then Jesus said, 'When you lift up the Son of man, then you will know that I am, and that I do nothing of my own accord,[5] but that I speak as the Father taught me. (29) And he who sent me is with me; he did not leave me alone; because I do the things that please him all the time.'

28. Jesus now says that the Jews[6] will one day have the answer to their question, 'Who are you?' This will be when they **lift up**, i.e. crucify,[7] **the Son of man**,[8] and so become the unconscious instruments of divine providence. For the death of

(ii) (cf. Lightfoot, p. 191). Of the various possible renderings of this as a statement, he favours, 'I am from the beginning what I tell you'. But it is questionable whether Jesus meant to give them an answer. Also if John intended to say 'from the beginning' he could have written ἀπ' ἀρχῆς, as in viii. 44; τὴν ἀρχήν can mean 'at first', but would require a verb in the aorist.

The reader must judge which interpretation best fits the context. [Cf. also B.-D. §§160, 300 (2), Turner, p. 49.—B. A. M.]

[1] Cf. iii. 31-34; v. 30; vii. 16. To 'hear' can also imply to 'obey', cf. p. 167, n. 7.

[2] See p. 129 n. 1.   [3] ἀληθής: see p. 75, n. 3.

[4] For the significance of the 'world' (κόσμος) in the FG see p. 76.

[5] ἀπ' ἐμαυτοῦ, literally, 'from myself' cf. v. 30; vii. 17, 28; viii. 42; x. 18; xiv. 10.

[6] Barrett (p. 284) objects that John knew that the Jews would not recognise the truth of Christ's claims even after the crucifixion, and so must be addressing his own readers here. But John, no less than Paul (cf. Rom. xi. 26), hoped for the eventual salvation of Israel, which, when it came, would be through the Cross. Christ will draw *all men* to himself (xii. 32). And many Jews did in fact believe, though before the crucifixion none achieved perfect faith.   [7] Cf. iii. 14; xii. 32-34.

[8] For the meaning of 'Son of man' in the FG see p. 106.

Christ will not only reveal him as the Saviour,[1] but, as the supreme example of his obedience to his Father,[2] will also demonstrate that his present actions and words are not the expression of his own self-will, but of his submission to the will of God (cf. v. 19, 30; vi. 38; vii. 16).

29. But the sending of the Son does not involve any separation from his Father (i.e. it must not be thought of in spatial terms). For the only way in which one can be separated from God is by sin, and this obviously does not arise in the case of the Son, who always pleases the Father (by never acting independently of him, verse 28), and so is not abandoned by him (cf. verse 16).[3]

(30) As he spoke these things, many believed in him.

Again, as in vii. 31, John records that **many . . . believed in** Jesus. He skilfully conveys the mounting tension of this period of controversy during the feast of Tabernacles by recording the alternation among Jesus' hearers of faith and hostility—both equally ineffective until the final crisis. Though he mentions the faith of the hearers, John was well aware that it was not wholly reliable (cf. ii. 23 f.), as the following passage here shows. It is therefore perhaps unjustified to say that this statement is 'anachronistic'.[4]

(31) Then Jesus said to the Jews who believed him, 'If you persevere in my word, you really are my disciples; (32) and you shall know the truth, and the truth shall set you free.'

31. Jesus now addresses a section of his audience, those **who believed him.** John does not say **believed _in_ him,** as in verse 30, perhaps to indicate that their belief did not amount to faith in the full sense.[5] There is indeed a hint of doubt in Jesus' opening words: they are only his **disciples if** they **persevere** in obedience to his teaching (cf. 2 John 9)—and the sequel shows

---

[1] Cf. iii. 17; xii. 32.   [2] Cf. x. 17 f.; xii. 27.

[3] It is possible that John records this saying in order to guard against any interpretation of Mark xv. 34, 'My God, my God, why hast thou forsaken me?', which took it to imply that God really had forsaken Jesus. A similar saying occurs in xvi. 32, in a context in which Jesus speaks of his disciples' coming desertion at the time of his death. See Bauer, p. 124. Lagrange (p. 240) and Barrett (p. 284) doubt this.   [4] See Barrett (p. 285, on viii. 31).

[5] For the distinction between 'believe' and 'believe in', see on ii. 22, p. 120, n. 1. John does, however, use the perfect tense here, on which see p. 198, n. 5.

that they do not. Both **persevere** (literally, 'stay') and **word** have a deeper significance—they suggest the abiding of the disciples with Christ, the Logos.[1]

32. Whereas unbelievers demand proof before they are prepared to believe,[2] true disciples proceed from obedience to knowledge (cf. vii. 17), from 'doing the truth' (iii. 21) to knowing it. And then to **know the truth,** i.e. to know all that Christ is and does, liberates them from sin. **Truth** is an important concept in the FG:[3] later, Jesus says that he is the truth (xiv. 6), and in verse 36 he speaks of the Son setting men free. We may therefore see here an anticipation of this. It is only here that the FG speaks of salvation in terms of freedom, which is a Pauline rather than a Johannine concept (cf. Rom. vi. 18; Gal. v. 1, etc.). It is a Stoic commonplace that only the wise man is free, but the FG probably owes nothing to Stoicism here. The idea that the truth sets men free from sin is congenial to other characteristic doctrines of the FG—e.g. the close connexion between truth and the Spirit (cf. iv. 24; xiv. 17; xv. 26; xvi. 13), and the freedom of the Spirit which is bestowed on those who are born of the Spirit (as is implied by iii. 8, though the terms employed there are different).

(33) They answered him, 'We are Abraham's seed, and have never been enslaved to anyone; what do you mean by saying,[4] "You shall become free"?'

Another characteristic misunderstanding. The Jews claim that their descent from Abraham through Isaac, the son of the free woman, guarantees that they are already free. Their nation may have lost its autonomy, but they are not individually or personally slaves.

(34) Jesus answered them, 'Amen, amen, I say to you[5] that everyone who commits sin is a slave. (35) Now the slave does not stay in the house for ever;[6] the Son does stay for ever.[6] (36) If then the Son sets you free, you shall be free indeed.'

34. Jesus explains why they are not free. They are sinners,

---

[1] For the significance of 'stay' (μένω) see on i. 38 f.; for that of 'word' (λόγος) see Introduction, p. 4.   [2] Cf. vi. 30, and see on viii. 25.
[3] See p. 83.   [4] Literally, 'How sayest thou?' Cf. vi. 42; xii. 34; xiv. 9.
[5] See on i. 51.   [6] εἰς τὸν αἰῶνα. See on iv. 14.

and **everyone who commits sin**[1] **is a slave.** All the authorities for the text, except D *b sin* Clement of Alexandria and Cyprian, add here *of sin*. But the omission of these words (if they formed part of the original text) is so improbable that they must be regarded as a gloss, introduced under the influence of Rom. vi. 17, 20. Moreover they distort the argument, which runs as follows:

A sinner **is a slave,** i.e. his attitude to God is a slave's, one of veiled hostility and reluctant service, unlike the willing obedience of a son. 35. A slave has no permanent place in the household: a son has. The slave can be expelled like Ishmael (cf. Gen. xxi. 10; Gal. iv. 30).[2] 36. (Here the argument is very compressed.) He can only attain a permanent place by becoming a son; men become children of God by faith (cf. i. 12), i.e. by that perseverance in Christ's word which leads to knowledge of the truth and to freedom (verses 31 f.). And to be freed by the truth is to be freed by the Son.

(37) 'I know that you are Abraham's seed; but you are seeking to kill me, because there is no room for my word in you.[3] **(38) I speak what I have seen at ⟨my⟩ Father's side; so you also do what you heard from ⟨your⟩ father.'**

37. Jesus' admission that the Jews are descendants of Abraham is as ironical as his admission that the Samaritan woman has no husband (iv. 18). Their murderous intentions (cf. v. 18; vii. 1, 25; viii. 40), which show that Jesus' word[4] has left them unaffected, indicate their true origin.

This sudden turn in the conversation is surprising, since there has been nothing since verse 31 to lead us to expect it. But Jesus knew men's thoughts (cf. ii. 25), and must have

[1] ὁ ποιῶν τὴν ἁμαρτίαν (cf. 1 John iii. 8) implies a habit of sin, as ὁ ποιῶν τὴν ἀλήθειαν (iii. 21) one of honesty.

[2] There may also be an allusion to the rule that a Hebrew who has sold himself into bondage must be released and sent away in the seventh year, cf. Lev. xxv. 40, which makes no provision for him to stay with his master if he wishes, unlike Exod. xxi. 5 f., Deut. xv. 16 f.

[3] ὁ λόγος ὁ ἐμὸς οὐ χωρεῖ ἐν ὑμῖν. The meaning of χωρεῖ is uncertain. That adopted here is the closest to that in the two other examples of the verb in the FG, ii. 6 and xxi. 25, in both of which it is used transitively, and means 'hold, have room for'. For the intransitive sense cf. the use of χωρεῖν as an impersonal verb in Mark ii. 2. 'There was no room.' Alternatively, it may mean here 'make progress' (cf. 2 Pet. iii. 9?).

[4] λόγος. See Introduction, p. 4.

realised that his denial of their proud claim to be free men had
caused grave offence. It now becomes increasingly clear that
the differences between Jesus and the Jews are deep and irrecon-
cilable. It is easy for the sceptical critic to assert that this episode
of controversy is artificial, and really echoes the disputes between
the Church and the Synagogue on the question which represented
the true Israel, but it must be remembered that these only arose
because there had previously been the conflict between Jesus
and his contemporaries. But John obviously records this controversy between Jesus and the Jews—inevitable even when the
latter were not at first hostile—because of his interest in that
between Church and Synagogue.

38. Conduct is the clue to paternity, both in the case of Jesus
and of the Jews. Jesus has **seen** his **Father** (vi. 46; cf. v. 19;
vii. 29), having been **at** his **side** (cf. i. 18, 'in the bosom of the
Father'), and gives his Father's message (cf. iii. 32): the Jews
have not seen[1] their father, but their attitude to Jesus shows
that they are responding to his prompting.

**(39) They answered and said to him, 'Our father is
Abraham'. Jesus said to them, 'If you are Abraham's
children, you were doing Abraham's works. (40) But now
you are seeking to kill me, a man who has spoken to you
the truth which I heard from God; this ⟨is⟩ not ⟨what⟩
Abraham did. (41) You are doing your father's works.'**

39. Puzzled, the Jews repeat the claim which Jesus has
apparently conceded (verse 37). So Jesus proceeds to repeat
in plainer terms what he has said already.

The text of his first sentence is uncertain. The inferior
authorities have the grammatically correct conditional sentence,
'If you were ..., you would do ...' (εἰ ἦτε ..., ἐποιεῖτε ἄν). But
while all the best authorities support **you are** (ἐστέ) in the
first clause, they are divided between 'you are doing' (ποιεῖτε,
which they probably take as the imperative 'do')—P⁶⁶ B * 700 ff²
vg sin—and **you were doing**—ℵ* D W Θ *vt eg*—in the second.
The latter is the more difficult reading, and is to be understood
as an ironical assumption—'If (as you claim) you are Abraham's

---

[1] The reading 'have seen' (P⁶⁶ ℵ D *lat sin pesh hl sah*) for 'heard' (B W Θ
fam 1 *fam* 13 *f hl*ᵐᵍ *boh*) is an unintelligent assimilation which obscures a real
distinction between Jesus and the Jews.

children, then (I suppose I must admit that) **you were doing**
what **Abraham** used to do (when you attacked me).' This fits
in well with what follows.

40. **'But,** as it is,[1] to attempt to murder **a man** for speaking
the truth which God has taught him cannot be regarded as a
thing **Abraham** would have done.'

That Jesus speaks **the truth** may be inferred from verses 31 f.;
that he has received his message **from God** has already been
stated in verse 26.

41. Thus their claim that Abraham is their father cannot be
true. But Jesus does not yet say who their father is. The gradual
revelation of the truth heightens the dramatic tension of the
scene.

**They said to him, 'We were not born ⟨as the result⟩ of
fornication; we have one Father, God'.**

Aware now that Jesus is denying that spiritually they are
children of Abraham, the Jews change their ground, and make
a higher claim, protesting that their spiritual filiation is above
reproach, since their Father is God (cf. Isa. lxiv. 8). They use
the term **fornication** in its familiar metaphorical sense of
idolatry (cf. Hos. i. 2), but may at the same time intend the
innuendo against Jesus himself which later became a standard
feature of Jewish anti-Christian polemic. John can of course
only intend his readers to appreciate this if he is himself aware
of the circumstances of Jesus' birth (cf. i. 13; vi. 42; viii. 19).
But whether or not John intends this allusion, it is obvious that
he appreciates the irony of the fact that the Jews make the same
claim as Jesus himself.

**(42) Jesus said to them, 'If God were your Father, you
would love me; for ⟨it is⟩ from God ⟨that⟩ I came forth
and am present ⟨among you⟩; for I have not come on my
own authority,[2] but he sent me. (43) Why do you not
recognise what I am saying?[3] Because you cannot heed[4]
my word! (44) The father whose ⟨sons⟩ you are is the**

---

[1] νῦν, cf. xv. 22 for this non-temporal sense.

[2] ἀπ’ ἐμαυτοῦ, literally, 'from myself', cf. v. 30; vii. 17, 28; viii. 28; x. 18;
xiv. 10.

[3] τὴν λαλιὰν τὴν ἐμήν; λαλιά (used also in iv. 42) means 'speech', λόγος
('word', in the next sentence) the meaning of what is spoken, i.e. Jesus'
message.   [4] For this sense of ἀκούω 'hear', cf. vi. 60.

Devil,[1] and ⟨it is⟩ your father's desires ⟨that⟩ you wish to do. He was a murderer from the beginning, and did not stand[2] in the truth, because there is no truth in him. Every lie that he speaks is of his own ⟨production⟩;[3] because he is a liar and the father of lying.[4] (45) But as for me, because[5] I am speaking the truth, you do not believe me. (46) Who of you convicts me of sin? If I am telling the truth, why do you not believe me? (47) He who is from God heeds[6] God's words; the reason why you do not heed[6] is that you are not from God.'

Jesus at last makes his meaning quite clear, demolishes the Jews' latest and boldest claim, and exposes the complete incompatibility, and the impossibility of communication, between himself and them. Much is repeated that has already been stated less explicitly, but the repetition again heightens the dramatic effect.

42. If the Jews were God's children, they would love Jesus (cf. 1 John v. 1), his representative (cf. iii. 17; v. 43; vii. 28), but, as Jesus has already said, they have no love for God (cf. v. 42).

43. Nor is there any possibility of their understanding him (cf. verse 37), since they do not want to do God's will (cf. v. 37; vii. 17). 44. They are children of **the Devil**, like Cain (1 John iii. 12),[7] and it is his will, not God's, that they are eager to do. This is proved by their repeated attempts to kill Jesus, for the Devil was a **murderer**[8] from the beginning, since it was by his envy that death came into the world (Wisdom ii. 24.)

And not only love is foreign to his nature (cf. 1 John iii. 15)

---

[1] Literally, 'You are of the father, the Devil'. The Greek could also mean 'of the father of the Devil', and was so taken by some Gnostic readers (see Bauer, pp. 127 f.).

[2] οὐκ ἕστηκεν (imperfect of στήκω), read by P⁶⁶ ℵ B* D W Θ etc., is superior to οὐχ ἕστηκεν (perfect of ἵστημι) read by C and the inferior MSS.

[3] Literally, 'Whenever he speaks the lie, he speaks of his own' (neuter plural, ἐκ τῶν ἰδίων—for τὰ ἴδια see on i. 11, p. 77.)

[4] ὁ πατὴρ αὐτοῦ; αὐτοῦ can be either masculine or neuter, but is more probably the latter, and refers to 'the lie' in the previous clause.

[5] ὅτι, which could also be taken as 'that' after 'believe'.

[6] ἀκούω, as in verse 43.

[7] Contrast the milder accusation of Rev. ii. 9; iii. 9 that the Jews are the synagogue of Satan.

[8] ἀνθρωποκτόνος, which occurs in the New Testament only here and in 1 John iii. 15.

but also **truth**[1] (cf. Rev. xii. 9, 2 Cor. xi. 3). That Satan **did not stand in the truth** may imply that once he had done so, i.e., that he had fallen before man fell. **45.** And so the Jews cannot **believe** Jesus, precisely **because** it is **the truth** which he speaks. This is another aspect of the contrast between light and darkness found in iii. 19 ff., and, like that, recalls the moral dualism so characteristic of the Dead Sea sect.[2]

46. Jesus sums up: he challenges his enemies to prove their accusations (cf. xviii. 23), knowing that he is without **sin** (cf. vii. 28), and so must be telling the truth (repeating verses 40 and 45). Nevertheless they **do ... not believe** him (cf. verses 43 and 45), **47.** because they **are not from God**, i.e., on God's side,[3] and so cannot recognise that his words are God's.

(48) The Jews answered and said to him, 'Are we not right in saying that you are a Samaritan and have a demon?'

By saying that Jesus is **a Samaritan** the Jews do not so much intend an insult, implying that Jesus is a heretic and schismatic, and outside the covenant, as the specific charge that he is possessed by **a demon,** like the Samaritan prophets Simon Magus (cf. Acts viii. 10) or Dositheus, who claimed to be Son of God[4]. Jesus shows that he regards the two charges as essentially one by his reply (verse 49). The Jews have already accused Jesus of having **a demon** (vii. 20), but there they mean only that he is mad (cf. x. 20). Here the charge is more sinister; the Jews are throwing back at Jesus his accusation against them of belonging to the devil, cf. Mark iii. 22, and so are guilty of the sin of blasphemy against the Holy Spirit (Mark iii. 29 f.). Unwittingly they confirm all that Jesus has said against them.

(49) Jesus answered, 'I do not have a demon, but I honour my Father, and you deny me my honour.[5] (50) But I am not seeking my own glory: there is ⟨one⟩ who seeks

[1] For the meaning of 'truth' in the FG, see on i. 14, p. 83.

[2] Cf. the passage in the *Manual of Discipline* (iii. 13–iv. 26) dealing with the spirits of truth and perversity (T. H. Gaster, *The Scriptures of the Dead Sea Sect* (1957), pp. 53–56).

[3] ἐκ τοῦ θεοῦ. ἐκ means first 'arising from' (e.g. iii. 31), then 'belonging to' (e.g. x. 26) and then (as here) 'on the side of'; cf. also ἐκ τοῦ κόσμου (xv. 19; xvii. 14, 16), ἐκ τῆς ἀληθείας (xviii. 37).

[4] Origen, *Contra Celsum*, VI. 11.

[5] ἀτιμάζετε, which corresponds to 'does not honour' (οὐ τιμᾷ) in v. 23.

and judges. (51) Amen, amen I say to you, if anyone keeps my word, he will never face [1] death at all.[2]'

49. Jesus turns from denunciation of the Jews to his own defence. All he does is due to his wish to **honour** God. The Jews, by denying him his honour, also deny God his, since honouring God involves honouring his Son (cf. v. 23). But though he expects the honour which is his due, i.e. the acknowledgement that he comes with God's authority, he is not merely **seeking** his **own glory,** acting from personal vanity (cf. vii. 18). Indeed, he knows that God will give him his due (cf. xvii. 1)— for it is God **who seeks and judges.** This appears to contradict v. 22, but in its context here is readily intelligible. Jesus appeals against those who do not accept his judgement to God, whose judgement they do profess to accept.

51. Jesus solemnly assures[3] the Jews that obedience to his **word** (cf. v. 24) will save them from **death** (cf. xi. 26). The sequence of ideas in verses 49-51 recalls that in v. 23 f.—honour, obedience, judgement, death.

(52) The Jews said to him, 'Now we know that you have a demon. Abraham died, and ⟨so did⟩ the prophets, and ⟨yet⟩ you say, "If anyone keeps my word, he will never taste death at all".[2] (53) You are not greater, are you, than our father Abraham, who died? (and the prophets died). Whom do you make yourself?'

52. Outraged, yet jubilant, the Jews seize on Jesus' last words as a proof of the truth of their accusation. With characteristic lack of understanding, they suppose that he is referring to physical death, and suggest that, if **Abraham . . . and the prophets died,** he can only offer immunity from death to his followers if he is in league with Satan, who was responsible for bringing death into the world (verse 44). 53. Just as the Samaritan woman could not imagine that Jesus was greater than Jacob (iv. 12), so now the Jews can only suppose Jesus guilty of inconceivable arrogance.

(54) Jesus answered, 'If I glorify myself, my glory is nothing; ⟨it⟩ is my Father who glorifies me, of whom you

---

[1] θεωρήσῃ. See p. 191.
[2] οὐ μὴ . . . εἰς τὸν αἰῶνα. See on iv. 14, p. 142 n. 3.
[3] For the formula, 'Amen, amen I say . . .' see on i. 51.

say that he is your God; (55) and you do not know him, but I do know him. And if I say that I do not know him, I shall be a liar like you. But I do know him, and I keep his word. (56) Abraham your father rejoiced to see[1] my day, and he did see it, and he was glad.'

54. Jesus repeats his assurance that he is not actuated by vanity and his claim that he will be vindicated by God (verse 50), to whom the Jews profess their allegiance, 55. though they **do not know him** as Jesus himself does (cf. vii. 28; viii. 19); if they did, he implies, they would recognise in him the faithful representative who keeps his word (cf. viii. 29).

56. He also points out that though they claim Abraham as their father, they do not follow his example (cf. viii. 39). **Abraham rejoiced to see** his **day, and he did see it, and he was glad.** For **my day** cf. 'one of the days of the Son of man' (Luke xvii. 22, cf. 30), and the Old Testament 'day of the Lord' (e.g. Amos v. 18 ff.): in Luke the 'day' is visualised as future, but it is characteristic of the eschatology of the FG that in it the **day** has now come.[2]

The second clause in this verse may appear to be redundant, and only added for emphasis. But this depends on the meaning of the first clause. If this means that **Abraham rejoiced,** during his lifetime, at the prospect of the coming of this **day,** revealed to him by God when he told him that all nations would be blessed in his seed (Gen. xxii. 18, interpreted, as in Gal. iii. 16, as an allusion to Christ), then the second clause ceases to be redundant, and means that **he also was glad,** when, in Paradise, **he did** in fact **see it** come in the incarnation of Jesus Christ. This interpretation accords with the belief, characteristic of popular, but not of official Rabbinic, religion in the time of Jesus, that the Patriarchs were still very much alive, and took an active interest in their descendants.[3] This belief is reflected in other sayings of Jesus, cf. Luke xvi. 23, and, most notably, Mark xii. 27.[4] Also it is not inconsistent with what is said in Luke x. 24 about the prophets and kings who desired to see the things which the disciples saw, and did not in fact see them,

---

[1] ἵνα ἴδῃ. See on iv. 34, p. 150 n. 5.   [2] See Introduction, pp. 13f.
[3] See Joachim Jeremias, *Heiligengräber in Jesu Umwelt* (1958), pp. 134 f.
[4] See Jeremias, *ibid.*, pp. 129 f.

i.e. they received the prophecies (cf. Heb. xi. 13), but their
longing to see them fulfilled in their own lifetime was not
satisfied.

In John xii. 41 the evangelist observes that Isaiah saw Christ's
glory: this is to be understood as the proleptic vision of the first
clause in viii. 56, rather than as the actual vision of the second.

The usual interpretation of this verse connects it with the
Rabbinic interpretation of Gen. xxiv. 1 (in which 'well advanced
in years' represents the Hebrew which may be translated
literally as 'went into the days'), as meaning that God gave
Abraham a vision of the whole future of his race, up to and into
the days of the Messiah.[1] Two things, however, tell against
this—the Rabbinic evidence is all much later than the date
of the FG[2]—to say nothing of Jesus' own lifetime—and it
allows no difference in meaning between the first and second
clauses.

**(57) So the Jews said to him, 'You are not yet fifty
years old—and have you seen Abraham?'**

A few inferior authorities read *forty* instead of **fifty** in order
to harmonise this statement with the Synoptic tradition about
the age of Jesus (Luke iii. 23), but this is mere pedantry.[3] The
Jews put Jesus' age as high as they can for a man obviously in
the prime of life, but even so he cannot be old enough to have
seen Abraham. Again some authorities fall victims to a pedan-
tic misunderstanding, and read *has Abraham seen you* (א *sin
sah*). But the Jews are asking what is Jesus' evidence for his
statement: he can only know that Abraham rejoiced if he has
seen him.

**(58) Jesus said to them, 'Amen, amen I say to you,[4]
before Abraham was, I am.' (59) So they picked up stones
to throw at him; but Jesus hid himself and went out of the
Temple.**

58. The long interval between Abraham and Jesus is irrelevant.
Just as Jesus appeared in time after John the Baptist, but was
first in relation to him (i. 30), so it is with Abraham. This is

---

[1] See Hoskyns, *op. cit.*, Vol. II, pp. 399 f., Dodd, *Interpretation*, p. 261,
Barrett, p. 291.   [2] See Strack–Billerbeck, II, pp. 525 f.
[3] For Irenaeus' speculations about Jesus' age, based on ii. 20 and viii. 57,
see p. 119, n. 2.   [4] See on i. 51.

brought out by the tenses of the verbs in Greek—the aorist γενέσθαι 'came into being', used of Abraham, is contrasted with the present εἰμί, which can express duration up to the present, 'I have been ⟨and still am⟩ [1]' as well as the simple present, 'I am'. Jesus claims that his mode of existence transcends time, like God's, and his **I am** is understood by the Jews as a claim to equality with God,[2] and, as blasphemy, 59. provokes the appropriate reaction, in an attempt to stone him (cf. Lev. xxiv. 16).[3]

The faith, such as it was, of verse 30 is quite forgotten, and the hostility, confined so far to attempts to arrest Jesus (vii. 30, 44), takes a more violent form. The tension steadily mounts, but the decisive moment has not yet come. Jesus quietly withdraws, as on an earlier occasion (Luke iv. 30), but not necessarily by supernatural means.

11. THE FIFTH SIGN, IN JERUSALEM, AND ITS CONSEQUENCES, ix. 1 – x. 42

ix. (1) And ⟨as he was⟩ passing by he saw a man blind from birth.

Here a new scene opens, with characteristic abruptness, and quite without circumstantial detail (cf., e.g., i. 19). But it is nevertheless carefully dovetailed into the preceding episode (cf., e.g., ii. 1), with which it is closely united by the common theme of the encounter between the light and the darkness. Jesus is the light (viii. 12; ix. 5, cf. i. 4, 9; iii. 19); the Jews represent the darkness which neither understood nor overcame the light (i. 5), and is condemned for rejecting it (iii. 19 f.), while the **man blind from birth** is an apt symbol of those who, helpless in a darkness they cannot escape by their own efforts, nevertheless accept illumination when it comes to them (i. 12).

[1] See p. 158, n. 4.
[2] It is not necessary to suppose that they saw in **I am** the Divine Name, though no doubt the evangelist would have his readers note the allusion; cf. viii. 24, 28, and see on iv. 26, pp. 148 f.
[3] Josephus, *Antiquities*, XVII. 215 f., records an incident in which some of Archelaus' soldiers were actually stoned in the Temple.

No interval of time is indicated between this verse and viii.
59. We are to suppose that Jesus saw the man while he was on
his way from the Temple, in the precincts of which beggars
(such as this man was, ix. 8) habitually gathered (cf. Acts iii. 2),
though it seems unlikely that a man who had just escaped
lynching would linger near the scene of the attempt. But John
is more concerned with the theological development of his story
than with the verisimilitude of its details.

Though in the formal pattern of the FG this is the second
sign in the second group of three signs, its closest affinity is not
to the second, but to the third sign (v. 1 ff.) in the first group.
The chronic character of the complaint resembles that of the
man in v. 5.

**(2) And his disciples asked him, saying, 'Rabbi, who
sinned, this man or his parents, for him to be born
blind?'**

The question illustrates the common belief of the time that
illness and other signal misfortunes were a punishment for sin,
as Job's 'comforters' also believed. Luke xiii. 2 and 4, also
illustrates the belief, and shows that Jesus did not share it.[1]

**(3) Jesus answered, '⟨This did⟩ not ⟨happen because⟩
this man or his parents sinned, but for the works of God
to be shown forth in him. (4) We must do[2] the works of
him who sent us while it is day. Night is coming when
nobody can work. (5) While I am in the world, I am ⟨the⟩
light of the world.'**

3. As in Luke xiii. 2 ff., Jesus refuses to discuss the cause of
the man's affliction; instead, he directs the disciples' attention
to the opportunity which it affords of showing forth **the works
of God**; cf. xi. 4.[3]

Here **the works of God** mean not only works of which God
approves (cf. the identical phrase in vi. 28), but also those

[1] For the connexion between sin and illness see on v. 15, p. 162.
[2] Literally, 'work' (as in vi. 28).
[3] The construction of the clause **for the works of God to be shown . . .**
is the same as that of **for him to be born blind**—ἵνα followed by the subjunctive, which normally indicates purpose. Purpose can, however, hardly be
attributed to the parents of a man born blind, and it is not intended in this
verse or in xi. 4. These are all instances of a characteristically Semitic refusal,
or inability, to distinguish the purpose and the consequence of an action. The
translation attempts to reproduce this ambiguity.

which God himself does (cf. v. 20), since Jesus proceeds to
complete God's work of creation (cf. iv. 34) by giving sight to
the blind man.

4. This is a general statement, though for the time being it
is only applicable to Jesus himself. He and his disciples must
seize their opportunity **while it is day,** i.e. while they have the
light (cf. xi. 9). But this rather obvious remark has a deeper
meaning, applicable only to the disciples, for the light which
enables them to see to do their work is Christ (verse 5). For the
symbolism of **night** cf. iii. 2; xiii. 30.

Though Jesus thus associates his disciples with his own work
and mission, they in fact do nothing during this episode. The
saying looks forward to xiv. 12, which promises that the believer will do the works of Jesus, and to xvii. 18; xx. 21, which
refer to Jesus' sending of his disciples, which may be deemed
equivalent to God's sending them, since Jesus always does
God's will (e.g. v. 30).[1]

5. **I am in the world** recalls i. 10; iii. 19, and **I am ⟨the⟩
light of the world** viii. 12, though the wording is slightly
different—I is not emphasised in the Greek, and **light** has no
article. It is less of a pronouncement, and more of a parable.

**(6) Having said this he spat on the ground, and made
mud of the spittle, and smeared[2] the mud on his eyes,
(7) and said to him, 'Go ⟨and⟩ wash in the pool of Siloam'
(which means 'Sent'). So he went away and washed,
and came seeing.**

6. Without waiting even to ask if the man wants to see (contrast v. 6, and Mark x. 51), Jesus at once proceeds to cure him.
The use of **spittle** as a means of healing usual in ancient times[3]
is strictly not relevant here,[4] since it was not the material means
of the cure, but was simply used to make **mud** (which would

---

[1] The text of this verse is uncertain. We and **us** are read by P⁶⁶ ℵ* W, **We**
and **me** by B D, **I** and **me** by the majority of the authorities. The last is an
obviously easier reading, that of B D probably a compromise, and the first
to be preferred as the most difficult. The attempts at emendation are probably
due to a desire to make the saying fit its context better than it does.

[2] ἐπέχρισεν, P⁶⁶ ℵ A D W Θ. B has the colourless ἐπέθηκεν (used in verse
15) preferred by some because ἐπέχρισεν also occurs in verse 11. This would
be more cogent if the other use of the word was earlier rather than later.

[3] For examples, see Barrett, p. 296.

[4] Contrast Mark vii. 33; viii. 23.

stick on the man's eyes) out of the dust of the ground, the material from which man was made (Gen. ii. 7). Jesus uses **mud** to complete the work of creation in the blind man (verse 3).

7. The cure is effected by the washing, as in the case of Naaman (2 Kings v. 10), and sending the man to the pool to wash is a challenge to his faith, as it was in Naaman's case.

The pool of Siloam symbolises the water of baptism,[1] as John indicates by giving the interpretation of **Siloam,** an obvious allusion to Christ, **'Sent'** for the salvation of the world (cf. iii. 17). John may also intend an allusion to Isa. viii. 6, the waters of Shiloah which the Jews refused to receive, as they refused Christ.

The pool still exists: it is to the south of the site of the Temple, and is fed by the overflow of the intermittent Virgin's Spring, brought (i.e. 'sent'—hence the name) by the tunnel which Hezekiah had made (2 Kings xx. 20).

The man obeyed (cf. v. 9) and was cured. John emphasises this by using for **seeing** the verb βλέπω throughout this passage (cf. 15, 19, 21, 25, 39, 41), since, unlike ὁράω, it is always used literally (cf. i. 29; v. 19; xi. 9; xiii. 22; xx. 1, 5; xxi. 9, 20).

(8) So the neighbours and those who perceived[2] that it was the man whom they had previously seen as a beggar,[3] said, 'This is the man, is he not, who sat and begged?' (9) Some said, 'This is ⟨the man⟩', others, 'No, but he is like him'. He said, 'I am ⟨the man⟩'. (10) So they said to him, 'How then were your eyes opened?' (11) He answered, 'The man called Jesus made mud and smeared my eyes and said to me, "Go to Siloam and wash"; so I went and when I had washed I received sight'. (12) And they said to him, 'Where is he?' He said, 'I do not know'.

This passage of dialogue establishes the genuineness of the cure. The question of its lawfulness is not yet raised.

12. For the man's ignorance cf. v. 13.

(13) They brought him, who had once been blind, to

---

[1] For the symbolic significance of water in the FG see p. 91, n. 2.
[2] θεωροῦντες. See p. 191.
[3] Literally, 'who perceived him previously, that he was a beggar'.

the Pharisees. (14) Now the day was Sabbath on which Jesus made mud and opened his eyes. (15) So the Pharisees also asked him again how he received sight. And he said to them, 'He put mud on my eyes, and I washed, and see'. (16) So some of the Pharisees said, 'This is not the man from God, because he does not keep the Sabbath'. Others said, 'How can a man ⟨who is⟩ a sinner do such signs?' And there was a division between them.

13. There is irony in the confrontation of the man **who had once been blind** with **the Pharisees**—who thought they saw. The words are by no means redundant (see Barrett, p. 298).

14. For the healing on **Sabbath** cf. v. 9.

15. In v. 10 ff., the interrogation of the man who had been healed is briefer and less formal, and **the Pharisees** are not mentioned there. They have, however, already made an appearance in vii. 32; viii. 13, and their presence, and the greater length and formality of the proceedings, are an indication of the exacerbation of the crisis.

16. The objection that Jesus **does not keep the Sabbath** is presumably based principally on the fact that it was a chronic disease which he had healed (cf. Luke xiii. 14), as was that of the man in v (see on vii. 21 ff.). The making of mud and the use of spittle are in comparison unimportant, cf. the carrying of the pallet in v. **So some** conclude from this that Jesus cannot be **the man from God,**[1] as he had claimed to be (vii. 29). **Others** object that he cannot be **a sinner,** since his actions appear to be approved by God. It is of course true that **signs** could be given which might even deceive the elect (cf. Matt. xxiv. 24), but the Pharisees sympathetic to Jesus here imply that they can discriminate between signs done in the power of God and those that are the result of collusion with the Devil (the explanation of his miracles given in Mark iii. 22). For the **division** which results from Jesus' presence among men cf. vii. 43, and Luke xii. 51.

(17) So they again said to the blind man, 'What do you

---

[1] The unusual order of words (οὐκ ἔστιν οὗτος παρὰ θεοῦ ὁ ἄνθρωπος) implies more than just, 'This man is not from God'.

say about his opening your eyes?[1]' And he said, 'He is a prophet'. (18) Then the Jews did not believe of him that he had been blind and had received sight, until they had called the parents of him who had received sight, (19) and asked them, saying, 'Is this your son, ⟨of⟩ whom you say that he was born blind? How then does he see at present?[2]' (20) So his parents answered and said, 'We know that this is our son, and that he was born blind; (21) but how he now sees we do not know, or who opened his eyes. We[3] do not know; ask him—he is old enough; he will speak for himself.' (22) His parents said these things because they feared the Jews; for the Jews had already agreed that if anyone were to confess him ⟨to be⟩ Christ, he was to be excluded from the synagogue. (23) This is why his parents said, 'He is old enough—ask him'.

17. The man's assertion that Jesus **is a prophet** is the same as that of the Samaritan woman (iv. 19), but not as that he is 'the Prophet' (vi. 14; vii. 40). Both this man and the Samaritan woman, however, soon reach a fuller faith (cf. ix. 38 and iv. 29).

The way in which this man stands up to the Pharisees, both now and later (verses 25 ff.) contrasts with the craven conduct of the other man whom Jesus healed, who simply told the Jews that it was Jesus who healed him, and said nothing in his defence (v. 15).

18 f. Unable to shake the man's conviction that Jesus was not a sinner, **the Jews**[4] try to resolve their dilemma by discrediting his evidence, and examine **his parents** to that end. 20. They, however, confirm the facts, but 21. refuse to commit themselves any further, 22. through fear of the consequences (cf. vii. 13).

---

[1] Literally, '. . . about this man, that (ὅτι) he opened thine eyes'. For the possibility that ὅτι is a mistranslation of the Aramaic d[e] and should be ὅς ('who'), see Black, pp. 56, 66, and Barrett, p. 298.

[2] ἄρτι. See p. 107, n. 3.

[3] **We** is emphatic: the pronoun ἡμεῖς is used here, but not in the two previous instances. This distinction is obscured by the usual punctuation, '. . . or who opened his eyes we do not know. Ask him . . .'

[4] John tends to lump all Jesus' opponents together as **the Jews**: but see on i. 19, and cf. 'Galileans' in iv. 45 with 'Jews' in vi. 41.

The decision **that if anyone were to confess him ⟨to be⟩ Christ, he was to be excluded from the synagogue** does not necessarily imply a formal excommunication, which would no doubt be an anachronism. But Luke vi. 22 shows that Jesus warned his disciples that they would be 'sent to Coventry', and this may be what is meant here and in xii. 42; xvi. 2. The confession that Jesus was the **Christ** need not mean more than that he is the Messiah of popular expectation, as in i. 41; vii. 41. The fact that Mark does not record any public admission that Jesus was the Christ is due to two causes—(i) that his evidence is in any case virtually confined to Galilee, and (ii) the dogma of the 'Messianic Secret'. The High Priest must have known that the opinion was current, as his question to Jesus shows (Mark xiv. 61). It is therefore not intrinsically improbable that the opponents of Jesus determined to silence his supporters in Judaea even during his ministry.[1]

(24) So they called a second time the man who had been blind, and said to him, 'Give glory to God; we know that this man is a sinner'.

They invite the man to confess that he has been deceiving them; cf. the words of Joshua to Achan (Joshua vii. 19), and Acts xii. 23, where it is said that Agrippa died because he did not give God the glory by dissociating himself from blasphemy. But the man is not impressed.

(25) So he answered them, 'If he is a sinner I do not know; one thing I do know, that I was blind and at present[2] I see'. (26) So they said to him, 'What did he do to you? How did he open your eyes?' (27) He answered, 'I told you once and you did not listen;[3] why do you want to hear again? You do not want to become his disciples as well, do you?'

25. The man, however, refuses to commit himself to an opinion on the merits of Jesus' action, and allows them no escape from their dilemma by reminding them of the facts which conflict with their preconceived ideas. 26. So they ask him to go over the facts again, hoping perhaps that he will

[1] But see Barrett, p. 299.   [2] ἄρτι. See p. 107, n. 3.
[3] ἠκούσατε, the verb translated 'hear' in the next clause. For the nuance cf. viii. 43; ix. 31, etc.

contradict himself and so enable them to discredit him. 27. But he avoids the trap, and ironically suggests that if they listen they may admit that Jesus is right after all.

(28) And they abused him and said, 'You are his disciple, but we are Moses' disciples; (29) we know that God has spoken to Moses, but ⟨as for⟩ this ⟨fellow⟩,[1] we do not know where he is from'.

The Jews in turn appeal to the facts as they see them, to the patent conflict between the law of Moses, to the divine authority of which they appeal, and this upstart whose origin and, in consequence, authority are unknown, and (as they imply) will not bear scrutiny.

In v. 39 ff. Jesus had appealed to Moses as evidence on his behalf, but the Jews did not accept his claim. Their assertion that they **do not know where he is from** contradicts, but only formally, the claim made by the Jews in vii. 27 that they know Jesus' place of origin, i.e. Nazareth, which they think proves that he cannot be the Christ (cf. vi. 42). In viii. 14 Jesus says that they do not know his origin—if they did they would accept his authority. Both the Jews' claims and their disclaimers are, ironically enough, true in a sense, but basically wrongheaded.

Jesus' own solution to their dilemma (Mark ii. 28) is of course quite unthinkable to them in their blind zeal (Rom. x. 2).

(30) The man answered and said to them, 'Well, this is a marvellous thing![2] You do not know where he is from, and he opened my eyes! (31) We know that God does not listen to sinners, but that, if a man is pious and does his will, this ⟨is the one to whom⟩ he listens. (32) It is quite unheard of[3] for anyone to open the eyes of one born blind; (33) if this man were not from God, he could not do anything.'

30. The man ridicules the ignorance of the experts, and draws the obvious conclusion. 31. **God does not listen to sinners** (cf. Isa. i. 15, and many other passages)—unless of

---

[1] τοῦτον, cf. οὗτος, vii. 15, and the note *ad loc.*
[2] Literally, 'in this is the marvellous ⟨thing⟩'.
[3] Literally, 'From the age (ἐκ τοῦ αἰῶνος) it was not heard . . .' See Bauer[5], s.v.

course they are penitent—and so, 32. since no one could have performed this unparalleled cure unless God *had* listened to him, Jesus cannot be a sinner, in spite of his breaking the Sabbath law, but 33. is **from God,** as Nicodemus had already seen (iii. 21).

(34) They answered and said to him, 'You were wholly¹ born in sins, and are you teaching us?' And they drove him out.²

The man has taken his side, and they take theirs. Blinded by their pride of learning (cf. vii. 15), they attribute the man's refusal to be persuaded by them to the **sins** in which he was born (cf. ix. 2), and give effect to the decision mentioned in verse 22. The examination had presumably taken place in a synagogue, for synagogues were used for many communal purposes besides public worship, and his expulsion brands him as an outcast from the community.

(35) Jesus heard that they had expelled him, and, when he had found him, said, 'Do you believe in the Son of man?'³ (36) He answered and said, 'Who pray is he, sir, for me to believe in him?' (37) Jesus said to him, 'You have indeed seen him, and it is he that⁴ is speaking with you'. (38) And he said, 'I do believe, Lord', and he worshipped him.

35. Jesus seeks out the man, as he did in v. 14, but not in order to utter a warning, as on that occasion, but to invite him to express the faith of which his conduct under examination has given proof. To **believe in the Son of man**⁵ is a turn of phrase without parallel, but is appropriate in a context in which the theme of Christ's judgement appears (cf. v. 27). See also on verse 37 below.

36. Since this is only a polite request for information the word Κύριε which the man uses cannot mean more than **sir** (cf. iv. 15).

37. Jesus' self-revelation resembles that in iv. 26, but it is

---

¹ ὅλος. For this adverbial use of the adjective cf. xiii. 10.

² Literally, 'threw him out'. Cf. vi. 37, p. 189, n. 2.

³ ἀνθρώπου, the reading of P⁶⁶ ℵ B D W *sin sah* etc. (RVᵐᵍ), is preferable to the easier, conventional reading 'of God', found in A Θ *fam* 1 *fam* 13 *lat pesh hl boh* and the majority of authorities.   ⁴ See p. 85, n. 2.

⁵ For the meaning of 'Son of man' in the FG see on i. 51.

noteworthy that on this occasion he claims only to be Son of man, the title which he normally uses in the Synoptic Gospels, and not Christ.[1]

38. Both by word and action the man shows that he acknowledges Jesus' claim. But it is not clear what he exactly understood by it. He again addresses Jesus as Κύριε, but this need not mean more than 'sir', as in 36. Equally **worshipped** (προσεκύνησεν) could mean only a rather extravagant gesture of respect, as in Matt. viii. 2; ix. 18; xviii. 26; xx. 20. But John most probably means us to take Κύριε as the divine title **Lord,** and **worshipped** in the full sense which it has in every other case in which it is used in the FG (iv. 20-24; xii. 20), in all of which God is the expressed or implied object of the verb.

For belief as the result of the sign cf. iv. 53.

(39) And Jesus said, 'For judgement I came into this world, for those who do not see to see, and for those who see to become blind'.

Jesus brings to expression the ironical consequences of his coming. He **came** as light (ix. 5), but also, and as the inevitable consequence, **for judgement** (cf. iii. 19; v. 22), **for**[2] the blind **to see** (cf. Isa. xxxv. 5), **and for those who see to become blind** (cf. Isa. vi. 9 f., quoted John xii. 40, and Matt. xiii. 14 f.).

(40) Some of the Pharisees who were with him heard these things, and said to him, 'We indeed are not blind, are we?' (41) Jesus said to them, 'If you were blind, you would not be sinners;[3] but now ⟨that⟩ you say, "We see", your sin remains'.

40. The Pharisees show their incredulity by the form of their question, which, beginning Μή . . . assumes that the answer will be 'No,' and so provoke 41. the blunt reply that their unfounded assumption that they do **see** proves the fact of their **sin** (cf. xv. 22, 24), which **remains,** like the wrath of God upon those who are disobedient to the Son (iii. 36). They are in the same condition as those who sin against the Holy Spirit (Mark iii. 29). If, however, they were blind, i.e. honestly

---

[1] See on iv. 26, p. 149 and x. 24 f.
[2] ἵνα, used in the same ambiguous fashion as in ix. 2, 3 (p. 237, n. 3).
[3] Literally, 'have sin' (εἴχετε ἁμαρτίαν), cf. xv. 22, 24.

ignorant, they **would not be sinners** (cf. Luke xxiii. 34). That
sin only counts as such when it is the conscious transgression
of a known command is a Pauline commonplace (cf. Rom. v. 13,
etc.), but it does not follow that the idea expressed in this verse
is derived from St Paul. For Jesus' accusation of spiritual
blindness against the Pharisees in the Synoptic tradition cf.
Matt. xxiii. 16, 17, 19, 24, 26.

Thus the lesson of Jesus' rejection at the feast of Tabernacles
is made explicit, and one would suppose that this episode had
now reached its natural climax and conclusion. But there is
only the modern chapter division to indicate that it is a new discourse which begins with x. 1. There is good reason for a new
chapter to start here, since there is an abrupt change of subject-
matter, but we have no grounds for supposing that John did not
intend x. 1-21 to be read as a continuation of the long controversy of vii-ix. We may, however, reasonably suspect, from the
abruptness of the transition from ix. 41 to x. 1, that John has
moved x. 1-21 from its original setting, though any restoration
of the order of his source cannot be more than conjectural.

The whole of vii–x (and much of xii) is a complex mosaic,
made up from one, or, more probably, more than one, of the
original author's sermons on the theme of Jewish disbelief, but
it is beyond the purpose of a commentary on St John to try to
restore the original order, since the present order of the
material is clearly intentional.

**x. (1) 'Amen, amen I say to you,[1] it is the one who
does not come in through the door into the fold of the
sheep, but goes up from another direction, that[2] is a thief
and a brigand. (2) But he who comes in through the door
is the shepherd of the sheep. (3) ⟨It is⟩ for this ⟨man
that⟩ the doorkeeper opens ⟨the door⟩, and the sheep
listen to his voice, and he calls his own sheep by name
and leads them out. (4) When he has driven out[3] all his
own ⟨sheep⟩,[4] he goes in front of them, and the sheep**

---

[1] See on i. 51.   [2] See p. 85, n. 2.
[3] Literally, 'thrown out', used of animals also in ii. 15. See also vi. 37,
p. 189, n. 2.
[4] τὰ ἴδια πάντα, P⁶⁶ BDW *fam* 1 *vt eg*, is preferable to 'his own sheep'
τὰ ἴδια πρόβατα AΘ *fam* 13 *vg*, etc.: 'his own' (τὰ ἴδια) ℵ* is probably due only
to an accidental omission of πάντα.

follow him, because they know his voice; (5) but ⟨as for⟩
a stranger, they will by no means follow ⟨him⟩, but will
run away from him, because they do not know strangers'
voice⟨s⟩.'

(6) This parable Jesus told them; but they did not
know what ⟨things they⟩ were that he was speaking
to them.

1. Jesus pictures a farmstead with an enclosed yard, entered
by a single **door,** so that a prospective sheepstealer had to get
in secretly or by force,[1] 2. while **the shepherd** could enter
openly, 3. since **the doorkeeper** (a domestic servant, cf.
xviii. 17) would know him, and open the door. The sheep also
know him, as well as he knows them—**he calls** them **by name,**
i.e. by their own names (cf. 3 John 14), which, according to
Lagrange (p. 276), was a custom still followed in Palestine in
his day. The description of the sheep as **his own** does not
necessarily imply that there are sheep belonging to other shepherds in the same yard, but simply emphasises the shepherd's
rightful position with regard to them, in contrast to the thieves
and strangers. 4. The shepherd first drives the sheep out of the
yard, and then puts himself at their head, and they **follow**[2]
at his call (with his dogs keeping an eye on stragglers),
5. not merely heedless of, but actively avoiding, anyone else.

6. John calls this vivid and accurately observed picture of
pastoral life a parable, παροιμία. He uses this word also in xvi.
25 and 29; in the Synoptic Gospels the word is παραβολή.
Both can translate the Hebrew *mashal*, which has a wide range
of meaning from 'riddle' to 'parable'; παροιμία stresses the
enigmatic character of the saying, and so is particularly appropriate in xvi. 25, 29, though even the Synoptic parables are
represented as having been no less of a puzzle to their hearers
than the Johannine (cf. Mark iv. 13).

John places the parable here in order to illustrate the contrast
between Jesus, the shepherd,[3] and the Pharisees who have

---

[1] A κλέπτης steals by guile, a λῃστής openly and by force: the words are
used respectively of Judas (John xii. 6, cf. Matt. vi. 19 f. etc.) and Barabbas
(John xviii. 40, cf. Mark xiv. 48).

[2] For the significance of 'following' Jesus see on i. 43 and xiii. 36.

[3] For the Messiah as shepherd elsewhere in the New Testament cf. Heb.
xiii. 20, 1 Pet. ii. 25; v. 4, and the use of the verb 'shepherd' ('rule' RV) in

just been denounced, and are now represented as thieves and brigands, who seek to exploit the flock for their own selfish ends. But it does not follow that this was its original meaning, if it may be assumed that it is a parable actually spoken by Jesus. It could well be such, since its imagery is not without parallel in the Synoptic Gospels, and there is nothing in it which obliges us to assume that it is nothing more than the evangelist's rehash of Synoptic themes.

The comparison of Israel to a flock of sheep, and of God to its shepherd, is familiar in the Old Testament (e.g. Ps. lxxiv. 1; lxxviii. 52; lxxix. 13; lxxx. 1; xcv. 7, Isa. xl. 11, Ezek. xxxiv, etc.). David also appears as the shepherd of God's flock (cf. Ps. lxxviii. 70, 72, Ezek. xxxiv. 23 f.; xxxvii. 24, Mic. v. 4), and so it is not surprising that in Mark xiv. 27 the shepherd of Zech. xiii. 7 is interpreted of the Messiah, or that in Matt. xxv. 32 the Messianic judgement is compared to a shepherd's sorting out of the sheep from the goats. In Mark vi. 34 Jesus is said to have had compassion on the multitude who are as sheep without a shepherd (cf. Num. xxvii. 17). In Matt. x. 6; xv. 24, he speaks of the lost sheep of the house of Israel, and in Matt. xviii. 12 f., Luke xv. 4-7, relates a parable of a lost sheep.

Thus in the original parable the sheep could represent Israel, God's flock, entrusted to his Messiah, but under attack from false Messiahs (cf. Mark xiii. 22), rather than from the Pharisees. No other flocks come into the picture—hence the interpretation given above of 'his own' in verse 3—and the door and door-keeper do not feature in the interpretation of the parable, which was not intended as an allegory, with every detail significant.

If this is so, then verses 7-18 should probably be regarded as a series of allegorising variations on themes from the original parable, composed by a Christian prophet, who was influenced by the Old Testament, particularly by Ezek. xxxiv, and who also incorporated other sayings of Jesus. The final result of his

Rev. ii. 27; xii. 5; xix. 15. It is unnecessary to look outside the Old Testamen for the source of the idea of Jesus as the shepherd. There are many parallels to this in Gnostic, Hermetic, and Mandaean literature, but they do not explain the Johannine usage. To quote them is, according to Lagrange (p. 284) 'une ostentation d'érudition puérile'.

work is something like the interpretations appended to Synoptic parables (cf. Matt. xiii. 37-43, Mark iv. 14-20).

(7) So Jesus said to them again, 'Amen, amen I say to you [1] **that I am the door of the sheep.** [2] **(8) All who came** [3] **are thieves and brigands; but the sheep did not listen to them. (9) I am the door:** [2] **through me anyone who enters** [4] **will be saved, will go in and go out, and will find pasture. (10) The thief only comes to** [5] **steal and slaughter** [6] **and destroy; I came for them to have life and have ⟨it⟩ in abundance.'**

7. If **the door of the sheep** here represents accurately what Jesus said then these four verses are in an almost intolerable state of confusion. But if the suggestion is adopted [7] that in an Aramaic original the accidental repetition of one letter (a *tau*) has caused *the shepherd* to be read as **the door,** then verses 7 and 8 give an interpretation consistent with the original parable, and the allegory does not begin until verse 9.

8. The **thieves and brigands** are pseudo-Messiahs, men of the type of Theudas and Judas (Acts v. 36 f.): this is indicated by the absolute use of **came,** i.e. claiming to be the 'coming one' (cf. Matt. xi. 3, Mark xi. 9). The reference cannot be to Moses, the prophets, or John the Baptist, for they all bore witness to Jesus (cf. v. 46; vi. 45; xii. 38). The pseudo-Messiahs had a certain success, but **the sheep,** i.e. those who were Christ's, **did not listen to them,** though Jesus has already foretold that others would do so (v. 43).

9. **I am the door** interprets allegorically an incidental feature of the original parable. The image is somewhat bizarre, though not much more so than 'I am the way' (xiv. 6). Both illustrate the truth that it is through Christ alone that men have

[1] See on i. 51.
[2] For these 'I am' sayings see on iv. 26; vi. 35.

This is the reading of P[45] ℵ* *lat sin sah*: P[66] ABDW *fam* 13 and the majority of authorities add 'before me'. That this is secondary is suggested by the fact that a few authorities (Θ *fam* 1 etc.) have 'before me' before 'came'.

[4] Literally, 'through me if anyone enters . . .'; 'through me' qualifies both clauses.
[5] Literally 'does not come if not in order to . . . .'
[6] θύσῃ, 'to slaughter for food' (cf. Acts x. 13).
[7] See Black, p. 193, n. 1. Barrett, however, does not accept this (p. 307).

access to God (cf. Heb. x. 20). Through Christ also men attain salvation (cf. iii. 17), and receive spiritual freedom and sustenance. To **go in and go out** is an Old Testament expression which suggests the freedom of movement enjoyed by a trusted servant (cf. David, 1 Sam. xviii. 13, 16). For freedom as the gift of Christ cf. viii. 36: for Christ as the source of spiritual food cf. vi. 35, and of spiritual drink, cf. iv. 14; vii. 37.

10. John returns to the contrast between **the thief** and **the shepherd,** but expounds this in the light of the lesson drawn from the allegory. The purpose of **the thief** is not merely selfish, but murderous, like that of the Devil (cf. viii. 44), and indeed, as **destroy** implies, fatal to the salvation of his victims, while that of **the shepherd** is not to take, but to give **life**— spiritual life (cf. iii. 15 f., 36) **in abundance** (περισσόν, literally, 'more than is really necessary'[1]). He gives of his 'fulness' (cf. i. 16), like God, who 'does not give by measure' (iii. 34).

(11) '**I am the good shepherd.**[2] **The good shepherd lays down his life**[3] **for the sake of the sheep; (12) but the ⟨one who is a⟩ hireling and no shepherd, who does not own the sheep,**[4] **perceives**[5] **the wolf coming and leaves the sheep and runs away (and the wolf seizes and scatters them), (13) because he is a hireling and is not concerned for the sheep.**'

11. Here John expounds a fresh aspect of the theme of the Messianic shepherd which is central to the original parable: he contrasts **the good shepherd,** not with the thieves, but with shepherds who are not worthy of the name. **The good** (καλός, i.e. the real, proper, rather than the morally good) **shepherd** shrinks from no sacrifice. He even **lays down his life.** The verb **lays down** (τίθησιν, literally, 'puts'[6]) is used consistently in the FG (cf. x. 15, 17, 18; xiii. 37, 38; xv. 13, cf. 1 John iii. 16), whereas Mark x. 45 =Matt. xx. 28, has 'give'.[7]

[1] Cf. 2 Cor. ix. 1, 'It is *superfluous* for me to write to you'.

[2] For the 'I am' sayings see on iv. 26; vi. 35.

[3] ψυχή, not ζωή, as in xii. 25; xiii. 37 f.; xv. 13. The ψυχή is the breath-soul, without which a body is dead, ζωή, that which ψυχή gives on the natural level, and πνεῦμα (spirit) on the supernatural level.

[4] Literally, 'whose own the sheep are not'. Contrast verse 3.

[5] θεωρεῖ. See p. 191.   [6] Used in xiii. 4 for 'taking off' garments.

[7] A few authorities read 'gives' for 'lays down' in this verse (P45 א* D *lat sin*), but they are most probably harmonising John to Matthew.

John's choice of verb may be meant to stress the freedom of Jesus' action (cf. verse 18). 'To *put* one's life in one's hand' is a common phrase in the Old Testament (Judges xii. 3; 1 Sam. xix. 5 etc.), and means 'to risk [rather than 'sacrifice'] one's life.' This would be a perfectly natural sense for the phrase to have in the FG, were it not for the sacrificial connotation of the preposition ὑπέρ, **for the sake of the sheep.** This preposition is used in vi. 51 and xi. 50 ff., and in Mark xiv. 24, Luke xxii. 19 f., Rom. v. 6-8. The death of Jesus is clearly visualised: he does much more than *risk* his life. The possibility of a shepherd dying in defence of his flock against wild beasts or robbers was a real one (cf. David's adventures, 1 Sam. xvii. 34 ff.), but is no part of the conventional picture of the shepherd-Messiah. It is Jesus' own distinctive contribution, and looks forward to xv. 13.

12 f. The description of **the hireling** recalls the attacks of the prophets on the leaders of Israel, Jer. xxiii. 1 ff., Ezek. xxxiv. 2 ff., Zech. xi. 16 f., as unworthy shepherds of God's flock. For **the wolf** as the enemy of the flock cf. Matt. x. 16, Acts xx. 29. For John **the wolf** is presumably the Devil (also pictured as a beast of prey in 1 Pet. v. 8), from whom **the hireling** fails to defend the flock. Thus, like the unworthy shepherds in the Old Testament, **the hireling** represents the religious leaders of Israel. The fact that he receives a wage is not the real point of the comparison. It is irrelevant to the Pharisees, and to the Rabbinate, which was not a paid professional body, while the priesthood (which was paid) does not seem to be under attack.[1] The point of comparison between **the hireling** and the Pharisees lies in their indifference to the fate of the ordinary people (cf. Matt. xxiii. 4 = Luke xi. 46), the 'sheep without a shepherd' of Mark vi. 34, for whom they felt no more concern than the hireling does for the sheep which he does not own.

(14) 'I am the good shepherd; and I recognise mine and mine recognise me, (15) just as the Father recognises me, and I recognise the Father; and I lay down[2] my life for the sake of the sheep.'

14. In a further elaboration of the theme of the original

---

[1] Hence there is no justification for using this text as an objection to a paid ministry.　　[2] P45, 66 ℵ* DW read 'give'. See on 11.

parable, John points to the mutual knowledge of the shepherd and the sheep, indicated in verses 3 and 4. This may be illustrated by Jesus' recognition of Simon (i. 42) and Nathanael (i. 47). 15. John finds a parallel to this in the mutual knowledge of the Father and the Son (cf. Matt. xi. 27).

(16) 'And I have other sheep, which do not belong to[1] this fold; I must lead them also, and they shall listen to my voice; and there shall be[2] one flock,[3] one shepherd'.

These **other sheep** are the scattered children of God who are to be brought together by Christ after his death and resurrection (cf. xi. 52; xii. 32). Thus this verse follows naturally after the allusion to Christ's death in 15, repeating 11. The **one flock** looks forward to the fulfilment of the prophetic hope that the Gentiles will be brought into God's flock (cf. Isa. xi. 10; xlix. 6; lx. 1 ff., etc.) under **one shepherd,** the Messiah (cf. Ezek. xxxvii. 24). The fact that Jesus during his ministry forbade his disciples to preach to the Gentiles (Matt. x. 5) does not necessarily imply that he did not expect them to be brought into the flock eventually.[4] It is quite as probable that he foresaw the gathering in of the Gentiles, in fulfilment of prophecy, as that this hope is read back into his teaching as a result of the activity of St Paul.[5]

(17) 'The reason why the Father loves me is[6] that I lay down my life, so as to take it up again. (18) No one takes[7] it away from me, but I lay it down of my own accord.[8] ⟨Just as⟩ I have authority[9] to lay it down, ⟨so⟩ also I have

---

[1] Literally, 'which are not out of (ἐκ) . . .'

[2] γενήσεται P⁶⁶ ℵ* A *fam* 13. Barrett (p. 312) prefers the plural, read by P⁴⁵ BDWΘ *fam* 1, etc. There is, however, probably little difference in meaning between them.

[3] The AV follows Jerome in reading *fold*. This was probably an unconscious alteration of Jerome's, preserved as fitting the institutional conception of the Church which was congenial to Western theology.

[4] A similar problem arises in the case of Jesus' activity in Samaria. See p. 153 (on iv. 40).

[5] As Bauer asserts (p. 141), and Barrett seems to imply (p. 312).

[6] Literally, 'For this the Father loves me', but 'this' refers to what follows.

[7] The aorist ἦρεν, read by P⁴⁵ ℵ* B, is preferable to αἴρει, the present, which has been assimilated to the tense of τίθημι. It is however to be translated by a present, since it is 'timeless', like the aorists εἶπον in x. 25, ἐβλήθη and ἐξηράνθη in xv. 6, cf. xv. 9, and possibly ἠγάπησα in xiii. 34; xv. 12.

[8] ἀπ᾽ ἐμαυτοῦ, literally, 'from myself'; cf. v. 30; vii. 17, 28; viii. 28, 42; xiv. 10.   [9] ἐξουσία; cf. i. 12; v. 27.

authority[1] **to take it up again; this ⟨is⟩ the command ⟨which⟩ I received from my Father.'**

The resurrection of Christ, now explicitly foreseen, is represented as the purpose of his death. His free acceptance of death and resurrection is the result, paradoxically enough, of his obedience to the Father's **command.** This obedience is the reason for the Father's love for his Son, and for his entrusting him with **authority** to dispose of his life, cf. v. 19 ff. The Son can **take up** his life **again** because, by the Father's design, he has life in himself (v. 26).

For the contrast of **lay down** and **take up** cf. xiii. 4 and 12, where the same verbs (τίθημι and λαμβάνω) are used of Christ taking off and putting on his garments.[2]

(19) A division again arose among the Jews because of these words. (20) And many of them said, 'He has a demon and is mad; why do you listen to him?' (21) Others said, 'These sayings are not ⟨those⟩ of one possessed by a demon; a demon cannot open blind men's eyes, can it?'

19. For **division** among Jesus' hearers, cf. vii. 43; ix. 16. The pattern continues, as it also does 20. in the repetition of the old charge that Jesus **has a demon** (cf. vii. 20; viii. 48 f., 52), though the further comment, that he **is mad,** added by way of explanation, may give it a less sinister turn.

21. Jesus' supporters appeal to common sense and experience, as did the man born blind (cf. ix. 31 ff.).

The final question serves to attach x. 1-21 to the previous episode. But this is somewhat artificial, since the subject of x. 1-21 has otherwise nothing to do with the man born blind. It looks like an editorial device made necessary by the extensive rearrangement which the material in vii-x has undergone. We seem to have reached an inconclusive, but dramatically not ineffective, end to the long series of disputes. The tension is unresolved, but before we move to the resolution of the tension by the violent action of Jesus' enemies, we have a further scene of disputation. The scene is the same, but the date is some three months later. Again we may detect the hand of the editor, arranging his material with an eye to its dramatic effect.

[1] See p. 252 n. 9 above.   [2] See p. 306.

(22) It was the ¹ Dedication in Jerusalem; it was winter; (23) and Jesus was walking in the Temple in Solomon's Portico.

22. John, as usual, gives the bare minimum of information to set the new scene—the date, the place, and the actors. There has been no note of time since vii. 37, and so we must conclude that the parable of the Good Shepherd was told on the last day of the feast of Tabernacles. But the controversy in x. 24-38 arises immediately out of the situation described in x. 19-21. The arrangement of the material is again artificial, but its lack of historical verisimilitude is concealed by its dramatic effectiveness. If we read *At that time* **it was** (ἐγένετο τότε) **the Dedication** it would indeed imply that x. 1-21 describes events at that festival, and so would overcome this difficulty—but only to create another, since John intended x. 1-18 to belong to the same context as chapter ix.²

The feast of the Dedication, *Chanukkah*,³ had been instituted by Judas Maccabaeus and his brethren to commemorate their cleansing of the Temple, on 25 *Kislev* B.C. 165, after its profanation by Antiochus Epiphanes, and lasted for eight days, from 25 *Kislev* (1 Macc. iv. 59). As the Jewish month *Kislev* covers parts of November and December, the feast coincided approximately in date, and also in the spirit of its celebration, with Christmas today. Since there is nothing in x. 22-42 which suggests any symbolic significance in the festival, it may be taken as a relic of genuinely historical information preserved when this section was moved to its present position by the editor of the FG, who wanted to bring all his controversial

¹ ἐγένετο τὰ . . . is read only by a very few authorities, including *fam* 1 565 and *a b*. Yet it is preferable, on grounds of transcriptional probability, to the alternatives ἐγένετο τότε τὰ . . . (P⁶⁶ BLW 33 *eg arm* RVᵐᵍ) and ἐγένετο δὲ τὰ . . . (א ADΘ *fam* 13 *lat pesh hl* RV). ΕΓΕΝΕΤΟΤΟΤΕΤΑ could easily arise by dittography from ΕΓΕΝΕΤΟΤΑ, and its secondary character is shown by the fact that elsewhere in the FG τότε always precedes the main verb (vii. 10; viii. 28; xi. 6, 14; xii. 16; xiii. 27; xix. 1, 16; xx. 8). If the true reading had been ΕΓΕΝΕΤΟΔΕΤΑ it would have resisted corruption more easily than ΕΓΕΝΕΤΟΤΑ, and the interpolation of ΔΕ is more likely than its omission. ΕΓΕΝΕΤΟ occurs first in the sentence three other times in the FG; in i. 6 there is no connecting word; in iii. 25 οὖν, in xix. 36 γάρ.

² See p. 246.

³ John's name Ἐγκαίνια is used to translate *chanukkah* in Theodotion's version of Dan. iii. 2. For details of the feast see Strack-Billerbeck, II, pp. 539 ff.

material into a single block. It is conceivable that in the original the Triumphal Entry and Cleansing of the Temple took place at *Chanukkah*, and were followed respectively by x. 24-42 and by the Jews' demand for a sign (ii. 18 ff.). There are grounds for thinking that John's Cleansing of the Temple is not in its original position,[1] and his account of the Triumphal Entry has some resemblance to the Maccabaean ascent to the Temple.[2] Certainly *Chanukkah* would be an effective time for such a demonstration.

If this is so, then in the source x. 24-42 corresponded to the controversy which in Mark xi. 18–xii. 34 follows the Cleansing of the Temple, though it may actually have occurred on the evening of the Triumphal Entry, and before the Cleansing. Mark xi. 11 alone records that the Cleansing was not on the same day. John may have put these two events at Passover— even though he separates them—because of his interpretation of Christ's death as the true Passover. But he preserves a relic of the original order of events in his source when he makes the raising of Lazarus the immediate motive for the decision to arrest Jesus (xi. 47-53). Finally, the Samaritan episode (iv. 4-42) may originally have come between *Chanukkah* and Passover,[3] and has been put in its present position for the sake of the dramatic contrast between the Samaritan woman and Nicodemus.[4]

The fact that **it was winter** may be mentioned either for the benefit of readers unfamiliar with the Jewish calendar, or in order to explain why 23. **Jesus was walking** under cover **in Solomon's Portico.** This was a part of the Temple (mentioned also in Acts iii. 11; v. 12) more ancient than the rest, and said to be a relic of the original fabric (Josephus, *Antiquities*, XX. 221). It was on the east side of the Temple area, immediately overlooking the Kidron valley, and may have been the place where Jesus was tempted to throw himself from the 'pinnacle' —i.e. the 'aisle' (πτερύγιον), not the roof—of the Temple into the valley beneath. And an appropriate time for this would be after either the Triumphal Entry or the Cleansing of the Temple.[5]

---

[1] See p. 121.　　　　[2] See p. 287.　　　　[3] See pp. 138 f.
[4] See pp. 137, 144.　　　　　　[5] See also p. 180 on vi. 15.

(24) So the Jews surrounded him, and said to him, 'How long are you keeping us in suspense?[1] If you are the Christ, tell us openly.'[2]

The Jews, having cornered Jesus in Solomon's Portico, do not intend to let him go until he has either satisfied or disavowed the expectations which he has aroused, by stating publicly whether he is the Christ or not. A similar demand was made, in almost identical terms, according to Luke xxii. 67, at Jesus' trial before the Sanhedrin. But it is unlikely that John has borrowed this from Luke.[3]

Their demand is understandable, since so far Jesus has only claimed to be the Christ to the Samaritan woman (iv. 26) and (less explicitly) to the man born blind (ix. 37), and his answer to the question, 'Who are you?' at viii. 25 had been evasive. He was in fact in a dilemma. He cannot deny that he is the Christ, and yet he cannot claim the title openly without inviting inevitable misunderstanding, since he is not the kind of Christ that the Jews want, and his attempts at enlightening them have so far failed. So again he tries to avoid a straight answer.

(25) Jesus answered them, 'I tell[4] you, and you do not believe;[5] the works which I do in my Father's name, these bear witness about me. (26) But you do not believe, because you do not belong to[6] my sheep. (27) My sheep listen to my voice, and I recognise them, and they follow me; (28) and I give them eternal life, and they shall never[7] perish, and no one shall snatch them from my hand. (29) ⟨They are⟩ the greatest gift of all which my Father has given me,[8] and no one can snatch ⟨anything⟩ from the

[1] Literally, 'How long are you raising our soul?' Barrett (p. 316) favours the meaning 'provoke', but in the context of the division of opinion just recorded, suspense is probably meant.

[2] παρρησίᾳ, in public (cf. vii. 4, 13, 26).

[3] Barrett, however, regards this as possible (p. 316). But see Introduction, p. 12.

[4] Εἶπον is to be taken as a 'timeless' aorist (cf. x. 18; xiii. 34; xv. 6). DΘ lat sin read Λαλῶ, a present.

[5] B reads the aorist ἐπιστεύσατε; but this is a mistaken assimilation to the tense of Εἶπον.

[6] Literally, 'you are not of (ἐκ) my sheep'.

[7] οὐ μὴ . . . εἰς τὸν αἰῶνα. See on iv. 14.

[8] Literally, 'My Father [nominative], that which he has given me is greater than all', ὁ πατήρ μου ὃ δέδωκέν μοι πάντων μεῖζόν ἐστιν, the reading

Father's hand. (30) I and my Father are one.'

25. Just as the Jews' demand in verse 24 resembles that in Luke xxii. 67, so too Jesus' reply uses similar words to that in Luke xxii. 67, 'If **I tell you, you** will **not believe.**' But again similarity does not necessarily imply literary dependence. It is inherent in the situation in each case.

If the Jews' demand is understandable from their own point of view, so is Jesus' reply from his. He meets their stubbornly repeated demand for clarification with the assurance that he has been telling them all the time, and still is telling them, who he is.[1] Much of what he goes on to say repeats what he has said already, and acts as a summary of the results of the long controversy now drawing to its close.

Since the Jews **do not believe** (cf. v. 38; vi. 64; viii. 45), they cannot appreciate that **the works which** he performs as his **Father's** representative (cf. v. 43) furnish the **witness** which they demand (cf. v. 36). His whole ministry is eloquent of what he is, as those who believe recognise (cf. vi. 68 f.).

26. The reason why the Jews **do not believe** is not any refusal on his part to enlighten them, but the fact that they **do not belong** to Jesus' **sheep, 27.** which **listen to** him (cf. x. 3), are known by him (cf. x. 14), and **follow**[2] him (cf. x. 3 f.). These allusions to a parable related some months before, and so only intelligible in the written Gospel, illustrate the artificial way in which the material in the FG is arranged.

28. A familiar theme is re-introduced, Jesus' gift of **eternal life** (cf. iii. 15 f., 36; v. 24; vi. 40, 47; x. 10; 1 John ii. 25; v. 11), which guarantees that his sheep will **never perish** (cf. iii. 16; vi. 37-40; xvii. 12), since **no one shall snatch them from** him (cf. x. 12).

29 f. The main lines of the argument are clear whichever of the two best attested readings is followed.[3] The verses explain

---

of B *lat boh.* For ὅ and μεῖζον most authorities, including P⁶⁶ *fam* 1 *fam* 13 *sin pesh hl sah* have ὅς and μείζων (masculine). These give excellent sense, but make it impossible to account for the harder reading, which is to be preferred. ℵ W have ὅ ... μείζων, ΑΘ ὅς ... μεῖζον (which Barrett favours, p. 317) and D ὁ δεδωκώς μοι πάντων μείζων. See also p. 258.

[1] This is the meaning of the 'timeless' aorist. See p. 256, n. 4.
[2] For the significance of 'following' Jesus see on i. 43 and xiii. 36.
[3] See p. 256, n. 8.

why no one can snatch Jesus' sheep from his hand. With the reading adopted above, it is because they are God's **greatest gift** to his Son, and, since **the Father** and the Son **are one**, and no one can take anything from the Father by force, it follows that no one can take anything from the Son. That God has given Christ his followers is shown by vi. 37; xvii. 6, but that they are God's **greatest gift** to him is not stated elsewhere. But it is clear that they are precious to Christ, since he gave his life for them (x. 11, 15; xv. 13).

If the other reading is adopted, 'The Father who gave me them is greater than all,' this point is lost. But the statement, though true, is so obvious that it did not need to be made. It is in fact intrinsically the inferior reading.

30. That the Son **and the Father are one** (ἕν, neuter, literally *one thing*), is not offered as a proposition in metaphysics, but simply as the explanation why an attack on the Son is also an attack on the Father, and so bound to fail. But the complete unity of Son and Father, which has already been expressed in other terms in i. 1; v. 17 ff., forms the basis and justification for the later orthodox affirmation of the unity of substance between the divine Persons.

(31) The Jews picked up[1] **stones, in order to stone him. (32) Jesus answered them, 'Many good**[2] **works have I shown you from the Father; for which work of these are you stoning me?' (33) The Jews answered him, '⟨It is⟩ not for ⟨any⟩ good**[2] **work ⟨that⟩ we are stoning you, but for blasphemy, and because you, who are a man, make yourself God'.**

31. The Jews have an answer that they can (they think) understand, and it provokes them to action, cf. viii. 59. 32. In reply to Jesus' ironical question 33. **the Jews** accuse him of

---

[1] ἐβάστασαν. The verb also occurs in John xii. 6; xvi. 12; xix. 17; xx. 15, but does not mean *pick up* in any of these passages, though that is its obvious meaning here. It may, however, mean that they were carrying stones, and had cornered Jesus with the prior intention of stoning him when they had forced him to make a confession.

After the verb most MSS., headed by P66 A, add οὖν πάλιν, an obvious conflation of οὖν (D 28 *lat*) and πάλιν (ℵ BW). A few MSS. (P45 Θ *ff*2 and one Vulgate MS.) have neither. Since there is no reason why either οὖν or πάλιν should have been omitted, the shortest reading is to be preferred.

[2] καλά, the adjective used for the *good* shepherd, on which see p. 250.

blasphemy, and of claiming divinity (cf. v. 18; xix. 7), which is
how they take verse 30.

Stoning was the proper punishment for blasphemy (Lev.
xxiv. 16), but on this occasion the Jews do not seem to be
proposing an execution following a trial, and observing the
proper legal forms,[1] but simply a lynching. It is, however,
hypercritical to argue[2] that this shows John's unfamiliarity with
Jewish practice. Lynching was not unknown among the Jews in
New Testament times (cf. Acts xxi. 31), and stones were handy
weapons for the purpose (cf. Acts xiv. 19). What a Gentile mob
could do to Paul at Lystra, could be done as well by Jews in
Jerusalem. And summary execution for blasphemy was in some
cases recognised by Jewish law.[3]

**(34) Jesus answered them, 'It is written in your[4] law,
is it not, "I said, You are gods"? (35) If it called "gods"
them to whom the word of God came (and the scripture
cannot be abrogated),[5] (36) are you saying of him whom
the Father sanctified and sent into the world, "You blaspheme", because I said, "I am the Son of God"? (37) If
I am not doing the works of my Father, do not believe
me. (38) But if I am doing them, even if you do not believe
me, believe the works; so that you may know and recognise[6] that the Father ⟨is⟩ in me, and I ⟨am⟩ in the
Father.'**

Jesus appeals to Scripture to clear himself of the charge of
blasphemy, and again uses the typically Rabbinic form of argument *from light to heavy* (cf. vii. 22 f.). 34. He quotes Ps. lxxxii.
6, attributing it to the **law,** meaning thereby *Scripture,* as in
xii. 34; xv. 25 (cf. 1 Cor. xiv. 21). For **your law** (if **your** is part
of the text), cf. viii. 17. In both passages **your** is emphatic,

---

[1] For the rules for trial and execution for blasphemy see Barrett, *The New
Testament Background* (1956), pp. 170-172.

[2] As Barrett does, p. 318.

[3] See Strack–Billerbeck, II, p. 542.

[4] ὑμῶν, which is omitted by P45 א* D Θ *vt sin,* perhaps rightly.

[5] λυθῆναι, cf. v. 18; vii. 23; for the meaning of λύω see p. 164, n. 2.

[6] γνῶτε καὶ γινώσκητε (an awkward phrase) is read by P45, 66 B Θ *fam* 1 *r*;
for γινώσκητε the majority of MSS., headed by א A *fam* 13 28 *f vg* have
the easier πιστεύσητε. D *sin* Tertullian and Cyprian read γνῶτε alone. Though
Barrett thinks this may be original (p. 321), it is an undeniably easier reading,
and it is difficult to see how γνῶτε καὶ γινώσκητε could have originated from it.

stressing that it is 'the **law** *to which you appeal in condemning me*' (as they eventually do, cf. xix. 7), and does not necessarily reflect the point of view of a period later than that of Jesus himself.[1]

35 f. To a reader conditioned by historical criticism to look for the original meaning of a text, this argument must seem unconvincing, but it is similar to others attributed to Jesus (cf. viii. 17 f., Mark ii. 25 f.; xii. 26 f.; Luke xiii. 15 f.), which conduct their appeal to Scripture in the fashion of his contemporaries, and, being purely *ad hominem*, is in the circumstances in which it is used quite legitimate. The original meaning of the verse is irrelevant to its use in the FG. It is sufficient that **gods** (*'elohim*) is part of the original.

35. The subject of **called** is not expressed in the Greek: it may be *he* (i.e. *God*), but **it** (i.e. the text just quoted) is perhaps more likely, in view of the parenthetic remark that **the scripture cannot be abrogated**: the scripture (ἡ γραφή) means a single text, cf. ii. 22:[2] **the word of God** is the statement **You are gods.** There is a certain irony in these words being spoken by the incarnate Logos.

36. The Son is **sanctified,** i.e. set apart for God's service, as 'the holy one of God' (vi. 69),[3] and is sent into the world as God's representative.[4] As such he can claim *a fortiori* to be **Son of God** if the men addressed in the psalm can be called gods (in the second half of the verse they are called 'sons of the Most High'), since, whoever they are, their status cannot be as high as his.

37 f. Jesus repeats the argument of v. 36; x. 25 (cf. xiv. 11; xv. 24). They can see what he is doing, and this should convince them of the truth of the claim which they find so offensive, **that the Father ⟨is⟩ in me, and I ⟨am⟩ in the Father.** This explanation of verse 30 suggests a more intimate association

[1] See p. 220.   [2] See p. 120.   [3] See p. 199, n. 2.
[4] iii. 17. See p. 129, n. 1. [Cf. also the discussions of this passage by J. A. Emerton, 'The Interpretation of Psalm lxxxii in John x', *J.T.S.*, n.s., Vol. XI, 1960, pp. 329-332, and 'Melchizedek and the Gods: Fresh Evidence for the Jewish Background of John x. 34-36', *J.T.S.*, n.s., Vol. XVII, 1966, pp. 399-401; A. T. Hanson, 'John's Citation of Psalm lxxxii', *N.T.S.*, Vol. XI, 1964-65, pp. 158-162; M. de Jonge and A. S. van der Woude, 'II Q Melchizedek and the New Testament', *N.T.S.*, Vol. XII, 1965-66, pp. 301-326.—B. A. M.]

than that claimed in viii. 16, 29, but looks forward to xiv. 10 f.,
20; xvii. 21, 23.

**(39) They again ¹ sought to arrest him; and he went out
of their hand⟨s⟩.²**

For previous attempts cf. vii. 30, 44; viii. 59. Jesus' enemies
are silenced, but not convinced. Now they can only resort to
force, but it is again unsuccessful.

**(40) And he went away again beyond the Jordan to the
place where John was first baptising; and he stayed³ there.
(41) And many came to him; and they said, 'John did not
do any sign, but all the things that John said about this
man were true'. (42) And many believed in him there.**

40. This quiet interlude between the controversies of vii–x
and the final sign in xi takes us back to the place where Jesus'
first appearance in the FG is recorded—at Bethany **beyond the
Jordan . . . where John was . . . baptising** (i. 28). The repetition of these words underlines the fact that the wheel has come
full circle. Here Jesus **stayed,** waiting upon his Father's will.

That **he stayed** and 41. that **many came to him** also recall
the first appearance of Jesus in the FG, when two disciples of
John the Baptist come to Jesus and ask where he is staying
(i. 38).⁴

There is no polemic against the Baptist implied by the remark
that he **did not do any sign;** the **many** were probably disciples
of his who, in giving their allegiance to Jesus, recognise that
John was a true prophet. This again echoes the witness of the
Baptist which marks the opening of Jesus' ministry.

42. In spite of failure, Jesus does win belief. The light has
shined, and has not been mastered. From its position in the
sentence, **there** is emphatic, and points the contrast with
Jerusalem, where belief, though not entirely absent (cf. vii. 31;
viii. 30), was submerged in the general hostility.

---

¹ The true reading may be that of P⁴⁵ א* D *lat,* which omits **again.** The
fact that the word does not occur in the same place in the other MSS. suggests
that it is an interpolation. In A L W *fam* 1 565 it occurs after, and in P⁶⁶ B Θ
before, **him.**

² Greek idiom has the singular where English has the plural.

³ The majority of the MSS. have ἔμεινεν (aorist); B *vt* have ἔμενεν, which
may be right, and means, 'was staying'.

⁴ For the significance of Jesus' 'staying' see p. 98.

12. THE SIXTH SIGN, IN JERUSALEM, AND ITS CONSEQUENCES, xi. 1-54.

Rejected in Jerusalem at the feast of the Dedication, Jesus spent an unspecified period of the winter in Transjordan, awaiting his Father's call to the next step. Humanly speaking, so far he had been a failure. But the climax of his ministry was at hand, in the raising of his friend Lazarus from the dead. This incident is peculiar to the FG, and raises the question of its historical value in its sharpest form. This will be considered in due course.

In the pattern of the FG the raising of Lazarus is the third and last of the second group of signs, and corresponds to the third of the first group, the healing of the man at Bethzatha (v. 2 ff.). They are linked by the theme of resurrection, which is a topic in the controversy which follows the healing (v. 21, 25, 28), and is now demonstrated in fact. The raising of Lazarus is thus the last sign which Jesus performs, and it points on to the final sign, the resurrection of Jesus himself.

xi. (1) Now there was a man who was ill, Lazarus of Bethany, the village of Mary and her sister Martha. (2) Now it was Mary who anointed the Lord with ointment and wiped his feet with her hair, whose brother Lazarus was ill.

1. **Lazarus** is known in the Synoptic Gospels only as the beggar in the parable of Luke xvi. 19 ff. Since the possibility of the raising of Lazarus is mentioned in this parable it is perhaps only what one would expect that critics who do not regard the historical value of the FG as very great should suggest that John borrowed the name from Luke's parable. But the characters in all the other parables attributed to Jesus are anonymous, while the names of two other persons upon whom miracles are performed are given (Jairus' daughter, Mark v. 22 ff., and Bartimaeus, Mark x. 46 ff.). It may therefore be that in telling the parable Jesus departed from his usual custom and deliberately used the name Lazarus ironically.[1]

Lazarus means 'God helps', but John gives no indication

[1] See Introduction, pp. 11 f.

that this is in any way significant. Since he could not expect Greek readers to pick up such allusions, he gives a translation when a proper name is intended to have a symbolical significance (cf. *Siloam*, ix. 7).

Bethany may be the same as 'Ananiah mentioned in Neh. xi. 32, the site of which was close to the modern el-'Azarîyeh, S.E. of Olivet, and about two miles from Jerusalem (xi. 18).

Mary and her sister Martha appear in Luke x. 38-42, inhabiting an unnamed village near Jerusalem. Again, it is suggested that John has borrowed them from Luke.

2. **Mary** is further identified as the woman **who anointed the Lord with ointment and wiped his feet with her hair.** John tells the story in xii. 1-8, but in Luke vii. 36-50 an unnamed woman who was a sinner washed Jesus' feet with her tears, wiped them with her hair, and anointed them with ointment. Again it is argued that John is borrowing from Luke. But Mark also has a story of an anointing of Jesus at Bethany, and the relationship of the three is by no means simple. This will be discussed more fully in connexion with xii. 1 ff.,[1] but it may be said now that the dependence of John on Luke is not demonstrable elsewhere,[2] which diminishes its plausibility here. The natural reference of this verse is to xii. 1 ff., and the aorist participles are used simply because the incident was past when John wrote, not because he is referring to an incident which was past at the time of xi. 2.[3]

These two verses are very clumsily expressed. That Lazarus was the brother of Mary and Martha comes in as an afterthought following the description of Mary which is not particularly germane to the present story. Elsewhere John, whose narrative style is usually straightforward, occasionally has difficulty in starting a story. In iv. 1-3 and vi. 22 f., this may be due to the fact that he had to alter the beginning of the stories because he had rearranged his material, and here also his clumsiness may be due to his introduction of the remark that Lazarus was Mary's brother, which he had not found in his source. But there may be another and more natural explanation.

---

[1] See pp. 283–286.　　　　　[2] See Introduction, pp. 10 ff.
[3] See J. N. Sanders, 'Those whom Jesus loved', *N.T.S.*, Vol. I, 1954–55, p. 36.

It is said that John introduces the sisters as if they were already well known to his readers, and this is used as an argument for his dependence on Luke, to whose narrative he is said to be alluding. But he (or his source) may give this impression simply because he is at last writing down a story which he had told many times already to listeners who knew it well, and then suddenly remembers to add for the benefit of his readers (who had not heard his stories before) that Mary anointed Jesus, and —of course!—that Lazarus was her brother. Thus the impression of clumsiness is only due to an old man repeating in an unfamiliar medium an oft-told tale.

(3) So the sisters sent to him, saying, 'Lord, see, your friend[1] is ill.'

The sisters appeal to Jesus' friendship for Lazarus to induce him to make the dangerous journey back into Judaea. But it was not simply out of friendship that he went.

(4) And when he heard, Jesus said, 'This illness is not fatal,[2] but ⟨is⟩ for the glory of God, in order that the Son of God may be glorified through it.'

One motive, in itself sufficient, for Jesus to go to Bethany is that it will be **for the glory of God,** i.e. the glory which God will bestow on his Son (cf. viii. 54), as the clause which follows makes clear. For the confidence that even illness falls within God's providential purpose cf. ix. 3. Jesus' answer, meant to be reported to, and to reassure, the sisters, is a further illustration of his clairvoyant power.[3] How far the knowledge went which he had by this means we cannot say, but the fact that his assurance that the illness would not be fatal was not fulfilled in the natural sense of the words (since Lazarus did actually die)[4] suggests that it was limited. But he knew at least that here was his call, and he followed it in confident obedience to his Father's guidance.

[1] Literally, 'he whom you love (φιλεῖς)'. φιλέω is also used in verse 36, whereas in verse 5 John uses ἀγαπάω. Barrett regards these words as synonymous (see p. 324), but see p. 130, n. 2 for the distinction between them. φιλέω describes a spontaneous affection—Jesus himself calls Lazarus 'our friend (φίλος)' in verse 11—and ἀγαπάω a love which is deliberate and voluntary, and does not depend on any attractiveness in its object except the need for love.

[2] Literally, 'to death'. The same expression (πρὸς θάνατον) is used in 1 John v. 16 f., with reference to sin.

[3] See p. 100.   [4] But see p. 274.

That it is in death that Jesus will be glorified has already been indicated.[1]

(5) Now Jesus loved Martha and her sister and Lazarus.

John adds this comment in order to avoid the suspicion that Jesus' delay in answering the sisters' call was due to indifference. But by his choice of the word ἠγάπα for **loved** he also shows that if love was Jesus' motive, it was not that which can be described as friendship, though he was Lazarus' friend, but the divine response to human need.[2]

In this verse also may be the clue to the identity of the disciple whom Jesus loved (ἠγάπα).[3]

(6) So when he had heard that he was ill, then indeed Jesus stayed for two days in the place where he was; (7) ⟨and only⟩ after that[4] did he say to his disciples, 'Let us go back into Judaea.'

John draws attention to Jesus' surprising delay by **then indeed** (τότε μέν) and **after that** (ἔπειτα μετὰ τοῦτο), both particularly emphatic. As in ii. 4, he acts only in his own time. But since Lazarus had been dead four days when he eventually arrived, he would not have found him alive if he had gone two days earlier.

(8) The disciples said to him, 'Rabbi, ⟨just⟩ now[5] the Jews were seeking to stone you, and are you going back there?'[6]

The disciples, remembering the events of Jesus' last visit to Jerusalem (cf. x. 31, 39), seem to imply, by using the singular **are you going** (ὑπάγεις), that, if Jesus chooses to run such a risk, they will not be there with him.

(9) Jesus answered, 'There are ⟨only⟩ twelve hours of the day, are there not?[7] If a man walks in the day, he does not stumble, because he sees the light of this world;

---

[1] See, on vii. 39, p. 215 n. 2.   [2] See p. 264, n. 1.

[3] See Introduction, pp. 31 f.

[4] For the significance of μετὰ τοῦτο see p. 131, n. 4.

[5] For νῦν referring to an event recently past cf. xiii. 31; xxi. 10.

[6] ἐκεῖ, in an emphatic position at the end of the sentence, cf. x. 40.

[7] The ancients divided the period of daylight into twelve hours, which thus altered in length throughout the year, and were only exactly equal to the modern fixed hour at the equinoxes.

(10) but if he walks in the night, he stumbles, because there is no light in him.'

Jesus replies by means of a parable. 9. He has only a limited time in which to do his Father's work (cf. ix. 4 f.), and he must use it to the full; no harm will come to him while he is doing his duty; 10. whereas the man who disregards his duty **walks in the night** and comes to harm.

For the significance of **this world**[1] cf. viii. 23; ix. 39; Jesus himself is the light of the world (viii. 12; ix. 5), but this is not an essential element in the parable here, though there can be no doubt that the thought was in John's mind as he wrote, since these verses clearly look forward to xii. 35 f. For the significance of **night**[2] cf. iii. 2; xiii. 30.

Black suggests that there may have been a play upon words in the original Aramaic, between $s^e qal$ ('stone') and $t^e qal$ ('stumble'), and notes the antithetic parallelism, characteristic of Hebrew poetry, in Jesus' words ([1]1946, pp. 128 f.).

(11) This he said, and after this[3] he said to them, 'Lazarus our friend is asleep; but I am going to wake him up'. (12) So the disciples said to him, 'Lord, if he is asleep, he will get better'. (13) But Jesus had spoken about his death; but they thought that he was speaking of actual sleep.[4]

11. The apparently clumsy mention, twice in the same sentence, of Jesus speaking is probably intended to imply that the disciples kept silent, and that Jesus then tried to appeal to them by describing Lazarus as **our friend,** and saying **I am going** (whether or not you come with me!). He explains that **Lazarus . . . is asleep,** and that he intends to **wake him up.**

Jesus' words are ambiguous, as John is careful to explain (verse 13), and 12. the disciples characteristically misunderstand him, saying (no doubt with relief, hoping that it will not now be necessary for Jesus to go into Judaea) that **if he is asleep, he will get better.** This remark also is ambiguous, though unintentionally so; **he will get better** translates $\sigma\omega\theta\acute{\eta}\sigma\epsilon\tau\alpha\iota$, which

---

[1] See p. 223.   [2] See pp. 122 f.

[3] $\mu\epsilon\tau\grave{\alpha}$ $\tauo\hat{\upsilon}\tauo$. See p. 131, n. 4.

[4] $\pi\epsilon\rho\grave{\iota}$ $\tau\hat{\eta}s$ $\kappao\iota\mu\acute{\eta}\sigma\epsilon\omega s$ $\tauo\hat{\upsilon}$ $\H\upsilon\pi\nuo\upsilon$. Both nouns mean 'sleep', $\H\upsilon\pi\nuos$ having the narrower sense of the physical state, and thus being less ambiguous than $\kappao\acute{\iota}\mu\eta\sigma\iota s$.

also means, 'He will be saved' (cf. x. 9). The disciples have
stumbled upon the truth that the raising of Lazarus is an acted
parable of the saving power of Christ, and have spoken better
than they knew—like John the Baptist[1] and Caiaphas (xi.
50).

**(14) So then Jesus said to them plainly,[2] 'Lazarus has
died;[3] (15) and I am glad for your sakes—so that you may
believe— that I was not there; but let us go to him.'**

14. Only now—**then** ($\tau \acute{o} \tau \epsilon$) is emphatic, being the first word
in the sentence (cf. verse 6)—does Jesus tell them the true state
of affairs, which again he must have learnt by supernatural means.
We need not suppose, however, that he had known this all the
time. **Lazarus has died,** 15. but Jesus is confident in God's
providence: it will be an opportunity for strengthening the disciples' faith. There are degrees of faith, and the disciples have
just revealed the immaturity of theirs by their reluctance to accompany Jesus. The opportunity is greater than it would have
been if Jesus had been with Lazarus, for then he would only
have healed him, and the disciples would not have seen his
resurrection. Jesus again appeals to them to go with him—
contrast **let us go** with 'I am going' in verse 11—and now his
confidence inspires one of his disciples to accept the challenge.

**(16) So Thomas (which means 'Twin') said to his
fellow-disciples, 'Let us also go, so as to die with him.'**

Thomas' words are very much in character: he has no
illusions about the dangers ahead, and, if his faith is not very
strong (cf. xx. 24 ff.), his loyalty is unquestioned, and he is as
ready **to die with** Jesus as the more sanguine and impetuous
Peter (cf. xiii. 37, Mark xiv. 31). At one period in his ministry
Jesus seems to have expected his disciples **to die with him**—
this is the natural meaning of Mark viii. 34—though afterwards
he realised that he was to die alone (cf. John xviii. 8). It is a
tribute to John's fidelity to the tradition that he preserves
Thomas' words.

**(17) So when Jesus arrived he found that he had already
been four days in the tomb. (18) Now Bethany was near**

---

[1] See p. 95.   [2] $\pi \alpha \rho \rho \eta \sigma \acute{\iota} \alpha$. See p. 201, n. 6.
[3] $\mathring{\alpha} \pi \acute{\epsilon} \theta \alpha \nu \epsilon \nu$. The aorist is explained by Black (p. 93) as the equivalent of a
Semitic perfect.

Jerusalem, about two miles[1] away; (19) and many of the Jews had come to Martha and Mary, to comfort them about their brother. (20) So when Martha heard that Jesus was coming, she went to meet him; but Mary was sitting in the house. (21) So Martha said to Jesus, 'Lord, if you had been here, my brother would not have died. (22) And I know that whatever you ask God, God will give you.'

17. Funerals were usually held on the day of death (cf. Acts v. 6, 10), so that Lazarus had been four days dead (xi. 39).

18. The proximity of **Bethany** to **Jerusalem** not only emphasises the danger in which Jesus was placing himself, but also explains 19. the presence of **many of the Jews**, i.e. men from Jerusalem. To pay a formal visit to comfort mourners was (like rejoicing at a wedding) a sacred duty, and an ancient custom (cf. 2 Sam. x. 2). There is no reason to doubt the sincerity of the visitors' motives, but 20. **Martha** may have gone to meet Jesus in order to put him on his guard, while **Mary** stayed behind to receive the condolences of their visitors, **sitting,** as etiquette required of mourners.[2]

The sisters' behaviour is consistent with their characters as shown in Luke x. 38 ff., but this may only mean that both John and Luke are using good sources.

21. Martha manages to imply a rebuke at the same time that she expresses a perfectly genuine confidence that Jesus would have healed Lazarus, if he had arrived in time, and, 22. having doubtless heard that Jesus had raised the dead, gives him a broad hint to do this for her, since she knows that his prayers have power with God (cf. ix. 31). Her last words anticipate closely what Jesus later says to his disciples about prayer (xv. 16; xvi. 23). John conveys a wonderfully lifelike portrait of a faithful, but rather managing, woman.

(23) Jesus said to her, 'Your brother shall rise again'. (24) Martha said to him, 'I know that he will rise in the resurrection on the last day'.

23. Jesus, disapproving, perhaps, of her tendency to assume

---

[1] Literally, 'fifteen stades', see p. 182, n. 1.

[2] Lagrange (p. 301) says that this was still the custom in Jewish families in Palestine in his time.

that he will do what she requires, answers truly, but noncommitally. His words can mean that Lazarus will be raised now, or in the general resurrection.

24. Martha, who had hoped for an unequivocal assurance, says, impatiently perhaps, that of course she knows **that he will rise in the resurrection on the last day** (but this is small comfort at the moment). She expresses orthodox Pharisaic doctrine, but in characteristically Johannine language, since the exact phrase **the last day** (ἡ ἐσχάτη ἡμέρα) occurs only in the FG (vi. 39, 40, 44, 54; xii. 48). But, so far as it goes, it is also a doctrine held by Jesus,[1] though he proceeds at once to modify it.

(25) Jesus said to her, 'I am[2] the resurrection and the life. Even if the man who believes in me dies, he shall live; (26) and everyone who lives and believes in me shall never die. Do you believe this?'

25. Jesus, the incarnate Logos, who is the principle of life in all that exists (i. 4), the Son, for whom it is the Father's purpose that men should attain eternal life through faith in him (cf. iii. 15, 36; v. 24; viii. 51, etc.), and the one who raises believers from the dead (v. 21, 28; vi. 39 f.), is **the resurrection and the life.** Since the believer has passed from the spiritual death of sin into life (v. 24; 1 John iii. 14), merely physical death cannot keep any hold over him, and, 26. if he does not happen to have succumbed to it before the general resurrection takes place, there is no reason why he should die at all.

This is the natural sense of the verse, and is consistent with the belief of the first generation of Christians that this would be the case with some, if not the majority, of their number (cf. 1 Cor. xv. 51). But this belief had faded as the first Christians gradually died, though some still clung to the hope that one at least of the first generation, the Beloved Disciple, would survive until the Lord's return. But John himself did not hold even this attenuated relic of the early faith (cf. xxi. 23), and so, though οὐ μὴ ἀποθάνῃ εἰς τὸν αἰῶνα is correctly translated **shall never die**[3] he cannot have understood the words to refer to physical death (whatever they meant to the compiler of his source), but rather

---

[1] See Introduction, pp. 13 f. and notes on v. 21, 25 f., 28 f., vi. 39.
[2] For the formula **I am . . . .** see p. 188, n. 7.   [3] See p. 142, n. 3.

to what he calls in Rev. ii. 11; xx. 6, 14; xxi. 8 'the second death,' i.e. the ultimate extinction of all that persevere in disobedience.

(27) She said to him, 'Yes, Lord, I am convinced[1] **that you are the Christ, the Son of God, who comes into the world'.**

Martha's confession consists of three affirmations, which echo respectively those of Andrew (i. 41), Nathanael (i. 49), and the men whom Jesus fed in Galilee (vi. 14), though these earlier confessions did not have the specifically Christian content which we must ascribe to Martha's. In content, though not in form, her confession has been anticipated by the Samaritan woman (iv. 29) and Peter (vi. 69). The clause **who comes into the world** has also been anticipated in its specifically Christian sense in i. 9, and looks forward to xii. 46.

Though Jesus has made no promise to raise Lazarus from the dead, Martha makes no further request or hint. She simply goes to fetch her sister. This is the natural consequence of faith in Jesus—Andrew fetches his brother to him (i. 41), and the Samaritan woman the men of her city (iv. 28 ff.).

(28) And when she had said this she went away, and called Mary her sister secretly, saying, 'The teacher is here, and calls you.'

Why **secretly?** Either from an excess of caution, because, knowing how dangerous it was for Jesus to be in Judaea, she wished to conceal his presence even from men whom she had no reason to suppose hostile to him, lest they should inadvertently betray him to his enemies; or, perhaps more probably, from tact, to enable Mary to escape from the visitors without giving offence.

In spite of the exalted titles which she has just ascribed to Jesus, when she speaks of him to her sister she simply calls him **the teacher,** the familiar title used by his disciples. It is no more surprising for her to use it now than it was for Nathanael to say, 'Rabbi, you are the Son of God' (i. 49).

John has not in fact said that Jesus had called Mary. Martha (used to arranging things for people) assumes that this is his wish.

(29) And she, when she heard, rose quickly, and went to him. (30) Now Jesus had not yet come into the village,

[1] πεπίστευκα. See p. 198, n. 5.

but was still in the place where Martha had met him. (31) So the Jews, who were with her in the house and comforting her, seeing that Mary got up quickly and went out, followed her, thinking that she was going to the tomb to weep there.

29. John may intend Mary's prompt response to Jesus' call to illustrate x. 3, and to point to the deeper significance there is in coming to Jesus (cf. iii. 21; v. 40; vi. 35, 37; vii. 37).

30. Martha's motives for secrecy could equally well have moved Jesus to stay outside the village. 31. But, if they wanted privacy, they were disappointed by the Jews, who followed Mary with the somewhat morbid relish which the spectacle of another's grief is liable to stimulate.

(32) So when Mary came where Jesus was, and saw him, she fell at his feet, saying to him, 'Lord, if you had been here, my brother would not have died'.

Mary has less self-control than Martha, but also less self-assertion. She echoes her sister's words in verse 21, but not 22.

(33) So when Jesus saw her weeping, and the Jews who had come with her weeping, his spirit was overcome with emotion, and he was troubled, (34) and said, 'Where have you laid him?' They said to him, 'Lord, come and see.' (35) Jesus burst into tears.

33. The words **his spirit was overcome with emotion** are an attempt to represent the meaning of ἐνεβριμήσατο τῷ πνεύματι. The verb ἐμβριμάομαι in the earliest example of its use describes the snorting of horses; later it is used metaphorically for the inarticulate groaning which indicates violent emotion, usually anger. But the addition of τῷ πνεύματι ('in spirit') seems to exclude any external expression. It is the equivalent of 'in himself' in verse 38. In the New Testament ἐμβριμάομαι occurs only in these two verses in John, and in Matt. ix. 30; Mark i. 43; xiv. 5. If it is assumed that anger is intended to be represented in all these passages, a great deal has to be read into the texts. In Mark xiv. 5 anger is most likely, though shocked surprise would be equally intelligible. In the other Synoptic passages, there is nothing to suggest anger.[1] In the present

---

[1] Except the variant reading ὀργισθείς, 'moved to anger', for σπλαγχνισθείς, 'moved with compassion', in Mark i. 41, D vt.

passage, the precise emotion intended (if precision is indeed intended) can best be determined from the context.

Jesus' emotion was occasioned by the weeping of Mary and the Jews, and later Jesus himself **burst into tears**[1] (verse 35). Also **he was troubled,** ἐτάραξεν ἑαυτόν.[2] The verb ταράσσω, which always expresses violent disturbance, is used again in xii. 27; xiii. 21; xiv. 1, 27. In the first two passages the subject is Jesus, and the verb describes his reaction to the appalling prospect of the Passion. We should perhaps recognise in the present passage that Jesus now realises that the miracle which he is about to perform will precipitate a final clash with the authorities, and so bring about his own death, a prospect from which he instinctively recoils. If so, the dominant emotion in the turmoil described by ἐνεβριμήσατο is no more likely to be anger than grief and horror. John's vivid, even grotesque, language, is not too strong to depict the agony of mind with which Jesus faces death and the despair which it brings, and recognises in death the enemy which he must soon face himself.[3]

34. Jesus' question shows that he has now made up his mind to raise Lazarus. 35. His sudden **tears** are probably not simply due to grief and compassion, but also the physical reaction to the crisis of his decision.

(36) So the Jews said, 'See, what a friend he was to

---

[1] This is the force of the aorist ἐδάκρυσεν. The verb used of Mary and the Jews is κλαίω.

[2] Literally, 'he troubled himself'. This means the same as ἐταράχθη τῷ πνεύματι in xiii. 21, and should not be pressed into meaning that this was a deliberate display, play-acting in fact. The variant reading ἐταράχθη τῷ πνεύματι ὡς ἐμβριμούμενος, 'he was troubled in spirit as by deep emotion' P⁴⁵, ⁶⁶ D Θ *fam* 1 *d p sah*), is an assimilation to xiii. 21, designed to avoid saying that Jesus actually ἐνεβριμήσατο, and must be rejected, in spite of its early attestation.

[3] For a discussion of the view that the two verbs are 'translation-variants' of the same Aramaic original, which implied deep emotional disturbance, and not necessarily anger, see Black, pp. 174 ff., and Barrett, pp. 332 f.

Another suggestion is that ἐνεβριμήσατο describes the violent physical effect of the expenditure of spiritual energy necessary for the performance of a miracle, when 'power went out of him' (Mark v. 30). This would fit Matt. ix. 30, Mark i. 43, and the present passage. See C. Bonner, 'Traces of Thaumaturgic Technique in the Miracles', *The Harvard Theological Review*, Vol. XX, 1927, pp. 171-181, and E. Bevan, 'Note on Mark i. 41 and John xi. 33, 38', *J.T.S.*, o.s., Vol. XXXIII, 1932, pp. 186-188.

him!'¹ **(37) But some of them said, 'This man, who opened the blind man's eyes, could have brought it about, could he not, even that this man should not have died?'**

36. Recognising in Jesus' tears something more than the ritual lamentation which convention required, **the Jews** attribute them to his friendship for Lazarus. Neither they nor the sisters really understand what is going on in Jesus' mind.

37. This question does not imply any hostility to Jesus, or even scepticism about his powers. The Jews accept the genuineness of the cure of the blind man (ix. 1 ff.), and say in effect precisely what Martha and Mary had said, since the form of the question² shows that they think that Jesus could have cured Lazarus if he had arrived in time to find him alive. Their only error is that they see in Jesus no more than an exceptionally powerful miracle-worker.

(38) So Jesus, again overcome with emotion,³ came to the tomb. Now it was a cave, and a stone lay upon⁴ it. (39) Jesus said, 'Lift⁵ the stone'.

38. Now that he actually faces the raising of Lazarus, Jesus is **again overcome with** the same **emotion** as before. If there was no reason to interpret this as anger before, nothing has happened in the meantime to justify the suggestion now. Jesus had in the past faced without anger misunderstanding much worse than that of the Jews in verse 37.

The **cave** (either natural or artificial) used for **the tomb** of Lazarus would either be a chamber behind a more or less vertical rock-face, with **a stone** in front of it, or in the side of a kind of pit or well, with the stone placed on top of it. The latter was the more common for private burials,⁶ and was probably the type used for the burial of Lazarus, and later for Jesus.

The dead man's sister Martha said to him, 'Lord,

---

¹ Literally, 'See, how he loved (ἐφίλει) him!' See p. 264 n. 1.

² Beginning Οὐκ . . . it expects the answer 'Yes': cf. iv. 35, and many other examples.   ³ ἐμβριμώμενος ἐν ἑαυτῷ. See pp. 271 f.

⁴ ἐπί (here, with the dative) could also mean 'against'; cf. the two senses of ἐπί (with the genitive) in vi. 19 and 21.

⁵ If ἐπί means 'against' in the previous verse, Ἄρατε must be translated 'Take away'. The same verb is used in xx. 1. The meaning depends on the type of tomb. See p. 420.   ⁶ See Lagrange, p. 306.

by now he will stink, for he has been four days ⟨dead⟩'.

Martha's horrified exclamation at Jesus' command shows that she has no idea of his intentions. That the corpse will already be decaying[1] is simply her inference from the fact that Lazarus has been dead for **four days.**

This observation is prompted by the reflexion that, though John doubtless wrote this narrative with the firm belief that Lazarus was indubitably dead, there is nothing in this verse to preclude the view that those whom Jesus is said to have raised from the dead were not, strictly speaking, dead at all.[2] Jesus himself is reported to have said this of Jairus' daughter (Mark v. 39), and there is nothing in the story to prevent us taking these words literally.[3] But she, like the widow's son at Nain (Luke vii. 12), would doubtless have been buried but for his intervention. The custom of burial on the day of death must have made premature burial a very real danger. Now if what Jesus in fact did on this occasion was to rescue Lazarus from premature burial, it would not mean either that there was nothing miraculous in his action, or that it lost its significance as a sign.

Lazarus had been seriously ill, and was indeed restored to life. Buried, he had been as good as dead. And his restoration could still be a sign. For if the objection is made that it would no longer be a parallel to the resurrection of Jesus, it can be said that even if Lazarus had been actually raised from death, this would not have been an exact parallel to the resurrection of Jesus either. For Lazarus, Jairus' daughter, and the widow's son did not anticipate the general resurrection on the last day, but in due course died (or died again). And the resurrection of the body, for which we must wait until the last day, and of which the resurrection of Jesus is the pattern, is not the same as the resuscitation of corpses, as St Paul is at pains to show (cf. 1 Cor. xv. 42 ff.).

---

[1] This does not mean that spices had not been used in the burial. This was the normal practice (cf. xix. 39), but the spices were not used in the Egyptian manner to arrest decay, but rather to mask the odour which it caused.

[2] This could not, however, be said in the case of Jesus himself. That a man should recover from the ordeal of crucifixion sufficiently to be able to walk within three days strains the credulity almost as much as the miracle, if not more.   [3] Cf. also John xi. 4.

(40) Jesus said to her, 'I told you, did I not, that if you would believe, you would see the glory of God?'

Not in these precise words: but he had said, in what he must have intended as a reply to the sisters' message that Lazarus was ill, that his illness was 'for **the glory of God**' (xi. 4), and the promise of return to life was implicit in his conversation with Martha (xi. 23-26) which had led up to her confession of faith. Now she is to **see,** in his return to life, the divine response to faith that will reveal **the glory** which **God** gives his Son.[1]

(41) So they lifted the stone. And Jesus lifted up his eyes and said, 'Father, I thank thee that thou didst hear me. (42) And I ⟨for my part⟩[2] knew that thou dost hear me every time;[3] but ⟨it was⟩ for the sake of the crowd standing round ⟨that⟩ I said ⟨it⟩, that they may believe that thou didst send me.' (43) And when he had said this, he shouted with a loud voice, 'Lazarus, come out!' (44) The dead man came out, with his feet and hands bound with bandages, and his face[4] bound round with a kerchief.[5] Jesus said to them, 'Undo him, and let him walk'.

41. The scene is set for the miracle. But first Jesus openly thanks his Father for hearing the prayer which he had (presumably) offered during the agony hinted at in verse 33.

42. His confidence at that time that God always hears him is the obverse of his own complete obedience to his Father's will (cf. v. 30). He prays aloud **for the sake of the crowd** (cf. xii. 30), not to impress them with his majesty, but to help them to understand that it is not as a talented wonderworker (which they believe him to be), but only as his Father's representative (cf. iii. 17;[6] v. 36, etc.) that he raises the dead.

43 f. The dead man hears the voice of the Son of God, lives, and comes out of the tomb (cf. v. 25, 28 f.).

[1] See on xi. 4, pp. 264 f.
[2] 'I' is emphatic in the Greek.   [3] πάντοτε. See p. 188, n. 6.
[4] ὄψις, 'face', as in Rev. i. 16. In vii. 24, it means 'appearance'. It is a Johannine word.
[5] Literally, 'bound ⟨as to ⟩ his feet and hands with bandages, and his face *was bound* round with a kerchief'. This construction, Semitic in character, is common in Revelation: cf. the description of the 'one like a son of man' in i. 13-16, which ends, '. . . and his face *shines* as the sun in its power'.
[6] See p. 129, n. 1.

These correspondences with chapter v underline the parallel-ism of the third and sixth signs.[1]

44. The corpse would have been placed on a strip of linen, wide and long enough to envelop it completely.[2] The feet would be placed at one end, and the cloth would then be drawn down over the head to the feet, the feet would be bound at the ankles, and the arms secured to the body with linen bandages, and the face bound round with another cloth to keep the jaw in place. This was the **kerchief** (σουδάριον, i.e. the Latin *sudarium*, 'sweat-cloth'), worn in life round the neck. It would seem that the body of Jesus was prepared for burial in the same way (see xix. 40; xx. 5, 7).

So bound up, a man could not possibly **walk**. Hence Jesus' final command, when Lazarus had struggled out of the tomb. But he could at least have shuffled to the entrance, and it is absurd to imagine that a subsidiary miracle was necessary to waft him from the tomb.

The story moves rapidly and dramatically to its climax. It is remarkably vivid and lifelike. Is this the vividness of remem-bered fact, or of a brilliant piece of fiction?

The objection to its historicity which is based on the conten-tion that the story is built up from data provided by Luke has already been shown to be open to question. A more serious one is that there is no trace of the miracle in the Synoptic tradition (if the Lucan parable[3] is not allowed to be such). This was serious indeed when it was still possible to assume that Mark provides a fairly accurate outline of Jesus' public ministry, un-distorted by theological considerations. But this is no longer the case.[4] Mark has his own distinctive theological presuppositions and his own historical perspective. For him, Galilee is the place of Jesus' ministry, Judaea of his death. A miracle of resurrection in Judaea so soon before the Passion (if he had known about it) might have seemed to him theologically inappropriate. Neither Mark nor John gives an exhaustive account of Jesus' miracles, and Mark has already told the story of the raising of Jairus'

---

[1] See p. 262.
[2] The 'Shroud of Christ' at Turin is approximately 1·4 by 4·2 metres, and would seem to have been used in the manner described above.
[3] See p. 262.   [4] See Introduction, pp. 17 f.

daughter. For his informant, and for the Galilean tradition in general, the raising of Lazarus would not have the particular interest that it had for John's, particularly if Lazarus was indeed the Beloved Disciple. And, while Lazarus lived, there may have been no great inclination on the part of his friends to give wide publicity to the story. And John may well be better informed than Mark about opinion in the Sanhedrin before the arrest of Jesus, and so better able to appreciate the importance of the raising of Lazarus in deciding them to act against Jesus.

The silence of the Synoptic tradition is not an insuperable obstacle to the credibility of the story. The real objection is to the miracle as John relates it. This may be met to some extent (for some readers perhaps) by the suggestion already tentatively put forward that the raising of Lazarus was not really different in kind from those of Jairus' daughter and the widow's son. But when the largest possible allowance has been made for John's conscious or unconscious enhancing of the miraculous features of the story, it does not seem entirely unreasonable to maintain that, if historical evidence can ever establish the credibility of any miracle, the story of the raising of Lazarus has as good a claim as any to rest upon the testimony of credible witnesses.

(45) So many of the Jews who had gone to Mary and had noticed[1] **what he had done, believed in him; (46) but some of them went off to the Pharisees and told them what Jesus had done. (47) So the highpriests and the Pharisees held a meeting, and said, 'What are we doing?**[2] **Because this man is doing many miracles,**[3] **(48) if we leave him like this,**[4] **all will believe in him, and the Romans will come and take away both our place and nation.'**

---

[1] θεασάμενοι. See p. 81, n. 3: P⁴⁵, ⁶⁶ D read ἑωρακότες, 'seeing', from iv. 45.

[2] The punctuation here is uncertain. 'Because . . . miracles' is in the Greek a subordinate clause, and can be taken either with the previous or the following sentence.

[3] σημεῖα, 'signs'; but Jesus' actions were not 'signs' (in John's meaning of the word) to Jesus' enemies. Hence the translation **miracles**.

[4] οὕτως. See on iv. 6, p. 140, n. 2. 'If we just leave him' may give the right sense here.

45. Faith is the natural result of Jesus' actions, cf. ii. 11, 23; iv. 53 etc. 46. They can, however, have the opposite effect in some cases (cf. vi. 52; viii. 43; ix. 16), and John would seem to imply that those who **went off to the Pharisees** did so with hostile intent, though he does not actually say so. They might have been so impressed themselves that they thought they could convince them of the truth of Jesus' claims. But whatever their intentions, the result of this publicity was (as Martha and Jesus himself had expected) to provoke Jesus' enemies to take action against him.

47 f. The leading members of the priestly aristocracy and the Pharisees who were members of the Sanhedrin,[1] on hearing the report, **held** (literally, 'assembled') **a meeting.**[2] This could have been either a regular meeting of the Sanhedrin (since John uses the word συνέδριον from which *Sanhedrin* was derived) or (as in the circumstances would not be unlikely) an informal meeting of leaders of the two parties to explore the possibility of a 'bipartisan' policy to put an end to their dangerous inactivity in the face of what they thought to be Jesus' growing popularity. Nothing had been done officially since the failure of the attempt to arrest Jesus at Tabernacles (vii. 32 ff.). 48. They were afraid that if they took no steps to check it, this messianic movement would be bound to provoke Roman intervention and lead to the destruction of the Temple[3] and the Jewish **nation.**[4]

The irony in this combination of political astuteness and spiritual blindness is sufficiently obvious. As John well knew, the Jewish policy brought about in the end the precise result which it was designed to avoid.

(49) But one of them, Caiaphas, who was Highpriest of that year, said to them, 'You do not know anything, (50)

[1] For this meaning of **the highpriests and the Pharisees** cf. vii. 32 (p. 210), and see on i. 19 (pp. 87 f.) for John's knowledge of Jewish parties and affairs.

[2] This is the only instance of συνέδριον without the definite article in the New Testament, with the exception of Matt. x. 17, Mark xiii. 9, where the reference is not exclusively to Jewish councils. τὸ συνέδριον always refers to the Sanhedrin.

[3] For this sense of ὁ τόπος cf. iv. 20, and Acts vi. 14; xxi. 28.

[4] ἔθνος, cf. xviii. 35. If any distinction is possible between ἔθνος and λαός ('people', xi. 50; xviii. 14) ἔθνος is narrower and more racialist.

nor do you consider that it is in your interest¹ that one man should die for the sake of the people and that the whole nation should not perish'. (51) But ⟨it was⟩ not of his own accord ⟨that⟩ he said this, but ⟨as⟩ being High-priest of that year he prophesied that Jesus was to die for the sake of the nation, (52) and not only for the sake of the ⟨Jewish⟩ nation, but so as also to assemble into one the scattered children of God. (53) So from that day they determined to kill him.

49 f. The way in which **Caiaphas** is mentioned, simply as **one of them,** suggests that this was not an official meeting of the Sanhedrin,² at which Caiaphas would have been in the chair. Probably Annas, Caiaphas' father-in-law (xviii. 13), had convened it, as leader of the Sadducees, and former Highpriest, whom many may well have regarded as still the lawful High-priest, since the office was intended to be for life. It was only Roman interference, much resented by the Jews, which had caused his retirement. John represents him as still influential—it is to his house that Jesus is taken after his arrest (xviii. 13)—and in this Luke seems to support him (cf. Luke iii. 2, Acts iv. 6).

Caiaphas had succeeded Annas about A.D. 18, and, though **Highpriest of that year** may seem to suggest it, it is not necessary to suppose that John was so ignorant as to think that the Highpriesthood was an annual appointment. He simply emphasises that he was **Highpriest of that** momentous **year** in which the Messiah was put to death—hence the repetition of the phrase in verse 51 and xviii. 13.

He speaks with brutal frankness, as the seriousness of the crisis demands: reasons of state require the death of Jesus, innocent or guilty.

51. But his words are an unconscious prophecy,³ uttered in virtue of his office,⁴ and John proceeds to elucidate and amplify

---

¹ συμφέρει ὑμῖν P⁴⁵, ⁶⁶ B D, etc. ἡμῖν A W Θ *fam* 1 *fam* 13 *syr*, etc. ℵ however, with some small support, reads συμφέρει alone, which may well be correct.

² See on verses 47 f., p. 278.   ³ Cf. John the Baptist, and see p. 95.

⁴ In ancient times the Highpriest prophesied by Urim and Thummim, but this had ceased at the Exile, as Neh. vii. 65 implies. Nevertheless, as God's representative, the Highpriest was still thought of as possessing powers of prophecy. Lagrange (p. 315) cites Philo, *de Spec. Leg.* IV. 192 in support

it. Caiaphas was prepared to sacrifice Jesus to save the Jewish nation from political suicide in a futile insurrection, as Jonah was sacrificed by the pagan crew to save them from shipwreck (Jonah i. 12 ff.). John agrees **that Jesus was to die for the sake of the nation,** but for its eternal salvation, not for its political survival. 52. And the benefits of his death were not limited to Israel. His destiny was **to assemble into one** (cf. xvii. 11) **the scattered children of God,** i.e. the 'other sheep' of x. 16, who would become children of God through believing in him (cf. i. 12), but had been hitherto dispersed through the world waiting for the light to shine (cf. iii. 21).

53. The Jews' wish to kill Jesus has already been repeatedly mentioned:[1] now they proceed to a definite decision, virtually a sentence of death. John does not record any later sentence of a Jewish court upon him, in contrast to Mark xiv. 64.

(54) So Jesus no longer showed himself[2] in public[3] among the Jews, but went away from there[4] into the district near the wilderness, to a city called Ephraim, and spent some time[5] there with the disciples.

Jesus withdraws from public life (cf. vii. 1): his public ministry is virtually over, and he waits in retirement, marking time, as it were, until his next move becomes clear, as he had done before the start of his Galilean ministry (iii. 22). The parallel is marked by the use of the verb διέτριβεν, **spent some time,** here and in iii. 22, its only occurrences in the FG.

of this. [C. H. Dodd, 'The Prophecy of Caiaphas', in *Neotestamentica et Patristica* (Supplements to *Novum Testamentum*, VI, 1962), pp. 134-143, argues that Philo is here speaking 'not of empirical priesthood, such as that of the temple at Jerusalem, but of ideal priesthood'; however, he cites evidence from Josephus and from *Tosephta Sota*, 13, 5-6 'that in popular belief prophetic powers were associated with the office of high priest'.— B. A. M.]   [1] See v. 18; vii. 1, 19, 25, 32, 45; viii. 40, 59; x. 31; xi. 8, 16.

[2] περιεπάτει, literally, 'walked'. See p. 200, n. 5.

[3] παρρησίᾳ. See p. 201, n. 6.

[4] ἐκεῖθεν. This is omitted by P45 D *lat sin*, etc., probably by accident, since the previous word (ἀπῆλθεν) ends with the same three letters.

[5] διέτριβεν is read by P45, 66 A D Θ *fam* 1 *fam* 13 33 *lat*. A few MSS., headed by ℵ BW, read ἔμεινεν. Since διατρίβω occurs only once elsewhere in the FG (iii. 22), while μένω is very common, the change is more likely to have been from ἔμεινεν to διέτριβεν than the other way round. (But see Barrett, p. 340.)

Ephraim is probably the Apherema ceded to Jonathan by Demetrius Nicator (1 Macc. xi. 34, Josephus, *Ant.*, XIII. 127), some five miles north-east of Bethel.[1]

C. THE PASSION AND RESURRECTION,
xi. 55–xx. 31

1. THE ANOINTING OF JESUS, AND HIS ENTRY INTO JERUSALEM, xi. 55–xii. 19[2]

(55) And the Jews' Passover[3] was near, and many went up to Jerusalem from the country before the Passover, in order to purify themselves. (56) So they were looking for Jesus and saying among themselves as they were standing in the Temple, 'What do you think? Surely not that he will come[4] to the feast?' (57) And the highpriests and the Pharisees[5] had given commands that anyone who knew where he was should inform them, so that they could arrest him.

55. According to Num. ix. 10 ff., anyone not in a state of ritual purity had to keep the Passover a month later, and, as the regulations were more stringent than in Hezekiah's time (2 Chron. xxx. 3, 17), pilgrims intending to keep the Passover arrived in good time to ensure that they were ritually clean; cf. xviii. 28.

56 f. The interest of the loiterers in the Temple in Jesus recalls that before the feast of Tabernacles (vii. 11). But now they

---

[1] See *The Westminster Historical Atlas to the Bible* (ed. F. V. Filson and G. E. Wright, 1946), Plate XII, A and D.

[2] This section of the FG and the next, xii. 20-50, form the transition between the signs and the story of the Passion, and it is not easy, in a work so closely articulated as the FG, to divide the sections exactly and to decide to which part of the work they belong. They bring the public ministry to a conclusion, but they also prepare so definitely for the Passion that it seems better to include them with it.

[3] For this phrase cf. ii. 13, and see p. 116.

[4] ὅτι οὐ μὴ ἔλθῃ; In statements οὐ μή is an emphatic negative (cf. vi. 35, 37; x. 5, 28; xiii. 8; xvi. 7). Here the οὐ expects the answer 'Yes' to the implied question '(You do think, don't you,) that he *won't* come?' But see Barrett, p. 341. [5] For this phrase, see p. 278, n. 1.

are much less confident that Jesus will appear. They assume, as do the authorities, that he is in hiding. The mention of the authorities' call for informers, in pursuance of their plan to kill Jesus (verse 53), prepares for the arrest of Jesus through the treachery of Judas (xviii. 2 ff.), already foretold (vi. 71). Mark xiv. 1 places the decision to arrest and kill Jesus rather later than John does, two days before the Passover (John xii. 1 is still six days before it). Mark's language may, however, be understood as implying that they were trying to put into effect a plan already formed.

After this interlude the second act of the FG opens with two scenes, the first showing Jesus in private among his friends, the second in public among the crowds, both of which have the common purpose of illustrating the inability of his supporters to understand his Messiahship. Their ignorant enthusiasm contrasts with the hostility of the authorities.

xii. (1) Then six days before the Passover Jesus went to Bethany, where was Lazarus, whom Jesus ⟨had⟩ raised from the dead. (2) So they made him supper [1] there, and Martha was serving, but Lazarus was one of those at supper [2] with him. (3) So Mary took a quantity [3] of valuable ointment—nard ⟨dissolved in oil⟩ of pistachio, [4] and anointed Jesus' feet, and wiped his feet with her hair. And the house was filled with the smell of the ointment.

1. According to the FG, [5] **the Passover** began on the following Friday evening (by our reckoning of the days), which (again by our reckoning) would make the day of Jesus' arrival in Bethany a Saturday. But since he is unlikely to have travelled on a Sabbath, we should probably reckon the **six days** in the ancient manner, i.e. *inclusively*. 2. Then the **supper** would have been on Sunday evening by our reckoning, but the first meal

---

[1] δεῖπνον, the main meal of the day, cf. xiii. 2. But 'the Last Supper' is so well established that it would be perverse to translate it, strictly more accurately, 'dinner'.

[2] ἀνακειμένων, literally, 'reclining'; in vi. 11 more probably 'sitting'.

[3] Actually λίτρα, which has no exact English equivalent. It is the Roman *libra*, approximately a pound Troy weight. As a liquid measure it was half a Hebrew *log*, ·27 of a litre.

[4] For this interpretation of νάρδου πιστικῆς see Black, pp. 159 ff.

[5] Cf. xiii. 1; xviii. 28; xix. 31, 42.

of the Monday by Jewish reckoning, according to which the day began at sunset. If so, the events of the second act of the FG occupy a week, Monday to Sunday; a week parallel to that with which the narrative of the FG begins, i. 19–ii. 11.[1] If then the meal did not take place immediately after the Sabbath had ended, but twenty-four hours later, the question whether or not it was connected with the *Habdalah*, the service which marked the end of Sabbath, does not arise, and there is no occasion for surprise that John does not mention it.[2]

Mark xiv. 1 ff. agrees that this meal took place in Bethany, but dates it two days, not six, before the Passover, and so after the Entry into Jerusalem, while Luke vii. 36 ff. places it in a Pharisee's house, presumably in Galilee, long before the Passion.

Who entertained Jesus is not clear from the FG. The reference to **Martha** suggests that it was in her house (cf. Luke x. 40), that to **Lazarus** as merely one of the party suggests the opposite. In Mark the meal is in the house of Simon 'the Leper' (xiv. 3), while according to Luke vii. 40 also the host was called Simon.[3]

3. Both Mark and Luke have 'an alabaster jar' where the FG has the **quantity**: all three have the same word for **ointment** ($\mu\acute{v}\rho o v$) while Mark and the FG have the striking agreement **nard of pistachio** ($\nu\acute{a}\rho\delta o v$ $\pi\iota\sigma\tau\iota\kappa\hat{\eta}s$): they also both call the ointment **valuable** (Mark $\pi o\lambda v\tau\epsilon\lambda o\hat{v}s$ for the FG's $\pi o\lambda v\tau\acute{\iota}\mu o v$). In Mark an unnamed woman anointed Jesus' head, meaning presumably by her action to make him Messiah, but Mark has a different verb from the FG. In Luke a woman who was a sinner wet Jesus' feet with her tears, wiped them with her hair, and then anointed his feet (anointing followed washing naturally enough). Luke uses the FG's verbs both for **anointed** and **wiped**. In the FG the action of **Mary** does not look so natural. She **anointed Jesus' feet,** and then **wiped** them **with her hair.** Moreover the repetition of **feet** looks clumsy,

[1] See p. 108.
[2] See Barrett, pp. 342 f., who places the meal on Saturday evening.
[3] One might suppose that Simon was a leper whom Jesus had healed—otherwise he would not be present at the meal. This would add point to Luke's parable of the Two Debtors (vii. 41 f.). But the FG has no hint of this.

especially if one compares this verse with xi. 2. It might be argued[1] that John originally wrote here '. . . anointed *Jesus*, and wiped his feet with her hair', and that the text which we have is due to harmonisation with Luke. But the repetition may be for emphasis, and a tacit correction of Mark. If the guests were in fact reclining on couches round the table, it would have been much easier to reach the feet than the head, and so the FG may be correct as against Mark. Mary had used quite a large amount of ointment, and, having made her demonstration, may have wiped it off to avoid inconvenience to her guest. Her intention may nevertheless have been to point out Jesus as Messiah, which Mark makes quite unmistakable by saying that she anointed his head. But this is of no importance to John. Incidentally, ointment would be easier to wipe with hair than tears would be.

The statement that **the house was filled with the smell of the ointment** is peculiar to John. It is often supposed to signify allegorically what Mark xiv. 9 states plainly, that the fame of her action would spread throughout the world. But John gives no hint that it is other than literal fact.

(4) But Judas Iscariot,[2] one of his disciples, who was going to betray him, said, (5) 'Why was this ointment not sold for three hundred shillings[3] and given to the poor?' (6) But he said this, not because he was concerned for the poor, but because he was a thief; he used to keep the money-box and filch[4] what was put in it.

4 f. In Mark xiv. 4 f. 'certain persons' make an almost identical complaint, but estimate the value of the ointment at *more than* **three hundred shillings.**

6. That Judas **was a thief** is not stated elsewhere. The avarice of which petty theft from his friends was a symptom may seem an inadequate motive for Judas' betrayal of Jesus. But if it was a fact that he did keep the common purse, it need

---

[1] As in fact I did in *N.T.S.*, Vol. I, 1954-55, p. 40.

[2] AΘ *fam* 13 and the majority of MSS. add 'son of Simon'. For **Iscariot** D has ἀπὸ Καρυώτου. See on vi. 71, p. 198, n. 6.

[3] Literally *denaria*. On this see p. 176, n. 3.

[4] ἐβάσταζεν. This also means, primarily, 'carry' (as in xix. 17). There is a double meaning here, which cannot be reproduced. But cf. the colloquial use of 'lift' = 'steal'. See also p. 258, n. 1.

not have been long before this accusation was made, to account for an almost inexplicable treachery.

The use of a common purse as a supreme example of mutual trust (even among thieves, cf. Prov. i. 14) is found not only in the case of Jesus and his disciples but also in the Qumran community and in the church of Jerusalem (Acts ii. 44 ff.), which presumably took Jesus for its precedent in this.

(7) So Jesus said, 'Let her be! ⟨She did this⟩ to keep it for the day of my burial. (8) For you have the poor with you all the time,[1] but you do not have me all the time.[1] '

There is again a close parallel to this passage in Mark xiv. 6-8, which, however, is fuller and much clearer in meaning than the FG, 'Let[2] her be! Why do you trouble her? She has done a good deed on me. For you have the poor with you all the time, and whenever you wish you can do them good, but you do not have me all the time. She did what she could; she anticipated the anointing of my body for burial.' If therefore John is here borrowing from Mark, he has not only abbreviated his source, but obscured its meaning in the process. His reference to Jesus' burial is particularly obscure.

Since it would have been contrary to the spirit of Mary's action to use only a part of the ointment, we cannot interpret verse 7 as, **'Let her . . . keep . . . ⟨what is left⟩ for the day of my burial'**. What Jesus appears to mean is that she has done now what she might have expected to do at his burial; **to keep it** means 'to have it ready'. This was not of course her intention. Jesus, however, though repudiating her anointing of him as *Messiah*, assures Mary that her action has a purpose which she had not realised, and that the ointment has not been wasted. He knew the usual fate of the bodies of executed criminals, and could not have foreseen that his body would be anointed before burial.

The relationship of the accounts of Jesus' anointing in Mark, Luke, and John is usually explained by supposing John to be dependent on Mark and Luke—and his own imagination. But elsewhere[3] parallels between Luke and John may be more

---

[1] πάντοτε. See p. 188, n. 6.
[2] In Mark the verb is plural, in John singular.
[3] See p. 263 and the Introduction, pp. 10 ff.

readily explained on the assumption that they are using a common source, and in the present case, since John has details independent of both Mark and Luke, it may be that the same explanation holds good, and that there were in the tradition used by the evangelists two independent stories, one of a penitent sinner who wept over Jesus' feet in the house of a Pharisee during the Galilean ministry, and another of a woman at Bethany who anointed Jesus' feet with ointment, and wiped them with her hair. Mark and John have alternative versions of the second story, of which John's may be the closer to the facts. Mark made the woman anoint Jesus' *head*, as more appropriate to the intention of the deed. Luke, who wished to avoid the Messianic implications of the second story, combined it with the first, but is an independent witness to the fact that it was Jesus' *feet* that were anointed.[1] There is thus no reason to identify Mary with Luke's anonymous sinner.

(9) Then the great crowd of the Jews got to know that he was there, and they came, not only because of Jesus, but also to see Lazarus, whom he had raised from the dead. (10) Now the highpriests had determined to kill Lazarus as well ⟨as Jesus⟩, (11) since because of him many of the Jews were going and[2] believing in Jesus.

9. This **great crowd** refers to the pilgrims who are mentioned as looking for Jesus in xi. 56 (cf. xii. 12). They are not hostile to Jesus (cf. xi. 45), but ignorant and curious, 10. in contrast to **the highpriests,** i.e. the hierarchy, whose determination to stamp out heresy had led to the decision **to kill Lazarus,** 11. who seemed to have been the cause for **many of the Jews** to transfer their allegiance to Jesus. But the popularity which they so much dreaded (cf. also xii. 19) was no more securely based than that which John has already noticed (ii. 23).

(12) The next day the great crowd which had come to the feast, hearing that Jesus was coming into Jerusalem,

---

[1] See S. Temple, *N.T.S.*, Vol. VII, 1960–61, p. 78.

[2] This use of ὑπάγω καὶ . . . to emphasise the main verb, and without necessarily implying motion (as in the English idiom), may be an equivalent to the auxiliary use of *'ªzal* ('go') in Aramaic (Black, p. 91), cf. John xv. 16. Alternatively, ὑπάγω may mean 'go away', i.e. 'become apostate', as in Jesus' question addressed to the Twelve (vi. 67).

(13) **took palm branches** [1] **and went out to meet him, and shouted, 'Hosanna! Blessed ⟨is⟩ he who comes in the name of the LORD!', and,** [2] **'The King of Israel!' (14) But Jesus, having found an ass, sat on it, as it is written, (15) 'Do not be afraid, daughter of Sion; behold, thy King is coming, sitting on an ass's colt.'**

The story of Jesus' entry into Jerusalem is told by the other three evangelists (Mark xi. 1-11, Matt. xxi. 1-11, Luke xix. 29-45) but with sufficient difference in detail to suggest that here also John is quite independent of them. Mark and Matthew place the entry before the anointing in Bethany.

12. Since the last day mentioned was that of the anointing, **the next day** must be the Tuesday (see on xii. 1 f.); **the great crowd** [3] is that of Jesus' ignorant supporters (or potential supporters) among the pilgrims in Jerusalem (cf. vi. 2; xii. 9).

13. Whereas in the other Gospels the entry is a demonstration prepared by Jesus, who had arranged for the ass to be ready for him, in the FG the demonstration was the spontaneous work of the crowd, and no more intended by him than the anointing in Bethany. It was rather an embarrassment to him, as his reaction to it showed.

Only John specifies **palm branches** (cf. 1 Macc. xiii. 51). Since palms did not grow in Jerusalem,[4] the crowds must have had them ready—they could not have cut them from the roadside trees. Now palm branches were used, with willow and myrtle branches, to make the *lulab* which was carried at the feast of Tabernacles, in obedience to Lev. xxiii. 40. It was the custom to shake the *lulab* when the word **Hosanna** occurred during the singing of Ps. cxviii at the feast, at verse 25. **Blessed ⟨is⟩ he who comes in the name of the LORD** also occurs in Ps. cxviii. 26, and the occurrence together of the **palm branches** and these quotations from the Tabernacles psalm lends colour to the suggestion that this demonstration took place, not before the Passover (though Ps. cxviii was also sung at Passover), but

---

[1] τὰ βαῖα τῶν φοινίκων. βαῖα alone means palm branches, so that τῶν φοινίκων is strictly redundant. But the phrase also occurs in *Testament of Naphtali*, v. 4 (Bauer, p. 160).

[2] καί may be used as 'that is to say', in which case there are not two slogans, but one. It is omitted by P⁶⁶ D Θ, etc., probably wrongly.

[3] ὁ ὄχλος πολύς, as in verse 9.   [4] Or so Bultmann says (p. 319, n. 7).

at Tabernacles, or perhaps at the Dedication, when the *lulab* was also used,[1] and that John has placed it here, not because he is following Mark, but because it is dramatically appropriate when in juxtaposition with the anointing.

Hosanna is a transliteration of the Aramaic (rather than the Hebrew) for, 'Save, we pray'. This cry for God's help and the blessing of the man **who comes in the name of the LORD** (i.e. as his representative, cf. v. 43; x. 25) as **King of Israel** indicate that they look to Jesus to restore the kingdom of David; cf. Nathanael, i. 49, and those whom Jesus fed in Galilee, vi. 14 f., and see the notes on these passages.

Only Luke xix. 38 agrees with John in recording that the crowd hailed Jesus as **King**: but he omits **Hosanna**, and has **Blessed ⟨is⟩ he who comes, the King, in the name of the LORD,** adding, 'In heaven peace, and glory in the highest'. Mark xi. 9 has **Hosanna . . . LORD** (as in John) and adds, 'Blessed ⟨is⟩ the coming kingdom of our Father David. Hosanna in the highest'; Matt. xxi. 9 has, '**Hosanna** to the Son of David. **Blessed . . . LORD.** Hosanna in the highest'.

14. Jesus' reaction was a prompt repudiation of the crowd's acclamations (cf. his turning the meaning of the anointing). He could not escape, as he had done after feeding the crowd in Galilee, and so, to show that he was not accepting the rôle of a military Messiah, but coming in peace, he **sat** on an **ass**[2] which happened to be available,[3] and so continued his journey.

There is no trace in the FG of the elaborate arrangements described (in somewhat legendary fashion) by the other Gospels to provide the ass beforehand, as if Jesus had intended to make a triumphal entry, or of any part played by his disciples in the demonstration,[4] while the other Gospels all describe Jesus' mounting the ass *before* the demonstration began.

If John is dependent on the Synoptic Gospels, or any one of them, he has drastically re-written the story. But if not, so far from being 'hardly possible as history' (Barrett, p. 347), his

---

[1] See p. 121, n. 2, p. 204, n. 3, and p. 255.

[2] ὀνάριον is diminutive in form, but, as often in *Koiné* Greek, probably without any diminutive force, cf. ὠτάριον, John xviii. 10.

[3] εὑρών, 'having found'. εὑρίσκω often means 'to come across' (by accident or providence) in the FG, cf. i. 41, 43; v. 14; ix. 35.

[4] Contrast particularly Luke xix. 37.

account may well reveal a better understanding than the other evangelists' of Jesus' dilemma, as 'Son of David' by right, and conscious of a mission to save Israel, yet refusing to adopt the only policy that the majority of his people would understand or accept.

John then notes that Jesus' action was a fulfilment of prophecy, and 15. quotes the passage, Zech. ix. 9, in an altered and abbreviated form. **Do not be afraid** is not part of Zechariah, but may be an instance of the unconscious conflation of prophetic testimonies, coming perhaps from Isa. xl. 9. It is frequently addressed to recipients of a divine visitation,[1] and as such would have seemed appropriate. John leaves out the description of the king as triumphant and victorious, as well as humble, and avoids the characteristic Hebrew idiom, 'an ass, and a colt the foal of an ass', which seems to have misled Matthew[2] (the only other evangelist to quote the passage) into supposing that two animals were involved.

(16) These things his disciples did not understand at first, but, when Jesus had been glorified,[3] then they remembered that these things had been written with reference to him, and that they had done these things to him. (17) This then was the witness borne by the crowd[4] which had been with him when he called Lazarus from the tomb and raised him from the dead. (18) This was a further reason why[5] the crowd met him, that they had heard that he had done this sign. (19) So the Pharisees said, for their part,[6] 'Do you realise[7] that you are not doing any good?[8] See, the world has gone after him!'

16. For the disciples' initial bewilderment and subsequent understanding cf. ii. 21 f. They are to be explained by vii. 39.

---

[1] E.g. Gen. xv. 1; xxi. 17, Luke i. 13, 30; ii. 10, etc.
[2] Matthew introduces the quotation at an earlier stage of the story.
[3] For the meaning of this, see on vii. 39.
[4] Literally, 'So the crowd bore witness'.
[5] Literally, 'Because of this also'.
[6] For this meaning of πρὸς ἑαυτούς see Black, pp. 77 f. He suggests that there (and in xx. 10) the phrase corresponds to the 'ethic dative' in Aramaic, and gives a better sense than the literal 'to themselves'.
[7] θεωρεῖτε. For the meaning of the word see p. 191. It can equally well be a statement or a command.
[8] ὠφελεῖτε. The word is used in the FG only here and in vi. 63 (which see).

Barrett allows here that probably 'John reproduced, intentionally or unintentionally, old and reliable tradition', but goes on to claim that the 'narrative is really self-contradictory' (p. 349). But is this so? The thing which the **disciples did not understand at first** was how Jesus could be a king in any sense if he was not the Messiah as popularly expected. It is not necessary to claim, as Barrett does, that the crowd might not have regarded Jesus as Messiah, and that John himself added **the King of Israel** to the slogan which they shouted. This is the result of assuming that John is dependent on Mark.

17 f. John is careful to record **the witness**[1] of the crowd to Jesus, though, like Caiaphas, they spoke better than they realised, and to stress yet again the importance of the raising of Lazarus.

19. The despair of **the Pharisees** at Jesus' apparent success is full of irony. By **the world** they simply mean 'everybody', cf. vii. 4; xiv. 22; xviii. 20. But **the world** has a deeper meaning in the FG (see on i. 9, p. 76). Yet they too are unconscious prophets, as the next scene in the FG suggests.

2. THE GENTILES AND THE JEWS, xii. 20-50

(20) Now there were certain Gentiles[2] among those who came up to worship at the feast; (21) these then approached Philip, who was from Bethsaida of Galilee, and asked him, saying, 'Sir, we wish to see Jesus'. (22) Philip went and told Andrew; Andrew and Philip went and told Jesus.

After the two contrasting scenes of the anointing of Jesus and his entry into Jerusalem there follows an episode which deals with the contrasting reactions of Gentiles and Jews to the impact of Christ on Jerusalem. Without any apparent discontinuity, it records the tentative approach of some Gentiles to

[1] For the theme of 'witness' in the FG see p. 75.

[2] Literally 'Greeks'; see vii. 35, p. 211, n. 3. The emphasis is on language rather than race, but implies that these were not Jews. The usual word for *Gentile* (ἐθνικός) is not found in the FG, where ἔθνος refers only to the *Jewish* nation (xi. 48-52; xviii. 35).

Jesus, which affords the occasion for a discourse by Jesus, into which is inserted (verses 37-43) a comment by the evangelist.

20. These Gentiles may be supposed to have been Galilean proselytes of some kind—at least men who 'feared God' (Acts xiii. 16). They would not be allowed to eat the Passover unless they had been circumcised,[1] but they could enter the Court of the Gentiles in the Temple and make certain offerings,[2] and so to some extent take part in the Temple worship, as did, e.g., the Ethiopian (Acts viii. 27), though he was debarred by the fact that he was a eunuch from becoming a full proselyte.

21. No explanation is given for their approach to Jesus, and none is perhaps necessary beyond a natural curiosity. If, however, in John's source the Cleansing of the Temple followed the entry into Jerusalem, the approach of the Gentiles may have been the result of this, and due to their gratitude for his making the Court of the Gentiles a more seemly place for worship. The transference of the Cleansing of the Temple to chapter ii[3] then left the present incident without its natural context. John presumably did not transfer it as well because it serves to illustrate verse 19, by showing symbolically the Gentile world seeking Jesus. There are not sufficient grounds for dismissing the episode as pure invention.

The deviousness of the Gentiles' approach (and indeed their curiosity) might well have been due to Jesus' reputation as a wonder-worker, to be treated with caution. Some of them may have known **Philip**[4] already, as he came from a town where Gentiles also lived, **Bethsaida of Galilee.**[5] He may, however, be so described to distinguish him from his namesake the evangelist, who had settled in Hierapolis, and so would be known to some of John's first readers.[6]

22. Philip's hesitation is natural enough. He must have known that Jesus had little to do with Gentiles, and no vocation to any ministry towards them (cf. Matt. xv. 24). **Andrew** is

---

[1] Exod. xii. 48.   [2] For details, see Strack–Billerbeck, II, pp. 548 ff.
[3] See pp. 117 and 121.   [4] Philip is also mentioned i. 44; vi. 5 ff.; xiv. 8.
[5] If Bethsaida Julias is meant, and not an otherwise unknown town, it was actually in the district of Gaulanitis, just over the border from Galilee. But such a mistake would not be surprising in a Jerusalemite source.
[6] There were probably two Philips, in spite of Polycrates. See Introduction, p. 43, and p. 177 (on vi. 5).

mentioned (in the same context as Philip) in vi. 8, but it is unreasonable to argue that this is why these are also mentioned together here.

(23) But Jesus answered them saying, 'The time[1] has come for[2] the Son of man to be glorified. (24) Amen, amen, I say to you,[3] unless the grain of corn falls to the earth and dies, it remains alone ⟨by⟩ itself;[4] but if it dies, it bears much fruit. (25) He who loves[5] his life[6] loses it,[7] and he who hates his life in this world shall preserve it for eternal life.[8] (26) If anyone serves me, let him follow me, and where I am there also shall my servant be; if anyone serves me, the Father will honour him.'

23. Jesus' words are not apparently an answer to anything that his disciples may be supposed to have said to him, but they are by implication, and negatively: this is not **the time** for interviews.[9] Positively, his words are a response to the evidence just given him, that, though Israel has misunderstood and rejected him, Gentiles are turning towards him. But they will only be able to 'see' him after his death and resurrection. **The time has** in fact come for his glorification, which it is now apparent is achieved by his death:[10] so far we have only been told that his time has *not yet* come (vii. 30; viii. 20).

For Jesus as **the Son of man** see pp. 105 f. (on i. 51).

24. Jesus now explains by means of a parable how his death will enable the Gentiles to see him: **the grain of corn** must be planted, and afterwards rot away, if it is to be fruitful. Other-

---

[1] Literally, 'hour'. See p. 107, n. 2, and p. 110 (on ii. 4).

[2] ἵνα. This may be an example of mistranslation of the Aramaic particle *dᵉ* which should have a temporal sense here. See Black, pp. 59-61. But the translation given above may preserve an intentional ambiguity.

[3] On this formula, see p. 105.

[4] αὐτὸς μόνος. This phrase also occurs in vi. 15, p. 180. The redundancy makes for emphasis.   [5] ὁ φιλῶν. See p. 130, n. 2.

[6] ψυχή (and in the parallel clause): for its distinction from ζωή see p. 250, n. 3.

[7] The present tense, attested by P⁶⁶ B W *ff²*, is preferable to the future, attested by A D Θ *fam* 1 *fam* 13 *lat*, etc., which is due to assimilation to the parallel clause.

[8] εἰς ζωὴν αἰώνιον. For this phrase see p. 142, n. 4, and pp. 185 f.

[9] So Lagrange *ad loc.* (p. 330). The Gentiles disappear from view even more promptly than Nicodemus in chapter iii.

[10] His death makes possible the gift of the Spirit (vii. 39), by which the Gentiles will be brought to see Jesus.

wise **it remains alone ⟨by⟩ itself,** i.e. does not reproduce itself. The language recalls the dying and rising corn-spirits of the pagan mystery cults, but has closer parallels in 1 Cor. xv. 36, and Mark iv. 8.[1] It could well have been used by Jesus himself, if we may allow that he expected his death, and meditated upon its results for mankind.

25. Mark viii. 35 = Matt. x. 39 and xvi. 25 = Luke ix. 24 and xvii. 33 has a saying similar to this in form and sentiment, but not in vocabulary. Both John and the Synoptic evangelists appear to have made their own additions and paraphrases to an original which was probably **He who loves his life loses it, and he who hates his life shall preserve it.** The plain contrast of **loves** and **hates** sounds more probably authentic than the Markan 'wishes to save' and 'loses', which tone down the paradox. To the original John or his source has added his characteristic contrast of the two orders of existence, **this world**[2] and **eternal life.**[3]

The saying is less particularised in its Johannine form (which is an argument for John's independence), and equally applicable to Jesus and to his would-be disciples, for whom, as the next verse makes clear, it is a warning to count the cost of discipleship.

26. Service to Christ means sharing his lot, whatever that may entail. Again, a similar thought is expressed in Mark viii. 34, 'If any man would come after me, **let him** deny himself and take up his cross and **follow me.'** In this case the plain warning that a disciple must be prepared to die with Christ[4] suggests that Mark has a more primitive form of the saying than John.

John then adds a further saying, unparalleled in Mark, to the effect that the disciple who shares Jesus' suffering will also share the honour[5] which God gives him, cf. xvii. 24.

[1] This verse has in common with John xii. 24 the words 'fall' (πίπτω) and 'fruit' (καρπός).

[2] For the meaning of 'world' (κόσμος) see, on i. 9, p. 76 and p. 223.

[3] For the meaning of 'eternal life' see, on iii. 15, p. 128.

[4] As Thomas professed to be willing to do, xi. 16. See p. 267.

[5] In viii. 49 Jesus claims that he honours God, but nowhere else in the FG is God said to honour anyone. The verb 'glorify', which is close to it in meaning, is however used with God both as object and subject. See viii. 54; xiii. 32; xvii. 4.

(27) 'Now my soul is troubled,[1] and what am I to say? "Father, save me from this time"? But this is the reason why[2] I came to this time. (28) Father, glorify thy name.'

Then there came a voice from heaven, 'I have both glorified it and will glorify it again'. (29) So the crowd which stood ⟨by⟩ and heard it said that it was a peal of thunder; others said, 'An angel has spoken to him.' (30) Jesus answered and said, '⟨It is⟩ not for my ⟨sake⟩ ⟨that⟩ this voice has come, but for yours.'

27. The prospect of his death, now seen to be imminent, fills the human **soul**[3] of Jesus with terror. His words echo most closely Ps. vi. 3.[4] This psalm continues with a prayer that the psalmist's life may be saved. It is natural for Jesus to pray in such a plight, but can he echo the psalmist's prayer? No, for it is in order to die that he **came to this time**, i.e. the time ($\H\omega\rho\alpha$) of verse 23.

28. His prayer must, as always, express his complete acceptance of his Father's will, and so he prays that through his death God may **glorify** his **name**. In the Old Testament both the glory of God and his **name** (which is virtually a synonym or periphrasis for God himself) are means whereby God is made known to be what he is[5] (e.g. Exod. xxxiii. 18-22). God will thus make himself known to men through the death of Christ. By obedience men can **glorify** God's **name** (cf. Ps. lxxxvi. 11 f.), and thus the supreme act of obedience is the supreme revelation of God.

There is a remarkable parallel between these verses and the story of Jesus' agony in Gethsemane in Mark xiv. 34-36. Jesus' **soul** was exceedingly sorrowful, and he prayed then that the **time** might pass from him, addressing God as 'Abba, **Father**', yet accepting whatever was God's will for him. There is no agony in Gethsemane in the FG, possibly because John felt

[1] τετάρακται. On this verb ταράσσω see p. 272.
[2] Literally, 'Because of this I came . . .'
[3] ψυχή, translated 'life' in verse 25. See p. 250, n. 3.
[4] vi. 4 in the LXX, which has both **soul** (ψυχή) and the verb, though the tense is different, ἐταράχθη (Aorist) LXX, τετάρακται (Perfect) John.
[5] Similarly to believe in Christ's **name** is to accept him for what he is: see on i. 12.

that it would be inappropriate after Jesus' prayer in chapter xvii. But it could also be because John's source did not know the story. The Beloved Disciple, who was not one of the Twelve, may not have been in the garden. But Jesus' reference to drinking the cup which his Father had given him (John xviii. 11) recalls Mark xiv. 36 [1] and this may support the suggestion that John is freely adapting Markan material. It does not, however, necessarily follow either that John is dependent on Mark, or that Mark is historically superior to John. For the words which are common to their accounts of Jesus' prayer at the prospect of death are those without which the story could hardly have been told at all, and the hypothesis of a common source, which gave no precise details of time or place, accounts for the facts as well, if not better. Moreover Mark's placing of the incident, though plausible, does raise one awkward question: who heard Jesus' prayer, when the Twelve were asleep?

The **voice from heaven** recalls those heard at Jesus' baptism (Mark i. 11 = Matt. iii. 17 = Luke iii. 22) and transfiguration (Mark ix. 7 = Matt. xvii. 5 = Luke ix. 35) as well as at Saul's conversion (Acts ix. 4).[2] It gives an assurance that Jesus' prayer has been heard. God has already **glorified** his name in and through the ministry of Jesus (cf. ix. 3; xi. 4, 40) **and will glorify it again** in his death.

29. The bystanders **heard** the sound (cf. Acts ix. 7) but explained it as **a peal of thunder,** while **others** (a section of the crowd, or perhaps the disciples) supposed it to be speech which they could not understand, and attributed it to **an angel** [3] (cf. Acts xxiii. 9).

30. It is not immediately obvious how the faith of the crowd could be stimulated or confirmed by a **voice** which they could not understand. It is not sufficient to say (with Lagrange, p. 334) that they could have asked; but it is also unnecessary to postulate (with Barrett, p. 355) a third group (perhaps the disciples) who did understand its message. In the Old Testament thunder is recognised as the voice of God (cf. Exod. xix.

---

[1] See below, p. 387.

[2] For later parallels, see W. James, *The Varieties of Religious Experience* (1902), e.g. pp. 69-71.

[3] That angels speak a different language from men may be inferred from 1 Cor. xiii. 1.

19, Ps. xxix. 3 ff.[1]) and if it had actually thundered just after Jesus had last spoken, this could explain the comments of the crowd, as well as Jesus' remark that he did not need such confirmation for his faith, even if the crowd did. The words of the voice are due to John's source, unless we are to suppose that Jesus told them to his disciples.[2]

(31) 'Now is the judgement upon this world; now shall the ruler of this world be driven out;[3] (32) and as for me, if[4] I am lifted up from the earth, I will draw all men to myself'. (33) Now by saying this he showed the kind of death which he was going to die.

31. Jesus continues his speech which had been interrupted by the voice from heaven. The repetition of **Now** (cf. verse 27) lays particular emphasis upon it. The moment of Jesus' death is that of **the judgement upon this world**—the *crisis* (for this *is* 'judgement'—κρίσις) of human history, whereby the power of evil is broken. By rejecting Jesus men condemn themselves, but this very act is made the means of their salvation, since judgement is not God's last word: he condemns only because he loves the world.[5]

The power of evil is personified, not because John is a metaphysical dualist, but because the only evil that really matters is moral evil, and moral evil involves persons. Hence **the ruler of this world,** ruler *de facto*, not *de jure*, because men have delivered themselves into his power by becoming slaves to sin. He is the Evil One (1 John v. 19), the Devil (John viii. 44), and Satan (John xiii. 27, Rev. xii. 9; xx. 2). St Paul (1 Cor. ii. 6, 8) speaks of 'the rulers of this age' (αἰών—virtually the equivalent of **this world**—κόσμος—in the FG),[6] who are the 'principalities' (literally 'rulers', ἀρχαί) of Rom. viii. 38, the 'world-rulers (κοσμοκράτορας) of this darkness' of Eph. vi.

---

[1] Gentiles also would recognise thunder as an omen. Thus in Vergil, *Aeneid*, II. 692 f., Jupiter acknowledges Anchises' prayer for help by a clap of thunder.

[2] It may have been a flash of lightning and a peal of thunder which precipitated St Paul's conversion, the physical shock breaking down his unconscious resistance to a conversion which had really happened already, and enabling him to apprehend the presence of the risen Lord.

[3] Literally, 'thrown out', cf. vi. 37, p. 189, n. 2.

[4] Literally, 'and I, if I . . .', but κἀγὼ ἐὰν . . . lays great emphasis on 'I'.

[5] Cf. iii. 16 ff. pp. 130 f. and (on 'world') p. 76 (on i. 10).

[6] See p. 223.

12, of whom the chief is 'the god of this age' of 2 Cor. iv. 4.[1]

32. In sharp contrast to Satan, Jesus for his part will be **lifted up.** This suggests exaltation in glory, but the word has a double meaning, and, as the next verse tells us, alludes to his crucifixion, which is indeed his glorification (verse 23).[2]

At vi. 44 it is God who is said to **draw** men,[3] but in this respect also Christ is God's agent. This power of attraction is what St Paul calls the grace of God, though 'grace' only occurs in John i. 14, 16, 17.

(34) So the crowd answered him, 'We have heard from the law that the Christ stays[4] for ever, and what do you mean by saying[5] that the Son of man must be lifted up? Who is this Son of man?'

Jesus is always being misunderstood. So now **the crowd** is misled by its own ideas of the Messiah. They had hailed Jesus as King of Israel, i.e. as Messiah (verse 13), and had heard him speak of the Son of man being glorified (verse 23). They had understood—correctly—that he was referring to himself, but they have been puzzled by his last remark that he **must be lifted up:**[6] they think it implies his *removal*, which is incompatible with what **the law** (i.e. Scripture, not only the Pentateuch[7]) says about **the Christ,** that he **stays for ever** (which is of course true, though in a sense which they cannot appreciate —see xv. 4 ff.). Texts which they may have had in mind are 2 Sam. vii. 16, Ps. xlv. 6, Isa. ix. 7. If then **the Son of man** is not the Christ, who is he? They want to know, not his identity, but the status and function which he claims.

---

[1] In Rabbinic Hebrew the term κοσμοκράτωρ ('world-ruler') was used (in transliteration) as a title for the Angel of Death, and the title 'Prince of the world' is also common, but does not refer to Satan. So Barrett (p. 355) objects that, 'At least at this point John does not seem to be in close touch with Hebrew and Jewish thought.' This may be true for Hebrew thought in the third century A.D. but not necessarily at an earlier period. The evidence on which he relies may be found in Strack–Billerbeck, III, p. 819 (on Rev. xvi. 5); the earliest is *circa* 220 A.D.

[2] Cf. iii. 14, pp. 127 f. and viii. 28, p. 225.   [3] See pp. 192 f.

[4] μένει. On Christ's 'staying' see on i. 38 f., p. 98.

[5] Literally, 'How sayest thou?' Cf. vi. 42; viii. 33; xiv. 9.

[6] That Jesus' 'lifting up' is also his 'glorification' may be traced to the LXX version of Isa. lii. 13, which uses both the FG's verbs ὑψωθήσεται καὶ δοξασθήσεται.   [7] So also in x. 34; see p. 259.

(35) So Jesus said to them, '⟨It is only⟩ for a little time longer ⟨that⟩ the light is ⟨to be⟩¹ in your midst. Walk² while you have the light, in order that the darkness may not overtake you;³ the man who indeed walks in darkness does not know where he is going. (36) While you have the light, believe in the light, in order that you may become sons of light.'

These ⟨were the things that⟩ Jesus spoke to them, and ⟨then⟩ he went away and hid himself.

35. In words which echo many previous statements Jesus gives the crowd only an indirect answer to their last question. He says in effect that he is **the light** (cf. i. 4; viii. 12), but will not be with them much longer (cf. vii. 33), so that this is their last chance of escaping **the darkness** (see i. 5; vi. 17; ix. 4 f.; xi. 9 f.). 36. This they can do by believing **in the light**, i.e. in himself, and so becoming **sons of light**,⁴ i.e. men who exhibit the same qualities as himself, cf. i. 12, where those who believe become children of God.

This is Jesus' final message to the crowd, of hope as well as warning, and after delivering it **he went away and hid himself**, cf. viii. 59. This marks the end of his public ministry, and John takes the opportunity of adding some general reflexions upon it. These fall into two parts, the first (verses 37-43) being his own comment on the rejection of Jesus by his people, and the second (verses 44-50) a summary of Jesus' teaching. Together they fulfil the same function of commenting on the action of the drama as the choruses in a Greek tragedy.⁵ The second passage follows logically after verse 36, and may have stood in that position in John's source, but there is no reason to suppose that its present position is not intentional.

(37) But though he had done so many signs before them they did not believe in him, (38) in order that the

---

¹ For this translation of the present tense cf. vii. 33, and see p. 210, n. 4.

² περιπατεῖτε. On the meaning of this see p. 200 n. 5, and cf. viii. 12; xi. 9 f.   ³ καταλάβῃ. On the meaning of this see p. 73 (on i. 5).

⁴ For the Hebraism 'sons of . . .' cf. 'the son of perdition' xvii. 12, and for the phrase itself cf. Luke xvi. 8, 1 Thess. v. 5, and Eph. v. 8. The *Manual of Discipline* refers to members of the Qumran Sect as 'sons of light' (i. 9).   ⁵ Cf. iii. 16 ff. and see p. 129.

word which Isaiah the prophet spoke [1] might be fulfilled, 'Lord, who believed our report? And to whom was the Lord's arm revealed?' (39) The reason why they could not believe was that [2] Isaiah said in another place, [3] (40) 'He has blinded their eyes and petrified [4] their heart⟨s⟩, in order that they should not see with their eyes and perceive with their heart⟨s⟩ and turn, and I should heal them.' (41) Isaiah said these things because [5] ⟨it was⟩ his glory ⟨that⟩ he saw, and about him ⟨that⟩ he spoke.

37. Though the purpose of Jesus' **signs** was, strictly, not to create but to confirm faith—hence his refusal to produce them on demand [6]—yet their significance was so overwhelmingly obvious to John that he could only explain the unbelief of the Jewish people (which is one of the major concerns of the FG) on the assumption that it was intended by God as part of his providential plan for man's salvation. There is great irony in a comparison between John's reference to the **signs** here and the comment by the authorities on them in xi. 47.

St Paul also sees Jewish apostasy as providential (cf. Rom. xi. 11 f.), and, like John, describes it in terms which suggest an absolute predestination to damnation. But Paul hopes that all Israel will be saved (Rom. xi. 26), John that Jesus will draw *all men* to himself (xii. 32), so that predestination to damnation is not necessarily their final word. Both recognise the paradox of grace and freedom in the relations between God and man; [7] a man can reject grace, and is to blame if he does.

38. Jewish unbelief was **in order that** (ἵνα) Isaiah's prophecy **might be fulfilled**: ἵνα implies purpose, but Hebrew

---

[1] Literally, 'the word of Isaiah the prophet which he spoke'.

[2] Literally, 'Because of this they could not believe, because . . .'

[3] πάλιν, 'again'.

[4] ἐπώρωσεν is read by A B* Θ *fam* 13 (the majority of authorities having the same verb, but in the perfect tense, by assimilation to 'blinded', τετύφ-λωκεν). But ἐπήρωσεν, 'maimed', read by P⁶⁶ ℵ and a few other authorities, has a claim to consideration, since ἐπώρωσεν may be the result of assimilation to Mark vi. 52; viii. 17, Rom. xi. 7.

[5] ὅτι is read by P⁶⁶ ℵ A B Θ 1 *e eg*; the alternative ὅτε, 'when', of D *fam* 13 and the majority is to be rejected as the easier reading. On Burney's view that ὅτι is a mistranslation of the Aramaic *dᵉ* (see p. 292, n. 2), which should have a temporal sense here, see Black, p. 60.

[6] Cf. ii. 18 and vi. 30, and see p. 113 (on ii. 11).

[7] See pp. 131 (on iii. 19 f.) and 190 (on vi. 37).

thought did not distinguish clearly between result and purpose,[1] and a foreseen result could very easily be represented as a purpose.[2]

John's first quotation is from Isa. liii. 1. This is a rhetorical question intended to draw attention to the extraordinary character of the revelation which follows. For John, it implies that nobody in fact believed it (cf. St Paul's use of it in Rom. x. 16).

39 f. They did not believe because they **could not**—because God prevented them, as is clear from Isa. vi. 10, which John quotes rather inexactly (probably from his memory of the Hebrew original). He has already alluded to this passage in ix. 39, and it is also used to prove the providential character of Israel's unbelief in Mark iv. 12 and Acts xxviii. 26 f.

41. John notes that the context in which this passage occurs is appropriate to the use which he makes of it to prove the providential character of the Jews' rejection of Jesus. For it is from Isaiah's account of his vision in the Temple, and John, who denies that any man has ever seen God (i. 18),[3] asserts that what Isaiah then saw was the glory of the Logos;[4] for, like Philo,[5] he believed that the Old Testament theophanies were appearances of the Logos.

(42) But for all that many even of the rulers believed in him, but because of the Pharisees they did not confess ⟨him⟩ so that they would not be excluded from the synagogue; (43) for they preferred[6] the ⟨good⟩ opinion[7] of men to the ⟨good⟩ opinion[7] of God.

42. John immediately modifies his sweeping condemnation of the Jews (cf. Rom. xi. 5) by remarking that Jesus had sympathisers even in the Sanhedrin—cf. Nicodemus (iii. 1 ff.; vii. 50 f.; xix. 39) and Joseph of Arimathea (xix. 38 ff.). The claim that there were **many** such may be exaggerated, but it is hyper-

---

[1] See p. 237, n. 3 (on ix. 3). The formula 'in order that the word [or 'scripture'] might be fulfilled' occurs also in xiii. 18; xv. 25; xvii. 12; xviii. 9, 32; xix. 24, 36.

[2] Cf. p. 130, n. 3 (on iii. 17 f.).   [3] See pp. 85 f.

[4] Black, p. 60 n. 5, notes that according to the Targum (the Aramaic paraphrase) of the Prophets Isaiah saw 'the glory of the Shechinah of the King of the Ages'.

[5] Cf. de Somniis, I. 229 f.   [6] Literally, 'loved . . . more'.

[7] δόξα, which of course also means 'glory'. John is aware of this double meaning, for which there is no precise English equivalent.

critical to doubt (as Barrett seems to do, p. 360) that there were some. The way in which Jesus' trial was conducted seems to suggest that his enemies were not sure that they had the whole Sanhedrin against him. John himself may well have been in a position to know the state of feeling at the time.[1] The reluctance of his sympathisers to declare themselves (cf. vii. 13), though pusillanimous, is intelligible enough in view of the decision which John has already noted (ix. 22) that Jesus' supporters should be excluded from the synagogue.[2] 43. For John's comment on their motive, cf. v. 44.

(44) But Jesus cried out and said, 'He who believes in me, does not believe in me, but in him who sent me, (45) and he who observes me [3] observes him who sent me. (46) I am come into the world ⟨as⟩ light, in order that everyone who believes in me may not stay [4] in darkness. (47) And if anyone hears my words and does not keep them,[5] it is not I who judge him; [6] for I did not come to judge the world, but to save the world. (48) He who sets me aside and does not accept my words has his judge—it is the word which I spoke that[7] will judge him on the last day. (49) Because I did not speak on my own behalf,[8] but the Father who sent me himself gave me a command what I was to say [9] and what I was to speak.[9] (50) And I know that his command is eternal life. This is why I speak as I do the things which the Father told me'.[10]

This short discourse is given without any indication of its context; it is in fact a concluding summary of Jesus' public

---

[1] See the Introduction, pp. 44 ff.

[2] See p. 242.　　　　　[3] ὁ θεωρῶν ἐμέ. See p. 191.

[4] For the significance of this word see on i. 38 (p. 98).

[5] John here uses φυλάσσω (which means 'preserve' in xii. 25; xvii. 12), but elsewhere τηρέω in this sense (viii. 51, etc.) See also on xvii. 12.

[6] ἐγὼ οὐ κρίνω αὐτόν. This translation is to bring out the emphasis there is on 'I' (ἐγώ).　　　　　[7] See p. 85 n. 2.

[8] ἐξ ἐμαυτοῦ, literally 'from myself'. Elsewhere John uses ἀπ' ἐμαυτοῦ (v. 30, etc.), and no difference may be intended. But it is odd that he uses ἐξ only once. For this sense of ἐξ cf. ἐκ τῆς ἀληθείας, 'on the side of the truth', xviii. 37.

[9] τί εἴπω and τί λαλήσω are 'deliberative' subjunctives—in direct speech, 'What am I to say?' (cf. xii. 27).

[10] Literally, 'Therefore the things which I speak, as the Father told me, thus I speak'.

teaching. As such, it necessarily repeats themes already handled. It stresses particularly Jesus' complete union with, and obedience to, his Father, and so the contrast between him and the Jews, whose unbelief is the topic of the previous section, verses 37-43.

44. Belief in Jesus is belief in his Father, cf. Matt. x. 40, and John v. 23, which expresses a similar idea negatively. 45. Cf. xiv. 9. 46. For Christ as **light** cf. i. 4 f., 9; viii. 12; ix. 5, dispelling the **darkness** cf. xii. 35 f. As light, Christ illuminates the faithful and shows up the disobedient, so that, 47. though the *purpose* of his coming was salvation, not judgement (cf. iii. 17), 48. judgement may indeed be its inevitable result (cf. iii. 18 ff.; viii. 15 f.).

The words **He who sets me aside** (ὁ ἀθετῶν ἐμέ), etc., recall Luke x. 16 and 1 Thess. iv. 8, which have the same verb (ἀθετῶ), found in the FG only in this passage.

There is a double meaning in **word** (λόγος), which John no doubt intended as an allusion to Jesus the Logos.[1] The judgement which is the result of the word spoken in Jesus' ministry is indeed his judgement (cf. ix. 39). It takes effect **on the last day,** cf. v. 29; vi. 39, etc.[2]

49. The reason why Jesus' ministry results in judgement is that his Father has entrusted him with this prerogative (cf. v. 22) because Jesus' word is not his own (cf. vii. 17; viii. 26, 28): in everything he obeys his Father (cf. v. 30; vi. 38).

50. God's **command is eternal life** (as the Jews themselves admit, cf. v. 39) since it is by it that Jesus himself lives, cf. iv. 34,[3] and xvii. 3. On the significance of **eternal life** see pp. 13 f. and 128.

3. THE LAST SUPPER, xiii-xvii

xiii. (1) But before the feast of the Passover Jesus, knowing that his time[4] had come to pass[5] from this

---

[1] See the Introduction, p. 4.   [2] See p. 190.
[3] See p. 150.   [4] Literally, 'hour': see pp. 107, n. 2 and 110 (on ii. 4).
[5] The same verb (μεταβαίνω) is used in v. 24 of passing from death to life.

world[1] to the Father, having loved his own ⟨while they were⟩ in the world, loved them to the end.

The break between this and the previous passage is so abrupt that the use of a connecting word is surprising, even in the FG. But, however, is probably meant to take us back to xii. 36, and would be more natural if xii. 44-50 had not been placed where it is.[2]

It appears from xviii. 28 that the supper was on the day **before the feast of the Passover,** i.e. on the evening (which on Jewish reckoning began the day) of the Friday, or, on our reckoning, on Thursday. Thus for John the meal was not the Passover, though according to Mark xiv. 12 it was, for the disciples' preparations were made on the day when they were sacrificing the lambs. Many attempts have been made to reconcile Mark and John, but Barrett (pp. 39 ff.) argues convincingly that the Synoptic tradition is self-consistent and is to be preferred to John's. A more recent attempt has been made[3] to argue that Jesus did not follow the official Jewish calendar, but the one also used by the Qumran community, and ate the Passover on the Tuesday night. Mark is therefore correct, and John was misled because he followed the official calendar, the only one known outside Palestine. But John may not be as ignorant as this makes out. It is conceivable that what Jesus in fact did was to observe as much of the Passover ritual as was possible twenty-four hours before the proper time, because he knew that by the proper time he would be dead (cf. Luke xxii. 15, which can mean

---

[1] See p. 223 (on viii. 23).   [2] See p. 298.

[3] See *La Date de la Cène. Calendrier biblique et liturgie chrétienne*, by Mlle A. Jaubert (1957), reviewed by Jeremias, *J.T.S.*, n.s., Vol. X, 1959, pp. 131 ff., and a further article by the same author in *N.T.S.*, Vol. VII, 1960–61, pp. 1-30. [Cf. also M. Black, 'The Arrest and Trial of Jesus and the Date of the Last Supper' in *New Testament Essays: Studies in Memory of T. W. Manson*, ed. A. J. B. Higgins (1959), pp. 19-33, a shortened form of which is printed as Appendix D, 'The Qumran Calendar and the Last Supper', in M. Black, *The Scrolls and Christian Origins* (1961), pp. 199-201; W. H. Cadman, 'The Christian Pascha and the Day of the Crucifixion—Nisan 14 or 15?', *Studia Patristica*, Vol. V, ed. F. L. Cross (Texte und Untersuchungen, Vol. 80, 1962), pp. 8-16; J. Finegan, *Handbook of Biblical Chronology* (1964), pp. 285-291—a full survey of the various theories advanced about the synoptic and Johannine chronologies; and the important and well documented essay by George Ogg, 'The Chronology of the Last Supper', *Historicity and Chronology in the New Testament* (S.P.C.K. Theological Collections, Vol. VI, 1965), pp. 75-96.—B. A. M.]

that it was not the Passover which Jesus was eating). This led Mark, and the Synoptic tradition with him, to date the meal on the actual day of the Passover, a mistake which John avoids.

The **time** of Jesus' passing recalls xii. 23; contrast Luke xxii. 53, 'This is *your* time ($\ddot{\omega}\rho a$)': for his going **to the Father** cf. xvi. 5: the mention of **his own** recalls the same phrase in i. 11, though there the reference is different: there they are the Jews who rejected Jesus, while here they are those (mentioned in i. 12) who accepted him, who, though **in the world,** are alien to it (cf. xv. 19). The hostility of the world is a dominant theme in the last discourses of Jesus, and contrasts with his love[1] for his disciples, which was shown both in his ministry, and also—and supremely—in his death (cf. xv. 13): **to the end** can indeed mean 'utterly', and John may intend the phrase to be taken in both senses. Indeed he may intend a further nuance: by mentioning **the end** so soon after **this world** he may allude to the 'end of the age' (cf. Matt. xiii. 39, etc.), since **this world** in the FG is virtually the equivalent of 'this age' in the Synoptic Gospels.[2] Consistently with his transvaluation of Synoptic eschatology,[3] it is the death of Jesus which brings to an end this age, and the rule of Satan (xii. 31).

Thus this verse forms the introduction, not just to the story of the supper, but to the whole Passion narrative proper.

(2) And during supper,[4] when the Devil had already put it into his heart that Judas Iscariot, ⟨the son⟩ of Simon,[5] should betray him, (3) ⟨Jesus,⟩ knowing that the Father had given all things into his hands, and that he came out from God and was going to God, (4) rose from supper and

---

[1] See pp. 129 f.   [2] See p. 223.

[3] See the Introduction, pp. 13 f.

[4] δείπνου γινομένου (present participle) is read by ℵ* B W and a few other authorities: the majority, headed by P66 A D Θ have the aorist, meaning 'after supper'. The latter may have found favour as seeming to make it easier to harmonise the gospels. But either text is compatible with the interpretation followed in this Commentary.

[5] In P66 ℵ B and a few other authorities **Judas** is the subject of the relative clause. The majority have Ἰουδᾶ (genitive, following 'heart'), which may be due to the accidental omission of 's' (ΙΟΥΔΑΣΙΜΩΝΟΣ for ΙΟΥΔΑΣΣΙ-ΜΩΝΟΣ). D (as at xii. 4) has ἀπὸ Καρυώτου for Ἰσκαριώτου (cf. ℵ*, etc., at vi. 71). See p. 198 n. 6.

took off his clothes, and taking a towel tied it round himself; (5) then he put water into the washbasin, and began to wash the disciples' feet and to wipe them with the towel which he had tied round him.

2. That it was the evening meal[1] (as in Mark xiv. 17) is shown by xiii. 30. It was normal for a servant to wash guests' feet before the start of a meal; for the host to wash them during (or, for that matter, after) it was unusual on two counts. Jesus assumes the rôle of the servant (cf. Luke xxii. 27) but whatever his motive was—an expression of his love for the disciples, or an object-lesson in humility, or something else—he might have been expected to act before the meal started. That he does not may suggest that his action was unpremeditated, and prompted by something which he had just noticed.

Either it was to silence the squabble about precedence which Luke xxii. 24 ff. records, or, as the mention of **the Devil** may suggest, an attempt to counter the wiles of Satan, and save Judas' soul (Jesus knew what was in men, ii. 25), though these are not mutually exclusive, and do not exclude other motives for his action.

John distinguishes two stages in the Devil's conquest of Judas—first, here, his suggestion that he should betray his master, and then his actual possession of Judas (verse 27, cf. Luke xxii. 3). It is noteworthy that John (who records no other instance of demon-possession) and Luke (who has no instance of it in his special material) are the only evangelists to ascribe Judas' betrayal to Satan.

The suggestion that one of Jesus' motives was to try to save Judas may seem inconsistent with his knowledge that Judas was to betray him,[2] and so in strict logic it may be. But Judas was not compelled to act as he did, and it is surely not incredible that Jesus should have given him the chance to save himself, even if he knew it would fail.[3]

3. The closest parallel to the statement **that the Father had given all things into his hands** is in Matt. xi. 27 = Luke x. 22 (cf. Matt. xxviii. 18): John v. 22, 26; xvii. 2 give particular examples of this, but John iii. 35 says something different.[4]

---

[1] See p. 282 n. 1 on δεῖπνον (xii. 2).   [2] Cf. vi. 64; xiii. 11.
[3] See p. 200 (on vi. 70 f.) and on xiii. 26 ff.   [4] See p. 136.

Though conscious of his authority, and of his divine origin and destiny (cf. vii. 28; viii. 42; xiv. 12; xvi. 28), 4. Jesus undertakes the proverbially menial task of washing the disciples' feet (cf. 1 Sam. xxv. 41). This states the theme of glory in humiliation which characterises the whole Passion.

That his action is also a symbolic representation of his death (cf. Mark x. 45) is suggested by the use of the word τίθησι (**took off**), which is used in x. 15 ff. for Jesus' *laying down* of his *life*. For dying symbolised by undressing, and resurrection as receiving a garment cf. 1 Cor. xv. 53 f., 2 Cor. v. 1-4, and (perhaps) Rev. vi. 11. The plural **clothes** (ἱμάτια) is surprising, but more consistent with the symbolism than the removing of a single garment would be.

The word for **towel** (λέντιον) is the Latin *linteum*. Suetonius (*Caligula* 26) records the humiliation which Gaius put upon the senators by having them attend him at dinner wearing a *linteum*: an ironic contrast.

5. For the significance of **water** as the vehicle of the spirit in the FG see p. 91, n. 2 and cf. xix. 34. Jesus' washing of **the disciples' feet** both illustrates the cleansing of the disciples achieved by his death and enables them to appropriate its benefits. It is a prophetic symbolic action like John's baptism (see pp. 90 f.)—though of greater scope—and an eschatological sacrament like the feeding of the crowd (see p. 181). It thus takes the place of the institution of the Eucharist, an action of precisely the same kind which John has attached to the miracle of feeding (see pp. 195 f.). He may have felt that the connexion between baptism and the death of Jesus (cf. Rom. vi. 3) made it appropriate to describe the washing at this place.

(6) So he came to Simon Peter; he said to him, 'Lord, are you washing my feet?' (7) Jesus answered and said to him, 'What I am doing you do not know at present,[1] but you shall understand after these things'.[2] (8) Peter said to him, 'Never shall you wash my feet'.[3] Jesus answered him, 'If I do not wash you, you have no share in me'.[4]

[1] ἄρτι. See p. 107 n. 3.

[2] μετὰ ταῦτα implies some lapse of time: see p. 131 n. 4.

[3] οὐ μὴ . . . εἰς τὸν αἰῶνα. See p. 142 n. 3.

[4] With 'to have a share in . . .' (μέρος ἔχειν μετά) cf. Deut. x. 9, Joshua xxii. 25, Rev. xx. 6; xxi. 8; xxii. 19.

(9) Simon Peter said to him, 'Lord, not my feet only but my hands and my head'.

6. Peter, perhaps the first to be approached, but in any case always ready to take the lead (cf. vi. 68; xviii. 10) questions Jesus' action. The present tense **are you washing** has a future sense, and does not mean that Jesus is already doing it (cf. vii. 33 f.; xiii. 27, 33; xiv. 3; xv. 27; xxi. 23).

7. Jesus explains that Peter will only understand what he is doing at some future time (cf. ii. 22; xii. 16)—which will be, as vii. 39 indicates, when he has received the spirit after Jesus' resurrection. (This does not look forward to Jesus' words in verses 12-16.)

8. But Peter only becomes more obstinate; he has not learnt that there is a generosity (sometimes harder to attain) in accepting as well as in giving. But when Jesus tells him that otherwise he will forfeit his **share** in him, 9. he has a sudden change of heart, and demands more than Jesus has offered to do.

Here it becomes evident that the washing of the disciples' feet is a symbol of baptism, which is necessary to salvation. It is in fact the institution of the sacrament. There is a parallel to the Eucharist since the actual washing in the one is as necessary as the actual eating and drinking in the other (cf. vi. 53).

(10) Jesus said to him, 'The man who has had a bath has no need to have anything but his feet washed, but is wholly¹ clean; (11) and you are clean, but not all'. (For he knew his betrayer²—this is why he said, 'You are not all clean'.)

10. This verse sets a difficult textual problem. Apart from minor variants, there is a choice between the longer reading followed above, ὁ λελουμένος οὐκ ἔχει χρείαν εἰ μὴ τοὺς πόδας νίψασθαι, found in the majority of authorities, headed by B W (with P⁶⁶ and D giving two different alternative forms of it), and the shorter reading, produced by the omission of εἰ μὴ τοὺς πόδας, **'The man who has had a bath has no need** to wash', found

¹ ὅλος, an adjective, is used with another adjective (**clean**) almost as an adverb. The closest analogy to this is in ix. 34, Ἐν ἁμαρτίαις σὺ ἐγεννήθης ὅλος, 'You were wholly born in sins'.

² τὸν παραδιδόντα: the present participle describes a permanent characteristic of the person.

in א, a few Old Latin MSS., the original text of the Vulgate, Tertullian, and Origen.

In spite of Barrett's persuasive arguments in favour of the shorter reading (p. 368), the longer is to be preferred, for the following reasons.

Jesus is persuading Peter to let him wash his feet, and so it seems necessary that there should be some explicit mention of them in his reply, especially since he is refusing to wash his hands and head. The clue to the interpretation of the passage is to take the reference to the **bath** as a metaphor for the effect of Christ's death in cleansing the faithful (cf. 1 Cor. vi. 11, Rev. i. 5 [1]). In virtue of this Peter can be described as 'bathed' (λελουμένος, perfect participle), though Christ is not yet dead —he, like the other disciples, is already **clean,** in principle, if proleptically. But he still needs the actual sacramental washing so that he may appropriate the benefits of the cleansing by Christ's death, just as in the other sacrament the actual eating of the flesh and drinking of the blood are necessary (see on verse 9). But he only needs **his feet washed**—not his head and hands as well (just as Jesus himself only needed his feet anointed to be ready for burial, xii. 7)—because this washing is a token, effectual only as such, and not by any virtue of its own (just as in the other sacrament the flesh, by itself, and apart from its value as a token, is of no use, vi. 63). But Jesus has already said that Peter cannot yet understand what he is doing, and so we should not expect this verse to be an explanation, but rather an implied demand for obedience. The very lucidity (not to say banality) of the shorter reading is in fact a condemnation of it.

11. The disciples **are clean,** not because they have had their feet washed (Jesus has not yet washed them all in any case) but because Christ is to die for them. But this does not avail for them **all**—it cannot help the **betrayer** (whom Jesus already **knew,** vi. 64, 70 f.), who has forfeited its benefits by his repudiation of his master, so that it was no use to him that he had his feet washed (cf. vi. 63 again).

(12) So when he had washed their feet and taken his

---

[1] Reading λούσαντι, 'washed' with P 046 g vg eg, etc. 'Washed us in his blood' is clearly metaphorical.

clothes and lain down[1] again, he said to them, 'Do
you realise what I have done to you? (13) You call me
"Teacher" and "Lord", and you speak correctly; for I am.
(14) So if I, the "Lord" and "Teacher", washed your feet,
you also ought to wash one another's feet; (15) for I have
given you a pattern, so that, as I did, you also may do. (16)
Amen, amen, I say to you,[2] the slave is not greater than his
lord, nor the emissary greater than he who sent him. (17)
If you know these things, you are blessed if you do them.'

12. Jesus' question does not imply that he is going to explain
the symbolic significance of his action, which they were not yet in
a position to understand (verse 7). Instead, he gives them a practical application. He is 'both a sacrifice for sin, and also an ensample
of godly life' (Collect for the Second Sunday after Easter).

13. A Jewish pupil never addressed his master by name, but
as 'My teacher and my lord' (*rabbi umari*[3]). Similarly Jesus is
always addressed by a title—'Rabbi' (i. 38, 49; iii. 2; iv. 31; vi.
25; ix. 2; xi. 8), 'Rabboni' (xx. 16), 'Lord' (some thirty times)
—and when speaking of him among themselves his disciples do
not use his name, cf. xi. 28; xx. 18, 25; xxi. 7. Jesus accepts this,
not just as the usage of polite society, but as expressing a fact.
Technically Jesus was not a Rabbi at all (vii. 15), but he is
Teacher and **Lord** *par excellence*.

14 f. A Jewish pupil could be expected to wash his master's
feet,[4] and so, if the master washes the pupils' feet, the pupils
must follow the **pattern** of his humble service in their dealings
with one another. A similar appeal is made in Phil. ii. 5 and
I Pet. ii. 21.[5] In I Tim. v. 10 to have washed the feet of the
saints is one of the qualifications for recognition as a 'widow
indeed.' It is noteworthy that none of these passages envisages
the extension of such humble service to those beyond the limits
of the Church.[6]

---

[1] ἀνέπεσεν. This probably means 'sat down' at vi. 10, but on this occasion
Jesus and his disciples were reclining on couches, as xiii. 25 shows. See also
on xii. 2.   [2] For this formula, see p. 105 (on i. 51).

[3] See Strack–Billerbeck, II, p. 558.   [4] See Strack–Billerbeck, II, p. 557.

[5] Peter uses ὑπογραμμόν for John's ὑπόδειγμα (pattern): ὑπόδειγμα is used
in John's sense in Heb. viii. 5; ix. 23, but for an example to be avoided in
Heb. iv. 11, Jas. v. 10, 2 Pet. ii. 6.

[6] See also pp. 129 f. (on iii. 16) for the scope of Christian love in the FG.

16. This verse both reinforces the appeal already made to follow Jesus' example, and also looks forward to verse 20, where we learn for the first time in the FG that the disciples are to be sent out by Jesus—as apostles in fact, though John never uses this word for them.[1] This is why it is better to translate ἀπόστολος here (cf. Phil. ii. 25) not as 'apostle' but as **emissary**.

For the actual saying (apart from the introductory formula) cf. Matt. x. 24 and its partial parallel in Luke vi. 40.

17. The form of this sentence, with two conditional clauses and the main clause between them, is designed to bring out that to know these things (i.e. that we are to imitate Christ's example) is necessary for salvation, but insufficient unless we actually put it into practice; cf. Matt. vii. 24, Jas. i. 25, and the Rabbinic saying that even if one has learnt the Scriptures and the Mishnah, but has not served the pupils of the learned, one is an '*am hā-'ārets*[2] (i.e. one who does not keep the law).

The word for **blessed** (μακάριος) is that used in the Beatitudes, Matt. v. 3-11.

(18) 'I am not speaking about you all; I know whom I chose; but—in order that the scripture[3] might be fulfilled —"He who eats bread with me[4] lifted his heel against me." (19) I am telling you at present,[5] before ⟨it⟩ happens, in order that you may believe, when it does happen, that I am. (20) Amen, amen, I say to you,[6] he who accepts whomsoever I send accepts me, and he who accepts me accepts him who sent me.'[7]

18. Jesus had not excluded Judas from the washing of the disciples' feet. But by his treachery he would exclude himself from the blessing which Jesus has pronounced, and Jesus breaks the thread of his discourse to give him what is in effect a final warning. Jesus has chosen Judas (cf. vi. 70 f.), but he had

[1] Apart from three instances in Revelation (ii. 2; xviii. 20; xxi. 14). But the cognate verb ἀποστέλλω and its synonym πέμπω ('send') are very common. See p. 129 n. 1. For ἀπόστολος = *shaliach* see p. 311 n. 3 (on verse 20).

[2] Quoted in Strack–Billerbeck, I, p. 527.

[3] ἡ γραφή means a single passage, cf. ii. 22, p. 120. See also p. 300, n. 1.

[4] μετ' ἐμοῦ, read by the majority of authorities, headed by P⁶⁶ ℵ D Θ, is to be preferred to μου, read by B *sah* and a few other authorities.

[5] ἀπ' ἄρτι is here not distinguishable from ἄρτι, on which see p. 107 n. 3. But see also on xiv. 7.   [6] For this formula, see p. 105 (on i. 51).

[7] On the sending of the Son see p. 129 n. 1.

broken their fellowship (of which the shared meal was a token) and spurned his friend, thus fulfilling Ps. xli. 9. John can be understood as meaning that Jesus **chose** Judas so that there would be someone to fulfil this prophecy. But it could also be that the necessity for Judas' action lay in his character, and not in divine predestination,[1] and that to foresee a result is not the same as intending it.[2]

19. Jesus' foreknowledge, even if it cannot help Judas, can be turned to some account in reassuring the faithful when the disaster happens (cf. xiv. 29). One must supply a predicate for **I am**—the Christ, in fact; cf. viii. 24, p. 224.

20. Jesus takes up again the thread of his discourse. As verse 16 has prepared us to expect, Jesus now speaks of his sending out his disciples, cf. xvii. 18; xx. 21. With this saying cf. xii. 44, Matt. x. 40, Luke x. 16.[3]

(21) When he had said these things Jesus was troubled in spirit and bore witness and said, 'Amen, amen, I say to you[4] that one of you shall betray me'.

Jesus apparently now realises that Judas is obdurate, and cannot refrain from sharing his grief with his companions. But he will do nothing to prevent Judas doing what he will, and so does not mention his name. For **troubled in spirit** cf. xi. 33 and xii. 27, in both of which the same verb (ταράσσω) is used.[5] The **spirit** is Jesus' human spirit (as in xi. 33) and virtually synonymous with 'soul' (ψυχή, xii. 27) and 'heart' (καρδία, xiv. 1, 27). That Jesus **bore witness** is said to stress the seriousness of his words, as does also the introductory formula **Amen, amen,** etc.

The same announcement is made in Matt. xxvi. 21 and Mark xiv. 18, the only difference being that they have one **Amen** instead of two, and that Mark adds, 'who is eating with me' (cf. verse 18 above). Luke xxii. 21 has a different form of words. The saying is in any case a memorable one, and it is not

---

[1] See pp. 198 and 200. [2] See pp. 299 f. on xii. 38.

[3] Cf. also the Rabbinic saying that 'a man's *shaliach* [an agent with full power to act on his principal's behalf] is as the man himself'. The word ἀπόστολος (used in verse 16) may be the equivalent of *shaliach*. See K. H. Rengstorf in *T.W.z.N.T.* s.v. ἀπόστολος, and Strack–Billerbeck, III, pp. 2-4.

[4] For this formula, see p. 105 (on i. 51).

[5] It is also used at xiv. 1 and 27, with 'heart' as the subject.

necessary to suppose that John took it from Mark, particularly since the rest of the story is told very differently in the two Gospels.

(22) The disciples looked at one another, at a loss ⟨to know⟩ of whom he was speaking.

In Matt. xxvi. 22 and Mark xiv. 19 the disciples at once ask Jesus in turn, 'It is not I, is it?' In Luke xxii. 23 they asked among themselves. It is as difficult to reconcile these statements with the stricken silence which John reports as it is to decide between them—a problem which often arises in the Passion story.

(23) ⟨There⟩ was reclining in Jesus' bosom one of his disciples, whom Jesus loved; (24) so Simon Peter beckoned to this man to enquire who it was[1] of whom he was speaking. (25) He just[2] leaned back against Jesus' chest and said to him, 'Lord, who is it?' (26) So Jesus answered him, 'It is the one for whom I shall dip the morsel and give it to him'. So having dipped the morsel he[3] gave it to Judas son of Simon Iscariot.[4] (27) And ⟨it was⟩ then,[5] after ⟨he had taken⟩ the morsel, ⟨that⟩ Satan entered into him. So Jesus said to him, 'What you are doing, do quickly'. (28) But no one of those at table[6] knew for what purpose he said this to him; (29) for some thought, because Judas had the money-box, that Jesus was saying to him, 'Buy what we have need of for the feast', or that he should give something to the poor. (30) So when he had received the morsel he immediately went out; and it was night.

23. It was the custom to recline at table propped on one's left elbow, and to lie at an angle of about 45° to the table. So

---

[1] For **to enquire who it was**, read by P66 *sin* and the majority of the authorities, B *lat* has *and said to him, 'Say who it is . . .'*, while ℵ conflates the two readings. While the B reading is simpler and in the style of the FG, both are clearly ancient, and the other fits the situation better.

[2] οὕτως. See p. 140 n. 2.

[3] B adds 'took and', which ℵ* D *lat sin* and most other authorities omit. Barrett (p. 373) suggests that it was added because Jesus *took* the bread in the institution of the Eucharist.

[4] ℵ B Θ etc. make **Iscariot** agree with **Simon**; P66 A W etc. with **Judas**; D has ἀπὸ Καρυώτου. See p. 198 n. 6, p. 284 n. 2, and p. 304 n. 5.

[5] τότε. The paraphrase is designed to bring out the emphasis laid on this word by its position in the sentence.   [6] Literally, 'of those reclining'.

the disciple with his back to Jesus could be described as **re-clining in Jesus' bosom,**[1] and when (verse 25) he wanted to speak to him without being overheard, he leaned back so that his head touched Jesus' chest.

The fact that Jesus and his disciples were reclining, and not sitting, suggests that this was the Passover meal, at which reclining was obligatory. But it is quite compatible with the suggestion that it was a substitute-Passover.[2]

If the disciple **whom Jesus loved** ($\dot{\eta}\gamma\acute{a}\pi a$) is neither an 'ideal figure' (i.e. a figment of the author's imagination) nor John the son of Zebedee, then he may perhaps be identified with Lazarus.[3]

Jesus and the Beloved Disciple were, relatively to one another, in the places customarily assigned to the principal guest and the host. So it is probable that either Jesus himself or the Beloved Disciple acted as host, for it is difficult to think that if Jesus was not the host, he was not the principal guest. The latter could have been the case if the meal took place in the house which afterwards became the apostles' headquarters, that belonging to Mary, the mother of John Mark (Acts xii. 12), and if John Mark himself is the Beloved Disciple.[4]

24. In the silence which followed Jesus' disclosure, Peter, not in a position to ask Jesus himself, **beckoned** to the Beloved Disciple to find out who was the traitor. If the majority reading is followed,[5] no word is spoken aloud until Jesus addresses Judas, and no disciple other than the Beloved is yet aware of the traitor's identity.

26. Jesus does not disclose his name, but promises to point him out, which he does in a way which only the Beloved Disciple can appreciate.

In Mark xiv. 20 Jesus replies to the question put by all the disciples by saying, 'One of the Twelve, who dips with me in the dish'. This could of course mean any of them, since all dipped in the dish together, Matt. xxvi. 23 appears to be paraphrasing Mark, while there is nothing equivalent in Luke. Once again there is a manifest discrepancy.

---

[1] $\dot{\epsilon}\nu$ $\tau\hat{\omega}$ $\kappa\acute{o}\lambda\pi\omega$ recalls i. 18, the only-begotten in the bosom ($\epsilon\dot{\iota}s$ $\tau\grave{o}\nu$ $\kappa\acute{o}\lambda\pi o\nu$) of the Father. See p. 86. Is this meant to suggest that as only Christ can reveal the Father, only the Beloved Disciple can reveal the Christ?
[2] See p. 303.   [3] See on xi. 5, and the Introduction, pp. 31 f.
[4] See the Introduction, p. 49.   [5] See p. 312 n. 1.

The sign was that Jesus would **dip the morsel** (ψωμίον)—
which he already held in his hand?—**and give it to him.** To do
this was a common courtesy (like taking wine with a fellow-guest)
and would by itself cause no comment. Jesus may have chosen
this course as a last reminder to Judas of the heinousness of
betraying one with whom he had eaten—and, not having been
unmasked publicly, Judas could still change his mind. The
morsel would most naturally be understood as bread,[1] but
Barrett (p. 373) suggests that it was the ritual bitter herbs dipped
in the *charosheth* sauce prescribed for the Passover, and so tells
against John's dating of the meal.[2] But the other explanation
seems more natural.

27. If Jesus was giving Judas a last chance, it was of no avail.
It was at this moment that **Satan entered into him.** We should
not suppose that Jesus was consigning him to Satan (cf. 1 Cor.
v. 5), or that Judas ate to his own condemnation (cf. 1 Cor. xi.
29). It was simply that this was the moment when Judas irrevoc-
ably committed himself by consenting to the tempter's suggestion (xiii. 2), and so giving him admittance to his soul. Luke
xxii. 3 puts this before the supper, but such a difference should
cause no surprise.

We must suppose that Jesus realised this, and spoke to Judas
at once. The present tense in **What you are doing** is best taken
in a future sense (cf. vii. 33 f.; xiii. 6, 33; xiv. 3; xxi. 23): **quickly**
is in fact comparative (τάχιον). It need not mean more than the
positive, or it could be superlative, 'as **quickly** as possible'. But
if a genuinely comparative meaning is intended, it may imply
'before anyone finds out what it is and tries to stop it'. Jesus has
done all he can for Judas; he expects death, in one way or
another; if Judas insists on being the means to it, then let there
be no delay.

28. All but the Beloved Disciple were unaware of what had
been happening, and he can be forgiven if he did not realise that
Jesus was bidding Judas put his plan into effect, and did not
know what to do. To call his inactivity incomprehensible, as
Barrett does (p. 373), is somewhat captious.

29. It is not surprising if the reasons which they found for

[1] The Modern Greek word for 'bread' is derived from ψωμίον.
[2] But not if it was a substitute-Passover, see p. 303.

Jesus' words are not very intelligent. Almsgiving at such a time was natural enough, but on any showing night was a curious time to buy what was needed for the feast. This may seem inconsistent with the interpretation of the supper as a substitute-Passover, but **the feast** could mean the whole Passover period, and need not be confined to the Passover meal.

30. Judas accepted **the morsel**—to refuse it would have drawn attention to himself—and **immediately went out,** before anyone had thought of stopping him.

John's concluding comment, **and it was night,** is extraordinarily impressive in its stark simplicity. It is more than a statement of fact: it recalls the **night** from which Nicodemus emerged (iii. 2), and symbolises the darkness which Judas preferred (cf. iii. 19 f.). In Rev. xxi. 25 and xxii. 5 there is no night in the heavenly Jerusalem.

(31) So when he had gone out, Jesus said, '⟨Just⟩ now[1] the Son of man[2] was glorified, and God was glorified in him; (32) if God was glorified in him,[3] God will also glorify him in himself, and will immediately glorify him.'

31. Jesus is referring to the washing of the disciples' feet as the event by which he has just been **glorified,** for it symbolised his death, the means of his glorification (cf. xii. 23). That a past event is intended is shown by the tense of the verbs (aorist).[4] But 32. what has just been prefigured in symbol will very soon be accomplished in fact, in the crucifixion.

For **him** and **himself** one could as easily read 'himself' and 'him' respectively: the difference, which is only in the 'breathing'—αὐτόν or αὑτόν, αὐτῷ or αὑτῷ—would not necessarily be apparent in a MS. written in uncials. And what we are meant to

[1] Νῦν is also used in referring to an event just past in xi. 8; xxi. 10.

[2] See p. 106 (on i. 51).

[3] The clause **if . . . him** is found in the majority of authorities, including A Θ *fam* 13 *vg* and Origen, but is absent from P⁶⁶ ℵ* B D W *vt sin*. The weight of the authorities for omission would be decisive were it not for the fact that the clause echoes the previous sentence, which suggests that at an early stage in the transmission a whole line was accidentally omitted. With a passage of this length, accidental omission seems more likely than accidental repetition. Moreover, there is no discernible motive for its interpolation, and, though strictly redundant, it is appropriate to the oracular style of the FG here.

[4] They could, however, also be taken as 'timeless' aorists; see p. 252 n. 7. The same verb (ἐδοξάσθη) is so taken in xv. 8.

understand is difficult to determine, because the glorification of
Father and Son is reciprocal; cf. i. 14 and xvii. 1, 4, 5.

**(33) 'Children,[1] I am ⟨to be⟩[2] with you ⟨only⟩ a little
longer; you will seek me, and, as I said to the Jews,
"Where I am going you cannot come", ⟨so⟩ for the
present I say to you also.'**

Jesus is beginning to break it to his disciples that he is to die
very soon. He repeats what he has already said **to the Jews**
(cf. vii. 33 f. and viii. 21), but with a significant modification.
Since it is to the Father that he is going (xvi. 5), the Jews cannot
follow Jesus because of their unbelief. The disciples also cannot
follow him **for the present**[3] but they will one day, as xiv. 3
implies. At one period of his ministry Jesus may have expected
that his disciples would in fact die with him,[4] and, if so, he is
now telling them that he is to die alone (cf. xviii. 8).

**(34) 'A new command do I give you, that you should
love[5] one another—that, as I love[6] you, you also should
love one another. (35) By this all will recognise that you
are disciples of mine, if you have love for one another.'**

34. For this **new command** cf. xv. 12, 17, 1 John ii. 8, 10.
Jesus puts into explicit and general terms what he had already
taught parabolically (verse 15). As the parabolic action of the
foot-washing shows, following Christ's example of love can lead
even to death (cf. xv. 13).

In one sense this command is not **new**[7] at all, for it appears in
Lev. xix. 18. But there it is apparently incidental to, and almost
swamped by, a mass of miscellaneous legislation. What makes

---

[1] τεκνία is diminutive in form, but the strict diminutive force is much
weakened in the *Koiné*. The word is not found elsewhere in the FG, but
occurs seven times in 1 John, always in the vocative, as here.

[2] For the use of the present tense in a future sense, cf. vii. 33 f.; xiii. 6, 27;
xiv. 3; xxi. 23.

[3] ἄρτι. See p. 107 n. 3.   [4] See p. 267 (on xi. 16).

[5] On **love** (ἀγάπη and ἀγαπῶ) in the FG see pp. 129 f. (on iii. 16).

[6] The tense of ἠγάπησα is aorist, and if this is given its most usual sense,
referring to a past event, it looks back to the foot-washing (cf. xiii. 1). But
there are other instances of 'timeless' aorists in the FG, cf. x. 18, 25; xv. 6,
and especially 9 and 12, where ἠγάπησα also occurs. See p. 252 n. 7.

[7] The adjective which John uses is καινός, 'fresh', its regular sense in
Revelation, where it is used eight times, cf. especially xxi. 5. Its only other
instance in the FG is in xix. 41, of the tomb in which Jesus was buried,
which was 'brand-new', a different nuance from that here.

it *fresh* is the fact that Jesus chose it as the one necessary and sufficient principle to guide his disciples (cf. Rom. xiii. 8-10).

In the context of the Last Supper, the **new command** to **love one another** must recall the new covenant, or testament, in Christ's blood (cf. 1 Cor. xi. 25), for it too is a kind of testament, given before Christ's death, while **love** as the subject of the **command** recalls the *Agapé*, the 'love-feast' of which the primitive Eucharist was an integral part.

35. It has already been remarked[1] that the FG appears to restrict the scope of Christian love to the circle of Christians. Nothing is said about loving one's enemies, and Matt. v. 46, which makes the point that loving those who love you is nothing remarkable, finds no echo in the FG. By the time that the FG and Epistles were written, the Church had been driven in upon itself. This did not mean, however, that it became indifferent to the world, which watched it not only with hostility (cf. xv. 18) but also with interest (cf. 1 Pet. iii. 15 ff.). It did not forget its mission (and xx. 21 shows that John did not either), but under the circumstances the mutual love of Christians, the *sine qua non* of the Christian life, was also the most effective witness which it could bear to the world of its faithfulness to its master. If Christians do not love one another, they will neither love, nor prove attractive to, anyone else.[2]

(36) Simon Peter said to him, 'Lord, where are you going?'

Peter, nettled perhaps by being put on a par with unbelievers (verse 33), and intrigued by Jesus' enigmatic words, interrupts him to ask for an explanation.

The fact that he puts this question here makes it difficult to understand Jesus' remark at xvi. 5, 'None of you asks me "Where are you going?"'. If, however, xiii. 31–xiv. 31 followed xvi,[3] that would be quite intelligible. This is one of the many indications that this part of the FG has been extensively rearranged. But there is no reason to suppose that the present order is not that intended by the editor.

[1] See p. 129.

[2] The second-century Apologists appreciate this point; cf. Tertullian, *Apologeticus* 39, 'See, they say, how they love one another' (*Vide, inquiunt, ut invicem se diligant*). But they also have the command to love one's enemies.

[3] See the Introduction, p. 4.

Jesus answered, 'Where I am going you cannot follow me now, but you shall follow me afterwards'.

Jesus does not answer Peter's question: he does not say that he is going, through death, to the Father until xvi. 5. Instead he repeats, to Peter individually, what he has already said to them all, adding, however, the explicit promise that Peter will **follow** him **afterwards** (cf. verse 33). This is a reference to Peter's death (cf. xxi. 18 f.), which he cannot yet appreciate.

To **follow** Jesus is the same as being a disciple;[1] it involves obeying him and accepting him as a pattern (verse 15).

(37) Peter said to him, 'Lord, why cannot I follow you at present?[2] I will lay down[3] my life[4] for your sake.'

Unconscious both of the irony in his bringing up the subject of death, and of the arrogance of his claim to be able to do for Jesus what Jesus is in fact to do for him, Peter obviously thinks that he is quite fit to follow Jesus at once. Possibly, if the fight which he tried to provoke (xviii. 10) had not been stopped by Jesus, Peter would, in the heat of the moment, have been as good as his word. But it is only when he has learnt what following Jesus really involves that he will really do as he says, and in a real sense die for Jesus' sake—as a martyr—and, like Jesus, glorify God by his death (xxi. 19). And before that must come the humiliation of his denial of Jesus.

(38) Jesus answered, 'You will lay down your life for my sake? Amen, amen, I say to you,[5] the cock will not crow until you have denied me three times.'

Jesus' question is completely non-committal, but his prediction of his denial exposes Peter's pretensions, and leaves him speechless.

The other three Gospels all record this episode. Mark xiv. 30 f. and Matt. xxvi. 34 f. have the prediction of the denial in words very similar to John's, but follow it with Peter's indignant assertion of his willingness to die *with* Jesus (cf. John xi. 16),

---

[1] See i. 43, p. 101 and the references there.

[2] ἄρτι. See p. 107 n. 3, and cf. verse 33.

[3] θήσω, future of τίθημι, used by Jesus, x. 15 ff. See also on xiii. 4, p. 306. Peter may have meant 'risk' rather than 'lay down'. See pp. 250 f.

[4] ψυχή. See p. 250 n. 3.   [5] On this formula see p. 105 (on i. 51).

and place the whole episode after Jesus and his disciples have
left the supper-room. Luke xxii. 33 f. has the same order and
placing of the two items as John, but his actual words are not
as close to John's as are Mark's and Matthew's. The most probable explanation for these facts seems to be that we have two
independent traditions of this episode rather than that John is
conflating Mark and Luke.

The question of the historical value of John's account of this
episode, and of the supper as a whole is not an easy one to answer.
Many critics think it cannot even be asked. But it involves the
important question of the testimony of the Beloved Disciple.
If it is possible to accept him as a historical and identifiable
person—at least in principle (though we may no longer be in a
position to identify him with certainty)—then John's account
of the supper is entitled to at least as much consideration as
Mark's. But if it is merely a tissue woven of threads taken from
the other Gospels, then the historicity of the Beloved Disciple as
well as the credibility of the narrative must come under grave
suspicion.

The omission of any reference to the institution of the
Eucharist is surprising. John knew of the Eucharist, as the
discourse in vi. 26-58 shows,[1] and his theology is generally
sacramental in character. His silence here is therefore to be
regarded as deliberate, and due neither to ignorance nor to
hostility to sacramentalism. Various explanations have been
given of this. The traditional explanation is that John is writing
a supplement to the other Gospels, and omits what they have
already adequately treated; but this will not do, for John is
substantially independent of the other Gospels, which he seems
to wish to supersede rather than supplement. Another explanation is that, writing as he is a book which he expects non-
Christians to read, he conceals the central Christian mystery
from possible misunderstanding and ridicule. But this does not
prevent him speaking of it in vi. 26-58. So perhaps his real
reason was to emphasise that the most important feature of the
supper was in the words of Jesus. To them the sacrament, important as it is, is subordinate, for it has no independent value
(vi. 63). There may have been some in Asia Minor who already

[1] See pp. 195 f.

held a view of the sacrament as magical in character, its efficacy depending solely on liturgical correctness.[1]

xiv. (1) 'Do not let your heart⟨s⟩[2] be troubled;[3] you believe[4] in God, believe in me as well. (2) In my Father's house are many places to stay in;[5] if there were not, would I have told[6] you that I am going to prepare[7] you a place? (3) And if I go and prepare you a place, ⟨it follows that⟩ I will come[8] back and take you to myself, in order that where I am you also may be. (4) And where I am going you know the way.'[9] (5) Thomas said to him, 'Lord, we do not know where you are going; how do we know the way?'

1. Jesus resumes the thread of his discourse after Peter's interruption, and explains the necessity for his departure, of which he has already spoken, vii. 33; viii. 14, 21; xiii. 33, 36, so that they may face without panic his impending arrest and death. To do this, they must have the same faith in him which they have in God. The unity of Father and Son which this implies (cf. v. 17 ff.; x. 30) is a recurrent theme in this part of the FG (cf. xiv. 7, 9, 11, 20; xvi. 15; xvii. 21-23).

[1] For this explanation of John's silence see E. Lohse, 'Wort und Sakrament im Johannesevangelium', *N.T.S.*, Vol. VII, 1960–61, pp. 110 ff.

[2] Singular in the Greek; English idiom requires the plural.

[3] ταρασσέσθω. On this verb see p. 272. The form of the prohibition implies that they are showing signs of anxiety. Cf. p. 115, n. 4.

[4] This could be Imperative, but the Indicative seems to give the better sense.

[5] μοναί. The only other occurrence of the word in the New Testament is in xiv. 23. It can mean a stopping-place on a journey (Latin *mansio*—hence the AV), but verse 23 suggests that it does not carry any implication of progress or development after death, as has been supposed. In both passages the word takes its meaning from the cognate verb μένω, on the significance of which in the FG see p. 98, on i. 39.

[6] This is often taken as a statement, 'I would have told . . .' If it is so taken, the following ὅτι (**that**) will have to be translated 'because'. The omission of ὅτι by the first hand of P⁶⁶ Θ and the majority of Greek MSS. is an obvious attempt to avoid the absurdity of saying, 'If there were not, I would have told you that I am going to prepare you a place'.

[7] Cf. Matt. xxv. 34, and contrast Matt. xx. 23, in both of which John's verb ἑτοιμάζω is used.

[8] ἔρχομαι; for examples of the present tense with a future sense cf. vii. 33; xiii. 6, 27, 33; xxi. 23 (p. 210 n. 4).

[9] The first hand of P⁶⁶ A D Θ *fam* 1 *fam* 13 *lat syr* have a longer reading '. . . you know, and you know the way', which may well be right—John's style is often diffuse. But if so, the meaning would be different. All that the disciples need to know is the way.

2. Jesus has already spoken of the **Father's house,** in which 'the Son stays for ever', in viii. 34 ff. He now tells them that they, as sons of God by faith (cf. i. 12), will also stay in the **Father's house,** in which there is ample room. The **house** is pictured as a king's palace, with many apartments.[1]

The next sentence has much more point as a question than as a statement. The objection may be made that Jesus has not in fact told his disciples that he is **going to prepare** them a **place,** but it might have been inferred from viii. 35 f. and xii. 26. The question is no more enigmatic than many other of Jesus' utterances in the FG.

3. Hitherto Jesus has only hinted at the possibility of the disciples following him (cf. xii. 26; xiii. 36). Following Jesus is virtually synonymous with being a disciple,[2] and involves following his example (xiii. 15), particularly in mutual love (xiii. 35). This is why the disciples can eventually be with Jesus, whereas the Pharisees cannot (vii. 33 f.; viii. 21; xiii. 33). But their eventual reunion with Jesus will only be accomplished by his return to them—not by their own efforts. The union of the disciples with Christ is the purpose of his mission (cf. xii. 26; xvii. 24). The precise occasion of Jesus' return (now mentioned for the first time) is not specified. It may be on the last day (cf. vi. 39, etc.), but is probably thought of as occurring primarily in the coming of the Paraclete (cf. xiv. 18), since his assistance will enable them to make their discipleship effective.

4. Jesus expects the disciples to **know the way,** for as men who believe in God (xiv. 1) they ought to know that **the way** to God is in the observance of his commandments, of the greatest of which Jesus has just reminded them (xiii. 34).

5. Thomas, more outspoken (though not necessarily more obtuse) than the others, expresses their bewilderment with characteristic bluntness (cf. xi. 16; xx. 25). They are as much at a loss as the Jews had been earlier (cf. vii. 35; viii. 22).

(6) Jesus said to him, 'I am[3] **the way and the truth and the life; no one goes to the Father except through me.**

---

[1] Cf. also the Jerusalem Temple, 1 Kings vi. 5 f. This is also 'God's house', Ps. xlii. 4.   [2] See p. 101 (on i. 43).

[3] See p. 188 n. 7 (on vi. 35) for this formula.

(7) If you know me, you will know my Father also.[1] **At present**[2] **you are getting to know him, and you have seen him.'**

6. Jesus is **the way,** just as he is the door (x. 9), as the sole means of access to the Father; for this cf. Matt. xi. 27 = Luke x. 22; Rom. v. 2; Eph. iii. 12; Heb. x. 20, etc. But to make a journey one needs not only a road, but directions for keeping to it, and the stamina to carry one to its end. As **the truth and the life** Jesus supplies these also. For **the truth** cf. 'full of grace and truth', i. 14;[3] and for **the life** cf. i. 4; vi. 35, 48; xi. 25. Jesus is all-sufficient because he is both God and man.

7. Because of this to **know** Jesus (which they can do as men since he is man) means that they **will know** God (since Jesus *is* God, i. 1, and one with the Father, x. 30). As a statement of fact this fits the context better than the variant reading,[4] which implies a reproach more appropriate to the Jews (cf. viii. 19) than to the disciples, dense as they are. And because they know Jesus, they **are** already **getting to know**[5] the Father, whom they **have seen** (though they do not realise it) in Jesus.

(8) Philip said to him, 'Lord, show us the Father, and satisfy[6] **us'.**

His request is understandable, cf. that of Moses, Exod. xxxiii. 18. Men hanker for the certainty which sight seems to give. But sight is not given us in this life—only faith, cf. 2 Cor. v. 7. And so the Father can only be seen through the Son, as Jesus at once explains. Philip's misunderstanding, like Thomas' above, helps Jesus to make his meaning plain. This is characteristic of the FG, cf. ii. 20; iii. 4; iv. 11; vi. 52, etc.

(9) Jesus said to him, 'Though the time is so long that

---

[1] This represents the text of P⁶⁶ ℵ D, etc.; A B Θ, etc. (with some minor variation) have, 'If you knew me, you would know my Father also'.

[2] ἀπ' ἄρτι should strictly be translated 'from the present, from now on', but in the only other instance of its use in the FG, xiii. 19, it is indistinguishable from ἄρτι, and is so taken here. See p. 107 n. 3 and p. 310 n. 5.

[3] See p. 83 for the meaning of **truth** in the FG.

[4] See note 1, above.

[5] γινώσκετε. The present tense properly has this meaning, as distinct from the perfect, which means 'know'. See also i. 48; ii. 24 f.; iii. 10; vii. 27, 49; viii. 43; x. 14 f., 27, 38; xiii. 12; xiv. 17; xv. 18; xvii. 3, 23; xxi. 17.

[6] Reading ἄρκει, the imperative. ἀρκεῖ is usually read and taken as the impersonal, 'It is sufficient for us', but there is no other clear example of this in the New Testament. In Matt. xxv. 9 there is a subject, unexpressed.

**I have been with you, do you not know me yet,[1] Philip?
He who has seen me has seen the Father; what do you
mean by saying,[2] "Show us the Father"?'**

Philip has already had ample opportunity to realise that to see
the Son is the same as seeing the Father. Indeed, Jesus has
already said as much, xii. 45, and has already claimed that he
and the Father are one, x. 30. But from the context of xii. 45,
and from the precise meaning of the verb $\theta\epsilon\omega\rho\epsilon\omega$[3] ('observe')
used in that verse, one would not necessarily infer what is stated
here. For xii. 44 f. can be understood to mean no more than that
believing in and observing Jesus entail believing in and observing
the Father. But now Jesus goes further than this, and states
that he is himself the fullest revelation of God available to man
(cf. i. 18). He is this simply because he is what he is—the image
of God, as St Paul says (2 Cor. iv. 4), who is otherwise invisible
(cf. Col. i. 15); cf. also Heb. i. 3.[4]

**(10) 'You believe, do you not, that I ⟨am⟩ in the Father
and the Father is in me? The words which I speak to you
I do not speak on my own authority;[5] but the Father staying in me does his works. (11) Believe me[6] that I ⟨am⟩ in
the Father and the Father ⟨is⟩ in me; but if ⟨you do⟩ not
⟨believe me⟩, believe because of the works themselves.'**

Here Jesus twice repeats the claim he has already made in
x. 38, and which he expects Philip to accept. He adds that he
does not make the claim **on** his **own authority** (cf. vii. 17; xii.
49),[7] but on that of the Father, and twice appeals to the evidence
of **his works** (cf. v. 36; x. 25, 37 f.; xv. 24). The relationship of
Father and Son is such that the works, hitherto attributed to
Jesus, can now be called his Father's.

There may seem to be a *non sequitur* in the transition from
words to **works** in verse 10. But both are vehicles of revelation,

---

[1] Literally, 'So long a time am I ($\epsilon\iota\mu\iota$) with you, and do you not know me?'
For this use of the present tense ($\epsilon\iota\mu\iota$) see p. 158 n. 4 (on v. 6).

[2] Literally, 'How do you say?' Cf. vi. 42; viii. 33; xii. 34.

[3] See p. 191 (on vi. 40).

[4] Thus the divinity of Jesus entails his humanity. Both John and the author
of Hebrews stress the humanity of Jesus, precisely because they are so
definite about his divinity.

[5] $\alpha\pi'$ $\epsilon\mu\alpha\nu\tau\upsilon\upsilon$, literally, 'from myself', cf. v. 30; vii. 17, 28; viii. 28, 42; x. 18.

[6] $\pi\iota\sigma\tau\epsilon\upsilon\epsilon\tau\epsilon$ $\mu\upsilon\iota$. For the difference between $\pi\iota\sigma\tau\epsilon\upsilon\omega$ and $\pi\iota\sigma\tau\epsilon\upsilon\omega$ $\epsilon\iota\varsigma$ see p. 120
n. 1.   [7] See the note on this passage, p. 301 n. 8.

and in both Jesus is his Father's agent (cf. viii. 28), while the **works** are in fact accomplished by the **words** of Jesus.

(12) 'Amen, amen, I say to you,[1] ⟨**as for the man**⟩ **who believes in**[2] **me, the works which I do he**[3] **also shall do, and greater than these he shall do, because I am going to the Father.'**

Just as Jesus does his works because he acts only in conformity with his Father's will (cf. iv. 34; v. 19, 30; vi. 38; viii. 29), so his disciples (whom he has already told to follow his example, xiii. 15) will also be able to do works, i.e. miracles, not merely like, but **greater than,** his own; **greater,** not intrinsically (a miracle is a miracle), but in the effect which they produce. The works of Jesus had apparently only a minimal effect. But the apostles were to gather in a great and increasing harvest; cf. v. 20, where Jesus speaks of the Father showing him **greater works** than those he had already done—again, greater in their effect.

The reason why the faithful disciple will be able to do this is **because** Jesus is **going to the Father** (cf. xiii. 3; xiv. 2 f.). For after Jesus' death he will possess the Spirit, which was not available before it (cf. vii. 39). And the coming of the Spirit is to be mentioned in verses 16 f.

(13) 'And whatever you ask in my name, this I will do, in order that the Father may be glorified in the Son. (14) If you ask me[4] **anything in my name,** ⟨**it is**⟩ **I** ⟨**who**⟩[5] **will do it.'**

13. While engaged in their work Jesus' disciples will be able to receive his help in answer to their prayers. To ask **in my name** does not mean to invoke the name of Jesus as a kind of magic spell, but to ask as his representative, while about his business.[6] This is what Jesus himself means when he speaks of himself as having come in his Father's name (v. 43, cf. x. 25), and Acts when it states that the apostles performed their miracles in Jesus' name (iii. 6, 16; iv. 10; xvi. 18).

---

[1] For this formula, see p. 105 (on i. 51).

[2] See the note on verse 11 above.   [3] ἐκεῖνος is emphatic. See p. 85 n.2.

[4] με is omitted by A D and some other authorities. This is an obviously easier reading. Some omit the whole verse, which must have been found puzzling as it stands.   [5] ἐγώ is emphatic.

[6] Thus it is not illogical to ask Jesus 'in his name' (verse 14), if the phrase is interpreted as suggested.

One would suppose, from the comparable passages xv. 16 and
xvi. 23, that it is to the Father that prayer is to be made, even
if it is Jesus who answers it, the purpose of this being **that the
Father may be glorified in,** i.e. by means of, **the Son** (cf.
xiii. 31 f.).

14. So it comes as something of a surprise to find it stated so
emphatically that it is to Jesus that prayer is to be made, and
that it is he who answers it. This is no doubt why some MSS.
omit either **me** or the whole verse.[1] But the contradiction
between this verse and xv. 16 and xvi. 23 is more apparent than
real, since the Father and the Son are effectively one (x. 30), and
the Father gives all things by means of the Son (iii. 35).

In the teaching on prayer attributed to Jesus in the Synoptic
Gospels (cf. Mark xi. 24, Matt. vii. 7-11, Luke xi. 9-13) there
is no hint that prayer is to be made to Jesus, but the practice
must have begun very soon, being a natural inference from the
conviction of his divinity.

**(15) 'If you love me, you will keep[2] my commandments,
(16) and I will ask the Father, and he will give you
another ⟨as your⟩ Champion, to be with you for ever, (17)
⟨namely⟩ the Spirit of truth, which the world cannot
accept, because it does not perceive[3] or recognise[4] him;[5]
you ⟨are to⟩ recognise him, because he ⟨is to⟩ stay with
you and be in you.'**

15. Love involves obedience, which is the criterion of its
reality (cf. verse 21), as **you will keep** implies, assuming, as it
does, a fact, which the imperative 'keep' does not do so clearly.[6]
In the same way Jesus obeys his Father and stays in his love,
and makes this relationship the pattern of that of his disciples to
himself (xv. 10). It is the disciples' obedience to Jesus' commandments, particularly to that to love one another (xiii. 34),

---

[1] See note 4, p. 324 above.

[2] The future is read only by BL *eg*, but fits best with the following **I will
ask**: P⁶⁶ ℵ have the aorist subjunctive (which only involves the change of one
letter); with this one must include this clause in the protasis—clumsy, though
not impossible. A D W Θ and the majority have the aorist imperative (again
with the change of one letter only).   [3] θεωρεῖ; see p. 191 n. 2 (on vi. 40).

[4] Literally 'get to know'. See on verse 7.

[5] αὐτό, though neuter to agree with πνεῦμα, must be translated **him**, here
and elsewhere in xiv-xvi when it refers to the Spirit, which is represented in
them as personal.   [6] See p. 320 n. 4.

which makes possible the continuance of their relationship with him after his departure. He now explains how this will be.

16. He **will ask the Father, and he will give** them **another** as their **Champion,** in whose person he himself is coming to them (verses 18-21). At xv. 26 and xvi. 7 Jesus says that he himself will send him, but the contradiction is only verbal.[1]

The word translated **Champion** is Παράκλητος, familiar in transliteration as Paraclete.[2] It is found in the New Testament only here and in xiv. 26; xv. 26; xvi. 7, and 1 John ii. 1. In 1 John it refers to Christ, but in the FG to the Spirit.[3] AV and RV translate it 'Advocate' in 1 John, 'Comforter' in the FG; RSV has 'advocate' in 1 John and 'Counselor' (an American synonym for 'advocate') in the FG. This reluctance to translate the word in these two documents by the same English word is due to a recognition that the functions of Christ and Paraclete are not identical, but is nevertheless misleading.

Etymologically, Παράκλητος is a passive verbal adjective derived from παρακαλέω, which means literally 'call to one's side'. Thus it corresponds exactly to the Latin *advocatus*, whence the translation 'Advocate' in 1 John ii. 1. But though the Latin *advocatus* pleaded another man's case for him in a Roman court, a Greek παράκλητος did not. A man before a Greek court had to plead his own case, but he brought his friends along as παράκλητοι to influence the court by their moral support and testimony to his value as a citizen. In the Empire the Roman custom may have prevailed, but it is perhaps significant that Tertullus (Acts xxiv. 1), who acts as an *advocatus*, is called an 'orator' (ῥήτωρ, not παράκλητος). Now one can call another to one's side either for him to give help, or to give help to him, and it is the latter which is the origin of the usual sense of the verb in the New Testament; cf. 'encourage, comfort'

---

[1] See the comment on verse 14 above.

[2] There is a case for using this in the translation, as RV^mg suggests in both 1 John and the FG, in the same way that Logos is used in this translation. But the cases are not exactly parallel. Logos has no precise equivalent in English, having a range of meaning found in no English noun, but this is not the case with Παράκλητος.

[3] Christ can be taken as being by implication himself a Παράκλητος in the FG only if the translation 'another Champion' is adopted. Why this should not be adopted is discussed below.

(e.g. 2 Cor. i. 4), and 'exhort' (e.g. Rom. xii. 1). This appears to have caused παράκλητος to have lost its passive sense at times, and to mean 'comforter'. Thus in Job xvi. 2, where the LXX has παρακλήτορες, the regular active noun for 'comforters', Aquila and Theodotion used παράκλητοι. After all, a man to whom one appeals for help does often turn out to be a comforter. This is the origin of the translation 'Comforter' in the FG.

But the verb παρακαλέω does not occur anywhere in the Johannine literature, and so one should perhaps be chary of using it to establish the meaning of the adjective. Παράκλητος is, however, found in Philo, and transliterated in the Talmud and Targums, precisely in the general sense of one who pleads for another; this may include, but is not confined to, an advocate in the strict forensic sense. So in spite of the fact that the Greek Fathers support the translation 'Comforter' in the FG, one should prefer a word which conveys the general sense of one who supports another by his presence and his words. This **Champion** does, and it is equally applicable in the FG and 1 John.[1]

He is, like Christ, **another**[2] representative of God, and, again like Christ, given or sent by God. But he has a distinctive function as **Champion,** helper and intercessor, which the FG does not ascribe to Christ.[3] By this distinction between these two personal representatives of the Father the FG set the Church on the way to the formulation of the doctrine of the Trinity.[4] Thus the translation **another ⟨as your⟩ Champion** is preferable to the linguistically possible (and perhaps more natural) **another Champion.**

John of course, the author of the Epistles, but only the editor of the FG, did regard Christ as our intercessor (1 John ii. 1),

[1] See LS⁹, Bauer⁵, *T.W.z.N.T.*, s.v., and Strack–Billerbeck, II, pp. 560 ff.; also E. K. Lee, *The Religious Thought of St John* (1950), pp. 213 ff., as well as the commentaries, particularly Bultmann's, pp. 437 ff.

[2] ἄλλος. This means 'another example of the same kind', as contrasted with ἕτερος, 'an example of another kind'; cf. the distinction in Gal. i. 6 f.

[3] Nor do the Synoptic Gospels. It is, however, a natural inference from Christ's function as sole intermediary between God and man ascribed to him, e.g., in Matt. xi. 27.

[4] 'The equality of substance between the Father and the Spirit is inferred from that between the Father and Christ.

and it is possible that he adopted the word Παράκλητος from
the source which he used for the FG, being no more worried
than St Paul was in attributing the same function to both Christ
and the Spirit (cf. Rom. viii. 26 and 34).

He is **to be**[1] **with** the disciples **for ever,** which Jesus, being
and remaining incarnate, cannot be. This is why it is expedient
for Jesus to leave them (xvi. 7), and why he can only come to
them in the Holy Spirit (verse 18).

17. He is **the Spirit of truth,**[2] i.e. who puts men in touch
with **truth** (cf. xv. 26; xvi. 13; 1 John iv. 6[3]), **which the world,**[4]
i.e. sinful mankind, **cannot accept, because it does not
perceive or recognise him,** any more than it does Christ or
the Father (cf. i. 10; v. 43; xv. 21; xvi. 3). This does not mean,
as the Gnostics held, that some men are by nature incapable of
receiving the Spirit, but only that they cannot do so unless they
abandon their hostility to God.

With the disciples, however, the case is different. They
recognise Christ (cf. x. 14), and Christ is to stay[5] in them (cf.
xv. 4 ff.), and be in them (cf. xvii. 23). In all these respects the
Spirit is comparable with Christ, except for the slight change
from 'stay *in*' to **stay with** (but cf. xiv. 23, 'we will make our
place to stay[6] *with* him ').

Barrett takes the tense of the three verbs in these last two
clauses as the simple present, reflecting the time at which John
wrote (p. 387). For at the time when Jesus is represented as
speaking the Spirit was not available, since Jesus was not yet
glorified (vii. 39).[7] But there are several examples in the FG of
present tenses with a future reference,[8] and these verbs are so
understood here.

[1] Black, pp. 58 f., regards this as an example of mistranslation from
Aramaic, ἵνα being used where ὅς ('who') is correct, and cites two Old
Latin MSS. in support. But Latin support may be illusory since *qui* ('who')
can have a final sense and so may be a loose translation of ἵνα.

[2] On the meaning of ἀλήθεια see p. 83.

[3] Cf. on xvi. 13 for the parallel with the language of the Dead Sea Scrolls.

[4] On the meaning of κόσμος see p. 76, on i. 9.

[5] On the significance of μένειν in the FG see p. 98 (on i. 38).

[6] μονή (derived from μένειν). See p. 320 n. 5.

[7] This is presumably why the majority of the authorities for the text here
(with the exception of B D* W *fam* 1 and a few others) read ἔσται ('shall be')
for ἐστίν ('is'), and why the Latin Vulgate takes μένει ('stays') as the future
μενεῖ.   [8] See p. 210 n. 4.

It is sometimes argued that the passages in which the Paraclete is mentioned are interpolations in the FG, a view which Barrett rightly regards as improbable. [1] But one cannot help but be struck by the fact that in each of these passages the references to the Spirit can be deleted without damage to their contexts, in which the only modification necessary is that the neuters have to be changed to masculines; [2] this suggests that they were put in by John when he edited his source. This hypothesis would account for two otherwise puzzling phenomena.

The first is that the masculine pronoun 'he' (ἐκεῖνος) is twice used after clauses introduced by the neuter relative pronoun (xiv. 26; xv. 26). This resumptive use of ἐκεῖνος is fairly frequent in the FG, [3] but these are the only two passages where it occurs in which a noun in apposition to the subject occurs between the subject and the resumptive pronoun.

The second is that it is only in the 'Paraclete-passages' that the Spirit is represented as personal. Though this could be explained if these passages were interpolations, it involves less disturbance in their contexts if only the parentheses identifying the Paraclete with the Spirit are regarded as interpolated.

The author of John's source appears to have refrained deliberately from the ambiguous half-personification of the Spirit which is characteristic of the rest of the NT, and, recognising that the activity of the Spirit is as personal as that of Christ, used a masculine noun for what later orthodoxy called the Third Person of the Trinity. [4] John, his editor, obscured the clarity of his distinction by his well-meant interpolations, designed to harmonise his source with his own more conventional theology.

Whence then did the author derive the term Paraclete? One answer is that it is an equivalent of *Jawar*, the 'Helper', one of the many semi-divine figures in the Mandaean mythology. [5] It

[1] Barrett, pp. 75 f. Bultmann also regards the *Paraclete* as belonging to John's source (p. 437).

[2] The passages interpolated are—'the Spirit of truth', xiv. 17 (the following ὅ ... αὐτό ... αὐτό being changed from ὅν ... αὐτόν ... αὐτόν); 'the Holy Spirit', xiv. 26 (the following ὅ being changed from ὅν); 'the Spirit of truth which comes out from the Father', xv. 26; and 'the Spirit of truth', xvi. 13. [3] For examples of this usage see p. 85, n. 2

[4] See also above, p. 327.

[5] See Bauer, p. 185, and Bultmann, pp. 437, 439 f.

may well be, however, that *Jawar* is in fact modelled on the
Paraclete, since the origin and originality of Mandaean mythology are still matters of dispute; but even if the FG were here
dependent on Mandaeism, all that it has borrowed is the name.
But sources nearer to hand than Mandaeism could have provided it. The word Paraclete was familiar in Judaism, though
apparently it was not actually used of the Spirit. But the Spirit
in Mark xiii. 11 plays the part of a Paraclete, and it only remained for the FG to make the combination of these two elements. The idea of a second intermediary between God and
man besides the Logos is not alien to Judaism, for Sophia has
this rôle in the Wisdom Literature. The degree of originality
shown in the conception of the Paraclete is no greater than that
in the identification of Christ with the Logos—and in the hunt
for origins one must not discount the possibility of originality
altogether.

**(18) 'I will not leave you bereaved; I am coming to
you.'**

Jesus returns to the theme of his coming to the disciples,
first mentioned in xiv. 3. He has meanwhile promised them that
they will have the Paraclete with them and in them. It is therefore presumably in virtue of this that they are not to be left
bereaved: the coming of Christ is in the coming of the Paraclete, and the mutual indwelling of Christ and Paraclete which
this implies is no more difficult to comprehend than that of
Christ and Father emphasised in this chapter (cf. xiv. 10, 20).

Barrett (p. 387) sees here a reference to the resurrection,
which certainly seems to be intended in the following verses.
But the two are not mutually exclusive, since the resurrection
and the coming of the Spirit (to say nothing of the Second
Coming) are closely linked together as moments in the same
eschatological drama of Christ's vindication and triumph. Moreover the resurrection did not mean Christ's return for ever.
Without the coming of the Paraclete the disciples would have
again been **bereaved** after the Ascension.

(19) 'A little longer and the world is to perceive¹ me no

---

¹ This verb, θεωρέω (see p. 191, n. 2) is strictly only appropriate to the
disciples, for though the world saw Jesus in his incarnate life, it was as blind
to his significance as it was to the Paraclete (verse 17). See also on xv. 24.

longer, but you are to perceive me, that I am living; and you also shall live. (20) On that day you shall know that I am in my Father and you ⟨are⟩ in me, and I ⟨am⟩ in you. (21) He who has my commandments and keeps them, he¹ is ⟨the one⟩ who loves me; and he who loves me will be loved by my Father, and I will love him and will make myself manifest to him.'

19. The first two verbs in the verse are present, but are to be taken as having a future reference, like those in verse 17.² Jesus is soon to die, and to disappear from the notice of mankind in general. But the disciples will be assured that he is alive when they see him risen from the dead, and thereby they will be assured of their own resurrection.

The translation of this sentence is uncertain. It is usually taken as either '. . . perceive me, because I am living and you shall live' or '. . . perceive me; because I am living you also shall live'; the word ὅτι can mean both 'that' and 'because'. There is, however, an exact parallel in construction to the alternative adopted above in ix. 8, which is, translated literally, 'who perceived him previously, that he was a beggar'. The same verb (θεωρέω) is used, with the subject of the subordinate clause as the object of the main verb, as it is here.³

20. **On that day,**⁴ i.e. the day of Christ's resurrection, they will realise that they have been taken into the divine society of the Father and the Son of which he had spoken in xiv. 10 (cf. xvii. 21-23). They will therefore live because they will share the divine life.

21. This is possible only for those who possess the divine quality of love, and show it by their obedience to Christ (cf. xiv. 15). Only they too will be capable of seeing the risen Christ.

---

¹ ἐκεῖνος. See p. 85, n. 2.

² See p. 210, n. 4.

³ Compare θεωροῦντες αὐτὸν . . . ὅτι προσαίτης ἦν (ix. 8) and θεωρεῖτέ με, ὅτι ἐγὼ ζῶ (xiv. 19).

⁴ ἐν ἐκείνῃ τῇ ἡμέρᾳ, cf. xvi. 23, 26. Mark xiii. 32 illustrates the eschatological significance of 'that day', which in the FG is also called 'the last day', cf. vi. 39, 40, 44. We are in fact drawn beyond the resurrection of Christ into the whole eschatological drama of which it is the first and decisive moment.

(22) Judas (not Iscariot) said to him, 'Lord, how is it[1] that ⟨it is⟩ to us ⟨only⟩ that you are about to make yourself manifest, and not to the world?'[2]

A **Judas** 'of James' appears in the lists of Apostles in Luke vi. 16 and Acts i. 13.[3] The natural assumption is that this means 'son', rather than 'brother, of James'.[4] It is unlikely, though not impossible, that he is the **Judas** named along with James and Joses among Jesus' 'brothers' in Mark vi. 3.[5]

His question recalls the challenge made to Jesus by his brothers in vii. 4 to show himself to the world, and reveals the same assumption about Jesus' Messiahship. If he is Messiah, he must surely want to vindicate himself before his enemies. Though the question betrays a failure to understand Jesus, it is natural enough, and it is unnecessary to suppose that it reflects the anxiety which was felt in the Church at the delay of the Second Coming, of which 2 Pet. iii. 4 is evidence.

(23) Jesus answered and said to him, 'If anyone loves me, he will keep my word, and my Father will love him, and we will come to him and make our home with him. (24) He who does not love me does not keep my words; and the word which you hear is not mine but that of my Father who sent me.'

23. Without directly answering Judas' question, Jesus repeats verse 21 with two changes. That of 'commandments' to **word** only widens the meaning of the sentence; Jesus' **word** is his message as a whole. The other modifies the meaning. He will be made manifest to the disciples because he and his Father **will make** their **home with** them; **home** is literally, 'place to stay in', used in the plural in xiv. 2.[6] Thus there will be realised

---

[1] BFBS[2] reads Κύριε, καὶ τί γέγονεν (καί expressing surprise), though καί is read only by ℵ W *fam* 1 *fam* 13 and a few other MSS. The reading may be due to a 'correction' of an accidental repetition of K̄Ē (Κύριε), viz. K̄ĒKĒ to K̄ĒKAI. See Barrett, p. 389. In ix. 36, which Barrett quotes as a parallel, καὶ τίς ἐστιν, κύριε, this could not have happened.

[2] There is great emphasis on **us** and **world**, which in the Greek are the first and last words in the clause.

[3] He replaces Thaddaios in Mark's list, Lebbaios in Matthew's, but there is no means of telling if he is the same person as either (or both) of them.

[4] In Luke vi. 14 Andrew is described explicitly as *brother* of Simon.

[5] John vii. 5 says that Jesus' brothers did not believe in him.

[6] See p. 320 n. 5.

the old prophetic hope of God dwelling among men (of which Rev. xxi. 3 announces the fulfilment), not just in a restored Temple (which is all that Ezek. xxxvii. 26 f. seems to suggest), but in terms of Isa. lvii. 15. For this the incarnation was the necessary preliminary (i. 14).

In this the answer to Judas is implicit. Jesus' Messiahship does not mean that he will force himself upon his enemies. His kingship is not anything to do with this world (xviii. 36), and does not involve using the world's methods.

24. Jesus then repeats in a negative form what he has just said in 23. It is the world which does not love him—it hates him (vii. 7; xv. 18, 24)—and so is incapable of having him made manifest to it.

Then Jesus again reminds the disciples of his dependence on his Father, cf. vii. 16; xii. 49.

(25) 'I have spoken these things to you while staying with you; (26) but the Champion, the Holy Spirit which the Father will send in my name, is the one who[1] **will teach you all things and remind you of all the things which I said to you.'**

25. The teaching which Jesus has given during his ministry on earth 26. is to be continued by the Paraclete, sent in his **name** (i.e. as his representative, cf. xiv. 14) who will guarantee that it is remembered and understood, but will not add any new revelation of his own (cf. xvi. 13 f.), since that given in Jesus is complete (cf. xiv. 9).

(27) '⟨It is⟩ peace ⟨that⟩ I am leaving you, my peace ⟨that⟩ I am giving you; ⟨it is⟩ not as the world gives ⟨peace that⟩ I am giving ⟨it⟩ you.'

Jesus is leaving his disciples, but not destitute (cf. xiv. 18). They have a legacy—his **peace** (cf. xvi. 33), based on the confidence they should have in his continuing protection. That **peace** is emphasised is shown by its position as first word in both clauses. It recalls the Hebrew greeting *shalom* (cf. xx. 19), but has much more than its conventional meaning. To give **peace** is a royal, and *a fortiori* a divine, prerogative (cf. Num. vi. 26, Ps. cxlvii. 14, Isa. xxvi. 12; xlv. 7, etc.), which Jesus bequeaths as God's Messiah, the Prince of Peace (Isa. ix. 6, cf.

---

[1] ἐκεῖνος. See p. 85 n. 2.

Ezek. xxxvii. 26). He gives it by the sacrifice of himself, now imminent (cf. Rom. v. 1, Eph. ii. 14 ff.), **not as the world gives** it, by coercion.[1]

'**Do not let your heart⟨s⟩ be troubled or cowardly.**'

Jesus again rebukes their manifest alarm (cf. verse 1[2]), and now adds that it is cowardice in face of the enemy soon to come upon them (verse 30).

(28) 'You heard me tell you, "I am going ⟨away⟩ and coming ⟨back⟩ to you". If you loved me, you would have rejoiced that I am going to the Father, because the Father is greater than I.'

The disciples had his assurance of his return (verse 3); their alarm is a sign of lack of love, for love involves faith (verses 21, 23). They should have **rejoiced . . . because the Father is greater than** Jesus, and so his departure to him does not mean any loss of power for Jesus, but rather the reverse. What is apparently a disaster is all part of the divine plan.

The statement that **the Father is greater than** the Son, torn from its context, became the subject of fierce controversy in the later phases of the Arian controversy.[3] But the dogmatic issues then raised are beyond the horizon of the FG, for which the inferiority of the Son is due to the fact that he is his Father's agent, fulfilling his will, and subordinating his own to it.

(29) 'And now I have told you before it happens, so that, when it does happen, you may believe.'

As when he foretold Judas' treachery (xiii. 19), Jesus' foreknowledge of events is a further ground for confidence on the part of the disciples (cf. also xvi. 4).

(30) 'I will no longer talk much with you, for the ruler of the world is coming; and, ⟨though⟩[4] he has no claim upon me,[5] (31) ⟨it is⟩ so that the world may know that I

---

[1] Cf. the bitter comment which Tacitus attributes to a British chieftain, 'Where they make a desert, they call it peace' (*Agricola* 30, ad fin.).

[2] See the notes, *ad loc.*

[3] See M. F. Wiles, *The Spiritual Gospel* (1960), pp. 122-125.

[4] This insertion is necessary to clarify the connexion of the ideas in this passage: **and** connects the previous clause and verse 31, with **he has no claim upon me** as a kind of parenthesis.

[5] Literally, 'He has nothing in me', corresponding to a Hebrew idiom (see Strack–Billerbeck, II, p. 563.)

love the Father, and as the Father commanded me, ⟨that⟩ I act like this.[1] Arise, let us be going from here.'

30. The time for words is past, and that for action has arrived. The enemy is at hand—**the ruler of the world**, i.e. Satan.[2] Jesus is ready to submit to his usurped power, in spite of the fact that **he has no claim upon** him, because he will thereby break his power (cf. xii. 31). 31. By this submission he will show the world his love for the Father by acting in obedience to his will. Thus at last he complies with the challenge of his brothers to show himself to the world (vii. 4), now that his time has come (cf. vii. 6).

He then bids his disciples rise and follow him against the enemy,[3] cf. Mark xiv. 42.[4]

These two verses plainly lead us to expect the account of their departure to follow at once. But it is deferred until xviii. 1, and instead we have two further chapters of discourse and the prayer of xvii. It seems reasonable to suppose that xiii. 31–xiv. 31 should follow xvi. 33, but for the fact that the present order seems clearly intentional, since the teaching on the Paraclete, for example, develops more naturally than it would if xiv followed xvi. xiii. 31–xiv. 31 and xv, xvi have much in common, and it is possible that they were originally alternatives, both of which were included in John's source, and the order of which he reversed when he edited his source.

xv. (1) 'I am[5] the real[6] vine, and my Father is the cultivator. (2) He takes away every branch in me which does not bear fruit, and prunes[7] every ⟨branch⟩ which

---

[1] οὕτως. See p. 140, n. 2.   [2] See pp. 296 f. (on xii. 31).

[3] The verb used for 'go' here (ἄγω) is particularly used of military operations. See LS[9], s.v. II. 2.

[4] The verbal parallel here between the FG and Mark (and others in their Passion narratives) is explained by S. I. Buse, 'St John and the Marcan Passion Narrative', *N.T.S.*, Vol. IV, 1957–58, pp. 215–219, as due to the use by John and Mark of a common source, that designated B by Vincent Taylor, *The Gospel according to St Mark* (1952), (Appendix J), to which, according to Vincent Taylor, Mark xiv. 32–42 belongs (p. 658).

[5] See p. 188, n. 7 on sayings in this form.

[6] ἀληθινή. On the adjectives ἀληθινός and ἀληθής see p. 75, n. 3.

[7] Note the play on the words for **takes away** (αἴρει) and **prunes** (literally, 'cleans' (καθαίρει)). This is unlikely therefore to be a translation from Aramaic.

does bear fruit,[1] so that it may bear more fruit. (3) Already you are clean through the word which I have spoken to you; (4) stay in me, and I ⟨shall stay⟩ in you. As the branch cannot bear fruit of its own accord, if it does not stay in the vine, so you cannot either if you do not stay in me. (5) I am the vine, you the branches. The one who stays in me (and I in him) is the one who bears much fruit, because apart from me you cannot do anything. (6) If anyone does not stay in me, he is thrown[2] out like the branch ⟨cut from the vine⟩ and withers,[2] and they collect them and throw them into the fire, and they burn.'

The abrupt opening of this chapter, in which it resembles chapter x, is a further indication that the original order has been disturbed—as is also probably the case in x.[3] If xv originally followed immediately after the account of the Last Supper, and if moreover the original account of the Last Supper included an account of the institution of the Eucharist, now utilised in the discourse of chapter vi,[4] then the reference here to **the real vine** would have followed closely on that to the bread of life, and its eucharistic reference (hardly appreciable in its present position) would have been unmistakable.

The analogy of the vine and its branches recalls that of the body and its members in Rom. xii. 5 ff., 1 Cor. xii. 12 ff.; this also may have a eucharistic significance, as 1 Cor. x. 17, 'We are one bread, one body', suggests.[5] The elimination of the account of the institution of the Eucharist from the Last Supper[6] may have been one of the motives for the transposition of xiii. 31–xiv. 31 and xv, xvi.

A further resemblance to x is in the allegorical character of the discourse. In x, however, the parable which is the basis for the allegorical exposition is preserved within it, and John specifically calls it a 'parable' ($\pi\alpha\rho o\iota\mu\iota\alpha$, x. 6), whereas here it would be difficult to reconstruct an actual parable out of the general

[1] These two clauses are literally, 'Every branch . . . he takes it away, and every ⟨one⟩ . . . he prunes it'.
[2] The tense of these two verbs is aorist ($\dot{\epsilon}\beta\lambda\dot{\eta}\theta\eta$ and $\dot{\epsilon}\xi\eta\rho\dot{\alpha}\nu\theta\eta$). See p. 252, n. 7.   [3] See p. 246.   [4] See p. 195, n. 7.
[5] There is nothing to suggest that John was at all influenced by Paul's analogy.   [6] For a discussion of John's motive for doing this see pp. 319 f.

comments on viticulture which are all that we have. This suggests that another basis for it has to be found, and this is probably in the Old Testament texts which speak of Israel as a vine or vineyard which God has planted (e.g. Ps. lxxx. 8 ff., Isa. v. 1 ff.; xxvii. 2 ff., Jer. ii. 21;[1] xii. 10 ff., Ezek. xvii. 5 ff., etc.).

1. Thus **I am the real vine** means in effect that it was about Jesus that Jeremiah and the other prophets were speaking; cf. the reference to Isaiah, xii. 41.

For the idea of God as **cultivator** cf. Matt. xv. 13, which shows that the imagery of the present allegory is not alien to the Synoptic tradition, or to Jesus himself, who uses it in a different way in Mark xii. 1 ff.

Thus Christ, **the real vine,** is the real Israel,[2] and 2. the branches of the vine are his disciples, as verse 5 states explicitly, and so the real Israelites.[3] Bearing **fruit** is a familiar image for living the Christian life, cf. Rom. vii. 4 f., Col. i. 6, 10, found also in the interpretation of the parable of the Sower, Mark iv. 14-20. There is a general resemblance to Paul's allegory of the olive in Rom. xi. 17 ff.; John is, however, not dependent on Paul, though he has had a similar experience of what Paul calls being 'in Christ'.

3. That the disciples are **clean**[4] recalls xiii. 10, and that they are so **through** Christ's **word** is because keeping Jesus' **word** is the prerequisite for the Father and the Son staying in him (xiv. 23). 4. This is a reciprocal relationship, which alone makes living the Christian life possible. Hence the command **stay in me,** which at last explains the significance of the earlier mentions of Christ staying in the disciples.[5]

The precise meaning of the words **and I in you** following the command **stay in me** is not so obvious here as it is in verse 5, where it follows a participle, equivalent to a relative clause. Had 4 followed 5, one would be inclined to suppose that they were a thoughtless addition in 4. They could mean **stay in me** ⟨as⟩ **I** ⟨in fact stay⟩ **in you,** but **and I** ⟨shall stay⟩ **in you** is more consistent with xiv. 23, which implies that obedience on the

---

[1] In the LXX here John's adjective **real** is also applied to the **vine,** but in the sense of 'genuine'.

[2] See p. 105.   [3] See p. 103.

[4] καθαροί, the adjective cognate to the verb καθαίρει in the previous verse. See p. 335 n. 7 above.   [5] See p. 98.

part of Christ's disciples is a condition of his staying in them, while 6. one can hardly suppose John to mean that Christ continues to stay in one who **does not stay in** him.

This warning to the apostate recalls the interpretation of the parable of the Tares in Matt. xiii. 37-42, but in the FG there is no reference to the end of the age or to the angel-reapers. John demythologises the apocalyptic imagery which he uses.[1]

(7) 'If you stay in me and my words stay in you, ask[2] whatever you wish, and it will happen for you. (8) ⟨It is⟩ in this ⟨that⟩ my Father is glorified,[3] ⟨namely⟩ in your bearing[4] much fruit and becoming[5] my disciples. (9) As the Father loves[6] me, I also love[6] you; stay in my love. (10) If you keep my commandments, you will stay in my love, just as I have kept my Father's commandments and stay in his love.'

In this passage, as elsewhere in xv and xvi, there is much repetition, and some variations, of themes already found, particularly in xiii. 31–xiv. 31.

7. Thus **my words stay in you** is another way of saying 'you keep my words' (cf. xiv. 15, 21, 23, 24), adopted possibly for the sake of the allusion to the fact that Christ himself is the Logos, even though **words** here is ῥήματα.[7]

The mutual indwelling of the disciples and Christ (cf. xiv. 23; xv. 3, 5) has the further consequence that their prayers (cf. xiv. 13) will be answered, for if the Father listens to (and answers) his prayers (cf. xi. 42), he will answer the disciples' prayers, which are in fact Christ's. They can **ask whatever** they **wish,** for they will not ask anything Christ would not ask.

8. The fruitfulness of their lives as Christ's disciples also

[1] See Introduction, pp. 13 f. and, on iii. 17, p. 130.

[2] αἰτήσασθε, read by B *fam* 13 *vt eg*, and corroborated by the meaningless αἰτήσασθαι (infinitive) of P66 A D, is preferable to the future indicative αἰτήσεσθε of ℵ Θ *vg*, etc.

[3] Another 'timeless' aorist, see p. 252, n. 7 and p. 315, n. 4.

[4] ἵνα . . . . φέρητε. For other examples of this use of ἵνα cf. iv. 34; viii. 56; xv. 13, and see p. 150, n. 5.

[5] γένησθε (aorist subjunctive), read by P66 (?) B D Θ and a few other authorities: the future indicative γενήσεσθε, read by ℵ A and the majority of authorities, gives a less smooth construction, and should perhaps be preferred for that reason.

[6] ἠγάπησεν and ἠγάπησα may be 'timeless' aorists; see n. 3 above.

[7] See the Introduction, p. 4.

glorifies **the Father,** as does Christ by his obedience to him (cf. xiii. 31; xiv. 13).

9. The continuance of this depends on the disciples keeping the bond of mutual love unbroken, as verse 10 explains. Love entails obedience (cf. xiv. 15, 21, 23).

For the love of the Father for Christ cf. iii. 35; x. 17; xvii. 23, 24, 26, and of Christ for the disciples xiii. 34; xv. 12. In these texts the tenses vary between the present, emphasising what is the case at the moment of speaking, in iii. 35; x. 17, and the aorist here and in the other texts. The aorist emphasises what is timelessly true,[1] cf. 'before the foundation of the world' in xvii. 24. In xiii. 34 and xv. 12, the aorists may refer to a past event (the washing of the disciples' feet), but also may be timeless.[2]

10. For Christ's keeping of his Father's commandments, cf. viii. 28 f.; xiv. 31, where 'I love the Father' corresponds to **I stay in his love** here.

(11) 'I have spoken these things to you[3] so that my joy may be in you and your joy may be fulfilled. (12) This is my commandment, that[4] you love one another, as I love[5] you. (13) No one can show[6] greater love than ⟨by⟩ this, by laying down[7] his life for his friends. (14) You are my friends, if you do what I command you. (15) I am no longer calling you slaves, because a slave does not know what his Lord is doing; but I have called you friends, because all that I have heard from my Father I have made known to you.'[8]

11. The mention of **joy** looks back to xiv. 28, 'If you loved me, you would rejoice'. The purpose of this whole discourse is

---

[1] See p. 252, n. 7.   [2] See p. 316, n. 6 (on xiii. 34).

[3] ταῦτα λελάληκα ὑμῖν echoes xiv. 25.

[4] ἵνα. This is another example of the extension of the use of ἵνα (see p. 150, n. 5), this time to express a command. See Moule, pp. 144 f.

[5] ἠγάπησα (aorist) as in xiii. 34 (see p. 316 n. 6); xv. 9.

[6] Literally, 'No one has . . .'

[7] ἵνα τις . . . θῇ. On this use of ἵνα see p. 150 n. 5.

[8] In this sentence **I have called** (εἴρηκα) is perfect, **I have heard** (ἤκουσα) and **I have made known** (ἐγνώρισα) are aorists. English idiom, however, requires the translation of the aorists by the English perfect, which does not coincide with the Greek. See Moulton, *Prolegomena*, pp. 135 f. They could also be taken as 'timeless' aorists (see p. 252, n. 7), but Jesus here seems to have in mind his whole ministry, now drawing to its end.

to reassure the disciples in face of the imminent death of Jesus. The disciples should echo the **joy** which the Baptist expressed at his coming (iii. 29), for his departure is but the prelude to his return (xiv. 3). This theme is developed more fully in xvi. 20 ff. The reason for Jesus' **joy** is his obedience to his Father and the love which subsists between them (verse 10).

Likewise the disciples' **joy** will **be fulfilled,** i.e. come to perfection, 12. from their obedience to Jesus' **commandment** to **love one another as** he loves them (cf. xiii. 34), and 13. from their realisation of the extent of that love.

He is about to give them the supreme proof of his love, **by laying down his life for** them.[1] If it is taken as a general principle, **No one . . . friends** is simply not true, as the example of Christ himself shows, who laid down his life for his enemies (cf. Rom. v. 8). But it is perfectly natural in its context here. Love is essentially reciprocal, so that God's love for the world (iii. 16) can only be effective if it evokes the response of love. And it is to those who have made this response, his **friends,**[2] that Jesus is talking.[3]

14. Friendship with Christ, like love for him, involves obeying his commandments (cf. xiv. 15 f.).

15. In this respect therefore there is no difference between friends and **slaves,**[4] and if Jesus **no longer** regards his disciples as **slaves,** it is not because he does not expect their obedience. A slave obeys from fear, and is left in ignorance of his lord's plans: 'Their's not to reason why, Their's but to do and die.' But Jesus throughout his ministry[5] has taken his disciples completely into his confidence, but has remained their lord (cf. xiii. 13). Many masters did in fact take their slaves into their confidence, and make friends of them, without necessarily altering their legal status. To modern man, this may be surprising, but it was not in the strongly authoritarian and patri-

---

[1] See pp. 250 f. (on x. 11) and 318 (on xiii. 37 f.).

[2] φίλοι is cognate with the verb φιλέω, which the FG uses as well as ἀγαπάω for 'love'. On the difference in meaning between them see p. 130 n. 2.

[3] On the meaning and scope of love in the FG see pp. 129 f. (on iii. 16) and p. 317 (on xiii. 35).

[4] Or between the slave and the son of the house. See pp. 227 f. on viii. 34 ff.

[5] This is implied if the tense of the verbs **I have heard** and **I have made known** is given the normal aorist force as referring to past events.

archal ancient world, Jewish, Hellenistic, and Roman alike. St
Paul's habitual description of himself as the slave of Jesus
Christ would not have seemed to anyone in the first century
A.D. incompatible with the FG here. In the same way the
principal officers of the Hellenistic kings, who adopted the
absolutism of their native oriental predecessors, were called the
King's Friends (cf. 1 Macc. ii. 18, etc.), but remained his
subjects.

That Jesus has **made known all that** he has **heard** contrasts oddly with the promise of further revelations to come in
xvi. 12 f. But the utterances of the Paraclete are to be understood (in the light of xvi. 14 f.) not as new revelations, but as
new insights into revelations already given.[1]

**(16) '⟨It was⟩ not you ⟨who⟩ chose me, but I ⟨who⟩
chose you,[2] and appointed[3] you to go and bear fruit, fruit
that should be permanent, so that the Father may give
you whatever you ask in my name.[4] (17) I am giving you
these commandments, so that you may love one another.'**

16. Disciples commonly chose their own teachers for themselves,[5] but Jesus claims emphatically that he has chosen his (cf.
vi. 70; xiii. 18). Some of them may indeed have thought otherwise (e.g. the two who approached him, i. 37). But even this
apparent initiative is really due to God (cf. vi. 37). The only
freedom open to a disciple is that of accepting or refusing Jesus'
choice.[6]

---

[1] This problem would not arise if the verbs were taken as 'timeless'
aorists. See previous note and p. 339 n. 8.

[2] This translation is designed to reproduce the emphasis in the Greek on
the pronouns **you** and **I**.

[3] ἔθηκα, aorist of τίθημι, literally 'place'. It is followed by a series of clauses
introduced by ἵνα, literally 'so that you should go and bear fruit, and that
your fruit should stay (μένῃ)'. There is no other example of this use of τίθημι
governing ἵνα in the New Testament. Its closest parallel is with the quotation
of Isa. xlix. 6 in Acts xiii. 47, where τέθεικά σε is followed by the infinitive
with the article (τοῦ εἶναί σε) expressing purpose: cf. the examples of the
infinitive following τίθημι in classical Greek cited in LS⁹ s.v. B.I.4. The process by which in modern Greek ἵνα has wholly replaced the infinitive was well
under way in the New Testament. It is hard to see why Barrett (pp. 398 f.)
says 'This use of τιθέναι is not Greek'.

[4] Literally, 'whatever you ask the Father in my name, he may give you'.

[5] Cf. the Rabbinic precept in *Pirke Aboth* i. 6, 'Get thyself a teacher'
(Strack–Billerbeck, II, p. 565).

[6] See pp. 200, 310 f. on the problem of predestination in the FG.

Jesus' choice of them lays on them the obligation **to go and bear fruit.** Here **to go and** may be an example of an Aramaic idiom in which **go** has no sense of motion, but intensifies the meaning of the following verb.[1] If so, the incongruousness of branches of a vine literally going to bear fruit is avoided. But more probably we should take **to go** in its literal sense, as a reference to the apostolic mission (cf. iv. 38; xiii. 20; xvii. 18; xx. 21); the **fruit** then refers to its results rather than to the allegory of the vine. For the permanence of this **fruit** cf. iv. 36, 'fruit to eternal life', from the metaphor of the harvest.

Finally, they are again assured that their prayers will be answered, cf. xiv. 13; xv. 7, for they will be acting **in Jesus' name,** i.e. as his representatives.[2]

17. Cf. xiii. 34; xv. 12. But the plural **these** makes it difficult to regard this verse simply as an echo of 12[3] (in which 'commandment' is singular). It should probably be understood as meaning that all that Jesus has commanded them is designed to teach them the lesson of mutual love, which they will realise in carrying out his commands.

(18) 'If the world hates you, recognise that it has hated me first in comparison with you. (19) If you were of the world, the world would love what belongs to it;[4] but because you are not of the world, but I chose you out of the world, for this reason the world hates you.'

18. We pass from the mutual love of the disciples to the hatred which the world[5] feels for them (cf. 1 John iii. 13). This hatred is a fact[6] to be recognised: **recognise**[7] (imperative) could be taken as indicative, but less appropriately; the disciples do not yet really understand what is happening. Jesus gives a similar warning according to the Synoptic Gospels, cf. Matt. x. 22, Mark xiii. 13. Jesus here explains that the world's

---

[1] Cf. xii. 11, and see p. 286 n. 2.   [2] See p. 324.

[3] In both verses there is a ἵνα clause. In 12 it expresses the content of the command, but here its proper sense of purpose (as in xv. 11; xvi. 1, 4). See Bauer, p. 193.

[4] τὸ ἴδιον, literally, 'its own', cf. i. 11.   [5] ὁ κόσμος. See p. 76.

[6] As the form of the conditional clause (εἰ + the present indicative) shows (contrast verse 19).   [7] γινώσκετε, cf. xiv. 7 and see p. 322 n. 5.

hatred for the disciples is due to its settled attitude[1] of hatred to himself (cf. vii. 7), which is to be explained by iii. 20. The rather cumbrous translation **first in comparison with you** is designed to bring out the absolute priority of Jesus to his disciples, as to John the Baptist (cf. i. 15,[2] where the same phrase occurs).

19. The phrase **of the world** (ἐκ τοῦ κόσμου) here means 'belonging to the world, on its side'.[3] Naturally the world **loves**[4] its adherents, cf. Matt. v. 46 f.

(20) 'Remember the word which I said to you, " The slave is not greater than his lord ". If they persecuted me, they will persecute you also; if they kept my word, they will keep yours also. (21) But all these things they will do to you on my account,[5] because they do not know him who sent me.'

20. Cf. xiii. 16, and Matt. x. 24. The two clauses **If they persecuted me . . .** and **if they kept my word . . .** may be taken to imply that while some of the Jews **persecuted** Jesus, others in fact **kept** his **word**[6] (cf. i. 11 f.). But if so, the second class has been forgotten by the next verse, for 21. **all these things** can only refer to the hatred and persecution which the disciples are to incur. Those who **do not know him who sent** Jesus can hardly be said to **keep** the disciples' **word.** So the second clause must be taken as a pure hypothesis, a condition which is not expected to be fulfilled, and is only mentioned ironically: cf. the way in which the conversation of Jesus with 'the Jews who believed in him' (viii. 31 ff.) ends in their complete rejection of him.

For the world's ignorance of God, cf. viii. 19; xvi. 3.

(22) 'If I had not come and spoken to them, they would

---

[1] As the perfect tense (μεμίσηκεν) implies (contrast **hates** in the conditional clause). This may, however, be an instance of the perfect with a present sense, as in i. 15 (κέκραγεν). See p. 83, n. 2.

[2] See p. 83, n. 3.

[3] See p. 232, n. 3.

[4] φιλέω not ἀγαπάω (as in verse 17). On the difference between them see p. 130, n. 2.

[5] διὰ τὸ ὄνομά μου, literally, 'because of my name', as in Matt. x. 22, Mark xiii. 13. The phrase does not occur elsewhere in the FG, but εἰς τὸ ὄνομα αὐτοῦ is used virtually as a periphrasis for 'in him' in i. 12.

[6] So Barrett, p. 401.

not be sinners;[1] but as it is[2] they have no excuse[3] for their sin. (23) He who hates me hates my Father also. (24) If I had not done among them works which no one else has done, they would not be sinners;[1] but as it is[2] they have both seen ⟨them⟩ and have hated both me and my Father. (25) But ⟨this happened⟩ to fulfil the saying[4] written in their law, "They hated me for nothing".[5]

22. Since sin is the deliberate refusal to obey a known command men cannot strictly be called sinners unless and until a command has been given (cf. Rom. v. 13). By his coming Jesus has shown mankind in its true colours, but 23. the response to this revelation has been not penitence, but hatred (cf. iii. 19 f.) for Jesus and so for his Father also. A man's attitude to Jesus determines his attitude to God (cf. v. 23; xii. 44 f.; xiii. 20; xiv. 7).

24. Jesus' revelation was not only by words, but also by his **works**, which are in fact his Father's (cf. x. 37 f.; xiv. 10), and sufficient to convince any reasonable person (cf. Matt. xi. 21-24). For the evidential value of Jesus' **works** in the FG cf. v. 36; x. 25, 38; xiv. 11.

It seems better to take **me and my Father** as the object of **have hated,** and to supply ⟨**them**⟩ (i.e. the works) as the object of **have seen,** since the Jews **have** not in fact **seen** the **Father,** since they had refused to believe in Jesus, through whom alone he could be seen (cf. xiv. 9).

The perfect tense of **have seen** again emphasises the settled attitude of the Jews to Jesus (cf. verse 18).

25. The fulfilment of specific prophecies is also noted at xii. 38; xiii. 18; xix. 24, 36, with the same formula as here,[6]

[1] ἁμαρτίαν οὐκ εἴχοσαν, literally, 'they did not have sin', cf. ix. 41. But since Jesus *had* come, they *were* sinners, and one would expect the particle ἄν (as in ix. 41) to make this clear. Its omission, however, may be meant to bring out that they were not in fact sinners until Christ came, though now that he has come, they are. For a similar construction, see xix. 11.

[2] νῦν, cf. viii. 40, and p. 230, n. 1.

[3] πρόφασις, found here only in the FG. Its basic meaning is 'motive or cause alleged', whether truly (as here) or not. Elsewhere in the New Testament it means 'pretence' (Matt. xxiii. 14 = Mark xii. 40 = Luke xx. 47, Acts xxvii. 30, Phil. i. 18) or 'disguise' (1 Thess. ii. 5).

[4] Literally, 'so that the saying might be fulfilled'.

[5] δωρεάν, literally, 'as a gift' (cf. Matt. x. 8, Rom. iii. 24, etc.), cf. Latin *gratis*.   [6] See pp. 299 f.

which is also used for the fulfilment of Scripture when no actual
text is quoted, at xvii. 12, and where the words are those of
Jesus, at xviii. 9, 32. **They hated me for nothing** occurs in
both Ps. xxxv. 19 and Ps. lxix. 4. The point of the quotation is
to show that the Jews' gratuitous hatred of Jesus is shown up
by their own Scripture (cf. v. 45 ff.), and thereby proved to be
within the providence of God. For **law** used of the Scripture
as a whole cf. x. 34; xii. 34; with **their law** cf. viii. 17; x. 34.[1]

(**26**) '**When the Champion comes whom I will send you
from the Father, the Spirit of truth which comes out from
the Father, ⟨it is⟩ he[2] ⟨who⟩ will bear witness about me:
(27) and you also are to bear witness,[3] because you have
been[4] with me from the beginning.**'

26. For **Champion** cf. xiv. 16,[5] where it is not Jesus but the
Father who sends him, though there is hardly any significance
in the change:[6] for his identification with **the Spirit of truth**
and the suggestion that **the Spirit of truth** etc. is an interpolation cf. xiv. 17:[7] for the masculine **he** (ἐκεῖνος), referring to
the Spirit (πνεῦμα, neuter) cf. xiv. 26.[8]

Here a further function is ascribed to the **Champion,** that of
witness, an important theme in the FG,[9] which comes in here
because in the previous verses Jesus has been warning the
disciples of the hostile reception which they will get from the
world when they **bear** their **witness** to Jesus before it.

This function is also ascribed to **the Spirit** in the Synoptic
Gospels, cf. Matt. x. 20, Mark xiii. 11. It is worth noting that
in this passage of the FG there are a number of parallels with
Matt. x and Mark xiii: in 18 f. with Matt. x. 22, Mark xiii. 13
('You will be hated by all men . . .'), in 21 with the same verses
('. . . on my account'); and in 20 with Matt. x. 24. There is little
if any evidence elsewhere in the FG of direct borrowing from
Matthew, and the most likely explanation of these parallels is

---

[1] See pp. 220, 259 f.   [2] ἐκεῖνος is emphatic; see p. 85 n. 2.
[3] μαρτυρεῖτε is present. For the present tense used with a future sense see
p. 210 n. 4. Lagrange, however, takes it as a genuine present—they are
already qualified to witness, but have not yet begun to do so (p. 414).
[4] ἐστέ is present. It is used in Greek for an action continuous up to the
present, for which English uses the perfect: cf. v. 6; xiv. 9.
[5] See pp. 326 ff.   [6] See p. 326.   [7] See p. 329.
[8] See p. 329 also.   [9] See p. 75.

that Matt. x uses some 'Q' sayings for the mission charge to the disciples, which are in part also incorporated into Mark xiii, and that the author of the FG in his turn applies them here. They probably had no indication of their historical context in the hypothetical source 'Q', and there is no means of telling which was their original context.

27. The witness of the apostles is complementary to that of the Spirit, cf. Acts v. 32. It is their essential function to bear witness to the facts of Christ's life, death, and especially resurrection, and to do this they had to be eyewitnesses of them, cf. the qualifications required of the man who was to replace Judas, Acts i. 21 f. The Spirit gives them the power to bear witness (cf. Luke xxiv. 49, Acts i. 8), inspires their utterance (cf. Acts vii. 55; xiii. 9), and controls their movements (cf. Acts xiii. 2; xvi. 6 f.; xix. 21).

xvi. (1) 'I have spoken these things to you so that[1] you should not be made to fall away. (2) They will exclude you from the synagogue; indeed,[2] the time[3] is coming when[4] every one who kills you will think that he is offering service to God. (3) And they will do these things[5] because they have not known the Father or me. (4) But I have spoken these things to you so that,[1] when their[6] time[3] comes, you may remember that I told you about them.'

These things refers back to the hatred of the world and the activity of the Spirit described in xv. 18-27; Jesus warns his disciples of what is to come **so that** in future adversity they

---

[1] See p. 342, n. 3.

[2] ἀλλ'; used here 'to introduce an additional point in an emphatic way', B.-D. § 448 (6). Cf. Turner, p. 330.   [3] ὥρα; see p. 107, n. 2.

[4] For the construction see B.-D. § 382 (1), Turner, p. 321. Cf. also Black, pp. 59-61, who argues that, though ἵνα may be due to mistranslation of the Aramaic particle d^e, which should have been taken in a temporal sense, it is also possible that the Greek word is used loosely here, like the English 'that'.

[5] ταῦτα ποιήσουσιν; ὑμῖν, 'to you', is inserted by א D *fam* 1 *fam* 13 565, a number of Old Latin MSS., some MSS. of the Vulgate, *hl sah boh ac²*, which have probably been influenced by the frequent appearance of the second person plural personal pronoun in the context.

[6] αὐτῶν, omitted by א* D *fam* 1 565 *a d ff² sin sah boh^{pt} ac²*; a second αὐτῶν in the verse two words later is omitted by א^c D *fam* 13 *lat sin sah boh^{pt} ac²*. It is simplest to suppose that both were originally included, the omissions being due to carelessness.

may remember what he has told them and **not be made to
fall away.** Cf. xiii. 19; xiv. 29; xv. 11. The experience of the
post-resurrection Church has inevitably influenced these discourses as Jesus addresses his followers through the mouth of
a Christian prophet,[1] though this does not mean that John loses
all sense of history (see further below, on verse 4b), or that these
sayings must always be interpreted solely in the light of circumstances at the end of the first century.

The verb translated **be made to fall away** (σκανδαλισθῆτε)
is found also at vi. 61 but does not appear elsewhere in the
Johannine literature, though the cognate noun σκάνδαλον is
found at 1 John ii. 10 and Rev. ii. 14. Both here and at vi. 61
apostasy is in view.

They will exclude you from the synagogue renders a
phrase which includes one word (ἀποσυνάγωγος) found also at
ix. 22 and xii. 42, but nowhere else in the NT. See pp. 242
and 301 for these passages, in which the word is used in a
different phrase which purports to describe conditions during
Jesus' ministry. The word does not appear in the LXX, and is
apparently not found in profane writers.[2] It is usually assumed
that what is described cannot have taken place before the last
quarter of the first century, when a determined attempt was
made to exclude Jewish Christians from the synagogue. Cf.
especially the Birkath ha-Minim (an insertion into the liturgy
designed to make it impossible for Christians to participate in
Jewish public worship[3]); it is commonly argued that the FG,
written at the end of the first century or beginning of the
second, reflects here conditions that obtained long after the
death of Jesus.[4] But while this is doubtless true, the Synoptic

---

[1] See p. 16 above, and cf. also A. R. Johnson, *The One and the Many
in the Israelite Conception of God* (1942) for a discussion of the idea of 'extension' of personality in Hebrew thought.

[2] LS⁹, s.v., refers to the FG only.

[3] 'May the Nazarenes and heretics (Minim) be suddenly destroyed . . .'
For the Birkath ha-Minim see C. K. Barrett, *The New Testament Background*
(1956), p. 167, no. 169.

[4] Cf., e.g., G. D. Kilpatrick, *The Origins of the Gospel according to St
Matthew* (1946), pp. 109-115, K. L. Carroll, 'The Fourth Gospel and the
Exclusion of Christians from the Synagogues', *Bulletin of the John Rylands
Library*, Vol. XL, 1957-58, pp. 19-32, and W. Schrage in *T.W.z.N.T.*, Vol.
VII, pp. 845-850.

Gospels also contain predictions of persecution and of death for the faith (cf., e.g., Mark xiii. 9, 12 f., Matt. v. 10; x. 17 f., 21 f.; xxiv. 9, Luke xii. 4, 11; xxi. 12, 16 f.) and it would have required little exercise of the imagination for Jesus to have foreseen that his followers would be persecuted by his enemies after his death. Although the final breach between Church and synagogue is probably to be dated after the fall of Jerusalem in A.D. 70, relations before this were by no means cordial; cf., e.g., Acts xviii. 5 ff. for Paul's secession from the synagogue at Corinth, and Josephus, *Antiquities*, XX. 9. 1 and Eusebius, *H.E.*, II. 23 for the martyrdom of James the Lord's brother in A.D. 62. While prophecy must be relevant for the situation in which it is delivered, on occasion material may be re-worked or re-presented in a fresh setting in which it acquires added significance.[1] This may have happened here, though Luke vi. 22a, 'Blessed are you when men hate you, and when they exclude you', also seems to hold the prospect of excommunication from the synagogue before the disciples; 'the prospect of such exclusion was before Christians of Jewish origin early enough, at least, to have entered into the common tradition behind both Luke and John'.[2]

The time for the disciples to suffer lies still in the future; cf. p. 110 and n. 2 for this word in the FG. **Their time** is the hour when the persecutors seem to be triumphant; cf. Luke xxii. 53b, 'this is your hour, and the power of darkness'. The disciples' enemies **will think that** they are **offering service to God;** they will be sincere in their opposition to what they regard as unspeakable blasphemy, though there is a sad irony in the fact that their **service to God** is expressed in this way. The word **service** ($\lambda \alpha \tau \rho \epsilon i \alpha$) conveys also the idea of worship; cf. the way in which in English a church 'service' is so named.

[1] Cf. P. R. Ackroyd, 'The Vitality of the Word of God in the Old Testament', *Annual of the Swedish Theological Institute*, Vol. I, 1962, pp. 7-23.

[2] C. H. Dodd, *Historical Tradition in the Fourth Gospel* (1963), p. 410. Dodd argues further that 'it is fair to say that there is nothing to suggest that the tradition which the Fourth Evangelist followed for predictions of the future of the disciples was formed in any environment but that of a Jewish-Christian community, absorbed in the task of witness before their fellow-Jews, and dreading, next to martyrdom, exclusion from the commonwealth of Israel' (*ibid.*, p. 413).

The cause of their hostility is that **they have not known the Father or me.** See the note on knowledge at xvii. 3. A parallel has sometimes been seen in the references to knowledge which appear in the Dead Sea Scrolls, but at Qumran the knowledge of God is knowing the knowledge which comes from God rather than knowing God, as in the FG.[1] For failure to know Christ or the Father, cf. i. 10; viii. 55; xvii. 25; this involves an inadequate apprehension of the true nature and activity of the Father and of Jesus, coupled with an inability to obey God's will.[2]

'I did not tell you these things from the beginning, because I was with you. (5) But now I am going to him who sent me, yet none of you asks me, "Where are you going?" (6) But because I have spoken these things to you, sorrow has filled your heart⟨s⟩.[3]'

I did not tell you these things from the beginning, because I was with you is an indication of the Church's apprehension of the earthly ministry of Jesus as an historical event which can be placed in a definite temporal setting and which is followed by a significantly different pattern of existence after Jesus has returned to the Father and the Paraclete has come. This outlook can be seen throughout the whole section. It is of course true that the FG's portrait of Jesus is coloured by the experience of the Church, but here there seems to be an authentic reminiscence of a moment of transition (cf. p. 215, on vii. 39, and xiv. 25 f.), accompanied by **sorrow** for the disciples, who, stupefied by the turn events are taking, do not ask Jesus where he is going. According to the present order of the FG, Peter and Thomas have already questioned Jesus on this point (xiii. 36; xiv. 5); it is simplest to suppose that two alternative accounts of Jesus' teaching at the Last Supper have both been included (see p. 335), this verse belonging to one of them and xiii. 36 and xiv. 5 to the other. As told in the

---

[1] H. M. Teeple, 'Qumran and the Origin of the Fourth Gospel', *Novum Testamentum*, Vol. IV, 1960, p. 15.

[2] Cf. Dodd, *Interpretation*, pp. 156-159.

[3] Cf. p. 320 n. 2 and Turner, p. 23: 'Contrary to normal Greek and Latin practice, the NT sometimes follows the Aram. and Heb. preference for a distributive sing.' The idiom is also found with this word at xii. 40; xiv. 1, 27; xvi. 22.

primitive church these verses try to recapture the moment when
the disciples were deprived of the physical presence of their
Master and present it as the beginning of the new life of the
Church (see on verses 20 ff. below).

For the sending of Jesus by the Father, cf. p. 129 n. 1; Jesus
will now **go** to him in death (cf., e.g., vii. 33; xiii. 33 and the
notes *in loc.*).

**(7) 'Nevertheless I tell you the truth, it is in your
interest that I go away. For if I do not go away, the
Champion** [1] **will not come to you; but if I go, I will send
him to you. (8) And when he comes he will convict the
world of sin, and of righteousness, and of judgement; (9)
of sin, because they do not believe in me; (10) of righteousness, because I am going to the Father, and you will
perceive me no longer; (11) of judgement, because the
ruler of this world is judged.'**

For the sending of the Spirit cf. xiv. 16, 26; xv. 26. The
Spirit could only be given after Jesus' death (vii. 39), but is to
remain with the disciples for ever (xiv. 16) and will teach them
things which they cannot grasp before the resurrection (xvi. 12).
As a result, a richer experience awaits the disciples, and **it is
in** their **interest** that Jesus goes away. A knowledge of Jesus
when he was on the earth is inferior to the possession of the
indwelling Spirit. Here, as at xv. 26, it is Jesus who sends
the Spirit, not the Father, as at xiv. 16, 26; cf. pp. 326, 345
above.

On **the world** in the FG, see p. 76. Cf. xv. 26 f. for the
testimony which the Spirit, together with the disciples, will
bear to Jesus; the more forceful verb 'to **convict**' (ἐλέγχειν)
used here is also found in the FG at iii. 20 (where the light
would expose the deeds of the evil man for what they are) and
viii. 46 (where Jesus asks who convicts him of sin).[2] Parallels in
the papyri have been cited for the meaning 'find guilty', while
an inscription gives the sense 'prosecute'; [3] as Barrett justly says,
'It is the activity of a judge and prosecuting counsel in one. The
Spirit . . . places the world in the position which it will occupy

---

[1] See above, pp. 326 f., for this translation of Παράκλητος.
[2] It is also found at Rev. iii. 19, where it means 'to punish'.
[3] Moulton and Milligan s.v.

at the last judgement.'[1] It has also been urged that the word
carries the connotation of educative discipline;[2] followed by the
preposition περί, as here, it means to convict or convince someone about something.[3] **Sin, righteousness** and **judgement**
are to be connected with the activity of the Spirit mounting an
offensive against **the world** through the Church, which alone
is able to receive him (cf. xiv. 17). They are also to be understood in the light of the imagery of the law-court, which controls the interpretation of verses 8-11.[4]

The subordinate clauses in verses 9-11 are introduced by ὅτι,
which can either be translated 'in that' or **because:**[5] it is perhaps more likely that the reasons for the world's conviction of
sin, righteousness and **judgement** are being given than that
these terms are being defined. **The world** is convicted **of sin
because** it failed to believe in Jesus;[6] the **sin** involved is
thus theological rather than moral in content, and this aspect
of the Spirit's work is a continuation of Jesus' ministry (cf. ix.
39-41; xv. 22, 24 and the notes *in loc.*).

If these verses set forth the themes of the apostolic preaching,
the **righteousness** is Jesus' own righteousness, vindicated by
his resurrection and ascension;[7] this interpretation is found in
sin, which reads 'his righteousness'. But the **world** can hardly
be convicted of **righteousness** in the same way as of **sin,** and
although the passage can be paraphrased in a number of different ways the legal overtones of the language in this section have
suggested that **righteousness** (δικαιοσύνη), found here only
in the FG, may signify 'justification' or 'acquittal'.[8] Although
this sense would not be appropriate in any of the other passages
in the Johannine writings where the word occurs (1 John ii. 29;
iii. 7, 10, Rev. xix. 11; xxii. 11), it is not impossible for a usage
which is normally considered Pauline to appear outside the
Pauline corpus, and the writer of the FG could know of the
word being used in this way from a number of possible sources

---

[1] Barrett, p. 76.   [2] F. Büchsel, *T.W.z.N.T.*, Vol. II, s.v. ἐλέγχω.
[3] Bauer[5], s.v.2.
[4] Cf. W. H. P. Hatch, 'The Meaning of John XVI, 8-11', *The Harvard
Theological Review*, Vol. XIV, 1921, pp. 103-105.
[5] Cf. Moule, p. 147.   [6] For belief in Jesus cf. p. 120, n. 1.
[7] So, e.g., E. C. Hoskyns, *op. cit.*, pp. 484 f.
[8] W. H. P. Hatch, *art. cit.*, p. 105.

—for example, his study of the Old Testament.[1] A parallel can be found in the Dead Sea Scrolls,[2] and the Pauline corpus also uses the word of moral uprightness,[3] showing that the word can be used in different ways in the same body of writings. If this is so, verse 10 refers to those who come to belief in Jesus, who are acquitted **because** of the new conditions which follow his departure from the earth.[4] The **judgement** is then the condemnation which is the alternative to acquittal and is based on the fact that **the ruler of this world is judged** already (cf. xii. 31; xiv. 30, and the notes *in locc.*; also xvi. 33, as the world can virtually be identified with its ruler, cf. 1 John v. 19. See further Luke x. 18). Thus the Spirit continues Jesus' work, which was directed towards the salvation of mankind, but which inevitably carried judgement with it (cf. iii. 16 ff.; xii. 47 f.). It would follow that more than the demonstration of the truth of certain propositions is involved; this is a picture of the Church's evangelistic work in progress, drawn as graphically as the description of Jesus' earthly ministry earlier in the gospel.

(12) 'I have still many things to tell you, but you cannot bear them at present.[5] (13) But when he who is the Spirit of truth comes, he will guide you into all the truth;[6]

[1] C. H. Dodd, *The Epistle of Paul to the Romans* (1932), pp. 9 ff. and C. K. Barrett, *A Commentary on the Epistle to the Romans* (1957), pp. 29 f. relate this idea in Paul's thought to his study of the Old Testament. It is not necessary to suppose with Hatch, *art. cit.*, that the author of the FG was familiar with Paul's use of δικαιοσύνη to indicate the sinner's acquittal, though he is right to claim that the doctrine has a different twist in its Johannine setting.

[2] Cf. M. Black, *The Scrolls and Christian Origins* (1961), pp. 125 ff., for the appearance of the 'Pauline' usage in the Dead Sea Scrolls; here too the thought draws on Old Testament sources.   [3] Cf. Bauer[5] s.v.

[4] This is not a reference to the advocacy of Christ in heaven, as W. H. P. Hatch argues (*art. cit.*); 1 John ii. 1 is no true parallel to what is described here, and seems to refer to sin committed by members of the Christian community. Cf. with the argument in the text the comment of Apollinarius, as summarised by M. F. Wiles, *op. cit.*, p. 150, n. 7: 'The Spirit will convict the world of δικαιοσύνη after Christ's ascension, because our justification is rooted in the ascension whereby σὰρξ ἐξ ἡμῶν καὶ εἶδος ἀνθρώπινον are on the throne.'   [5] ἄρτι; see p. 107, n. 3.

[6] εἰς τὴν ἀλήθειαν πᾶσαν, read by A B 054 *a e f q r*[1] and (with inversion of τὴν ἀλήθειαν and πᾶσαν) by *fam* 13; ἐν τῇ ἀληθείᾳ πάσῃ is read by ℵ D W *fam* 1 *b d ff*[2] *sin pesh hl* and (with inversion of τῇ ἀληθείᾳ and πάσῃ) by Θ and is preferred by Barrett as having better attestation (p. 407), though he does not account for the variant with εἰς. He adds, 'The difference in meaning

for he will not speak on his own authority,[1] but will speak whatever he shall hear[2] and will disclose to you the things that are to come. (14) He will glorify me, for he will take what is mine[3] and disclose it to you. (15) All that the Father has is mine; that is why I said, "He takes what is mine[3] and will disclose it to you."[4]'

12. The disciples are not yet ready to receive further teaching from Jesus (cf. xiii. 7), 13. but they will be instructed by the Spirit after Jesus has returned to the Father. With **he will guide you into all the truth**, cf. Philo, *Life of Moses* ii. 265, which speaks of a divine spirit guiding (τὸ ποδηγετοῦν) the mind to the truth; parallels have also been noted in the Hermetic Literature,[5] but the source of this quite natural expression is probably to be found in the Old Testament. Cf. especially Ps. xxv (xxiv). 5, 'lead me in thy truth' (LXX ὁδήγησόν με ἐπὶ τὴν ἀλήθειάν σου) and Ps. cxliii (cxlii). 10, 'let thy good spirit lead me' (LXX τὸ πνεῦμά σου τὸ ἀγαθὸν ὁδηγήσει με) and Isa. lxiii. 14 LXX. Note further that Jesus is 'the way' (ἡ ὁδός, xiv. 6) and see Rev. vii. 17, Acts viii. 31.

The Spirit of truth (τὸ Πνεῦμα τῆς ἀληθείας) is a term found also at xiv. 17 and xv. 26. At 1 John iv. 6 the spirit of truth is

between the two readings is slight, but whereas εἰς τ. ἀλ. suggests that, under the Spirit's guidance, the disciples will come to know all truth, ἐν τ. ἀλ. suggests guidance in the whole sphere of truth' (*ibid.*); the reading with ἐν could easily be due to the influence of the LXX, in which ὁδηγέω is frequently followed by ἐν, but also results in the removal from the text of a thought which could have appeared theologically dangerous.

[1] ἀφ' ἑαυτοῦ, literally 'from himself'; cf. p. 205, n. 7.

[2] ἀκούσει, read by B D W Θ; the present ἀκούει, read by ℵ L 33, is less well attested and is probably due to the dogmatic preconceptions of a later age, which thought in terms of the eternal relations of the Persons of the Trinity. John thinks rather of the future activity of the Spirit (Lagrange, p. 422).

[3] ἐκ τοῦ ἐμοῦ. It is highly probable that this idiom has a Semitic origin; cf. Black, p. 251.

[4] The omission of verse 15 by P⁶⁶ and ℵ* is probably an accident due to the fact that its last three words are identical with the conclusion of the preceding verse. 'He takes what is mine . . .' (introduced by ὅτι in Greek) could equally well be taken as indirect speech ('I said that he takes . . .'). This is not an exact quotation since the tense of **takes** is present here but future in verse 14; however, it is doubtful whether the change is significant (Barrett, p. 409).

[5] For details see the references in Bauer⁵ s.v. ὁδηγέω and Dodd, *Interpretation*, p. 223.

contrasted with the spirit of error (τὸ πνεῦμα τῆς πλάνης) and
1 John v. 7 states that 'the Spirit is the truth'. It is often argued
that this usage has its background in the language of the *Manual
of Discipline* iii. 13–iv. 26,[1] where reference is made to 'the
spirits of truth and of wickedness' (*ruhoth ha'emeth weha'awel*).
This is of course not to claim that **the Spirit of truth** is a concept borrowed in its entirety from the Qumran sect; in the FG
Jesus sends the Spirit (xv. 26) and it is to Jesus that the Spirit
will bear witness (*ibid.*). Compare also the following parallels in
the *Testaments of the Twelve Patriarchs*: 'The inclination of the
good man is not in the power of the deceit of the spirit of Beliar
(ἐν χειρὶ πλάνης πνεύματος Βελίαρ), for the angel of peace
guideth (ὁδηγεῖ) his soul', *Test. Benj.*, VI. 1; 'two spirits wait
upon man—the spirit of truth and the spirit of deceit (τὸ τῆς
ἀληθείας καὶ τὸ τῆς πλάνης). . . . And the spirit of truth testifieth (μαρτυρεῖ) all things, and accuseth (κατηγορεῖ) all', *Test.
Judah*, XX. 1, 5.[2] The Johannine vocabulary comes out of a
milieu in which such terminology is current coin, but cannot be
pinned down more closely than this. It is, however, interesting
to note that **the Spirit of truth** bears witness (μαρτυρήσει, xv.
26) and guides the disciples (ὁδηγήσει, xvi. 13[3]), both verbs
being used in the quotations from the *Testaments of the Twelve
Patriarchs* given above (though there 'the angel of peace' once
replaces the spirit of truth as subject). 1 John iv. 6 provides the
closest parallel to this non-canonical literature, but in the FG
the world cannot receive **the Spirit of truth** (xiv. 17) just as in
the *Manual of Discipline* there is inveterate hostility between
'the generations of truth' and 'the generations of wickedness',

[1] Cf., e.g., W. F. Albright, *art. cit.*, pp. 168 f. Translations of this passage
may be found in P. Wernberg-Møller, *The Manual of Discipline* (1957),
pp. 25 ff., M. Black, *op. cit.*, pp. 131 ff., and G. Vermès, *The Dead Sea Scrolls
in English* (1962), pp. 75-78.

[2] The translations are those of R. H. Charles, *The Testaments of the
Twelve Patriarchs* (1908); cf. R. H. Charles, *The Greek Versions of the
Testaments of the Twelve Patriarchs* (1908), and note the variant reading at
Test. Judah, XX. 5, involving the omission of 'testifieth all things and'.
Barrett claims that the passage cited from the *Testament of Judah* is not
relevant since 'the "spirits" seem to be the good and evil "inclinations"'
(p. 386), but the evidence from the *Manual of Discipline* perhaps suggests
that these references cannot be discounted so easily.

[3] διηγήσεται, supported by some Old Latin MSS., the Vulgate, Eusebius,
and Cyril of Jerusalem, seems to be a deliberate 'improvement' of the text.

the latter being those who abhor the truth (cf. especially iii. 23 f.; iv. 17 f., 24). In the *Manual of Discipline* the spirit of truth illuminates the mind, though its primary function in so doing is to produce right behaviour (iv. 2-6); in the FG **the Spirit of truth** has a didactic function (xvi. 13). In the FG the Spirit comes to aid the disciples (cf. xiv. 16, 18, and the notes *in loc.*), and in the *Manual of Discipline*, iii. 24 f., iv. 21 the spirit is given to help in the conflict with darkness and to cleanse from evil deeds. Thus, despite the differences, there are sufficient parallels between the immediate contexts in which the phrase **Spirit of truth** is found in the FG and the appearance of the same or related expressions in non-canonical literature for it to be likely that the Johannine term is a development from the usage of sectarian Judaism.

The function of the Spirit is to **guide** the disciples **into all the truth;**[1] that is to say, he will quicken their understanding about Jesus, who is the truth (xiv. 6) and who came to reveal what was true (i. 14, 17; viii. 31 f., 40, 45 f.), and will continue the work which Jesus had begun. There is no question here of completely fresh revelations (cf. xiv. 26 and the note *in loc.*); **he will take what is mine and disclose it to you** may be illustrated by the comments at ii. 22; xii. 16. The authority of the Spirit lies behind the theological development which is expressed in the FG—or so John would have argued. With the disclosure of **the things that are to come** (τὰ ἐρχόμενα), cf. the citation from the *Preaching of Peter* in Clement of Alexandria, *Stromateis*, VI. 6, where the apostolic preaching is said to have included 'showing clearly what would take place (τὰ μέλλοντα)', so that 'they who heard and believed should be saved; and that those who believed not, after having heard' should have no excuse.[2] Cf. Isa. xliv. 7 LXX; here, however, the reference is not simply to prophecy (though this is not excluded) but to the interpretation of the life and death of Christ and the declaration of the new order which follows his departure to the Father.

---

[1] See above, p. 352, n. 6, for the reading adopted here.
[2] A translation may be found in the *Ante-Nicene Christian Library*, Vol. XII, pp. 331 f. Also in E. Hennecke, *N.T. Apocrypha*, ed. W. Schneemelcher, ii (E.T., 1965), p. 101.

Like Jesus, the Spirit **will not speak on his own authority**
(cf. v. 30; vii. 17; xii. 49; xiv. 10); further, his work will **glorify**
Jesus: cf. xvii. 1, 4 f. and the notes *in loc.* for the same verb used
of the mutual relationship of the Father and the Son. With **all
that the Father has is mine,** cf. xvii. 10; the whole of verse
15 indicates further the close relationship that exists between
Jesus, the Father, and the Spirit.

**(16) 'A little while and you will perceive[1] me no more,
and again a little while and you will see[2] me.'[3] (17) So
some of his disciples[4] said to one another, 'What is this
that he says to us, "A little while and you will not perceive[1] me, and again a little while and you will see[2] me",
and, "Because I am going to the Father"?' (18) So they
said, 'What is this that he says,[5] "A little while"? We do
not know what he means.'**

16. The word translated **a little while** (μικρόν) is found
seven times in verses 16-19, which are built around its use, but
appears apart from this only four times in the FG (vii. 33; xii.
35, where it is used as an adjective with the noun 'time' (χρόνος),
and xiii. 33; xiv. 19, where, as here, the neuter of the adjective
is used as a substantive). This section takes up these earlier
appearances of the word and, by giving it considerable emphasis,
conveys further teaching as Jesus is shown predicting his death
but looking beyond this to the resurrection. The stress laid on
this point suggests that the writer felt it important to give clear
teaching on the necessity of the death of Christ as the inaugura-
tion of the new life of the Christian Church; it is only after
Christ has died and the disciples have suffered through being
deprived of him that they will be able to share in the joy of which

---

[1] θεωρεῖτε; cf. p. 191, n. 2.   [2] ὄψεσθε; cf. p. 191.

[3] So P⁵. ⁶⁶ ℵ B D W *vt sah boh*ᵖᵐ *ac²*; ὅτι (+ ἐγὼ 33 *al*) ὑπάγω πρὸς τὸν
πατέρα (+ μου *sin*) is added by A Θ *fam* 1 *fam* 13 *vg sin pesh boh*ᵖᵗ, probably
because the clause is found in verse 17, it being assumed that the disciples
are simply repeating what Jesus has just said. But this idea is not taken up
again in verse 19, and it is likely that in verse 17 John wishes to resume in a
single statement two different aspects of what is to happen shortly after the
Last Supper, reintroducing a theme frequent in these discourses (cf. the
references cited on p. 428) and last alluded to at verse 10, lest sight of it be
lost.   [4] ἐκ τῶν μαθητῶν αὐτοῦ; cf. p. 353, n. 3 and Turner, pp. 208 f.

[5] ὃ λέγει is omitted by P⁵. ⁶⁶ ℵ* D* W *fam* 13 1 565 579 *vt sah* and the
shorter reading has much to commend it. It is easy to see how ὃ λέγει could
have been added under the influence of the preceding verse.

he goes on to speak (cf. verses 19-22). It has been said earlier that in a little while the world will see Jesus no more, though the disciples will be able to see him (xiv. 19); here and in verses 17 and 19 the theme of seeing is reintroduced. There is no need to suppose that the two different Greek words translated **perceive** and **see** are used to contrast different sorts of sight, though it is likely that there is here a play on the two meanings of physical sight of Jesus and true insight into the nature of his person and work: the double meaning lies in both words.[1] 17. Not surprisingly, the disciples fail to understand Jesus (cf. xiii. 36; xiv. 5, 8, 22), and they ask each other what he means. In a similar way, vii. 33 f. is followed by an identical reaction on the part of the Jews (vii. 35 f.). The warning of vii. 33 f. and the challenge to believe of xii. 35 f. are stated in terms of the impending departure of Jesus (cf. xiii. 33), though now a further step forward is taken: though both Jews and disciples must be left behind by Jesus (xiii. 33), the latter will see him again (xiv. 19), and therefore (despite the fact that they do not question him directly) Jesus clarifies the issue for them (as he did not do for the Jews, vii. 35 f.). Dodd argues that the simple metaphors used in the two cryptic sayings mentioned in verse 17 were variously understood when the evangelist wrote as predictions either of the death and resurrection of Christ, or of an apocalyptic appearance at the end of the age. The FG insists that the former is the true interpretation, and although this is an expression of John's own theology it is not unreasonable to suppose that 'the earliest tradition of all contained predictions in broad, general terms of the death of Jesus and of renewed life and activity after death' which later came to be understood in different ways; thus, 'John is here reaching back to a very early form of tradition indeed, and making it [his] point of departure . . . the oracular sayings which he reports have good claim to represent authentically, in substance if not verbally, what Jesus actually said to his disciples.'[2]

(19) Jesus knew that they wanted to question him, and he said to them, 'Are you discussing among yourselves

---

[1] On 'seeing' in the FG cf. further Dodd, *Interpretation*, p. 167 and n. 3.
[2] C. H. Dodd, *Historical Tradition in the Fourth Gospel* (1963), pp. 419 f. See further *ibid.* pp. 413 ff.

what I said, "A little while and you will not perceive[1] me, and again a little while and you will see[2] me"? (20) Amen, amen,[3] I say to you, you will weep and lament, but the world will rejoice; you will be sorrowful, but your sorrow will turn into joy. (21) When a woman is in labour she is in pain,[4] because her time[5] has come; but when she is delivered of the child she no longer remembers the anguish for joy that a man has been born into the world. (22) Accordingly you are sorrowful[6] now, but I will see you again, and your heart⟨s⟩[7] will rejoice, and no one will take[8] your joy from you.'

19. It is hardly necessary to attribute Jesus' knowledge of the disciples' desire to question him to omniscience;[9] anyone sensitive to the feelings of an audience of friends could recognise their disquiet at something that has been said. The quotation of Jesus' words here and at verse 17 differs from the original statement of verse 16 by substituting **not** (οὐ) for **no more** (οὐκέτι); such minor variations are found elsewhere in the FG when words are repeated, but the meaning is unaffected. Cf. also p. 353, n. 4. 20. With **you will weep**, cf. xx. 11, 13, 15, and also Mark ii. 20 = Matt. ix. 15 = Luke v. 35. The picture is of the grief of the disciples whose Master has been killed, contrasted with the rejoicing of the world, glad to have put him out of the way. Cf. verse 6 for the disciples' **sorrow**; however, **joy** will once again be their lot, after the resurrection (cf. xx. 20).

[1] θεωρεῖτε; cf. p. 191, n. 2.

[2] ὄψεσθε; cf. p. 191.

[3] See p. 105.

[4] λύπην ἔχει, which could also be translated 'is sorrowful'. Cf. verses 20, 22; the play on words cannot be brought out in English.

[5] ὥρα; ἡμέρα, read by P[66] D vt sin pesh ac[2], perhaps introduces a reference to the 'day of the Lord' under the influence of the eschatological language of this section.

[6] λύπην ἔχετε, read by P[22] ℵ* B W[c] fam 1 fam 13 aur c f ff[2] q vg syr; the future ἕξετε, read instead of the present by P[66] ℵ[c] A D W* Θ a b d e r[1], is to be rejected as a pedestrian 'improvement' of the text (so Barrett, p. 411).

[7] See p. 349, n. 3.

[8] This verb is in the present tense but has a future meaning; cf. p. 210, n. 4. The future ἀρεῖ, read by P[5] B D* a aur c d ff[2] r[1] vg sah boh, is best taken as a correction.

[9] So, e.g., A. J. B. Higgins, The Historicity of the Fourth Gospel (1960), pp. 65 f.

A parallel to the simile of the woman in travail has been seen in a passage from one of the Qumran Thanksgiving Psalms.[1] This imagery is frequent in the Old Testament (cf., e.g., Mic. iv. 9 f.; v. 3, Jer. iv. 31, Isa. xxvi. 17 f.), and it has been argued that the writer of the psalm draws on this symbolism to depict the woes which will precede the appearance of the Messiah.[2] However, on the one hand the Messianic interpretation of this passage has been challenged,[3] and on the other it has been claimed that it refers, not to an individual, but to 'the emergence through trial and suffering of the redeemed Israel'.[4] Cf. also Rev. xii. 1 ff. However, it is not necessary to suppose that the **woman . . . in labour** represents 'the true Israel whose sufferings give birth to the resurrected Christ'.[5] It can hardly be thought that the resurrection is due in any way to the disciples' suffering;[6] the imagery employed here is graphic, and in the context of the Last Supper the words could only mean that the disciples' deep grief would be turned into great joy after the resurrection. Just as Israel suffers before being delivered, so will the disciples. Yet the appearance of this imagery is specially appropriate here, for it also hints at the secondary meaning that the beginning of the Messianic woes does not lie after Jesus' death but in it: everything that follows is simply the outworking of what is here set in motion.

Her time (ἡ ὥρα αὐτῆς, cf. p. 107, n. 2) may well be intended to hint at Jesus' death, the 'time' for which is indicated by the

---

[1] I Q H iii. 7-11. For translations of this passage, see T. H. Gaster, *op. cit.*, p. 140, and G. Vermès, *op. cit.*, p. 157.

[2] Cf., e.g., John V. Chamberlain, 'Another Qumran Thanksgiving Psalm', *Journal of Near Eastern Studies*, Vol. XIV, 1955, pp. 32-41.

[3] Cf., e.g., Lou H. Silberman, 'Language and Structure in the *HODAYOT* (IQH3)', *Journal of Biblical Literature*, Vol. LXXV, 1956, pp. 96-106, E. Lohse, *Die Texte aus Qumran* (1964), p. 288 nn. 10, 11. Svend Holm-Nielsen, *Hodayot* (1960), p. 64, holds that there is here a description of present salvation already realised within the community.

[4] M. Black, *op. cit.*, p. 150. Cf. also O. Betz, 'Die Geburt der Gemeinde durch den Lehrer', *N.T.S.*, Vol. III, 1956-57, pp. 314-326.

[5] W. H. Brownlee, 'John the Baptist in the New Light of Ancient Scrolls', in *The Scrolls and the New Testament*, ed. K. Stendahl (1957), p. 255 n. 29. Cf. also the same writer, *ibid.*, pp. 50 f. for a similar exegesis of this Thanksgiving Psalm. So too Stendahl, *ibid.*, p. 12.

[6] The opposite view appears to be taken by John V. Chamberlain, *art. cit.*, p. 41, and W. H. Brownlee, 'Messianic Motifs of Qumran and the New Testament', *N.T.S.*, Vol. III, 1956-57, p. 29.

same word; cf. p. 110 and n. 2. These verses indicate the
way in which the early Christians faithfully remembered
how their joy in the Christian gospel was born out of sorrow
and **anguish** (for this word see on verse 33); it is a **joy** that
no one will take from the disciples, even under persecution,
for it is the settled possession of the Christian Church.

(23) **'And on that day you will ask me no questions.
Amen, amen,**[1] **I say to you, if you shall ask the Father for
anything, he will give it you in my name. (24) Until the
present moment**[2] **you have asked nothing in my name;
ask, and you will receive, that your joy may be fulfilled.'**

23. **On that day** no doubt refers here and at verse 26, as
does xiv. 20, to the day of Christ's resurrection, but there seems
to be an unmistakable eschatological overtone, not merely on
account of the NT evidence cited by Barrett (p. 412), but more
particularly because of the OT usage; cf., e.g., Isa. ii. 11, 17,
20; iii. 7, 18; iv. 2, Hos. ii. 16, 18, 21, Amos viii. 3, 9. It accords
well with the teaching of the FG for both these ideas to be
present. **You will ask me no questions** could equally well be
translated, 'you will ask me for nothing', as the verb ἐρωτάω
has the same range of meaning as the English 'to ask'. However,
in context the translation given seems the more probable;[3] under
the guidance of the Spirit the disciples will learn all that they
need to know, and so they will **ask** Jesus **no questions** (cf.
verse 19).

Amen, amen introduces a new saying about petitionary
prayer, in which a different Greek word for **ask** (αἰτέω) is used.
For asking **in** Jesus' **name,** cf. xiv. 13 f.; xv. 16; xvi. 26 and p.
324. Such requests can only be made after Jesus is glorified, for
only then will the appropriateness of such prayer be evident;
until the present moment the disciples **have asked nothing in** Jesus' name. **Ask, and you will receive** does not
imply the automatic granting of any request that one may
choose to make, but only of those genuinely asked **in** Jesus'
name (cf. further xv. 7 and the note *in loc.,* 1 John iii. 22, v.

[1] See p. 105.
[2] ἕως ἄρτι; see p. 107, n. 3.
[3] Moulton, *Prolegomena,* p. 66, n. 1; Bauer[5] s.v.

14 f., also Mark xi. 24 = Matt. xxi. 22, and especially Matt.
xviii. 19 f., where the prayer of those gathered in Christ's name
is answered because he is present with them). In verse 23 'if
you shall ask the Father for anything in my name, he will give
it you' is read by P²²ᵛ¹ᵈ A D W Θ *fam* 1 *fam* 13 *lat syr boh*,
but the more difficult reading adopted here, which inverts the
order of **in my name** and **he will give it you,** though only
supported by Pˢᵛ¹ᵈ ℵ B *sah ac*², is possibly original. It is in
his Father's name that Jesus has come (v. 43) and does his
works (x. 25), and it is in Jesus' name that the Spirit is sent
(xiv. 26); thus verse 23 illustrates the fundamental unity of the
Son with the Father as verse 24 shows the disciples united with
the Son. It is easy to see how a text which was hard to understand was simplified by rearranging the word-order to bring it
into line with a phrase found frequently in these discourses
(see above). With **that your joy may be fulfilled,** cf. iii. 29;
xv. 11; xvii. 13, 1 John i. 4, 2 John 12; emphasis is laid on joy
as brought to the highest degree.

(25) **'I have spoken these things to you in parables;
the time is coming when I will no longer speak to you
in parables but will tell you plainly of the Father.'**

For **parables** (παροιμίαι) cf. x. 6 and p. 247. During
Jesus' earthly ministry much that he said to the disciples was
enigmatic (cf. xiii. 36; xiv. 5, 8, 22; xvi. 17 f.), but **the time is
coming** (i.e. after the resurrection) when Jesus will be able to
speak to them **plainly** (παρρησίᾳ, cf. p. 201, n. 6 and xi. 11-14).
For **the time** (ὥρα) cf. p. 107, n. 2 and p. 147. **I . . . will tell
you . . . of the Father** as a summary of Christ's teaching is
consistent with what has been said earlier about his work (i. 18;
xiv. 6 f., 9). Cf. also xvi. 23a and the note *in loc.*; at xiv. 17 f. the
rôles of Spirit and Son cannot be disentangled, and we are
perhaps to think here also of the Spirit instructing the disciples
(cf. xvi. 12-15).

(26) **'On that day you will ask in my name, and I do not
say to you that I will pray to the Father for you; (27) for
the Father himself¹ loves you, because you have loved
me and have believed that I came out from God. (28)**

---

¹ αὐτός; cf. Moule, p. 121, Turner, pp. 40 f.

I came out from the Father[1] and have come into the world; again, I am leaving the world and going to the Father.'

For **on that day**, cf. on verse 23, p. 360. **You will ask in my name** takes up again the theme of xiv. 13 f.; xv. 16; xvi. 24; the same word for **ask** (αἰτέω) is used, though **I will pray** translates ἐρωτήσω (for which see on verse 23). This latter verb is used at xiv. 16 of Jesus' prayer to the Father that the Spirit be given to the disciples, and at xvii. 9, 15, 20 in Jesus' prayer for the disciples and for all future disciples; presumably one is to understand that in the age of fulfilment, when the Spirit is given, there will be an intimate relationship between the Father and the disciples that will make such prayer unnecessary. **27.** With **for the Father himself loves you, because you have loved me** (in which the verb used is φιλέω), cf. xiv. 21, 23 (where the verb is ἀγαπάω). For a summary of the teaching conveyed by these verbs in the FG, see pp. 129 f. and p. 130, n. 2. With **I came out from God**, cf. viii. 42; xiii. 3; xvi. 28, 30; xvii. 8; in fact, though Jesus says that the disciples **have believed** this about him, it soon becomes plain that as yet their belief remains imperfect (verses 30 f.). The perfect of πιστεύω, 'to believe', is also found at iii. 18; vi. 69; viii. 31; xi. 27; xx. 29. At viii. 31 it seems clear that the belief of the Jews is incomplete, and the same is true of the content of the affirmations made by Peter and Martha at vi. 69 and xi. 27. Faith is not fully reached till xx. 28 f. **28.** There follows a brief description of Jesus' ministry: he has **come into the world** and will now **go to the Father** in death. This provides an opportunity for

---

[1] ἐξῆλθον ἐκ τοῦ πατρός, omitted by D W b ff² sin ac², which render verses 27 b and 28 a: 'You have believed that I came out from God and have come into the world.' Barrett argues that this may well be the original reading, claiming that 'the shorter reading is somewhat clumsy and the expansion "improves" it' (p. 414). But the text adopted here is fully consistent with John's style, and it may be better to regard the omission as an accident. If this is so, **from God** (παρὰ θεοῦ) is to be read in verse 27 with P⁵·⁶⁶ᵛⁱᵈ ℵ* A Θ (παρὰ τοῦ θεοῦ W fam 1 fam 13, παρὰ θεοῦ or παρὰ τοῦ θεοῦ lat sin pesh hl), and 'from the Father' (παρὰ τοῦ πατρός), supported by (ℵᶜ) B D sah boh ac², is normally taken to be due to the influence of the next verse. Since D ac² read 'from the Father' at verse 27 but omit it in verse 28 the problem may however be more complex than this; does this fact support the longer reading? In the longer reading, ἐκ is read by B 33 pesh hl, παρά by P⁵· ²² ℵ A Θ fam 1 fam 13, probably by assimilation to the preceding verse.

the disciples to interrupt (this is the only occasion on which
they address Jesus in this account of the teaching given at
the Last Supper, though that contained in xiii–xiv includes
several comments and questions), and Jesus then brings it to a
close.

(29) His disciples said, 'Why,[1] **now you are speaking
plainly and are telling no parable! (30) Now we know
that you know everything and have no need of anyone to
ask you; because of this**[2] **we believe that you came out
from God.'**

29. The disciples' interjection, **now you are speaking
plainly** (ἐν παρρησίᾳ) **and are telling no parable** (παροιμία),
is a claim to possess already that understanding which Jesus
declared at verse 25 would only be available after his resurrection. They think they have at last discerned his meaning, 30.
and confidently say **we know that you know everything**
and add that there is **no need of anyone to ask** (ἐρωτᾷ) Jesus
(cf. verse 23), because he has already revealed all they need to
know. However, **we believe that you came out from God**
is belief in only a part of what Jesus was declaring at verse 28,
though their faith is sincere and as far as it goes it is correct.
It is perhaps also defective in that the word **God** is used instead
of the more expressive term 'Father', which is normally found
on Jesus' lips in these discourses (but cf. verse 27). It is only
later that questions will be unnecessary (verse 23). Cf. xvii. 8
and the note *in loc*. **From** translates ἀπό here, but παρά in verse
27 and ἐκ in verse 28; no significance seems to lie in the use
of these three different prepositions.

(31) Jesus answered them, 'Do you believe at present?[3]
**(32) Behold, the time is coming and has already come
when**[4] **you will be scattered, every one to his home, and**

---

[1] Literally Ἴδε, 'see!'

[2] ἐν τούτῳ; the causal use of ἐν is found in the papyri, but there is a
strong possibility of Semitic influence. Cf. Moulton-Howard, p. 463, B.-D.
§ 219 (2), Turner, p. 253.

[3] Ἄρτι; see p. 107, n. 3. A possible alternative translation is, 'You do believe
at present' (cf. B.-D. § 440); if this is adopted, the meaning is, 'While *at
present* you do believe, your faith will soon be shaken.' But in context the
statement that 'the time is coming *and has already come*' for the disciples'
flight seems to suggest that a question here is more probable.

[4] See p. 346, n. 4.

**will leave me alone; yet I am not alone, because the
Father is with me. (33) I have spoken these things to you
so that in me you should have peace. In the world you
have[1] tribulation; but take courage, I have overcome the
world.'**

31. Jesus challenges the disciples' affirmation of their faith;
it is only later that full faith will be possible for them (cf. xx. 8,
29, 31). For faith as the response to Jesus' words and actions
earlier in his ministry, cf. the passages cited on p. 120 and the
notes on these passages. 32. **The time** for the disciples' flight
is at hand; for the omission of an account of this in the FG, see
p. 386. Although two disciples followed Jesus (xviii. 15 ff.),
Peter denied him and, effectively, Jesus was left **alone**—upheld
only by the presence of **the Father,** with whom every action
of the Son is perfectly united. Cf. viii. 16, 29 and p. 226 and n. 3.
But **the time** (ὥρα) is also the term used for the hour of Jesus'
glorification; cf. p. 107, n. 2 and p. 147. Earlier in the FG, for
example at vii. 30 and viii. 20, it has been said that Jesus' hour
has not yet come, but at xii. 23 and xiii. 1 the imminence of this
hour is asserted; now stress is laid on the fact that it **is coming
and has already come.** As at iv. 23 and v. 25, what (from one
point of view) still lies in the future is already realised in the
world's life by the presence of Jesus. Cf. further xvii. 1. **You
will be scattered** (σκορπισθῆτε) recalls the use of Zech. xiii.
7 ('strike the shepherd, that the sheep may be scattered') at
Mark xiv. 27 = Matt. xxvi. 31. But, while Mark and Matthew
cite Zechariah, there is no explicit quotation here in the FG;
also the FG adds **every one to his home** (εἰς τὰ ἴδια; cf.
Bauer[5] s.v. ἴδιος), which, if taken literally, is hardly consistent
with xx, unless it is expressed from the point of view of a Jerusalem disciple. The argument that the FG is drawing on the
use of Zechariah by Mark is improbable; the resemblance lies
only in a single word (διασκορπισθήσονται in Mark), and even
though this is a variant reading in the LXX the correspondence
is most probably due to 'the existence of non-septuagintal
versions of the "testimony" passages, which Christian writers
might quote without any suspicion of borrowing from one

---

[1] ἔχετε; ἕξετε, read by D *fam* 13 *lat*, is another 'correction' of the
text.

another'.[1] It has also been argued that the FG is using an early
tradition that underlies the use of this *testimonium* by Mark and
Matthew, and which, like the *Gospel of Peter* vii. 26 (cf. xiv.
58 ff.),[2] told of the flight of the disciples to Galilee.[3] But it may
be that the real point of contact here is the frequent use of this
section of Zechariah for purposes of comment on the passion
by the early church;[4] thus it has been argued that Zech. xiii. 7
was used to answer the objection, 'If the Messiah's death was
God's plan, predetermined in Scripture, why did his followers
desert him?'[5] If so, it is not necessary to hold that the allusion to
this passage in the FG is connected with a prediction of a flight
to Galilee. Note also the same verb at x. 12, and cf. τὰ διεσκορπι-
σμένα, xi. 52; see further x. 1 ff. and xxi. 15 ff.

33. Cf. xiii. 19; xiv. 29; xv. 11; xvi. 1. For **peace** cf. xiv. 27
and the note *in loc.* **Tribulation** (θλῦψις) is the disciples' lot
in the world; cf. verse 21 (where the word is rendered 'anguish'), and also Rev. i. 9; ii. 9, 10, 22; vii. 14. The thought of
the tribulations of the last days is here combined with a quite
general reference to persecution.[6] For **the world** cf. p. 76.
It has *already* been **overcome** by Jesus; cf. xii. 31; xvi. 11 and
the notes *in loc.* and p. 14. For the verb (νενίκηκα), which
occurs in Revelation but is not found elsewhere in the FG, see
1 John ii. 13 f.; iv. 4; v. 4 f. The confidence of the Church is
based on Christ's victory.

Chapter xvii contains a prayer of Jesus for his disciples and
for those who will believe in him through them. The tone of
serene confidence which pervades it (cf. especially verse 24,
where petition passes into desire—the Son's will is identical

---

[1] C. H. Dodd, *Historical Tradition in the Fourth Gospel* (1963), p. 58 n. 1.
A verbal parallel (again consisting of one word only) between Mark xiv. 27 and
John xvi. 1 can once more hardly be enough to support the theory of borrow-
ing from Mark: in this instance Dodd, *ibid.*, p. 57, points out that 'the verb
σκανδαλίζεσθαι . . . appears to be deeply rooted in the vocabulary of primitive
Christianity'.

[2] E.T. in E. Hennecke, *New Testament Apocrypha*, ed. by W. Schneemelcher,
E.T. ed. by R. McL. Wilson, Vol. I (1963), pp. 185, 187.

[3] P. Gardner-Smith, *Saint John and the Synoptic Gospels* (1938), p. 55.

[4] For discussions of the use of Zechariah by the evangelists see F. F.
Bruce, 'The Book of Zechariah and the Passion Narrative', *Bulletin of the
John Rylands Library*, Vol. XLIII, 1960–61, pp. 336–353; B. Lindars, *New
Testament Apologetic* (1961), pp. 110 ff.

[5] B. Lindars, *ibid.*, p. 132.   [6] Cf. Barrett, p. 416,

with the Father's) contrasts strongly with the narrative of the Agony in the Garden which the Synoptic Gospels place immediately before the arrest (Mark xiv. 32-42, Matt. xxvi. 36-46, Luke xxii. 39-46). Nowhere else do the gospels relate a prayer of Jesus at such length, and it has been suggested that the writer may have been influenced by the liturgical practice which he knew.[1] However, despite unquestioned similarities to chapter x of the *Didache*,[2] there is little evidence on which to rely, and although the stress laid on the communion which unites the Church with Jesus and the mention made of the way in which it owes its origin to his sacrificial death on behalf of his own have led to the view that this chapter is a substitute for the synoptic account of the Institution of the Eucharist, so much that has previously been said in the FG is summed up here that it would be unwise to define the origin or purpose of xvii too narrowly. The prayer illustrates in action that unity of Father and Son which has been manifested throughout Jesus' ministry and in which the disciples are now to share; yet, however theologically appropriate this may be as the conclusion of Jesus' witness to his followers before the crucifixion, the exalted style does not fit the actual situation in the Upper Room. This is rather an ideal construction (which may well incorporate traditional material) that presupposes a full comprehension on the disciples' part which they did not then possess. But if later developments in Christian thought may be noted (cf. the proper name 'Jesus Christ' at verse 3), the prayer preserves the standpoint of one about to die and those before whom it is uttered are the disciples assembled with Jesus in the Upper Room (cf. especially verse 20, where the scope of the prayer is enlarged to include later believers); past and present are inextricably inter-

---

[1] Contrast the view of O. Cullmann, *Early Christian Worship* (1953), p. 111: 'The so-called high-priest's prayer (chap. 17) is a typical eucharistic prayer. It differs, however, from later eucharistic prayers in that only Christ himself who surrenders himself to death can utter it.'

[2] Cf. with verse 11, *Didache*, x. 2, 'we give thee thanks, holy Father (πάτερ ἅγιε) for thy holy name (ὑπὲρ τοῦ ἁγίου ὀνόματός σου) which thou didst cause to dwell in our hearts', and with verses 15, 23, and 26, *Didache*, x. 5, 'Remember, O Lord, thy Church to deliver her from all evil (ἀπὸ παντὸς πονηροῦ) and to perfect her in thy love (τελειῶσαι αὐτὴν ἐν τῇ ἀγάπῃ σου)'; the passage goes on to speak of the Church as 'the sanctified' (τὴν ἁγιασθεῖσαν, cf. John xvii. 17, 19).

twined in the author's thought. The prayer forms a fitting culmination (in Johannine terms) to Jesus' earthly ministry and leads on to the cross.

xvii. (1) When Jesus had spoken these ⟨words⟩, he looked up[1] **to heaven and said, 'Father, the time has come; glorify thy Son, that the Son may glorify thee, (2) since thou gavest him authority over all flesh, to give eternal life to all whom thou hast given him. (3) (And this is eternal life, that they know thee, the only true God, and Jesus Christ, whom thou didst send.)'**

1. **When Jesus had spoken these ⟨words⟩** is probably an artificial link constructed to bind Jesus' prayer to the preceding discourses. **He looked up to heaven** is the conventional Jewish attitude of prayer;[2] cf. xi. 41 (where the verb is $\alpha i\rho\omega$), Luke xviii. 13, and Enoch xiii. 5 (where, as here, the verb $\epsilon\pi\alpha i\rho\omega$ is used), and Mark vi. 41; vii. 34, Matt. xiv. 19, Luke ix. 16 (where the verb is $\dot{\alpha}\nu\alpha\beta\lambda\epsilon\pi\omega$). For **Father** as a title of God on Jesus' lips, cf. pp. 86, 117; for **the time has come** cf. xvi. 32 and the note *in loc.*: the phrase is used here to suggest that the time determined by God for the crucifixion has now arrived. The theme of 'glorification' is very prominent in this chapter; see p. 82 and p. 215 and n. 2 for discussions of the noun 'glory' and the verb 'to glorify'. For the mutual glorification of Son and Father, cf. xiii. 31 f.; Jesus' glory is from the Father (cf. viii. 54), and the Father is glorified in the Son (xiv. 13).

2. The **authority** ($\dot{\epsilon}\xi o\upsilon\sigma i\alpha$) of Jesus **over all flesh** (i.e. 'over everyone'[3]) is given him by the Father; cf. the authority given to the Son by the Father to judge (v. 27) and to lay down and take up his life (x. 18), and the authority of Pilate over Jesus given him from above (xix. 10 f.). In each case emphasis is laid on the Father as the source of authority; both Jesus and Pilate are permitted to exercise certain prerogatives, though Jesus alone is conscious of this. Cf. further iii. 27, 35; xiii. 3, and also Matt. xi. 27 = Luke x. 22, Matt. xxviii. 18. Both Father

---

[1] Literally, $\dot{\epsilon}\pi\dot{\alpha}\rho\alpha s$ $\tau o\dot{\upsilon}s$ $\dot{o}\phi\theta\alpha\lambda\mu o\dot{\upsilon}s$ $\alpha\dot{\upsilon}\tau o\hat{\upsilon}$, 'having lifted up his eyes'.

[2] Cf. Strack–Billerbeck, II, pp. 246 f.

[3] **All flesh** ($\pi\hat{\alpha}\sigma\alpha$ $\sigma\dot{\alpha}\rho\xi$) is a Semitism found also in the LXX's literal translation of the Hebrew כָּל־בָּשָׂר.

and Son will be glorified in the exercise of this **authority,** in virtue of which **eternal life** (on which see p. 128, and cf. p. 5 for Jesus as the source of life) will be given **to all whom** the Father has **given** to the Son; see pp. 190, 198 for a discussion of this thought. The construction at the end of the verse is not smooth, but this is deliberate[1] and hints at a major theme of the prayer; 'the conception of a single corporate whole is placed in sharpest prominence by the phrase πᾶν ὃ δέδωκας αὐτῷ, "that entire unity which Thou hast given him", followed immediately by the plural, "that to them he might give eternal life"'.[2]

3. **Eternal life** is further described as knowing the Father and **Jesus Christ;** whereas the characteristic Old Testament usage was to regard man's knowledge of God as future, it is here asserted to be a present possession of believers.[3] Cf. p. 77 for 'knowledge' in the FG, and see i. 10; viii. 55; x. 14; xiv. 7, 9; xvi. 3; xvii. 25 for 'knowing' (or 'not knowing') Jesus or the Father. Note that **Jesus Christ** is a proper name here and at i. 17; elsewhere in the FG **Christ** is always a title. This contrasts with the Pauline usage, for which 'Christ' is merely a proper name, largely on account of the Gentile environment in which Paul was writing. Because of the status given to Jesus in the FG, it can be said that the required knowledge is of **the only true God, and Jesus Christ;** for the sending of the Son by the Father, cf. p. 129, n. 1.

After this definition of **eternal life** in parenthesis, the prayer continues: **(4) 'I glorified thee on the earth, having com-**

---

[1] For the suggestion that the complicated syntax is due in part to an attempt to translate the indeclinable Aramaic particle *dᵉ*, cf. Moulton-Howard, pp. 424, 437, Black, pp. 61 f., B.-D. §§ 138 (1), 282 (3), Turner, pp. 21, 40, 317. See also p. 190 and compare the similar construction in verse 24.

[2] W. F. Howard, *Christianity According to St. John* (1943), p. 133.

[3] Cf. Dodd, *Interpretation*, pp. 163 ff., and see *ibid.* p. 151 for the background in contemporary thought to 'knowing God'. W. D. Davies, 'Paul and the Dead Sea Scrolls: Flesh and Spirit', in *The Scrolls and the New Testament*, ed. K. Stendahl (1958), p. 282 n. 86, contrasts the knowledge of God which preserves a distinction between creature and creator, found here and at 1 Cor. xiii. 12 and in the *Manual of Discipline*, iv. 22 ff., with the suggestion of absorption in God implied by the same term in Hellenistic sources. Cf. *ibid.* for further discussion of 'knowledge' in the Dead Sea Scrolls.

pleted the work which thou hast given me to do; (5) and now, Father, glorify thou me in thy own presence with the glory which I had with thee before the world existed.'

4. For the completion of Jesus' work or works, cf. iv. 34; v. 36, and also xix. 28, 30, and the notes *in loc.* This task has been entrusted to Jesus by the Father (cf. iv. 34; v. 36; x. 25, 37), and its fulfilment results in the Father's glorification. 5. The converse of this is that Jesus resumes the glory proper to the pre-existent Son, given him by the Father; cf. above on verse 1. For the pre-existence of Jesus, cf. i. 1 f.; viii. 58; xvii. 24, and also iii. 13; viii. 38; i. 18. Though it has been held that the glory prayed for here and referred to at verse 24 is 'the glory of the eternal Word, the glory which is His by nature and right', while the glory prayed for in verse 1 is 'the glory of self-sacrificing love, as manifested by Him throughout His ministry and, supremely, in His death',[1] too sharp a distinction should not be drawn; the one is the expression of the other. Cf. especially i. 14.

(6) 'I made thy name known to the men whom thou gavest me out of the world. They were thine, and thou gavest them to me, and they have kept thy word. (7) Now they know that everything which thou hast given me is from thee; (8) for I have given them the words which thou gavest me, and they received them and knew truly that I came out from thee; and they believed that thou didst send me.'

6. For the verb **I made ... known** (ἐφανέρωσα) used of the manifestation of Jesus, or his glory, or God's works, cf. i. 31; ii. 11; ix. 3; xxi. 1, 14. Only at vii. 4 is 'the world' brought into relation with this verb (cf. the note *in loc.*), and Jesus declines his brothers' challenge to show himself to it. Similarly here it is to those given Jesus by the Father (cf. on verse 2 above) **out of the world** that Jesus, by his words and deeds, makes known God's **name**, i.e. his character and person.[2] The disciples had

---

[1] R. H. Lightfoot, *op. cit.*, pp. 300 f.

[2] Cf. J. Pedersen, *Israel: Its Life and Culture*, I-II (1926), pp. 245 ff. for a full discussion of the 'name' in Hebrew thought, and Moulton and Milligan s.v. ὄνομα 2.

always belonged to the Father—this is part of John's teaching about predestination—and they are given to Jesus not only because of the authority mentioned at verse 2, but also because all that the Father has belongs to the Son (xvi. 15; xvii. 10). Just as Jesus keeps the Father's word (viii. 55), so the disciples have kept Jesus' word (cf. xiv. 23; viii. 51 f.—the standpoint of the prayer is that of the post-resurrection Church), which is the Father's word (xiv. 24). Cf. p. 332 and 1 John ii. 5; Rev. iii. 8.

Verse 7 declares the total faith which the disciples partially affirm at xvi. 30; the entire ministry of Jesus with all that this involves **(everything which thou hast given me)** is recognised as the Father's gift. 8. Jesus' words are the Father's words (iii. 34; vii. 16; xii. 49 f.; xiv. 10, 24), and they are received by the disciples, though not by the Jews (v. 47; vi. 68; viii. 47; xii. 47 f.). With they **knew truly that I came out from thee,** cf. xvi. 27. This verse in the prayer might seem to imply that the disciples' affirmation at xvi. 30 was adequate after all, but Jesus here limits himself to a statement of his divine origin that is not intended as a full account of the Christian faith, but recognition of which is basic to its acceptance. Both during Jesus' earthly ministry and throughout the history of the Church this issue has been fiercely contended; in context Jesus does not merely mean that he is Messiah, far less that he is a superman, one of the divine heroes of the ancient world, but that his claims to pre-existence (cf. verse 5) are justified. It is the unique ministry of this Jesus that has the authority of God behind it, and this is far more than the rulers of the Jews are earlier thought by some to know truly (vii. 26), as it is far more than the disciples assert at the Last Supper. The knowledge and belief referred to here are part of the life of the worshipping Church, which can participate in the mutual life of the Father and the Son (verse 21). On the sending of the Son by the Father, cf. p. 129, n. 1.

(9) 'I am praying for them; I am not praying for the world, but for those whom thou hast given me, because they are thine.'

The antithesis between the disciples and **the world,** which is hostile to God, is maintained. While the FG is emphatic that God loved the world and sent his Son to save it (iii. 16 f.), just as there is a peculiar quality of mutual love between Christians (xiii. 34), so Jesus prays for those who can share in the mutual love of Father and Son (verse 26); he is not indifferent to the needs of the rest of mankind, but they are not capable, unless they come to belief (verse 20), of sharing in the things for which he asks. Cf. on verse 2 for the recurrent theme of **those whom thou hast given me,** and on verse 6 for **they are thine.**

(10) 'And all things that are mine are thine, and thine are mine, and I am glorified[1] in them.' Cf. xvi. 15. **All things** is neuter in gender, and the intention is to include more than the disciples in the thought; 'there is a complete mutuality of interest and possession between the Father and the Son'.[2] **In them** can either be neuter, referring to **all things,** or, if verse 10a is understood as parenthetic, it could be masculine, referring to **those whom thou hast given me** (verse 9). In context the latter interpretation seems the more appropriate, for verses 9 and 11 both speak of the disciples; at xv. 8 and xxi. 19 actions of disciples are said to glorify God; and the Father's glorification *in* the Son at xiii. 31 f.; xiv. 13 provides a suitable parallel. As the prayer continues it explains how Jesus is **glorified in** the disciples.

(11) 'And I am no longer in the world, but they are in the world and I am coming to thee. Holy Father, keep them in thy name which thou hast given me, that they may be one, as we are.'

Jesus is represented as looking forward to his imminent departure (cf. xiii. 1), when the disciples will be left exposed to the hostility of the **world** (cf. xv. 18 ff.; xvii. 14, and p. 76). Cf. xvi. 1-5a for an alternative presentation of some of the themes of this verse. For the complete unity of the Son and the Father see the note on x. 30; the unity of believers is modelled on the shared purpose and character of the Father and the Son (see further verses 21-23 below) and is therefore rightly expressed in the phrase **keep them in**[3] **thy name** (for **thy**

---

[1] Perfect tense, δεδόξασμαι.   [2] Barrett, p. 423.
[3] It is less likely that the ἐν is instrumental and means 'by the power of'; for ἐν τῷ ὀνόματι αὐτοῦ at xx. 31, sometimes cited as a parallel, see the note *in loc.*

name see the note on verse 6). The prayer is that the relationship with the Father which is the disciples' because they have accepted Jesus' declaration to them of the Father's character (cf. verses 6, 12, and 26) should be preserved after Jesus' departure. Cf. xiv. 10, 20. That it was Jesus' mission to reveal the Father in this way is expressed by the phrase **which thou hast given me** (cf. v. 43; x. 25). The Greek which this translates ($\mathring{\omega}$ δέδωκάς μοι) is strongly attested, and the variant ὃ δέδωκάς μοι, which has the same meaning and is supported by D* and a few other MSS., is best understood as an 'improvement' designed to avoid the attraction of the relative pronoun to the case of its antecedent. The reading '*those whom* thou hast given me' (οὓς δέδωκάς μοι), supported by D^c and a few other MSS., *aur f q vg sah^{mss} got eth geo^2*, reintroduces a thought found already in verses 2, 6, and 9 and is probably a deliberate 'correction' of a text which appeared unintelligible. A similar motive may lie behind the omission of **which thou hast given me, that they may be one, as we are** by *a b c e ff^2 r^1 sin ac^2*, though P^{66}* omits only from **that they may be one** to the end of the verse. Cf. further the textual notes on verse 12.

Any thought of the institutional church is at best secondary, though there are clear hints of the snares which lie in the disciples' path (cf. verse 15) and may lead some away from the truth; attention is focused on what is primary, namely on what is demanded from believers (cf. especially verse 26), and the way in which this expresses itself is not considered, even though it is no doubt at the back of the writer's mind. The adjective **holy** (ἅγιος), applied here only in the FG to the **Father,**[1] introduces a theme which is taken up by the use of the cognate verb 'to sanctify' (ἁγιάζειν) in verses 17 and 19. Holiness is that which distinguishes God from man, and the sanctification of the disciples mentioned later in the prayer is a necessary part of their unity with each other and with God; see further on verse 17 below.

(12) 'When I was with them I kept them in thy name

---

[1] W. F. Howard, *op. cit.*, p. 59, notes how here and at verse 25, in this prayer 'where the perfect trust of the Son in the Father finds its completest expression, twice over in direct appeal the most sacred title of confident intimacy is qualified by an adjective'.

which thou hast given me,[1] **and I preserved**[2] **them, and none of them is lost except for the son of perdition, in order that the scripture might be fulfilled.'**

This statement of Jesus' care for his own while he was on the earth, which leads on naturally from verse 11b and forms a prelude for the emphasis laid yet again in verse 13a (cf. verse 11a) on Jesus' coming to the Father, also enables the writer to explain why Jesus chose Judas (a problem felt acutely in the early church): it was not due to an error on Jesus' part, or to ignorance of Judas' real character, but was **in order that the scripture**[3] **might be fulfilled.** Here and at xiii. 18 and xv. 25 this formula is placed on the lips of Jesus, though elsewhere in the FG it appears plainly as the deposit of the reflection of the early church on Jesus' ministry in the light of the Old Testament (xii. 38; xix. 24, 36). There seems no good reason for supposing that Jesus did not use Scripture in this way, though in a chapter which it is more natural to take as the creation of the post-resurrection church it is highly likely that the theme of xiii. 18 (for which see pp. 310f.) is reintroduced because difficulties were felt in a later period over the fate of Judas. For **in order that** ($\H{\iota}\nu\alpha$), cf. pp. 299 f. and p. 385, n. 4 (on xviii. 9). That **none of them is lost** (cf. vi. 39; x. 28 f.) came to have the status of a prophecy (xviii. 9, cf. the note *in loc.*) before the FG received its final form; Jesus' words, or the words of a Christian prophet spoken in his name, could have the same validity as the Old Testament (cf. ii. 22; xviii. 32). This is natural in view of the fact that Jesus' words are the Father's words (xiv. 24). Although this verse has a wider significance, the scene in the Garden exemplifies what is intended. The Semitism **son of**

---

[1] 'Those whom thou hast given me' ($o\H{\upsilon}s\ \delta\H{\epsilon}\delta\omega\kappa\acute{a}s\ \mu o\iota$) is read by AD Θ *fam* 1 *fam* 13 *lat pesh hl got eth geo*², but the more difficult reading $\H{\phi}\ \delta\H{\epsilon}\delta\omega\kappa\acute{a}s\ \mu o\iota$ is to be preferred. The whole phrase is omitted by P⁶⁶ᵛⁱᵈ ℵ*sin*; cf. the textual note on verse 11. Although xviii. 9 in citing this verse reads $o\H{\upsilon}s\ \delta\H{\epsilon}\delta\omega\kappa\acute{a}s\ \mu o\iota$, no attempt is made to provide an exact quotation; 'those whom thou hast given me' simply gives a suitable introduction to the saying, and it is likely that in some authorities this verse has been assimilated to xviii. 9 since the variant reading is more strongly established here than in verse 11.

[2] $\epsilon\phi\acute{\upsilon}\lambda\alpha\xi\alpha$; cf. p. 301, n. 5. The verb is found elsewhere in the FG only at xii. 25, 47, and is here probably a synonym for $\tau\eta\rho\acute{\epsilon}\omega$, although it can have a very much stronger meaning.

[3] The singular $\H{\eta}\ \gamma\rho\alpha\phi\acute{\eta}$ implies that a particular passage was in mind (cf. p. 120)—perhaps Ps. xli. 9, as at xiii. 18.

perdition,[1] which means 'man destined for perdition', is also found in the NT at 2 Thess. ii. 3, where it stands for the Antichrist. **Perdition** (ἀπώλεια) is not found elsewhere in the FG, though the cognate verb be **lost** (ἀπόλλυμι), with which there is a play on words here, does occur; cf. iii. 16; vi. 39; x. 10, 28; xii. 25; xviii. 9. There seems to be an undoubted predestinarian overtone in this passage, where **is lost** may well mean 'lost eternally'; cf. iii. 16; x. 28.[2]

(13) **'But now I am coming to thee, and I am speaking these things in the world so that they may have my joy fulfilled in themselves.'** Cf. xv. 11, with which there is a close link in vocabulary and thought, and pp. 339 f.; see also xvi. 24 and the note *in loc.* (14) **'I have given them thy word, and the world has hated them, because they are not on the side of**[3] **the world, as I am not on the side of**[3] **the world.**[4]**'** With **I have given them thy word** cf. verses 6 and 8 and the notes *in loc.*; though verse 8 uses ῥήματα and λόγος is used here and in verse 6, the meaning is basically the same. The rest of the verse repeats themes found at xv. 18 f. (on which see pp. 342 f.), though here **has hated** renders an aorist (ἐμίσησεν); the tense reflects the Church's experience of the hostility of its enemies. The overlap with material found in the Last Discourses supports the view that this prayer was developed like them by a Christian prophet; this does not exclude the possibility that words actually spoken by Jesus at the Last Supper are recorded, but it would be difficult to disentangle them.

(15) **'I do not pray that thou shouldest take them out of the world, but that thou shouldest keep them safe from the Evil One. (16) They are not on the side of**[3] **the world, as I am not on the side of**[3] **the world.'**

Despite the hostility of **the world** (underlined by the repetition of verse 14b at verse 16), the task of the disciples is to continue to live in it, aided by the sustaining power of God.

---

[1] Cf. p. 298, n. 4, Moulton-Howard, p. 441, Moule, p. 175, Turner, p. 208.

[2] Bauer[5] s.v. ἀπόλλυμι.

[3] See p. 232, n. 3 for this translation of the preposition ἐκ.

[4] **As I am not on the side of the world** is omitted by P⁶⁶* D *vt sin*. This is perhaps due to the repetition of the phrase **on the side of the world**; the scribe's eye has jumped to the end of the verse.

Though the Greek could be taken either way, **the Evil One**
(ὁ πονηρός) is probably intended by the writer, rather than
'evil' (τὸ πονηρόν); elsewhere in the FG the word is only used
adjectivally (iii. 19; vii. 7), but 1 John ii. 13 f.; iii. 12; v. 18 f.
suggest that a personal force of evil is meant.[1] Cf. pp. 296 f.

(**17**) **'Sanctify them by the truth;**[2] **thy word is truth.'**
Since holiness is a quality which belongs to God alone, he is the
only one who can **sanctify** men. Here, as at x. 36 (where the
word is used of Jesus and is coupled with the fact that he is sent
into the world, cf. verse 18), it means 'set apart for God's
service'. Cf. the *Manual of Discipline*, iv. 20 f., 'God will then
purify every deed of Man with his truth. . . . He will cleanse
him of all wicked deeds with the spirit of holiness; like puri-
fying waters He will shed upon him the spirit of truth';[3] however, in the FG it is God's **word** which **is truth** that is the
means of sanctification (cf. xv. 3). See p. 83 for **truth** in the
FG; here the Father's **word** is characterised as the revelation of
ultimate reality. Similarly the incarnate Logos is 'full of . . .
truth' (i. 14), and Jesus is **the truth** (xiv. 6); equally **the truth**
sets free those who persevere in Jesus' word (viii. 31 f.). Cf. also
verse 14 for the Father's **word** given to the disciples by
Jesus.

(**18**) **'As thou didst send me into the world, so I sent
them into the world.'** Cf. xx. 21, and, for the sending of the
Son by the Father, p. 129, n. 1. See also iv. 38; xiii. 20. The
disciples are to continue Jesus' mission. (**19**) **'And for their
sake I sanctify myself,**[4] **so that they too may be sanctified
by truth.'**[2] In the LXX the verb to **sanctify** (ἁγιάζω) is used
both for the setting apart of an offering for God (Exod. iii. 2;
Deut. xv. 19) and for the consecration of men to God's service
(Jer. i. 5, of a prophet; Exod. xxviii. 41, of priests). The preposition used in the phrase **for their sake** (ὑπὲρ αὐτῶν) has a
sacrificial connotation elsewhere in the FG (see p. 194, on vi.

---

[1] See Bauer[5] s.v. πονηρός for a full discussion of this word in the New
Testament.
[2] The presence or absence of the article with the noun **truth** in verses 17
and 19 is probably not significant; cf. Moule, p. 112, Turner, p. 177.
[3] Cited from the translation by G. Vermès, *The Dead Sea Scrolls in
English* (1962), p. 77.
[4] ἐγὼ ἁγιάζω ἐμαυτόν ; ἐγώ is omitted by P66 vid ℵ AW 700.

51), and Christ, who is both the Son and representative man, goes to his death as both priest and victim for the disciples' sake, **so that they too may be sanctified by truth.** Christ's perfect self-offering (cf. x. 18) is the means by which the disciples whom he is sending into the world are dedicated in obedience to God. Compare the thought of, e.g., Heb. ii. 11; x. 10.

The scope of the prayer is now extended. **(20) 'But it is not for these alone that I pray, but also for those who will believe**[1] **in me through their word, (21) that they may all be one, as thou, Father, art in me and I in thee, that they also may be**[2] **in us, so that the world may believe that thou didst send me.'** Cf. the note on verse 11; the heavy stress laid on the unity of the Church shows that this had become a problem, and no doubt the expansion of the Christian community meant that it came to include very diverse elements which it was difficult to hold together. During his earthly ministry faith as well as division was produced **through** Jesus' **word** (iv. 41; x. 19); now, **through** the disciples' **word** a company of believers is being created, which, because of its participation in the divine character, must necessarily **be one** (cf. x. 16; xi. 52). The relationship between the Father and the Son which Jesus continually declared was one of love and trust and unity of purpose (cf. x. 38; xiv. 10 f., 20), and his followers are required both to abide in him (xv. 4 f.) and to show the quality of his love for them in their dealings with each other (xiii. 34 f.). The primary interest of the writer does not lie in the Church as an institution but in those characteristics which are peculiarly distinctive of the Christian fellowship. It is by the expression of these that the world can come to see the results of Jesus' activity and believe that the Father sent him.[3]

These themes are further developed. **(22) 'And the glory which thou hast given me I have given them, that they**

[1] τῶν πιστευόντων, a present participle denoting a future action (probably an Aramaism); cf. B.-D. § 339 (2b), Turner, p. 87, Black, p. 254.

[2] ὦσιν; ἐν is inserted before this word by ℵ A Θ *fam* 1 *fam* 13 *lat pesh hl boh*[pt] Clement, probably by assimilation to the same phrase earlier in the verse.

[3] For the sending of the Son by the Father see p. 129 n. 1. Cf. p. 86 for the title **Father** in the FG.

**may be one as we are one; (23) I in them and thou in me,
that they may attain perfect unity, so that the world may
know that thou didst send me and didst love**[1] **them as
thou didst love me.'**

22. The renewed mention of **glory**[2] brings to mind a rich
complex of ideas. Jesus is glorified in the disciples (verse 10),
who will like him glorify God (cf. xv. 8) by doing the work
appointed for them (cf. verse 4), even if their obedience involves humiliation and suffering (cf. verse 1 and xxi. 19). The
mutual glorification of Father and Son (for which see on verse 1
and cf. verses 4 f.) implies a unity in which the disciples are to
share. 23. Christ and the disciples are to be one as he is one with
the Father (cf. xiv. 20), **that they may attain perfect unity**
(ἵνα ὦσιν τετελειωμένοι εἰς ἕν); cf. the use of the same verb
in verse 4 to describe the completion of Jesus' work, by which
he has glorified the Father. The close connexion of faith and
knowledge in the FG may be illustrated by a comparison of
so that the world may know that thou didst send me with
verse 21b (cf. further p. 77), though here is added **and didst
love them as thou didst love me.** Cf. pp. 129 f. and p. 130,
n. 2 for a summary of the FG's teaching on love. The verb
love (ἀγαπάω) is first introduced into the prayer here, in preparation for the climax reached in verse 26; **didst love** (ἠγάπησας), as in verses 24 and 26, is a 'timeless' aorist (for the
significance of which see p. 339). It is implied, with a glance
back to xiii. 34 f.; xv. 12, 17, that only as the disciples love each
other can it be known that the love the Father has for the Son
(cf. iii. 35; x. 17; xv. 9; xvii. 24, 26, and also v. 20, where the
verb is φιλέω) is available for the disciples too (cf. xiv. 21, 23,
and also xvi. 27, where the verb is φιλέω), and therefore may be
appropriated by any who leave the world's side to join the
disciples of Jesus.

**(24) 'Father, I desire that those men also whom thou
hast given me may be with me where I am, so that they
may behold**[3] **my glory which thou hast given me because**

---

[1] ἠγάπησας. The variant ἠγάπησα is chiefly a Western reading (D *a b r*[1] *z gat*)
and is probably the result of an attempt at easing the thought; it appeared
difficult to believe that the Father loved the disciples in the same way that
he loved the Son.   [2] Cf. p. 82 for this word in the FG.

[3] θεωρῶσιν; cf. p. 191 and n. 2.

thou didst love me before the foundation of the world.'

Translated literally, the opening of the verse would read: 'Father, that which thou hast given me, I desire that where I am they also may be with me' (Πατήρ, ὅ δέδωκάς μοι, θέλω ἵνα ὅπου εἰμὶ ἐγὼ κἀκεῖνοι ὦσιν μετ᾽ ἐμοῦ); it has been suggested that the complicated syntax[1] is due to problems arising from the translation into Greek of the indeclinable Aramaic particle *d*[e], but as Black says, 'the *casus pendens* gives emphasis to the Johannine neuter phrase, and the employment of the neuter is not ineffective as a generalization—Thy gift to me—explained more fully in the sequel.'[2] Moreover, this mode of expression is not alien to the theme of oneness found elsewhere in the prayer; 'the gift is depicted first in its unity = ὅ, then individually = κἀκεῖνος'.[3] Cf. the note on verse 2. With **so that they may behold my glory** (commonly taken as an eschatological expression) cf. i. 14; ii. 11; xi. 4, 40; xii. 41. It is not unlikely that an experience of the disciples in this life is in mind, though the thought may well move on more than one level: in the FG the **glory** of Christ is manifest throughout his earthly ministry, and now Jesus has been glorified by the Father (cf. on verse 1) and has resumed the glory which belongs to the pre-existent Son (verse 5); further, the glory given to Christ by the Father during his ministry is given by him to the disciples (verse 22). Thus the wish **that those men also whom thou hast given me** (for which phrase cf. on verse 2) **may be with me where I am** is a reformulation of the prayer for the unity of the disciples with Christ, who has now been glorified by God in his death (cf. verse 1) and is now once more, as it were, in the presence of the Father (verse 5). See xii. 26; xiv. 3 and the notes *in loc*. The love of the Father for the Son (for which see further on verse 23) **before the foundation of the world** is given prominence to stress the verities which transcend the temporal order. Cf. on verse 5 for further references to pre-existence in the FG.

---

[1] οὕς is read instead of ὅ by A (Θ) *fam* 1 *fam* 13 *lat pesh hl sah boh* ᵐˢ; this seems to be a deliberate 'improvement' of the text, and the more difficult reading is to be preferred.

[2] Black, p. 62. Black does, however, think that there is much to be said for the view that the Greek neuter reflects Aramaic influence. Cf. Moulton-Howard, pp. 424, 437.

[3] Turner, p. 21.

(25) 'O righteous Father, although¹ the world did not know thee, yet I knew thee, and these knew that thou didst send me. (26) And I made known to them thy name, and I will make it known, that the love with which thou didst love me may be in them, and I in them.'

25. In the FG the adjective **righteous** (δίκαιος) is applied elsewhere only to judgements (v. 30; vii. 24), and it is possibly used here to characterise the **Father** as the just judge in the situation in which **the world** fails to recognise either the Father or the Son who has come to reveal him (cf. i. 10; xvi. 3), though the disciples have come to know that the Father sent Jesus; cf. verse 8 and the note *in loc.*—there is once again a close connexion between 'knowing' and 'believing'. For Jesus' knowledge of the Father, cf. viii. 55; x. 15.

26. The verb **I made known** (ἐγνώρισα) is found in the FG in this verse and at xv. 15; the thought is the same as that of verse 6, with the addition of **and I will make it known** (καὶ γνωρίσω): the disciples are still to be kept in the Father's **name** (cf. verses 11 f.) so that the love which the Father has for the Son **may be in them** (cf. verse 23) and Jesus himself may abide in them (cf. verses 21, 23). This is the climax of the prayer, and describes the Christian ideal.

4. THE ARREST AND TRIALS OF JESUS,
xviii. 1 – xix. 16a

It is clear that this section of the gospel, as much as any other, presents a religious and theological interpretation of the events

---

¹ καί (omitted by D *vt*); Barrett describes the word as 'obscure', but thinks (as Turner, p. 335) that 'it was probably intended to co-ordinate the statement about the world and the disciples' (p. 430), though Moule (p. 167) queries this conclusion and treats the word as an apparent displacement. The difficulty appears to be caused by the combination of the καὶ . . . . δέ construction with the καὶ . . . καί construction used to introduce a contrast (cf. Bauer⁵ s.v. καί 1. 6), giving the sequence καὶ . . . δὲ . . . καί, rendered in the translation **although . . . yet . . . and.** There is then no need to regard ἐγὼ δέ σε ἔγνων as a parenthesis.

that are recorded. Thus Winter is right to say that to the people who transmitted the reports, 'the trial of Jesus was part of his Passion—not an object for legal, or historical, enquiry but an experience of intense religious import'.[1] But it is meditation on real happenings that has produced the Passion story in the four gospels, and so the reader has to ask continually not only what the evangelist teaches, but also what, if anything, can be discovered from his record about what actually took place. These questions, together with the connected problem of the relationship of the Johannine and Synoptic accounts of the arrest and trials, are the main issues raised by this passage.

xviii. (1) When he had said this Jesus went out with his disciples across the brook Kedron,[2] where there was a garden, which he and his disciples entered. (2) Now Judas, his betrayer,[3] also knew the place, because Jesus often met there with his disciples.

That **Jesus went out with his disciples** is paralleled by Luke xxii. 39b, 'and the disciples followed him', but not by Mark or Matthew. The place of the arrest is called a **garden** (κῆπος) only in the FG, here and at xviii. 26. It is perhaps too ingenious to imagine that this is intended to bring the Garden of Eden to mind.[4] Mark xiv. 32 and Matt. xxvi. 36 use the term 'a piece of land' (χωρίον) and give its name, 'Gethsemane'; it has been pointed out that Luke and John do not use this name. Mark xiv. 26, Matt. xxvi. 30 and Luke xxii. 39 all state that Jesus went out to the Mount of Olives. Both here and at Luke xxii. 40 the word **place** (τόπος) is used, though it is hard to agree that this correspondence is significant.[5] It is too common a word in the FG, where it occurs 17 times, for its appearance

[1] Paul Winter, *On the Trial of Jesus* (1961), p. 6.

[2] Reading τοῦ κεδρών with A *pc lat sin pesh Diat*, and regarding it as a trans-literation of the Hebrew Kidrôn. τῶν κέδρων, read by א[c] BCL Θ *fam* 1 *fam* 13 *pl boh*[pt] Origen, and τοῦ κέδρου, read by א* DW *a b d r*[1] *sah boh*[pt] *ac*[2], are both rationalisations of a text that was no longer understood, deriving the word from κέδρος a cedar tree. There was no 'cedar brook' near Jerusalem, as far as is known, while there is ample evidence (e.g. in Josephus) for the existence of the Kedron. χείμαρρος, **brook**, is literally 'winter torrent, wady', a stream that flows abundantly in the rainy season.

[3] See p. 307 n. 2.

[4] For this idea see, e.g., A. Loisy, *Le Quatrième Évangile* (1903), *in loc.*, and cf. below on xix. 41.

[5] So, e.g., S. I. Buse, *N.T.S.*, Vol. VII, 1960–61, p. 70.

here to be important,[1] and is in any case a natural word to use when referring back to a locality mentioned in the previous verse. So far all the resemblances noted between John and the Synoptic Gospels could well be purely accidental and do not imply that the FG was at this point dependent on the Synoptics for its information.

Far more important than the slight verbal agreements is the support given to the statement that **Jesus often met there with his disciples** by Luke xxii. 39, where it is said that it was 'customary' ($\kappa \alpha \tau \dot{\alpha} \ \tau \dot{o} \ \check{\epsilon} \theta o s$) for Jesus to go to the Mount of Olives. Similarly Luke xxi. 37 adds that during Jesus' last visit to Jerusalem he spent the nights on the Mount of Olives. Mark, however, suggests that Jesus stayed at Bethany (xi. 11 f.; cf. xi. 19 f., xiv. 3) and is followed by Matt. (xxi. 17 f.; xxvi. 6), though both gospels associate the Apocalyptic Discourse with the Mount of Olives (Mark xiii. 3, Matt. xxiv. 3). It therefore seems probable that Luke and the FG are drawing on a common tradition at this point; John xii. 1 does not necessarily mean that Jesus stayed at Bethany, though it would be natural for him to visit there, and xii. 9 need only refer to the evening on which Jesus arrived. Indeed, in view of the reception which he received on the following day (xii. 12 ff.) it is not unlikely that Jesus would stay away from Bethany because the presence of Lazarus there only stirred up popular excitement, and this was not wanted by Jesus (see the notes on xii. 9-19). Bethany and the Mount of Olives both lay to the east of Jerusalem, though at different distances from the city; it is easy to see how confusion could have occurred in the tradition (cf. Mark xi. 1, Luke xix. 29), more especially as Jesus was known to have visited Bethany.

There is no hint of the Agony in the Garden at this point in the FG, and it has been supposed that the writer omitted the incident because he did not wish to draw attention to what might appear a moment of weakness on the part of Jesus.[2] It has already been suggested that the omission may possibly be due to a feeling that the narrative would be inappropriate after Jesus' prayer in chapter xvii, or to ignorance of the story by

[1] J. A. Bailey, *The Traditions Common to the Gospels of Luke and John* (1963), p. 53.
[2] E.g. by G. H. C. Macgregor, *The Gospel of John* (1928), *in loc.*

John's source.[1] But xviii. 11 shows that the themes of Geth-semane are not wholly removed from the writer's mind, and it may be that they were introduced more fully at xii. 27 f. so that a theological interpretation of the significance of the arrest could be made more explicit.

(3) So Judas, taking[2] the company ⟨of Roman soldiers⟩ and some temple-police[3] sent by the highpriests and Pharisees, came there with lanterns and torches and weapons.

The rôle of Judas in the FG is to guide the soldiers and police to where Jesus could be found; cf. verse 2, which emphasises that Jesus frequented the garden. As a result of his treachery, the Jewish authorities are able to arrest Jesus in the absence of the crowds; cf. xi. 57, and Mark xi. 18, Luke xix. 47 f.; Mark xii. 12, Matt. xxi. 46, Luke xx. 19; Mark xiv. 1 f., Matt. xxvi. 4 f., Luke xxii. 2; Luke xxii. 6. There is no kiss of betrayal in John, though in Mark xiv. 45 and Matt. xxvi. 49 it is perfectly clear that Judas kissed Jesus to identify him to the soldiers. It is difficult to be sure whether Luke thought that Judas actually kissed Jesus; Luke xxii. 47 f. may simply mean that Jesus re-proached Judas for betraying him with a kiss, whereupon Judas' nerve failed him.[4] John is concerned to show how Jesus was in complete control of the situation at the arrest, and it is con-sistent with this that Jesus gives himself up while Judas stands by ineffectively (see below on verse 5). Luke may have been aware of a tradition of the arrest which did not mention the kiss—and certainly Acts i. 16 refers to Judas simply as the guide of those who arrested Jesus—and if this is so the difficulty in interpreting Luke xxii. 47 f. is due to the fact that he was trying to combine two incompatible traditions. However, attention should be paid to what M. Black, in a slightly different con-nexion, describes as 'a principle of contemporary historiography, which paid less attention to an ordered and orderly account of events than to conveying or portraying an impressive dramatic sequence . . . the principle is that of the artist making the best

---

[1] Supra, pp. 294 f.
[2] λαβών, but having rather the meaning 'with', B.-D. §§ 418 (5), 419 (1), Turner, p. 154.   [3] See p. 210 n. 3.
[4] See J. A. Bailey, *op. cit.*, p. 47, n. 2, for a discussion of this point.

use of his canvas and colours rather than that of the historian
seeking to account for every stage and step in a process.'[1] In the
writer's anxiety to draw out an interpretation of the arrest, the
kiss becomes irrelevant.

Company (σπεῖρα) is a technical term for a unit of the
Roman army; it can mean a cohort, usually 600 strong, or a
maniple, 200 strong, and is usually taken to be the former here.
But in the darkness and confusion it would be difficult to tell
precisely how many soldiers were present, and it may be that
no exact indication of numbers is intended. **The highpriests
and Pharisees** is John's usual expression for the Sanhedrin;[2]
highpriests is a word used in the plural in the New Testament
and Josephus for members of the Sanhedrin who belonged to
highpriestly families.[3] It would appear from the FG that there
were negotiations between the Jewish and Roman authorities
before the arrest took place. This is by no means unlikely; the
Jews wanted Pilate to dispose of Jesus for them, and Pilate
would be glad to have a trouble-maker delivered to him. His
task of keeping order was doubly difficult at the Passover, and
he would not be surprised to hear that there was in Jerusalem someone claiming to be King of the Jews. He permits the
Jewish leaders to hold Jesus during the night so that they might
prepare the charges which they would bring against him in
the governor's court the following morning. Although the
Synoptics contain no suggestion that Roman soldiers were
present at the arrest (Mark xiv. 43, Matt. xxvi. 47, Luke
xxii. 47, 52) this is no reason why the FG may not be
correct.

**(4) So Jesus knowing all that was to happen to him
went out and said to them, 'Whom do you seek?' (5)
They answered him, 'Jesus the Nazoraean.' He said to
them, 'I am he.'**

Jesus, fully aware of what was to happen to him, takes the
initiative even in his arrest. This incident cannot be harmonised
with the Synoptics. Mark xiv. 45 f. and Matt. xxvi. 49 f. both

---

[1] 'The Arrest and Trial of Jesus and the Date of the Last Supper', in
New Testament Essays, ed. A. J. B. Higgins (1959), p. 25.

[2] Cf. vii. 32, 45; xi. 47, 57, and the note on xi. 47, above.

[3] Bauer[5], s.v.

relate how Judas' kiss was followed immediately by Jesus'
arrest (in Matthew, after a brief speech by Jesus). Then comes
the attack on the servant of the Highpriest (Mark xiv. 47, Matt.
xxvi. 51). But in the FG and in Luke xxii. 47-54 the arrest
comes at the end of the scene in the Garden. Force is here used
in the attempt to prevent his arrest, not to free him, as in Mark
and Matthew. Although Luke shows a Jesus in control of the
situation to a limited extent, since he is able to heal the servant
and rebuke his captors before he is seized, he does say 'This is
your hour' when addressing them (Luke xxii. 53), and is less
decisively in control than in John. There is no reason why the
order of events common to Luke and the FG should not be
historical, and it is reasonable to suppose that Luke here combines Markan material with other traditions which John also
knew. Westcott may be right to say that Jesus was not recognised in the uncertain light, and that the soldiers would
not suppose for a moment that he would come to meet
them.[1]

The title **the Nazoraean** (ὁ Ναζωραῖος), found also in the
FG at xviii. 7 and xix. 19, is sometimes explained as equivalent
to 'from Nazareth' (cf. τὸν ἀπὸ Ναζαρέθ, i. 45 and the note
in loc.). But Nazoraean cannot be derived from Nazareth, and
Black[2] suggests that this title was originally given to the
Christians through their popular identification with the movement inaugurated by John the Baptist. This would derive
Nazoraean from the Hebrew *naṣar*, 'to guard, to observe', comparing the name *naṣorayya* given to the Mandaean sect. Black
argues that it would be consistent with what is known of the
Baptist and his movement if this designation, meaning 'keepers'
or 'guardians' of a strict religious tradition, or 'observers of
certain rites', were given them. Dr H. Chadwick points out that
there may be some sort of analogy in the origin of the term
'Methodist'. This name may then have survived as a description of the Mandaeans, who may have been connected with the

---

[1] *The Gospel According to St. John* (1882), p. 252.
[2] Black, pp. 143-146. Cf. also W. F. Albright, 'The Names "Nazareth"
and "Nazoraean"', *Journal of Biblical Literature*, Vol. LXV, 1946, pp. 397-
401, who argues that Nazoraean can be derived from Nazareth, and, especially, O. Cullmann in *The Interpreter's Dictionary of the Bible*, Vol. III (1962),
p. 523.

Baptist movement,[1] and also as the name of a sect described by Epiphanius. In Acts xxiv. 5 it is used as a name for the Christians. In Jesus' lifetime it may have been difficult for contemporaries to distinguish his movement from that of the Baptist, and it is significant that according to Josephus John the Baptist was arrested for raising Messianic expectations in the people.

Jesus' reply, **'I am he'** (Ἐγώ εἰμι), is the divine name, but would have been quite natural under the circumstances and simply serves to identify Jesus. But an overtone is probably intended by the evangelist (cf. pp. 148 f., and the notes on vi. 20; viii. 24, 58).

And Judas also his betrayer[2] stood with them. This may be intended to emphasise the passive rôle of Judas in the arrest, but it probably also records a quite accurate description of the situation: Judas, the disciple who has betrayed his master, identifies himself with the powers of darkness that have arisen against Christ. This is the last mention of Judas in the FG, and is dramatically effective.

(6) So when he said to them, 'I am he', they drew back and fell to the ground. This incident certainly emphasises the divine majesty of Jesus,[3] though it may have a basis in fact: if Jesus had the popular reputation of being a magician, his pronouncing the divine name, itself a most potent spell, might have been enough to deter the most hardy from laying hands on him. It should also be remembered that previously in the FG the temple-police had failed to arrest Jesus (vii. 30, 44 ff.; x. 39); it is possible that similar difficulties were experienced in the Garden.

(7) So he asked them again, 'Whom do you seek?' And they said, 'Jesus the Nazoraean.' (8) Jesus answered, 'I told you that I am he; if then it is I whom you seek, let these men go,' (9) so that[4] the word might be fulfilled which he spoke, 'As for those whom thou hast given me, of them I have not lost one.'

Here and at xviii. 32 John uses the fulfilment-formula not

---

[1] But cf. Dodd, *Interpretation*, p. 124 and n. 2 and pp. 127 f., for the contrary view.

[2] See p. 307 n. 2.   [3] Cf. also p. 199.

[4] ἵνα; for the grammar of this word here, see Moule, pp. 144 f., and the references cited there; cf. Turner, pp. 95, 304.

with reference to the Old Testament, but of the prophetic words of Jesus himself. The reference is to xvii. 12; cf. vi. 39; x. 28; xvii. 2, 6. See the note on xvii. 12. In Mark xiv. 50 and Matt. xxvi. 56 the flight of the disciples is recorded, but although Luke xxii. 32 and John xvi. 32 both seem to be aware of this event it is not recorded explicitly in either gospel. From the FG it would almost seem that Jesus gave himself up on condition that the disciples should be allowed to go away free, and this is a legitimate theological interpretation of what happened; but quite apart from this, Jesus knows that he must die alone and is therefore anxious both to facilitate his disciples' escape and to ensure that there should be no resistance or provocation. Jesus' intervention may have been required to prevent a blood-bath, and it is his action in giving himself up and dismissing his disciples that causes them to flee. The FG focuses attention on the decisiveness of Jesus' act. Later reflection on the incident saw it as prophesied by Christ himself; cf. ii. 22; xii. 16; xviii. 32.

(10) So Simon Peter, who happened to have a sword, drew it and struck the Highpriest's slave and cut off his right ear; the slave's name was Malchus. (11) So Jesus said to Peter, 'Put the sword in the sheath; the cup which my Father has given me, am I not to drink it?'

This incident occurs in all the gospels; cf. Mark xiv. 47, Matt. xxvi. 51 f., Luke xxii. 49-51. But there is insufficient agreement between the FG and any of the Synoptic Gospels in the vocabulary used for any significant relationship to be asserted.[1] The only important parallel is the agreement of John xviii. 10 and Luke xxii. 50 that it was the slave's **right ear** that was cut off. But this is a trivial detail, and if the FG were copying Luke here a greater degree of correspondence would be expected. It is quite unthinkable that any writer should choose isolated words and phrases from the three Synoptic accounts of the incident and work them up into another account of the same happening. It is better to regard the different narratives as independent developments of the tradition, which may of course have reacted on each other. The FG alone has the name of the

[1] *Pace* S. I. Buse, *N.T.S.*, Vol. IV, 1957-58, p. 217, and P. Borgen, *N.T.S.*, Vol. V, 1958-59, pp. 249 f.

disciple and the slave involved; if different traditions of the same event are in question, the silence of the Synoptics is no reason for thinking that John is wrong. He may very well be correct.[1]

The reference to the **cup** may well echo the story of Gethsemane (cf. Mark xiv. 36, Matt. xxvi. 39, Luke xxii. 42), though the same idea also appears at Mark x. 38 f. = Matt. xx. 22 f. Jesus confidently accepts his destiny.

(12) So the company and the tribune and the Jewish temple-police arrested Jesus and bound him, (13) and led him first to Annas. For he was the father-in-law of Caiaphas, who was Highpriest of that year. (14) Now it was Caiaphas who advised the Jews that it was expedient for one man to die for the sake of the people.

The repetition of **company** (see on verse 3 above) and the use of **tribune** ($\chi\iota\lambda\iota\alpha\rho\chi\sigma$, a Roman officer commanding a cohort[2]) confirm that the writer thought that Roman soldiers were present in the Garden (see above).

The verbs translated **arrested** and **led** are also found in Luke xxii. 54, but Mark xiv. 46 and Matt. xxvi. 50 use different words for the arrest. However, Mark xiv. 53 and Matt. xxvi. 57 use a compound of 'to lead' when they describe Jesus led to the Highpriest, and Luke xxii. 54 uses another compound of the same verb at this point. It is very doubtful whether these isolated correspondences signify literary relationship between John and Luke; the words are, in any case, natural ones to use.

For **Highpriest of that year,** see on xi. 49; with verse 14, cf. xi. 49 ff. and the notes *in loc.*

The order of events at this point in the FG is at variance with the tradition followed by Mark and Matthew, which is also represented in Luke. Mark xiv. 53 ff. relates a formal trial of Jesus before the Sanhedrin, held during the night. This is followed by another meeting of the Sanhedrin in the morning, but no business is recorded apart from the delivery of Jesus to Pilate (Mark xv. 1). Matthew follows Mark (Matt. xxvi. 57 ff.;

---

[1] Cf. p. 10.

[2] But cf. A. N. Sherwin-White, *Roman Society and Roman Law in the New Testament* (1963), pp. 124, 136 f., for the same term used of Herod's officers at Mark vi. 21. See also Rev. vi. 15; xix. 18.

xxvii. 1 f.), and adds the name of the Highpriest to whom Jesus was taken, Caiaphas (xxvi. 57). However, in Luke, although Jesus is taken after his arrest to the Highpriest's palace (xxii. 54), no trial takes place until the morning (xxii. 66 ff.), after which Jesus is taken to Pilate (xxiii. 1). In John, Jesus is taken to the house of Annas, where he is not tried but interrogated (xviii. 13, 19 ff.); he is then sent bound to Caiaphas (xviii. 24), but no trial is recorded before Jesus is taken to the praetorium (xviii. 28). These phenomena would be adequately accounted for if Luke and John were drawing on common tradition here, Luke combining this with Markan material.

Annas appears elsewhere in the New Testament only at verse 24, Luke iii. 2 and Acts iv. 6. These two passages supply independent testimony that he was still an important person. He was himself Highpriest A.D. 6–15, and his family held the Highpriesthood as a virtual monopoly till A.D. 41.[1] Although he had been deposed from office by the Romans, it is not *a priori* incredible that Jesus should have been taken to him.

In the FG sentence has already been passed on Jesus (see xi. 53 and the note *in loc.*), and what follows now is an examination to collect evidence to put before the Roman governor. It cannot be harmonised with Mark, but preserves an independent Jerusalem tradition. Thus it may be possible to escape Barrett's scepticism about John's account here,[2] which is based on the assumptions that the FG is using the Synoptic Gospels and is describing a trial. Difficulties in the Synoptic account of the Jewish trial have often been noted,[3] and it has also been argued, on the basis of the Johannine record and the absence of a verdict from Luke xxii. 71, that while the Synoptics are correct in much of what they say happened, they are wrong to turn it into a trial.[4] The Jewish leaders may have genuinely expected resistance when Jesus was arrested. This would have given them a cast-iron case to lay before Pilate; now they have to draw up an indictment. Ultimately, Caiaphas is sufficiently

[1] E. Mary Smallwood, 'High Priests and Politics in Roman Palestine', *J.T.S.*, n.s., Vol. XIII, 1962, p. 16. The tenures of the only two men chosen from other families in this period were brief.

[2] Barrett, p. 438.   [3] See, e.g., M. Black, *art. cit.*, p. 20.

[4] O. Cullmann, *The State in the New Testament* (1957), pp. 44 ff.

cynical to hand Jesus over to the Romans for being what he had consistently refused to be.

Certain difficulties have been noted in the order of events in this section, and sometimes rearrangements of the material are suggested. But the order of the verses in the Sinaitic Syriac (13, 24, 14, 15, 19-23, 16-18) and in 225 (13a, 24, 13b, 14-23) merely shows that the problem was felt at an early date; it does not provide manuscript authority for changing John's presentation. The main awkwardness in the narrative is said to be the fact that in verse 13 Jesus is taken to Annas, but that verses 15, 19, and 22, with their references to the Highpriest, presuppose that he was then in fact appearing before Caiaphas. However, the title 'Highpriest' could be given to ex-highpriests as well as to the Highpriest in office,[1] and so the issue is really whether John's record of the Jewish 'trial' is inherently probable.

It has also been said that the second part of the story of Peter's denial (verses 25-27), which comes after the statement that Jesus was sent bound to Caiaphas, suggests that throughout Jesus was in Caiaphas' house, where all three denials took place. But Barrett notes on verse 24 that '"sending" need not imply movement from one building to another',[2] and it may also be that the story of Peter's denial has been divided into two for dramatic reasons to bring out more forcefully the way in which Jesus stands alone before his accusers.

(15) And there followed Jesus Simon Peter and another disciple. And that disciple was known to the Highpriest, and went in with Jesus into the Highpriest's courtyard, (16) but Peter stood by the door outside. So the other disciple who was known to the Highpriest went out and spoke to the Portress, and brought Peter in. (17) So the maid who kept the door said to Peter, 'Are you also not one of this man's disciples?'

It is perhaps most likely that the other disciple is to be

---

[1] H. St. J. Thackeray and R. Marcus, *A Lexicon to Josephus*, Part II (1934), p. 87b, state that in Josephus the plural of ἀρχιερεύς includes, 'besides the acting h.p., ex-high-priests and members of the privileged families from which the h.priests were drawn.' Cf. p. 383 above. But the word is also used deliberately in the singular by Josephus to denote an ex-highpriest; cf. E. Schürer, *Geschichte des Jüdischen Volkes im Zeitalter Jesu Christi*, II (³1898), p. 221.   [2] Barrett, p. 441.

equated with the Beloved Disciple; cf. xx. 2, 3, 4, 8, and the notes *in loc*. Barrett[1] suspects that he may have been invented to provide a means of introducing Peter to the scene of the trial, to which (some might object) he would not have otherwise been admitted; however, this verdict rests on the theory that John was here dependent on Mark. As the story develops it combines a basic agreement on the main outline of the synoptic record with considerable divergence on minor points of detail which it is difficult to account for on the hypothesis that John was editing Mark.

The Sinaitic Syriac brings the FG into closer accord with the Synoptics here by reading 'Porter' for **Portress** in verse 16, and 'the female slave of the Porter' for **the maid who kept the door** in verse 17. Black[2] points out that one would normally expect a man to be in charge of the door of the Highpriest, especially on such an occasion as this, and notes that the Greek text could result from dittography of a ⊓ in Aramaic. He suggests that this may be the original reading.

The word translated **known** ($\gamma\nu\omega\sigma\tau\acute{o}s$) can mean 'friend' or 'intimate' or 'acquaintance',[3] though C. H. Dodd goes beyond this and argues that 'it means that the person so described was a member of the High Priest's circle, possibly a kinsman and himself of priestly birth, or at any rate one who stood in intimate relations with the governing high priestly family.'[4] Unless Riesenfeld's conjecture is correct[5] this disciple was not John the son of Zebedee. Eisler[6] thinks he was the John of Acts iv. 6, who eventually became John of Ephesus and who was Highpriest A.D. 37–41. It is not necessary to distinguish the Beloved Disciple and the Other Disciple,[7] though it would be possible to do so and to claim that the latter was from Jerusalem and may conceivably have been John Mark.[8] Macgregor[9] points out

[1] Barrett, pp. 438 f.

[2] Black, pp. 192 f. M. É. Boismard, 'Importance de la critique textuelle pour établir l'origine araméenne du Quatrième Évangile', in *L'Évangile de Jean*, Recherches Bibliques III (1958), p. 46, notes that the reading of the Sinaitic Syriac is supported by Tatian and the Ethiopic version.

[3] Bauer[5], s.v. [4] *Historical Tradition in the Fourth Gospel* (1963), p. 87.

[5] See above, p. 30. [6] *The Enigma of the Fourth Gospel* (1938), pp. 39–45.

[7] See p. 32 above.

[8] See p. 49 and pp. 50 ff. for theories connecting John Mark with the FG.

[9] *Op. cit.*, pp. 330 f.

that if the Other Disciple was a Jerusalem disciple, he may well have moved in priestly circles and be the basis of Polycrates' tradition about the *petalon*.[1] If the implications of verse 16 are accepted they could explain the intimate knowledge of the Sanhedrin and affairs in Jerusalem shown by the FG.

The motive of Peter in following Jesus is obscure. The suggestion that it was curiosity hardly meets the situation. But note how his courage in doing this brings him to the tragedy of his denial.

(18) He said, 'I am not'. There were standing ⟨there⟩ the slaves and the temple-police,[2] who had made a charcoal fire because it was cold, and were warming themselves; and Peter also was standing with them and warming himself.

'I am not' is not the form of Peter's reply in the Synoptic Gospels (Mark xiv. 68, Matt. xxvi. 70, Luke xxii. 57) nor does John record a withdrawal from the firelight after the first challenge (Mark xiv. 68, Matt. xxvi. 71). But all four gospels agree that the first challenge came from a woman and use the same word to describe her (παιδίσκη). She spoke to Peter—no doubt quite idly—after he had reached the fire; however, after a time this rouses the curiosity of the slaves and temple-police about the newcomer, and the story continues in verses 25-27. Verse 25 repeats verse 18b; this arrangement of the material may be intended to mark a lapse of time, but is also dramatically effective (see above).

(19) So the Highpriest asked Jesus about his disciples and about his teaching.

This is an interrogation before Annas whose purpose is to provide evidence that could later be used against Jesus. In the Synoptic Gospels the trial turns on the question of the person of Jesus. In the FG that has long been a subject of dispute, and the Highpriest has already made up his mind. It is possible that the trials of Christians may be reflected in John's account, though this does not mean that it is not also to be understood as a basically-factual record of what actually happened. It is also possible that the Synoptic tradition has read back into its trial scene features of the dispute between church and synagogue,

[1] See above p. 43.   [2] See p. 210 n. 3.

in which claims made for Christ by the Christians *were* blasphemy. It was, of course, never blasphemous to claim to be Messiah, and Son of God was simply a Messianic title; although some of Jesus' contemporaries may have wondered whether he might not be claiming a quasi-divine status, this was never fully explicit, and it was more his attacks on vested interests in religion and the possibility of armed uprising caused by his work that forced the Jewish authorities to act. In the circumstances further enquiries might produce useful information about his followers' activities and his own subversive propaganda.

(20) Jesus answered him, 'I spoke in public[1] to the world; I taught all the time[2] in synagogue and in the temple, where all the Jews congregate, and I said nothing in secret.'

The world simply means 'all and sundry' here, though the term has a further nuance in the FG; cf. the note on xii. 19. For the thought cf. Jesus' speech at the Arrest, 'I was with you daily teaching in the Temple', Mark xiv. 49 and parallels. While Jesus did of course give teaching in private (cf. xiii-xvi), this was not in secret meetings of conspirators. There may also be an allusion to the fact that in the FG Jesus was known as Messiah from the outset.

(21) 'Why do you ask me? Ask those who heard what I said to them: see, these know what I said.'

Jesus protests against the attempt to incriminate him and appeals for witnesses. It is probable that the 'false witnesses' of the Synoptic trial (Mark xiv. 55-59, Matt. xxvi. 59-61) are also part of the historical scene; they are false in the sense that they witness against Jesus, not in the sense that they are dishonest. If the affair had been prearranged it is hard to see why the necessary testimony failed to emerge. As well as examining Jesus the Jewish authorities examine witnesses to see if damaging information can be collected. There is an honest attempt to collect the necessary evidence for contriving Jesus' execution in as legal a fashion as possible; in most people there is a curious combination of principle and expediency that produces results that are not always fully consistent with themselves.

(22) And when he had said this one of the temple-police

---

[1] παρρησίᾳ; see p. 201, n. 6.   [2] πάντοτε; see p. 188, n. 6.

standing by struck Jesus a blow, saying, 'Is that the way to answer the Highpriest?'

The **blow** ($\dot{\rho}\acute{\alpha}\pi\iota\sigma\mu\alpha$) is literally 'a blow on the cheek with the open hand';[1] cf. xix. 3 and Mark xiv. 65 for the word [2] and Acts xxiii. 2 for the incident. Jesus' refusal to answer a leading question annoys the court.

(23) Jesus answered him, 'If I spoke wrongly, testify of the wrong; but if rightly, why do you strike me?'

Jesus is undeterred by violence. On this protest the examination ends, though John may have known more of what occurred than he tells in the gospel. He selects an incident that reveals Jesus dealing boldly with his enemies, and in so doing indicates the significance of what took place.

(24) So Annas sent him bound to Caiaphas the Highpriest. This was presumably so that Caiaphas could keep him in custody until he could be taken to Pilate. There is no trial before Caiaphas in John (see above, p. 280).

(25) Now Simon Peter was standing and warming himself. So they said to him, 'Are you not also one of his disciples?' He denied and said, 'I am not.' (26) One of the slaves of the Highpriest, who was a relation of the man whose ear Peter cut off, said, 'I saw you in the garden with him, didn't I?' (27) So Peter denied it again, and at once a cock crowed.

John tells the story most objectively. There is no mention of Jesus looking at Peter as he left the court (Luke xxii. 61) or of Peter remembering Jesus' words and weeping (Mark xiv. 72, Matt. xxvi. 75, Luke xxii. 61b, 62). In the Synoptics, the second challenge to Peter was given by an individual (Mark xiv. 69, Matt. xxvi. 71, Luke xxii. 58), though there is no agreement about who this individual was; the second challenge is not a direct question (Mark xiv. 69, Matt. xxvi. 71, but cf. Luke xxii. 58); and the third challenge is based on the fact that Peter is a Galilean (Mark xiv. 70, Matt. xxvi. 73, Luke xxii. 59). That **a relation of the man whose ear Peter cut off** challenged him, and that he claimed to have seen Peter in the garden, are details peculiar to John (cf. Mark xiv. 70, Matt. xxvi. 73, Luke

---

[1] Moulton and Milligan, s.v.
[2] Though the translation of this latter passage is doubtful, Bauer[5], s.v.

xxii. 59 for Synoptic differences at this point). It is surely most unlikely that John is here editing any of the Synoptic Gospels; the minor variations between the accounts suggest that different forms of the story circulating independently have been preserved in Mark/Matthew, Luke and John.

(28) So they took Jesus from Caiaphas into the praetorium; and it was morning; and they themselves did not enter the praetorium, in order that they should not be defiled but should eat the Passover.

The praetorium is Pilate's official residence. **It was morning,** i.e. just before 6 a.m.; Roman courts started business at dawn. **The Passover** was to be eaten that evening (which, by Jewish reckoning, was the beginning of the next day); for John's dating of the crucifixion see above, pp. 303 f. Gentile homes were *ipso facto* unclean for the orthodox Jew. In view of what they were doing, the punctiliousness of the Jewish leaders is ironical. Barrett[1] questions the historical basis of their scruple, and states that any uncleanness contracted could be removed by a bath before evening. But according to some authorities a seven-day impurity would be caused.[2]

(29) So Pilate went out to them and said, 'What accusation do you bring against this man?'

This is the correct formal opening to a Roman trial.[3]

(30) They answered and said to him, 'If this ⟨fellow⟩[4] were not an evil-doer, we would not have handed him over to you.'

According to Luke xxiii. 2, when Jesus was brought before Pilate formal charges were laid against him. But Mark xv. 2 f. and Matt. xxvii. 11 f. put the charges laid against Jesus after Pilate's question, 'Are you the King of the Jews?' In John too it is *Pilate* who first raises the question of Jesus' kingship (verse 33). In view of the desire of the Jews to act within the letter of the law, and as they had no real evidence for their charges, it is surely reasonable to suppose that here they try to avoid the issue. Jesus' death is to be brought about through the

---

[1] Barrett, p. 444.
[2] Strack-Billerbeck, II, pp. 837 ff.
[3] A. N. Sherwin-White, *op. cit.*, p. 47.
[4] οὗτος; see p. 205 n. 1.

Romans, but on the basis of a prior understanding with Pilate rather than as the result of a direct accusation now. It is only when this attempt fails that accusations are laid; they are hinted at in xix. 12. Barrett argues that this remark cannot reveal an understanding between the Jews and Pilate 'because Pilate in referring the case back to the Jews shows that he did not understand that a capital sentence was required'.[1] He thinks that the verse represents an attempt to incriminate the Jews. But it is possible that when Pilate first saw Jesus he suspected that the Jews had misled him.

(31) So Pilate said to them, 'Take him yourselves, and judge him according to your law.' The Jews said to him, 'We are not allowed to kill anyone,' (32) in order that[2] the word of Jesus should be fulfilled which he spoke, showing by what kind of death he was to die.

Pilate tries to get out of his understanding with the Jews; there is thus no parallel with Gallio (Acts xviii. 14 ff.). It is possible that the Jews' desire that Jesus should be crucified was intended to discredit him as Messiah in view of Deut. xxi. 23, 'he that is hanged [on a tree] is accursed of God'. But this would seem at best to be a subsidiary motive. The Jews' claim that they were not allowed to inflict capital punishment, though it has been widely questioned, does seem justified,[3] although this may not be the vital issue here. Jesus had much popular support, and the Jewish leaders (as Barrett observes)[4] needed Pilate's help if they were to dispose of Jesus. What the Jews may be saying in effect is that *they* could not kill Jesus since they were only a minority. Either or both of these factors may have been operative. In any case, the upshot of the matter is that Jesus is discredited with his supporters because he is not the sort of king they wanted, while he is also misrepresented before Pilate, who becomes profoundly suspicious of

---

[1] Barrett, p. 444.   [2] See on xviii. 9 above.

[3] See Barrett, pp. 445 f., and A. N. Sherwin-White, *op. cit.*, pp. 35-43, and 'The Trial of Christ', in *Historicity and Chronology in the New Testament* (S.P.C.K. Theological Collections, Vol. VI, 1965), pp. 97-116, for a full discussion; also J. Jeremias, 'Zur Geschichtlichkeit des Verhörs Jesu vor dem Hohen Rat', *Z.N.W.*, Vol. 43, 1950–51, pp. 145-150, G. D. Kilpatrick, *The Trial of Jesus* (1952), J. Blinzler, *The Trial of Jesus* (1959), pp. 157-163, Paul Winter, *op. cit.*, pp. 9-15, 75-90.   [4] Barrett, p. 445.

the Jews' motives and decides to interrogate Jesus apart from his accusers.

For **the word of Jesus** cf. iii. 14 f.; viii. 28; xii. 32 f., and see the note on xviii. 9.

(33) So Pilate went back into the praetorium and summoned Jesus and said to him, 'You are the King of the Jews?'

You is emphatic; Pilate cannot believe this claim could be made by or on behalf of the man in front of him. He had presumably been told about Jesus' Messianic claims before the arrest. Cf. i. 49; vi. 15; xii. 13, and the discussion on p. 104 for the theme of Jesus' kingship.

(34) Jesus answered, 'Do you say this of your own accord, or did others say it to you about me?'

Jesus wants to know the background to the question. If it is the basis of the charge against him, he must explain in what sense he is king.

(35) Pilate answered, 'I am not a Jew, am I? Your nation¹ and the highpriests handed you over to me. What did you do?'

Pilate is impatient at the situation that has developed. He tacitly admits that the charge has been made, but asks what Jesus has done to cause the Jewish authorities to wish him out of the way. Pilate's suspicion of the highpriests is already apparent.

(36) Jesus answered, 'My kingship is not anything to do with this world;² if my kingship were to do with this world, my servants would be fighting, so that I should not be handed over to the Jews; but as it is³ my kingship is nothing to do with it.'

Jesus denies the charge and explains the nature of his kingship. Cf. iii. 3, 5. He puts into words for Pilate's benefit the dilemma in which he has been throughout his ministry—though conscious of an absolute authority, and of Davidic descent, he has known that to assert his authority by force would ruin the purpose for which he had come.

¹ ἔθνος; see p. 278 n. 4.

² κόσμος; see on i. 9, p. 76. Cf. the Synoptic ἐν τούτῳ τῷ αἰῶνι, Matt. xii. 32; cf. Luke xvi. 8, xx. 34. And see p. 223.

³ νῦν δέ; see p. 230 n. 1. See also M. E. Thrall, *Greek Particles in the New Testament* (1962), p. 31.

(37) So Pilate said to him, 'You are a king then, are you not?'[1]

Pilate in some sense recognises Jesus' claim and attempts to press him further, but he will not commit himself further. Instead, **Jesus answered, 'It is you**[2] **who say that I am a king. The purpose for which I was born and have come into the world is to bear witness to the truth; everyone who is on the side of**[3] **truth listens to my voice.'** On **the truth** (ἡ ἀλήθεια) see p. 83. It means 'reality' here. Jesus finds such a formulation of the purpose of his mission less misleading than the idea of kingship. **It is you who say** is probably intentionally ambiguous; Pilate and Jesus mean different things by kingship, so a direct answer is not possible.[4] With **listens to my voice,** cf. x. 3, 4, 16, 27.

(38) Pilate said to him, 'What is truth?' (a question administrators would be well advised not to ask). He thereby showed that he was not **on the side of truth.** This is the last mention of truth (ἀλήθεια) in the FG; the answer to Pilate's question is given in the rest of the story. As in the Synoptic Gospels, Pilate has a certain sympathy with Jesus. He sees that they are both victims of a plot, and wants to free both Jesus and himself if he can do so without danger in the explosive period of the Passover (cf. Mark xv. 10, 14, Matt. xxvii. 18, 23, Luke xxiii. 4, 14, 20, 22).

And when he had said this he went out again to the Jews, and said to them, 'I find no guilt at all in him. (39) But it is your custom that I should release you one ⟨prisoner⟩ at the Passover; do you wish me then to release you the King of the Jews?'

Pilate admits Jesus' innocence and attempts to secure his release. The references in the Synoptic Gospels just cited support the historicity of this portrayal of Pilate. But the Synoptics do not account for Pilate's attitude; John does this by his record of Pilate's conversation with Jesus. It is conceivable that this is simply an ingenious invention on the part of John, but it can

---

[1] Reading οὔκουν. Turner, B.-D. § 451 (1), and Bauer⁵, s.v. οὐκοῦν, all read οὐκοῦν; Turner, p. 337, claims 'The interrogative . . . may be Pilate's ipsissimum verbum'. For a discussion, see Moule, p. 165.

[2] Σύ is emphatic; Turner, p. 37, paraphrases, 'you have said it, not me'.

[3] ἐκ τῆς ἀληθείας; see p. 232, n. 3.   [4] M. E. Thrall, *op. cit.*, pp. 75 f.

also be historically true, and so explain what the other gospels leave unexplained. It is unlikely that such a conversation would be without witnesses; the FG, as the Jerusalem gospel, is the most likely to contain authentic tradition on this point. In addition, the FG suggests that Pilate had been tricked by the Jews, who had negotiated with him before the arrest; Pilate is now anxious to escape from his undertaking to the Sanhedrin, and appeals over the heads of the Jewish leaders to the crowd. There is no evidence outside the gospels for the custom of releasing a prisoner at Passover, but there is no reason to doubt that such a practice existed. Mark xv. 6 (=Matt. xxvii. 15, cf. Luke xxiii. 18) and John are probably independent witnesses to it, and the Romans were shrewd enough to appreciate the value of such a safety-valve. Pilate offers Jesus as the Passover prisoner to be released. Barrett[1] wonders why Pilate calls him **the King of the Jews,** since he has already decided that Jesus is not king in any ordinary sense of the word, and the title would not commend Jesus to the Jews, who were using it as the basis of a charge against him. Barrett allows that 'John has probably taken the title straight out of the earlier tradition', by which he means Mark. But it is surely equally plausible to suggest that Pilate is here appealing over the heads of the highpriests and Pharisees to the crowd, to whom the title may well appeal. At the same time Pilate is using it sarcastically, and John records it in irony: Pilate proclaims the true King of Israel.

(40) So they again shouted saying, 'Not this ⟨fellow⟩,[2] but Barabbas.' Now Barabbas was a bandit.

Again (πάλιν) is pointless as it stands. According to Barrett[3] it is borrowed from Mark xv. 13. There is a variant reading 'all' (πάντες, presumably a correction) supported by G K *fam* 1 *fam* 13 33 *al vt*, while P66vid A Θ, some late Greek MSS. and *vg* conflate the two readings. But if **again** is the genuine reading, it may be due to a rearrangement of his material by John to give an effective climax to the scene with the apostasy of the Jews at xix. 15. **They again shouted** logically follows the series of shouts in xix. 6, 12, 15. Also, the scourging (xix. 1) should follow the sentence as the first part of the punishment. This

---

[1] Barrett, pp. 448 f.   [2] τοῦτον; see p. 205 n. 1.
[3] Barrett, p. 449.

suggests that in John's source, after the conversation with Jesus (xviii. 33-38a) Pilate came out and declared him innocent (38b). The Jews then appealed to their law (xix. 7-14), and on Jesus' appearance with Pilate shouted, 'Crucify him' (xix. 6). Pilate replied, 'Take him and crucify him yourselves, for I find no guilt in him.' They repeated, 'Crucify' (xix. 15), and Pilate then offered Jesus as the Passover prisoner to be released (xviii. 39). On the crowd's demand for Barabbas (xviii. 40) Pilate had Jesus scourged (xix. 1 ff.—the second 'Behold your King' is then sheer irony) and handed him over to be crucified (xix. 16). There may be some reduplication in this (e.g. the bringing out of Jesus *twice* to the crowd), though Luke is also a witness to three protestations of Jesus' innocence on the part of Pilate (John xviii. 38, xix. 4, 6; Luke xxiii. 4, 14, 22). Another possibility is that John has put together *two* independent stories.

The present arrangement of the material gives a formal but dramatically effective pattern. There are six scenes: 1. Jesus handed to Pilate, xviii. 28-32. 2. First hearing, 33-38. 3. Jesus or Barabbas? 39 f. 4. Scourging and exhibition of Jesus, xix. 1-7. 5. Second hearing, 8-12a. 6. Condemnation of Jesus, 12b-16a. These form two groups (xviii. 28–xix. 7 and xix. 8-16), each culminating in a presentation of Jesus to the crowd and the demand for his crucifixion. Such a formal pattern also appears in the FG in its treatment of the signs in the ministry. John's order is intentional, culminating in the apostasy of the Jews.

Mark xv. 7 and Luke xxiii. 19 give fuller information about Barabbas and support John's description of him as a **bandit** (λῃστής); it is the common description of nationalists given by an occupying power. Barabbas was in fact what Jesus was accused of being. Hence, when the crowd saw the chance of the release of a prisoner they called for Barabbas and spoilt Pilate's plan. Cf. Mark xv. 6-11, where the crowds ask Pilate for the release of a prisoner; Matt. xxvii. 15-18, 20 f. and Luke xxiii. 18 f. are not clear on the point.

xix. (1) So then Pilate took Jesus and scourged him. A Roman scourging was invariably associated with other punishments. Luke xxiii. 16, 22 refers to a less severe grade of corporal punishment that could stand by itself.[1] Thus the scourging here

---

[1] A. N. Sherwin-White, *op. cit.*, pp. 27 f.

is clearly out of place in the present order of events in the FG.
The rearrangement suggested above would bring the FG into
line with Mark xv. 15 = Matt. xxvii. 26, where the scourging
takes place after the sentence. It was a savage punishment, and
would materially hasten the death of the crucified man.

**(2) And the soldiers plaited a crown out of thorns and
put it on his head, and put a scarlet cloak round him, (3)
and kept coming to him and saying, 'Hail, King¹ of the
Jews!', and struck him with their hands.**

All this is in mockery, and, like the scourging, presupposes
that sentence has been passed. It is highly probable that the
thorns were palm fronds (cf. xii. 13), woven into the caricature
of a radiate crown, which was intended to indicate the divine
status of its wearer.² It is a symbol of divine kingship rather
than an instrument of torture, and the **scarlet cloak** (which
was part of the Roman uniform) is a mock-royal robe of purple.
For **struck him with their hands,** see on xviii. 22; the blows
replaced the kiss of homage. Jesus, the King of the Jews, is
dressed up as a king and given mock homage. The shame and
irony of the scene are evident. Cf. Mark xv. 16-20, Matt. xxvii.
27-31.

**(4) And Pilate again went out and said to them, 'See, I
am bringing him out to you, in order that you may know
that I find no guilt in him.' (5) So Jesus went out, wearing
the crown of thorns and the scarlet cloak. And he said to
them, 'See, the man!'³**

One would expect, 'See, your King' here, as Jesus comes out
arrayed in a parody of royal attire. This showing of Jesus may
well be a doublet of verses 13 f. But as it stands **the man**
(ὁ ἄνθρωπος) has a deeper meaning, being the equivalent of
'the Son of man', a Greek translation of an Aramaic periphrasis
for man,⁴ and here representing the Man, made in God's
image; Pilate, like Caiaphas, is an unwitting prophet. At the
same time he is having a bitter revenge on the Jews, who them-

---

¹ ὁ βασιλεύς, articular nominative for vocative; Moulton, *Prolegomena*, p.
70.
² H. St J. Hart, 'The Crown of Thorns in John 19, 2-5', *J.T.S.* n.s.,
Vol. III, 1952, pp. 66-75.
³ This sentence is omitted by some ancient authorities: P⁶⁶* *a e ff²* r¹ ac².
⁴ On the Son of man see p. 106.

selves first suggested that Jesus was a king. The one whom
they claim to be king is shown to them in a mockery of royal
dress.

**(6) So when the highpriests and the temple-police saw
him, they shouted, saying, 'Crucify, crucify.'** Cf. Mark
xv. 13 f., Matt. xxvii. 22 f., Luke xxiii. 21 ff. **Pilate said to
them, 'Take him yourselves and crucify him. For I do
not find any guilt in him.'**

This is of course sarcasm. The Jews did not in any case
crucify.

**(7) The Jews answered him, 'We have a law, and
according to that law he ought to die, because he made
himself Son of God.'**

They cynically admit that their motive is not rejection of
Jesus as King, but as Son of God, although they are not prepared to stop pressing the political charge. Pilate could not take
cognisance of the true accusation, but he is still committed to
accepting the one he knows to be false.

A law, i.e. the enactment against blasphemy, Lev. xxiv. 16,
though T. F. Glasson[1] thinks there may also be the further
suggestion here of the incompatibility of Christ and the Torah;
cf. i. 17.

For **he made himself Son of God,** cf. v. 18; viii. 58 f.; x.
30 ff., and the notes *in loc.*

**(8) So when Pilate heard this account ⟨of the matter⟩,
he became more afraid, (9) and entered the praetorium
again and said to Jesus, 'Where are you from?' But Jesus
did not give him an answer.**

Pilate's fear may be superstitious, or it may be a recognition
of the nature of the trap in which he has been caught. **More
afraid** is probably best rendered 'exceedingly afraid', **more**
($\mu\hat{a}\lambda\lambda o\nu$) having the force of a superlative. With Pilate's question, cf. the question of Luke xxiii. 6 whether Jesus was a
Galilean, and with Jesus' refusal to answer, Mark xv. 5 = Matt.
xxvii. 14, and Luke xxiii. 9. But the circumstances are different
in each case, so that it is unlikely that John derives either incident from the other gospels. Jesus' silence in John is due to the
impossibility of giving Pilate an answer he will understand.

---

[1] *Moses in the Fourth Gospel* (1963), p. 92.

(10) So Pilate said to him, 'Do you not speak to me?[1] You know, do you not, that I have authority to release you and I have authority to crucify you?' (11) Jesus answered, 'You had no authority in my case—and would not have it now—if it had not been given you from above.'

Pilate's **authority** (ἐξουσία) is his imperial power (his *imperium*), which he thinks absolute. But it is in fact derivative (cf. Rom. xiii. 1 ff.). The grammatical construction of Jesus' answer (οὐκ εἶχες . . . εἰ μὴ ἦν) is represented by the paraphrase. For the omission of ἄν here see p. 344, n. 1.[2] Jesus himself has power (ἐξουσία) over his own life (x. 18), given him by God. He continues, **'That is why he who handed me over to you has a greater sin '**—because he causes Pilate to abuse his God-given authority. **He who handed me over to you** is probably Caiaphas rather than Judas.

(12) In consequence of this[3] Pilate began to try[4] to release him; but the Jews shouted, saying, 'If you do release this ⟨fellow⟩[5] you are not Caesar's friend;[6] everyone who makes himself a King opposes Caesar.'

This attempt to release Jesus should surely come earlier in the record. The highpriests play their trump-card. In the reign of Tiberius, whose suspicion was pathological, a whisper in Rome that Pilate condoned *maiestas* would be fatal to him, particularly if the crucifixion is to be dated *c.* A.D. 33, after the fall of Seianus, Pilate's patron, on the same charge of *maiestas*. Pilate bows to the inevitable.

(13) So when Pilate heard these words, he led Jesus out, and sat on the judgement-seat in a place called Lithostrōton, but in Aramaic[7] Gabbatha. (14) It was the Day of Preparation of the Passover; it was about the sixth hour; and ⟨Pilate⟩ said to the Jews, 'See, your King!'

Sat on the judgement-seat (ἐκάθισεν ἐπὶ βήματος) could

---

[1] Ἐμοί is emphatic.
[2] Reading εἶχες with B W Θ *fam* 1 *pm*; ἔχεις is read by ℵ A *fam* 13 565.
[3] ἐκ τούτου; see p. 198 n.2.   [4] ἐζήτει.
[5] τοῦτον; see p. 205 n. 1.
[6] On this phrase, cf. E. Bammel, 'φίλος τοῦ Καίσαρος', *Theologische Literaturzeitung*, Vol. LXXVII, 1952, cols. 205-210; it may well represent an honour conferred rarely on those of equestrian status which Pilate had been given.   [7] See p. 158 n. 3.

equally well be translated 'set *him* (i.e. Jesus) on the judgement-seat', as the verb can be either transitive or intransitive. Justin, *Apology* i. 35, and the *Gospel of Peter*, iii. 7, give the former sense, though the verb is usually intransitive in the NT, as in its other appearance in the FG at xii. 14 (cf. viii. 2).[1] If this verse is to be placed at an earlier stage of the trial in John's source, it may be that it was originally transitive, though as it stands it is more likely to be intransitive, implying that Pilate now sentences Jesus to death. But despite this it could still be seen as a savage joke; **'See, your King!'** certainly implies contempt for the Jews. Pilate has been manoeuvred into a false position by the highpriests, and takes his revenge.

The judgement-seat was in the open air, as was usual in Roman courts. There is considerable dispute over the location of the praetorium; it may have been at the Tower of Antonia or at the Old Palace of Herod.[2] If the former alternative is accepted, the **Lithostrōton** is the great court of the Tower of Antonia, which was about 2,500 square metres in area. **Lithostrōton** could mean either 'an area paved with blocks of stone', or 'a tessellated pavement'.[3] **Gabbatha** is an Aramaic word whose meaning is uncertain,[4] though it has been linked with the word 'gabbetâ', 'ridge'; the Tower of Antonia originally stood on a rocky elevation rising above the adjacent terrain.[5]

With **the sixth hour,** i.e. noon, cf. Mark xv. 25, which puts the crucifixion itself at 9 a.m. Barrett[6] points out that this divergence may have arisen from a confusion of two similar Greek

[1] See Moulton-Howard, p. 409.

[2] For presentations of these two viewpoints, see L.-H. Vincent, 'Le Lithostrotos Évangélique', *Revue Biblique*, Vol. LIX, 1952, pp. 513-530, and P. Benoît, 'Prétoire, Lithostroton et Gabbatha', *Ibid.*, pp. 531-550.

[3] Bauer[5], s.v.   [4] Bauer[5], s.v.

[5] See, e.g., W. F. Albright, *The Archaeology of Palestine* (1960 edition), p. 245, and 'Recent Discoveries in Palestine and the Gospel of St. John', in *The Background of the New Testament and its Eschatology*, ed. W. D. Davies and D. Daube (1956), pp. 158 f. See also G. E. Wright, *Biblical Archaeology* ([2]1962), Figs. 164 and 166 for the Tower of Antonia and the Pavement, which may be seen by the modern visitor to Jerusalem beneath the convent of the Sisters of Zion, and L.-H. Vincent and M.-A. Stève, *Jérusalem de l'Ancien Testament*, Vol. I (1954), pp. 216-221.

[6] Barrett, p. 454. For a conjectural attempt to harmonise John and Mark, reviving an older view that the two gospels used different methods of reckoning time, cf. Norman Walker, 'The Reckoning of Hours in the Fourth Gospel', *Novum Testamentum*, Vol. IV, 1960, pp. 69-73.

numerals, or from the use of a Hebrew sign that had a different
value at different periods. He also notes that Mark had as much
reason to alter the time of the crucifixion as did John. While
Barrett is surely correct in saying that the FG notes the time
here either to show that the 'hour' of Jesus had now come, or
because he later wishes to represent Jesus' death as that of the
true Paschal lamb, slain in the afternoon on the Day of Preparation, it may well be that John is only drawing out the inner
significance of what actually happened.

**(15) So they shouted, 'Take him! take him! crucify
him!' Pilate said to them, 'Am I to crucify your King?'
The highpriests answered, 'We have no King but Caesar.'
(16) So then he handed him over to them to be crucified.**

15. The highpriests' answer is the ultimate blasphemy; God
alone is the true King of Israel.

16. This cannot mean that Pilate handed over Jesus to the
Jews for them to crucify him. Barrett[1] notes the difficulty of the
verse as it stands, and thinks that perhaps John has borrowed
handed . . . over from Mark xv. 15 without noticing that he
had introduced an absurdity by the addition of **to them.** But
in the original order of the source the antecedent of **to them**
was probably the soldiers (xix. 2), who certainly carried out the
execution.

It has been claimed above in the commentary on xviii. 1–
xix. 16a that the FG preserves much reliable information about
the arrest and trials of Jesus. Although events that also appear
in the Synoptic Gospels are being recorded, there is no solid
basis for the view that John is here editing and elaborating their
account. Much information is given that does not appear in the
Synoptic record, and it is hard to believe that the FG picks
isolated snippets—often words or phrases only—from their
narrative, and works them up into a very different presentation.
It is highly probable that at some points John was drawing on a
tradition known also to Luke, and that elsewhere he represents
an authentic Jerusalem tradition. Theological issues are presented skilfully, but this is always done within the existing
narrative, which preserves an accurate historical record. On
some points (e.g. the presence of Roman soldiers in the Garden),

[1] Barrett, p. 454.

John may be more informative than the Synoptics. In his account of the trial before Pilate, on which interest is focused in the FG (at the expense perhaps of the appearance before the Sanhedrin) John may well have in mind the trials of Christians, and holds up Jesus as their example. But it does not follow that there is any distortion due to an apologetic motive. Pilate comes out no better in John than he does in Mark.

5. THE CRUCIFIXION AND BURIAL OF JESUS, xix. 16b-42

So they took Jesus; (17) and carrying his cross by himself he went out to the place called 'A Skull',[1] which is called in Aramaic[2] Golgotha, (18) where they crucified him, and with him two others, one on each side, and Jesus in the middle.

That Jesus carried his own cross contradicts the Synoptic Gospels (Mark xv. 21, Matt. xxvii. 32, Luke xxiii. 26), though it would not be difficult to harmonise the two accounts by supposing that Jesus set out carrying his own cross but that it was later transferred to Simon of Cyrene. John's statement here is perhaps meant to emphasise that Jesus needed no help in the world's redemption, perhaps to counter the view later held by Basilides that it was Simon who died on the cross.[3] The writer may have in mind a parallel between Christ and Isaac (cf. Gen. xxii. 6) that is drawn in the Epistle of Barnabas 7, but he may simply be emphasising that Jesus died the death of an ordinary criminal. C. H. Dodd has recently suggested that John followed a branch of the tradition into which the story of Simon of Cyrene had not been introduced, and points out that in any case it is perfectly reasonable to suppose that Jesus set out carrying his own cross, but later had to be relieved of it.[4]

Golgotha may perhaps be an unusual formation from an

---

[1] Κρανίου, epexegetic genitive.   [2] See p. 158 n. 3.

[3] Irenaeus, *Adv. Haer.*, I. xxiv. 4.

[4] C. H. Dodd, *Historical Tradition in the Fourth Gospel* (1963), p. 125 and n. 2.

Aramaic word equalling the Hebrew *gulgōleth*, a skull.[1] Probably it was named from its appearance. Its site is uncertain, though traditionally it was to the north-west of Jerusalem, just outside the walls.[2]

For the **two others** (probably companions of Barabbas) cf. Mark xv. 27, Matt. xxvii. 38, Luke xxiii. 32 f. There is no hint of the story of the Penitent Thief (Luke xxiii. 39 ff.) in the FG.

(19) And Pilate also wrote a placard and put it on the cross; there was written, 'Jesus the Nazoraean the King of the Jews'. (20) So many of the Jews read this placard, because the place where Jesus was crucified was near to the city; and it was written in Aramaic,[3] Latin, and Greek.

Pilate takes his revenge on the Jews. The placard was customary; the use of the three languages secured maximum publicity. Cf. the variant 'in letters of Greek and Latin and Hebrew' at Luke xxiii. 38, which has strong support[4] and may be a genuine parallel rather than a gloss based on John.

(21) So the highpriests of the Jews said to Pilate, 'Do not write "The King of the Jews", but that "He said, I am King of the Jews".' (22) Pilate answered, 'What I have written, I have written.'

Their objection was understandable; what Pilate wrote amounted to a confession of high treason on their part when they had just protested their loyalty to Caesar, and was a studied insult as well. But Pilate is the unwitting witness to the truth.

(23) So when the soldiers had crucified Jesus, they took his clothes and divided them into four parts, a part for each soldier, and ⟨left out⟩ the shirt. And the shirt was

---

[1] Bauer[5], s.v.

[2] For a discussion see A. Parrot, *Golgotha and the Church of the Holy Sepulchre* (E.T. 1957 by E. Hudson of *Golgotha et Saint-Sépulcre*), and K. M. Kenyon in Hastings' *Dictionary of the Bible* ([2]1963), ed. F. C. Grant and H. H. Rowley, p. 475b. See also K. M. Kenyon, 'Excavations in Jerusalem, 1963', *Palestine Exploration Quarterly*, 1964, pp. 14, 16, for evidence that the Church of the Holy Sepulchre is in fact outside the line followed by the city walls at the time of the crucifixion. This of course does not mean that the site is necessarily authentic.   [3] See p. 158 n. 3.

[4] It is read by ℵ* A C[3] D W Θ *fam* 1 *fam* 13 *lat pesh hl* and some codices of *boh*.

seamless, woven from top to bottom in one piece. (24) So they said to one another, 'Let us not tear it, but toss up for it whose it shall be', in order that[1] the Scripture might be fulfilled, 'They divided my garments among themselves, and cast lots upon my vesture.'

For the division of Jesus' garments by casting lots see Mark xv. 24, Matt. xxvii. 35, Luke xxiii. 34b. The passage of scripture quoted is Ps. xxii. 18, and it has been supposed that John misunderstands the nature of Hebrew poetry and refers the two parallel descriptions of the division of the clothing to different happenings. However, it has recently been argued[2] that John knew the meaning of this verse, but purposely chose to take it literally. This is because he is interested in the **shirt** ($\chi\iota\tau\omega\nu$), which, like that of the Highpriest,[3] was **seamless**: it therefore has symbolical significance and is to be connected with controversy over Jesus' Highpriesthood. There may also be the ironical thought intended that Jesus, the true Highpriest, is stripped of his priestly vestment when he offers himself in sacrifice. But it is not necessary to believe that the incident is an ideal creation of the author, though it is always possible to suppose that John worked up the incident from the prophecy—if that is how his mind worked.

This then is what the soldiers did. (25) And there stood by the cross of Jesus his mother and his mother's sister, Mary the wife of[4] Clopas and Mary of Magdala.

This list has been read as referring to two, three or four persons. A comparison with Mark xv. 40 would suggest that **his mother's sister** was Salome, the wife of Zebedee (cf. Matt. xxvii. 56) and that **Mary the wife of Clopas** was the mother of James the Less and Joses. It is odd that Mark does not mention Mary the mother of Jesus, unless perhaps James here and Joses were his brethren. With **Clopas,** cf. the Cleopas of Luke xxiv. 18; there is no proof that these are the same person, though **Clopas** is a Semitic name and Cleopas a genuine Greek name which evidently takes the place of the similar

---

[1] See on xviii. 9 above.

[2] Barnabas Lindars, *New Testament Apologetic* (1961), pp. 91, 267 f.; on p. 114 it is argued that Matt. xxi. 2, 7, often cited as a parallel misunderstanding, is not a naive deduction from Zech. ix. 9.

[3] Josephus, *Antiquities*, III. 161.   [4] Literally $\dot{\eta}$ τοῦ Κλωπᾶ.

Semitic name.[1] Hegesippus mentions a Clopas as a brother of Joseph.[2] According to the Synoptic Gospels, Mary Magdalene was a witness of the crucifixion (Mark xv. 40, Matt. xxvii. 56) and of the resurrection; cf. also Luke viii. 2. There is no conclusive evidence for regarding her as the sister of Martha and Lazarus, or as the woman of Mark xiv. 3, Matt. xxvi. 7, or of Luke vii. 37. She is called **of Magdala,** a town probably to be located in Galilee, to distinguish her from the other Maries. While the presence of Salome may be an argument for the identification of the Beloved Disciple with John the son of Zebedee, it may be urged against this that it would have been so natural for Mary to go to her sister's that Jesus would hardly need to suggest it. In the Synoptic Gospels the women stand at a distance (Mark xv. 40, Matt. xxvii. 55, Luke xxiii. 49), though it has been argued that the preposition used in the FG, **by** (παρά), means here 'by, *beside* . . . not of immediate neighbourhood.'[3] There is a dramatic contrast here between the soldiers who crucified Jesus and the women, Jesus' friends, who come to behold his death.

(26) So Jesus, seeing his mother and the disciple whom he loved standing by ⟨her⟩, said to his mother, 'Woman, see, your son.' (27) Then he said to the disciple, 'See, your mother.' And from that time the disciple took her into his house.[4]

The historicity of this incident is widely doubted. But Jesus' brethren did not believe in him (see vii. 5), and if they were the sons of Joseph by a former wife it is unlikely that they would be kindly disposed to his mother after he had been crucified. Jesus therefore makes provision for the care of his mother after his death. For **Woman,** see on ii. 4.

(28) After this[5] Jesus, knowing that all things were already accomplished, in order that the Scripture might be fulfilled, said, 'I am thirsty'.

In Mark xv. 36, Matt. xxvii. 48, the giving of a drink to Jesus follows the Cry of Dereliction, which John omits. In Luke xxiii. 36 the offering of vinegar is part of the soldiers' mockery;

---

[1] Bauer[5], s.v. Κλεοπᾶς.   [2] Eusebius, *H.E.*, III. xi.
[3] Turner, p. 273.   [4] εἰς τὰ ἴδια; cf. i. 11.
[5] See p. 131 n. 4. The phrase implies immediate succession.

here it is an act of mercy. But John relates it to the fulfilment of prophecy, using the same word for **were accomplished** (τετέλεσται) as will be used later in verse 30 for Jesus' last utterance. **Might be fulfilled** translates a similar word (τελειωθῇ), which is only used here in this phrase (cf. verse 24, 'might be fulfilled', πληρωθῇ, the usual word). The allusion may be to Ps. xxii. 15, but is more likely to be to Ps. lxix. 21, 'for my thirst they gave me vinegar to drink'. But the reference here is not so much to the fulfilment of one particular prophecy as to the perfect completion by Jesus in his life and death of all that had been prophesied about him. The word is usually used in the FG for the accomplishment by Jesus of his Father's work (iv. 34; v. 36; xvii. 4). For thirst in the FG, see iv. 13-15. John may wish to point to the irony of Jesus' thirst by contrast with this passage.[1] At the same time he rules out docetism by emphasising the human weakness of Jesus.

(29) There stood there a jar full of sour wine.[2] So they put a sponge full of wine on hyssop and brought it to his mouth.

John does not specify the identity of those who did this. **Hyssop** is a plant that would not be at all suitable for holding a wet sponge to the lips of a crucified man. For **hyssop** (ὑσσώπῳ) 'javelin' (ὑσσῷ) has been conjectured; in an early MS. in which no gaps were left between words ΥΣΣΩΠΕΡΙΘΕΝΤΕΣ could easily have become ΥΣΣΩΠΩΠΕΡΙΘΕΝΤΕΣ, and one late minuscule, 476, (probably by accident) does read 'javelin'. Moreover, Mark xv. 36, Matt. xxvii. 48 use 'staff' (καλάμῳ). But **hyssop** is the more difficult reading, and may be used here because it was prominent in the Passover ritual (cf. Ex. xii. 22). There are important Paschal overtones in this section of the gospel, and as John is setting forth Jesus as the true Paschal Lamb (see below) it might be natural to use **hyssop** here. Barrett[3] thinks that the evangelist was not concerned about the appropriateness of the term used. C. H. Dodd, however, argues strongly that a primitive corruption has resulted in the reading **hyssop**, and that 'javelin' is the true reading.[4]

---

[1] Barnabas Lindars, *op. cit.*, p. 268.
[2] ὄξος; this was cheaper than ordinary wine, and a favourite drink of soldiers.   [3] Barrett, p. 460.
[4] C. H. Dodd, *Historical Tradition in the Fourth Gospel* (1963), p. 123, n. 2.

(30) So when Jesus had accepted the vinegar he said, 'It is accomplished', and bowing his head gave up his spirit.

For **'It is accomplished'**, cf. on verse 28 above. The reference is neither purely theological nor purely chronological; the verb means both that the life of Christ on earth is at an end, and that he has accomplished all that he came to do. It is essentially a cry of victory. Cf. 'to the end' ($\epsilon\dot{\iota}s\ \tau\acute{\epsilon}\lambda os$), xiii. 1.

With **gave up his spirit,** cf. Luke xxiii. 46, 'Father, into thy hands I commit my spirit'. Jesus' death is a voluntary act to the very end (cf. x. 18). Because of xx. 22 (see note *in loc.*) this phrase cannot refer to the giving of the Holy Spirit to the Church.

In John's record of the crucifixion the tendency of the narrative is to emphasise the majesty of Jesus, the true King of the Jews, who fulfils the Scriptures that must be fulfilled by him, makes disposition for his mother, and finally declares the completion of his work and voluntarily gives up his spirit. Jesus is represented as the true Highpriest (verse 23) and as Passover victim (verse 14, and see below), and throughout the dramatic and allusive element is prominent. There is no emphasis on Jesus' agony, there is no mockery while he is on the cross, and there is no Cry of Dereliction. John, like the other evangelists, was not writing a factual account of all that transpired, but was drawing out the inner significance of the crucifixion by relating actual events, which he describes in such a way as to make his meaning plain.

(31) So the Jews, since it was the Day of Preparation, in order that the bodies should not remain on the cross⟨es⟩ on the Sabbath, since that Sabbath-day was a great day, asked Pilate to have their legs broken and ⟨their bodies⟩ removed.

Deut. xxi. 22 f. requires the removal of the body of a man hanged on a tree before nightfall, and is the basis of the Jews' request. What was objectionable in normal circumstances would have been doubly objectionable if, as the FG supposes, the Sabbath was also 15th Nisan, the first Passover festival day.[1]

---

[1] Even if the Synoptic dating is preferred, the title 'great' is still appropriate.

The breaking of the legs (*crurifragium*) was sometimes an independent form of capital punishment and sometimes the accompaniment of crucifixion.

(32) So the soldiers came, and broke the legs of the first, and of the other who was crucified with him; (33) but when they came to Jesus, and saw that he was already dead, they did not break his legs, (34) but one of the soldiers pierced his side with a spear, and there came out at once blood and water.

For the significance of **they did not break his legs,** see below on verse 36. With the early death of Jesus recorded in the FG (victims of crucifixion sometimes lived for some days), cf. the surprise of Pilate at Jesus' rapid death, Mark xv. 44. The incident of the spear-thrust is obviously of great importance to John (see on verse 35). It is peculiar to the FG, Matt. xxvii. 49b being clearly an interpolation from John.[1] The whole section, verses 31-34, leads up to the flowing of water and blood from the side of the dead Christ, which is important for John because of its symbolic significance. But this does not mean that the incident was created to produce the symbolism. It is fundamental to the evangelist's purpose to show how real events have a hidden, deeper meaning, and his task is to make this meaning plain. It would be possible for blood and water to flow from a corpse, and John describes what was seen by an eye-witness (see on verse 35, below). Barrett[2] points out that the Synoptic Gospels have no room for the incident—the centurion himself observes Jesus' death and informs Pilate, Mark xv. 39, 45—and argues that if Jesus was already dead there was no necessity for the lance-thrust. But Mark xv. 45 would go after John xix. 38 if an attempt were made to harmonise the two records, so the two points are in fact only one, which may be met by supposing that it was desired to make absolutely certain that Jesus was dead—unless, indeed, as Barrett says, it was done out of mere spite or casual cruelty. Verse 34 certainly excludes docetism in its insistence that Jesus' death was a real death, but its wider significance lies in the symbolism of the blood and water. For **blood,** cf. vi. 53 ff.: from the crucified Christ there flows life

---

[1] It is read by ℵ B C L *vg*codd. But in Matthew at this point Jesus is not yet dead.   [2] Barrett, p. 462.

made available in the Eucharist. For **water**, cf. iv. 14; vii. 38 f.;
iii. 5; xiii. 5: there may possibly be an allusion to baptism, but
more probably (in view of the order of the words—baptism
would be expected to precede the Eucharist) to the gift of the
Spirit, given in the crucified Jesus to his Church. Scarcely is
Jesus dead when it is shown how, in Eucharist and Spirit-filled
community, he will be present with his own, and this is to be as
real as was the blood and water which flowed from his side.
Throughout the FG the death of Jesus has been represented as
the glorious achievement of all he came to bring for his own,
and as soon as he has died the reality of this is emphasised.

**(35) And he who saw is the witness of this, and his
witness is reliable, and he knows that he speaks the
truth, that you also may believe.**

This verse claims eye-witness authority for the incident just
described. There is very slight textual authority for omitting the
verse, but this is probably not significant.[1] As the Beloved
Disciple is mentioned standing by the cross, xix. 25 ff., he is
presumably **the witness** referred to in this verse. This conclusion is supported by the fact that the phrase **his witness is
reliable** recurs at xxi. 24,[2] where it clearly refers to the Beloved
Disciple. The verse comes from John of Ephesus, and is a trace
of his activity as a preacher. The crux here is the identity of the
he (ἐκεῖνος) who **knows that he speaks the truth.** It may
be the eye-witness just mentioned, resuming **his** in the previous
clause, and this seems the best explanation; but it could refer to
Jesus or God (although this seems overinterpretation of the
text as it stands) or to the writer speaking of himself in the third
person (which seems a more difficult rendering).[3] **That you
may believe** makes clear that the **blood and water** of verse
34 is not only a physical happening, but is charged with a pro-

---

[1] It is omitted by *e* and Codex Fuldensis of the Vulgate. The comment of
B.-D. § 291 (6) is strange: '*Everything* . . . is critically uncertain in this verse
. . . It is only due to a total neglect of textual criticism that so many scholars
have erected their theories of the origin of the Fourth Gospel upon this verse
and its customary interpretation'.

[2] This holds despite the use of ἀληθής in the second passage and ἀληθινή
here. See p. 458 n. 1 below.

[3] Turner, p. 46, notes that the meaning of ἐκεῖνος 'is often weakened
(especially in Jn) to *he* or *they* . . . So it is inadvisable to build any theories
of authorship on the notorious ἐκεῖνος' here.

found significance. The **witness** presented in the FG from John the Baptist on is intended to lead to belief in Christ (cf. i. 7). Both John the Baptist and Jesus have seen and borne witness (i. 34; iii. 11), and this also is the function of the Church. Cf. xx. 29 and the note *in loc.* on seeing and believing. What has been seen is witnessed to so that belief may be produced.

(36) For this happened that the Scripture might be fulfilled, 'A bone of him shall not be broken'. (37) And again another Scripture says, 'They shall look at him whom they have pierced'.

It is not clear which Old Testament passage is intended by verse 36. Exod. xii. 10 (LXX), xii. 46, and Num. ix. 12, are all possible sources, and all refer to the Passover Lamb, but there is also Ps. xxxiv. 20, which shares a passive verb with John against the active verb of the other passages, though John's words are closer to those of Exodus. Probably two sources have influenced each other to give the present form of the quotation.[1] The interest here is in bringing out a reference to the Paschal Lamb, whose bones also were not broken. Passover allusions form one of the themes with which John is concerned at this point, and the dating of the crucifixion at the time of the killing of the lamb (verse 14) is part of this presentation. For Jesus as the Paschal Lamb, cf. also 1 Cor. v. 7 and perhaps 1 Pet. i. 19. Many have thought that the incident of the *crurifragium* has been developed from reflection on this text, but it is apposite to note with C. H. Dodd that crucifixion itself (unlike, for example, stoning) did not involve the breaking of bones, and that therefore it is simplest to treat the happening as the cause of the use of the testimonium, and not the other way round.[2] Moreover, the climax of the unit 31-34 is the blood and water, and not the *crurifragium*, which is in a sense incidental even though it is used theologically by John; it is hard to see the blood and water as a development from this text.

The Scripture of verse 37 is Zech. xii. 10, cited in a form more akin to the Massoretic Text (which, however, reads 'me' for 'him') than the LXX. It is impossible to say where this rendering originated. **They shall look** is not intended as a

[1] Barnabas Lindars, *op. cit.*, pp. 95 f.
[2] C. H. Dodd, *Historical Tradition in the Fourth Gospel* (1963), pp. 131 f.

reference to **he who saw** (verse 35); the subject of the verb is the opponents of the pierced one, and it is on the future occasion of Christ's return that his enemies will gaze on him. Only the piercing is already fulfilled by the Roman soldiers. **Shall look at him** means seeing him vindicated and seeing themselves correspondingly in the wrong. Cf. Matt. xxiv. 30, Rev. i. 7.[1]

(38) Now after this[2] Joseph of Arimathaea, who was a disciple of Jesus (though a secret one for fear of the Jews), asked Pilate if he might take away the body of Jesus; and Pilate gave permission.

Joseph of Arimathaea was a member of the Sanhedrin, who was 'a good and righteous man, who had not consented to their (i.e. the Sanhedrin's) purpose and deed, and he was looking for the kingdom of God' (Luke xxiii. 50 f.); cf. also Mark xv. 43, Matt. xxvii. 57. **Arimathaea**[3] was a city in the province of Judaea. For **secret** disciples, cf. xii. 42, and also vii. 13. With great bravery (cf. Mark xv. 43) Joseph requested permission to bury Jesus properly; bodies of crucified men were commonly left to the vultures. That such men as Joseph and Nicodemus (see on the next verse) were willing to show openly their support for Jesus' cause after his death strongly supports the substantial historicity of xii. 42 (see note *in loc.*).

So he came and took away his body. (39) Nicodemus also, who came to him by night the first time, came bringing a mixture of myrrh and aloes, about a hundred pounds[4] ⟨in weight⟩. (40) So they took the body of Jesus, and bound it in linen cloths with the spices, as is the custom of burial among the Jews.

John alone mentions **Nicodemus** here. On **Nicodemus,** see iii. 1 ff.; vii. 50 f., and pp. 122 f., 217 f. He is another sympathiser with Jesus among the Sanhedrin. Already Jesus is drawing all men to himself, cf. xii. 32. John contrasts Nicodemus now with his first visit **by night;** see pp. 122 f. The **linen cloths**

---

[1] C. F. D. Moule, *J.T.S.* n.s., Vol. X, 1959, p. 258, n. 3; *Novum Testamentum*, Vol. V, 1962, p. 182, n. 4.

[2] See p. 131 n. 4; μετὰ ταῦτα implies an interval of unspecified length.

[3] Cf. J. Simons, *The Geographical and Topographical Texts of the Old Testament* (1959), p. 307; it is identical with Ramah, Samuel's home (1 Sam. vii. 17), on the edge of the hill country of Ephraim.

[4] λίτρας, see p. 282 n. 3.

are bound round the corpse, and the spices are inserted into this covering. For the reference to Jesus' burial in xii. 7, cf. p. 285. Cf. the notes on xi. 44 for the Jewish mode of burial. There is no suggestion in the FG that the burial of Jesus was provisional or incomplete. According to the Synoptic Gospels, the body of Jesus was not anointed before burial, and this was known to the women who followed Jesus (Mark xv. 46–xvi. 1, Luke xxiii. 53, 55 f., xxiv. 1, cf. Matt. xxvii. 59-61).[1] But despite the immense amount of spices used according to the FG—the quantity involved has doubtless been exaggerated, **about a hundred pounds ⟨in weight⟩** seeming appropriate in view of who it was that was buried—it is at least as plausible to suppose that the corpse was properly buried as that it was not. Whatever the need for haste (see verse 42), there had been plenty of time to make the necessary preparations while Jesus was on the cross. Luke alone goes so far as to state that the women 'saw . . . how his body was laid' (Luke xxiii. 55), and it may well be that the story of the women bringing spices contained in Mark and Luke is a later elaboration of the tradition,[2] better historical material being preserved in the FG. There is an *a priori* presumption that Joseph and Nicodemus did what they had to do properly.

(41) Now in the place where he was crucified was a garden, and in the garden was a new tomb, in which no one had ever been laid. (42) So on account of the Jews' Day of Preparation, because the tomb was near, they laid Jesus there.

With **in which no one had ever been laid,** cf. Luke xxiii. 53. While it is possible that here once more John and Luke are drawing on a common stock of tradition, Matt. xxvii. 60 also records that it was a new tomb. It is appropriate that Christ should be buried in an empty tomb. John alone notes that the crucifixion and burial took place in a **garden** (κῆπος); it is

---

[1] Though Bultmann, p. 517 n. 1, thinks Mark xv. 46 implies that the burial was complete and that the women were introduced into the story merely to link the narratives of the burial and of Easter, which were originally distinct.

[2] For example, how could the women have failed to realise that the stone had to be removed from the entrance of the tomb? Mark xvi. 3 seems to be introduced simply to provide an effective preparation for xvi. 4.

unlikely that an allusion to the Garden of Eden is intended, as then one would expect the word used in the LXX ($\pi\alpha\rho\dot{\alpha}\delta\epsilon\iota\sigma\sigma$) to be used.[1] The burial had to be rapid because of the approaching sabbath rest. It is understandable that John should not mention the women in this narrative, as he is bringing out the way in which Jesus' death led to increased discipleship on the part of Joseph and Nicodemus.

6. THE RESURRECTION, xx

As xxi is an epilogue added to the FG to meet a particular need after an earlier draft of the gospel had been completed (cf. xx. 30 f. and pp. 440 ff.), xx. 1-29 has first to be compared with the resurrection narratives of the Synoptic Gospels and the appearance of Jesus to the disciples in Galilee must be treated separately. The primary purpose of the evangelists (cf. xx. 31 and the note *in loc.*) is satisfied without a full account of all that Jesus did after his resurrection, and in comparing the various available records the limitations imposed by the circumstances under which the traditions have been handed down must be clearly recognised. It is likely that originally isolated units— each in itself sufficient to convey the Christian conviction that Christ had triumphed over death—were transmitted independently, and the fact that each has its own history of development helps account for the difficulty felt when these come to be combined. In the FG there is no doubt that the tradition has been shaped to suit the theological purposes of the writer, though equally one can by no means regard the stories contained in the Synoptic Gospels as totally uncontaminated by the interests of the early church. It is therefore not surprising that while one must necessarily ask about the worth of the resurrection narratives as history, the task of complete historical reconstruction is impossible. Certainly all the available data cannot be harmonised.

---

[1] Though Aquila and Theodotion do use $\kappa\hat{\eta}\pi\sigma$ here, and in this they may be following an early tradition of translation, which could have been current in the first century A.D.

xx. (1) Now on the first day of the week Mary of Magdala came to the tomb early, while it was still dark, and saw that the stone had been taken away from the tomb. (2) So she ran and came to Simon Peter and to the other disciple (the one whom Jesus loved), and said to them, 'They have taken away the Lord out of the tomb, and we do not know where they have laid him.'

The Synoptic Gospels state that **Mary of Magdala** was one of the women who discovered that the tomb was empty (Mark xvi. 1, Matt. xxviii. 1, Luke xxiv. 10) when they visited it **on the first day of the week** (Mark xvi. 2, Luke xxiv. 1, cf. Matt. xxviii. 1). Mark xvi. 1 and Luke xxiv. 1 state that the purpose of this visit was to anoint Jesus' body (cf. the *Gospel of Peter*, 50-54), but even if this had already been done (see the note on xix. 39 f.) there is no improbability in the women going to weep at the tomb (cf. xi. 31). The other women do not appear in the Johannine account because later (xx. 11-18) attention is to be focused on **Mary of Magdala** (for whom see further on xix. 25), though the plural verb **we do not know** at xx. 2 suggests acquaintance with a tradition which told of several women at the tomb. For the type of tomb used, see p. 273 and on xx. 5 below.

Though it is widely held that the story of the empty tomb was not part of the earliest tradition of the resurrection, St Paul's statement that Christ was raised on the third day (1 Cor. xv. 4) does at least imply that the tomb did not contain his body then; further, **'They have taken away the Lord out of the tomb, and we do not know where they have laid him'** would be a natural assumption if it were discovered that the corpse had vanished. Mary's actions as recorded in the FG are intrinsically plausible; cf. Luke xxiv. 9-11, which tells how the women related their experiences 'to the eleven and to all the rest.' Matt. xxviii. 8, 'So they departed quickly from the tomb with fear and great joy, and ran to tell his disciples', is often thought to be an arbitrary editorial alteration of Mark rather than genuine tradition, and in any case it would be hazardous to base much on a parallel taken from a section of the gospel that is heavily charged with legendary elements. But unless the FG shares a common tradition with Luke here—an explanation made more probable if Luke xxiv. 12 (for which see on xx. 3 below) is not an interpolation based on John—the two gospels provide independent confirmation of each other. It is less likely that John wrote with Luke's narrative in mind; the account given in the FG has been less subject to the addition of legendary elements than the synoptic parallels,[1] and this is all the more intelligible when account is taken of the part played in the composition of the gospel by **the other disciple (the one whom Jesus loved),** whoever he may have been.[2] It should be noted that, despite considerable similarities, the Synoptic Gospels themselves differ markedly from each other in this pericope; it seems that a basic tradition telling of the finding of an empty tomb on the Sunday morning has been used in a distinctive way in each of the four gospels.

(3) So Peter set out with the other disciple, and they went to the tomb. Luke xxiv. 12, which tells of a visit of Peter to the tomb, is normally considered to be an interpolation based on John xx. 3-10,[3] though it has recently been strongly argued that it is Luke which represents the earlier form of a tradition that is elaborated in the FG.[4] The possibility that both gospels are using a common source should perhaps not be dismissed too readily.[5] Cf. further the statement of Luke xxiv. 24, em-

---

[1] See below, on xx. 11-13, for the mention of angels in the FG.

[2] Barnabas Lindars, 'The Composition of John xx', *N.T.S.*, Vol. VII, 1960–61, pp. 142-147, does not seem to regard the Beloved Disciple as a real figure involved in these happenings, and his analysis of the chapter depends on the view that John is working on a tradition whose basic outlines are preserved in the Synoptic Gospels. He shows that, although there are contacts in vocabulary with the synoptic resurrection narratives, the material has been recast in a Johannine mould, and concludes that traditions lying behind the Synoptic Gospels have been very freely developed to convey what John wishes to teach. But if xx can contain reliable information which does not appear in the Synoptic Gospels—a matter made more likely by the disagreements of the synoptic resurrection narratives among themselves—a different estimate of the sources used by the evangelist is possible. It is of course conceded that the material has been reworked, but not so drastically as Lindars suggests.   [3] Cf., e.g., J. A. Bailey, *op. cit.*, p. 85 n. 3.

[4] K. Aland, 'Neue Neutestamentliche Papyri II', *N.T.S.*, Vol. XII, 1965–66, pp. 205 f. Luke xxiv. 12 (which is found in P75) is only omitted by D *a b d e l r*1, by some manuscripts of the Palestinian Syriac, Marcion, the Diatessaron and (presumably) one form of the tradition known to Eusebius. Aland does not discuss whether Luke is John's source, or whether both depend on a common tradition.

[5] Cf., e.g., K. H. Rengstorf, *Das Evangelium nach Lukas* (1949), p. 269. It

bedded in the Emmaus story, that after they had heard the women's news some of the disciples went to the tomb. The view that xx. 3-10 is a free composition of the Fourth Evangelist, based on some such hint as this, is perhaps less plausible than the assertion that Luke and John preserve related traditions.[1] It is inherently probable that some at least of the disciples would go to the tomb if they heard that it was empty; moreover, if the story was created to serve a specific purpose, it is strange that this does not shine through more clearly. An accurate record is being presented, albeit with a theological motive.[2]

(4) And the two men were running together, but the other disciple ran ahead faster than Peter and came first to the tomb; (5) and stooping down, he saw the linen cloths lying ⟨there⟩, though he did not go in. (6) Then Simon Peter also came, following him, and entered the tomb; and he saw the linen cloths lying ⟨there⟩, (7) and the kerchief, which had been on his head, not lying with the linen cloths but rolled up separately in a place by itself. (8) So then the other disciple who had come first to the tomb also entered, and he saw and believed; (9) for they did not yet know the scripture, that he must rise from the dead. (10) Then the disciples for their part[3] went away again.

is hazardous to follow A. R. C. Leaney, 'The Resurrection Narratives in Luke (xxiv. 12-53)', *N.T.S.*, Vol. II, 1955-56, pp. 110-114, and *A Commentary on the Gospel According to St. Luke* (1958), pp. 28-31, in his attempt to reconstruct this source; his conclusions are based on the assumption that John xx. 3-10 represents a form of the tradition which has been considerably developed, and also involve reading ᾔδει (supported only by אֲ* *vt*) for ᾔδεισαν at xx. 9, though the singular is more probably due to assimilation to xx. 8 (so Bultmann, p. 531 n. 1).

[1] In any case it is hardly possible to make Luke xxiv. 12 dependent on a passage which in its turn depends on Luke xxiv. 24.

[2] Some scholars have found unevennesses in the narrative, and J. A. Bailey, *op. cit.*, pp. 91, 96 f., thinks in terms of editorial revision of an already-existing record. However, unless Bailey's position is adopted, the more difficult it is to find a coherent story in xx. 3-10, the more likely it is that what actually happened is being related.

[3] πρὸς αὑτούς. Cf. Black, pp. 77 f.; this verse shares with Luke xxiv. 12 a difficult construction in which the preposition πρός is used after the verb ἀπέρχομαι, and Black plausibly connects this with the Aramaic ethic dative, claiming that both verses 'may go back to the same piece of Aramaic tradition'.

Viewed as historical narrative, the story is not intrinsically implausible; if two men run to a given destination at top speed one may easily arrive before the other, and it would not be unnatural for **the other disciple** to hesitate for a moment before entering the tomb. **Stooping down,** a necessary action to see through the small entrance of the tomb-cave whether or not it was approached by way of a shallow pit or well, **he saw the linen cloths lying ⟨there⟩.** However, **Peter** at once **entered the tomb,** and it has frequently been conjectured that his temperament is consistent with such an action; cf., e.g., vi. 68; xviii. 10. Cf. p. 276 for details of the Jewish mode of burial. In view of what is said there, the fact that **the kerchief** was **rolled up separately in a place by itself** would seem to rule out all theories that the writer thought that the body of Jesus had passed through the grave-clothes, leaving them as they were. The point is rather that the corpse has vanished but the grave-clothes remain, laid out in an orderly manner.

The Synoptic Gospels do not mention the discovery of grave-clothes by the women in the empty tomb, and the implication is that they were not there (Mark xvi. 6, Matt. xxviii. 6, Luke xxiv. 3, 23). Their presence is, however, essential to the purpose of the FG, for who would take away a corpse and leave the grave-clothes neatly folded? The only rational explanation of the evidence is that the body has been raised from the dead, and it is the intuitive recognition of this that distinguishes **the other disciple,** who **saw and believed,** from Mary, who still thinks in terms of a body that has been removed (verses 2, 13, 15). The delay between the arrival of **the other disciple** at the tomb and his reaching faith in the resurrection, which is stressed—**then** (τότε) is emphatic[1]—is readily explicable on this hypothesis[2]; time was needed for realisation of the true state of affairs to dawn.

For further discussions see Bauer⁵, s.v. ἀπέρχομαι and Barrett p. 469. Note, however, that at Num. xxiv. 25 ἀπῆλθεν πρὸς ἑαυτόν—the same phrase as is found at Luke xxiv. 12—does not translate an ethic dative in the Hebrew. Cf. p. 289 n. 6.   [1] Cf. p. 267.

[2] The alternative is to adopt some such explanation as that advanced by E. C. Hoskyns, *The Fourth Gospel* (ed. F. N. Davey, 1947), p. 541: 'Perhaps the reader is intended to detect the love of the Beloved Disciple in the speed with which he reached the tomb; and his entrance is delayed in order that his faith may form the climax of the narrative.'

The FG also shows knowledge of the tradition that all traces of the burial had vanished when it tells later how Mary looked into the tomb (verse 11). A similar action need not be implied by verse 2—the fact that a tomb was open presupposed that it was empty. If xx. 3-10 contains authentic historical information it could hardly have circulated without some introduction of the type provided by xx. 1 f., and it is possible that xx. 1-10 and 11-18 are to be seen as independent though related units connected in some way with the synoptic accounts of the discovery of the empty tomb, the influence of which is to be seen in particular in xx. 11-13. See pp. 424 f. for the view that this tradition contains substantial secondary elements. While it may be agreed that the FG combines two stories which do not fit well together, xx. 1 f. is silent on the crucial point of what precisely the women did and is open to several widely differing interpretations.

Although **Peter** plays a prominent rôle in the FG, when he appears with **the other disciple** (whom verse 2 identifies with the Beloved Disciple[1]) he takes second place. Thus, at the Last Supper it is the Beloved Disciple who sits in the place of greater honour and whom Peter has to ask to discover the identity of the traitor (xiii. 23 f.); Peter is unable to obtain entry to the Highpriest's courtyard on his own (xviii. 15 f.); after Peter's denial it is the Beloved Disciple who, standing at the foot of the cross, is entrusted with the care of Jesus' mother (xix. 26 f.); when Jesus appears to the disciples in Galilee the Beloved Disciple identifies Jesus to Peter (xxi. 7); and after Peter is commissioned, he is rebuffed when he asks about the Beloved Disciple's task (xxi. 20 ff.). In this passage it is stressed that **the other disciple ran ahead faster than Peter and came first to the tomb** (verse 4, cf. verse 8, **So then the other disciple who had come first to the tomb also entered),** and it has also been held that the phrase **following him** (i.e. **the other disciple)** at verse 6 may be intended to underline Peter's subordinate rôle;[2] moreover it is implied that **the other disciple, who saw and believed,** came to a faith in the resurrection which Peter had not yet attained. Cf. the assertion of Luke xxiv. 12 that Peter 'went away . . . wondering at what had happened'.

---

[1] For an alternative point of view see pp. 29 f.   [2] Barrett, p. 468.

Bultmann regards **Peter** and **the other disciple** as figures standing for Jewish and Gentile Christianity respectively, and thinks that the story clearly assumes that **Peter** also came to faith in the resurrection at the empty tomb; the significance of the narrative is then that, as the Beloved Disciple ran to the tomb more quickly than Peter, so the Gentiles have a greater capacity for faith than the Jews.[1] Another suggestion which ascribes a purely representative function to the Beloved Disciple is that he stands for the prophetic ministry which the FG gives a higher authority than the local pastoral ministry represented by Peter.[2]

However, the point of the incident is brought out by verse 9, **for they did not yet know the scripture, that he must rise from the dead.** Although the use of proof-texts was to assume great importance in the life of the early church and was a powerful argument in an age of fundamentalism (cf., e.g., Acts xvii. 2 f., 11 f., 1 Cor. xv. 3 f., Luke xxiv. 44-46), it was only after more reflection that the disciples were able to relate the happenings of Jesus' life to the Old Testament. Cf. xii. 16 and the note *in loc.* Despite the absence of scriptural proof[3] the Beloved Disciple becomes the first believer. Just as xx. 24-29 stresses the unimportance of physical contact with the risen Christ, this section shows how the disciple whose relationship with Jesus during his earthly ministry was such that he could legitimately be called the Beloved Disciple perceives without need of further demonstration what has happened to his Lord. The incident is included because the writer knows that faith is primarily a matter of insight, and it is for this reason that the tradition of the empty tomb assumes a surprising importance in the FG.

Thus the Beloved Disciple is the type of the perfect believer. Like those pronounced blessed at verse 29, he has not seen Jesus and yet has believed. But even though the incident has a basis in history, there seems to be a deliberate attempt to denigrate Peter in the way in which it is presented. This may

---

[1] Bultmann, pp. 530 f.

[2] A. Kragerud, *Der Lieblingsjünger im Johannesevangelium* (1959).

[3] **The scripture** (τὴν γραφήν) is possibly Ps. xvi. 10, 'For thou dost not give me up to Sheol, or let thy godly one see the Pit'; in any case the singular in the Greek implies that a specific passage is in mind (see p. 120).

perhaps most plausibly be accounted for in terms of tensions and conflicts within the early church, of a similar kind to those reflected in 3 John, though in this case set on a larger stage.[1] Is there here an expression of resentment at the attitude adopted by a church claiming to derive its authority from Peter towards a church which had till a comparatively recent date included no less a figure than the Beloved Disciple?

(11) But Mary stood at the tomb outside, weeping. So while she was weeping, she stooped to look into the tomb,[2] (12) and saw two angels in white[3] sitting, the one at the head and the other at the feet, where the body of Jesus had lain. (13) And they said to her, 'Woman,[4] why are you weeping?' She said to them,[5] 'They have taken away my Lord, and I do not know where they have laid him.' (14) When she had said this she turned round and saw Jesus standing ⟨there⟩, but did not know that it was Jesus.

These verses skilfully introduce a quite separate incident, which is mentioned elsewhere in the NT only in the spurious 'longer ending' of Mark (Mark xvi. 9 f.[6]), though there are superficial similarities to Matt. xxviii. 8-10. The statement that **she stooped to look into the tomb** (cf. verse 5) and Mary's reply to the angels, **'They have taken away my Lord, and I do not know where they have laid him'** (cf. verse 2), link

---

[1] Note also the attitude towards the Corinthians adopted in 1 Clement, which was written around the same time as the FG.

[2] παρέκυψεν εἰς τὸ μνημεῖον. Although παρακύπτω is used with εἰς in the LXX with the meaning 'to peep into' (Prov. vii. 6, Sirach xxi. 23), it originally signified 'to stoop for the purpose of looking' (LS⁹, s.v.), and as Mary's act necessitates stooping (see on verse 5 above, where the same verb is used) the translation given is legitimate. It is further supported by the *Gospel of Peter* 55 (παρέκυψαν ἐκεῖ καὶ ὁρῶσιν) and 56 (παρακύψατε καὶ ἴδατε), where the usage is probably dependent on the FG or Luke xxiv. 12; the translation 'look in' (so M. R. James, *The Apocryphal New Testament* (1924), p. 93) is less adequate than 'stoop down' (so, e.g., L. Vaganay, *L'Évangile de Pierre* (1930), pp. 326 ff.). Cf. also Bauer⁵, Moulton and Milligan, s.v. παρακύπτω.

[3] ἐν λευκοῖς; for the meaning of the adjective cf. p. 151 n. 7, and for the ellipse of ἱμάτιον, see Turner, p. 17, Moule, p. 96, and Bauer⁵, s.v. λευκός.

[4] γύναι; see p. 110.

[5] ὅτι here either introduces direct speech or is the first word of the reply and means 'because'.

[6] These verses may be based on John xx, unless both go back independently to a common oral source.

this story to what has preceded, just as mention of the **two angels** relates it to the synoptic narratives of the discovery of the empty tomb. According to Mark, the women enter the tomb and see 'a young man *sitting* (καθήμενον) on the right side, dressed in a *white* robe (στολὴν λευκήν)' (Mark xvi. 5).[1] Luke says that when the women entered the tomb it was empty, and that 'while they were perplexed about this, behold, *two* men (ἄνδρες δύο) stood by them in dazzling apparel' (Luke xxiv. 4). Luke xxiv. 23 further identifies these men by the phrase 'a vision of *angels*' (ὀπτασίαν ἀγγέλων), and it is presumably the same '*two* men . . . in *white* robes' (ἄνδρες δύο . . . ἐν ἐσθήσεσι λευκαῖς) who reappear at Acts i. 10. According to Matthew, the women 'went to see the sepulchre. And behold . . . an *angel* of the Lord (ἄγγελος γὰρ κυρίου) descended from heaven and came and rolled back the stone, and *sat* (ἐκάθητο[2]) upon it. His appearance was like lightning, and his raiment *white* (λευκόν) as snow' (Matt. xxviii. 1-3).[3]

It would be difficult to base any theory of literary dependence on such slight parallels, and it is notable that the Synoptic Gospels differ markedly from each other. However, the FG seems to know some form of the tradition of the appearance of an angel or angels to the women at the tomb, even though the use it makes of it is highly distinctive. Contrast Mary's calmness on discovering the angels with the reaction of the women in the Synoptic Gospels (Mark xvi. 5 f., 8, Luke xxiv. 5, Matt. xxviii. 5, 8); moreover, in the FG the angels do not deliver a message (which is their most important function in the Synoptic Gospels, Mark xvi. 6 f., Luke xxiv. 5-7, 23, Matt. xxviii. 5-7), but are merely a device used to draw out Mary's expression of the reason for her grief (verse 13). **Angels** are rarely mentioned in the FG (see p. 105), and the way in which the tradition is handled at this point suggests that it may be secondary.

[1] Possible parallels to the FG in these quotations are indicated by the use of italics. Note that different verbs for 'sitting' are used in Mark and the FG, and cf. p. 423 n. 3 above for the way in which the FG uses the adjective 'white' here.   [2] The same verb as in Mark.

[3] The further development of such legendary material is to be found in the *Gospel of Peter* 35 ff., where, e.g., the stone rolls away of its own accord from the mouth of the tomb to admit two young men who descend from heaven, though this gospel's account of the visit of the women to the tomb (55-57) seems rather to depend basically on Mark xvi. 1-8.

It is, however, possible that the original account of the discovery of the empty tomb contained no mention of angels (cf. verses 1 f.), and that their appearance in the synoptic narratives is a later development in the tradition. It has to be frankly admitted that the material available to the writer has been freely manipulated to forge a link between verses 1-10 and 14 ff.; not only are there repetitions of phrases from the previous section (see above, p. 423), but a contrast is drawn between Mary and the Beloved Disciple, who has already been brought to faith at the empty tomb (verse 8), and the statement **'I do not know where they have laid him'** forms a dramatically appropriate introduction to the fact that Mary **saw Jesus . . . but did not know that it was Jesus.** But the writer seems to have been working over traditions already available to him (namely the story of the women at the tomb, also represented in verses 1 f., and the story of the vision of angels), and if his treatment of them in the interests of producing a good coherent narrative results in some distortion of history, we may sympathise with the difficulties he experienced in fitting two different stories together.

It is normally held that Jesus' appearance to Mary cannot be considered good history because (i) it is not mentioned elsewhere in the NT and (ii) there is a strong tradition that Jesus appeared first of all to Peter (1 Cor. xv. 5, Luke xxiv. 34). But these arguments do not exclude the possibility of other resurrection appearances, and it is likely that individual units of tradition about the resurrection, whether stories or lists of selected appearances, circulated independently of each other until a relatively late date, by which time it was difficult to combine them into one self-consistent narrative. One should not expect too great an agreement between different parts of what is on any showing a very varied tradition. Moreover, apart from the meagre contacts with the traditions known to the Synoptic Gospels noted above, the nearest parallel to this incident is Matt. xxviii. 8 f., where, after having heard the angel's message, the women were running from the tomb to tell the news of the resurrection to the disciples when they met (and recognised) Jesus. This is so different from the account in the FG that one must either suppose the author is drawing freely on his imagination, or that he is relating something which did in fact take place. The latter alternative may well be the less incredible.[1]

Mary's failure to recognise Jesus is a feature found elsewhere in the resurrection narratives (xxi. 4, 7, 12, Luke xxiv. 16 ff., Matt. xxviii. 17, cf. Luke xxiv. 37-41) and may have a simple psychological explanation if one takes into account the great emotional upheaval which had been caused by the crucifixion. However, it is used with great dramatic effect by the writer.

(15) Jesus said to her, 'Woman,[2] why are you weeping? Whom are you looking for?' She, thinking that he was the gardener, said to him, 'Sir, if it is you who have carried him away,[3] tell me where you have laid him, and I will take him away.' (16) Jesus said to her, 'Mary.' She turned and said to him in Aramaic,[4] 'Rabbuni!' (which means 'Teacher'). (17) Jesus said to her, 'Stop touching me,[5] for I have not yet ascended to the Father; but go to my brothers and say to them, "I am ascending to my Father and your Father, and my God and your God"'. (18) Mary of Magdala went and announced to the disciples,[6] 'I have seen the Lord', and that he had said this to her.

15. In characteristic Johannine style, the story continues with Jesus repeating and elaborating the angels' question to Mary.[7] If history is being reported, the mode of presentation is the evangelist's own. Similarly, just as earlier in the FG Jesus'

---

[1] See also the comments of C. H. Dodd, 'The Appearances of the Risen Christ: An Essay in Form-Criticism of the Gospels', in *Studies in the Gospels*, ed. D. E. Nineham (1955), pp. 19 f.   [2] γύναι; see p. 110.

[3] εἰ σὺ ἐβάστασας αὐτόν; σύ is emphatic.   [4] See p. 158 n. 3.

[5] μή μου ἅπτου; an alternative translation would be, 'Do not try to touch me'. The negative with the present imperative is used to signify that something already existing is to stop, and Mary has therefore already either touched Jesus or attempted to do so. Cf. B.-D. § 336 (3), Moulton, *Prolegomena*, p. 125, Turner, p. 76.

[6] ὅτι is used once only in this sentence, but introduces both direct and indirect speech. The variants from the text translated here can all be explained as attempts to improve the style; thus instead of ἑώρακα, ἑώρακεν is read by A D Θ *fam* 1 *fam* 13 *vt pesh boh*^pt and ἑωράκαμεν by S 33, while for ταῦτα εἶπεν αὐτῇ the reading ταῦτα εἶπέν μοι is presupposed by *ff*² *vg sah*^pm *boh*^pc *ac*² and ἃ εἶπεν αὐτῇ ἐμήνυσεν αὐτοῖς is supported by D *c* (*e*) *sin eth*.

[7] The addition of τίνα ζητεῖς; at verse 13, supported by D (69) 579 *ff*² *sin*, is presumably by assimilation to this verse. The verb ζητέω is also used (rather differently) in the synoptic narratives, Mark xvi. 6, Matt. xxviii. 5, Luke xxiv. 5.

words are frequently misunderstood at first by his hearers, their full meaning only becoming apparent later,[1] so now Mary fails to understand whom she is addressing. Note also the double meaning of the word translated **Sir** (κύριε) which can also indicate the divine status of Christ. Each time the term appears in this chapter (verses 2, 13, 15, 18, 20, 25) there is an overtone derived from the belief of the Christian community, until finally it is used by Thomas in his confession of faith (verse 28; see the note *in loc.*). Mary speaks more truly than she knows.

16. It is enough for Jesus to utter Mary's name; the good shepherd 'calls his own sheep by name and leads them out . . . and the sheep follow him, because they know his voice' (x. 3 f.). That **she turned** (στραφεῖσα) to address Jesus need not mean that Mary had turned away from the supposed gardener to the grave, and now turns back to him.[2] It is also unnecessary to claim that the Greek text is the result of mistranslation from an Aramaic original;[3] the rendering of *sin*, 'and she recognised him', is probably only designed to remove an imagined difficulty. In fact, though the Greek verb used can mean 'to turn right round' (as at verse 14, ἐστράφη εἰς τὰ ὀπίσω), it can also describe a partial turning of the body, as it clearly does elsewhere in the NT when it is used of an action occurring in the course of a conversation (Matt. xvi. 23, Luke ix. 55). Mary now faces Jesus directly and greets him as **Rabbuni,** an **Aramaic** word meaning 'my lord' or 'my master', found only here and at Mark x. 51 in the NT. Although other vocalisations of the Aramaic are known, the one represented in the NT is found in the Palestinian Pentateuch Targum, whose language dates back to at least the first century A.D., and in which the term is invariably used of a human lord.[4] Cf. i. 38, where **'Teacher'** (διδάσκαλε) is given as the translation of 'rabbi' (and see also the note *in loc.* and iii. 2). Mary thus shows her intention of resuming her former attitude to Jesus. Further, 17. she seizes

---

[1] Cf. p. 119.   [2] So Barrett, p. 469.

[3] So Black, pp. 189 f., and M. É. Boismard, *art. cit.*, p. 47, who provides further textual evidence for the theory.

[4] Black, pp. 20 f., who also notes that 'in Jewish literature generally the word is usually reserved for the Divine Lord.' Cf. Strack–Billerbeck, II, p. 25.

hold of him,[1] and although this may be taken as a natural expression of joy—a comparison has been drawn with the reception of Alexander the Great by his army when he had been believed dead, 'some touching his hands, some his knees, some his garment'[2]—the command **'Stop touching me'** has more significance than this for the writer. There is no verbal parallel with Matt. xxviii. 9, where the women meet Jesus as they are running from the tomb to give the angel's message to the disciples 'and took hold of his feet ($\dot{\epsilon}\kappa\rho\dot{\alpha}\tau\eta\sigma\alpha\nu$ $\alpha\dot{\upsilon}\tau o\hat{\upsilon}$ $\tau o\dot{\upsilon}s$ $\pi\dot{o}\delta\alpha s$) and worshipped him',[3] and in the FG the story moves on a quite different level.

Mary may not touch Jesus because he has **not yet ascended to the Father.** This seems to imply that after the Ascension it will be possible to touch Jesus, and it has been noted that later Thomas is invited to do so (verse 27). Moreover, the coming of the Spirit is said in the FG to be consequent upon the departure of Christ (xvi. 7), but according to verse 22 the Spirit is given to the disciples on the evening of the day on which Jesus appeared to Mary. It has therefore been supposed that the writer thought the Ascension took place some time during Easter Sunday. But this is perhaps to mistake his intention.

The return of Jesus to the Father is usually expressed in the FG by the verbs $\dot{\upsilon}\pi\dot{\alpha}\gamma\omega$ (vii. 33; viii. 14, 21; xiii. 3, 33, 36; xiv. 4, 28; xvi. 5, 10, 17[4]) and $\pi o\rho\epsilon\dot{\upsilon}o\mu\alpha\iota$ (xiv. 2, 12, 28; xvi. 7, 28[4]); in these passages it is primarily the death of Jesus that is in view, but 'by naming the Father as the goal of the journey [Jesus] is predicting the death, the resurrection, the ascension drawn together as in a single act.'[5] The FG has no real interest in the Ascension as a separate event, though it does not doubt that the process of Jesus' glorification will be completed when he has **ascended to the Father;** the verb used here ($\dot{\alpha}\nu\alpha\beta\alpha\dot{\iota}\nu\omega$) is only found with this meaning in two other places in the FG

[1] See p. 426 n. 5 above.

[2] Arrian, *Anabasis of Alexander* VI. 13. 3, cited by Bauer[5], s.v. $\ddot{\alpha}\pi\tau\omega$; the quotation is from the translation by E. I. Robson in the Loeb Classical Library (1933).

[3] To claim that the verb $\ddot{\alpha}\pi\tau\omega$ may possibly have been found in a source used by the FG and Matthew (so B. Lindars, *art. cit.*, p. 145) is at best precarious.   [4] See the notes *in loc.*

[5] A. M. Ramsey, 'What Was the Ascension?' Bulletin II of the *Studiorum Novi Testamenti Societas* (1951), p. 48.

(iii. 13; vi. 62 [1]). For John the regulative idea is rather that of the departure of Christ.

The message which Jesus gives Mary, **'I am ascending to my Father . . .'**, employs a verb in the present tense ($\dot{\alpha}\nu\alpha\beta\alpha\dot{\iota}\nu\omega$) with 'the meaning of "to be in the process of going . . ." for which reaching the destination still lies in the future.'[2] Thus what is conveyed is that any attempt to recapture the past, such as is expressed in word and action by Mary, is doomed to failure; the resurrection appearances are only a temporary phase in the Church's experience, leading on to a fresh relationship with Christ. Contact with him will then be of a different kind, and the next pericope (verses 19-23) perhaps suggests something of what this will be like (see the notes *in loc.*); but the imminence of the time when Jesus will no longer appear in the world in physical form is the presupposition of the remainder of xx, which looks forward beyond the era of bodily touch. The meaning of the verb 'to touch' is transmuted, just as in vi the verb 'to eat' is given a new connotation.

Mary is sent to Jesus' **brothers,** i.e. the Christian Church (cf. xxi. 23), not the unbelieving members of his family mentioned at vii. 3, 5, 10, cf. ii. 12. In the synoptic resurrection narratives the word only appears at Matt. xxviii. 10, where Jesus says to the women 'go and tell ($\dot{\alpha}\pi\alpha\gamma\gamma\epsilon\dot{\iota}\lambda\alpha\tau\epsilon$—cf. John xx. 18, $\dot{\alpha}\gamma\gamma\dot{\epsilon}\lambda\lambda o\upsilon\sigma\alpha$) my brethren ($\tauo\hat{\iota}\varsigma\,\dot{\alpha}\delta\epsilon\lambda\phi o\hat{\iota}\varsigma\,\mu o\upsilon$) . . .', though the content of the message is different and the verbal similarities with the FG are probably fortuitous. The parallelism **my Father and your Father, my God and your God,** stresses that there is kinship between Jesus and his **brothers,** though this does not involve the loss of the unique identity of 'the only-begotten, who is in the bosom of the Father . . . that revealed him' (i. 18)[3]; the disciples are given by Christ 'authority to become children of God' (i. 12).[3]

(19) Now when it was evening on that day, the first day of the week, and the doors were locked where the disciples were for fear of the Jews, Jesus came and stood among them and said to them, 'Peace be with you.'

---

[1] See the notes *in loc.*
[2] B.-D. § 323 (3), cf. Turner, p. 63.
[3] See the notes *in loc.*

(20) And when he had said this he showed them his hands and his side. Then the disciples rejoiced when they saw the Lord.

Apart from the traditions contained in the 'longer ending' of Mark (cf. Mark xvi. 14-18) and the bare mention of an appearance 'to the twelve' at 1 Cor. xv. 5, the only parallel to this narrative is Luke xxiv. 36 ff., where Jesus shows himself to 'the eleven . . . and those who were with them' (Luke xxiv. 33), who have just been joined by the two disciples who had encountered Jesus on the road to Emmaus. The Twelve as a group do not seem to possess great significance for the FG,[1] and it is impossible to say who **the disciples** referred to here were thought to be. They stand for all those who joyfully accept the Risen Christ as their **Lord.**

At the conclusion of Luke xxiv. 36 'and he said to them, "Peace be with you"' is read by all authorities except D *a b d e ff*[2] *l r*[1]; similarly Luke xxiv. 40, 'and when he had said this he showed them his hands and his feet' is omitted by D *a b d e ff*[2] *l r*[1] *sin cur* Marcion. It is usual to regard these two passages as interpolations based on the FG,[2] though it has recently been strongly argued that they form part of the original text of Luke.[3] But even if this were not the case there are clear contacts here between the Lucan and Johannine traditions; cf. he **stood among them** (ἔστη εἰς τὸ μέσον) with 'he stood in their midst' (ἔστη ἐν μέσῳ αὐτῶν, Luke xxiv. 36) and **then the disciples rejoiced** (ἐχάρησαν) with 'they disbelieved for joy' (ἀπὸ τῆς χαρᾶς, Luke xxiv. 41), and especially **he showed them his hands** (τὰς χεῖρας) **and his side** with 'See my hands and my feet' (τὰς χεῖράς μου καὶ τοὺς πόδας μου, Luke xxiv. 39)—only here in the gospels is it implied that Jesus was nailed to the cross.[4] Thus it is possible that a common source is

[1] See p. 199.

[2] Cf. J. A. Bailey, *op. cit.*, p. 86 n. 2; K. H. Rengstorf, *op. cit.*, *in loc.*

[3] K. Aland, *art. cit.*, pp. 206-8; Aland also discusses the other variant readings at Luke xxiv. 36 and finds them secondary.

[4] 'The condemned person was sometimes fastened to the cross with cords and sometimes with nails', J. Blinzler, *The Trial of Jesus* (E.T. by I. and F. McHugh of *Der Prozess Jesu*, 1959), p. 250. Cf. *ibid.*, pp. 264 f., for a full discussion of the evidence in the case of Christ; Blinzler concludes that 'it does not seem permissible to doubt that Jesus was nailed.'

being drawn upon by Luke and the FG, though each develops the material in a different way.[1]

It would be understandable if **the doors were locked where the disciples were for fear of the Jews** (cf. vii. 13; xix. 38), but mention of this is not intended to encourage speculation about the nature of Jesus' resurrected body, which is in any case by definition unique. When **he showed them his hands and his side** it was solely to demonstrate that the one who had been crucified was once more present with them, and it is the fact of this presence—despite a barred door—that the writer wishes to bring out. Cf. Matt. xviii. 20, the influence of which may be seen in a variant reading at verse 19.[2] Further, it is significant that **it was evening on that day, the first day of the week,** when Jesus **came and stood among** his disciples; by the time the FG was written Sunday was observed as the festival of the resurrection,[3] though neither Jewish nor pagan employers would have been likely to permit Christians to share in communal worship during the day. There may therefore be more than a hint here of Jesus being specially present with the Christian community as it meets for worship; cf. verse 26 and the note *in loc.*, and also Luke xxiv. 30, 35, where there are possible eucharistic overtones. Acts xx. 7 ff. illustrates how early Christian practice involved worship in the evening.

'Peace be with you' is a conventional Jewish greeting (cf. Judges vi. 23; xix. 20, Dan. x. 19 Theodotion, Tobit xii. 17), but the emphasis given by its repetition at verses 21 and 26 suggests a reference back to xiv. 27 and xvi. 33 (see pp. 333 f.). Stress on the genuine appearance of the real Jesus to the disciples is shared with Luke;[4] see further on verses 25 ff., where the development

---

[1] Cf. xix. 34 for the FG's interest in the wound in Jesus' side.

[2] After **where the disciples were**, συνηγμένοι, 'gathered together', is read by Θ *fam* 1 *fam* 13 *vt* some manuscripts of the Vulgate and Cyril.

[3] On the development of the Christian observance of Sunday cf. H. Riesenfeld, 'Sabbat et Jour du Seigneur', in *New Testament Essays*, ed. A. J. B. Higgins (1959), pp. 210-217 (not all of whose interpretations are adopted here).

[4] Cf. P. Vielhauer in E. Hennecke's *New Testament Apocrypha*, ed. by W. Schneemelcher (E.T. ed. by R. McL. Wilson), Vol. I (1963), pp. 128-130 for a discussion (with translation of the texts, which are conveniently printed in K. Aland, *Synopsis Quattuor Evangeliorum* (1964), p. 503) of Jerome, *de viris inlustribus* 16 and Ignatius, *ad Smyrn.* III. 1 f., which refer to an appearance to Peter and others in the course of which Jesus invites the disciples to

of the theme of 'seeing' in this chapter is also discussed.
Cf. on xv. 11; xvi. 20-24; xvii. 13 for the rejoicing of the disciples.

**(21) Then Jesus said to them again, 'Peace be with
you. As the Father has sent me, so I send you.' (22) And
when he had said this he breathed on them[1] and said to
them, 'Receive the Holy Spirit.[2] (23) If you forgive anyone's[3] sins, they are forgiven;[4] if you retain anyone's[3]
⟨sins⟩, they are retained.'[5]**

21. Matt. xxviii. 18 ff. records a commissioning of the
disciples by Jesus in Galilee (cf. Mark xvi. 14-18, part of the
'longer ending', where the scene is presumably Jerusalem),
while Luke, despite his divergence from the FG about the
scheme of events in the post-resurrection period (for which see
p. 433 below), relates the preaching of 'repentance and forgiveness of sins' (cf. verse 23) to the resurrection (Luke xxiv. 46 f.).
It is appropriate for the future to be considered here in a
similar (if characteristically Johannine) way. Just as Jesus has
been sent into the world with the authority of **the Father**

handle him so that they may be assured that he is no 'bodiless demon'. They
do touch him, and believe. It is likely that the sole basis for these traditions
is to be found in Luke xxiv. 36 ff.

[1] Literally, 'he breathed', ἐνεφύσησεν, which must be taken absolutely,
unless the αὐτοῖς later in the verse belongs also to this verb. Cf. Bauer[5], s.v.
ἐμφυσάω. After ἐνεφύσησεν, αὐτοῖς is inserted by D W *sin pesh sah boh* to ease
the grammar.

[2] Πνεῦμα Ἅγιον. The absence of the article is not significant; cf. vii. 39,
where the word appears twice, once with and once without the article.

[3] τινων. The singular τινος, supported by B *a e f syr*, could be an error
due to faulty hearing, ω and ο being pronounced alike and frequently confused, or the result of the scribe holding a clause in his memory while copying
it down; cf. B. M. Metzger, *The Text of the New Testament* (1964), pp. 190-
193, for these types of mistake.

[4] ἀφέωνται, the perfect passive, is supported by ℵ[c] A D L *fam* 1 *fam* 13 565
and provides a good parallel to κεκράτηνται, **they are retained**, to which
Jeremias, *T.W.z.N.T.* Vol. III, p. 753 n. 88 thinks the form has been
assimilated. The present ἀφίενται is read by W Θ *aur b c f vg boh geo* Origen,
and ἀφείονται, read by B*, is probably a variant form of the present (though
Barrett, p. 475, thinks B* may support ἀφέωνται, ιο having been written for
ω); if the present is the true reading it has a future meaning (cf. B.-D. § 323
(1), Turner, p. 63, both citing Jeremias, *art. cit.*, p. 753). The future ἀφεθήσεται,
read by ℵ* with some support from the versions, is presumably to be taken
as a reverential passive, with God as the implied subject of the act.

[5] Or, 'Whoever's sins you forgive … whoever's [sins] you retain.' On the
construction with ἄν here, cf. Moule, pp. 151 f.

behind his mission, so the disciples are sent to continue his work. This marks the establishment of the Christian Church.[1] Cf. especially v. 23; xiii. 20; xvii. 18 and the notes *in loc.*

22. That **he breathed on them** recalls Gen. ii. 7 (cf. Wisdom xv. 11) and perhaps also Ezek. xxxvii. 9. A new creative act of God is being described, as significant as the breathing of the breath of life into Adam's nostrils. The FG is explicit that the **Spirit** (Πνεῦμα—which also means 'breath') will only be given after Jesus' glorification (vii. 39) and that he will be sent by Jesus after Jesus has returned to the Father (xvi. 7); moreover, the placing of the gift of the Spirit on Easter Day can hardly be harmonised with the accounts given by Luke (cf. Luke xxiv. 49, Acts i. 4 f., 8; ii. 33). But, as Barrett points out, 'The existence of divergent traditions of the constitutive gift of the Spirit is not surprising; it is probable that to the first Christians the resurrection of Jesus and his appearances to them, his exaltation (however that was understood), and the gift of the Spirit, appeared as one experience, which only later came to be described in separate elements and incidents.'[2] It should also be remembered that although Acts i. 3-10 describes an Ascension after a forty-day period during which Jesus appeared to the disciples, Luke xxiv. 51 (whatever the correct reading in the latter part of the verse) describes an equally decisive parting on Easter Day; if this is tolerable within the writings of one person, too much should not be made of the differences between Luke and the FG here.[3]

23. Cf. Matt. xviii. 18; xvi. 19. In view of the fact that 'to forgive sins' (ἀφιέναι ἁμαρτίας) and 'to retain' (κρατεῖν) are expressions not used elsewhere in the FG and not found in the Matthean parallels, it is unlikely that this verse is an adaptation

[1] **I send** translates πέμπω, **has sent** ἀπέσταλκεν; it is likely that these verbs are used synonymously in the FG (cf. p. 129 n. 1, and for a different view K. H. Rengstorf in *T.W.z.N.T.*, s.v. ἀποστέλλω). It is doubtful whether deductions about ecclesiastical institutions can be based on this verse; while the noun ἀπόστολος is important in any discussion of the origins of the Christian ministry, it is not the cognate verb ἀποστέλλω but πέμπω which is used of the sending of the disciples.

[2] Barrett, p. 475.

[3] For the Spirit in the FG, cf. pp. 93-97 and the notes on the passages cited in p. 96 n. 5.

from Matthew or a free invention of the Fourth Evangelist.[1] It has frequently been noted that Matt. xvi. 19 recalls Isa. xxii. 22, and it has been plausibly suggested that if the Matthean and Johannine sayings are variants of a common original (which one might reasonably suppose was composed in Aramaic), this may well have followed Isaiah in describing the authority conferred in terms of opening and shutting, but without defining it further. Matthew and John then provide different interpretations of what was said, the Johannine version developing naturally out of an ambiguity in the Aramaic; אחד, 'to shut', can also mean 'to seize or hold', and פתח, 'to open', could well have suggested the meaning 'to release, let loose, set free'. One merit of this hypothesis is that it satisfactorily accounts for the verb 'to retain', which is not used here in any of its normal Greek senses, as a Semitism.[2]

The authority conferred is connected with the gift of the Spirit;[3] cf. on xvi. 8-11 for the continuation of Jesus' ministry by the Spirit, and also Luke xxiv. 47, which speaks of the preaching to all nations of 'repentance and forgiveness of sins' ($\mu\epsilon\tau\acute{a}\nuοιαν$ $\epsilon\acute{i}s$ $\acute{a}\phi\epsilon\sigmaιν$ $\acute{a}\mu\alpha\rhoτιῶν$). Matt. xxviii. 19 (and also Mark xvi. 16) mention baptism in a comparable position, and it is likely that the immediate reference in the FG is to the remission of sins which accompanies conversion and baptism, and the retention of the sins of those who reject the apostolic preaching. It would not, however, be impossible for there to be a secondary reference to the situation which arises when a person who has been excommunicated wishes to be readmitted to the Christian community.[4] In any case, 'the controversy

---

[1] C. H. Dodd, *Historical Tradition in the Fourth Gospel* (1963), pp. 347-9, though ἀφιέναι ἁμαρτίας is found at 1 John i. 9; ii. 12 and κρατεῖν (used admittedly in a different sense) appears 8 times in Revelation.

[2] J. A. Emerton, 'Binding and Loosing—Forgiving and Retaining', *J.T.S.* n.s., Vol. XIII, 1962, pp. 325-331.

[3] C. K. Barrett, 'The Holy Spirit in the Fourth Gospel', *J.T.S.* n.s., Vol. I, 1950, pp. 3 f., notes that in the FG 'the consequence [of the gift of the Spirit] is not inspired utterance but ... the permanent authority and mission of the Church'. He compares Mark xvi. 17 f., according to which very different 'signs will accompany those who believe', and Luke xxiv. 49, the significance of which is brought out in Acts, and comments, 'the continuator of Mark and the author of Luke–Acts are looking back upon an already half-legendary past.'

[4] F. W. Beare, 'The Risen Jesus Bestows the Spirit: A Study of John 20:

whether the commission is given to the Church as a whole or to the apostles is irrelevant. There is no distinction here between the Church and the ministry; both completely overlap.'[1]

(24) Now Thomas (which means 'Twin'), one of the twelve, was not with them when Jesus came. (25) So the other disciples told him, 'We have seen the Lord'. But he said to them, 'Unless I see in his hands the mark[2] of the nails and put my finger into the place left by the nails[3] and put my hand into his side, I will not[4] believe'.

24. Thomas is included in lists of **the twelve**[5] at Mark iii. 18, Matt. x. 3, Luke vi. 15 and Acts i. 13, but apart from this story is mentioned elsewhere in the NT only at John xi. 16; xiv. 5; xxi. 2. See pp. 267, 321. Cf. on verse 19 for the difficulties of the evidence about those to whom Jesus appeared on Easter Day; that Thomas was absent is material peculiar to the FG. **25.** With **'We have seen the Lord'**, cf. Mary's announcement to the disciples, 'I have seen the Lord' (verse 18), which is only possible because, after having seen Jesus and failed to recognise him, he revealed himself to her (verses 14-16). Similarly 'the disciples rejoiced when they saw the Lord', but only after 'he showed them his hands and his side' (verse 20). Up to a point, Thomas is only demanding what the other disciples had already been given, though he does ask in addition for physical contact with Christ. In the event, when this is offered he does not need it (verses 27 f.), though his requirement shows that he will not be content with less than the truth. It has been

19-23', *Canadian Journal of Theology*, Vol. IV, 1958, p. 99, thinks the two meanings are intended equally, and argues that the force of the perfects rendered **are forgiven** and **are retained** is that the apostolic sentence 'is effective as soon as spoken'. Cf. the Roman Catholic writer P. Niewalda, *Sakramentssymbolik im Johannesevangelium?* (1958), pp. 6 f., who thinks there is no doubt that the institution of the sacrament of penance and nothing further is recorded here.

[1] E. C. Hoskyns, *The Fourth Gospel* (ed. F. N. Davey, 1947), p. 545.

[2] τὸν τύπον; the plural is read by P[66] 565, and τὸν τόπον, which differs by only one letter and also appears later in the verse, is supported by N f q sin. It is easy to see how this reading could have arisen.

[3] τὸν τόπον τῶν ἥλων; τύπον is read instead of τόπον by B ℵ[c] D L W Γ Δ fam 1 fam 13 sah boh (cf. the previous note), and for the whole phrase τὴν χεῖρα αὐτοῦ is read by ℵ*.

[4] οὐ μή, an emphatic negative; cf. Bauer[5], s.v. μή, Moulton, *Prolegomena*, p. 191, Turner, p. 97.

[5] For **the twelve** in the FG, see p. 199.

claimed that there is 'legendary embroidery of the crudest type' in Luke's story of the appearance of Jesus to the disciples in Jerusalem because it contains (for example) an invitation to handle him (Luke xxiv. 39);[1] there is, however, a certain sophistication about this story in the FG, which balances the narrative of verses 1-10.

The Beloved Disciple knows that his Lord has risen when he sees the grave-clothes lying in the tomb; 'he saw and believed' (verse 8, see p. 420). Thomas, by contrast, should have come to faith through the witness borne to Jesus by the Christian community, which ought to have been sufficient for him; the importance of the testimony to Christ of the first generation of Christians is heavily stressed in the Johannine literature (i. 14; xix. 35; xxi. 24, 1 John i. 1-3), and it is in the Church that Jesus now makes himself known (cf. the notes on verses 19 and 26).

Matt. xxviii. 17 may possibly claim that some of the eleven doubted at an appearance of Jesus to them in Galilee (cf. Luke xxiv. 37 f., 41), while Luke xxiv. 11, 23-25 tells how the disciples did not believe the women who gave them the angels' message that Christ was risen and Mark xvi. 11, 13 f. (part of the 'longer ending') says that they disbelieved those to whom Jesus appeared after his resurrection. The point of this story is to show how even more far-reaching doubt was overcome.[2] The narrative culminates in a blessing pronounced by Jesus on all those who, though they have not seen him, nonetheless believe (verse 29); heightened emphasis is given to this statement by the fact that it formed the climax of the FG before xxi was added,

[1] F. W. Beare, *The Earliest Records of Jesus* (1962), p. 245.

[2] C. H. Dodd, *Historical Tradition in the Fourth Gospel* (1963), p. 145 n. 2, points out how, in almost all the narratives of the appearances of the Risen Christ, 'some degree of doubt or uncertainty seems to be implied . . . The "longer ending" of Mark (the latest treatment of the theme, probably, in the N.T.) is pervaded with the contrast of belief and unbelief . . . This may be taken as indicating the way in which narratives of the Christophanies were employed in the early Church for paraenetic purposes', the point being, as in Mark xvi. 16, 'He who believes and is baptized will be saved; but he who does not believe will be condemned'. But it is not perhaps essential to follow Dodd (*ibid.*, pp. 145 f.) in his view that the story of Doubting Thomas is 'a dramatization (in our author's manner) of the traditional motive of the incredulity of some or all of the disciples.'

being at that time the last recorded utterance of Christ in this gospel.

(26) And after eight days his disciples were again indoors, and Thomas was with them. Jesus came though the doors were locked and stood among them and said, 'Peace be with you.' (27) Then he said to Thomas, 'Reach out your finger here and see my hands, and reach out your hand and put it into my side, and stop being faithless, but believing.' (28) Thomas answered and said to him, 'My Lord and my God!' (29) Jesus said to him, 'Is it because you have seen me that you have believed?[1] **Blessed are those who have not seen and yet believe.'**

26. Cf. verse 19 and the notes *in loc*. There is no mention in the rest of the NT of an appearance in Jerusalem **after eight days,** i.e. on the Sunday after Easter Day;[2] once again there may be a conscious attempt to depict Jesus present with the assembled Church. Bearing in mind that the Feast of Unleavened Bread lasted for a week after Passover, it is possible that the continued presence of the disciples in Jerusalem was due, if not to the exceptional circumstances of this particular Passover, then to their duty as pious Jews.[3] Cf. further on xxi. 1 for the locale of the resurrection appearances. 27. **Stop being faithless, but believing** has to be interpreted in the light of verses 30 f. and of one's understanding of the purpose of the gospel as a whole; see the notes *in loc*. and pp. 52 ff. The context provided by the rest of the verse seems to contain an unmistakable anti-docetic element, and to this extent the incident may be related as a corrective for Christian belief, though 28. Thomas' response, **'My Lord and my God!'**, which embodies the faith of the Church in Jesus, may well in addition be polemic

---

[1] The earliest MSS. are not punctuated, but 700 *al* treat this clause as a question. The Textus Receptus regards it as a statement and Barrett comments (p. 477) that 'in this solemn and impressive pronouncement Jesus does not ask questions, but declares the truth', though it may be that the situation is summed up in a question which confronts the listener with the vital issue involved before the blessing which forms the climax to the whole is pronounced. Cf. also i. 50.

[2] The figure is reckoned inclusively, in accordance with ancient practice; cf. the addition of a gloss corresponding to τῇ μιᾷ ἑτέρων σαββάτων in *sin*.

[3] C. F. D. Moule, 'The Post-Resurrection Appearances in the Light of Festival Pilgrimages,' *N.T.S.*, Vol. IV, 1957–58, p. 59.

directed against the imperial cult. Domitian (A.D. 81–96) affected the title 'Our Master and our God' (*Dominus et Deus noster*),[1] and a reference to this may be intended; **Lord** is a title used by the earliest Christian community after the resurrection to express its veneration for Jesus,[2] but the NT evidence for calling him **God** is at best sparse.[3] See, however, i. 1; v. 18; x. 33, and p. 85, n. 1 for the variant reading at i. 18. Yet **29. a still wider meaning is implied**; the gospel was written to supply the place of sight (cf. verse 31), being inspired in part by a missionary purpose, and those who attain to faith are hailed as **blessed** by Christ. For the reasonableness of Thomas' demand for evidence, cf. on verse 25; the value of the story is that it shows how the disciples did not accept the news of the resurrection uncritically, and the way in which doubt was overcome demonstrates that good evidence was available. The circumstances under which Mary is told to stop touching Jesus are quite different; cf. the note on verse 17. At the same time this apologetic is subordinated to the idea that the requirements made by Thomas are now unnecessary, the witness of the first generation of Christians being a sufficient basis for faith (cf. on verse 25); Thomas is a part of this generation (cf. verse 24) and his testimony is recorded for the sake of **those who have not seen.**

(30) Now there were many other signs which Jesus also performed in front of his disciples,[4] but they are not written in this book; (31) but these are written in order that you may believe that Jesus is the Christ, the Son of God, and that, so believing, you may have life in his name.

Cf. pp. 52 ff. It is not surprising to be told that a deliberate process of selection (cf. xxi. 25) lies behind a book as carefully

---

[1] Suetonius, *Domitian* 13; 'the custom arose of . . . addressing him in no other way even in writing or in conversation', *ibid.*, trans. by J. C. Rolfe, *Suetonius*, Loeb Edition, Vol. II (1950), pp. 367-9.

[2] Cf. V. Taylor, *The Names of Jesus* (1953), pp. 38-51.

[3] Cf. V. Taylor, 'Does the New Testament Call Jesus God?', *The Expository Times*, Vol. LXXIII, 1961–62, pp. 116-8; see also N. Turner, *Grammatical Insights into the New Testament* (1965), pp. 13-17, for a different evaluation of the evidence.

[4] αὐτοῦ is read by P⁶⁶ ℵ C D L W Γ Θ *fam* 1 *fam* 13 and a number of the versions.

constructed as the FG. Each incident has its place in the overall
scheme, which is designed to present Christ's life in such a
way that the reader **may believe.**

Signs play a somewhat ambiguous rôle in the gospel; at
times the word seems to be a synonym for 'the working of a
miracle' (iv. 48; xi. 47), and this can lead to an imperfect form
of faith (ii. 23; iii. 2; vi. 2, 14; cf. also vii. 31; ix. 16; xii. 18).
Jesus refuses to give a sign which would compel faith (ii. 18 f.;
vi. 30), though the signs which he did provide ought to have
led men to believe (vi. 26; xii. 37). However, stated exactly, their
function was to *confirm* faith (cf. ii. 11; iv. 50-54), and so they
were **performed in front of his disciples** who must now bear
witness to what they have seen. The **signs** form the core of the
FG (see p. 5), and it is not unreasonable to suppose that,
whatever the precise public for which the gospel was written, it
was designed to meet the needs of those who had at least close
contact with the Church. This contention is perhaps strengthened if the sermons of a Christian prophet lie behind much of
the FG.[1]

The fact that the gospel was **written in order that** men
may believe that Jesus is the Christ suggests that it may in
part be intended to reach a Jewish audience, for which such a
formulation would have meaning; Jesus claims this title for
himself (iv. 26), and during his ministry others apply it to him—
Andrew (i. 41), John the Baptist (iii. 28), the woman of Samaria
(iv. 29), some of Jesus' hearers in Jerusalem (vii. 31, 41), and
Martha (xi. 27). Furthermore, confession that **Jesus is the
Christ** leads to excommunication (ix. 22). **Son of God,** in
origin a Messianic title (cf. on i. 49), has to be understood here
in its full Christian sense and includes within its scope all the
FG's teaching on Jesus' Sonship.

For Jesus as the source of **life,** cf. p. 5; **in his name**
could be paraphrased 'in him' (cf. iii. 15), the **name** standing
for the person who is named.[2] Cf. xiv. 20; xv. 4 f. for being or

---

[1] See p. 16.
[2] Cf. E. Jacob, *Theology of the Old Testament* (E.T. by A. W. Heathcote
and P. J. Allcock of *Théologie de l'Ancien Testament*, 1958), pp. 82-85 for the
Name of God as a manifestation of God, and also A. R. Johnson, *The One
and the Many in the Israelite Conception of God* ([2]1961), pp. 3 f., 17 ff. Bauer[5]

abiding in Christ, which is necessary if one is to share in the **life** which Christ offers.

In order that you may believe, whatever reading is adopted,[1] could refer either to the conversion of unbelievers or to the deepening and instructing of the faith of those who already believe, or to both of these at once.[2] It is perhaps most likely that the writer did not consciously restrict himself to any one aim, but endeavoured to assist all who came within his sphere of influence to a fuller appreciation of the significance of Christ for human life.

D. EPILOGUE, xxi

It is generally agreed that xx. 30 f. marks the conclusion of the FG in its original form, and it would seem to follow that xxi was added to meet a need which was not felt earlier. In view of the relationship between Peter and the Beloved Disciple in this narrative (cf. verses 7, 20, 22) it is not likely that the primary motive for its composition was the re-establishment of Peter's authority or the commendation of this (written) gospel at Rome where Peter was honoured, and it seems more probable that the writer's chief concern was to explain the Beloved Disciple's death (cf. verse 23 and the note *in loc.*). The Church need not be alarmed—Jesus had not prophesied that this disciple would live until the parousia. The chapter is evidence for a lively expectation of the Second Coming at the time when the FG was completed; it also stresses the dual commissioning of the disciples as evangelists (verses 6, 8, 11) and pastors (verses 15-17), to show that a continued period of church life was foreseen and

---

s.v. ὄνομα argues that the ἐν here is instrumental, meaning 'through the name', comparing xvii. 11 f. (on which see the note *in loc.*). It is hardly possible to take ἐν τῷ ὀνόματι αὐτοῦ with πιστεύοντες since this verb is regularly followed in the FG by the preposition εἰς; cf. p. 127, n. 2.

[1] πιστεύητε is read by B ℵ* θ 0250 892, πιστεύσητε by all other MSS.

[2] The force of the tenses should not be pressed too closely; cf. Dodd, *Interpretation*, p. 9. 1 John v. 13, which shows strong similarities to this verse, is definitely addressed to those already within the Christian fellowship.

provided for by Jesus.¹ Just as the disciples may have expected
the parousia to take place in Galilee (cf. on verse 1) but had to
adjust themselves to a new way of life and a new relationship
with Jesus, so the Church had to become accustomed to settled
institutions.

At the same time verse 24 may be significant; no gospel
explicitly states its author's name, but here heavy emphasis is
laid on the veracity of the testimony to Jesus borne by the
Beloved Disciple. This point may have especial weight if
Aland's theory that anonymity was the norm for early Christian
writing is to be accepted,² and could show that the FG was
expected to provoke controversy. In view of the tension between Peter and the Beloved Disciple which xxi shares with the
rest of the gospel, perhaps the influence of the circle which produced the finished book was already being resisted. See above,
pp. 422 f., for the possible significance of this atmosphere of conflict for the church history of the period.

Barrett (pp. 479 f.) discusses the contrast between the style
and vocabulary of i-xx and xxi and concludes that, in view of
the resemblances which are also found, the differences are insufficient to show that xxi is by another author, although they
would confirm the view that anyone adding fresh material to his
own book would not be likely to do so in such a clumsy way.
The fact that even the enthusiasm of C. C. Torrey was unable
to lead him to believe that xxi had an Aramaic original³ is an
instance of the contrast between this chapter and the rest of the
FG which most readers feel instinctively. Contacts in thought
with i-xx and the fact that xxi. 1-14 may in part draw on a tradition known also to Luke, as may certain sections of i-xx, need
mean no more than that xxi could suitably be considered as the
product of a 'Johannine circle'—which in any case its position
at the conclusion of the FG seems to make certain. However, if
it was composed subsequently to i-xx to meet specific urgent
needs, it may be that the author (or editor) of the FG had not

¹ However foreign it may be to our way of thinking, the commissions
given in Galilee are seen by the writer as complementary to xx. 21-23.
² K. Aland, 'The Problem of Anonymity and Pseudonymity in Christian
Literature of the First Two Centuries,' *J.T.S.* n.s., Vol. XII, 1961, pp. 39-49.
³ C. C. Torrey, *The Four Gospels: A New Translation* (1933), p. 331.
Torrey did of course think that i-xx had originally been written in Aramaic.

meditated on these themes as fully as on those contained in the original draft, which was intended to be complete, and that this accounts for the lack of polish here.

xxi. (1) **After this** [1] **Jesus showed himself again to the disciples by the Sea of Tiberias; and he showed ⟨himself⟩ in this way.** (2) **Simon Peter and Thomas (which means 'Twin') and Nathanael, who was from Cana in Galilee, and the sons of Zebedee, and two others from among his disciples were together.** (3) **Simon Peter said to them, 'I am going fishing'. They said to him, 'We too will come with you.' So they went out and got into the boat, but that night they caught nothing.**

1. It is sometimes argued that there are two contradictory traditions of where the Church began, Galilee being supported by Matthew, Mark, and John xxi, Jerusalem by Luke and John xx. Mark xiv. 28 = Matt. xxvi. 32 reports Jesus as saying on the night of his betrayal, 'But after I am raised up, I will go before you to Galilee', and Mark xvi. 7 = Matt. xxviii. 7 tells how the women were given by the angel at the tomb as part of their message for the disciples that Jesus 'is going before you to Galilee; there you will see him'. Similarly Matt. xxviii. 10 states that Jesus said to the women when he met them on their way back from the tomb, 'go and tell my brethren to go to Galilee, and there they will see me'. It has been suggested that the disciples returned to Galilee—as in any case they would naturally do after the feast [2]—expecting the parousia to take place there; if this is so it might explain why the Beloved Disciple, who, whatever his identity, is presumably a Jerusalem disciple, was with them on this occasion. [3] Even if 'Luke is determined that the gospel shall start from Jerusalem and no-where else' [4] the FG provides independent testimony to resurrection appearances in Jerusalem; cf. on xx. 22 for a justification

---

[1] μετὰ ταῦτα, on which see p. 131, n. 4; an interval of unspecified length is implied.

[2] C. F. D. Moule, 'The Post-Resurrection Appearances in the Light of Festival Pilgrimages', *N.T.S.*, Vol. IV, 1957–58, pp. 58–61.

[3] Alternatively, it has been suggested that he may have found Jerusalem dangerous after the crucifixion, and may also have been concerned for Mary's safety.

[4] A. R. C. Leaney, *A Commentary on the Gospel According to St. Luke* (1958), p. 292.

of the mode of presentation adopted in Luke xxiv and John xx, which is perfectly comprehensible in the light of the disciples' experience. If Jesus appeared to the disciples in Jerusalem but they anticipated that the parousia would occur immediately afterwards in Galilee, it would not be surprising if, when yet another resurrection appearance took place, confusion in the traditions resulted. The point of resurrection appearances in Galilee is that the disciples may be assured that Jesus is present with them wherever they may happen to be, and it is worth noting that the writer of xxi saw no incongruity in adding it to xx.

It has been claimed that Luke v. 1-11 combines the tradition of the call of the disciples recorded in Mark i. 16-20 with that of the post-resurrection appearance described in John xxi. 1-14[1]; cf. pp. 449 ff. below. For **Thomas** in the FG, see on xx. 24; elsewhere in the NT he appears only in lists of the twelve. **Nathanael** is only mentioned in the NT here and at i. 45-49; cf. p. 101, n. 3. The double name **Simon Peter** is relatively common in the FG but rare in the Synoptics, though it is found at Luke v. 8.[2] The only other disciples named in Luke v. 1-11 are 'James and John, sons of Zebedee' (υἱοὺς Ζεβεδαίου, Luke v. 10), and here is the only reference to **the sons of Zebedee** (οἱ τοῦ Ζεβεδαίου[3]) in the FG. The **two others from among his disciples** may be deliberately introduced in this way to disguise the identity of the Beloved Disciple—who of course need not be one of them.

3. There is no need to be surprised that the disciples went fishing. They had after all to earn their living somehow or other; there is as yet no full-time paid ministry. Barrett suspects that Peter's words may be intended by the writer 'to have a double meaning and refer to the apostolic mission of "catching men"',[4] though the verb used (ἁλιεύειν) is found only here in the NT;

---

[1] Cf., e.g., A. R. C. Leaney, 'Jesus and Peter: the Call and Post-resurrection Appearance', *The Expository Times*, Vol. LXV, 1953-54, pp. 381 f.; *op. cit.*, pp. 54-57.

[2] Σίμων alone is read here by D W *fam* 13 *vt sin*, but since it is not until Luke vi. 14 that the writer records that Simon was named Peter by Jesus the longer reading is the more probable.

[3] For this construction, cf. B.-D. § 162 (1) and Turner, p. 207.

[4] Barrett, p. 482.

Mark i. 16 f.=Matt. iv. 18 f., with its pun on the cognate noun 'fishermen' (ἀλεεῖς), has no precise parallel in Luke, where a quite different phrase is used for the catching of men (Luke v. 10), even though the word 'fishermen' does occur earlier in the narrative (Luke v. 2). In the FG Peter has not yet received his commission,[1] and it is unlikely that his speech carries an overtone; moreover, the whole point of the story is to show how the disciples' evangelistic task is only made possible by the command and aid of Jesus. With **but that night they caught nothing** cf. Luke v. 5, 'we toiled all night and took nothing'; there is, however, no significant verbal correspondence. The *Gospel of Peter*, 60 is probably dependent in part on this passage.[2]

(4) Just as day was breaking[3] **Jesus stood on the shore, though the disciples did not know that it was Jesus. (5) So Jesus said to them, 'Children, you have no fish, have you?'**[4] **They answered him, 'No.' (6) He said to them, 'Cast the net on the right side of the boat, and you will find ⟨some⟩.' So they cast ⟨it⟩, and they were no longer able to haul it in because of the large number of fish.**

4. With **the disciples did not know that it was Jesus,** cf. the note on xx. 14. The theme is developed further in verses 7 and 12, and verse 14 makes clear that an important feature of the story is to show how Jesus revealed himself to his disciples in Galilee; he was there with them, even though they did not

---

[1] xx. 21-23 notwithstanding; cf. the introduction to this section.

[2] 'But I, Simon Peter, and my brother Andrew took our nets and went to the sea. And there was with us Levi, the son of Alphaeus, whom the Lord . . .' (cited from the translation by Chr. Maurer in E. Hennecke's *New Testament Apocrypha*, ed. by W. Schneemelcher, E.T. ed. by R. McL. Wilson, Vol. I, 1963, p. 187). The text breaks off abruptly at this point. If this gospel is simply 'a further development of the traditional material of the four canonical Gospels' (*ibid.*, p. 180), the fact that the disciples return home without having seen the risen Jesus (cf. the *Gospel of Peter*, 59) does not provide independent support for the view that John xxi tells how disillusioned disciples resumed their former occupation. See further the argument of L. Vaganay, *L'Évangile de Pierre* (1930), pp. 331-5, that the apocryphal writer's characteristic interests are decisive for his handling of the material at this point.

[3] πρωΐας δὲ ἤδη γινομένης, supported by AB *al boh*, though it would be possible to read γενομένης with ℵ DW θ *fam* 1 *fam* 13 *pm*.

[4] μή τι προσφάγιον ἔχετε; cf. B.-D. § 427 (2) and Bauer⁵ s.v. μήτι. For the noun προσφάγιον, see Bauer⁵ s.v.

perhaps expect him to be present in quite this way (cf. on verse 1). 5. **Children** (Παιδία), which, according to Moulton, is used as a form of address to adults in modern Greek,[1] indicates that the speaker feels he is on terms of fatherly intimacy with those who are addressed;[2] cf. 1 John ii. 18. Jesus knows the predicament of his disciples (there can hardly be any connexion here with Luke xxiv. 41), and they are impotent without him (cf. verse 3 and xv. 5); 6. however, on obeying his instructions, they at once achieve success.[3] Although the detail of the story is worked out in a very different way, Luke v. 4-7 also tells how a great draught of fish is caught in obedience to a word of Jesus after a fruitless night's work.[4]

(7) So that disciple whom Jesus loved said to Peter, 'It is the Lord!' So Simon Peter, when he heard that it was the Lord, put on his outer garment (for he was stripped)[5] and jumped into the sea. (8) But the other disciples came in the boat, dragging the net ⟨full⟩ of fish, for they were not far from the land, only about a hundred yards[6] away.

For the contrast drawn between **Peter** and the **disciple whom Jesus loved** in the FG, see p. 421. It is the Beloved Disciple who intuitively recognises the figure standing on the shore, after which **Peter** at once rushes to join **the Lord,** followed at a more sedate pace by **the other disciples.** The miraculous catch of fish reveals Jesus (cf. verse 14), and it appears that when his disciples obeyed him they did not know who he was (verse 4); contrast Simon's speech in Luke v. 5, 'Master . . . at your word I will let down the nets.' This somewhat improbable feature of the Johannine narrative may perhaps best be explained if the interpretation of the genesis of the story suggested on pp. 450 f. below is adopted.

(9) So when they got out on land they saw a charcoal

---

[1] Moulton, *Prolegomena*, p. 170, n. 1.   [2] Bauer[5], s.v. παιδίον.

[3] Though **the right side of the boat** is the lucky side (Bauer[5] s.v. μέρος), Barrett (pp. 482 f.) is probably correct to claim that the writer's concern is rather to bring out the implicit obedience of Jesus' disciples.

[4] In the FG after Jesus' speech in verse 6, there is an insertion based on Luke v. 5 read by P⁶⁶ᵛⁱᵈ ℵ¹ g² *eth* Cyr.

[5] γυμνός, i.e. not wearing **his outer garment** (τὸν ἐπενδύτην); for this meaning see LS⁹ s.v. γυμνός, 5.

[6] πηχῶν διακοσίων, literally 'two hundred cubits'; the cubit was approximately 18 inches long.

fire there,[1] with fish lying on it, and bread. (10) Jesus said to them, 'Bring some of the fish which you have just[2] caught'.

As breakfast is ready when the disciples land, it is strange that Jesus should say 'Bring some of the fish which you have just caught'. This command introduces verse 11, which is chiefly significant for its symbolism—the catch plays no further part in the story—and the unevennesses in xxi lead one to suspect the presence of a number of different elements which have not been combined with the thoroughness and polish characteristic of the FG. Luke v. 1-11, whatever its relation to this narrative, is evidence for the circulation of similar accounts of a miraculous draught of fish in the early church, and it is possible that two such stories have been run together here; the point of the one is expressed in verse 11, of the other in verse 14. An additional theme is introduced with the **fish** and **bread** supplied by Jesus (cf. verse 13 and the note *in loc.*), and it may be that a third strand of tradition has been worked in.[3] But although xxi. 1-14 appears to be composite, it does not seem possible to reconstruct the original form of any of its components.

(11) **Simon Peter went aboard and hauled the net to the land, full of large fish, a hundred and fifty-three ⟨of them⟩; but, though there were so many, the net was not torn.**

Cf. Luke v. 6 f., where the nets do break under the strain, and two ships are so heavily loaded with the catch that they begin to sink; in the FG it is emphasised that **the net was not torn, even though there were so many,** and they were **large fish.** Moreover, while in Luke v. 8 Peter says to Jesus, 'Depart from me, for I am a sinful man, O Lord,' in the FG he rushes out of the boat to his Lord (verse 7), and then goes at Jesus' command

---

[1] ἀνθρακιὰν κειμένην; *incensos* is read by *vt* for κειμένην, presupposing καιομένην in the Greek. The phrase would then mean 'a pile of burning charcoal'.   [2] νῦν; cf. p. 265, n. 5.

[3] Cf. Barrett's suggestion that 'two stories have been combined, in one of which the disciples caught and brought the fish, while in the other Jesus provided the meal' (p. 483), and the view of D. M. Smith, Jr., *The Composition and Order of the Fourth Gospel* (1965), p. 235, that 'minor obscurities' are 'to be expected in a traditional story that has perhaps grown by accretion'.

to land the catch. It is perhaps significant that it is **Peter** who hauls the net ashore, not the other disciples, who have already disembarked (verse 9); once again he takes the lead. See the note on verse 3 for the commission to catch men in the Synoptic Gospels; the symbolism seems to demand a reference to this theme here, fuller mention of which may have been suppressed because another account using a different image was known and was to be utilised in verses 15 ff. The number **a hundred and fifty-three** has attracted much attention, though unfortunately Jerome's statement that Latin and Greek naturalists thought there were 153 species of fish does not seem reliable and hence cannot be used to explain this passage.[1] As far back as the time of Augustine it was noted that 153 is the sum of the numbers from 1 to 17; it is thus a triangular number since 153 dots can be arranged as an equilateral triangle with 17 dots on the base line.[2] However, many of the mathematical explanations which have been advanced are too arbitrary to be allowed to stand, and have insufficient relevance when seen in context. A relationship has sometimes been noted between this verse and Ezek. xlvii. 10, 'Fishermen will stand beside the sea; from En-gedi to En-eglaim it will be a place for the spreading of nets; its fish will be of very many kinds, like the fish of the Great Sea,' and it has been suggested on the basis of this that it was observed that the numerical values of the Hebrew consonants of Gedi and Eglaim add up to 17 and 153 respectively, and that these figures are mathematically related.[3] This explanation based on the principle of gematria is more plausible than many other attempts to find Hebrew or Greek words whose letters have a numerical value of 153, but it is perhaps still most probable that the number 'represents the full total of those who are "caught" by the Christian fishermen', for, in addition to those features of 153 noted above, '17 itself is the sum of 7 and 10, both numbers

---

[1] R. M. Grant, '"One Hundred Fifty-Three Large Fish" (John 21: 11)', *The Harvard Theological Review*, Vol. XLII, 1949, p. 273.

[2] Cf. the diagram in E. C. Hoskyns, *The Fourth Gospel* (ed. F. N. Davey, 1947), p. 553.

[3] J. A. Emerton, 'The Hundred and Fifty-Three Fishes in John xxi. 11,' *J.T.S.*, n.s., Vol. IX, 1958, pp. 86-89; cf. P. R. Ackroyd, 'The 153 Fishes in John xxi. 11-A Further Note,' *J.T.S.*, n.s., Vol. X, 1959, p. 94, and J. A. Emerton, '*Gematria* in John xxi. 11,' *J.T.S.*, n.s., Vol. XI, 1960, pp. 335 f.

which even separately are indicative of completeness and perfection. The fish then represent the full total of the catholic and apostolic Church.'[1] That they are **large fish** means they are a worthwhile catch, and that **the net was not torn** means that **Peter,** whose rôle is emphasised, is able to bring them safely **to the land.** There is probably also an allusion here to the perfect unity which ought to characterise the Church.

(12) Jesus said to them, 'Come and have breakfast.' None of the disciples dared to ask him, 'Who are you?' They knew it was the Lord. (13) Jesus came and took the bread and gave to them, and the fish in the same way. (14) This was now the third time Jesus appeared to the disciples when he was raised from the dead.

That Jesus **took the bread and gave to them, and the fish in the same way** ($\lambda\alpha\mu\beta\acute{\alpha}\nu\epsilon\iota$ $\tau\grave{o}\nu$ $\check{\alpha}\rho\tau o\nu$ $\kappa\alpha\grave{\iota}$ $\delta\acute{\iota}\delta\omega\sigma\iota\nu$ $\alpha\mathring{\upsilon}\tauo\hat{\iota}s$, $\kappa\alpha\grave{\iota}$ $\tau\grave{o}$ $\mathring{o}\psi\acute{\alpha}\rho\iota o\nu$ $\mathring{o}\mu o\acute{\iota}\omega s$) recalls the fellowship meal (also by the Sea of Tiberias) during Jesus' ministry when (vi. 11) he 'took the loaves, gave thanks, and distributed them . . . and in the same way as much of the fish as they wanted' ($\check{\epsilon}\lambda\alpha\beta\epsilon\nu$ . . . $\tauo\grave{\upsilon}s$ $\check{\alpha}\rho\tauo\upsilon s$ . . . $\kappa\alpha\grave{\iota}$ $\epsilon\mathring{\upsilon}\chi\alpha\rho\iota\sigma\tau\acute{\eta}\sigma\alpha s$ $\delta\iota\acute{\epsilon}\delta\omega\kappa\epsilon\nu$ . . . $\mathring{o}\mu o\acute{\iota}\omega s$ $\kappa\alpha\grave{\iota}$ $\mathring{\epsilon}\kappa$ $\tau\hat{\omega}\nu$ $\mathring{o}\psi\alpha\rho\acute{\iota}\omega\nu$ $\check{o}\sigma o\nu$ $\mathring{\eta}\theta\epsilon\lambda o\nu$). Cf. pp. 178 f. The importance of the restoration of table fellowship is suggested by Acts x. 40 f., 'God raised [Jesus] on the third day and made him manifest . . . to us who were chosen by God as witnesses, who ate and drank with him after he rose from the dead.' Luke xxiv. 42 f. relates how Jesus ate 'a piece of broiled fish' before his disciples to prove to them that he was no ghost, while at Emmaus 'when he was at table with [Cleopas and his companion], he took the bread and blessed, and broke it, and gave it to them'; the two disciples then return to Jerusalem and tell the eleven and those who were with them 'how [Jesus] was known to them in the breaking of the bread' (Luke xxiv. 30, 35). It is highly likely that there is a eucharistic reference both in this last incident and here in the FG. On both occasions Jesus shows

---

[1] Barrett, p. 484. Cf. Grant, *art. cit.*, pp. 274 f.: 'The significance of seventeen is due to its being the sum of the two most sacred numbers, and . . . this significance is multiplied when the number is triangulated. In the gospel, however, the emphasis does not fall on the components of the number but on its size. . . . The number must stand for the perfect unity of the church, into which the fish are gathered by the disciples.'

how he will continue to be present with his disciples, but first they have to become used to the fact that the expectations of the past are at an end. The eschatological sacrament which took place in Galilee (cf. p. 181) is linked with this meal, which, however, marks a period of transition in the disciples' experience. The awkwardness they felt is expressed by, **None of the disciples dared to ask him, 'Who are you?'**[1] **They knew it was the Lord.** Something completely different was anticipated, and they had to become adjusted to the new situation.

It is this that marks the story as containing at least some accurate historical information; the rough edges of the situation have not been smoothed away in the interests of the symbolism. The way in which **Jesus appeared to the disciples when he was raised from the dead** was as important to the first believers as the fact that they could still meet him in the eucharist. And as the settled life of the Church developed, many of the uncertainties and perplexities of the very early days of its history remained close at hand. Barrett notes that 'a fish occurs along with bread in some early representations of the eucharist,'[2] and it may well be that this is due to the appearance of fish here and in vi. On both occasions Jesus presided at a meal which had profound significance, though not every detail carries a sacramental allusion. It is pertinent to add that in Luke xxiv. 30, 35 the eucharistic symbolism is more prominent, and in addition that there Jesus acts as host although one would expect him to be the guest; it may be that there is a greater sobriety here in the FG's recording of events.

The points of contact and difference with Luke v. 1-11 have been noted above as occasion offered; it is fairly clear from the limited amount of common material that the one narrative

---

[1] It seems far less probable that this question means, 'What sort of a person are you?' (so Bauer[5] s.v. τίς, comparing i. 19; viii. 25). The problem lies rather in recognising Jesus, cf. verses 4 and 7.

[2] Barrett, p. 484, who also comments that 'fish-symbolism was very widespread in early Christianity.' Aileen Guilding, *The Fourth Gospel and Jewish Worship* (1960), p. 222, n. 1, adds that 'in primitive Christian representations of the eucharist . . . the number of apostles present is sometimes shown as seven, as in this chapter, sometimes twelve, as in the feeding of the five thousand,' though Niewalda, *op. cit.*, p. 168, points out that a connexion is not demonstrable since it was Roman practice to have seven dining together.

cannot be an edited version of the other,[1] though it is possible
that both draw on traditions which were circulating in the early
church. The argument that 'it is exceedingly unlikely that Jesus
performed two such similar miracles at different times. One of
the two accounts must be secondary'[2] perhaps fails to reckon
with this view. Just as a definite motive inspires fishermen's
yarns, so something must lie behind what is described here:
either Jesus performed a miracle[3]—and this type of miracle,
which meets no urgent need of the disciples and is virtually
opposed to the expected natural course of events, does not strike
many today as inherently probable—or legendary material with
no basis in fact has attached itself to Jesus because he was
known as a wonder-worker, or there is a theological development originating either in some Old Testament passage such as
Ezek. xlvii. 10 (for which see on verse 11 above), or in the idea
of the disciples as fishers of men. This theme is found in two
different forms in the Synoptic Gospels (see on verse 3) and
seems to be present in the FG also (see on verses 10 and 11).
May the evangelist not be drawing here on a meditation cast in
historical form which, starting from this notion, shows the
plight of the disciples without Christ and the results of their
obedience to him?[4]

However, as F. W. Beare, commenting on Luke v. 1-11,
rightly points out, 'In the Lucan as in the Johannine form, this
is clearly the story of an epiphany. [In Luke] Jesus reveals himself as a divine being, and therefore Simon is seized with terror
and with the sense of sinfulness which makes him unfit to bear
the divine presence.'[5] Although the presentation of the FG is
different the general tenor of the narrative is sufficiently

---

[1] Unless the editor was willing to make drastic alterations.

[2] J. A. Bailey, op. cit., p. 16.

[3] It is better to avoid rationalistic explanations, e.g. that Jesus 'noticed
from the shore that a shoal of fish was gathering at the farther side of the
boat' (J. H. Bernard, A Critical and Exegetical Commentary on the Gospel
According to St. John (1928), p. 696).

[4] This does not affect the claim that the evangelist set out to write history
if there is no reason to doubt that he believed the material was historically
true. The Testament of Zebulun VI. 6, which speaks of large catches of fish
given as a divine reward, provides a partial parallel in the thought of the
period. The presence of the Beloved Disciple in the story does not complicate
the issue if it is recognised that a number of elements have been combined
by an editor.   [5] Op. cit., p. 51.

explicit to support this conclusion even if the verb φανερόω—translated 'showed himself' at verse 1 and **appeared** at verse 14—did not carry overtones of revelation.[1] If it be conceded that there was a post-resurrection appearance in Galilee in which Jesus revealed himself to the disciples on the shore of the lake, it is not impossible to see how this could come to be expressed through the medium of a wonder-story which was already in existence. The Lucan version then represents a parallel development from the same basic meditation, set, however, in the context of the ministry and linked naturally enough with Peter's initial call, just as the FG draws in addition on a somewhat similar tradition of the giving of a commission when it relates this post-resurrection appearance.

If the evangelist's intention was to relate a miracle, is there an eighth sign here? Against this it has been argued that what took place was not an act of Christ but of his Church, aided by him, though one may be on safer ground to observe with C. H. Dodd that 'xxi, whether the work of the evangelist or of another, has the character of a postscript, and falls outside the design of the book as a whole.'[2] The editorial note that **this was now the third time Jesus appeared to the disciples** presumably refers only to the two appearances to groups of disciples recorded in xx.

(15) So when they had breakfasted, Jesus said to Simon Peter, 'Simon son of John, do you love me more than these?' He said to him, 'Yes, Lord, you know that I love you'. He said to him, 'Feed my lambs'. (16) He repeated to him a second time, 'Simon son of John, do you love me?' He said to him, 'Yes, Lord, you know that I love you'. He said to him, 'Tend my sheep'. (17) He said to him for the third time, 'Simon son of John, do you love me?' Peter was distressed because he said to him for the third time, 'Do you love me?', and he said to him, 'Lord, you know everything, you know that I love you.' Jesus said to him, 'Feed my sheep'.

The symbolism here is different to that of verses 1-14, and it is possible that **so when they had breakfasted** is an artificial

---

[1] Cf. the note on xvii. 6 and Bauer[5] s.v.
[2] Dodd, *Interpretation*, p. 290.

link. Cf. on x. 1-16 for Jesus as the shepherd and for a discussion of the Old Testament background to this theme; by a
three-fold call Jesus associates Peter in the closest possible way
with his own ministry. See also 1 Pet. v. 2, Eph. iv. 11 and Acts
xx. 28; the reference is primarily to the charge of a congregation,
though that there are 'other sheep, which do not belong to this
fold' but which must be brought within it (x. 16) suggests that
the task of evangelism is also implied. Though used around the
time of Jesus of the Davidic King-Messiah who would deliver
his people,[1] the term has now acquired a different nuance by
being set in a fresh context. Cf. the Damascus Document xiii.
9, which applies the image of the shepherd to the 'overseer of
the camp.'[2]

Though xxi may well be composite, attempts to isolate the
sources from which the material was taken result in so many
equally plausible yet mutually exclusive theories that the enter-
prise does not seem worthwhile. Play has sometimes been made
(as in many other speculations about the resurrection narratives) with the conjectured 'lost ending' of Mark, thought by
some to be utilised by the FG here, and it has also been suggested that this dialogue is from the record of the first of all the
resurrection appearances, that to Peter, mentioned in the New
Testament (1 Cor. xv. 5, Luke xxiv. 34), but nowhere described.
However, as the story now stands it is the Beloved Disciple and
not Peter who recognises Jesus (verse 7), and this is not the first
appearance; more important, Jesus does not appear to Peter
alone. If part of the author's purpose is to define Peter's position
in relation to that of the Beloved Disciple, though he may conceivably be combining independent strands of tradition, it is
perhaps inherently more probable that he is using polemically a
story which reached him in substantially its present form.

It has sometimes been thought that the exegesis of this

[1] The *Psalms of Solomon* xvii. 40, 'tending (ποιμαίνων) the flock of the
Lord faithfully and righteously'.
[2] It is however difficult to build much on this reference as the translation
of CD xiii. 9 is disputed; cf., e.g., C. Rabin, *The Zadokite Documents* (1954),
pp. 64 f., G. Vermès, *Discovery in the Judean Desert* (1956), p. 180, A. Dupont-
Sommer, *The Essene Writings from Qumran* (E.T. by G. Vermès of *Les
Écrits esséniens découverts près de la mer Morte*, 1961), p. 157, E. Lohse, *Die
Texte aus Qumran* (1964), pp. 94 f.

passage depends on the meaning of the verbs translated **love**.[1]
Jesus twice asks ἀγαπᾷς με, and Peter replies φιλῶ σε; however,
the third time both of them use φιλέω. Nonetheless to distinguish between ἀγαπάω and φιλέω here may be unduly
subtle[2] as their use may simply be due to the FG's fondness
for synonyms.[3] Cf. further **Feed** (βόσκε) **my lambs** (ἀρνία)
with **Tend** (ποίμαινε) **my sheep** (προβάτια) and **Feed** (βόσκε)
my sheep (προβάτια); these phrases also have been given
the most intricate interpretations, probably without just
cause.[4]

Jesus' first question is either, **'do you love me more than**
⟨you love⟩ **these** ⟨things⟩?'**, taking **these** (τούτων) as neuter
(cf. the NEB's interpretation, 'more than all else'), or, more
probably, **'do you love me more than these** ⟨disciples
do⟩?'**, taking **these** as masculine and comparing Mark xiv. 29,
Matt. xxvi. 33, for Peter's boast that he did. Significantly,
Peter's reply avoids the comparison, and Jesus then drops it
from the question. Since Peter's denial is prophesied in Mark
xiv. 30, Matt. xxvi. 34, immediately after his claim about himself, it is not unlikely that there is a reference to the denial here.
But the main point of the story is the commissioning of Peter,
not his rehabilitation; cf., however, Luke xxii. 32-34, where, in
the setting of the Last Supper, a commission is given but is
linked with prediction of the denial. See also xiii. 36 ff.,

---

[1] Cf., e.g., E. Evans, *art. cit.*

[2] The Vulgate translates by *diligo* and *amo* respectively, though Augustine
(*de Civ. Dei* xiv. 7) claims there is no distinction in meaning here and *a* and
e use *amo* throughout; perhaps significantly, the Syriac versions recognise no
distinction in meaning.

[3] Cf., e.g., Edwin D. Freed, 'Variations in the Language and Thought of
John', *Z.N.W.*, Vol. LV, 1964, pp. 167-197.

[4] e.g. J. H. Bernard, *op. cit.*, p. 706 argues that πρόβατα (supported by
ℵ D W* θ *fam* 1 *fam* 13) should be read instead of προβάτια (supported by
A B C Wᶜ) in verse 17, and that 'the charge to Peter first entrusts to his care
the *lambs*, then the *young sheep*, and lastly the *whole flock*, young and old'.
But Bernard, who does regard the two verbs 'to love' and also the verbs 'to
feed' and 'to tend' as synonyms, offers his interpretation tentatively and also
draws some support for his view from Burkitt's study of the Syriac versions;
examples of far more extreme exegesis could be cited. It is likely that the
reading πρόβατα (also read by ℵ A D W θ *fam* 13 for προβάτια in verse 16) is
an assimilation to x. 2 ff., 7 f., 11 ff., 15 f.; in verse 15, it is read instead of ἀρνία
by C* D *vt.* Ἀρνίον and προβάτιον are not found elsewhere in the FG, though
the former word is frequent in Revelation.

where a protestation by Peter is linked with the prophecy of his denial and also of his future death, taken up in verses 18 f.

The attempts of Goguel and Bultmann[1] to disassociate verses 15-17 from the story of Peter's denial are not perhaps wholly convincing. Granted the absence of any explicit reference to Peter's repentance or to the giving of absolution, there is an allusive quality about the FG which forbids too tight an exegesis. But it is possible that the connexion seen by most commentators between the three-fold questioning of Peter and the fact that he had denied Jesus three times is not well-founded, and that the quasi-liturgical pattern of verses 15-17 is designed rather to give Jesus' charge heavy emphasis.[2] Peter is entrusted with the leadership of the Christian community (cf. Matt. xvi. 17-19, Luke xxii. 31 f.), and it is notable that stress is laid on his position in the Church (cf. also verses 10 f.), whatever may be said about his rôle *vis-à-vis* the Beloved Disciple.

(18) 'Amen, amen, I say to you,[3] while you were young you girded yourself and used to go where you pleased; but when you are old you will stretch out your hands, and someone else will gird you and bring ⟨you⟩ where you do not wish ⟨to go⟩.' (19) (Now he said this to show by what kind of death he would glorify God.) And when he had said this he said to him, 'Follow me'.

The thought moves on two levels, as often in the FG. Superficially the picture—conceivably based on a proverb contrasting youth with old age—is of the impulsive Peter (cf. verse 7, where 'he put on' is διεζώσατο, found here in its simple form and translated **girded** and **will gird**) dependent on another in the future when he is no longer able to look after himself. But,

---

[1] M. Goguel, 'Did Peter Deny His Lord? A Conjecture', *The Harvard Theological Review*, Vol. XXV, 1932, pp. 1-27, and *Jésus* ([2]1950), pp. 390-392; Bultmann, pp. 551 f.

[2] Cf. M. H. Pope, *The Interpreter's Dictionary of the Bible*, Vol. III (1962), p. 564, 'Next to the number SEVEN, the number most frequently used in connection with sacred matters is three . . . Tripartite composition occurs in a number of striking cases without mention of the number' (though he does not cite this passage).   [3] See on i. 51.

as the editorial note in verse 19a indicates, this is a veiled reference to Peter's death;[1] although Bauer[2] thinks that, in view of
the order in which the events are described, **you will stretch
out your hands, and someone else will gird you** must
refer to binding the prisoner to the cross-beam which he has to
carry to the place of execution, there seems no reason to doubt
that **you will stretch out your hands** could refer to crucifixion,[3] and Tertullian writes, 'Then is Peter girt by another,
when he is made fast to the cross'.[4] Lagrange argues that this
is the true interpretation and that the sequence of events has
unavoidably been displaced because of the basic image used,[5]
though the difficulty would vanish if **bring ⟨you⟩ where you
do not wish ⟨to go⟩** is referred to the raising of the body on
the cross.

For the significance of '**Follow me**' cf. on i. 43 and xiii. 36.
By what kind of death is reminiscent of xii. 33; xviii. 32, and
Peter will **glorify God** by his death in the same way that Jesus
did (cf. especially xvii. 1, 4); for the significance of the verb 'to
glorify' in the FG see p. 215, n. 2 and the notes on the passages
cited there. It has been argued that, in the light of x. 11, 15,
17 f., where Jesus' work as shepherd culminates in his death,
Peter's martyrdom is the summit of his pastoral ministry, to
which it is organically related: '[Peter] follows [Jesus] as shepherd, he follows him in his death, he follows him in glorifying
God by his death'.[6]

**(20) Peter turned and saw the disciple whom Jesus
loved following; this was the one who leant back against
his chest at the supper and said, 'Lord, who is it who will
betray you?' (21) So Peter, seeing him, said to Jesus,
'Lord, what about this man?' (22) Jesus said to him, 'If I**

---

[1] Cf. O. Cullmann, *Peter: Disciple, Apostle, Martyr* (E.T. by Floyd V.
Filson of *Petrus*, [2]1962), pp. 71-156, for a discussion of the problems connected with the death of Peter. See also the annotated bibliography in A. A.
de Marco, *The Tomb of Saint Peter* (1964).

[2] Bauer, p. 232.

[3] See Bauer[5], s.v. ἐκτείνω.

[4] *Scorpiace* 15: 'Tunc Petrus ab altero cingitur, cum cruci adstringitur.'
Cf. the Ante-Nicene Christian Library, Vol. XI, p. 414, and see p. 430 n. 4
above for the tying of condemned persons to the cross.

[5] Lagrange, pp. 531 f.

[6] Bishop Cassian, 'John xxi', *N.T.S.*, Vol. III. 1956–57, pp. 132-6.

want him to remain until I come, what is it to you? Follow me!'

While Peter has to be commanded to follow (verse 19), the Beloved Disciple is already **following**[1] Jesus of his own accord. The reference back to his privileged position at the Last Supper (cf. xiii. 23 ff.) further points the contrast between the two men. When Peter asks about the Beloved Disciple's fate, he is firmly told to mind his own business and is commanded once again, **'Follow me!'** The form of this injunction (σύ μοι ἀκολούθει, in which σύ ('you') is emphatic[2]) both focuses attention on Peter's task and distinguishes him from the Beloved Disciple; the crucial thing for any disciple is that he should be a faithful follower of Christ, though equally it is not unlikely that tensions within the Church are also reflected. Despite the importance which Peter assumes in xxi, there is an insistence that he occupies no exclusive place at the head of the Christian community which is perhaps related to the FG's comparative neglect of 'the Twelve' (see p. 199 above). On the one hand it is claimed that the passing over of Peter's authority to the Beloved Disciple is being described here,[3] on the other that they are being entrusted with different commissions since 'one is to govern the Church, the other to reveal to it the mind of the Lord'.[4] However, it may be simpler to see a reflection of conflicts about authority that are otherwise hidden from us in the obscure period of church history when xxi was written; the Church of which the Beloved Disciple was a member demands a rightful place for him, and hence for itself.

At the same time, the incident is related so that a current misunderstanding could be corrected: **(23) So this saying went out among the brethren, that that disciple would not die;[5] but Jesus did not say to him that he would not die,[5] but, 'If I want him to remain until I come, what is**

[1] **Following** (ἀκολουθοῦντα) is omitted by ℵ* W *ff*[2] *boh*[pt].

[2] Cf. Turner, p. 37.

[3] Bultmann, p. 547. This is further related to the establishment of the authority of the FG in the early church, *ibid.*, p. 555.

[4] E. L. Allen, 'On This Rock', *J.T.S.* n.s., Vol. V, 1954, p. 62.

[5] ἀποθνῄσκει, the present tense; cf. Moulton, *Prolegomena*, pp. 114, 120, Turner, p. 63. For the present tense carrying a future sense see p. 210 n. 4.

it to you?' The ambiguity of Jesus' rebuff to Peter[1] has caused problems which were perhaps brought to a head shortly before xxi was written by the death of the Beloved Disciple. For the popular belief involved, cf. p. 269, and note the strength of futurist eschatology in the circles to which the FG was directed.

As xxi now stands, we have to imagine that what is described in verses 15-22 took place while those concerned were walking by the lake after breakfast. Yet attention is concentrated exclusively on the dialogue, which is theologically significant; the only action described is Peter's turning to see the Beloved Disciple following (verse 20), and this is important for the thought of the passage. It is just as likely that the narrative details have been whittled away as that themes important to the writer have been developed in an ideal construction; in either case equally statements that are heavily charged with meaning are presented to the reader with emphasis. The evidence is so sparse it is impossible to reach any firm conclusion about the process of composition, though it may reasonably be held that several units of tradition which were already in existence have been built together to form this chapter.

(24) This is the disciple who bore witness about these things, and wrote these things, and we know that his witness is true. (25) And there are many other things which Jesus did: if these were written down one by one, I do not think that the world itself would hold the books which would be written.

Cf. pp. 47 f. for a discussion of these verses. That **the disciple who bore witness about these things** is the Beloved Disciple, who enjoyed a special intimacy with Jesus, may be mentioned to emphasise the great weight that belongs to the

---

[1] Cf. B.-D. § 373 (1), '$\dot{\epsilon}\grave{a}v$ $a\dot{v}\tau\grave{o}v$ $\theta\acute{\epsilon}\lambda\omega$ $\mu\acute{\epsilon}v\epsilon\iota v$ is safeguarded by the author in *v.* 23 against the interpretation "if, as is to be expected" which is the only possible one in Att., and is also a conceivable one in Koine'. The explanation of this saying as the result of a misunderstanding of some such word as Mark ix. 1 (=Matt. xvi. 28, Luke ix. 27), 'there are some standing here who will not taste death before they see the kingdom of God come with power' (so, e.g., J. A. T. Robinson, *Jesus and His Coming* (1957), p. 91) is at least no more plausible than the view that the FG records a genuine *logion*, albeit one which falls within the same general range of ideas. Cf. p. 31 for the contention that the identification of the Beloved Disciple with Lazarus is more plausible in view of the popular understanding of this saying.

FG's testimony; similarly it is stressed that **his witness is true.** Cf. xix. 35;[1] D. E. Nineham traces the FG's interest in eye-witness testimony to its apologetic against docetism and notes how the particular incident in the passion which is attested would validate the Christological and sacramental position of the writer.[2] It is possible that some other apologetic concern (see above, p. 441) controls the appeal to such witness here.[3] Cf. also i. 14 and 1 John i. 1-3. The hyperbole of verse 25[4] closes the gospel in its final form as xx. 30 f. closed it in its original form.

APPENDIX

THE WOMAN TAKEN IN ADULTERY
vii. 53 – viii. 11

vii. (53) And they went each to his own house, viii. (1) but Jesus went to the Mount of Olives. (2) And early in

---

[1] 'True' in xix. 35 is ἀληθινή but in xxi. 24 it is ἀληθής. Attempts have been made to distinguish the meaning of the two words (cf. p. 75 n. 3), but recently G. D. Kilpatrick has argued that the FG uses ἀληθής predicatively and ἀληθινός attributively; this involves several textual emendations, including reading ἀληθής at xix. 35 with ℵ 124 Chrys, and Kilpatrick suggests that scribes who were not aware of the FG's usage may have altered the text to preserve a contrast in meaning between the two words which they themselves recognised. For the FG the two words possess an identical meaning which ranges from 'true' to 'genuine, real' (*The Bible Translator*, Vol. XI, 1960, p. 174). Kilpatrick has also argued that the same distinction is observed in the Johannine Epistles, though 7 times in Revelation and 3 times elsewhere in the NT the idiom is not maintained (*J.T.S.* n.s., Vol. XII, 1961, pp. 272 f.). But if the words can possess identity of meaning, may they not be used as synonyms?

[2] D. E. Nineham, 'Eye-Witness Testimony and the Gospel Tradition. III,' *J.T.S.* n.s., Vol. XI, 1960, p. 254.

[3] C. H. Dodd, 'Note on John 21, 24', *J.T.S.* n.s., Vol. IV, 1953, pp. 212 f. reads verse 24 with verse 23 and thinks it means that the true understanding of Jesus' statement about the fate of the Beloved Disciple rests on the authority of that disciple himself, who put it in writing and whose evidence is to be accepted.

[4] Though verse 25 is omitted by ℵ*, it is inserted subsequently by the same hand. This could mean that ℵ was copied from a MS. which ended the FG at xxi. 24, if accidental omission is thought to be unlikely, though the textual tradition is at best weak.

the morning he arrived again in the Temple, and all the people came to him; and he sat down and taught them. (3) And the scribes and the Pharisees brought a woman who had been detected in adultery; and when they had placed her in the midst, (4) they said to him, 'Teacher, this woman has been detected in the very act of committing adultery. (5) Now in the Law Moses commanded us to stone such women; now what do you yourself say?'[1] (6) But they said this to put him to the test, so that they might have charges to bring against him. And Jesus bent down and wrote with his finger on the ground. (7) But when they persisted in questioning him,[2] he straightened himself and said to them, 'The one without sin among you, let him be the first to cast a stone at her'. (8) And bending down again he went on writing on the ground. (9) And when they heard[3] they went out one by one, beginning with the older men, and he remained alone, together with the woman who was in the midst. (10) Then Jesus, straightening himself, said to her, 'Woman, where are they? Did no one condemn you?' (11) And she said, 'No one, sir.' And Jesus said, 'Neither do I condemn you; go away, and from now on sin no more'.

This passage cannot be part of the original text of the FG. It is inserted after John vii. 52 by D and several Old Latin MSS. (b^* c e ff[2] j l[c] z), but it is lacking in the best Greek MSS. (P[66, 75] $\aleph$ (A) B (C) L N T W X Δ Θ Ψ 33 157 565 892 1241 et al.), and it is significant that of the other Greek MSS. which do include it (E F G H K M S U Γ Λ Π 28 579 700 1579 et al.) some mark it with an obelus (e.g. S) or an asterisk (e.g. E M Λ). It is

---

[1] This conveys the force of the Greek, σὺ οὖν τί λέγεις;

[2] On the Greek construction here, cf. Turner, pp. 159, 226.

[3] The addition of καὶ ὑπὸ τῆς συνειδήσεως ἐλεγχόμενοι, 'convicted by their conscience', by E, some other Greek MSS. and boh at this point is an interpretation of the incident rather than an original part of the text. Cf. the explanatory additions after τῶν πρεσβυτέρων in this verse, which fall into the same category: ὥστε πάντας ἐξελθεῖν is read by D 1071 d, ἕως τῶν ἐσχάτων by S U Λ 69 118 209 700, πάντες ἀνεχώρησαν by c ff[2]. The presence of such phrases in the text-tradition of this passage (other examples in verses 6 and 8 are noted below, and further instances, especially in verse 10, could be given) illustrates how the story was used by the Church; this sort of detail could readily be added to give increased vividness as the narrative was related.

attested by Ambrose, Ambrosiaster, and Augustine, though there is no allusion to it in Tertullian's and Cyprian's discussions of the admission of adulterers to penitence; also, it is mentioned by no Greek Church Father (even by those who, like Origen, Chrysostom, or Nonnus dealt with the FG verse by verse) until the early twelfth century. Jerome, who knew both Greek and Latin MSS. containing the pericope, included it in the Vulgate, and it is also found in the Palestinian Syriac. However, it is omitted by *syr sah boh*^{pt} *ac*^{2} *arm got* and by other Old Latin MSS. (*a b^c f l* q*). 225 places it after vii. 36, *fam* 1 1076 1570 after xxi. 24, and *fam* 13 after Luke xxi. 38, while in a revision of the Old Georgian version it appears after vii. 44.

On the basis of this evidence it is usual to regard the pericope as a piece of floating tradition, and Vincent Taylor treats it as a Pronouncement-Story which, he thinks, circulated orally.[1] However, if this is so it is difficult to see why the narrative should begin with two verses which appear to relate the conclusion of a previous incident. Although there are many textual variants in this pericope, the omission of vii. 53 by *ff* ^{2} is the only evidence we have for a different opening to the story. This suggests a process of literary transmission.

As has been frequently argued, the evidence of vocabulary and style is opposed to Johannine authorship of this section.[2] It is therefore of interest to find that *fam* 13 has inserted it after Luke xxi. 38. Westcott and Hort comment, 'The Section [John vii. 53 – viii. 11] was probably known to the scribe exclusively as a church lesson, recently come into use; and placed by him here on account of the close resemblance' between Luke xxi. 37 f. and John vii. 53 – viii. 2. They continue, 'Had he known it as part of a continuous text of St John's Gospel, he was not likely to transpose it'.[3] This is very reasonable, but it may be that there is here a further clue to the original setting of the story.

---

[1] V. Taylor, *The Formation of the Gospel Tradition* (^{2}1935), pp. 83 f.

[2] Cf., e.g., J. H. Bernard, *A Critical and Exegetical Commentary on the Gospel According to St. John* (1928), Vol. II, p. 715; E. C. Hoskyns, *The Fourth Gospel* (ed. F. N. Davey, 1947), p. 565.

[3] B. F. Westcott and F. J. A. Hort, *The New Testament in the Original Greek: Notes on Select Readings* (1881), p. 63.

The Mount of Olives (mentioned nowhere else in the FG) is, according to Luke xxi. 37, the place where Jesus spent the nights during his last visit to Jerusalem; again, the Lucan statement that Jesus was 'teaching in the temple' (ἐν τῷ ἱερῷ διδάσκων) and that 'all the people used to get up very early in the morning' (πᾶς ὁ λαὸς ὤρθριζεν) to come to listen to him may be compared with Jesus' appearance **in the temple** (εἰς τὸ ἱερόν) **early in the morning** (Ὄρθρου) when **all the people** (πᾶς ὁ λαός) came and he **taught** (ἐδίδασκεν) them.[1] The probability of a relationship between the pericope and this Lucan summary of Jesus' activity is strengthened if (as will be argued later to be the case) the subject-matter of the incident fits well with the happenings of Jesus' last days. Barrett also notes a parallel between the abrupt opening of this paragraph and Mark xi. 11 f., 19 f., which forms part of the Marcan narrative of the last week in Jerusalem.[2] Cf. too Luke xix. 47 f.

E. F. F. Bishop has argued that this pericope formed part of the Third Gospel at an early stage in the development of the gospel tradition,[3] though others rely rather on Eusebius' statement (*H.E.*, III. xxxix. 17) that Papias 'has adduced another story of a woman who was accused of many sins before the Lord, which is contained in the Gospel according to the Hebrews' and think it highly probable that the source of the narrative is either the Gospel according to the Hebrews or Papias's *Expositions of the Lord's Oracles*.[4] This evidence has been variously estimated,[5] and in the present state of our knowledge it would be hazardous in the extreme to claim too much on the basis of it. The suggestion that, if this incident is found in the Gospel according to the Hebrews, it is easy to see why more orthodox churchmen should treat it with suspicion, is

---

[1] The omission of viii. 2 from **and all the people** to the end of the verse by *fam* 13, involving a slightly shorter insertion in Luke, does not affect the issue.

[2] Barrett, p. 491.

[3] E. F. F. Bishop, 'The Pericope Adulterae: A Suggestion', *J.T.S.* o.s., Vol. XXXV, 1934, pp. 40-45.

[4] So B. F. Westcott and F. J. A. Hort, *op. cit.*, p. 88.

[5] Cf. P. Vielhauer in E. Hennecke's *New Testament Apocrypha*, ed. by W. Schneemelcher (E.T. ed. by R. McL. Wilson), Vol. I (1963), pp. 121 f.; J. H. Bernard, *op. cit.*, p. 716; E. C. Hoskyns, *op. cit.*, p. 566.

perhaps less plausible than Augustine's view that it was omitted because its teaching seemed too lenient.[1] Indeed, the striking thing is that, 'in face of all the 2nd-century tendencies to turn the Christian ethic into a morality of rules and precepts, [it] asserted its claim to a place in the canon'.[2]

It is highly probable that this story is an authentic piece of early tradition. It is precious as a piece of information which has circulated (whether primarily in Syria[3] or in certain parts of the Western Church[4]) independently of the canonical gospels and which therefore gives some insight into the nature of documents which have now perished (cf., e.g., Luke i. 1). Despite close resemblances to the style of Luke,[5] it is not possible to say whether it ever formed part of an earlier draft of this gospel, as Bishop claims, or even whether it may have been a unit of Caesarean tradition, as Vincent Taylor tentatively suggests.[6] But that there is a close link with the tradition represented in Luke xxi. 37 f. can hardly be doubted, even though the nature of this connexion cannot be defined more precisely.

Barrett draws attention to the evidence of Eusebius cited above and to a similar story (taken from the third-century Syriac *Didascalia*) in the *Apostolic Constitutions* II, 24 (where it is told to caution bishops against dealing too severely with penitents) and comments, 'It may be that stories on this theme were current in several forms at an early date . . . and that the story as we know it came into the fourth gospel because at some time it was combined with it (as originally non-biblical material) in a

---

[1] Augustine, *de conj. adult.*, ii. 6: 'Some of little faith, or rather enemies of the true faith, I suppose from a fear lest their wives should gain impunity in sin, removed from their MSS. the Lord's act of indulgence to the adulteress.' It is the struggle with pagan promiscuity which is in fact significant.

[2] H. Chadwick, *Encyclopaedia Britannica* [1964], s.v. 'John, Gospel According to and Epistles of Saint'. For the reading of D at Luke vi. 5 (an insertion of a saying about sabbath observance into the text of the Third Gospel), cf. especially C. F. D. Moule, *The Birth of the New Testament* ([2]1966), p. 49 and n. 2.

[3] H. Riesenfeld, 'Perikopen de adultera i den fornkyrkliga Traditionen', *Svensk exegetisk årsbok*, Vol. XVII, 1953, p. 108. I am indebted to my colleague Mr D. R. Ap-Thomas for his kindness in translating this article for me.

[4] B. M. Metzger, *The Text of the New Testament* (1964), p. 224.

[5] Barrett, pp. 491 f.

[6] Taylor, *op. cit.*, p. 84, n. 1.

lectionary.'[1] It has been suggested that its appearance at this point is due to the mention of the theme of judgement at vii. 24 and viii. 15,[2] and the reading that places it after vii. 36 may be due to an accidental error;[3] its insertion between xxi. 24 and the last verse of the FG by *fam* 1 etc. is presumably due to the mention of the many other things not recorded in the FG in xxi. 25.

The scribes and the Pharisees is a phrase found nowhere else in the FG, but is common in the Synoptic Gospels. The motive in bringing **a woman who had been detected in adultery** to Jesus is to trap him; the situation is such that his questioners think that whatever ruling he gives he will do himself harm. They explain (verse 4) that there is no doubt of the woman's guilt,[4] and, addressing Jesus as **Teacher,** invite his opinion on a point of law: **Moses commanded us to stone such women,**[5] which is undoubtedly true (cf. Lev. xx. 10, Deut. xxii. 22-24), but Jesus may have another view of the matter. Cf. especially Mark x. 2 ff. = Matt. xix. 3 ff., where a legal question about divorce is put to Jesus by Pharisees 'to put him to the test' ($\pi\epsilon\iota\rho\acute{a}\zeta o\nu\tau\epsilon\varsigma$ $a\grave{\upsilon}\tau\acute{o}\nu$—the phrase found in this

---

[1] Barrett, p. 491. J. H. Bernard, *op. cit.*, p. 716, relates the acceptance of the story into the canon at a late date to the relaxation of ecclesiastical discipline in the fourth century. The whole question is discussed at length by Riesenfeld, *art. cit.* For the transmission of this unit, contrast Isa. ii. 2-4 = Mic. iv. 1-3; O. Eissfeldt, *The Old Testament: An Introduction* (E.T. by P. R. Ackroyd of *Einleitung in das Alte Testament*[3], 1965), p. 318, thinks this 'a passage of anonymous origin which was at one time attributed to Isaiah and at another to Micah', being on each occasion taken over from a collection (or perhaps two different collections) of songs intended for cultic recitation.

[2] E. C. Hoskyns, *op. cit.*, p. 564, where it is also suggested that the insertion may have been due to 'homiletic purposes', the incident being used in illustration of these texts.

[3] So B. F. Westcott and F. J. A. Hort, *op. cit.*, p. 84. But if the insertion of the pericope into the canonical gospels developed out of its use as lectionary material, this may have had some influence in producing a varied text tradition.

[4] Jewish law required an eye-witness if adultery were to be punished, cf. Deut. xxii. 22.

[5] Cf. Strack–Billerbeck, II, pp. 519-521 for a discussion of this in the light of Jewish practice, and the argument that this mode of execution implies that the woman was engaged but not yet married. But Bauer[5] s.v. $\gamma\upsilon\nu\acute{\eta}$ rightly queries this conclusion, which is possible but not necessary; see E. C. Hoskyns, *op. cit.*, pp. 568 f. Cf. also the full discussion by J. Blinzler, 'Die Strafe für Ehebruch in Bibel und Halacha: Zur Auslegung von Joh. viii. 5', *N.T.S.*, Vol. IV, 1957–58, pp. 32-47, who concludes that at the time of Jesus the mishnaic code was not in force on this point.

story in verse 6), and where Jesus roundly condemns the position adopted in the Law in no uncertain terms.¹ But it is unlikely that all that is involved here is an attempt by Jesus' enemies (who know his merciful attitude towards sinners) to obtain a judgement from him which will enable them to accuse him as a transgressor of the Law.² It is perhaps more plausible to interpret the story on the same lines as that involving the giving of tribute to Caesar (Mark xii. 13 ff. and parallels).

If the Jews were not allowed to inflict capital punishment in this period,³ Jeremias may be right in supposing⁴ that the dilemma put before Jesus was whether to support the sentence demanded by the Mosaic Law (but which could not legally be carried out in Palestine then⁵), and so lay himself open to an accusation of revolutionary activities, or whether to fall into line with current Jewish practice and so lose favour with the people. In the event, Jesus adopted neither alternative.

At least as far back as the time of Jerome (*Contra Pelagium*, ii. 17), some have supposed that Jesus **wrote with his finger on the ground** the sins of the woman's accusers; some MSS. (U Π) add 'the sins of each one of them' (ἑνὸς ἑκάστου αὐτῶν τὰς ἁμαρτίας) at the end of verse 8. Others have thought that he was setting down some relevant quotation from the Old Testament.⁶ Eisler supposed that the learned **scribes and Pharisees** would

---

¹ For other interpretations of this Pronouncement-Story, cf. V. Taylor, *The Gospel According to St. Mark* (1952), pp. 415 ff. The verb πειράζω is sometimes used in the Synoptic Gospels when attempts are being made by Jesus' opponents to find something that can be used against him; cf., for example, Matt. xxii. 35, where a legal matter is involved (but contrast the parallels in the other Synoptic Gospels) and the story concerning the giving of tribute to Caesar (Mark xii. 15 = Matt. xxii. 18). Cf. Bauer⁵, s.v. Cf. also (but without this verb) Luke xi. 53 f.

² So E. C. Hoskyns, *op. cit.*, p. 569.

³ See above, p. 395 and n. 3 for some recent discussions of this topic.

⁴ J. Jeremias, ' Zur Geschichtlichkeit des Verhörs Jesu vor dem Hohen Rat', *Z.N.W.*, Vol. 43, 1950–51, pp. 148 f. His assertion is more convincing if it is argued on other grounds that the Jews did not then possess the *ius gladii* than if this incident is used as evidence for that conclusion.

⁵ A. N. Sherwin-White, *op. cit.*, p. 42, points out that under the Roman system of toleration it would be possible to have such a local custom ratified, though the *lex Iulia de adulteriis* did not treat adultery as a capital crime.

⁶ Cf., e.g., J. D. M. Derrett, 'Law in the New Testament: The Story of the Woman Taken in Adultery', *N.T.S.*, Vol. X, 1963–64, pp. 16 ff. He adds, *ibid.*, p. 18, 'the writing was symbolic of divine "legislation" (cf. Ex. xxxi. 18;

see in Jesus' action a reflection of Jeremiah xvii. 13, with its reference to apostates being 'written in the earth' (LXX ἐπὶ τῆς γῆς γραφήτωσαν);[1] however, it is hard to believe that the significance of the gesture would be immediately appreciated by even such an audience. A more common conclusion, found in the addition of the words 'taking no notice' (μὴ προσποιούμενος) by some MSS. (E G H K) at the end of verse 6, is that Jesus' action 'was simply a studied refusal to pronounce judgement'.[2]

One plausible suggestion is T. W. Manson's view that Jesus was modelling himself on the practice of Roman judges, who first wrote down the sentence and then read it aloud; thus Jesus says in effect by his action, 'If you want me to usurp the functions of the Roman Governor, I will do so in the correct Roman manner'. Then he stoops down and pretends to write the sentence, after which he reads it out: **'The one without sin among you, let him be the first to cast a stone at her'.** Jesus thus defeats the plot by going through the form of pronouncing sentence according to the correct Roman procedure, but wording it so that it cannot be executed.[3] It may be added in support of this conjecture that Jesus must have been aware that he would be compelled to give some sort of answer, and that although he may have been preoccupied with his own thoughts,[4] it is unlike him to lose the initiative in such a situation.

The Law required the witnesses whose evidence had secured the conviction to take the lead in carrying out the sentence (Deut. xiii. 9, xvii. 7; cf. Acts vii. 58). Jesus' ruling is that any of his questioners may cast the first stone—provided that he is **without sin.** This does not refer to sins of the flesh, even in the limited sense of lust or sensuality, but to any form of sin at all;[5] Jesus uses the incident to teach the presumption of sitting in judgement in the place of God.[6] Cf. Paul's argument in Rom.

---

[1] R. Eisler, 'Jesus und die ungetreue Braut', *Z.N.W.*, Vol. 22, 1923, pp. 305-307.   [2] Barrett, p. 492.

[3] T. W. Manson, 'The Pericope de Adultera (Joh. 7₅₃-8₁₁)', *Z.N.W.*, Vol. 44, 1952-53, pp. 255 f., and *Jesus and the Non-Jews* (1955), pp. 10 f.

[4] J. H. Bernard, *op. cit.*, p. 719.   [5] Cf. E. C. Hoskyns, *op. cit.*, pp. 571 f.

[6] Cf. Riesenfeld's summary of the point of the story, *art. cit.*, p. 107: 'Only the Messiah, who himself is free of sin, can combine radical judgement on sin with healing mildness towards the sinner.' Compare with this Mark x. 18 = Luke xviii. 19.

ii. 1, 22. By raising the level of the discussion to this plane Jesus has also escaped from the predicament in which the scribes and Pharisees had hoped to place him. They admit defeat, and leave Jesus alone with the woman. The crowd has hardly vanished during the incident (*pace* Barrett)—indeed it would have been more likely to have grown in size—but attention is focused on Jesus and **the woman who was in the midst,** and the setting of the scene is no longer relevant. It is Jesus' judgement which counts, and it was to preserve this that the story continued to be told.

Jesus' statement **'Neither do I condemn you; go away, and from now on sin no more'** seems to have caused difficulties for some readers; thus a tenth-century Armenian MS. reads instead, 'Go in peace, and present the offering for sins, as in their law is written', while the Syriac paraphrase of Barsalibi merely says, 'Go thou also now and do this sin no more'.[1] The difficulty of this verse certainly favours the authenticity of the incident recorded. The point is that the court has withdrawn from the scene, and Jesus will not set himself up as judge (cf. Luke xii. 14). However, his pronouncement stigmatises the woman's conduct as sin; he demands right behaviour for the future, but does not condone the past. The question of forgiveness is not raised explicitly, and there is no hint of the woman's repentance; one should, however, note that Jesus' attitude to her is one of mercy, and that this story was recorded to teach the Church to behave according to its Founder's example.

[1] J. H. Bernard, *op. cit.*, p. 721.

INDEX OF NAMES AND SUBJECTS

467

INDEX OF AUTHORS

INDEX OF GREEK WORDS AND
PHRASES DISCUSSED

ἐὰν αὐτὸν θέλω μένειν, 457n
Ἑβραϊστί, 158n
Ἐγκαίνια, 254n
Ἐγώ εἰμι, 148, 183, 188n, 224, 236, 385
ἔθνος, 278n, 290n
εἰκών, 23
εἰμί, 84, 345n
εἶπον, 252n, 256n, 301n
εἰς τὸν αἰῶνα, 142n, 186
εἰς τὰ ἴδια, 77, 364
εἰς τὰς χεῖρας, 136
εἶτα, 107n
ἐκ, 232n, 252n, 256n, 301n, 343, 353n, 356n
ἐκ τούτου, 198n
ἐκάθισεν ἐπὶ βήματος, 402f
ἐκεῖνος, 85n, 96, 329, 345, 412
ἐκτείνω, 455
ἐλέγχω, 350f
ἔλεος, 82
Ἕλληνες, 211n
ἐμβριμάομαι, 271f, 273n
ἐμφυσάω, 432n
ἐν, 363n, 371n
ἐν ἐκείνῃ τῇ ἡμέρᾳ, 331n
ἐν συναγωγῇ, 195n
ἐν τῇ χειρὶ αὐτοῦ, 136
ἕν, 258, 377
ἐνέργεια, 163n
ἐξηγέομαι, 86
ἐξουσία, 77, 367, 402
ἑορτή, 121n, 203n
ἐπί, 105n, 182n, 183, 273n
ἐπὶ τῇ προβατικῇ κολυμβήθρᾳ, 159n
ἐργάζομαι, 163n
ἔρχομαι, 76, 320n, 355
ἐρωτάω, 360, 362, 363
ἐσθίω, 194n
ἐσχάτη ἡμέρα, 269
ἐσχάτη ὥρα, 28n
ἕτερος, 327n
εὐλογέω, 178f
εὑρίσκω, 288n
εὐχαριστέω, 178

ζητέω, 426n
ζωή, 70n, 250n
ζωὴ αἰώνιος, 14, 128, 142n

θαυμάζω, 207n
θεάομαι, 81n

(ὁ) θεός, 70
θεωρέω, 191, 323, 330n, 331
θλῖψις, 365
θύω, 249n

ἴδιος, 77, 99n, 164n, 231n, 342n
Ἱεροσόλυμα, 87n
Ἱερουσαλήμ, 87n
ἵνα, 72n, 150n, 237n, 245n, 292n, 299f, 328n, 338n, 339n, 341n, 342n, 346n, 385n
Ἰουδαῖος, 133
ἰχθύς, 177n

καθαίρω, 335n
καθαρός, 337n
καί, 379n
καὶ ὁ γράψας ταῦτα, 48
καινός, 316n
καιρός, 202n
καλός, 250, 258n
καρδία, 311
καταβαίνω, 188, 193
καταλαμβάνω, 73, 123n
κατεσθίω, 117
Κεδρών, 380n
κῆπος, 380, 415f
Κλεοπᾶς, 407f
κλέπτης, 247n
Κλωπᾶς, 407f
κοιλία, 212n
κοίμησις, 266n
κόλπος, 86, 313n
κοσμοκράτωρ, 296f
κόσμος, 76, 223, 296
κόφινος, 179
κράζω, 83n
κρατέω, 432ff
κρίσις, 169n, 296
Κύριος, 23, 28n, 188n, 244, 245, 427

λαλέω, 301n
λαλιά, 230n
λαμβάνω, 253, 382n
λαός, 278n
λατρεία, 348
λέντιον, 306
λευκός, 151n, 423n
λῃστής, 247n, 399
λιθόστρωτος, 403
λίτρα, 282n